SANDER'S FISHING GUIDE 2

The Finger Lakes Region

John M. Sander

published by Sander's Fishing Guide
& Service Directory, Inc.
P.O. Box 0624, Amherst, NY 14226

Also available from Sander's Fishing Guides

Sander's Fishing Guide & Service Directory - Western New York
Edition. A comprehensive guide to 200 lakes and streams in
Western New York.

Cover Design: Rose Hoth
Cover Photo: Rich Newberg (left) of Channel 4 News, Buffalo and
his father Marvin Newberg of Long Island, New York were fishing
with Capt. Vince Pierleoni when they caught these salmon. The
largest fish weighed 31 lbs. 15 ozs. and won the Shakespeare Fall
Derby media award for 1986.

Acknowledgments

I would like to thank the following organizations for their cooperation in the preparation of this book:

—The New York State Department of Environmental Conservation, regions 7 and 8.

—The publications office of the Department of Environmental Conservation.

—The State University of New York at Buffalo - Department of Geography.

—The New York State Sea Grant Institute

—The United States Fish and Wildlife Service

—The United States Department of Agriculture - Forest Service

—Empire State/Lake Ontario Trout & Salmon Derby, Inc.

I would also like to thank the following individuals for their contributions to this project:

Chuck Annis, Capt. Tony Arlauckas, Debra Bauman, Dominick Bello, Rob Birchler, Mike Bleech, Capt. Tony Buffa, Barton Butts, Donnie Davenport, Fred David, Gordy Dekdabrun, Capt. Charles Denoto, Red Devan, John Fik, Dr. John Forney, Dr. Jim Haynes, Earl Holdren, Mike Keller, Capt. Bill Kelley, Mike Kennan, Capt. John Kowalczyk, Rick Kustich, Gene Leonard, Len Lisenbee, Roger Lowden, John McGough, John McKinnis, Craig Nelson, Jay Nelson, Janet Rengert, Chuck Rogers, Dr. Gaylord Rough, Dick Schleyer, Rick Schleyer, Clarence Smith, Capt. Randy Snyder, Capt. Joe Swift, Jerry Turfano, Dr. Michael Violand and Jake Warnken.

Finally, special thanks go out to Susan Prefontaine, Karen Angelo and Carla Santino for typing the manuscript, Vince Mecca and Ellen Smith for proofing sections of the text, Ken Gravelle for working on much of the photography, Rose Hoth for her work in designing the cover, John Boyd of Heather Printing for his efforts in preparing negatives, Cheryl McCaffery and Greg Theisen for designing and producing most of the maps, Judy Scott, Bob Scott and Jane Burke of J.A.S. Complete Composition for their undying patience in the typesetting and layout of this book, the personel of DEC regions 7 and 8 (Cliff Creech, Les Wedge, Tom Chiotti, Shelly Riter, Lucy Hinell, Carl Widmar, Bill Abraham, Dave Kosowski, Gene Lane, Fred Angold and Ron Schroeder) whose input, guidance and especially patience can not be overstated, to J. Michael Kelly and C. Scott Sampson, whose articles, photographs and work in reviewing the text were instrumental in the preparation of this book, and for many reasons to my parents.

Forward

John M. Sander

In the three years since I published Sander's Fishing Guide to Western New York I've received hundreds of letters asking for information on other parts of New York State. The vast majority of these requests were for a book on the Finger Lakes Region. Looking at a map of New York State the reason for this becomes obvious. The area is uniquely endowed with an abundance of lakes and streams. The Finger Lakes, Oneida Lake, Lake Ontario, Naples Creek and Catharine Creek are known across the county for the quality of their fishing.

The region also hosts many lesser waters that offer superior angling opportunities, many of which are unknown or under-utilized by the fishing public. For although Central New York has a wealth of water, until now a comprehensive guide to what is available has never been written. This book, which covers 250 lakes and streams, is an attempt to remedy that situation.

As was the case with my first book, I allowed this guide to evolve as it progressed. This resulted in a number of important changes being made in its original design,which initially was for a book only on where to go fishing. The most significant change was the inclusion of local techniques used to fish the major lakes. It quickly became obvious in my research of the Finger Lakes and Oneida Lake that they are individually and collectively very unique. Where else can you find large numbers of smallmouth bass suspended out in deep water, take northern pike in 90 feet of water or catch lake trout spawning in 4 feet of water?!!

Because of the peculiarities of these lakes I tried to provide the reader with information on local methods that have proven to be effective on these waters. I was helped in this task by two noted outdoor writers, C. Scott Sampson, and J. Michael Kelly. Their articles on how to fish several of the Finger Lakes are valuable additions to this book. I was also fortunate to obtain permission to reproduce many of the chapters from Earl Holdren's book, "Fishing New Yotk State Lakes for Fabulous Trout and Salmon". These chapters are a wealth of information on techniques designed specifically for the Finger Lakes.

A second major change was in the review process used to check the accuracy of the information contained in this book. Essentially every article was reviewed by at least two readers intimately familiar with the area in question.This was done to insure the highest possible degree of accuracy. Their corrections of errors of omission or commission, as well as other re-commendations, were then incorporated into the text. However any inaccuracies that may have crept into this book are solely the fault of this author.

Good Luck Fishing!

Table of Contents

Italicized Numbers Indicate Maps

13. Wayne County 140

Streams & Rivers

Lakes & Ponds

14. Yates County 156

Streams & Rivers

Part II - Major Waters

15. The Finger Lakes 161

16. Oneida Lake .... 254 - 267
17. Lake Ontario.................. 268 - 310

A Quick Guide to The Fish
of Central New York .... 311 - 323

Log Sheets

Italicized Numbers Indicate Maps

How to Use Your Fishing Guide

This book was designed to be a comprehensive introduction to the wide range of angling opportunities available in the Finger Lakes Region. While some of this area's streams and lakes are heavily fished, many go virtually unnoticed because few people realize that they exist. To remedy this situation, we have endeavored to provide you with 3 basic categories of information; 1) how to locate a particular stream or lake on a map, especially topographical maps; 2) how to access the site in the field; and 3) what general set of conditions and facilities to expect when you get there. While most of the information contained in this guide is self-explanatory a number of points should be clarified in order for you to fully utilize the information provided.

A. **Map Coordinates** — These coordinates are provided for each lake and stream. In the case of a stream or river, the coordinates correspond to the location of the stream mouth. These make it possible to locate the position of the stream or lake on any map that is delineated in terms of latitude and longitude, such as a topographical map (see below), regardless of whether or not the name of the stream or lake appears on the map.

B. **USGS map(s)** — U.S. Geological Survey topographical maps are by far the best field maps available, and when purchased will provide you with a wealth of information on alternative access sites, terrain, the locations of tributaries and much more. With regard to streams and rivers, the first map refers to the topographical map that covers the most downstream portions of the stream and the stream mouth. The maps that follow cover progressively upstream sections until the final map, which covers the head waters of the stream.

C. **Access** — For each lake, all launch sites that we were able to locate and verify were open to the general public are listed, as are all principle roads surrounding the lake. For streams and rivers, naturally we could not list every road or bridge crossing. Instead, usually only one access is given. Keep in mind that these are only recommendations. The ability to access a stream via a particular road crossing can change abruptly, such as by posting by land owners. Therefore, it would be a good idea to always have an alternate access road in mind before you head for a particular stream.

For streams that are stocked, the given access road will always put you onto a section of the stream that is stocked.

D. **Notes** — A very important aspect of this guide is the note space left at the end of each entry. This space was provided in order for you to: 1) keep a record of any important additional information (alternate access sites, data on a particular hole etc.) not found in this guide; 2) to keep an updated record of any major changes that take place on a stream or lake; and 3) to note any errors of omission or commission that may have occurred in the writing of this guide. This will enable you to maintain your guide as a reliable source of information for many years.

E. **Log Sheets** — The log sheets found at the end of the book will help you to record the one thing that no book can provide you with - experience. If used faithfully, logs can turn even an unsuccessful fishing trip into a learning experience and increase your chances becoming a successful angler.

WEST RIVER

map coordinates	42º 39' 59" 77º 21' 29"
USGS map(s)	Middlesex, Canandaigua Lake Rushville
location (township)	Italy
access	see below
principle species	largemouth bass, bullhead, chain pickerel, panfish

The West River is a large warm water stream that empties into the south end of Canandaigua Lake. The majority of the fishing that is available here is found downstream of the crossing at South Hill Road, which runs off Route 245. This fishable reach is about 2.5 miles long. Averaging about 100 feet in width in the summer, the West River is heavily encroached upon by trees, weeds and snags, but is nevertheless navigable by full size bass boats. The only area where there might be a navigation problem is at the junction with Naples Creek, where there is excess sedimentation.

Largemouth bass are the most important species found in the West River, and the fishing for them can be extremely good. There are extensive weed beds along the river, scattered patches of lily pads and numerous snags, providing prime bass habitat. Bass can also be found in a cut known as "The Duck Channel," which is a short, 40 foot wide channel that starts near Canandaigua Lake and runs southeast. Originally constructed as a waterfowl habitat, this navigable channel has some fine fishing for largemouth bass.

Chain pickerel can also be found in the West River, but their numbers are considerably less than those of the largemouth. Also available are panfish, particularly crappie, which can be found here in good numbers in the spring. A proven hot spot for spring crappie is at the old marina, now owned by the DEC, off Route 245. Shore fishermen can fish either the waters of the marina itself, or the access channel that leads to the river. Both have very good spring crappie fishing. Bullhead are also found throughout the river, especially in the spring.

The entire West River is open to public fishing, as the fishable reach flows through the High Tor Wildlife Management Area. Boat access is provided by three state owned launch sites:

1. The DEC fishing access and boat launch site, along Route 21, on Canandaigua Lake, at Woodville. Hard surface ramp — no charge.
2. The old marina, off Route 245, downstream of South Hill Road. This property is now owned by the DEC and boats can be launched from a dirt ramp — no charge.
3. The DEC fishing access and boat launch site, just off Route 245 on South Hill Road. Hand launch site for cartop and canoes — no charge.

The West River is not stocked.
See also — High Tor Wildlife Management Area.

NOTES: _____

_____

_____

PART I
COUNTY WATERS

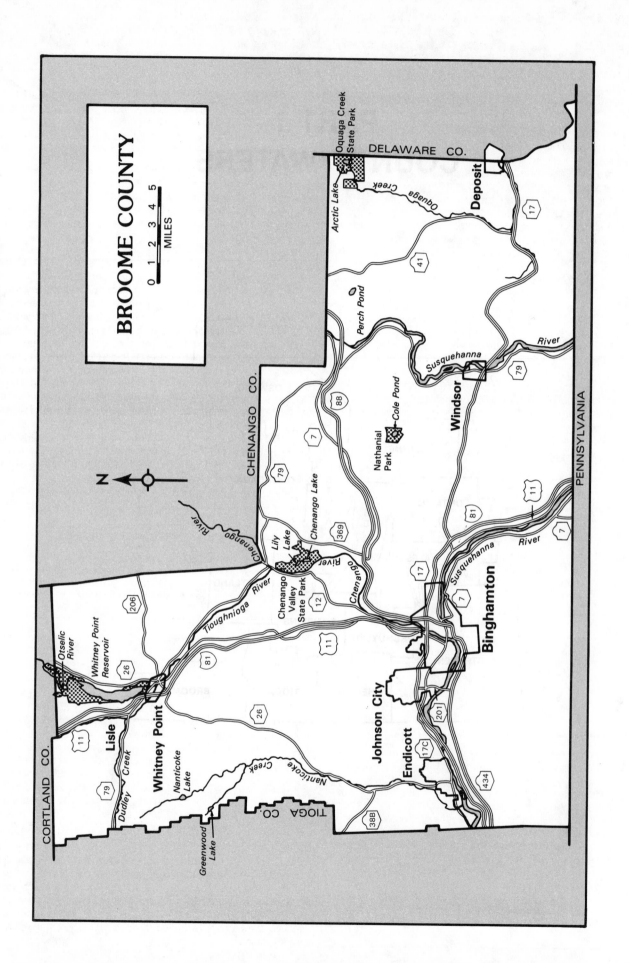

BROOME COUNTY STREAMS & RIVERS

CHENANGO RIVER (Broome County Section)

map coordinates.......... 42º 05' 32"   75º 55' 05"
USGS map(s)............. Binghamton West, Castle Creek, Chenango Forks, Greene
location (township)....... Dickinson, Chenango, Fenton
access.................. see below
principle species .... smallmouth bass, walleye, northern pike, panfish

The Broome County portion of Chenango River is a small version of the Susquehanna River, but not nearly as productive. Flowing through a narrow, picturesque valley, this river ranges up to several hundred feet in width, is a bit turbid, though not excessively, and has a fair amount of aquatic vegetation. The flow in the Chenango River is constant all year long, but it can be a bit low during the summer. The major problem on this river is the general lack of habitat. The very lower reach is dredged and much of the river above the dredged section, at least upstream to Chenengo County, lacks deep pools or strong riffs. There are some exceptions, however, and the fishing, if one is persistent, can be rewarding. Smallmouth bass predominate in the Broome County portion of the river, followed by walleye. Occasionally, northern pike and (at least according to rumors) muskellunge are taken here, but their numbers are few and they don't contribute much to the fishing. Concentrate on the stretch of water between Chenango Bridge and the county line for the best bass and walleye fishing. Reportedly, the section of the river near Chenango Bridge is very good for walleye and panfish.

Access to the Chenango River is rather limited. Shore access can be found at Otsiningo Park on the west side of the river, north of Binghamton, off Route 11. But the best way to fish the Chenango would be from a small boat or canoe. The river has a low gradient for most of its length and is very amenable to drift fishing. This would give you a chance to check out the major pools.

Small boats and canoes can be put in on the lower reach of the Tioughnioga River at Chenango Forks Elementary School, on Route 79, and its a short run to the Chenango River (boats must be carried across the school's athletic field to access at this point). Small boats can also be put in at the private campground on the east side of Route 12, about 1 mile upstream of the junction of Route 12 and 79, or at Otsiningo Park.

NOTES: _____

_____

DUDLEY CREEK

map coordinates.......... 42º 21' 21"   76º 00' 08"
USGS map(s)............. Lisle, Richford, Harford
location .... Lisle
access.................... parallelled and crossed by Route 79
principle species .... brown trout (stocked)

A tributary of the Tioughnioga River, Dudley Creek is a small, mediocre quality brown trout stream. Averaging about 15 feet in width, it has a good year round flow of clear water over a bottom of unstable gravel and is fishable all season long. The stream flows through pasture land and could be fly fished, but you're likely to take quite a few chubs. Only 2.6 miles of Dudley Creek is classified as trout water, and the fishing in this section is entirely sustained by stocked fish. In the spring, the stream is stocked with 200 trout yearlings, from the crossing at Howland Hill Road upstream to the crossing at Route 79 (Catskill Turnpike).

NOTES: _____

_____

NANTICOKE CREEK

map coordinates.......... 42º 05' 03"   76º 05' 07"
USGS map(s)............. Endicott, Maine, Lisle
location (township)....... Union, Maine, Nanticoke
access.................... the lower section is parallelled and crossed by Route 26; the stocked section is roughly parallelled by Caldwell Hill Road and Nanticoke Road
principle species .... brown trout (stocked), smallmouth bass, panfish

The lower reach of Nanticoke Creek is a medium size, warm water stream. Right at the mouth of the stream there is fair quality fishing for smallmouth bass and rock bass, but above the mouth, as far upstream as the village of Maine, the stream has little to offer other than chubs, bluegills, rock bass and very small smallmouth bass.

Above Maine, Nanticoke Creek is classified as a trout stream, at least as far upstream as the village of Nanticoke. Nanticoke Creek is a mediocre quality trout stream. It averages 20 feet in width, has a gravel and rubble bottom and flows through abandoned farmland and residential areas. The stream is badly washed by floods, resulting in limited holding areas for fish. This, combined with fairly heavy fishing pressure, means that few fish will survive through the summer in this stream. Though much of the stream is open, fly fishing is difficult, or at least aggravating, due to the number of chubs found here. There are enough to drive a fisherman batty. Above the village of Nanticoke, the stream is not classified as trout water, but some wild brook trout can be found in the east branch of the stream which enters Nanticoke Creek below the village of Nanticoke.

In the spring, Nanticoke Creek is stocked with 2,000 brown trout yearlings, from the mouth of the east branch of Nanticoke Creek (about one tenth mile upstream of Cross Road) upstream 7 miles to the village of Nanticoke.

In addition, 960 brown trout yearlings are stocked in the east branch of Nanticoke Creek each spring, in the 3 mile reach below the hamlet of Glen Aubrey.

NOTES: _____

_____

_____

_____

OQUAGA CREEK

map coordinates.......... 42º 03' 28"   75º 25' 23"
USGS map(s)............. Deposit, North Sanford
location (township)....... Sanford
access.................... parallelled by Route 17 (Southern Tier Expressway) between Deposit and McClure — see below
principle species .... brown trout (stocked), brook trout (wild), american eel, smallmouth bass, panfish

Oquaga Creek is Broome County's best, if not only, real trout stream. Originating near Arctic Lake in the northeast corner of the county, the stream flows through farmland and abandoned farmland for 15 miles before emptying into the Delaware River at Deposit. Oquaga Creek averages 25 feet in width, has a bottom of gravel, rubble and silt and a good year-round flow. Streamside cover is fairly good between McClure and Deposit, but above McClure, bank cover is limited. It does pick up somewhat above North Sanford.

The most productive section of Oquaga Creek is the stretch between Deposit and McClure. The fishing for stocked brown trout is good throughout the reach and there are several pools up to six feet deep that are exceptionally good. Keep in mind that special regulations apply to part of this section. A no kill policy is in effect from the old Route 17 bridge, east of McClure, downstream 3 miles to the new Route 17 bridge, west of Deposit. Trout can be taken here all year long on artificial lures only. Be sure to check for current regulations.

Warm water species are also found in the lower reach of Oquaga Creek. Smallmouth bass, green sunfish, rock bass, and american eels are all found here in good numbers. The members of the bass family are well distributed throughout the stream below McClure, while the eels are most often taken from the same deep pools that harbor brown trout. Just above McClure the quality of this stream deteriorates significantly, for a short stretch, but as you move upstream toward Sanford, the quality picks up. Stocked brown trout predominate in this section of Oquaga Creek, but wild brook trout are taken occasionally. Above North Sanford, upstream to Arctic Lake, quality again declines. There is limited fishing for brown trout in the uppermost reaches of the stream, but several of the upper tributaries in the vicinity of Arctic Lake hold good populations of wild brook trout. These brookies aren't large, but they are numerous and seldom get any attention from local anglers.

To guarantee public access to Oquaga Creek, the state has purchased a total of 4.19 miles of public fishing easements on this stream and one public parking area (currently underdeveloped). A short (210 ft.) easement has also been obtained on Fly Creek, which enters Oquaga Creek near McClure.

In the spring, Oquaga Creek is stocked with 2,300 brown trout yearlings, from Deposit upstream 4.5 miles to the mouth of Fly Creek near McClure. An additional spring stocking of 900 brown trout yearlings takes place between the mouth of Fly Creek and the village of Sanford. In the fall, Oquaga Creek is stocked with 2,100 brown trout fingerlings, from the village of Sanford upstream to the hamlet of North Sanford. The lower 2.5 miles of Fly Creek is stocked in the fall with 1,400 brown trout fingerlings.

NOTES: _____
_____
_____
_____

OTSELIC RIVER — see Cortland County streams and rivers

SUSQUEHANNA RIVER (Broome County Section)

map coordinates . . . .
USGS map(s) . . . . Afton, Gulf Summit, Belden, Windsor, Binghamton East, Binghamton West, Endicott
location (township) . . . . Colesville, Windsor, Conklin, Binghamton, Vestal
access . . . . see below
principle species . . . . smallmouth bass, walleye, muskellunge, northern pike, channel catfish, bullhead, tiger muskellunge, pickerel, panfish

The Susquehanna River is one of Broome County's best kept secrets, at least as far as fishing is concerned. Although it flows through a very populous, urbanized region for much of its length, it is generally underutilized, in spite of the fact that the fishing for walleyes and smallmouth bass is downright excellent.

The river is large. It generally runs between 200-300 feet in

width, but there are sections that range up to 600 feet wide. With the exception of the spring runoff period, the Susquehanna River is a shallow, slow moving waterway. Its slightly turbid waters flow over a bottom of rubble and gravel that is, for the most part, lacking in deep holes. The surroundings range from abandoned farmland to the urbanized area of Binghamton, Endicott and Johnson City.

The following is a run down on the great fishing that is available in the Susquehanna, from the Chenango/Broome County line downstream to the Broome/Tioga County line, including the portion that flows through Susquehanna County, Pennsylvania.

Walleye: found throughout most of the Susquehanna downstream of the town of Windsor, walleye are probably the single most sought after species in the river. The DEC has determined that the Broome County portions of the river serve as a spawning area for the species. Most of the fish taken in this section, from opening day until the beginning of October, will be juveniles, averaging 12-14 inches long. The larger, adult fish have been known to migrate downstream, well into Pennsylvania. Few walleye, 20 inch or larger, will be taken during this period, but smaller fish are plentiful, at least as far upstream as the village of Oakland, in Pennsylvania.

In the fall, the larger fish return to the New York portion of the river. Beginning around the first week of October, tremendous numbers of adult walleye will congregate in the Broome County section of the Susquehanna River, especially between the Tioga county line and the village of Endwell. These fish will average about 6 pounds, but walleye from 9-12 pounds are not at all uncommon.

While walleye can be found throughout much of the river, there are a number of notable hotspots. As indicated above, the stretch between the Tioga county line and Endwell is excellent for adult walleye in the fall.

Further upstream, there are a series of very deep pools near Murphy's Island, just downstream of the Goudey Station Dam. These pools hold a variety of species, including trophy muskellunge, but walleye predominate. Below the dam at Goudey Station you will find outstanding fishing for juvenile walleyes. A good fisherman could pick up 30-40 walleye here in the spring. Many of the fish will be sublegal in size, but they can be a lot of fun. Upstream in Binghamton is the Rock Bottom Dam. Spawning walleye are known to congregate below this dam, often times providing some truly outstanding fishing.

Above the Rock Bottom Dam is a still water section stretching for several miles. There is some fair to good walleye fishing in this reach, as well as in the Susquehanna County, (PA) section of the river.

Smallmouth bass: old bronzeback is the predominent game species in the Susquehanna River, and are even more ubiquitous than the walleye. They are found in good numbers throughout the Broome County portion of the river, including the eastern section.

Exceptionally productive areas include: the water below the Goudey Station Dam; the stretch of stillwater above the Rock Bottom Dam; from the state line upstream to Oakland; and the reach that runs through the town of Windsor. The last mentioned area has a higher gradient that the downstream sections, and is extremely good for smallmouth. There are a number of very large deep pools in this reach, especially below Windsor, that offer some of the best bass fishing in Broome County.

Muskellunge: two strains of muskie are found in the Susquehanna River; the natural strain and the hybrid tiger muskie. Although approximately 4,500 tiger muskies are stocked in the Broome County portion of the river, few of them are taken by fishermen, at least within the borders of the county. For reasons unkown, most of these fish are caught downstream in Tioga County. An overwhelming majority of the muskie taken here are the natural strain. Their numbers are limited, and really constitute a bonus when caught. Naturally, most muskies will be caught in the deeper sections of the river, which are quite limited. One area known to hold a fair number of these toothsome torpedoes are the series of deep pools downstream of Goudey

Station Dam, near Murphy's Island.

Rounding out the fishing opportunities found in the Susquehanna River are limited numbers of northern pike, pickerel, channel catfish, (fishing for catfish is good above Owego), bullhead (there are good populations of bullhead here, but they are isolated; for fast spring action try the waters around Murphy's Island or the Endwell area), and panfish, including yellow perch, white crappies, rock bass and sunfish.

Access to the Susquehanna River is adequate, but not great, especially in the western section. The eastern section of the river is parallelled by Route 79, from near the Chenango County line downstream to Oakland in Susquehanna County (this route changes to 92 in Pennsylvania). Boat access is available at several locations. An informal cartop access site is located on Route 79, between the ice cream stand and the car wash directly across from the Route 17 east exit. Follow the road directly back to the river. This is private property and the owners rights must be respected to insure his continued cooperation.

Further downstream, one mile below the state line is a Pennsylvania Fish Commission access site on Route 92 (NY 79), where small boats can be launched. Other Pennsylvania access sites are located on Harmony Road. This road is also known as legislative Route 57063 and is the first left turn off Route 11 after crossing the Susquehanna River. One access site is located 2 miles upstream of the Route 11 crossing, while another is located only ½ mile upstream at the crossing of Interstate 88.

In the Tri-City area (Binghamton, Johnson City, Endicott) bank access is available at several county parks (Grippen Park on Grippen Avenue and Riverside Park off Riverside Drive) and from Sandy Beach off Route 7, William H. Hill Park behind Westover Plaza, or the county park north of Bevier Street. Small boats or canoes can be launched from all of the above sites, but caution should be exercised with special diligence in this reach of the river due to the presence of dams at Goudey Station and Rock Bottom Station.

An excellent map of the water covered in this article can be obtained by contacting the Broome County Department of Parks and Recreation, P.O. Box 1766, Binghamton, New York, 13902, 607/772-2193.

See also — Tioga County streams and rivers.

NOTES: _____

_____

_____

_____

TIOUGHNIOGA RIVER - see Cortland County

An assortment of warm water flies — leech patterns, pike streamers, Wooly Buggers, Matukas and Zonkers.

BROOME COUNTY LAKES & PONDS

ARCTIC LAKE

map coordinates.......... 42° 01′ 11″ 75° 27′ 14″
USGS map(s)............. Deposit
location .... township of Sanford, in Oquaga
Creek State Park
access .... off Sanford Road

Physical Characteristics

area .... 134 acres
shoreline .... 1.9 miles
elevation .... 1572 feet
maximum depth .... 35 feet
mean depth .... approximately 14 feet
bottom type .... gravel, muck

Chemical Characteristics

water clarity .... clear
pH....................... alkaline
oxygen.................. oxygen is good throughout the
lake all year

Plant Life

There is minimal rooted aquatic vegetation in Arctic Lake. Algae blooms are not a serious problem here.

Species Information

largemouth bass.......... common; growth rate fair
rainbow trout............. common; seasonal (spring, summer)
brown bullhead........... common; growth rate very good
pumpkinseed .... common; growth rate fair

Boat Launch Sites

There are no formal launch sites on this lake. Small cartop boats or canoes could be hand launched here. Check with park officials for current regulations.

General Information

Arctic Lake is located in Oquaga Creek State Park. Also known as Oquaga Lake, it is an impoundment of Oquaga Creek. Rainbow trout are the single most important species here, but recent gillnettings indicate that there is probably a significant population of fair size largemouth bass here, as well. The fishing for large bullhead and pumpkinseeds is also reportedly good. Also present is a remnant population of sea-run lamprey. These are fish that were trapped in the upper reaches of Oquaga Creek when it was dammed to form the lake. These lamprey do not spawn successfully and should die out within the next few years.

Arctic Lake is stocked each spring with 2,500 rainbow trout yearlings.

NOTES: _____

_____

_____

_____

CHENANGO LAKE

map coordinates.......... 42° 12′ 38″ 75° 50′ 13″
USGS map(s)............. Chenango Forks
location .... township of Fenton, in Chenango
Valley State Park
access .... off Route 369

Physical Characteristics

area .... 40 acres
shoreline .... 1.8 miles
elevation .... 885 feet
maximum depth .... 19 feet
mean depth .... 7 feet
bottom type .... gravel, muck

Chemical Characteristics

water clarity .... clear
pH....................... alkaline
oxygen.................. oxygen is good throughout this
lake all year

Plant Life

There is a moderate amount of rooted aquatic vegetation scattered throughout the lake. Algae blooms are not usually a problem here.

Species Information

rainbow trout............. common; seasonal (spring, summer)
largemouth bass.......... uncommon; fair
yellow perch .... uncommon; poor
pumpkinseed .... uncommon; poor

Boat Launch Sites

1. Private boats are not allowed in Chenango Lake. However, the park does rent row boats between Memorial Day and Labor Day. No motors, fee. Contact Chenango Valley State Park at 607-648-5251 for current regulations.

General Information

Located in Chenango Valley State Park, this small lake is a glacial kettle hole. Its waters are kept clear and cool all year long by a large influx of cold spring water near the north end of the lake. This makes the lake ideal for rainbow trout. Chenango Lake is heavily stocked in the spring, and there is intense fishing pressure here in the spring and summer. Also present are populations of stunted largemouth bass, yellow perch and pumpkinseeds.

Chenango Lake is stocked with a total of 9,100 rainbow trout yearlings in March, April and May.

NOTES: _____

_____

_____

_____

_____

GREENWOOD LAKE

map coordinates.......... 42° 17′ 15″ 76° 05′ 37″
USGS map(s)............. Lisle
location .... township of Nanticoke, in Greenwood County Park
access .... off Greenwood Road

Physical Characteristics

area .... 25 acres
shoreline .... N.A.
elevation .... 1300 feet
maximum depth .... 25 feet
mean depth .... 8 feet
bottom type .... gravel, muck

Chemical Characteristics

water clarity .... moderately clear
pH....................... alkaline
oxygen.................. oxygen is deficient at the bottom
of this lake in the later summer
months

Plant Life

Significant weed beds are found scattered throughout this lake.

Species Information

rainbow trout............. common; seasonal (spring, early summer)
largemouth bass.......... common; fair
pumpkinseed .... common; fair

Boat Launch Sites

Private boats are not allowed on Greenwood Lake. Row boats can be rented in the park from Memorial Day to Labor Day. For current regulations contact the park at: (607) 862-9933.

General Information

Greenwood Lake is located in Greenwood Park, Broome County's most complete park. The park offers a wide variety of outdoor activities including camping, picnicking, cross-country skiing, orienteering and fishing. Greenwood Lake has good fishing in the spring and early summer for rainbow trout and fair to good fishing for largemouth bass and panfish in the summer. This lake is stocked each spring with 2,000 rainbow trout yearlings.

NOTES: _____

_____

_____

Species Information

chain pickerel	common; growth rate good
largemouth bass	common; growth rate good
pumpkinseed	common; growth rate fair
brown bullheads	common; growth rate fair

Boat Launch Sites

1. No boats are allowed on this lake.

General Information

Located in Chenango Valley State Park, this small lake has an excellent population of chain pickerel. Unfortunately, most of them are safe from anglers. Due to the lack of boat access and the extreme amount of weed growth here, fishing is very difficult. Contact Chenango Valley State Park for current regulations (607) 648-5251.

NOTES: _____

_____

_____

_____

LILY LAKE

map coordinates	42° 12' 49" 75° 50' 20"
USGS map(s)	Chenango Forks
location	township of Fenton in Chenango Valley State Park
access	off Route 369

Physical Characteristics

area	19.2 acres
shoreline	1.2 miles
elevation	895 feet
maximum depth	8 feet
mean depth	5 feet
bottom type	muck

Chemical Characteristics

water clarity	clear
pH	alkaline
oxygen	oxygen is good throughout the lake all year

Plant Life

There is a significant amount of rooted aquatic vegetation throughout the lake, including patches of lily pads.

Chain pickerel are found in many of Broome County's lakes and ponds. Photo courtesy J. Michael Kelly.

NANTICOKE LAKE

map coordinates	42° 20' 00" 76° 05' 37"
USGS map(s)	Lisle
location	township of Lisle
access	off Squedunk Road

Physical Characteristics

area	46 acres
shoreline	N.A.
elevation	1400 feet
maximum depth	21 feet
mean depth	N.A.
bottom type	gravel, some muck

Chemical Characteristics

water clarity	turbid
pH	alkaline
oxygen	oxygen levels are reduced in the summer, but this does not appear to effect any species of fish.

Plant Life

Limited rooted aquatic vegetation is found in this lake.

Species Information

rainbow trout	common; seasonal (spring)
crappies	common; growth rate good
brown bullhead	common; growth rate good
pumpkinseeds	common; growth rate good
chain pickerel	common; growth rate good

Boat Launch Sites

The DEC has a hand launch site on Squedunk Road, 4 miles south of hamlet of Center Lisle. Parking for 15 cars. No motors, 400 yard carry to water - no charge.

General Information

An impoundment of Nanticoke Creek, this lake was originally intended to be a trophy brook lake in a wilderness setting. These plans were upset, however, when local anglers released crappies, chain pickerel, pumpkinseeds and brown bullhead in the lake. The stocking policy was then changed to brown trout and finally to rainbow trout.

In the spring Nanticoke Lake is stocked with 2,300 rainbow trout yearlings.

NOTES: _____

_____

_____

NATHANIEL COLE PARK POND

map coordinates	42° 08′ 30″ 75° 42′ 29″
USGS map(s)	Belden
location	in Nathaniel Cole Park, township of Colesville
access	off Farm to Market Road in County Park

Physical Characteristics

area	53 acres
shoreline	N.A.
elevation	1260 feet
maximum depth	40 feet
mean depth	approximately 15 feet
bottom type	sand, gravel, muck

Chemical Characteristics

water clarity	clear
pH	alkaline
oxygen	oxygen appears to be adequate throughout this lake all year long.

Plant Life

There is relatively little plant life in this lake. Weed beds are sparse and algae blooms are not a problem.

Species Information

smallmouth bass	common; growth rate fair to good
brown bullhead	common; growth rate fair
yellow perch	common; growth rate fair
bluegills	common; growth rate fair

Boat Launch Sites

Private boats are not allowed on this lake. Row boats, pedal boats, canoes and sailboats can be rented at the park. For current regulations contact the park at (607) 693-1389.

General Information

Nathaniel Cole Park offers a wide variety of outdoor activities including picnicking, swimming, cross country skiing and fishing. The park's 53 acre pond offers fair quality fishing for smallmouth bass and panfish. This pond is not stocked.

NOTES: _____

_____

_____

_____

PERCH POND

map coordinates	42° 10′ 29″ 75° 33′ 26″
USGS map(s)	Afton
location	township of Sanford
access	off Perch Pond Road

Physcial Characteristics

area	25.6 acres
shoreline	0.8 miles
elevation	1471 feet
maximum depth	19 feet
mean depth	12 feet
bottom type	muck

Chemical Characteristics

water clarity	some turbidity due to algae
pH	alkaline
oxygen	oxygen levels are often poor below 15 feet in the summer

Plant Life

There is a moderate amount of rooted aquatic vegetation in this lake. There is a recurrent problem with algae blooms here.

Species Information

rainbow trout	common; seasonal (spring)
yellow perch	common; poor
brown bullhead	common; fair

Boat Launch Sites

Cartop boats and canoes can be hand launched on the west side of the lake. There are no formal public launch sites here.

General Information

Perch Pond is privately owned, but land owners currently allow fishermen access to the pond. Until 1985 this pond was stocked with both brook and rainbow trout. However, the DEC changed the stocking policy to rainbow trout in 1986, feeling that the rainbows would have a better survival rate in this relatively warm body of water. The trout fishing is quite good here in the spring, but quickly deteriorates in the summer.

Perch Pond is stocked with a total of 2,600 rainbow trout yearlings in April and May.

NOTES: _____

_____

_____

_____

WHITNEY POINT RESERVOIR

map coordinates	42° 20′ 21″ 75° 57′ 54″
USGS map(s)	Willet, Whitney Point
location	townships of Triangle & Lisle
access	off Route 26 - see below

Physical Characteristics

area	1200 acres
shoreline	N.A.
elevation	1010 feet
maximum depth	35 feet
mean depth	approximately 8 feet
bottom type	muck, gravel

Chemical Characteristics

water clarity	turbid (clay)
pH	alkaline
oxygen	oxygen depletion occurs in depths greater than 15 feet

Plant Life

Rooted aquatic vegetation is present, but the growth of large weed beds is inhibited by the drawing down of the reservoir in the fall.

Species Information

white crappies	abundant; growth rate excellent
smallmouth bass	common; growth rate fair
largemouth bass	uncommon; growth rate good
yellow perch	common; growth rate fair
northern pike	uncommon; growth rate very good
striped bass/white bass hybrid	common; growth rate good
walleye	uncommon; growth rate very good
tiger muskellunge	common; growth rate N.A.

Also available are minor populations of black crappies, bluegills and pumpkinseeds.

Boat Launch Sites

1. Dorchester Park, off Route 26, 1 mile north of dam. Hard surface ramp, parking for 40 cards and trailers, - no charge.

2. Upper Lisle Park, off Route 26, at north end of reservoir. Launching for cartop boats and canoes.

3. Informal access for shore fishing and the hand launching of small boats or canoes is available on the west side of the Reservoir via the road that runs from Route 11 north to Lisle Park.

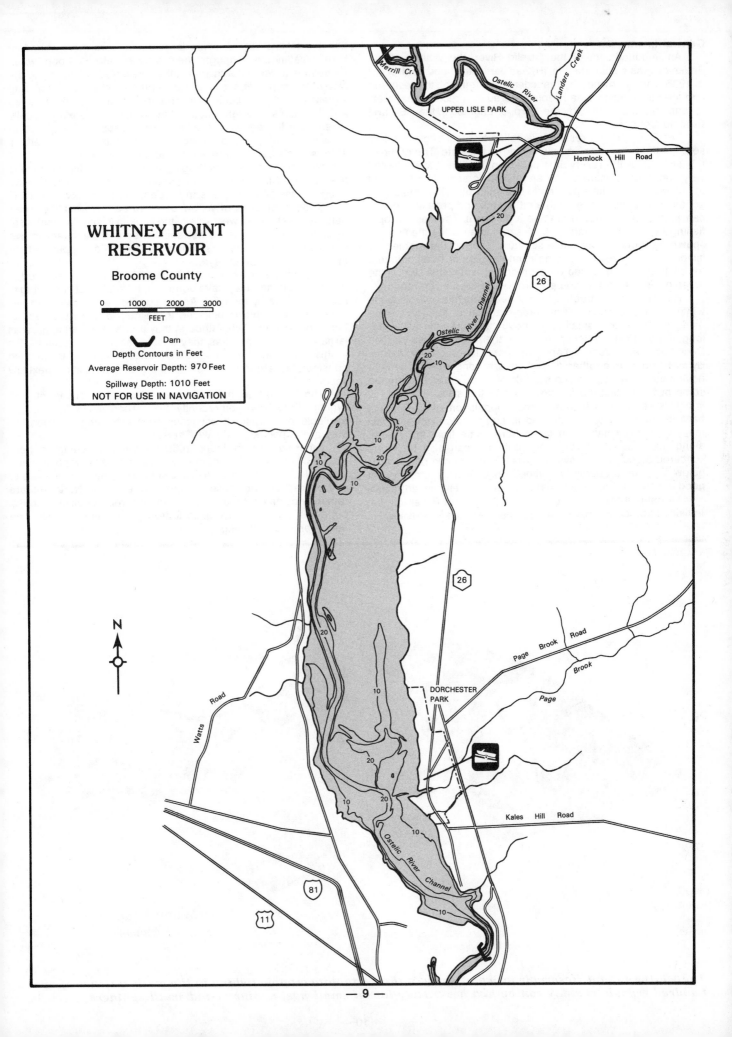

WHITNEY POINT
RESERVOIR

Broome County

0   1000   2000   3000
FEET

Dam
Depth Contours in Feet
Average Reservoir Depth: 970 Feet
Spillway Depth: 1010 Feet
NOT FOR USE IN NAVIGATION

Merrill Cr.

Ostelic River

Landers Creek

UPPER LISLE PARK

Hemlock Hill Road

26

20

Ostelic River Channel

20
10

N

20

10

20

10

10

20

Page Brook Road

Brook

26

Page

10

DORCHESTER
PARK

Watts Road

20

Kales Hill Road

20

10

20

10

Ostelic River Channel

81

11

10

General Information

An impoundment of the Otselic River, the Whitney Point Reservoir was constructed in 1942 as part of the flood control Act of 1936. Though owned by the federal government, the reservoir and the surrounding area is administered as a recreational area, though joint agreement, by the Corp. of Engineers, the DEC and Broome County.

The Point, as the reservoir is called by local anglers, offers some of the best white crappie fishing in the state. The origin of this species in the reservoir is unknown, but they have adapted very well here. Because they are a pelagic schooling fish, you might have to do a little hunting to find them, but when you do the action can be incredible. With a bit of luck and persistence, you can land over a hundred crappie a day here. The best crappie fishing occurs in the spring (May-early June) when the fish are spawning. Work any available structure, such as the submerged islands on the west side, using minnows, jigs or small spinners for best results. The steep drop-off on the north-east side of the reservoir is also a top crappie producing area in the spring.

Another very productive time of year for white crappie is the winter. Bushel baskets full of crappie are taken through the ice using minnows and small jigs. Though crappie feed all winter long, the best fishing occurs just after the reservoir ices up (late December - early January) and just prior to ice-out (early March). By noticing where other fishermen are congregated, even a novice fisherman can locate schools of crappie and experience some of the fastest ice-fishing action in the state.

This reservoir also has a good population of smallmouth bass, though this is not reflected in angler catch rates. A vast majority of the smallmouth taken here come from the rip-rap along the base of the dry dam, but they can also be found scattered along the old river channel. Their growth rate is a bit below par, due probably to competition from white crappie, but good catches of smallmouth bass can be had here, nevertheless.

Largemouth bass are found in Whitney Point Reservoir, but in limited numbers. Their population has declined from its level in the mid to late 1960's, when largemouth were more abundant than smallmouth. Though their growth rate is good when compared to largemouth from other New York State lakes, the size of the population is limited by a number of factors, including excessive turbidity, fluctuating pool levels, and a lack of rooted aquatic plants. The largemouth that are landed here are usually taken from the edges of available weed beds by anglers using lures that employ sounds or vibrations, such as large spinnerbait. This is necessary due to the turbidity of the water.

One of the more encouraging aspects of the fishing here is the apparent increase in the numbers of yellow perch being caught in the past few years. In a recent gillnet sampling, the DEC found the population of yellow perch to be quite healthy. Their nets were set on the west side of the sunken islands, indicating at least one potential perch hot spot. They can be taken on live minnows, worms, small spinners or small jigs tipped with a mousey grub or perch eye.

Recently, striped bass/white bass hybrids were stocked in this reservoir, and they have done well here, at least according to recent nettings by the DEC. Angler success with this hybrid has been low, and this is believed to be due to a general lack of familiarity with this fish. Although they aren't expected to grow as large as in southern lakes, they should reach a respectable size in this reservoir, and fish up to 20 inches have been taken. Fish considerably larger are expected to be taken here in the next few years.

The hybrid tiger muskellunge was also introduced into the Whitney Point Reservoir recently (1985). There isn't sufficient data available to determine how successful this stocking has been, but they are expected to do well here.

Other species are found in the reservoir, including northern pike, bullhead, bluegills, pumpkinseeds and black crappies, none of which are found in significant numbers. The only species of any interest among these are the northern pike. Northerns are rather uncommon here, due to very low reproductive success, but those that do survive grow to trophy size, and provide some very memorable fishing.

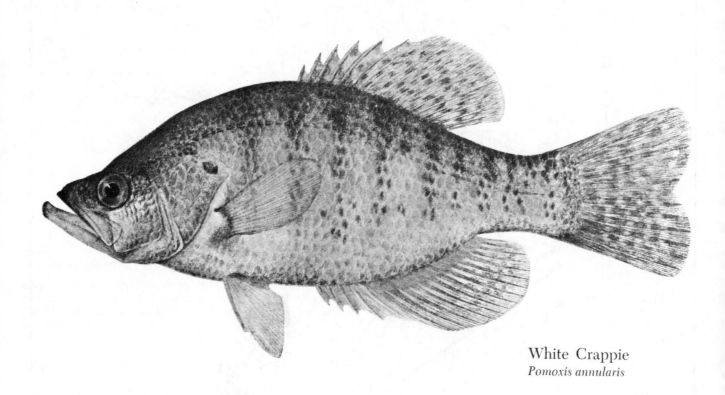

White Crappie
Pomoxis annularis

The Whitney Point Reservoir provides some of the best white crappie fishing in the state. Catches of over a hundred crappie per day can be had here. They hit on small jigs, minnows and small spinners.

Due to the quality and popularity of ice fishing on the Whitney Point Reservoir, an annual crappie derby was initiated by the Whitney Point Sportsmens Association in 1974. Today, this derby has grown to become one of the premier ice fishing events in the state, drawing anglers from every corner of New York. For further information on this derby contact:

Broome County Department
of Parks and Recreation
P.O. Box 1766
Binghamton, NY 13902
(607) 722-2193

NOTES: _____

_____

_____

_____

In addition to the lakes and ponds listed above, numerous small ponds have been constructed in Broome County. While the primary purpose of many of these ponds is flood control, most are open to the public and provide fair to good fishing for a wide variety of species. Because many of these ponds are not on current editions of USGS topographical maps, map coordinates have been deleted.

LITTLE CHOCONUT #1

location . . . . in Johnson City, one mile north of Route 17C
access . . . . just west of Reynolds Rd.
area . . . . 5 acres
principle species . . . . rainbow trout

This small pond has a maximum depth of 18 feet. It has been stocked annually with rainbow trout since 1976 (500-1000 yearling per year). Because it was recently drained by the Broome County Soil and Conservation District, species other than trout are relatively scarce.

NOTES: _____

_____

_____

_____

LITTLE CHOCONUT #2

location . . . . township of Dickinson, one mile east of Johnson City
access . . . . Airport Road
area . . . . 4.7 acres
principle species . . . . brown bullhead, largemouth bass, pumpkinseeds, black crappies, channel catfish

With a maximum depth of 7 feet, fishing in this pond is limited to warm water species. The quality of the fishing is further limited by the fact that this pond is drained rather frequently. After it is drained in 1987, it will probably be restocked with largemouth bass, catfish and panfish.

NOTES: _____

_____

_____

LITTLE CHOCONUT #2A

location . . . . township of Dickinson
access . . . . off East Main Road
area . . . . 4 acres
principle species . . . . brown bullhead, largemouth bass, black crappies, pumpkinseeds

The maximum depth of this pond is 7 feet, limiting available fish to warm water species. The fishing for bullhead is very good here. Recent netting studies indicate that the average bullhead in this pond is close to 10 inches. Black crappies and pumpkinseeds are abundant, but stunted. Largemouth bass have been stocked here and provide a limited fishery.

NOTES: _____

_____

_____

_____

LITTLE CHOCONUT #2B

location . . . . township of Maine, 2 miles north of Johnson City
access . . . . along Airport Road
area . . . . 4 acres
principle species . . . . northern pike, largemouth bass, brown bullhead, black crappies, pumpkinseeds, channel catfish

This pond has a maximum depth of 8 feet and available fish are limited to warm water species. Netting studies in 1984 indicated that there was an abundance of pumpkinseeds and black crappies here, while largemouth bass and brown bullhead were less than common. This led to the decision to stock an additional predatory species in this pond. In 1985 6 male and 2 female adult northern pike were stocked here. If they spawn successfully, they could greatly improve the quality of fishing in Little Choconut 2B.

NOTES: _____

_____

_____

_____

LITTLE CHOCONUT # 2C

location . . . . township of Maine, 2.5 miles north of Johnson City
access . . . . off Stella Ireland Road
area . . . . 4.7 acres
principle species . . . . largemouth bass, black crappies, yellow perch, pumpkinseeds

The maximum depth of this pond is 14 feet. At presently only warm water species are present. However, there are indicators that this pond could support rainbow trout. The DEC is currently studying Little Chocnut 2C to see if a trout stocking policy should be implemented.

NOTES: _____

_____

_____

_____

LITTLE CHOCONUT # 2E

map coordinates . . . .
USGS map(s) . . . .
location . . . . Township of Chenengo, 2 miles
                                   northeast of Johnson City
access . . . . off Dimmock Hill Road
area . . . . 1.2 acres
principle species . . . . rainbow trout, largemouth bass,
                                   brown bullhead, black crappies

Although this pond has a maximum depth of only 7 feet, its dissolved oxygen content and temperature profile are very suitable for rainbow trout. The DEC has implimented a stocking policy here, calling for 200 rainbow trout yearlings per year. This pond has good fishing for brown bullhead and limited fishing for black crappies and largemouth bass.

NOTES: _____

_____

_____

_____

PALMERS POND

location . . . . on the north edge of the village of
                                   Deposit
access . . . . off Pine Street
area . . . . 1.9 acres
principle species . . . . rainbow trout, largemouth bass,
                                   brown bullhead, yellow perch,
                                   bluegills.

This is a relatively new inpoundment, having been constructed in 1982. Over 50% of Palmers Pond (it is also known as Deposit Pond #1) is at the maximum depth of 10 feet and it may have the potential to sustain rainbow trout. A stocking policy, initiated in 1986, calls for the planting of 200 rainbow trout yearling per year here. Recent gillnet studies indicate limited populations of warmwater species.

NOTES: _____

_____

_____

_____

NANTICOKE #7A

location . . . . township of Maine, 2 miles north of
                                   the village of Maine
access . . . . off Bailey Hollow Road
area . . . . 11 acres
principle species . . . . rainbow trout, pumpkinseeds,
                                   bluegills, brown bullhead, white
                                   suckers.

Nanticoke #7A has a maximum depth of 20 feet and is believed to be capable of supporting stocked rainbow trout. The DEC has plans to study this pond to see if a stocking policy should be implemented here. If approved, the policy will call for the stocking of 500 rainbow trout yearlings per year. Recent netting studies showed that white suckers and pumpkinseeds were common here, but that bluegills and brown bullhead were uncommon.

NOTES: _____

_____

_____

_____

NANTICOKE #7B

location . . . . 4.5 miles north of the village of
                                   Maine
access . . . . off Myers Road
area . . . . 4 acres
principle species . . . . brown bullhead, white suckers,
                                   pumpkinseeds, largemouth bass,
                                   northern pike, channel catfish.

This pond has a maximum depth of 8 feet and available fish are limited to warm water species. In the fall of 1985 the pond was completely drained to repair damage done by beaver activity. Prior to this, Nanticoke # 7B had good populations of largemouth bass, pumpkinseeds, white suckers and brown bullheads. Northern pike and channel catfish were stocked here in 1985 and 1984, respectively. The DEC plans to restock largemouth bass and panfish here.

NOTES: _____

_____

_____

_____

NANTICOKE # 9A

location . . . . 3 miles north of the village of
                                   Nanticoke
access . . . . pond is ½ mile west of Cadwell Hill
                                   Road
area . . . . 6 acres
principle species . . . . largemouth bass, pumpkinseeds.

The maximum depth of this pond is 10 feet. Fishing is generally limited to warm water species, primarily largemouth bass and pumpkinseeds. However, trout occasionally drop down from tributary # 22 of Nanticoke Creek into the pond. Nanticoke # 9A gets little attention from anglers because of the long walk-in from Cadwell Road. The DEC is recommending restocking this pond in 1987 with largemouth bass.

NOTES: _____

_____

_____

_____

NANTICOKE # 9C

location . . . . 3 miles north of the village of
                                   Nanticoke
access . . . . just east of Cadwell Hill Road
area . . . . 13 acres
principle species . . . . largemouth bass, yellow perch,
                                   brown bullhead, pumpkinseeds,
                                   black crappies, chain pickerel,
                                   channel catfish, northern pike,
                                   white suckers.

This pond has a maximum depth of 9 feet. Recent gillnetting studies indicate that all of the species listed above are present, but in limited numbers. To improve the quality of fishing here, the DEC introduced channel catfish in 1984 and northern pike in 1985.

NOTES: _____

_____

_____

_____

NANTICOKE # 13

location . . . . 2 miles north of Endwell
access . . . . off Harrington Road
area . . . . 11.2 acres
principle species . . . . black crappies, pumpkinseeds, bluegills, brown bullhead, largemouth bass, channel catfish, northern pike.

Nanticoke # 13 has a maximum depth of 12 feet. The pond was completely drained in the fall of 1985 and the spring of 1986. The DEC is recommending that largemouth bass and panfish be restocked here in 1987. Also, if northern pike again become available, they will probably be stocked here.

NOTES: _____

_____

_____

_____

PATTERSON # 1

location . . . . 2 miles north of Endwell
access . . . . off Strubell Road
area . . . . 7.6 acres
principle species . . . . rainbow trout, pumpkinseed, brown bullhead, white suckers.

This pond has a maximum depth of 13 feet. In the 1970's and early 1980's brook trout were stocked here with considerable success. Beginning in 1985, rainbow trout have been stocked here. Gillnet studies indicate that the rainbows survive in this pond through the summer. The stocking policy calls for 800 rainbow trout yearlings per year. Pumpkinseeds are abundant here and brown bullheads, bluegills and white suckers are common.

NOTES: _____

_____

_____

_____

PATTERSON # 2

location . . . . 2 miles north of Endicott
access . . . . off Taft Avenue
area . . . . 5.8 acres
principle species . . . . channel catfish, largemouth bass, pumpkinseeds, brown bullhead, bluegills, black crappies, yellow perch, northern pike.

Located on Brixius Creek, this pond has a maximum depth of 5 feet. Recent gillnettings indicated that brown bullhead, black crappies, bluegills and pumpkinseeds are abundant. Largemouth bass and yellow perch are common. Adult channel cat fish were introduced here in 1984, and northern pike were stocked in 1985. It is hoped that the northern pike will increase the quality of fishing for all species in this pond.

NOTES: _____

_____

_____

Bullhead are found in many of Broome County's ponds and rivers. Excellent tablefare, they can be taken in great numbers in the spring. Be careful not to get stung by the sharp barbs on their fins. Photo courtesy New York State DEC.

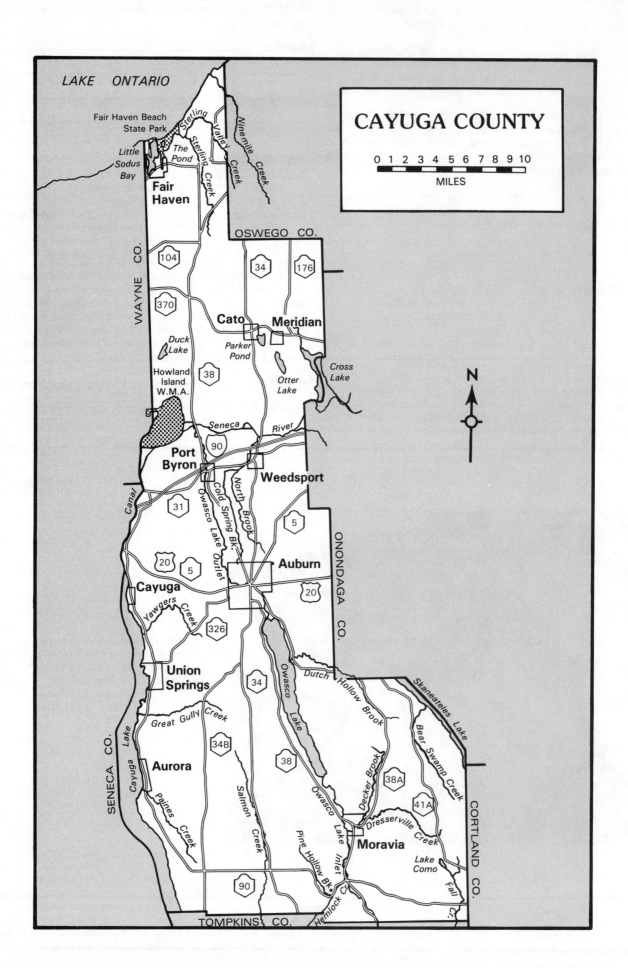

LAKE ONTARIO

Fair Haven Beach
State Park

Little
Sodus
Bay

Sterling

Sterling Creek

Valley Creek

Ninemile Creek

The Pond

Fair
Haven

WAYNE CO.

OSWEGO CO.

104

370

34

176

Cato

Meridian

Duck
Lake

Parker
Pond

38

Howland
Island
W.M.A.

Otter
Lake

Cross
Lake

Seneca

River

90

Port
Byron

Weedsport

Canal

31

Cold Spring Bk.

Owasco Lake Outlet

North Brook

5

ONONDAGA CO.

20

5

Auburn

20

Cayuga

Yawgers Creek

326

Union
Springs

34

Owasco Lake

Dutch Hollow Brook

Skaneateles Lake

Bear Swamp Creek

Great Gully Creek

Cayuga Lake

SENECA CO.

34B

Aurora

38

Decker Brook

Dresserville Creek

38A

41A

CORTLAND CO.

Paines Creek

Salmon Creek

Owasco Lake Inlet

Pine Hollow Bk.

Moravia

Lake
Como

Fall C.

90

Hemlock Cr.

TOMPKINS CO.

CAYUGA COUNTY

0 1 2 3 4 5 6 7 8 9 10
MILES

N

—14—

CAYUGA COUNTY STREAMS AND RIVERS

BEAR SWAMP CREEK

map coordinates	42º 49′ 25″ 76º 19′ 50″
USGS map(s)	Spafford, Sempronius
location (township)	Niles, Sempronius
access	crossing at Curtin Road
principle species	brook trout (wild), rainbow trout (wild)

Entering Skaneateles Lake at Carpenter Point, Bear Swamp Creek offers fair quality trout fishing throughout most of its 6.5 mile length. There is a falls about three-quarters of a mile upstream of its mouth, and this lower section, though of generally poor habitat, does see a small run of wild rainbows from Skaneateles Lake every spring.

Further upstream, above the village of New Hope, the creek wanders through a swamp. There are isolated pockets of brook trout throughout this section, and some of these fish are quite respectable in size. However, because of the terrain, most of these brookies will never see a hook. The area is very difficult to travel by foot or canoe, and few if any of the beaver impoundment are near roads.

Bear Swamp Creek is not stocked.

NOTES: _____

_____

_____

_____

SALMON CREEK - see Tompkins County Streams and Rivers

COLD SPRING BROOK

map coordinates	43º 04′ 13″ 76º 33′ 36″
USGS map(s)	Weedsport, Auburn
location (township)	Mentz, Throop
access	crossings at Jacobs Road and Ryer Road
principle species	brown trout (stocked), brook trout (wild)

Although only a fair quality trout stream, the importance of Cold Spring Brook is amplified by its proximity to Auburn area anglers. Surrounded by farmlands, this stream averages 20 feet in width and has excellent bank cover. Stream flow is diminished in summer, but it does not dry to pools. It does, however, have a slight problem with turbidity due to its silt and clay bottom. There are also occasional fish kills due to agricultural malpractices.

The only portion of Cold Spring Brook that is considered to have good trout habitat is the stocked section, which runs from Jacobs Road 3.8 miles upstream to Ryer Road. In the fall, this area is stocked with 1,200 brown trout fingerlings. These stocked fish are augmented by a small number of wild brook trout.

NOTES: _____

_____

_____

_____

DECKER BROOK

map coordinates	42º 42′ 56″ 76º 24′ 38″
USGS map(s)	Moravia, Owasco
location (township)	Niles, Moravia
access	crossing at Jugg Street
principle species	rainbow trout (wild), brown trout (wild), brook trout (stocked and wild)

A major tributary of Dresserville Creek, Decker Brook is a good quality trout stream. Nearly six miles in length, it averages eight to ten feet in width, has a bottom of bedrock and gravel and good, but intermittant bank cover. Surrounded by farmlands and woodlands, Decker Brook usually has a constant flow of cool, clear water. In the middle section, however, there is a problem with flow in dry years, and it can dry to pools.

Decker Brook is a tertiary tributary of Owasco Lake (by way of Owasco Lake Inlet and Dresserville (Mill) Creek). About one-quarter mile upstream of its junction with Dresserville Creek there is a large waterfall. Below the falls the stream is dominated by runs of fish from Owasco Lake. Wild rainbows make runs here in the spring and fall, and wild browns also make an appearance here in the fall. (Check for current Finger Lakes tributary regulations when fishing below the falls.)

Above the falls, Decker Brook is a good quality brown trout stream shading to brook trout the further upstream you go. This section of the stream has open sections that could be fly fished, but its not classic fly fishing water. There are few deep pools on Decker Brook, but those you do find are usually quite productive, though most of the fish taken here will be on the small side.

In the fall, the lower 2.5 miles of Decker Brook is stocked with 2,000 brown trout fingerlings. In addition, the first tributary of Decker Brook above the falls receives a stocking of 600 brown trout and 600 brook trout fingerlings each fall.

To increase the access to Decker Brook, the state has purchased 2.95 miles of public fishing rights and two foot path right-of-ways on the stream.

NOTES: _____

_____

_____

_____

DRESSERVILLE CREEK

map coordinates	42º 42′ 56″ 76º 24′ 39″
USGS map(s)	Moravia, Sempronius
location (township)	Moravia, Sempronius
access	parallelled and crossed by Dresserville Road; see also below
principle species	brown trout (wild), rainbow trout (wild), brook trout (wild)

Dresserville Creek is also known as Mill Creek after it is joined by Decker Brook near Moravia. Fourteen miles in length, this stream averages only six feet in width, but the lower sections are upwards of twenty feet wide. It has a good year round flow of cool, clear water over a bottom of silt, gravel and rubble. Surrounded primarily by farmlands and woodlands, there is generally excellent bank cover on this stream, but sections are sufficiently open to allow for fly fishing. Dresserville creek has a moderate to steep gradient, a good riff-pool ratio and some of these pools are up to four feet deep. The habitat is further improved by the numerous improvement structures that have been built here.

Dresserville Creek is divided by an impassible falls in the village of Moravia. The quarter mile stretch of the creek below the falls is dominated by migrating fish from Owasco Inlet which Dresserville Creek empties into in Moravia. In the spring there is a very good run of Owasco Lake rainbow trout, and this run is repeated to a lesser extent in the fall. In addition to rainbows, large (15 - 16 lb.) Owasco Lake brown trout can also be taken in this section in the fall.

Above the falls, Dresserville Creek is a high quality inland trout stream. This is one of the few streams in the area that has good fishing for wild resident rainbows. These fish are found throughout most of the stream above the falls, but the best fishing seems to be just below the small hamlet of Dresserville. Wild brown trout are also found throughout Dresserville Creek and in the extreme upper reaches, brightly colored wild brook trout can be taken with regularity.

The resident trout found in Dresserville Creek are usually a bit on the small side, about 10 inches, but their abundance and willingness to take a well presented fly or small spinner makes this a very popular stream with local anglers. To facilitate access to Dresserville Creek, the state has obtained 4.3 miles of public fishing right-of-ways on the stream, between the mouth of Decker Brook and the hamlet of Dresserville. In addition, the state reports that an underdeveloped parking area has been obtained, as have six foot paths, two of which are presently developed.

Be sure to check the current regulations for Finger Lakes tributaries when fishing on this stream.

Dresserville Creek is not stocked.

NOTES: _____
_____
_____
_____

DUTCH HOLLOW BROOK

map coordinates	42° 51' 14" 76° 30' 41"
USGS map(s)	Scipio Center, Owasco, Spafford
location (township)	Owasco, Niles, Skaneateles (Onondaga County)
access	crossing at Cream Hollow Road
principle species	landlocked salmon, rainbow trout (wild), brown trout (wild), brook trout (wild), smallmouth bass, smelt

A relatively minor tributary of Owasco Lake, Dutch Hollow Brook wanders for eighteen miles through the farmlands and woodlands of Cayuga and Onondaga Counties. The lower half of the stream, roughly from the village of Niles on down, is strongly influenced by the migration of fish from Owasco Lake. These fish provide essentially all of the angling opportunities in this section on the stream. In the spring there are good runs in succession of smelt, rainbow trout, and smallmouth bass, though most of the smallmouth will be out of the stream by the opening of bass season. Your best bet for success in the spring might be to

The YELLOW WOOLY WORM effective, depending upon its size, for steelhead and salmon to bluegills and crappies.

concentrate on some of the large, deep pools in the mid-section of the stream. The pools usually hold good numbers of large rainbows, and small spinners or fliers should prove to be productive. There is also a fall run of rainbows here, as well as a run of landlocked salmon.

Aside from the runs of Owasco Lake fish, Dutch Hollow Creek holds good populations of native rainbows, browns and brook trout. These fish can be found in the section of the creek from Niles upstream to Burdock Road. The stream averages six to ten feet in width here and is mostly brush lined, making fly fishing difficult.

Dutch Hollow Creek is not stocked.

NOTES: _____
_____
_____
_____

FALL CREEK - see Tompkins County Streams & Rivers

GREAT GULLY CREEK

map coordinates	42° 48' 31" 76° 42' 30"
USGS map(s)	Union Springs
location (township)	Springport
access	road crossing at State Route 90
principle species	rainbow trout (wild), smelt

Only a short section of Great Gully Creek is fishable, from the falls just above State Route 90 to its mouth at Cayuga Lake. There is an intense fishery for lake run rainbows in the spring, and smelt can also be taken nearer the creek mouth. There is a smaller, but adequate run of rainbow trout here in the fall. Be sure to check for current Finger Lakes tributary regulations when fishing Great Gully Creek.

The stream is not stocked.

NOTES: _____
_____
_____
_____

HEMLOCK CREEK

map coordinates	42° 39' 33" 76° 25' 44"
USGS map(s)	Moravia, West Groton
location (township)	Locke
access	parallelled by Creek Road and State Route 90; see also below
principle species	rainbow trout (wild), brown trout (wild), brook trout (wild)

Flowing northeast for five miles before emptying into Owasco Inlet at the village of Locke, Hemlock Creek averages only about eight to twelve feet in width. The lower half of the stream has a constant flow of cool, slightly turbid water, while the upper reaches often dry to pools in the summer. The bottom ranges from gravel to bedrock, there is good, but intermittant bank cover, and the surroundings consist primarily of farmlands.

Hemlock Creek is a fairly productive fishery. In the summer a large pool will typically hold up to 50 juvenile rainbows and numerous brown trout, several of which will likely be 12 to 14 inches. In the upper reaches, where the stream dries to pools, brook trout are occasionally taken.

Because it is a tributary of Owasco Inlet, Hemlock Creek shares in the spawning runs of Owasco Lake rainbow trout in the spring, and rainbows and brown trout in the fall. The runs here are generally 10 to 15 days later than in other area streams and generates a moderate amount of angling pressure. To facilitate access to this stream, the state has purchased 1.2 miles of public fishing rights and one foot access right-of-way (undeveloped).

Check for current Finger Lakes tributary regulations when fishing Hemlock Creek.

This stream is not stocked.

NOTES: _____

_____

_____

_____

NINE MILE CREEK - see Oswego County Streams & Rivers

NORTH BROOK

map coordinates . . . . 43° 02' 30"   76° 34' 49"
USGS map(s) . . . . Weedsport, Camillus
location (township) . . . . Throop, Brutus, Mentz
access . . . . crossings at Manrow Road and Mills Road — see below
principle species . . . . brown trout (stocked & wild)

North Brook, like Cold Spring Brook, derives its importance more from its proximity to Auburn area anglers than from the overall quality of its fishing. Fourteen miles in length and averaging 15 to 20 feet in width, this stream has a fairly constant flow of cool clear water over a bottom of sand and gravel. The surroundings are sparsely residential, and the bank cover is generally good, consisting of overhanging willows and mature hardwoods. The stream has a moderate gradient, a good mixture of riffles and pools, undercut banks and several stream improvement structures.

The trout section of North Brook is only 4.2 miles long, from the crossing at Mills Road upstream to the mouth of tributary #11, .4 miles upstream of the crossing at Manrow Road. This section is stocked each fall with 700 brown trout yearlings. Wild brown trout are also taken from North Brook, though infrequently, and few fish reach a size of 20".

To increase access to this stream, the state has purchased a total of 2.51 miles of public fishing easements on North Brook.

NOTES: _____

_____

_____

_____

OWASCO INLET

map coordinates . . . . 42° 45' 19"   76° 27' 50"
USGS map(s) . . . . Owasco, Moravia, West Groton, Groton
location (township) . . . . Moravia, Locke (Cayuga County), Groton (Tompkins County)
principle species . . . . brown trout (stocked & wild), rainbow trout (stocked & wild), landlocked salmon, largemouth bass, smallmouth bass, rock bass

Owasco Inlet is one of the finest flyfishing streams in central New York. Beginning near Peruville in Tompkins County (where it

is known locally as Peruville Creek), this stream meanders for over 20 miles through farmland and woodlands before emptying into Owasco Lake. It ranges from sixty feet in width near its mouth down to only ten feet in its upper reaches. It has a good constant flow of cool, somewhat turbid water over a bottom of gravel, rubble and clay. Although the stream is fairly shallow, it does have a good number of pools, some of which are up to six feet deep. There are some old stream improvement structures on Owasco Inlet and there is a lot of instream rip-rap, providing ideal fish habitat.

The stream can be divided into cold and warm water sections at the Route 38 crossing at Moravia. Below this point Owasco Inlet is a fair quality warm water stream. It gets a good migration of largemouth bass, smallmouth bass and rock bass from Owasco Lake, and these fish will often run well upstream of Moravia.

Trout can also be taken in the lower portion of Owasco Inlet. This stream gets excellent runs of rainbow trout and brown trout in the fall, as well as a few land locked salmon. Most of the rainbows that run up this stream from the lake are wild fish and spawn primarily in the spring, though many fish will be taken in the fall as well. These fish run well up into the upper reaches of the stream and many of its tributaries (see Hemlock Creek, Decker Creek, Dresserville Creek and Pine Hollow Creek).

Above Moravia Owasco Inlet has an excellent resident trout population, one of the best, in fact, of all the Finger Lakes tributaries. Wild rainbow trout can be found throughout the stream as far up as the town of Groton in Tompkins County. Wild brown trout can be taken right into the headwaters of the stream (Peruville) Creek). (Don't ignore Peg Mill Creek, a small tributary that enters Owasco Inlet just downstream of Groton. It gets a good run of Owasco rainbows in the spring, and has a fair population of resident wild rainbows). A unique aspect of Owasco Inlet is the size of the brown trout taken here. Because of the good carry over of stocked fish and their excellent growth rate in this stream, fish of seven or eight pounds are not uncommon, and occasionally fish substantially larger than this are taken.

Mike Kelly of Marcellus, New York holds a 10 pound rainbow taken from an Owasco Lake tributary. Many of the streams that feed into Owasco Lake have good to excellent runs of rainbow trout and brown trout. Photo Courtesy of J. Michael Kelly.

In the fall, Owasco Inlet is stocked with 20,000 rainbow trout fingerlings. The stream is also stocked with 3,000 brown trout yearlings, from the crossing at Long Hill Road upstream 8.5 miles to the town of Groton.

Access to Owasco Inlet is readily found along Route 38 upstream of Moravia. The state has purchased 10.3 miles of public fishing rights on this stream in Cayuga Rounty, and 3.0 miles in Tompkins County. The state has also obtained two fisherman parking areas (undeveloped), and eight foot path right-of-ways, six of which are developed.

NOTES: _____

_____

_____

_____

OWASCO LAKE OUTLET

map coordinates . . . . 43º 04' 36"   76º 38' 55"
USGS map(s) . . . . Montezuma, Weedsport, Auburn
location (township) . . . . Mentz, Throop
access . . . . parallelled and crossed by Route 38
principle species . . . . rainbow trout, brown trout, lake trout, smelt, yellow perch, smallmouth bass, largemouth bass, walleye, bullhead

Owasco Lake Outlet meanders north for 17 miles before entering the Seneca River at Mosquito Point. Averaging 50 feet in width, this stream has a fairly constant flow of warm, turbid water over a bottom of silt, clay, sand and rubble. The stream, however, suffers somewhat from inadequate discharge from Owasco Lake and from pollution from the city of Auburn.

The flow of water in Owasco Outlet is regulated by the state dam at the north end of Owasco Lake and significant numbers of fish escape from the lake through the dam system, including lake trout, brown trout, rainbow trout and smelt. The fish are generally schooled up at the pool below the dam and at times can provide an intense fishery. Apparently, the fall provides the best angling opportunities here. This pool really constitutes the major fishery in Owasco Outlet. The remainder of the stream has a lot of slow moving, weedy stretches that provide fair fishing for yellow perch, bullhead, largemouth bass and walleye (in the lower sections). Faster moving, rubble bottomed portions of the outlet have populations of smallmouth bass and rock bass. But legal size fish are the exception here, and the stream does not warrant much attention.

Owasco Outlet is not stocked.

NOTES: _____

_____

_____

_____

PAINES CREEK

map coordinates . . . . 42º 44' 16"   76º 42' 18"
USGS map(s) . . . . Sheldrake, Genoa
location (township) . . . . Ledyard
access . . . . crossing at Route 90
principle species . . . . rainbow trout (wild), smelt

Paines Creek is a tributary of Cayuga Lake, which it enters just south of the village of Aurora. There is an impassable falls about one mile upstream of the lake and only the section below the falls is fishable. This is not a significant fishery, but there is a fair run of wild rainbows here in the spring and, to a lesser extent, in the fall. Smelt can also be taken here in the early spring. This stream gets only light to moderate fishing pressure and could be worth trying if you are in the area, but it is not worth a special trip.

Paines Creek is not stocked.

NOTES: _____

_____

_____

_____

PINE HOLLOW BROOK

map coordinates . . . . 42º 38' 43"   76º 26' 44"
USGS map(s) . . . . Moravia
location (township) . . . . Locke, Genoa
access . . . . parallelled by State Route 90
principle species . . . . rainbow trout (wild)

A tributary of Hemlock Creek, which it joins near the junction of State Route 90 and North Lansing Road, Pine Hollow Brook is a small, brush lined stream averaging 10 to 15 feet in width. It has a good flow of cool, clear water in the spring and fall (it goes underground in the lower reaches in summer) over a bottom of bedrock, gravel and rubble. The surroundings are primarily woodlands.

Reportedly, there are wild rainbows in the stream all year. But the main fishery is the spring run of adult wild rainbows from Owasco Lake, via Owasco Inlet and Hemlock Creek. This run provides good fishing for trout ranging from 1-1/2 to 5 pounds. Fly fishing would be difficult on Pine Hollow Brook, but small spinners, streamers of nymphs will work well. On occasion this stream also gets a fair fall run of adult rainbows, but this run is inconsistant.

Pine Hollow Brook is not stocked.

NOTES: _____

_____

_____

_____

SENECA RIVER - see Onondaga County Streams & Rivers

STERLING CREEK

map coordinates . . . . 43º 20' 14"   76º 41' 43"
USGS map(s) . . . . Fair Haven, Victory
location (township) . . . . Sterling, Victory, Conquest
access . . . . via Fair Haven Beach State Park, off Route 104A
principle species . . . . rainbow trout (stocked), brown trout (stocked), coho salmon, chinook salmon, lake trout, smallmouth bass, largemouth bass, northern pike, grass pickerel, bullhead, panfish, smelt

Sterling Creek, known locally as the west branch of Sterling Creek to differentiate it from Sterling Valley Creek, is Cayuga County's principle (if not only) tributary of Lake Ontario. Though flowing northward for 21 miles before emptying into "the pond" at Fair Haven Beach State Park, only the lower three miles, between "the pond" (known locally as Sterling Pond) and the dam at Sterling are really worth fishing. Below Sterling, the stream averages about 50 feet in width, has a good, constant flow of water over a bottom of gravel, silt and clay with pools up to four feet deep. Much of the surroundings are marshland and consequently large sections of the stream exhibit the lush vegetation generally associated with marshes; channels lined with cattails and tall grasses, extensive patches of lily pads and often dense submerged aquatic vegetation.

Spawning trout and salmon from Lake Ontario constitute what is probably the principle fishery in Sterling Creek. In the spring rainbow trout, brown trout, lake trout and coho salmon can all be found in varying concentrations in the near shore areas of Lake Ontario off the entrance to "the pond". Brown trout, moving in to feed on bait fish (smelt and alewives) can be found in "the pond" and in Sterling Creek, and there is a fair spring run of adult rainbows here as well. In the fall there are significant runs of coho and chinook salmon, followed by runs of brown trout and rainbow trout. Exceptional fishing for trout and salmon can be found between Old State Road and Sterling Dam, where the stream takes on characteristics of a large trout stream. Snagging is presently allowed on this portion of the stream from August 15 to November 15. Be sure to check for current snagging regulations.

Sterling Creek also has better than average warm water fishing in its lower reaches. In the spring there are exceptionally strong runs of Lake Ontario smallmouth bass. While most of these fishes will be out of the stream by the opening of bass season, there are usually enough "bronzebacks" holding in the stream in the early part of the season to make a trip to Sterling Creek worthwhile. And be prepared for a fight. Most of the smallmouth taken in this stream are very much on the large size.

Other species that run Sterling Creek in the spring include rock bass, bullhead and smelt, all of which provide excellent fishing opportunities. There are also small resident populations of largemouth bass, northern pike, grass pickerel and panfish associated with the lower most reaches of Sterling Creek and "the pond".

NOTES: _____

_____

_____

_____

STERLING VALLEY CREEK

map coordinates .... 43° 20' 56"   76° 39' 57"
USGS map(s) .... Fair Haven, Hannibal, Cato
location (township) .... Sterling
access .... Fraden Road
principle species .... rainbow trout (stocked), brown trout (stocked), coho salmon, chinook salmon, smallmouth bass, largemouth bass, northern pike, grass pickerel, northern pike, bullhead, pan fish

This stream is known locally as the east branch of Sterling Creek. It joins the west branch (i.e. Sterling Creek) about one and one-half miles below the crossing at Fraden Road. In most respects Sterling Valley Creek is a carbon copy of Sterling Creek, but on a smaller scale. The stream gets the same runs of trout and salmon, smallmouth bass and rock bass as Sterling Creek and snagging is allowed from August 15 to November 15 from Fraden Road upstream to the impassable barrier at Route 104A.

This stream is not stocked.

NOTES: _____

_____

_____

_____

YAWGERS CREEK

map coordinates .... 42° 53' 10"   76° 42' 32"
USGS map(s) .... Cayuga, Union Springs, Scipio Center
location (township) .... Springport
access .... road crossing at State Route 90
principle species .... rainbow trout (wild), smelt, bullheads

Yawgers Creek is a fairly large (25 feet wide) partially open stream that enters Cayuga Lake about two miles south of the village of Cayuga. This stream is well known locally for its spring run of wild rainbows from Cayuga Lake. The best fishing for these rainbows takes place in the mile or so just above State Route 90, and the fishing pressure on this stretch can be intense. There is also a fall run of wild rainbows in Yawgers Creek, but it is usually insignificant in terms of angling opportunities. There is a run of smelt and bullhead here in the early spring as well. There is no summer fishing in Yawgers Creek. Be sure to check for current Finger Lakes tributary regulations when fishing on this stream.

NOTES: _____

_____

_____

_____

The lower reaches of many Lake Ontario tributaries, such as Sterling Valley Creek, offer fishing for a wide variety of warm water species. Photo courtesy New York State DEC.

CAYUGA COUNTY LAKES & PONDS

CROSS LAKE

map coordinates	43° 08' 32" 76° 29' 05"
USGS map(s)	Jordan, Lysander, Cato
location	townships of Elbridge, Cato and Lysander
access	see launch sites below

Physical Characteristics

area	2086 acres
shoreline	12.4 miles
elevation	373 feet
maximum depth	65 feet
mean depth	N.A.
bottom type	muck, gravel, marl
mean thermocline depth	30 feet

Chemical Characteristics

water clarity	turbid
ph	alkaline
oxygen	Severe oxygen depletion occurs in depths greater than 30 feet in late summer.

Plant Life

Extensive weed beds exist around the perimeter of the lake.

Species Information

white perch	very common; growth rate good
white crappie	very common; growth rate good
northern pike	common; growth rate good
walleye	common; growth rate good
channel catfish	common; growth rate good
smallmouth bass	common; growth rate good
largemouth bass	common; growth rate good
yellow perch	common; growth rate good

Also present are populations of bluegills, pumpkinseeds and bullhead.

Boat Launch Sites

1. The only formal launch site on Cross Lake is Cross Lake Marina, at the north-west end of the lake, off Jordan Road. Single hard surface ramp, parking — fee.

2. Additional launch sites are available on the Seneca River, most notably Quimbey's Marina, located about one mile west of Cross Lake, on the east side of the first bridge crossing at River Road.

General Information

Cross Lake is a relatively deep, bowl-shaped body of water. The lake stratifies in the summer and there is a serious problem with oxygen depletion below 30 feet. Thus, the central portion of the lake is dominated by pelagic species, most notably white perch and white crappie, which are probably the most abundant species in Cross Lake. The shallow periphery of the lake, however, is dominated by a variety of game fish, and is strongly influenced by the influx of fish from the Seneca River.

Early in the season, there is very good fishing for large (15 lbs. and up) northern pike in the south-west corner of the lake, near the inlet. Northern pike can also be taken in the summer by slowly trolling along the weed beds on the west side of the lake with red and white Daredevles or Mepps spinners. The weed beds are located primarily south of the inlet.

In the fall, schools of walleye often congregate right in the mouth of the inlet. The fishing is good, but not great, and walleye up to 10 pounds are taken on occasion. Additional walleye fishing can be found just downstream (east) of Cross Lake in the Seneca River, at the bend known as Jack's Reef.

Channel catfish are found in good numbers in Cross Lake, but a majority of those caught are taken incidentally while fishing for other species. The best fishing for catfish is found around Big Island and Little Island. They are also found in good numbers in the inlet and outlet of Seneca River. A humid summer night is the best time to take these hard fighting and good tasting fish.

Largemouth bass are found in Cross Lake in the shallow, weedy areas. The best bass fishing is probably found in the shallow bays of the north end. Smallmouth bass are found primarily in the fall, when they congregate near the inlet.

The Department of Transportation draws Cross Lake down in the winter to such an extent that ice fishing is precluded.

NOTES: _____

_____

_____

_____

DUCK LAKE

map coordinates	43° 08' 49" 76° 41' 24"
USGS map(s)	Victory
location	Township of Conquest
access	off Duck Lake Road

Physical Characteristics

area	217 acres
shoreline	2.8 miles
elevation	396 feet
maximum depth	8 feet
mean depth	5 feet
bottom type	muck

Chemical Characteristics

water clarity	turbid
pH	neutral
oxygen	oxygen depletion is a problem on this lake, particularly in the winter.

Plant Life

Weed beds are found throughout Duck Lake.

Species Information

northern pike	common; growth rate poor
largemouth bass	common; growth rate fair
tiger muskellunge	new introduction; data not available
bullhead	abundant; growth rate poor
yellow perch	abundant; growth rate poor
bluegills	abundant; growth rate poor

Chain pickerel and black crappie have been reported here.

Boat Launch Sites

Public access is limited to the pavilion on the west side of the lake where small boats can be ramp launched.

General Information

Duck Lake is a shallow, weedy pond showing evidence of eutrophication. All of the game species found here have signs of environmental stress — poor growth rates, winter kills, etc. The recent introduction of tiger muskie into the lake will hopefully improve the future quality of fishing here. Until then, Duck Lake offers only mediocre fishing at best.

NOTES: _____

_____

_____

_____

HOWLAND ISLAND STATE WILDLIFE MANAGEMENT AREA

map coordinates	43° 05' 01" 76° 40' 45"
USGS map(s)	Montezuma
location (township)	Conquest
access	Howland Island Road
principle species	largemouth bass

The Howland Island Wildlife Management Area is composed of three units (Way-Cay, Bluff Point and Howland Island) totalling

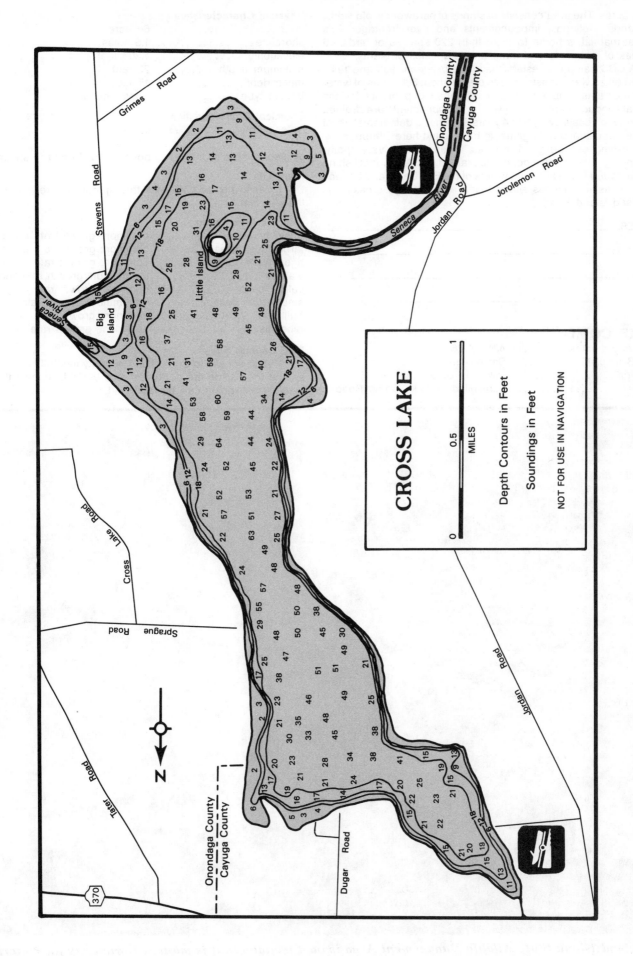

CROSS LAKE

Depth Contours in Feet

Soundings in Feet

NOT FOR USE IN NAVIGATION

MILES

0   0.5   1

3,602 acres. The area consists of stands of hardwoods, old fields, farmlands, wetlands, impoundments and river frontage. This diverse habitat is home to more than 220 species of birds, 46 species of mammals and innumerable species of plants.

A CCC camp was established here between 1933 and 1941, and 18 dikes were constructed to create about 300 acres of water impoundments. The entire area is managed primarily for the natural production of waterfowl. The impoundments are drained on a rotation basis every 3 to 4 years. This has a detrimental effect on the populations of largemouth bass found here. Although the bass fishing can be good at times, it can also be very spotty, depending upon when a pond was drained last. Additional fishing can be found in the adjacent waters of the Erie Canal and Seneca River. A fishing access site is found at the bridge crossing at Howland Island Road.

NOTES: _____

_____

_____

_____

LAKE COMO
map coordinates......... 42º 40' 26"   76º 17' 52"
USGS map(s)............. Sempronius
location................. township of Summer Hill
access.................. parallelled by Lake Como Road

Physical Characteristics
area .... 64 acres
shoreline .... 1.5 miles
elevation .... 1,309 feet
maximum depth .... 22 feet
mean depth .... 15 feet
bottom type .... gravel, muck

Chemical Characteristics
water clarity .... fair
pH .... alkaline
oxygen................... poor below 15 feet in summer

Plant Life
Extensive weed beds exist throughout the lake in depths less than 10 feet.

Species Information
chain pickerel .... common; growth rate good
largemouth bass .... common; growth rate good
tiger muskellunge......... common; growth rate good
walleye .... uncommon; growth rate very good
yellow perch .... common; growth rate poor
smallmouth bass.......... uncommon; growth rate good
bullhead .... common; growth rate fair
bluegills................. abundant; growth rate fair

Boat Launch Sites
Public access to Como Lake is pretty much limited to a site behind the bar on the northwest side of the lake, near the inlet, where small boats can be launched.

Howland Island State Wildlife Management Area is vast wetland that is managed primarily for waterfowl. Some of the impoundments have good fishing for largemouth bass. Photo courtesy of New York State DEC.

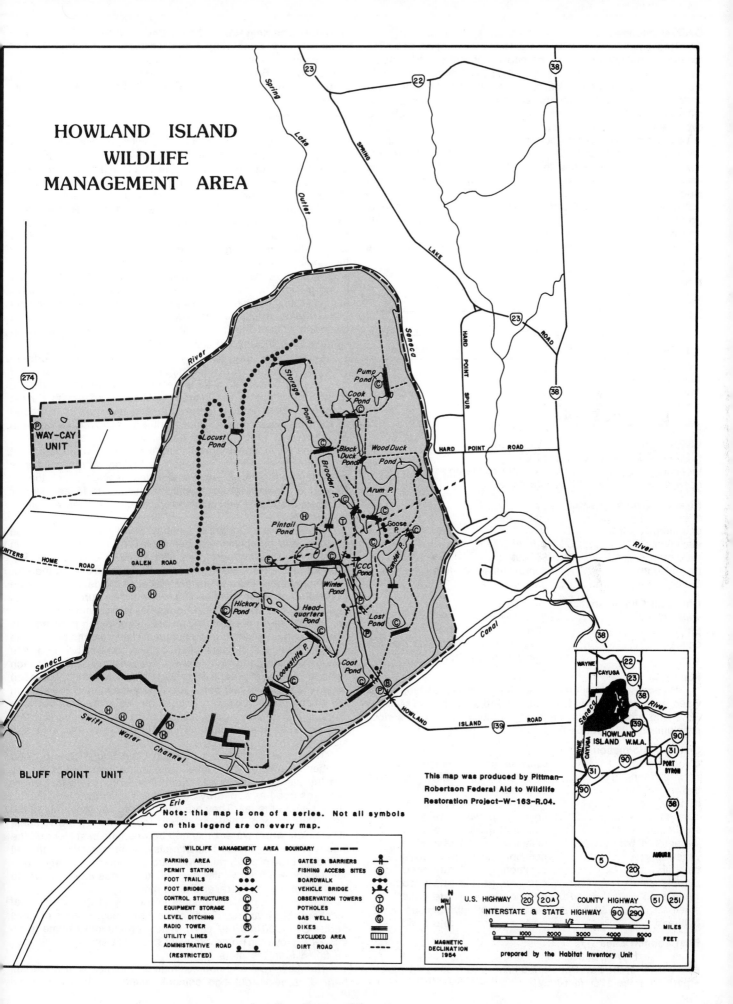

HOWLAND ISLAND WILDLIFE MANAGEMENT AREA

WAY-CAY UNIT

Pump Pond
Cook Pond
Locust Pond
Storage Pond
Black Duck Pond
Wood Duck Pond
Brooder P.
Arum P.
Pintail Pond
Goose P.
Gander P.
CCC Pond
Winter Pond
Hickory Pond
Head-quarters Pond
Lost Pond
Loosestrife P.
Coot Pond

GALEN ROAD
HUNTERS HOME ROAD
HARD POINT SPUR
HARD POINT ROAD
HOWLAND ISLAND 139 ROAD

Seneca River
Spring Lake Outlet
Seneca River
Swift Water Channel
Erie Canal

BLUFF POINT UNIT

274
23
22
38
23
38
38

Note: this map is one of a series. Not all symbols on this legend are on every map.

This map was produced by Pittman-Robertson Federal Aid to Wildlife Restoration Project-W-163-R.04.

Inset map

WAYNE
CAYUGA
22
23
38
Seneca River
39
HOWLAND ISLAND W.M.A.
90
31
PORT BYRON
31
90
90
38
AUBURN
5
20

Legend

WILDLIFE MANAGEMENT AREA BOUNDARY	— — —
PARKING AREA	(P)
PERMIT STATION	(S)
FOOT TRAILS	● ● ●
FOOT BRIDGE	✕✕✕
CONTROL STRUCTURES	(C)
EQUIPMENT STORAGE	(E)
LEVEL DITCHING	(L)
RADIO TOWER	(R)
UTILITY LINES	— ● —
ADMINISTRATIVE ROAD (RESTRICTED)	● ●
GATES & BARRIERS	
FISHING ACCESS SITES	(R)
BOARDWALK	●●●
VEHICLE BRIDGE	
OBSERVATION TOWERS	(T)
POTHOLES	(H)
GAS WELL	(G)
DIKES	
EXCLUDED AREA	▦
DIRT ROAD	— — —

N
MN
10°
MAGNETIC DECLINATION
1954

U.S. HIGHWAY 20 20A   COUNTY HIGHWAY 51 251
INTERSTATE & STATE HIGHWAY 90 290

1/2
0 1000 2000 3000 4000 5000
MILES
FEET

prepared by the Habitat Inventory Unit

General Information

This small, weedy lake has a highly developed shoreline (cottages) and offers little or no public access to the shore.

The most common species of game fish found here are chain pickerel. The average pickerel runs about 16" and larger specimens are not uncommon. Largemouth bass are the second most prevalent predator and many fish weighing 3 pounds and over are taken here each year. Tiger muskie, which are stocked in Lake Como, also do very well here. A muskie of 10 pounds is not an unusual fish, and a 29 pound muskie has been taken from this lake. Lake Como has lesser populations of walleye and smallmouth bass. The average walleye taken here averages close to 6 pounds.

In the winter, Lake Como is intensively ice fished, providing good catches of chain pickerel, yellow perch (small but plentiful) and occasionally a bonus walleye or muskie.

This lake is stocked each year with 300 tiger muskie fingerlings.

NOTES: _____

_____

_____

_____

LITTLE SODUS BAY

map coordinates	43° 20' 03" 76° 42' 32"
USGS map(s)	Fair Haven
N.O.A.A. Chart #	14803
location	township of Sterling
access	see below

Physical Characteristics

area	750 acres
shoreline	N.A.
elevation	246 feet
maximum depth	36 feet
mean depth	approximately 25 feet
bottom type	gravel, muck

Chemical Characteristics

water clarity	generally clear
ph	alkaline
oxygen	oxygen is good throughout this embayment all year long

Plant Life

Weed beds are found in waters less than 12 feet deep. Large weed beds are found in the southern end of the bay, in Meadow Cove and around Grass Island. Algae blooms are not a serious problem on Little Sodus Bay.

Species Information

chinook salmon	seasonal (fall); common
coho salmon	seasonal (spring and fall); uncommon
brown trout	seasonal (spring and fall); common
rainbow trout	seasonal (spring and fall); uncommon
northern pike	common; growth rate good
smallmouth bass	common; growth rate good
largemouth bass	common; growth rate good
yellow perch	common; growth rate good
bluegills	common; growth rate good
pumpkinseeds	common; growth rate good
white perch	common; growth rate good
smelt	seasonal (spring); common
bullhead	common; growth rate good

Boat Launch Sites

1. Fair Haven Beach State Park, off Route 104A, at north-east corner of the bay. Double width, hard surface ramp, parking - park user fee after mid-May.

2. Foot of King Road, off West Bay Road. Single hard surface ramp, parking along King Road, adjacent to Chinook Harbor Marine - no charge.

3. Foot of Bell Avenue, off Fancher Avenue. This is a steep, single hard surface ramp adjacent to Little Sodus Inn - no charge.

General Information

Little Sodus Bay provides anglers with excellent fishing for a wide variety of cold and warm water species. Largemouth bass can be found in nearly all of the shallow areas of the bay. Exceptionally good fishing for largemouth bass is found between Eldridge Point and Pearson Point, where numerous docks provide classic holding areas. Another productive area is Grass Island. The shallows around this patch of emergent weeds offer some of the best bass fishing in the bay, but caution is advised when fishing in this area. When water levels are low in the bay this shoal is very close to the surface and can be a dangerous and expensive navigational hazard. Largemouth can also be found in significant numbers in Meadow Bay. Smallmouth bass are also found in Little Sodus Bay, though they are less significant than largemouth bass. A majority of the smallmouth are taken in the north end of the bay, near the piers. These are big Lake Ontario bass that periodically enter the bay to feed.

Little Sodus Bay has an excellent population of northern pike. They don't grow quite as large as in North Sandy Pond, but they are good size fish. Like largemouth bass, northerns can be found throughout the bay in areas that have weed growth. But the most productive areas is in the south end, from Fox Point around to the Fair Haven Yacht Club. Northerns can also be taken in Meadow Bay. Many anglers have reported success in taking northerns while downrigger fishing along deep weed lines, but most northerns seem to be taken by trolling with long flatlines along the 10 foot mark. There is excellent fishing through the ice for northern pike in the south end. Fishing in 10 to 14 feet of water between Eldridge Point and the yacht club is often extremely productive.

Panfish are abundant in this bay. Shortly after ice-out large bluegills and pumpkinseeds can be taken in great numbers in Mission Bay. Yellow perch are also found in Little Sodus Bay. Most of these are Lake Ontario fish that winter-over in the bay, spawn and then return to the lake. Because it is dependant on the population of perch in Lake Ontario, which is currently depressed, the perch fishing in Little Sodus Bay is presently not as good as it has been in the past. When the yellow perch population is up, they can be taken in good numbers right from the piers in the spring. In the fall, anglers often do very well still fishing with minnows in the deep water betwen Grass Island and the launch ramp at Fair Haven Beach State Park. When the perch population is large, catches of 100 perch are not uncommon in this area. In the winter, perch are taken through the ice in the area between Grass Island and the due east shore of the bay. Other panfish that can be taken here include white perch, brown bullhead and smelt.

Trout and Salmon are taken in Little Sodus Bay in good numbers. Brown trout are taken from the northern end of the bay and the piers as late as mid-June. The fishing is good, but not nearly as good as at nearby Sodus Bay. Brown trout can also be taken here in the fall. They are found in the bay, primarily in the deep northern end. They can also be found off the piers. A plume of relatively warm water builds up between the east pier and the mouth of Sterling Creek. This attracts a great many fish in the fall including brown trout, rainbow trout, chinook salmon and coho salmon. Brown trout winter over in Little Sodus Bay and can be taken from the northern end all winter long.

Chinook salmon congregate in the bay in the fall in great numbers. They are stocked in the north-east corner of Little Sodus Bay (200,000 per year). Returning chinooks home in on this area, providing some excellent salmon fishing. They can also be taken from the piers.

Rainbow trout and coho salmon are not nearly as abundant here as brown trout and chinook salmon. They do stray on

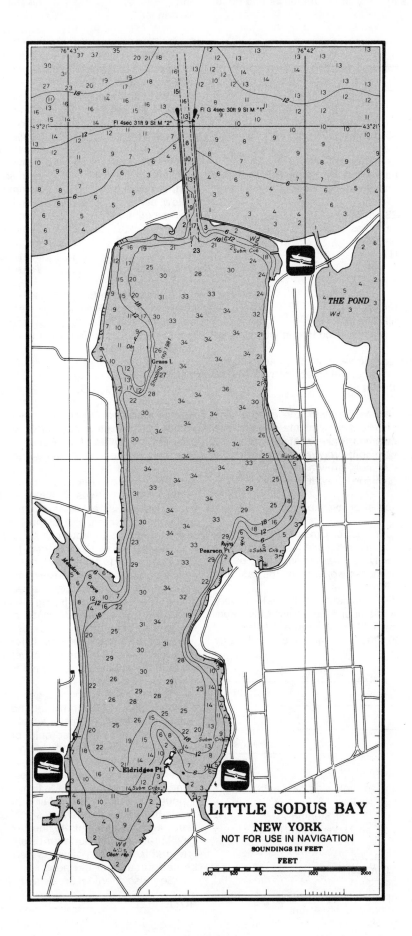

LITTLE SODUS BAY

NEW YORK

NOT FOR USE IN NAVIGATION

SOUNDINGS IN FEET

FEET

occasion into the bay, but a majority of the rainbows and coho are taken from the piers.

NOTES: _____

_____

_____

OTTER LAKE

map coordinates	43° 08′ 21″ 76° 31′ 59″
USGS map(s)	Cato
location	township of Cato
access	parallelled by Bonta Bridge Road and Short Cut Road

Physical Characteristics

area	282 acres
shoreline	3.6 miles
elevation	396 feet
maximum depth	N.A.
mean depth	5 feet
bottom type	muck

Chemical Characteristics

water clarity	turbid
ph	alkaline
oxygen	oxygen is good throughout this lake

Plant Life

This lake is rimmed with aquatic vegetation. Rooted aquatic vegetation is severely limited in the central portion of the lake due to the excessive turbidity of the water.

Species Information

largemouth bass	common; growth rate good
northern pike	common; growth rate good
walleye	common; growth rate good
bullhead	common; growth rate good
yellow perch	common; growth rate fair
bluegills	common; growth rate fair

Boat Launch Sites

There are no public launch sites available on this lake.

General Information

Otter Lake lies 3 miles northwest of Cross Lake. Approximately 40% of the shoreline is developed (cottages) and much of the remaining shoreline is low lying swampland. Thus, public access is rather poor. The best access would be on the east side of the lake, off Bonta Bridge Road.

Generally speaking, the fish population of this lake is very healthy. Largemouth bass of 4 to 5 pounds are commonly taken. Northern pike occasionally reach 10 to 12 pounds. Walleye are stocked here by the DEC (1,300,000 fry per year) and also do fairly well.

NOTES: _____

_____

_____

_____

THE POND

map coordinates	43° 20′ 29″ 76° 41′ 43″
USGS map(s)	Fair Haven
location	township of Sterling
access	via Fair Haven State Park

Physical Characteristics

area	83 acres
shoreline	3.0 miles
elevation	246 feet
maximum depth	approximately 10 feet
mean depth	approximately 4 feet
bottom type	muck

Chemical Characteristics

water clarity	clear
ph	alkaline
oxygen	oxygen is adequate all year throughout The Pond

Plant Life

The Pond has extensive beds of rooted aquatics throughout, with patches of lily pads in the bays. There are no serious problems with algae blooms here.

Species Information

chinook salmon	seasonal (fall); common
coho salmon	seasonal (fall); common
rainbow trout	seasonal (spring and fall); common
brown trout	seasonal (spring and fall); common
largemouth bass	common; growth rate good
smallmouth bass	common; growth rate good
northern pike	common; growth rate good
yellow perch	common; growth rate good
brown bullhead	common; growth rate good
bluegills	common; growth rate excellent
black crappie	uncommon; growth rate good
smelt	seasonal (spring); abundant
white perch	seasonal (spring); common

Boat Launch Sites

1. Fair Haven Beach State Park, off Route 104A. Single hard surface ramp, parking —park user fee after mid-May. Boats can be trailer launched here, but access to Lake Ontario via the mouth of The Pond is limited to small boats due to low bridge.

General Information

The Pond is also known as Sterling Pond, in reference to its main tributary, Sterling Creek. Emptying into Lake Ontario just east of Little Sodus Bay, The Pond has a good mix of cold and warm water species. Because its shallow waters are so much warmer than Lake Ontario, the effluent serves as an attractant to a number of species in the lake. A warm plume of water builds up between the mouth of the Pond and the east pier at Little Sodus Bay. This plume attracts large numbers of rainbow trout, brown trout and coho salmon in the spring. In the fall you will find the above species as well as chinook salmon. A good number of fall rainbows and browns will move into The Pond and Sterling Creek, as well as a few stray chinook. This can result in some pretty good fishing, but at present, it is highly underutilized. Lesser numbers of trout can be found here in the spring.

Other Lake Ontario species that contribute to the fishing in The Pond include smallmouth bass, brown bullhead, white perch, yellow perch and smelt. Large numbers of smallmouth bass move into The Pond to spawn, and a good number of them are usually still in The Pond or in Sterling Creek when bass season opens. Relatively few smallmouth bass are taken here, however. The spring also sees a large influx of white perch, brown bullhead, yellow perch (when their population is up) and smelt. The fishing for large, lake-run bullhead is exceptionally good throughout The Pond in the spring. Equally good is the smelt fishing right at the mouth of The Pond.

The Pond also has a good population of resident fish. Northern pike are found throughout The Pond and the lower reach of Sterling Creek, which is known as "the moat." Largemouth bass are also quite common, and can be found at least as far upstream as the McIntyre Road crossing on Sterling Valley Creek (this crossing is posted) and the crossing of Route 104A on Sterling Creek. For those who enjoy panfishing, The Pond and "the moat" provide fishing for bluegills that often reach 1 pound in weight, and a fair number of crappies.

In the winter, ice-fishing is good on The Pond, but most hard water anglers concentrate their efforts on nearby Little Sodus Bay. Ice-fishing for northern pike is very good in the north-east bay, and fair catches of yellow perch, bluegills and crappies can be had throughout the pond.

See also Sterling Creek and Sterling Valley Creek.

NOTES: _____

_____

_____

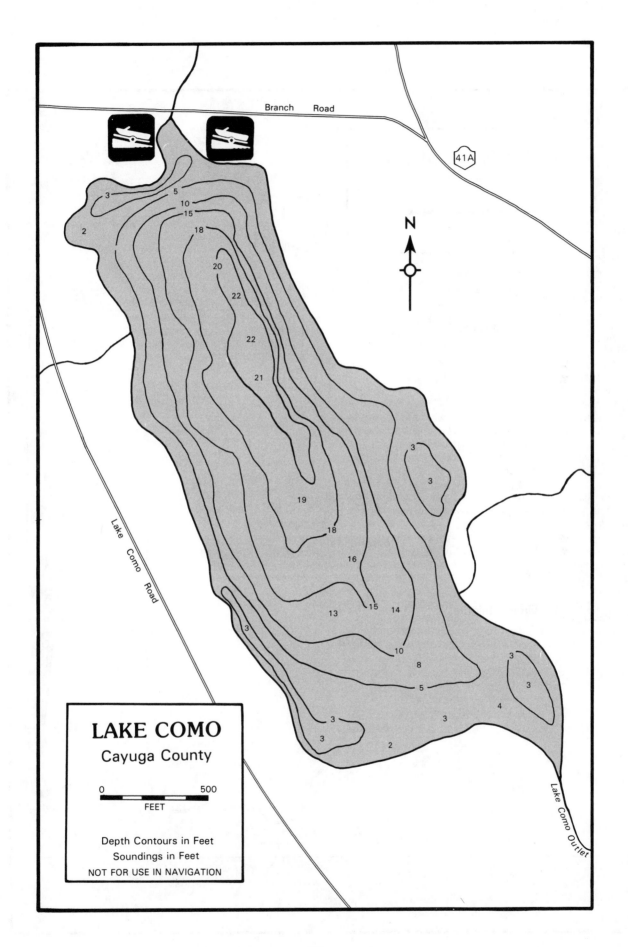

Branch   Road

41A

N

3
5
10
15
2
18
20
22
22
21

3
3

19

18

16

15   14
13
3

10
8

5

3

3

2

3
3
3
4

Lake Como Road

Lake Como Outlet

LAKE COMO

Cayuga County

0   500

FEET

Depth Contours in Feet
Soundings in Feet
NOT FOR USE IN NAVIGATION

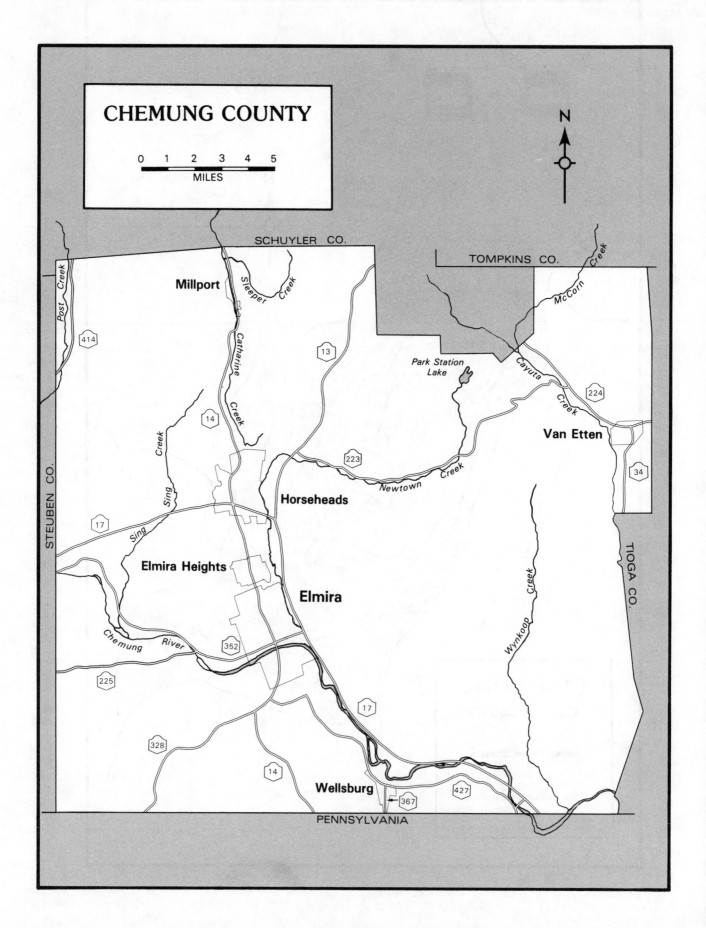

CHEMUNG COUNTY

0 1 2 3 4 5
MILES

N

SCHUYLER CO.

TOMPKINS CO.

Post Creek

Millport

Sleeper Creek

Catharine Creek

McCorn Creek

414

13

Park Station Lake

Cayuta Creek

224

Van Etten

14

STEUBEN CO.

Sing Creek

223

Newtown Creek

34

17

Sing Creek

Horseheads

Elmira Heights

Elmira

Wynkoop Creek

TIOGA CO.

Chemung River

352

225

17

328

14

Wellsburg

367

427

PENNSYLVANIA

CHEMUNG COUNTY STREAMS & RIVERS

CATHARINE CREEK - see Schuyler County streams & rivers

CAYUTA CREEK - see Tioga County streams & rivers

CHEMUNG RIVER

map coordinates.........	41° 55' 19" 76° 30' 57"
USGS map(s).............	Waverly, Wellsburg, Elmira, Seely, Caton, Corning
location (township).......	Chemung, Ashland, Elmira, Big Flats (Chemung County), Corning (Steuben County)
access...................	parallelled by Route 17 (Southern Tier Expressway) see below
principle species.........	smallmouth bass, walleye, channel catfish, rock bass, bullhead, panfish

The Chemung River is the principle warm water fishery in Chemung County. Ranging between 60 and 200 feet in width, this diverse river flows through urban and residential areas, farmlands and a scenic valley.

Combining the waters of several major rivers (the Cohocton, Tioga and Canisteo), the Chemung River has a gravel and rubble bottom, with some areas of siltation, extensive streamside vegetation, numerous deep runs and a significant amount of aquatic vegetation in the deeper pools. Although the water quality is generally quite good, water releases from the Tioga-Hammond and Cowanesque Dams do cause some turbidity. These releases also cause moderate fluctuations in water levels which can be dangerous to wading fishermen.

The most numerous game fish in the Chemung River is the smallmouth bass. They can be found in nearly every environment of the river, from deep pools to shallow riffles. Smallmouth hot spots include: The Bottcher's Landing area; the stretch of river above the Walnut Street Bridge in Elmira; and the Wellsburg-Lowman Crossover area. You might also find it worthwhile to check out the mouth's of some of the tributaries of the Chemung River, such as Wyncoop Creek, Sing Sing Creek and Newton Creek. Most will hold modest numbers of feisty smallmouth.

The most commonly used baits for Chemung smallmouth are Tony's Dobsons, Mister Twisters, Rapalas and worms. Recently there has been an increase in the popularity of fly fishing for bass on this river. The heads and tails of riffles appear to be the productive areas. Most local fly fishermen are doing well using fairly large hair-bodied flies or streamers. Chuck Annis, a local outdoorsman, and the source for much of the information in this article, reports good success using a deer hair mouse.

One heartening aspect of the Chemung River is the development over the past decade of a strong walleye fishery. Walleye certainly are not new to this river. The current state record (15 lbs. 3 oz.) was taken from the Chemung in 1952. But they were in decline for a long time. They are not nearly as numerous as smallmouth, but their numbers are good and definitely on the way up. The walleye are currently running 16-20 inches, but fish of 7-8 lbs. are taken on occasion. The fishing for walleye here is best in the spring and the fall. Local hot spots include: The Patterson Bridge area, just west of Corning; just below the dam in downtown Elmira; and near the state line just west of Waverly. As with bass, jigs, Rapalas, and worms are popular local baits. Rounding out the available fish found in the Chemung River are the ubiquitous rock bass, an occasional largemouth bass, which are found in limited numbers in some of the larger back-eddies and slack-water areas, channel catfish, a fairly new arrival, some of which are tipping the scales at 12 lbs., and bullhead, a spring time favorite.

Formal access to the Chemung River is limited, but the situation is improving. The state has recently completed a launch site on the south bank of the river, off Mossy Glen Road, just south of the village of South Corning. The Chemung County Federation

Smallmouth bass are the most abundant game fish in the Chemung River and can be found in almost every environment the river has to offer. They hit well on traditional bass hardware, as well as on large hair-bodied flies and streamers. Photo courtesy J. Michael Kelly.

of Sportsmen has developed three launch sites. They are located as follows: At Bottcher's Landing, off Route 352, on Corning Road; Fitches Bridge launch site, off Route 352, on Hendy Creek Road; and at the White Wagon Bridge, off the end of County Road 56, in Chemung. All four of the above listed sights are designed for car-top boats and canoes. The Chemung River is too shallow for the safe navigation of larger vessels. Additional access can be found at Dennison Park, off Route 225, in Corning, and at Brand Park, off Maple Avenue in Elmira. Because posting is minimal on this river, informal access can also be found at numerous road crossings.

The Chemung River is not stocked.

NOTES: _____

_____

_____

_____

McCORN CREEK

map coordinates.........	42° 15' 33" 76° 37' 31"
USGS map(s).............	Alpine, West Danby
location (township).......	Cayuta (Schuyler County), Van Etten, (Chemung County)
access...................	there are extensive areas of public fishing rights on this creek in the lower end (9/10 miles). This section is accessible via an old jeep trail off Decker Road near Jackson Road.
principle species.........	brown trout (wild)

This creek is a secondary tributary of Cayuta Creek. Averaging ten feet in width, with a gravel and rubble bottom, good bank cover and excellent water quality, McCorn Creek flows through a totally isolated area. Fishable all season long, there are good numbers of wild brown trout throughout its length, but there is some posting in the upper reaches.

McCorn Creek is not stocked.

NOTES: _____

_____

_____

_____

NEWTON CREEK

map coordinates	42° 05′ 10″ 76° 46′ 51″
USGS map(s)	Elmira, Horseheads, Erin
location (township)	Elmira, Horseheads, Erin
access	Latta Road, off South Main Street in Horseheads
principle species	brown trout (stocked), smallmouth bass

The section of this stream that is stocked with brown trout is in the vicinity of the town of Horseheads. The upper reaches of Newton Creek go dry in the summer and the lower portions give way to a limited fishery for smallmouth bass that migrate in from the Chemung River. the trout section is 20-30 feet wide, with a gravel/rubble bottom and good bank cover. Primarily a spring fishery, this stream is stocked with 1,400 brown trout each spring in the 1.5 mile section immediately below Route 17.

NOTES: _____

_____

_____

_____

POST CREEK - see Steuben County streams & rivers

SING SING CREEK

map coordinates	42° 05′ 47″ 76° 55′ 14″
USGS map(s)	Seeley Creek, Big Flats, Beaver Dams
location (township)	Big Flats, Catlin
access	parallelled by Carpenter Road and and crossed by Sing Sing Road, just east of Whitney Cemetary
principle species	brown trout (stocked & wild)

Except for the very lowest reaches, this stream is a good quality brown trout stream. Sing Sing Creek averages fifteen to twenty feet in width, has a gravel and rubble bottom and good bank cover. It flows through a partially developed valley and some sections are posted. The uppermost reaches of Sing Sing Creek provide a moderate fishery for wild brown trout. Just below Route 17, Sing Sing Creek gets a good shot of cold water from a spring-fed pond. This results in some pretty good trout fishing in the stretch immediately down stream of the expressway.

In the spring a 2.4 mile section of Sing Sing Creek below Route 17 is stocked with 1,340 brown trout yearlings. The extreme lower reaches of this creek has a fair population of smallmouth bass that move up from the Chemung River.

NOTES: _____

_____

_____

SLEEPER CREEK

map coordinates	42° 17′ 11″ 76° 50′ 38″
USGS map(s)	Montour Falls
location (township)	Veteran
access	road crossing at Route 14, north of Millport
principle species	rainbow trout (wild)

Sleeper Creek is the most notable tributary of Catharine Creek (see Schuyler County) in Chemung County. This stream averages about ten feet in width, has a gravel and rubble bottom, good bank cover and very good water quality.

In the spring, Sleeper Creek gets a good influx of wild rainbows from Catharine Creek.

This stream is not stocked.

NOTES: _____

_____

_____

_____

WYNKOOP CREEK

map coordinates	42° 00′ 07″ 76° 35′ 41″
USGS map(s)	Waverly, Wellsburg, Van Etten
location (township)	Chemung, Baldwin, Erin
access	roughly parallelled by Wyncoop Creek Road
principle species	brown trout (stocked & wild)

Wyncoop Creek is a mediocre trout stream that gives every indication of improving in quality. A meandering, riffle-pool type stream, Wyncoop flows through a developed valley and is surrounded by residential areas and farmlands. It averages fifteen to twenty feet in width, has a gravel and rubble bottom and generally good bank cover.

A recent (1985) D.E.C. survey of Wyncoop Creek indicated that the population of wild brown trout was increasing, and wild fish can now be found scattered throughout the stream. This development has caused the D.E.C. to lower the number of fish being stocked here. In the spring this stream is now being stocked with 400 brown trout yearlings, between Thayer Road and Porter Hill Road.

NOTES: _____

_____

_____

_____

A well tied YELLOW STONE FLY is very effective when fished in riffles and rocky runs.

CHEMUNG COUNTY LAKES & PONDS

PARK STATION LAKE

map coordinates..........	42° 09' 17" 76° 43' 27"
USGS map(s)	Erin
location (township).......	Erin
access	off Park Station Road

Physical Characteristics

area	100 acres
shoreline	1 mile
elevation	1145 feet
maximum depth	25 feet
mean depth	10 feet
bottom type	muck, gravel

Chemical Characteristics

water clarity.............	often some turbidity due to algae
pH......................	alkaline
oxygen..................	oxygen appears to be good throughout this lake all year long

Plant Life

Extensive weed beds are found in the shallower areas of the lake. Algae blooms occur periodically, causing some turbidity.

Species Information

rainbow trout.............	common; growth rate not available
largemouth bass	common; growth rate good
yellow perch	common; growth rate fair
chain pickerel	common; growth rate fair
black crappie.............	common; growth rate fair
brown bullhead..........	common; growth rate good

Boat Launch Sites

1. A gravel ramp is found on the north side of the lake. A boating permit is required (free) and can be obtained at the park's office, 217 Madison Avenue, Elmira, New York 14902. Row boats and paddle boats can be rented at the lake. Motors are not allowed.

For current regulations, contact the park at (607) 739-9164 or (607) 737-2907.

General Information

The following information was contributed by Chuck Annis, of Elmira, New York.

"Park Station Lake is approximately 100 acres in size. It was constructed as part of the Newtown-Hoffman Creek Watershed Project. It was developed as a recreation area with boating, camping, swimming, hiking and picnic facilities.

"Park Station Lake has been developed as a fishery thanks to the Chemung County Federation of Sportsmen. The federation has stocked largemouth bass, yellow perch, crappies, and rainbow trout in the lake. A two story fishery has developed with the lake supporting both warm and cold water species. After two years of angler surveys, both the Chemung County Federation and the Catharine Creek Chapter of Trout Unlimited gathered enough information to convince the DEC that the trout stocked were "holding over." After studying the water chemistry the DEC agreed to develop a stocking policy for the lake. Park Station Lake will begin receiving 1840 rainbow trout yearlings in the spring of 1987. Park Station Lake has also received spent breeder rainbow trout in the past.

"If you plan on fishing at Park Station Lake, watch your regulation book this fall. Trout Unlimited and the Chemung County Federation of Sportsmen have proposed a regulation change that should be in effect in the fall of 1987. The regulation change would open the trout season to year round and establish a five fish limit. This was done to allow ice fishing in the lake which is currently not allowed.

"Trout are not the only species doing well in this lake. Yellow perch, crappies, bullhead and often panfish are abundant. The largemouth bass population is doing well with bass in the 3 to 4 pound range being caught fairly regularly.

"Park Station Lake is the only lake in Chemung County of any size and is rapidly becoming a favorite fishing spot."

NOTES: _____

_____

_____

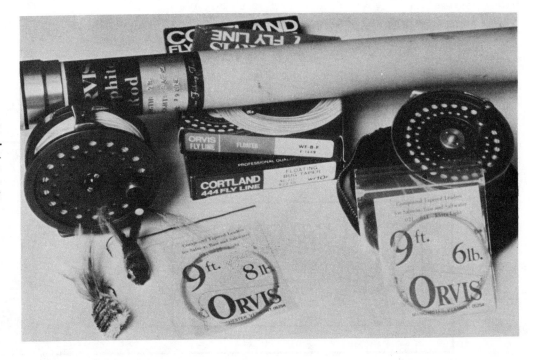

Fly fishing is not restricted to trout streams. The equipment shown at left is designed for bass fishing. The fly rods are designed for casting large poppers and flies.

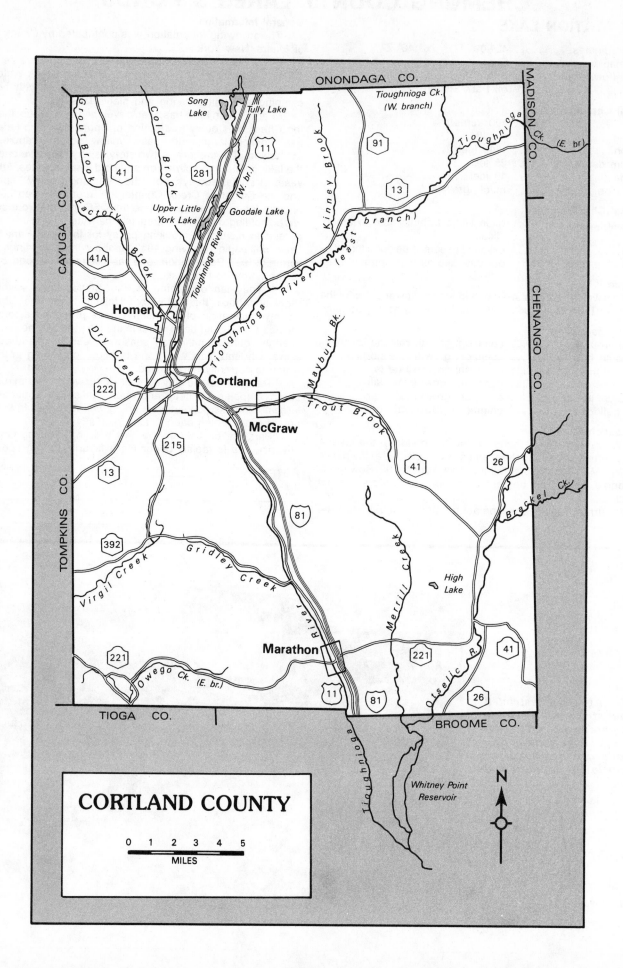

ONONDAGA CO.

Tioughnioga Ck.
(W. branch)

Grout Brook

Song
Lake

Tully Lake

Cold Brook

Tioughnioga Ck. (E. br)

MADISON CO.

41

281

11

91

Kinney Brook

13

Tioughnioga River (W. br.)

(east branch)

Tioughnioga

CAYUGA CO.

Factory Brook

Upper Little
York Lake

Goodale Lake

41A

90

Homer

Tioughnioga River

Dry Creek

222

Cortland

Maybury Bk.

Trout Brook

McGraw

CHENANGO CO.

215

13

41

26

81

Brackel Ck.

392

Virgil Creek

Gridley Creek

Merrill Creek

High
Lake

TOMPKINS CO.

221

Marathon

221

41

River

11

81

Otselic R.

26

TIOGA CO.

BROOME CO.

Tioughnioga

N

Whitney Point
Reservoir

CORTLAND COUNTY

0 1 2 3 4 5
MILES

CORTLAND COUNTY STREAMS AND RIVERS

BRACKEL CREEK

map coordinates	42° 31 49" 75° 54' 12"
USGS map(s)	Cincinnatus, Pitcher, East Pharsalia
location (township)	Cincinnatus (Cortland County), German, Pitcher, Pharsalia (Chenengo County)
access	roughly parallelled by Brackel Road
principle species	brook trout (stocked & wild)

Flowing through farmlands from the village of Lower Cincinnatus upstream to its headwaters near the Pharsalia Wildlife Management Area, Brackel Creek is a small, medium quality trout stream. It is a gravel and rubble bottomed stream with alternating brush-lined and exposed banks. The water is clear, and summer flows are generally good, making Brackel Creek fishable all season. It would not be considered a fly fishing stream.

There is a good population of wild brook trout in this stream, which is augmented by a number of small (3 to 4 foot) tributaries that also hold brookies. There are also stocked fish in Brackel Creek. The stream is stocked in the fall from Cincinnatus Road in Cortland County upstream 3.3 miles to County Road 12 in Chenengo County with 700 brook trout fingerlings.

This stream is not heavily posted (most of the posting in Chenengo County is against deer hunting, not fishing), and it receives only light fishing pressure.

NOTES: _____

_____

_____

_____

COLD BROOK

map coordinates	42° 40' 50" 76° 09' 54"
USGS map(s)	Homer, Otisco Valley
location (township)	Homer, Scott
access	parallelled by Cold Brook Road
principle species	brown trout (stocked), brook trout (wild)

The quality of fishing in Cold Brook's 8.6 miles of trout water is mediocre at best, and the best section is posted. Averaging 10 to 12 feet in width, this gravel bottomed stream has very poor bank cover and very low water levels in summer. The lower reaches go nearly dry in some summers, making Cold Brook fishable only in the spring.

This is not a fly fishing stream. Live baits and small spinners offer the best chances for taking the brown trout that are found in the lower reaches of Cold Brook, and the brook trout that are found in the reaches above the crossing at Long Road. Fishing pressure on this stream is very light, and it would be worth investigating if you are in the area, but it is not worth a special trip.

In the fall, Cold Brook is stocked with 1,000 brown trout fingerlings, from the first crossing of Cold Brook Road, going north out of Pratt Corners, upstream to just north of the hamlet of East Scott, a distance of 2.5 miles.

NOTES: _____

_____

_____

DRY CREEK

map coordinates	42° 36' 35" 76° 10' 55"
USGS map(s)	Cortland, Homer, Sempronius
location (township)	Cortlandville, Homer
access	roughly parallelled by Kinney Gulf Road
principle species	brook trout (stocked)

Dry Creek is a very small (8 to 10 feet wide) tributary of the west branch of the Tioughnioga River, which it enters at Cortland. The name is appropriate, for the lower one-mile section of this stream goes nearly dry in summer. There is some brush along Dry Creek, but the banks are generally exposed. It gets very little fishing pressure and is too small for fly fishing.

In the fall, 300 brook trout fingerlings are stocked in a 1.8 mile section of the creek, just above crossing at Sweeny Road, near its junction with Kinney Gulf Road.

NOTES: _____

_____

_____

_____

FACTORY BROOK

map coordinates	42° 38' 31" 76° 10' 31"
USGS map(s)	Homer, Sempronius
location (township)	Homer, Scott
access	crossed by Route 41 north of Homer; see below
principle species	brook trout (wild), brown trout (wild)

Though small and heavily fished, Factory Brook certainly rates as Cortland County's premier trout stream. Slightly over seven miles long, this small (average width - 12 feet) gravel and rubble bottomed stream flows primarily through open fields, emptying into the west branch of the Tioughnioga River in Cortland. Its cold, high quality water has a constant, even flow all year long, making it fishable all trout season. It takes an extremely hard rain to muddy the waters of Factory Brook.

Factory Brook is managed by the Conservation Department as a wild trout stream. While brook trout predominate in the upper reaches (this stream is fishable right up into its headwaters) and brown trout in the lower reaches, both are found throughout Factory Brook in very good numbers. Indicative of the number of trout in this stream, one angler recently took 38 browns and brookies in an evening, and many of these were fish over 12 inches.

Because there is little bank cover on some sections, it is very fly fishable. The stream is noted for its mayfly and caddisfly hatches. The angler mentioned above strongly recommended using a pale evening dun (38 fish make for a very persuasive argument).

As of 1986, the Department of Environmental Conservation had 2.29 miles of public fishing rights secured along Factory Brook, as well as two public right-of-ways, making this a very easily accessed stream. Be sure to watch for signs indicating public use areas, as some sections are posted against fishing.

Factory Brook is not stocked.

NOTES: _____

_____

_____

_____

Much of Factory Brook can be fly fished, but this stretch, off Route 41 in Homer, is worm drifting water. Fishable all trout season, Factory Brook is Cortland County's premier wild trout stream. Brook trout are found in the upper reaches of the stream, while brown trout predominate in the lower end.

A major tributary of Skaneateles Lake, Grout Brook is a small, gravel and rubble bottomed stream averaging about twelve feet in width. Slightly over six miles long, it flows primarily through farmlands and has alternating open and brush lined banks. Although it has a fairly constant year round flow of cold, high quality water, there is no significant summer fishery in this stream.

Grout Brook is renowned for its spring run of adult wild rainbow trout from Skaneateles Lake. The rainbows generally run small in this stream; A fish of 20 inches is considered large, but they are plentiful and will run right up into the headwaters of the stream. There is a lesser run of smaller, primarily male rainbows, in the fall, and every couple of years a minor run of wild landlocked salmon also takes place in the fall. On occasion you might take a brown trout or brook trout from Grout Brook, but they do not contribute much to the fishery. Rounding out the angling opportunities, chain pickerel can be taken in the very lowest reaches of this stream, especially in June and July.

For the most part, Grout Brook is too small for fly fishing. Drifting salmon eggs on the bottom is a proven technique for taking the hard fighting rainbows found here.

Because of the intense amount of use that this stream gets during the spring trout run, the state conservation department has purchased 1.86 miles of public fishing rights on Grout brook. To further facilitate access, the state has also purchased three fisherman parking areas, two of which are currently developed. One is located on Glen Haven Road, about one-fifth of a mile west of Route 41 near the hamlet of Scott. The second is also located on Glen Haven Road, approximately 100 yards north of Sweeny Hill Road.

Grout Brook is not stocked.

NOTES: _____

_____

_____

_____

GRIDLEY CREEK

map coordinates	42° 29' 25" 76° 04' 21"
USGS map(s)	Marathon, McGraw, Cortland
location (township)	Virgil
access	parallelled by Route 392 west of Messingerville
principle species	brook trout (stocked)

Gridley Creek is a mediocre quality, rubble-bottomed brook trout stream. Averaging 10 - 12 feet in width, it flows through a deep, scenic gorge, and some sections can be fly fished. The principle source of water for this stream is surface runoff, and in very dry summers portion of Gridley Creek can go completely dry. Spring and fall are thus your best times to fish for brookies here.

In the fall, a five-mile section of Gridley Creek, from the mouth of tributary #3 in the village of East Virgil, upstream to the mouth of tributary #8, one-half mile above the Page Green Road crossing, is stocked with approximately 900 brook trout fingerlings.

NOTES: _____

_____

_____

_____

KINNEY BROOK

map coordinates	42° 41' 53" 76° 02' 26"
USGS map(s)	Truxton, Tully
location (township)	Truxton
access	Foster Road crossing
principle species	brook trout (stocked)

Kinney Brook, known also as Wescott Brook, is a very small, brush lined, gravel bottomed trout stream, averaging about eight feet in width. Although over six miles long, only the middle section is trout water, and this provides essentially a put and take fishery in the spring. There are some small pools that hold an occasional wild fish, but fly fishing would not really be feasible here.

In the fall, Kinney Brook is stocked with 600 brook trout fingerlings, from tributary #2, located about three-fifths of a mile below the crossing of Foster Road, upstream 2 miles to the mouth of tributary #3, located about one-half mile upstream of the Truxton-Tully Hill Road crossing.

NOTES: _____

_____

_____

_____

GROUT BROOK

map coordinates	42° 45' 52" 76° 16 23"
USGS map(s)	Spafford, Sempronius, Homer, Otisco Valley
location (township)	Scott
access	Glen Haven Road - see below
principle species	rainbow trout (wild), landlocked salmon (wild), chain pickerel

If the trout stream you planned to fish is too high or muddy due to recent rains, try fishing the upper reaches of the stream or one of its tributaries. These waters usually clear up first.

Mike Kelly holds a 19 inch rainbow trout that he coaxed from Grout Brook. This stream is renownded for its spring runs of rainbows from Skaneateles Lake. A lesser run also occurs in the fall. Most of these fish will be a bit on the small side for lake run rainbows, but they're plentiful and can be found the entire length of the stream. Grout Brook also has a minor run of landlocked salmon in the fall.

MAYBURY BROOK

map coordinates	42° 35' 54" 76° 03' 45"
USGS map(s)	McGraw, Truxton
location (township)	Solon
access	parallelled by Maybury Road
principle species	brook trout (stocked & wild)

A tributary of Trout Brook, this is a very small (4 - 6 feet wide) gravel and rubble-bottomed stream. But do not let the size fool you. This stream has a very respectable population of beautifully colored wild brook trout, especially in its upper reaches. The stream is open in the upper section and has intermittant bank cover in the lower sections. Maybury Brook might be a bit too small for fly fishing, but bait and spinners are both productive methods here.

In the fall, this stream is stocked with 300 brook trout fingerlings, from the crossing at Route 41 upstream one mile to Widger Road.

NOTES: _____
_____
_____
_____

MERRILL CREEK

map coordinates	42° 24' 09" 75° 58' 18"
USGS map(s)	Willet, Cincinnatus, McGraw
location (township)	Marathon, Freetown (Cortland County), Triangle (Broome County)
access	brook trout (wild), brown trout (stocked)

Emptying into the Otselic River near the Whitney Point Reservoir in Broome County, Merrill Creek is a long (10.9 miles), gravel-bottomed, fair quality trout stream that suffers somewhat from temperatures that are a bit on the warm side. Its brush-lined banks abutt mainly to farmlands. Averaging fifteen feet in width, Merrill Creek has a fairly constant flow of water in the summer and should be fishable all season.

Merrill Creek has a good population of wild brook trout, stocked brown trout and lots of shiners. Trout up to eighteen inches are taken here each year. Fly fishing would be very difficult on this stream, so be sure to have spinners or bait with you. The fishing pressure on Merrill Creek is very light.

In the spring a 3.9 mile section of Merrill Creek is stocked with 800 brown trout yearlings, from its mouth upstream to the crossing at Route 221. In the fall, another 300 brown trout fingerlings are stocked in the one-mile section just above Route 221.

NOTES: _____
_____
_____
_____

OTSELIC RIVER - (Chenengo County line to Whitney Point Reservoir)

map coordinates	42° 19' 50" 75° 57' 57"
USGS map(s)	Whitney Point, Willet, Cincinnatus, Pitcher
access	roughly parallelled by Route 26 from Whitney Point Reservoir to the Chenengo County line - see below
principle species	brown trout (stocked & wild), brook trout (wild), walleye, northern pike, smallmouth bass, panfish

Approximately 15 miles of the Otselic River are located in Cortland County. This portion of the river averages sixty feet in width, has a gravel and silt bottom and a good year-round flow. Due to mild seasonal flooding, much of the river lacks any significant bank cover. The lower Otselic River flows through farmland and small hamlets.

The hamlet of Lower Cincinnatus marks the division of cold and warm water habitats in the Otselic River. Above the hamlet, in fact right to the headwaters in Madison County, the river is a good brown trout stream. Wild brook trout are also found throughout this portion of the river, and many of its tributaries, especially those in Chenengo County, have good populations of small, wild brookies. Fly fishing is definitely an option on this river (there is a good hatch of Stenonema Vicarium here in early April) but salted minnows are more often the choice of local anglers for taking brown and brook trout from the Otselic.

Below Lower Cincinnatus the river begins to warm and non-trout species begin to make up a significant portion of the fishery, primarily smallmouth bass and northern pike (there are some smallmouth above Cincinnatus). By the time the Otselic River flows through Willet, these species predominate. Worms, drifted crabs and #1 gold spinners are most commonly used for smallmouth. Spinners, light spoons, and jigs should all be productive for northern pike, some of which tip the scale at 20 pounds. Further down stream, near the Whitney Point Reservoir, smallmouth bass still predominate, but walleye can be found in some of the larger pools (there is a spawning run of walleye out of the reservoir into the river). A few largemouth bass are also taken on occasion, and a local hot spot for smallmouth bass and bullhead is found at the mouth of Merrill Creek.

Below the Whitney Point Reservoir, the river flows for about one mile before emptying into the Tioughnioga River. This short stretch of the Otselic has an excellent population of walleye. These fish average 16 inches and fish up to 10 pounds are taken every year. There are also numerous northern pike and smallmouth bass. In the pool below the dam you find large numbers of northern pike, white crappies (escapees from the reservoir) and a few perch and bullhead.

The Otselic River is ideally suited to canoes and cartop boats. Access to the lower river is generally good. It is parallelled by Route 26, but the road is rather far from the river in many places, making the launching of even small cartop boats difficult except at bridge crossings.

There are three convenient launch sites. The first is found on Landers Corners Road, approximately one-half mile west of Route 26 in Willet (parking for 7 cars, hand launch). Further downstream, at Upper Lisle, there is a good hand launch site at the Hemlock Road bridge crossing, in the Whitney Point Multiple Use Area. Lastly, a hard-surface ramp is available at Dorchester Park on Whitney Point Reservoir (boats are limited to 7.5 hp).

An overwhelming majority of this river is on state or federal property. The state has acquired 6.4 miles of public fishing rights on the Cortland County portion of the Otselic above Cincinnatus. Most of the river below Cincinnatus is on property owned by the Army Corp of Engineers. It is used as a flood control project (thus the reservoir) and the surrounding property is leased to the state as a wildlife managment area and is open to recreational purposes. Be aware that some of this property is sublet by the state to local farmers.

Between March and May a 4.1 mile section of the Otselic River in Cortland County is stocked with 4,300 brown trout yearlings, from the mouth of Brackel Creek near Lower Cincinnatus, upstream to the mouth of Mud Creek near the village of Pitcher.

NOTES: _____
_____
_____
_____

OWEGO CREEK (east branch) - see Tioga County Streams & Rivers

TIOUGHNIOGA RIVER (main stream)

map coordinates	42° 14' 12" 75° 50' 36"
USGS map(s)	Chenengo Forks, Greene, Whitney Point, Lisle, Marathon, McGraw, Cortland
location (township)	Baker, Triangle, Lisle (Broome County), Marathon, Lapeer, Virgil, Cortlandville (Cortland County)
access	parallelled by Route 11 between the city of Cortland and the village of Lisle-see below
principle species	brown trout (stocked), rainbow trout (stocked), smallmouth bass, walleye, northern pike, bullhead, chain pickerel, panfish

The main stream of the Tioughnioga River flows from the city of Cortland down to Chenengo Forks in Broome County, a distance of 35 miles, where it empties into the Chenengo River. The average width of the river in Cortland County is 75-80 feet, and up to 100 feet in the Broome County portion. The bottom runs the gamut from gravel and rubble to heavily silted areas. There is a good constant flow all year long. Though the water is generally slow moving and turbid, some stretches between Blodgett Mills and Messengerville are listed as intermediate class canoeing water, so care should be taken when considering using a small boat or canoe here. This is especially true during the spring when run off waters cause mild seasonal flooding on the Tioughnioga.

An important aspect of the Tioughnioga River, at least to this angler, is the scenery. It ranges from residential and farmland to near wilderness. The gorge through which much of the river flows was formed by glacial melt waters at the end of the last ice age. The resulting narrow, steep-sided ravine is crowned with mature hardwoods giving the lower portions of the river a character usually found only in vastly more remote areas.

The type of fishing found in the Tioughnioga is as diverse as the surroundings through which it flows. Because of the input of sewage, the fishing between Cortland and Blodgett Mills is rather poor, but below Blodgett Mills the quality picks up. It is not unusual to find brown trout, rainbow trout, bass, pickerel, walleye and northern pike all inhabiting the same large, deep pool. There are a number of pools where a 7 pound brown trout is as likely to be taken on a spinner or drifted worm as an 8 pound walleye is. An example of such a honey hole is Hoxie Gorge pool, 2 miles below Blodgett Mills, off Route 11.

Further downstream, between Messengerville and Marathon, the water quality continues to improve, as does the fishing. Pools are also more frequent in this stretch of the river. (note: it should be pointed out that the term "water quality" is relative. Throughout most of the Tioughnioga River the fish are tainted with a pollutant of undetermined origin; it could be man made or from a natural source. The D.E.C. is currently studying this problem. The fish caught here have a noticeable smell and flavor similar to kerosene, and this has resulted in the D.E.C. reducing the number of fish stocked in the river).

Wild trout are rare in the Tioughnioga River, but the Cortland County portion of the river is stocked. In the spring, 1,800 brown trout and 1,100 rainbow trout are stocked in a 4.5 mile stretch of river, from the mouth of Hunts Creek in Marathon, upstream to the mouth of Gridley Creek, near Messengerville.

The Cortland County portion of this river gets only moderate pressure from anglers. While most of the locals rely on jigs, spinners and live baits, fly fishing is certainly a viable option, especially on some of the larger pools.

Shortly below Marathon, the Tioughnioga enters Broome County. From the county line to its junction with the Chenengo River, with the exception of the dredged section in the village of Whitney Point, this is an excellent quality warm water fishery. There are numerous, well defined riffs and pools good for drift fishing (you might have to do a bit of canoe dragging in some of the shallower stretches). Throughout this lower section is found a good mixture of walleye, smallmouth bass, panfish and bullhead. On occasion some of the pools give up northern pike. Some of the more productive reaches include: Killawog to Lisle; Whitney Point to Itasca, (very good for walleye and bullhead); and at the mouth of the Otselic River in Whitney Point, (good for walleye, smallmouth bass and some northern pike).

Access to the Tioughnioga River is facilitated by the parallelling, for most of its length, of Route 11. In addition, there are 3.97 miles of public fishing areas located on the Cortland County section. Its parallelled by Route 70 between Lisle and Chenengo Forks in Broome County. This is an excellent river for drift fishing, and for those who choose to fish from a canoe or cartop boat, access can be found at numerous bridges found all along this river.

NOTES: _____

_____

_____

_____

TIOUGHNIOGA RIVER (east branch)

map coordinates	42° 36' 15" 76° 09' 33"
USGS map(s)	Cortland, Homer, Truxton, Cuyler, Erieville
location (township)	Cortlandville, Homer, Truxton (Cortland County), De Ruyter (Madison County)
access	parallelled and crossed by Route 13 between Cortland and De Ruyter
principle species	smallmouth bass, walleye, pickerel, largemouth bass, northern pike, brown trout (stocked), brook trout (stocked), pan fish

Originating in southwestern Madison County, the east branch of the Tioughnioga River is a long and diverse waterway offering a wide variety of angling opportunities.

The village of Truxton is a convenient point to divide this stream into cold and warm water habitats. From its mouth in the city of Cortland, upstream to Truxton, the east branch of the Tioughnioga River is a good quality warm water stream averaging about 50 feet in width. It has a good constant flow of slightly turbid water (due to clay and algae) over a bottom of silt and gravel. The stream flows primarily through farmlands and is generally lined with brush and mature hardwoods. There is a significant amount of rooted aquatic vegetation, especially in the many deep, slow moving stretches.

The lower most reaches of the east branch provide good fishing for smallmouth bass, pickerel and pan fish. Brown trout can also be taken from this section of the stream, and while not at all uncommon, the brown trout that are taken are often "lunkers". With the exception of brown trout, all of the above mentioned species of fish can also be found, in varying degrees of availability, above the village of East Homer. But they must compete with walleye, largemouth bass and northern pike, which find good habitat in the deep, slow moving sections found between East Homer and Truxton. The northern pike fishing is very good in this reach and fish of 8 to 10 pounds are not uncommon.

While warm water species predominate in the middle reaches of the stream, some very fine trout fishing can be found in the south flowing tributaries that feed this section of the east branch. Streams such as Haights Gulf Creek, Albright Creek, Wescott Creek, Morgan Hill Creek and Tripoli Creek are all small, high quality tributaries that hold impressive numbers of wild brook and brown trout. Chenengo creek, a major north flowing tributary that joins the east branch of the Tioughnioga River three miles south of Truxton, also has some excellent brook trout fishing in its upper most reaches.

As you move upstream toward the village of Truxton, trout begin to dominate the stream. The further upstream you go, the better the trout fishing gets. Brown trout are the principle species, but brook trout can be found in the Madison County sections. The stream is sufficiently open above Truxton to allow for fly fishing, and both dry and wet flies should be quite productive. Be prepared for more than a minor test of your angling abilities when fishing in the Cuyler area. There are several deep, meandering pools in that area that hold some very large, very feisty brown trout.

With the possible exception of the very headwaters of the stream, wild trout are rare, if not completely absent from the east branch. Large portions of the stream, however, are heavily stocked with trout, as are several of its tributaries. The lower 7.1 miles of the stream, from its mouth upstream to the mouth of Trout Brook, is stocked with 6,600 brown trout yearlings each spring. From the mouth of Trout Brook upstream to the road crossing at Crains Mills Road, the east branch of the Tioughnioga is too warm to support a trout population and, therefore, is not stocked. Between Crains Mills Road and the crossing of Route 13 at Cuyler, a distance of three miles, the stream is stocked in the spring with 2,800 brown trout yearlings. In the Madison County portion, brown and brook trout are stocked in tributaries that act as nursery streams for the east branch of the Tioughnioga River.

There is no formal public access to this stream, but stream access is quite good in most areas. Though much of the east branch of the Tioughnioga River gets a lot of attention from local anglers, some sections are underutilized. Canoeing down the middle and lower reaches could put you into some lightly fished, but very promising areas.

NOTES: _____

_____

_____

_____

TIOUGHNIOGA RIVER (west branch)

map coordinates	42° 36' 15" 76° 09' 33"
USGS map(s)	Cortland, Homer, Otisco Valley
location (township)	Cortlandville, Homer, Preble
access	parallelled and crossed by Route 11
principle species	brook trout (wild), brown trout (stocked), chain pickerel

The west branch of the Tioughnioga River runs from Tully Lake down to its junction with the east branch in the city of Cortland. It averages 15 to 20 feet in width, has a gravel bottom and good flow all year long. The stream is tree and brush-lined for the most part, but some sections that run through residential areas have little or no cover.

The principle species found in the west branch are brown trout and brook trout. Though there can be some good trout fishing right at the mouth of the creek as late as July, the trout section actually starts just above the village of Homer and continues up to Tully Lake. The best brook trout fishing in the stream is from Goodale Lake upstream to Preble Crossroads. Unfortunately, this stretch is leased by a private fishing club and is not open to the public. There are, however, wild brook trout scattered throughout the stream.

Above Preble the stream runs through a swamp. There are fairly good numbers of brook trout in this section, as well as chain pickerel, but this is a difficult area to fish because of the surroundings. The best part of the stream for public fishing would probably be the section from the mouth of Cold Brook down to Homer. A very popular spot is the park in Homer. There is a good population of brown trout in this stretch as well as a few brookies.

The west branch of the Tioughnioga River is a good fly fishing stream, and it is well known for its excellent mayfly and caddisfly hatches.

In the spring, this stream is stocked with 900 brown trout yearlings, from 0.5 miles below the mouth of Factory Brook upstream 1.4 miles to Seven Valley Pond.

NOTES: _____

_____

_____

_____

TROUT BROOK

map coordinates	42° 34' 54" 76° 08' 05"
USGS map(s)	Cortland, McGraw, Cincinnatus
location	Cortlandville, Solon
access	parallelled by Route 41
principle species	brook trout (stocked and wild)

Trout Brook is a high quality brook trout stream. Averaging 10 to 12 feet in width, it has a gravel bottom and a year round flow of cold, clear water. From the headwaters to the mouth of tributary #7 at Stillwell Road, Trout Brook is quite overhung with alders. Salted minnows, worms and small spinners will attract the attention of the unusually brightly-colored brook trout that inhabit this stream. Below Stillwell Road the stream is generally open, and fly fishing becomes a viable option. Most of the larger fish, through, are holed up above Stillwell Road.

Most of the fishing on Trout Brook takes place between the hamlet of Solon and the village of McGraw. Below McGraw the stream suffers from minor seasonal flooding, siltation and generally poor trout habitat. The one exception is the spring hole at the mouth of Trout Brook, which usually holds a few fish. Native brook trout can also be found in several of the south flowing tributaries of this stream, primarily Maybury Brook (see above) and tributary #11, which enters Trout Brook at Solon.

In the fall, 1,300 brook trout fingerlings are stocked in Trout Brook, from Stillwell Road upstream 2.7 miles to 0.5 miles above the mouth of Pritchard Brook.

Fishing pressure on this stream is light to moderate, and much of the stream is posted.

NOTES: _____

_____

_____

_____

VIRGIL CREEK - See Tompkins County Streams & Rivers

The RED MATUKA streamer is effective for Trout and bass.

Near the Cortland County line, Virgil Creek is a wide, turbid stream. Most of the trout taken here are stocked browns, but wild trout can be found here as well. Browns up to 6 pounds can be taken in some of the larger pools found along this reach.

CORTLAND COUNTY LAKES & PONDS

GOODALE LAKE

map coordinates.......... 42° 42' 29" 76° 08' 44"
USGS map(s) .... Homer
location .... townships of Homer and Preble
access .... parallelled by Route 11

Physical Characteristics

area .... 45 acres
shoreline .... 1.5 miles
elevation .... 1,150 feet
maximum depth .... approximately 18 feet
mean depth .... approximately 6 feet
bottom type .... muck

Chemical Characteristics

water clarity .... fairly clear
pH .... alkaline
oxygen................... oxygen levels are good throughout the lake all year long

Plant Life

Submerged aquatic plants and beds of lily pads are found throughout most of this lake.

Species Information

largemouth bass .... abundant; growth rate good
chain pickerel .... common; growth rate good
yellow perch .... common; growth rate fair
brown trout .... uncommon; growth rate good
bullhead .... common; growth rate good
bluegills................. abundant; growth rate very good

Also present are small populations of carp and suckers.

Boat Launch Sites

1. Goodale Lake is actually an arm of Upper Little York Lake, connected by a small strait that runs under Route 81. Boats can be launched at Dwyer Memorial park at the north end of Upper Little York and taken under Route 81 (cartop boats and canoes only — larger boats won't be able to go under the road).

2. On the east side of Goodale Lake there is a private pull-off on Route 11. The landowner usually allows access to the lake from this point (be sure to ask permission). Cartop boats and canoes could be hand-launched from this site.

General Information

Goodale Lake is a very productive little lake. Most of it is very shallow and very weedy, but there is a roughly 7 acre area in the north end that is up to 18 feet deep. This is an excellent largemouth bass lake. Bass up to 4 pounds are fairly common, and lunkers up to 6 pounds are taken annually. Chain pickerel are also common here, but large specimens are uncommon. Most of the pickerel taken here are young fish, sublegal in size. A 20 inch pickerel is very rare from Goodale Lake. Why older and larger pickerel are not found here is unknown. Bluegills are very abundant here and their growth rate is exceptional. Very popular with local anglers, good catches of keeper size bluegills are taken in the summer and through the ice. The best catches seem to come at the start of the ice-fishing season and at the very end.

Early in the spring, big brown trout can be taken at the mouth of the inlet (i.e. the west branch of the Tioughnioga River). Many of these browns will tip the scales at between 6 and 12 pounds. Bullheads are taken in large numbers in the spring from the shore along the railroad bed. Goodale Lake is very popular with ice fishermen, primarily for large bluegills, but yellow perch, chain pickerel and an occasional trout can be taken here as well.

NOTES: _____

_____

_____

_____

HIGH LAKE

map coordinates.......... 42° 29' 32" 75° 57' 08"
USGS map(s) .... Willet
location .... township of Cincinnatus
access .... off Gee Brook Road

Physical Characteristics

area .... 45 acres
shoreline .... 1.0 miles
elevation .... 1,348 feet
maximum depth .... approximately 20 feet
mean depth .... approximately 6 feet
bottom type .... muck, some gravel

Chemical Characteristics

water clarity .... somewhat turbid
pH .... acidic
oxygen................... severe oxygen depletion occurs periodically

Plant Life

Extensive weed beds are found around the perimeter of the lake.

Species Information

chain pickerel .... common; growth rate fair
largemouth bass .... common; growth rate good
yellow perch .... common; growth rate fair
pumpkinseed .... common; growth rate fair
bullhead .... common; growth rate fair

Boat Launch Sites

There is a gravel launch ramp, off Gee Brook Road, on the north side of the lake. Motors are not allowed on High Lake.

General Information

High Lake is also known as Papish Pond or Glover Pond. It is located entirely on state owned property, in a very picturesque stand of woods. The original lake was a 19 acre bowl-shaped pond. This pond was flooded to its present size by a low dam. The rising waters inundated a ring of button bushes and hemlocks that ringed the pond. This flooded shelf is now littered with old stumps and brush, providing good habitat for chain pickerel and

Actually an arm of Upper Little York Lake, Goodale Lake is separated from the main lake by Route 81. Despite its small size, Goodale Lake has healthy populations of many warm water species. The fishing for large sunfish is especially good.

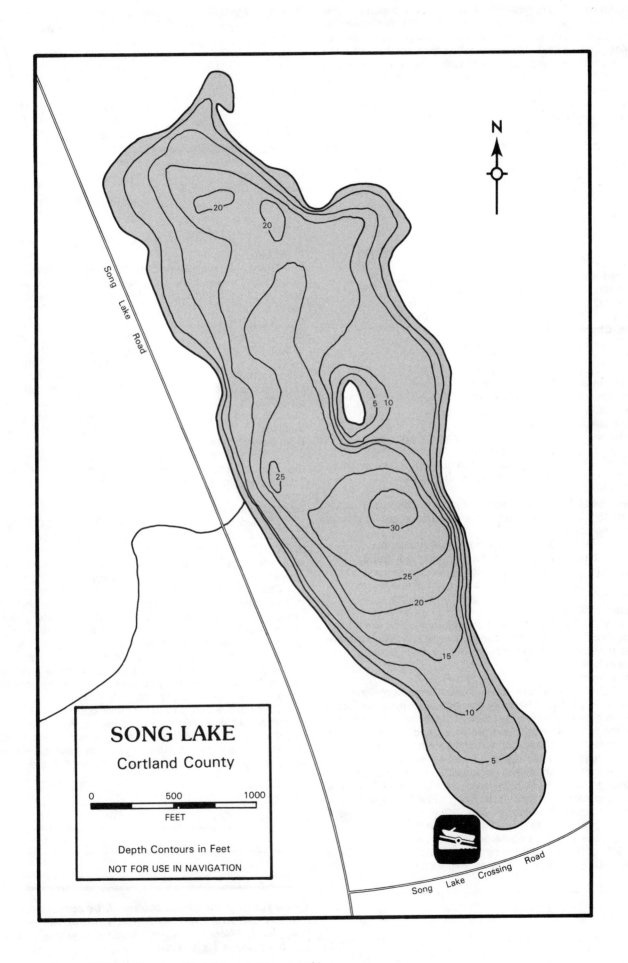

SONG LAKE

Cortland County

0   500   1000

FEET

Depth Contours in Feet

NOT FOR USE IN NAVIGATION

Song Lake Road

Song Lake Crossing Road

N

20
20
5 10
25
30
25
20
15
10
5

largemouth bass. Chain pickerel are the dominant predator in this lake. The average pickerel is sublegal in size, but some do manage to attain a length of up to 17 inches. Largemouth bass fair a bit better in High Lake. Most bass taken here are legal size and there are some very big largemouth taken here on occasion. In the winter, High Lake is fairly heavily ice-fished, primarily for chain pickerel and small yellow perch.

High Lake is an ideal place for family picnicking and for introducing children to the pleasures of fishing.

NOTES: _____

_____

_____

_____

SONG LAKE

map coordinates	42° 46' 08" 76° 08' 50"
USGS map(s)	Otisco Valley
location	township of Preble
access	off Song Lake Crossing

Physical Characteristics

area	109 acres
shoreline	2.2 miles
elevation	1190 feet
maximum depth	32 feet
mean depth	15 feet
bottom type	gravel, marl, muck

Chemical Characteristics

water clarity	slightly turbid in summer
pH	alkaline
oxygen	Oxygen depletion occurs in deepest water in summer.

Plant Life

Weed beds are found throughout much of the lake in water less than 15 feet, but there are areas of exposed gravel shoals.

Species Information

chain pickerel	common; growth rate fair
largemouth bass	common; growth rate good
yellow perch	common; growth rate good
pumpkinseed	abundant; growth rate fair
walleye	rare; growth rate good

Boat Launch Sites

1. There is a piece of county-owned property off Song Lake Crossing Road. Between this county property and the lake, there is a narrow strip of private property where small boats can be hand launched.

General Information

This small, weedy lake has a well-balanced population of predators and panfish. The most common predator is the chain pickerel, but their growth rate leaves something to be desired. Most of the pickerel caught here are young and sublegal in size. The largemouth bass fare somewhat better here. The average bass runs approximately 12 to 14 inches in Song Lake, but substantially larger fish are not uncommon. Yellow perch provide good fishing, especially early in the ice fishing season. There is a remnant population of walleye in Song Lake. Walleye haven't spawned successfully here in over 20 years. What walleye remain are big, old, 9 to 10 pound individuals.

Song Lake is very popular with local residents. Approximately 50% of the shoreline is developed (cottages). The lake is used for swimming and boating as well as fishing.

NOTES: _____

_____

_____

TULLY LAKE

map coordinates	42° 46' 40" 76° 08' 07"
USGS map(s)	Otisco Valley
location	township of Preble
access	off Saulsbury Road at Friendly Shores Drive

Physcial Characteristics

area	230 acres
shoreline	6.1 miles
elevation	1,195 feet
maximum depth	37 feet
mean depth	12 feet
bottom type	marl, muck

Chemical Characterics

water clarity	somewhat turbid
pH	alkaline
oxygen	oxygen depletion occurs in water over 30 feet deep in summer.

Plant Life

There are extensive patches of weeds (lily pads, rushes etc.) along some areas of the shallow fringe of the lake. An island of emergent vegetation (cattails, bulrushes) is found in the center basin of the lake.

Species Information

chain pickerel	common; growth rate good
largemouth bass	common; growth rate good
walleye	uncommon; growth rate good
yellow perch	uncommon; growth rate good
black crappie	uncommon; growth rate good
bluegills	abundant; growth rate good
pumpkinseed	abundant; growth rate good
bullhead	common; growth rate good

Boat Launch Sites

1. The state maintains a hand launch site in the south end of the middle basin, off Saulsbury Road on Friendly Shores Drive. Trailer launching is prohibited and motors are limited to 7.5 horse power.

General Information

Located on the border between Onondaga County and Cortland County, Tully Lake is the main source of the west branch of the Tioughnioga River. Composed of three separate spring-fed glacial kettle holes, this lake has luxuriant weed growth along much of its shallow fringe.

Chain pickerel and largemouth bass are the major predators in Tully Lake. Pickerel are typically 18 inches, but fish up to 24 inches are not uncommon. Largemouth bass are generally 12 inches, but bass of 6 to 8 pounds are taken here on occasion. There is a small population of large, old walleye in the lake, and walleye fingerlings have been stocked here in recent years. The stocking has been discontinued because of low survival rates. This is not a lake where you would go to fish specifically for walleye. They are a bonus fish in this lake.

Tully Lake is very popular. It offers opportunities for boating, swimming, water skiiing as well as fishing. Although there are a lot of skiers in the lake, they are not nearly the problem to fishermen as on Upper Little York Lake. Ice fishing is very popular here, and good catches of pickerel and panfish are common in winter.

NOTES: _____

_____

_____

_____

When fishing for chain pickerel, be sure to use a steel leader or 6 to 8 inches of heavy monofilament above your lure. Their teeth are razor sharp and will easily cut through a light line.

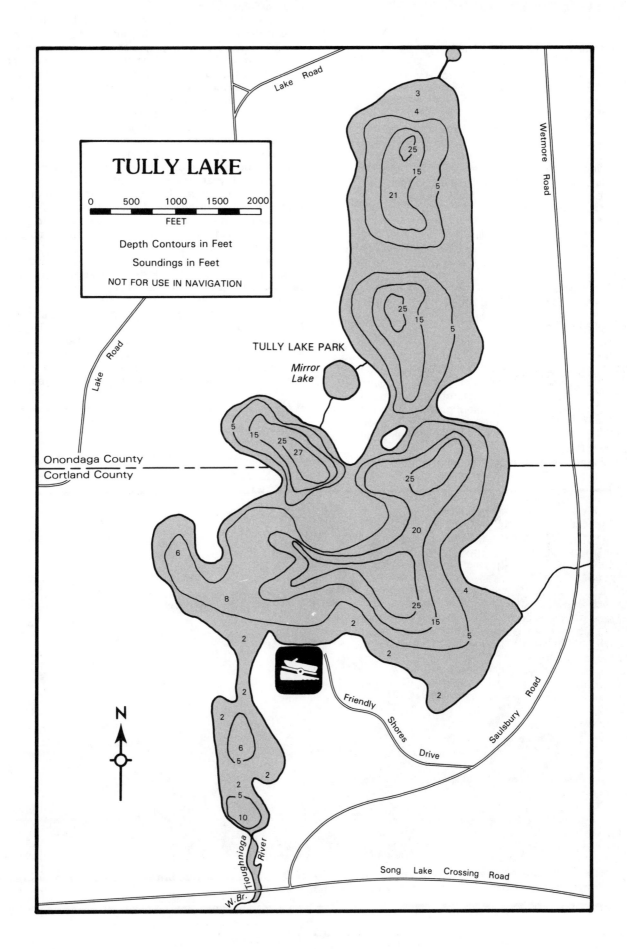

TULLY LAKE

0   500   1000   1500   2000
FEET

Depth Contours in Feet

Soundings in Feet

NOT FOR USE IN NAVIGATION

Lake Road

Wetmore Road

3

4

25

15

5

21

25

15

5

TULLY LAKE PARK

Mirror Lake

Lake Road

5

15

25

27

Onondaga County
Cortland County

25

25

20

4

6

8

25

15

5

2

2

2

2

Friendly Shores Drive

Saulsbury Road

2

2

6

5

2

2

5

10

Tioughnioga River

W. Br.

N

Song Lake Crossing Road

UPPER LITTLE YORK LAKE

map coordinates..........	42º 42' 07" 76º 09' 21"
USGS map(s).............	Homer
location	townships of Homer and Preble
access	via Dwyer Memorial Park, at north end of lake

Physical Characteristics

area	150 acres
shoreline	1.4 miles
elevation	1,150 feet
maximum depth	78 feet
mean depth	approximately 35 feet
bottom type	marl, muck

Chemical Characteristics

water clarity	clear
pH	alkaline
oxygen..................	oxygen is adequate throughout the lake year round.

Plant Life

Tall weed beds are found intermittently along the shallow fringe of the lake. Extensive weed beds are found in the shallow bays on the north east side of the lake.

Species Information

brown trout	uncommon; growth rate very good
rainbow trout.............	common; growth rate good
largemouth bass	common; growth rate good
chain pickerel	common; growth rate good
yellow perch	common; growth rate good
bluegills.................	common; growth rate good
pumpkinseed	common; growth rate good
bullhead	common; growth rate good

Boat Launch Sites

This is a gravel ramp at Dwyer Memorial Park, on the north end of the lake, off Route 281.

General Information

Often referred to simply as Little York Lake, this pond is essentially two lakes in one. It consists of a large glacial kettle hole surrounded by a fringe and shallow water and weedy bays. The deep central basin is a typical coldwater lake. A forage base of alewives supports a population of stocked and wild brown trout and stocked rainbow trout. The brown trout are not very common, but they do grow well here. Brown trout of 6 to 7 pounds are taken here each year and occasionally a specimen of up to 12 pounds is reported. Good fishing for brown trout and rainbow trout can be had in the spring by concentrating on the mouths of tributary streams. This is one of the few lakes in the region where trout can be taken through the ice using tip-ups. Trout can be taken here all year, any size, 10 per day.

The fringe of Upper Little York Lake and the bays on the north east side are more typical of shallow, weedy lakes. Extensive weed beds rent with open water channels provide good habitat for large populations of largemouth bass and chain pickerel, as well as for numerous panfish.

This lake is heavily fished all year long. In the winter, a considerable amount of ice fishing takes place here, primarily for yeallow perch, but catches of trout and pickerel are not uncommon.

The best access to Upper Little York Lake is via Dwyer Memorial Park, at the north end of the lake. The large park has ample parking areas, shelters and facilities for picnicking, a launch ramp, a short fishing pier and a food concession.

Upper Little York Lake is stocked annually with 5,000 rainbow trout yearlings and 1,000 brown trout yearlings.

NOTES: _____

_____

_____

_____

Upper Little York Lake, seen from Dwyer Park, off Route 281. The park has many facilities, including a boat launch site, parking areas, a food concession and picnic shelters.

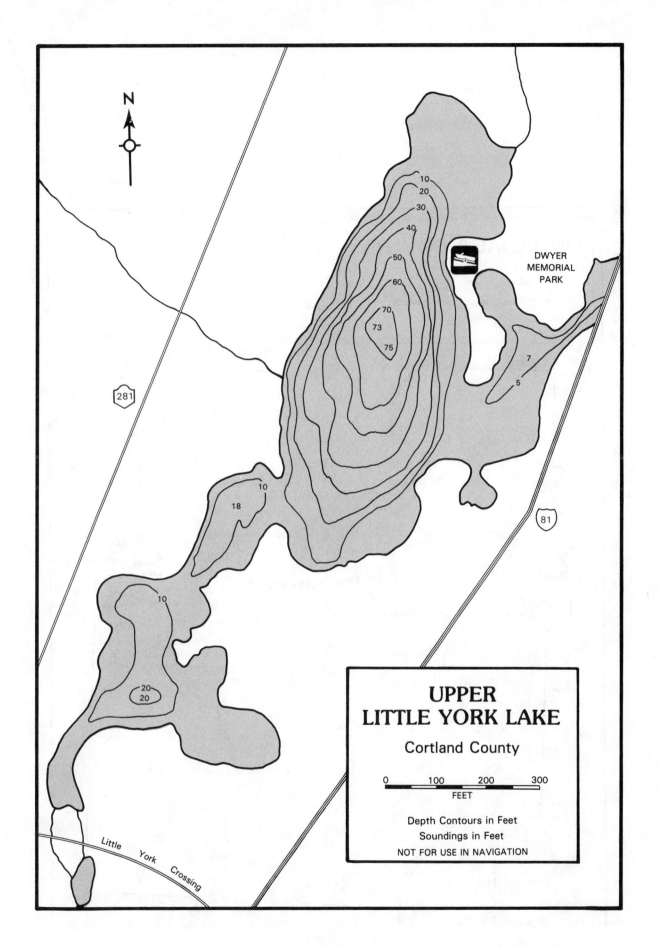

N

281

DWYER
MEMORIAL
PARK

10
20
30
40
50
60
70
73
75

7
5

81

10
18

10

20
20

**UPPER
LITTLE YORK LAKE**

Cortland County

0   100   200   300
FEET

Depth Contours in Feet
Soundings in Feet
NOT FOR USE IN NAVIGATION

Little   York   Crossing

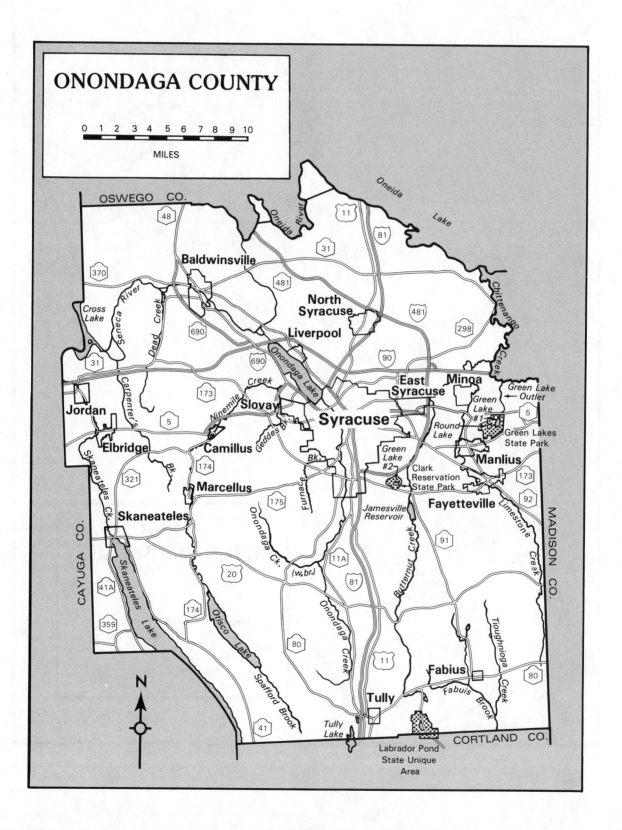

ONONDAGA COUNTY

0 1 2 3 4 5 6 7 8 9 10
MILES

OSWEGO CO.

48

370

Baldwinsville

Cross Lake

Seneca River

Dead Creek

690

31

Carpenter's Creek

Jordan

5

Elbridge

Bk.

321

174

Marcellus

Skaneateles Ck.

Skaneateles

41A

359

Skaneateles Lake

Otisco Lake

174

20

41

Oneida River

11

481

North Syracuse

Liverpool

690

Onondaga Lake

173

Ninemile Creek

Slovay

Camillus

Geddes Bk.

Green Lake #2

175

Onondaga Ck.

(w.br.)

Furnace

Bk.

Jamesville Reservoir

11A

81

80

Onondaga Creek

11

Tully

Tully Lake

Spafford Brook

Oneida Lake

81

31

481

298

90

East Syracuse

Syracuse

Minoa

Green Lake Outlet

Green Lake #1

5

Round Lake

Green Lakes State Park

Manlius

Clark Reservation State Park

Fayetteville

173

92

Limestone Creek

91

Butternut Creek

Chittenango Creek

MADISON CO.

Tioughnioga Creek

Fabius

80

Fabius Brook

Labrador Pond State Unique Area

CORTLAND CO.

CAYUGA CO.

N

—46—

ONONDAGA COUNTY STREAMS & RIVERS

BUTTERNUT CREEK

map coordinates	43° 05' 53" 76° 00' 00"
USGS map(s)	Manlius, East Syracuse, Jamesville, Tully
location (township)	Fabius, Lafayette, Dewitt, Manlius
access	roughly parallelled above Jamesville by Apulia Road - see below
principle species	brown trout (stocked & wild), brook trout (stocked), northern pike, largemouth bass, bullhead, pickerel, walleye, panfish

Originating near the Onondaga/Cortland County line, Butternut Creek provides 15 miles of very high quality trout fishing above the Jamesville Reservoir, and a mixed bag of cold and warm water species between the reservoir and the junction with Limestone Creek, just north of Minoa.

Beginning with the extreme upper reaches of the stream, above Apulia Station, Butternut Creek is a very small, brush-lined stream that has very good fishing for stocked brook trout. Too small for fly fishing, these headwaters are best fished with bait. Because the stream is heavily fished in the spring, there is little carry-over of stocked fish and the fishing slows considerably in the summer.

Below this, the stream flows for about three miles, primarily through woodland. The stream is still fairly small in this section and has a high gradient with a good ratio of riffles to pools. There is an excellent population of brown trout here, both stocked and wild. Very dark colors characterize the trout found here. They are most often taken on bait or small spinners, but limited areas in this reach could be fly fished.

Not far below Apulia Station is an old, abandoned dam site, and beginning here the streams gradient gradually flattens out briefly before flowing through a heavily wooded area. From this point to the Jamesville Reservoir the surroundings are mostly farmland, and the stream has a significant amount of bank cover, mostly alders and willows. Brown trout are the predominant species in this reach, but the closer you get to the Jamesville Reservoir the greater the chances are of picking up a few largemouth bass or pickerel. Because of the bank cover, fly fishing is limited, and as with the upper reaches of the creek, the fishing slows in summer due to high fishing pressure in the spring.

Downstream of the Jamesville Reservoir, Butternut Creek is a medium size stream running over limestone ledges, small cascades and falls. The stream is very pretty in this section, but it starts to flow through more developed areas. Trout can still be found below the reservoir, and what they lack in numbers they make up for in size. Some of the brown trout caught here are 16 to 18 inches in size, and will be found mainly in the larger pools. Because of the high gradient, between the reservoir and Dewitt, the population of warm water species in this section is very limited.

Just downstream of the crossing of Route 290, near East Syracuse, Butternut Creek undergoes a big change in character. The stream becomes very deep, sinuous and sluggish. Ranging up to 60 feet in width, with a silt bottom, warm water species dominate the remainder of the fishing. Even in this section, though, is mediocre at best. The "wide waters" section near the Erie Canal Park has a limited fishery for largemouth bass, northern pike, walleye, bullhead and panfish. Brown trout are also taken in this section. There are not very many—they are down right scarce— but typical of brown trout taken from this type of water, they are big. Access to this portion of Butternut Creek is poor because it runs through a developed area. But if a specialist in large brown trout got permission to fish this water, he would probably do fairly well, if he has patience, using minnows or small Rapalas. The D.E.C. reports that most of the browns found here are in the three to six pound class.

To facilitate access to the trout section above the Jamesville Reservoir, the state has purchased just over eight miles of public fishing rights, located intermittently between the reservoir and Apulia Station. In addition, eleven parking areas have been purchased, four of which have been developed. They are located as follows: On the west side of Clark Hollow Road, three-fifths of a mile north of Berry Road; on the east side of Clark Hollow Road,one and one-half miles north of Verry Road; on the south side of Cascade Road, two-fifths of a mile east of Clark Hollow Road; on the north side of Dodge Road, one-tenth of a mile east of Jamesville-Apulia Road. Nine foot path right-of ways have also been purchased, but none have been developed to date.

In the fall, a 2.2 mile section of Butternut Creek just above Apulia Station is stocked with 300 brook trout fingerlings. A further 1,100 brook trout fingerlings are stocked in the 2.1 mile stretch of water below Apulia Station. Brown trout are also stocked in this stream, above the Jamesville Reservoir by Onondaga County. This stocking amounts to about 6,600 brown trout.

NOTES: _____

_____

_____

CARPENTER'S BROOK

map coordinates	42° 50' 25" 75° 57' 28"
USGS map(s)	De Ruyter, Oram
location (township)	Elbridge, Marcellus
access	road crossing at Route 5
principle species	brook trout (wild), brown trout (stocked)

A tributary of the Seneca River, Carpenter's Brook provides anglers with about eight miles of good quality trout fishing. The stream can be divided by the crossing at Route 5 into a high quality section and a fair quality section. The upper portion of Carpenter's Brook is a small, brush-lined stream flowing through a heavily wooded area. Some of the tributaries of this section hold good numbers of wild brook trout, and a few brookies can also be found in Carpenter's Brook itself. There are also some remarkably large brown trout in upper Carpenter's Brook. However, the overall productivity of this stretch of the stream is not very high. Add to this difficult terrain, an abundance of mosquitos and enough snags to drive even the most patient fisherman daffy, it's easy to understand why the upper sections of Carpenter's Brook get only light pressure from local anglers.

Near Elbridge, Carpenter's Brook gets a heavy infusion of cold ground water, and the quality of the stream improves considerably, to the point where it can supply the water for the Onondaga County Fish Hatchery. The stream is still fairly small, though some sections below route 5 are up to 30 feet in width. The water is clear and cold, and there are many deep, still water areas. As with the upper sections, unusually large brown trout can be found here, but their numbers are considerably greater. Bait fishing is the most apropo technique on Carpenter's Brook, but some stretches could be fly fished with difficulty. Getting to these spots is not easy, though, because of the swampy, tangled surroundings. Because of this, and because of posting between the hatchery and route 5, access is rather limited.

The lower most tributary of Carpenter's Brook is stocked by the state with 200 brown trout fingerlings in the fall. An additional stocking of approximately 1,500 brown trout is made in Carpenter's Brook by the Onondaga County Fish Hatchery.

NOTES: _____

_____

_____

CHITTENANGO CREEK
(Onondaga County Section)

map coordinates . . . . 43º 11' 01" 75º 59' 37"
USGS map(s) . . . . Cleveland, Manlius
location (township) . . . . Manlius, Cicero
access . . . . bridge crossing at Route 31
principle species . . . . walleye, brown trout (stocked), northern pike, silver bass, white perch, bullhead, panfish

The lower reaches of Chittenango Creek run for about 15 miles along the Onondaga/Madison County line. For the most part, this portion of the stream is a deep, sluggish, turbid, low gradient mess (the gradient does pick up a little near Bridgeport). As you might suspect, this is primarily a warm water habitat, and a mediocre one at that. The stream does benefit from runs of fish from Oneida Lake, primarily walleye, silver bass and white perch. A popular spot for early season walleye is the bridge crossing at Route 31 in Bridgeport. The fish can be found as far upstream as the thruway crossing at North Manlius, and are taken on small rapalas, jigs or worms. Bullhead fishing is very good in the spring, close to Oneida Lake, and northern pike are occasionally taken in the lower most reaches of the stream in spring as well.

Above the mouth of Limestone Creek, the Onondaga County portion of Chittenango Creek has a sparse brown trout population. As with many deep, marginally warm waterways, the few brown trout found here are generally large. Bait fishing, either with worms or minnows fished at night, should prove to be effective to the patient angler.

The state does not stock this part of the stream, but Onondaga County does. About 650 brown trout are stocked in the lower portion of Chittenango Creek each year.

NOTES: _____
_____
_____
_____

DEAD CREEK

map coordinates . . . . 43º 09' 20" 76º 22' 42"
USGS map(s) . . . . Lysander, Jordan
location (township) . . . . Van Buren, Elbridge
access . . . . brown trout (stocked & wild)

This is a small, fair quality trout stream fishable from Laird Corners to the Seneca River. Above the thruway it is known as White Bottom Creek. Dead Creek has a very low gradient, runs through a swampy area, has poor transparency, lots of bank cover and is so uniformly deep that one gets the impression it was at one time dredged. Aside from road crossings, access to Dead Creek is poor.

The best fishing on Dead Creek is found in the lowermost reaches near the Seneca River. While the fishing is not great, the wild brown trout found here are very beautifully colored.

This stream is stocked yearly with brook trout by the County of Onondaga.

NOTES: _____
_____
_____
_____

For information on nearly 200 lakes and streams in the western portion of New York State, obtain a copy of "Sander's Fishing Guide - Western New York edition".

*FABIUS BROOK

map coordinates . . . . 42º 48' 03" 75º 57' 41"
USGS map(s) . . . . De Ruyter, Tully
location (township) . . . . Fabius, Pompey
access . . . . crossings at: Routes 90 & 81; Chaffee Mills Road; Bardeen Road; Keeney Road — see below
principle species . . . . brook trout (wild), brown trout (wild), burbot, american eel

Fabius Brook is an incredible little stream. In terms of numbers, it has what is probably the best resident fish population of any inland trout stream in the Finger Lakes region. Unfortunately, most of these fish will never see a hook. Fabius Brook is, for much of its length, a fisherman's waking nightmare of swamps, tag alders and remote beaver ponds.

This stream flows for nine miles through south eastern Onondaga County before emptying into the west branch of the east branch of Tioughnioga Creek, south of the village of Fabius. Above Fabius it is a typical wild brook trout stream. The gradient is fairly high, the stream is about 10 feet wide and has a bottom of pea gravel and rubble. Despite its high gradient, it is choked with alders, except where you encounter beaver ponds. Access to this section of Fabius Brook is difficult, due in part to the lack of roads close to the stream.

At Fabius the stream runs through swamp land. Below these swamps the stream channel is better defined, but the stream is heavily infested with beavers, and as a result, there are numerous beaver ponds. The stream itself widens out to 20 to 25 feet, has a silt and rubble bottom and is fairly slow moving and deep. It could be waded, but it is so slow and flat that ripples seem to go on forever, and as above Fabius, it is choked with alders. There are numerous good size pools on the lower reaches of Fabius Brook, and all of them invariable hold 3 or 4 brown trout over 14 inches. Fish substantially larger than this, both brook and brown trout, are also taken on occasion, but you are really going to have to work to find them because of the terrain. The beaver ponds mentioned above are known to hold some nice brook and brown trout as well, but few are near enough to a road to make access feasible.

As you might guess, much of Fabius Brook is so swampy and tangled that there is little opportunity for fly fishing. In sections where a fly rod can be employed, though, your success can be spectacular. The Hendrickson brown caddis and light cahill dry fly patterns are reportedly very effective from early May to late June.

As far as Fabius Brook is concerned, a more productive method than fly fishing (if for no other reason than that you can fish more of the stream) is the old fashioned technique of drifting a worm or minnow under overhanging brush, log jams or through deep pools. You might hang up a lot, but your efforts will be well rewarded. Most of the fish you take will be small brookies under ten inches, but they are abundant!

While you are drifting your worm or minnow through a deep, rubble bottomed pool, you might encounter a unique aspect of Fabius Brook — burbot. These fresh water cod are occasionally found in small tributaries of the Susquehanna River drainage system, and their presence in Fabius Brook has been confirmed by the DEC. Most often caught at night, burbot are usually disdained by anglers. But they are tough fighters reaching 30 inches in length and are good table fare. As if burbot were not odd enough residents of a trout stream, Fabius Brook also has a fair population of american eels. This is a strange stream indeed!

Although much of this stream is essentially inaccessible, the state has purchased 1.4 miles of public fishing rights on Fabius Brook, and one foot path right-of-way (see map). It is not stocked by the state, but Onondaga County annually stocks this stream with brook trout.

The following article, written by John Fik of West Henrietta, New York, gives you a first hand impression of this remarkable little stream.

"Fabius Brook is located 8 miles east of Tully, New York. Bailey and East Keeney Road parallel this stream for most of its 9 mile length. Access along this stream is very good.

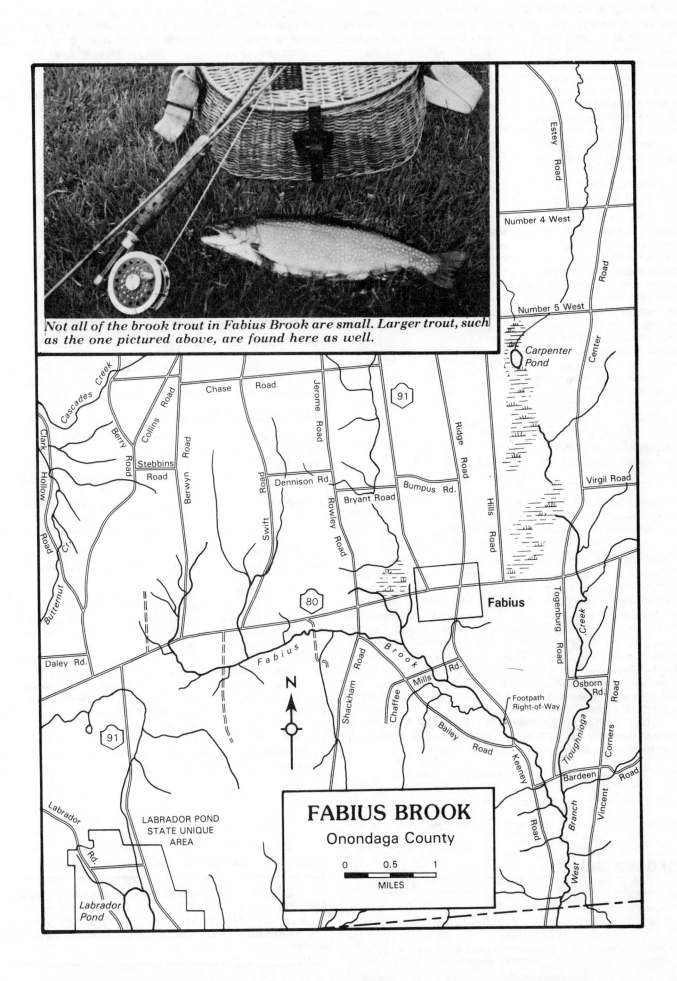

Not all of the brook trout in Fabius Brook are small. Larger trout, such as the one pictured above, are found here as well.

FABIUS BROOK
Onondaga County

0   0.5   1
MILES

A very good friend of mine, John Wheeler of Tully, showed me this stream several years ago and told me of the promise this stream showed. John is a classic work dunker and has caught numerous brown and brook trout up to 17" long in this log jam infested and brush tangled stream.

Although this stream is nearly impossible to fish with a fly, there are some accessible areas near all the bridges. Hare's ear nymph works best, with most catches in the 6"-10" range. Ultralight tackle is preferred on this stream with spinners, worms and minnows the preferred bait.

The bigger fish seem to be found closer to the mouth of Fabius before it enters the west branch of the Toughnioga Creek.

If you enjoy fishing small strems with little pleasure, big surprises and naturally reproducing trout than this stream is not to be missed."

*The upper reaches of Fabius Brook consists of several branches. These branches generally flow southeast toward the confluence with Tioughnioga Creek just south of Bardeen Road in the town of Fabius. One brance flowes east before bending south along Bailey Road; the other main branch (not usually shown on county maps) begins along Cemetary Road and flows south along the west side of Route 91 to meet the other branch just downstream of the village of Fabius. Both branches offer good fishing.

NOTES: _____

_____

_____

_____

FURNACE BROOK

map coordinates	43º 01' 07" 76º 09' 47"
USGS map(s)	Syracuse West, South Onondaga
location (township)	Onondaga
access	Elmwood Park
principle species	brook trout (stocked & wild), brown trout (stocked & wild)

Short in length and averaging only about 10 feet in width, Furnace Brook, nevertheless, offers area anglers some fine fishing opportunities. The stream has been tamed — some selections have no bank cover due to the banks being lined with stone and concrete, and the most productive reaches flow through Elmwood Park — but this does not seem to have affected the fish populations. It is gravel bottomed and surrounded primarily by mature hardwoods. The stream generally lacks significant pools, and this has a deleterious effect on the growth rate of the brown trout found here. But what they lack in size, they make up for in numbers. Brook trout are also found throughout Furnace Brook, and they are beautifully colored.

This stream is not currently stocked by the state. It is, however, stocked annually by Onondaga County with 300 brook trout fingerlings.

NOTES: _____

_____

_____

_____

GEDDES BROOK

map coordinates	43º 04' 40" 76º 13' 51"
USGS map(s)	Syracuse West
location (township)	Camillus
access	via Shove Park or from Fairmount Fair
principle species	brown trout (stocked & wild), brook trout (wild)

People often believe that if a stream runs through a heavily populated area, it cannot be a good quality trout stream. Geddes Brook proves the falseness of this assumption. This often overlooked stream begins inauspiciously near the former Onondaga County garbage dump. There is not much fishing in the upper reaches, but just above Route 173 the stream gets a strong influx of cold ground water and quickly grades to a high quality trout stream. Geddes Brook is very small and mostly open. It has a flow problem in summer until it reaches Fairmount. In Fairmount it flows past a shopping plaza (Fairmount Fair). From this point on the stream holds large numbers of wild brook and brown trout, and good fishing can be had right behind the plaza. The fish are commonly eight to nine inches, but due to the hold over of stocked fish, trout over twelve inches are often encountered.

Below Fairmount Fair, there is a lot of development along the stream, but high quality fishing can be expected as far downstream as Solvay. Below Solvay the stream has been hit with a lot of industrial pollution, but it still rates as a good trout stream.

In the fall, Geddes Brook is stocked by the state with 500 brown trout fingerlings in the one-mile section just above Route 173.

The stream is also stocked by Onondaga County.

NOTES: _____

_____

_____

_____

GREEN LAKE OUTLET

map coordinates	43º 05' 00" 75º 57' 49"
USGS map(s)	Manlius
location (township)	Manlius
access	Green Lakes State Park; Erie Canal State Park
principle species	brown trout (stocked & wild), rainbow trout (stocked) northern pike, panfish

Known also as Lake Brook, this is a good quality trout stream for most of its 2.8 mile length. It is small, averaging only 15 feet in width, but there are several good size pools, some up to 40 feet across. Most of the stream is brush lined (fly fishing is not an option here), and gravel bottomed, with pockets of rubble and silt. Because Green Lake Outlet is very fertile, there is some in stream vegetation in areas where there is sufficient light penetration. It has a good ratio of riffles to pools.

Most of the fish taken here are brown trout. There is good carry-over of fish resulting in some very large browns being taken by the relatively few anglers who try their luck here. Also fairly abundant are northern pike and panfish, which probably originate in Chittenango Creek and move up into Green Lake Outlet. Most of the northerns taken here are on the small side. Occasionally anglers are surprised by large hatchery breeder rainbows stocked by the state in green lake, which escape into the outlet. Some of these fish can weigh up to several pounds.

NOTES: _____

_____

_____

_____

Northern pike and muskellunge are similar in appearance, but they are easy to differentiate if you know what to look for. Northerns have 5 or fewer sensory pores on the underside of the lower jaw; muskies have 6 to 9 pores.

LIMESTONE CREEK

map coordinates . . . . 43° 06' 12" 75° 58' 34"
USGS map(s) . . . . Manlius, Syracuse East, De Ruyter, Erieville
location (township) . . . . Manlius, Pompey, Fabius (Onondaga County) Cazenovia (Madison County)
access . . . . parallelled in parts by Pompey Hollow Road—see below
principle species . . . . brown trout (stocked & wild), brook trout (stocked & wild)

Limestone Creek has a long standing reputation as a very high quality trout stream. While it is not quite as good as its reputation, this stream is an important resource to area fishermen, providing approximately 28 miles of good trout water.

Beginning in the Madison County township of Cazenovia, Limestone Creek (the name is a misnomer—there is very little limestone on this stream, most of it being downstream of Fayetteville) starts out as a very high quality wild brown trout stream. There is also a limited population of wild brook trout in the very uppermost reaches of the stream, as well as in most of its tributaries. The Madison County portion of Limestone Creek is too small and brush lined for fly fishing, but drifting worms should work well.

The most heavily fished section of this stream lies between the village of Manlius and the Onondaga/Madison county line. Above Route 20, this section is still fairly small, but not as brushy as in Madison County. Below Route 20, the stream begins to widen and eventually grows to 60 feet in width, and is quite deep. This section is heavily stocked with brown trout, and there is good carry over of fish. There are a lot of fallfish here to try your patience if your bait fishing, but with a little persistence, lunker brown trout can be taken with fair regularity.

An angler tries his luck on Ninemile Creek, just outside of Syracuse. One of the finest trout streams in the state, it is also one of the most heavily fished. Photo courtest of J. Michael Kelly.

Below Manlius, Limestone Creek has a very low gradient and becomes a very slow moving, sinuous and deep stream. It also becomes turbid (this actually begins two miles above Manlius). There are not a lot of trout below Fayetteville, but those found here are big. An unusual aspect of this lower portion of Limestone Creek is the natural reproduction of brown trout that the Department of Environmental Conservation has observed taking place right in the village of Fayetteville.

Access to the middle reaches of Limestone Creek is very good. There are numerous road crossings and parking areas. The state has purchased 1.6 miles of public fishing rights on the stream. These access areas are found intermittantly between the crossings of Routes 20 and 80.

In the fall, Limestone Creek is stocked by the state from its mouth upstream four miles to the crossing of Route 173, with 2,400 brown trout fingerlings. Many of its tributaries are also stocked with brook trout and brown trout, but these tributaries serve principally as nursery streams. In Madison County, nearly the entire stream is stocked with 2,800 brown trout fingerlings each fall. In addition to the state stocking program, there is a massive stocking in the middle reaches of Limestone Creek by Onondaga County.

NOTES: _____

_____

_____

_____

NINEMILE CREEK

map coordinates . . . . 43° 05' 20" 76° 13' 47"
USGS map(s) . . . . Syracuse West, Camillus, Marcellus
location (township) . . . . Camillus, Marcellus
access . . . . parallelled by County Route 174 —see below
principle species . . . . brown trout (stocked & wild), brook trout (stocked & wild), rainbow trout (stocked), smallmouth bass, panfish

Ninemile Creek is unquestionably one of the top trout streams in Central New York. This fact, along with its proximity to the metropolitan area of Syracuse, makes this stream extremely popular with anglers. The following article was written by J. Michael Kelly of Marcellus. Long familiar with this stream, his article provides a wealth of first hand information on Ninemile Creek.

A D.E.C. creel census conducted on Ninemile Creek in 1978-80 showed fishing pressure on a prime one-mile stretch of the stream averaged 2,432 man-hours per acre, per year. State biologists called that level of popularity "remarkable," but local fishermen who can't find a place to park along their favorite pools in April or May use stronger language to describe the situation.

There are two reasons for this intense pressure. First, of course, is Ninemile's proximity to Syracuse and its metropolitan population of half a million people. Second, and more important, is the creek's own population of wild and holdover brown trout.

An average Ninemile brownie is fat, colorful, 10 to 12 inches long, and prone to vault out of the water at the first touch of a hook. He's the primary reason many knowledgeable anglers in the Syracuse area rate Ninemile as the best trout stream in their region and one of the best in state.

The same state report that described Ninemile angling pressure as remarkable referred to its productivity as "awesome." Although the stream receives annual stockings of about 20,000 browns, brooks and rainbows, approximately half the trout caught from Marcellus Falls downstream to Camillus during the study period were found to be of wild origin, and growth rates of the wild fish were rated as excellent. Three-year old browns captured by D.E.C. electrofishing crews ranged from 12-15 inches in length, and four-year olds ran from 16 to 18 inches.

Yet Ninemile fishing is far from easy, and newcomers to the creek should take pains to learn its special quirks if they hope to have consistent success.

The first thing anglers ought to know about Ninemile is that it is physically the opposite of most trout waters. Instead of being fed by cool tributaries near its source and warming as it flows toward its mouth, Ninemile begins as the warmwater outlet of Otisco Lake.

For its first eight miles, between the Otisco Dam and the crossroads at Marcellus Falls, Ninemile (which is actually about 16 miles long) is characterized by a predominately muddy bottom and summer water temperatures that are, at best, marginal for trout. Carp, rock bass, black crappies, sunfish and mostly sub-legal smallmouth bass compete with a sparse population of stocked and holdover trout in this section.

Just upstream from the falls, however, the first in a series of large limestone springs replenishes the creek with icy cold water. From this point down to the swamp that borders the village of Camillus, water temperatures seldom climb above the low 60's, even on the hottest summer days, and trout thrive.

There is also good trout habitat through Camillus and, intermittently, downstream to Amboy. Below the hamlet of Amboy to its confluence with Onondaga Lake, Ninemile is badly polluted by chloride waste seeping from the former Allied Chemical Corp. property.

Ninemile is readily accessible to anglers over most of its length. Although there are just two short stretches marked by D.E.C. "public fishing" signs, 19 bridges span the creek, and few posted signs are to be seen. The troutiest sections of Ninemile are paralleled by county Route 174, and well-trod footpaths point the way from the road.

Like other Onondaga County streams, Ninemile gets its annual transfusions of trout from the county-owned Carpenter's Brook Hatchery, rather than from state-operated rearing stations. The 6 to 9 inch trout are unloaded at bridges from Otisco Lake to Camillus in late March, April and early May, so that early season anglers have a good shot at catching at least a couple of trout no matter where they choose to fish. The bait fishing and spinning upstream from the South Street bridge, just south of the village of Marcellus, can be surprisingly good in April, and hardly a season passes without some local youngster hauling a three or four pound brownie out of one of the deep holes inside the village limits.

However, serious trout fishermen can't be bothered with the small panfish and chubs that constantly peck away at their worms and flies in this part of the stream, and concentrate their efforts in the picturesque pocket water around Marcellus Falls or the deep pools between the Martisco railroad crossing and Camillus.

Walking along the creek bank just upstream from the Martisco Paper Mill at Marcellus Falls, you'll see the bubbling springs that magically change Ninemile from an ordinary put and take fishery into a classic wild trout stream. From here to Amboy, butter-flanked browns and an occasional native brook trout fatten on a smorgasbord of mayfly, caddis and stonefly nymphs, midges, minnows and terrestrial insects. But the staple of their diet, especially in early season, is the scud, a shrimp-like crustacean found by the millions on Ninemile's rocky bottom. The scuds give a bright orange-red hue and a particularly sweet taste to the flesh of Ninemile trout, and spur their rate of growth.

From the paper mill dam, Ninemile tumbles through a short stretch of rocky pools, slows briefly behind another dam, and then pours over Marcellus Falls, one of the most-photographed spots in Onondaga County. The next quarter mile of pocket water offers some of the most challenging fishing in the entire stream. There are big browns here —like the 23½ inch fish I was lucky enough to nail on April 1, 1986 — but most are exceedingly wary, and few freshly-stocked fish survive long in these frothy whitewater pools. Those who can fish a nymph without drag on a weighted leader prosper here, at times; so do bait fishermen who fish the side-eddies with worms on opening date or after a summer shower.

The D.E.C. parking area and public fishing section just below

This brown trout was taken from Ninemile Creek on a nymph. The trout in this stream feed heavily on scuds, which give the fish a bright orange-red hue and exceptional flavor. Photo courtesy J. Michael Kelly.

here, three bridges downstream from Marcellus Falls, is the most popular spot on the creek, but only because few fishermen are willing to hike far from their automobiles. The relatively thin water doesn't provide nearly as much cover as the pockets upstream or the shaded pools in the swamp above Camillus, but it's close to Route 174 and heavily stocked early in the season. A long, shallow riffle that parallels Route 174 about 100 yards below the public access is a favorite of dry fly fishermen because of its even currents, dependable hatches and abundance of 9-10 inch risers. The pool is also favored by local bait fishermen in April, yet is so shallow and sunlit in July that few fish remain.

Several deep pools at bridges and bends harbor some nice trout in the next quarter mile, before Ninemile slides under the Martisco Railroad culvert, just above Route 174's junction with Route 321, and sweeps into a wooded, boggy area known to locals as "The Flats."

Fifteen or 20 years ago, the Flats harbored more brookies than browns, and I vividly remember a limit catch of 9-13 inch natives my father snaked out of this stretch one opening day, when there was still a carpet of snow on the ground. In the fall, we could hike up Windfall Brook, a tributary which winds along Route 321, and watch hundreds of red-bellied brook trout on their spawning grounds.

Today, however, the brook is clogged with silt and deadfalls, and heavy fishing pressure has decimated the ranks of the gullible brookies. Although you may still be surprised by a 10 or 11 inch native now and then, there are 10 or more browns for every brookie in the Flats.

Like those brookies of yesteryear, the browns are wild, and they patrol every pool and riffle from the railroad crossing to Amboy, in sizes ranging from three or four inches to several pounds. The big ones aren't easy, but any veteran Ninemile angler can assure you, they are indeed there.

Every sort of fisherman has his innings on Ninemile. Worms, particularly the 1-2 inch "pinkies" found in your garden's cool spring soil, can't be beat in April or after a summer freshet. I've also watched more than one opening day limit of nice browns succumb to salted minnows, patiently jerked across the pocket water on a hand-twist retrieve. Ultralight spinning tackle can be deadly, too, and gold Phoebes and Hildebrandt Flickers in the smaller sizes are local favorites.

Yet Ninemile is best known as a fly fisherman's stream, with good reason. Its average 20-30 foot width and moderate currents are ideal for the nymph or wet fly, and heavy hatches in May and June bode well for the dry fly man. Later, the brushy banks of the Flats and the thick grass and towering black willows along the Amboy stretches are alive with ants and other terrestrial insects.

Good fly fishing begins on the creek in mid or late April, as water temperatures edge into the low 50's. At this time a dead-drifted Hendrickson, Gold-ribbed Hare's Ear, Cased Caddis or Dark Stonefly nymph can always be counted on to draw a few strikes.

Although there are light hatches of Blue Winged Olives and Blue Duns in the early weeks of the season, surface action doesn't really get underway until the Hendrickson hatch in mid-May, and the dry fly fishing normally peaks between May 20 and June 10, while the Pale Evening Duns, or sulfurs, are emerging.

More dedicated hatch-matchers might disagree with the strategy, but I have always fished both the Hendrickson and Sulfur hatches with the same dry fly, a size 14 Hendrickson comparadun, and have done quite well on browns up to 15 inches. For that matter, a dark brown nymph will outproduce any dry most of the time during these or any other hatches on Ninemile.

A variety of caddis in size 16 to 18 come off the water throughout the day in late May, June and on into July. There are also good fishing hatches of March Browns (about June 110), Light Cahills (the second half of June) and big, size 10 Cream Variants (at dusk in late June). In July, fair numbers of Dun Variants, or Isonychia, may emerge in the evening, and you can also expect to see tiny, size 18-22, Bluewinged Olives almost any summer day. However, these hatches do not seem to elicit much interest from Ninemile trout, which tend to hug the bottom more and more as the water level shrinks and the summer sun beats down.

When I feel like dry fly fishing on a summer evening, I forget about hatch-matching and tie on a size 12 Ausable Wulff or similar attractor pattern. The Wulff doesn't look like much of anything, but as it dances over the pockets and riffles, has a definite hint of life, and often brings up a 12 or 13 inch brown.

Despite its dependably cold water, Ninemile fishes poorly during mid-day in July and August, and your best chances for a good fish at this time of year come in the first two hours of daylight, or, if you're one of that special breed of night fishermen, after midnight. Don't pass up a chance to hit the stream with worms or nymphs after a cool summer rain, however.

Some of the most enjoyable Ninemile angling occurs after Labor Day. A new emergence of Isdonychia begins about then, and the wild and holdover trout attack a tumbling nymph with fury on chilly afternoons. The fish are moving, too, stacking up in deep pools as they edge toward favored spawning areas.

Best of all, the crowds are gone, and the Ninemile regulars can end their season in peace and blessed solitude.

NOTES: _____

_____

_____

_____

ONEIDA RIVER - see Oswego County streams & rivers

ONONDAGA CREEK
map coordinates . . . . 43° 04′ 04″ 76° 10′ 42″
USGS map(s) . . . . Syracuse West, South Onondaga, Otisco Valley
location (township) . . . . Otisco, Tully, Lafayette, Onondaga
access . . . . Newell Avenue, roughly parallelled above the Onondaga Indian Reservation by Route 11A
principle species . . . . brown trout (stocked)
                                     brook trout (wild).

Onondaga Creek is a sorry story, indeed. Originally a very high quality trout and salmon stream, it is now riddled with problems, all of them man-made. The stream originates in Tully Valley near Vesper, and its here where the problems begin. There is a large brine field nearby which leaks brine and silt into Onondaga Creek. From this inauspicious beginning the stream flows northward and is parallelled by a brine line for most of its length. This line leaks in several places, and the result is 83 documented fish kills to date. There are also sewage overflows that cause the stream to go completely anoxic at times.

Given the above circumstances, one finds it amazing that trout can still be taken from Onondaga Creek. Yet, it's reported that as far downstream as the Syracuse city line large brown trout are taken at night on spinners and black streamers. Above the Onondaga Indian Reservation (fishing is not allowed on the reservation) browns can be taken, primarily using live bait or small spinners.

Quality wise, the best part of Onondaga Creek is the uppermost six miles, from tributary #22, found two miles below the crossing at Tully Farms Road (some posting above, mostly open below), to the stream's source. This section is stocked in the fall with 3,200 brown trout fingerlings.

NOTES: _____

_____

_____

_____

ONONDAGA CREEK (WEST BRANCH)
map coordinates . . . . 42° 55′ 42″ 76° 10′ 53″
USGS map(s) . . . . South Onondaga, Jamesville
location (township) . . . . Onondaga
access . . . . crossed and parallelled by Cedarvale Road
principle species . . . . brown trout (stocked & wild)

This 25 feet wide stream has a good year round flow over a bottom of gravel and rubble (there is some siltation in the larger pools). The surroundings are farmland and the bank cover is generally very good. There are several very large pools on the stream, and consequently, some very large brown trout. Because it gets little fishing pressure, these browns are pretty spooky, so be especially quiet when approaching the stream. As with most streams in this area, the tributaries will have nice populations of native brook trout, though very few will be found in the west branch of Onondaga Creek itself. The stream is very productive, and some sections, especially the larger pools, are marginally fly fishable. Some sections of this stream are posted, but land owners will usually give permission to fish here.

In the fall, the lower 6.5 miles of this stream is stocked by the state with 2,000 brown trout fingerlings.

NOTES: _____

_____

_____

_____

SENECA RIVER
map coordinates . . . . 43° 12′ 05″ 76° 16′ 52″
USGS map(s) . . . . Baldwinsville, Brewerton, Camillus, Lysander, Jordan, Weedsport, Montezuma
location . . . . Onondaga County, Cayuga County
access . . . . numerous launch sites are located along the river—see below
principle species . . . . largemouth bass, smallmouth bass, northern pike, bullhead, channel catfish, panfish

The Seneca River is the longest of Central New York's three major rivers (the other two being the Oneida and Oswego). An integral part of the New York State Barge Canal System, the Seneca River starts near the Howland Island State Wildlife Management Area, north of Cayuga Lake. It flows slowly for a distance of 47 miles, primarily through rural and light residential areas, before joining the Oneida River to form the Oswego River, near Baldwinsville.

The Seneca is typical of many large, flatland rivers. The current is minimal, the water turbid, and the bottom is composed primarily of silt and muck. The sections maintained as part of the canal system are dredged to a minimum of 12 feet. Consequently, there is little or no aquatic vegetation or riprap in the main channel. However, there are a great many back waters and loops along the river that are choked with lily pads, arrow root and cattails. These backwater sections are usually fairly shallow, but there are some holes over 15 feet deep. Overhung by black willows and alders, these areas provide some of the best fishing on the Seneca River.

The best fishing in the Seneca River is found upstream of the outlet of Onondaga Lake. Despite its appearance, the water quality in the upper sections of the river is good. The D.E.C. feels that the most popular and productive fishing here is for channel catfish. Though most often found in fast moving water, such as below dams and spillways, these tasty, hard fighting fish can be found in many parts of the Seneca River. Preferring deeper water with little or no weed cover, channel catfish are most often taken on hot summer nights by fishing on the bottom with cut bait or live minnows. A known hotspot for channel catfish is at Mosquito Point, off the eastern end of Haiti Island, where Route 38 crosses the river, and at Jack's Reef, downstream of Cross Lake.

A close relative of the channel catfish, the brown bullhead, is also popular with Seneca River fishermen. They too, can be found throughout much of the river, but are more closely associated with submerged weed beds than are catfish. Bullhead fishing is very popular with local anglers, who are very successful using worms, doughballs and small crabs. Mosquito Point is a top bullhead area, but don't fail to check out such areas as the eastern sides of Maloney Island, Forbes Island and Big Island. All of these have the type of habitat sought out by spring bullhead.

Walleye are another species popular with local anglers. Seneca River walleye are not quite as common as the aforementioned fish, but they do occur in good numbers, and some walleye manage to attain a very respectable size here. They are probably found throughout the dredged sections of the Seneca River, but there are a number of areas known to be especially productive for walleye. The stretch from Bonta Bridge downstream to Cross Lake has an abundant population of walleye. Further downstream the loop of the river that was bypassed by the state ditch cut is also very good for walleye. In the late spring, the water just below the Baldwinsville Bridge is a real hotspot. Local anglers do well using black and white jigs, small spinners or worm/spinner combinations.

Northern pike provide some of the most exciting fishing found in the Seneca River. The most productive reach for northerns is the section of the river that flows around Howland Island. The fishing is especially good from the northern tip of Howland Island to Mosquito Point, on Haiti Island. By drift fishing this stretch of water in the summer and early fall, you can be sure to experience some of the best northern pike fishing in the region. If you do not have a boat, try fishing from the shore at Mosquito Point. Small red and white spoons, golden shiners and Mepps spinners are all good for taking northerns in the morning here. Further downstream, trophy size northern pike can be taken in the deep channel between Bonta Bridge and Cross Lake. There are not a lot of northerns in this stretch, but they are big! When fishing for northerns in the Seneca River, do not limit yourself to the areas just mentioned. There are many submerged weedbeds along the river that almost certainly hold a few of these toothsome torpedos. Patience and practice are sure to pay off.

Largemouth bass, and to a much lesser extent, smallmouth bass, also contribute to the fishing in the Seneca River. This is not really good habitat for smallmouth bass, and most of them will be taken in the dredged channel. Largemouth bass, on the other hand, are very common and very well distributed. Look for water choked with vegetation and overhang by black willows or alders for the best action. The river, from the northern tip of Howland Island to Mosquito Point is very good for largemouth. This stretch of the river is ideally suited to fishing from a small cartop boat or canoe and can be extremely productive when fished in late June, July and August. But there are many other areas of the Seneca River that almost certainly hold good populations of largemouth. Try the waters around Haiti Island, the downstream end of the loop bypassed by the state ditch cut and the shallow weed beds around Forbes Island for good action.

Rounding out the fishing in the Seneca River upstream of Onondaga Lake are good populations of bluegills, white perch, yellow perch, black crappie and white crappie.

Due to the fact that the Seneca River is a part of the New York State Barge Canal System, the water levels here are artificially maintained. In the winter the water level is drawn down, but only about two feet. This has a minimal effect on the fish or their habitat. Thus, fishing here in the winter, which at present is almost nonexistent, should be a very viable possibility.

As indicated earlier in this article, the best fishing in the Seneca River is found upstream of the outlet of Onondaga Lake. The reason for this is the very poor quality of the water that the Lake feeds into the river. Very saline and full of organic pollutants, this outflow severely diminishes the quality of the habitat in the river, from Onondage Lake to its mouth at Three Rivers. The waters are so different in fact, due to differences in temperature and salinity, that the river below the outlet actually stratifies. There are few game fish found in this lower section of the river. The principle species consist of blue gills, white perch and rough fish such as sheepshead and suckers.

The Seneca River is very popular with pleasure boaters, canoeing enthusiasts and fishermen, though, with regard to fishing, the river is rather underutilized. This could be due, in part, to the fact that foot access to much of the Seneca River is generally poor. But, boat access is good. The following is a list of commercial marinas where launch ramps and other marine services are available:

1. Cold Springs Harbor — 3642 Hayes Road, Baldwinsville. Single hard surface ramp, parking - fee.

2. Cooper's Marina, Inc. — West Genesee Street, Baldwinsville, at upper level of lock 24. Single hard surface ramp, parking - fee.

3. J & S Marine — 3558 Hayes Road, Baldwinsville. Single hard surface ramp, parking - fee.

4. Motor Car & Marine — 8½ Syracuse Street, Baldwinsville, at lock 24. Single gravel ramp — fee.

5. Quimby's Marine — on River Road, one mile west of Cross Lake.

6. Rainbow Harbor — 3520 Hayes Road, Baldwinsville. Hard surface ramp — fee.

7. Howland Island Wildlife Management Area — off Route 38, 3½ miles north of Port Byron. Hard surface ramp, parking — no charge.

8. Bonta Bridge Road crossing — 2 miles east of Weedsport. Hand launch only — no charge.

9. Jack's Reef — bridge crossing 2 miles east of Cross Lake.

10. Mercer Park — off Charlotte Street in Baldwinsville.

11. Onondaga Lake Park — at north end of Onondaga Park. Launch ramp is off of Long Branch Road.

NOTES: _____

_____

_____

_____

— 54 —

SKANEATELES CREEK

map coordinates . . . . 43° 04' 39" 76° 30' 39"
USGS map(s) . . . . Weedsport, Jordan, Skaneateles
location (township) . . . . Cato (Cayuga County), Elbridge,
Skaneateles (Onondaga County)
access . . . . Route 31C — see below
principle species . . . . brown trout (stocked & wild),
rainbow trout (stocked)

A very high quality trout stream, Skaneateles Creek does not receive nearly as much attention as does Ninemile Creek, which is only a few miles to the east. This oddity is explained in the following article by J. Michael Kelly.

The amazing thing about Skaneateles Creek is its lack of popularity. Why is it that you can have this pretty little stream all to yourself on balmy May and June evenings when Nine Mile Creek, just six miles away, is crowded with anglers?

Maybe the answer lies in the fact that Skaneateles, now one of the best trout streams in the Syracuse area, wasn't a trout stream, at all, until the early 1970's. Before then it was so fouled by sewage and industrial effluent that it held few fish of any kind.

Then, one by one, the towns and manufacturers along the creek began to eliminate their deadly discharges, with prodding from state and federal agencies.

Experimental stockings of browns, rainbows and brookies followed, and Skaneateles now has provided more than a decade of good fishing to its comparative handful of devotees.

The creek has been reclassified as a C(T) stream —capable of supporting trout — for its entire 13-mile length.

Today the creek offers generous put and take fishing for stocked rainbows and browns, and shelters some heavyweight holdovers in its deeper pools. I have taken browns up to 21 inches in the stream, and one local angler took a fish of 24½ inches in April, 1986. Better than the lunkers to many fishermen are the tiny brown trout fingerlings that occasionally latch onto a dry fly or nymph drifted through the crystalline pools. They are proof of successful spawning, and a sure sign of the stream's bright future.

Skaneateles has its shortcomings, to be sure. For one thing, its average depth is barely a foot, and it runs only 10-12 feet wide in most places. Long stretches of shallow water and naked bedrock bottom limit its fish-holding capacity, and its water temperatures are only marginally suitable for trout during July and August.

Don't let these things discourage you, however. Although there are no marked "public fishing" sections on the stream, there are few "no trespassing" signs, either. Skaneateles is parallelled by paved roads for all but the last two miles of its journey from Skaneateles Lake to the Seneca River, and is criss-crossed by 18 bridges. It's barely 20 minutes from both Auburn and Syracuse. It has an abundance of aquatic insects and is full of black-nosed dace, chubs and sucker minnows. Its trout will never go hungry.

In some ways, it is an easy stream to fish. The annual stockings of 6,000 to 7,000 browns and rainbows from the Carpenter's Brook Hatchery are, if anything, too generous, and the choice pools are crowded with 8-9 inch fish in April and May. In-stream cover is sparse, compared to Ninemile Creek, Limestone Creek and other major trout streams in the Syracuse area, and the stocked fish tend to congregate in deep pools where they are readily accessible to patient worm and minnow anglers. The predominantly shallow flow may be one reason that Skaneateles Creek trout are prone to feed on the surface. They are absolute suckers for dries during the Hendrickson, Pale Evening Dun and March Brown hatches in May and June.

Big fish are not so easy to take on Skaneateles, of course. The holdover 14 to 20 inch browns typically seek out the thickest snags, and manage to disappear completely when careless anglers thrash about in the shallows or cast their shadows on the stream.

The lunker browns can be taken with some dependability, however, by anglers who arrive on the stream just after a spring or summer shower. As the water colors up, the browns leave their hideouts and move up to the riffly heads of Skaneateles Creek pools, where they will nab a dead-drifted worm, minnow, streamer fly or nymph. Capture of these two or three-pound browns and you'll likely find it has gorged on dace and sucker minnows. That 21-incher I mentioned earlier had four suckers in his stomach, one of them nearly six inches long.

Sean Kelly tries his angling skills out on Skaneateles Creek. Until the early 1970's Skaneateles Creek wasn't much more than an open sewer. Today rainbow trout and brown trout crowd its waters and provide some of the finest trout fishing in the Syracuse area. Photo courtesy J. Michael Kelly.

In the first seven miles of the creek, from the dam at Skaneateles Lake to the crossing at Hamilton Road near Route 5, bait fishing is a preferred method simply because heavy bank cover and the narrow channel tends to limit fly casting. Yet a careful flyfisher can pick and choose his spots on any stream, and nymphs, fished on a short line, are very effective in the larger pools around bridges and bends. One especially beautiful stretch of fly water in this part of the creek may be found above and below the Welch-Allyn Co. plant, near the intersection of Jordon and Stump roads, four miles downstream from the village of Skaneateles.

Below Elbridge, Route 31C takes you along some superb flyfishing water. For two miles, the creek cuts a channel through a steep-sided gorge, then flows placidly past half a dozen homes and into the village of Jordon. Unfortunately, a good share of this stretch is posted, and you should obtain permission from the landowners before trying your luck.

Within the Jordan village limits are some of the most productive pools in the entire stream. I like to fish them with worms in April and match the hatch later on.

Downstream from Jordan, the creek eases under the Thruway and finally empties into the Seneca River. Although there are some trout in this stretch, you should also expect to run into carp, suckers, occasional rock bass or smallmouths, and even a northern pike or two. Many of these fish come up from the river in warm weather.

You can count on good dry fly fishing from the second week of May into July on Skaneateles. Hendricksons and Pale Evening Duns (sulfurs) emerge from about May 10 to June 15, and March Browns show from the last week of May into the second week of June. Numerous caddis species hatch sporadically throughout May, June and July.

The sulfur fishing is perhaps the highlight of the season. At dusk, swarms of mating spinners can be so thick that trout have a hard time spotting your imitation amid the naturals drifting on the surface. A size 14 creme-yellow comparadun imitates the dun, and rusty-bodied, hen-winged spinner patterns, also size 14, should bring up a trout or two just before darkness sets in.

March Brown hatches are quite heavy on Skaneateles, particularly on the riffly sections around the Stump Road and Irish Road crossings. These big mayflies, imitated with a size 10 or 12 fly, tend to emerge sporadically all day long, but their heavy spinner flights may not begin until an hour before sunset.

Once the March Brown hatches are over, Skaneateles trout rise dependably to attractor patterns like the Ausable Wulff or Badger Bivisible until about mid-May. At that time, afternoon water temperatures climb into the mid-70's, trout migrate to the spring holes, and fishing becomes an early morning or after-the-rain proposition until September.

NOTES: _____

_____

_____

_____

SPAFFORD BROOK

map coordinates	42° 50' 13" 76° 14' 57"
USGS map(s)	Otisco Valley
location (township)	Spafford, Tully
access	crossing at Church Road
principle species	brown trout (stocked & wild), rainbow trout (wild)

Spafford Brook is the principle inlet of Otisco Lake. Only seven miles in length, this is a stream of contrasts and can be divided into three distinct sections. The lower most section, from Otisco Lake upstream to Church Road, is a sluggish, swampy, beaver dominated waterway that is marginally warm and not especially good for any particular species. Some good browns can be found in the section between Church Road and Sawmill Road, but this is

a fair fishery at best. This lower reach does not appear to benefit from a strong run of fish from Otisco Lake, either.

From Church Road upstream to Bromley Road, Spafford Brook is a good quality trout stream. This section averages about 10 feet in width and is surrounded by mature hardwoods. There is a lot of clay substrate, resulting in some turbidity. The stream has a moderate gradient and good riffle/pool ratio. There are plenty of stocked and wild brown trout in this middle reach, and there is a good deal of carry over, so the chances of hooking into a lunker brown are promising.

Above Bromley Road, Spafford Brook is threaded, or highly channeled. Surrounded by mature hardwoods, the gradient in this section is rather high, and the stream is brush lined. About all of the fish found here are wild brown trout, augmented by a sprinkling of native rainbow trout. The rainbows are all brightly colored and non-migratory; they do not move down into Otisco Lake, but remain in the headwaters of Spafford Brook.

In the fall, Spafford Brook is stocked with 1,300 brown trout fingerlings.

NOTES: _____

_____

_____

TIOUGHNIOGA CREEK
(west branch of east branch)

map coordinates	42° 44' 41" 75° 57' 15"
USGS map(s)	Cuyler, De Ruyter
location (township)	Cuyler (Cortland County), Fabius (Onondaga County)
access	crossings at Bardeen Road and Harris Road
principle species	brook trout (wild), brown trout (wild), burbot

This is a unique, above average trout stream that despite its productivity, gets relatively little attention from local anglers. The stream averages about 40 feet in width, has a gravel bottom and is surrounded by farmlands, and above Fabius, cedar swamps. There are flow problems in the upper reaches during dry summers, but below Fabius there is a year round flow of cool, clear water. Much of the adjacent land is grazed, and as a result most of the stream is quite open.

The village of Fabius is a convenient point to divide this stream. Aboved Fabius brook trout are by far the predominant species. Access is only fair due to a general lack of roads (there is a crossing at Pompey Center Road) and swampy terrain. The brook trout are numerous and you do not have a great deal of fallfish and other competitive species to deal with.

Below Fabius (actually the crossing at Route 80) the fish population becomes more diverse. There are good numbers of native brook and brown trout as far down stream as the hamlet of Keeney near the Cortland County line. Unfortunately, there are large populations of fallfish, creek chubs, and oddly enough burbot. These freshwater cod, which are very fine table fair, are occasionally found in some of the smaller tributaries of the Susquehanna River drainage system. Because of the large numbers of fall fish and creek chubs, bait or spinner fishing would be difficult, but the stream is sufficiently open to fly fish. Below Keeney the stream quickly grades to warm water, but the flow does not become significant warm water fishery until well below its junction with the east branch of Tioughnioga Creek.

This stream is not stocked.

NOTES: _____

_____

_____

ONONDAGA COUNTY LAKES AND PONDS

GREEN LAKE #1

map coordinates	43° 02' 02" 75° 57' 59"
USGS map(s)	Manlius
location	Green Lake State Park
access	off Route 5 on Route 290 in township of Manlius

Physical Characteristics

area	150 acres
shoreline	1.8 miles
elevation	418 feet
maximum depth	192 feet
mean depth	N.A.
bottom type	marl, bedrock

Chemical Characteristics

water clarity	extremely clear
pH	neutral
oxygen	This lake is meromictic — see general information.

Plant Life

Extremely limited, even in shallow water areas.

Species Information

rainbow trout	common; put and take only

There are also very insignificant populations of sunfish, largemouth bass and northern pike in Green Lake.

Boat Launch Sites

Row boats are rented in the park.

General Information

Green Lake was formed as a melt water plunge pool at the end of the last glacial retreat, about 11,000 years ago. Because of its great depth (192 feet), relatively small surface area, and protection from the wind, this lake does not experience mixing and turnover, thus there is no oxygen in the lower layers of water. Such lakes are known as meromictic. Eleven such lakes exist in the United States, 2 of which are located in Green Lake State Park (Green Lake and Round Lake).

The only significant fishing in this lake is for rainbow trout, which are stocked here by the Onondaga County fish hatchery. Excess breeder trout are also stocked here occasionally by the state. This is strictly a put-and-take fishery, with the best action occuring in the spring.

Trout can be taken from Green Lake from April 1 to November 30, any size, 10 fish per day.

NOTES: _____

_____

_____

_____

GREEN LAKE #2

map coordinates	42° 59' 45" 76° 05' 30"
USGS map(s)	Jamesville
location	township of Dewitt, in Clark Reservation State Park
access	off Route 173

Physical Characteristics

area	8 acres
shore line	0.4 miles
elevation	570 feet
maximum depth	62 feet
mean depth	N.A.
bottom type	primarily bedrock, rubble

Chemical Characteristics

water clarity	very clear
pH	alkaline
oxygen	good except in the deepest parts of the lake

Plant Life

There is minimal rooted aquatic vegetation in Green Lake. Algae blooms are not a problem here.

Boat Launch Sites

Boats are not allowed on this lake.

Species Information

walleye	common; growth rate fair
largemouth bass	uncommon, growth rate fair
chain pickerel	uncommon; growth rate fair
bullhead	common; growth rate fair
pumpkinseeds	common; growth rate fair

General Information

Located in the 290 acre Clark Reservation State Park, Green Lake, known also as Round Lake, is the remnant of a large glacial plunge pool. A number of fish species are found here, but because there is relatively little actual habitat, their numbers are limited. Probably the most important species here is the walleye. Walleye are stocked in Green Lake at the rate of 20,000 fry per year.

In addition to fishing, Clark Reservation has numerous hiking trails, unique geological formations and a wide variety of rare plants. For further information contact the park at (315) 492-1500.

NOTES: _____

_____

_____

_____

JAMESVILLE RESERVOIR

map coordinates	42° 58' 57" 76° 04' 12"
USGS map(s)	Jamesville
location	township of Lafayette
access	Jamesville Beach County Park on the west side of lake. Parallelled by Route 91 on the east side of lake.

Physical Characteristics

area	333 acres
shoreline	3.2 miles
elevation	640 feet
maximum depth	38 feet
mean depth	22 feet
bottom type	gravel, silt

Chemical Characteristics

water clarity	slightly turbid
pH	alkaline
oxygen	oxygen depletion occurs in the deep water near the dam in the summer, but not to a serious degree.

Plant Life

There is relatively little rooted aquatic vegetation in this reservoir.

Species Information

walleye	common; growth rate good
largemouth bass	common, growth rate good
smallmouth bass	common; growth rate good
rock bass	common; growth rate good
tiger muskellunge	uncommon; growth rate good
brown trout	uncommon; growth rate good
yellow perch	common; growth rate good
bluegills	common; growth rate good
bullhead	common; growth rate good

Boat Launch Sites

1. Small boats can be hand launched at Jamesville Beach Park. The boat must be carried a short distance to the water.

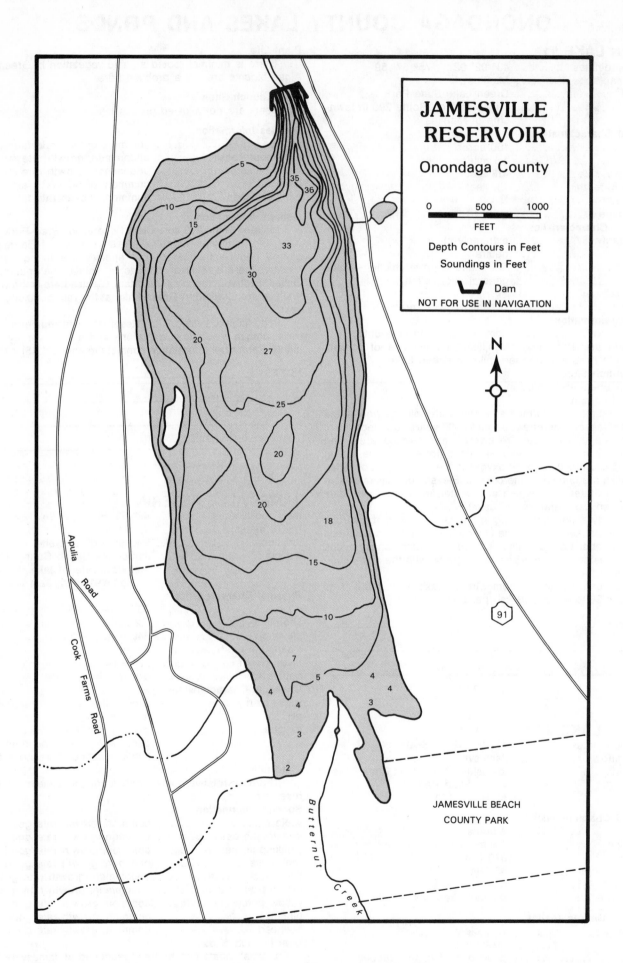

JAMESVILLE
RESERVOIR

Onondaga County

0   500   1000
FEET

Depth Contours in Feet
Soundings in Feet

⊔ Dam
NOT FOR USE IN NAVIGATION

N

5
35
36
10
15
33
30
20
27
25
20
20
18
15
10
91
7
5
4
4
4
4
3
3
2

Apulia Road

Cook Farms Road

Butternut Creek

JAMESVILLE BEACH
COUNTY PARK

General Information

An impoundment of Butternut Creek, Jamesville Reservoir was created in the mid-nineteenth century as part of the barge canal feeder system. A stable pool level is now maintained and the reservoir serves primarily as a recreational resource. Most of the impoundment is a relatively steep, gravel-sided basin, grading to silt in the southern end near the inlet. The reservoir was last drained in 1978 to repair the dam, and the population of fish has not yet fully recovered. Though population levels are down, there is a well balanced mix of warm water species. Included is a small population of blue spotted sunfish. These beautifully colored fish are normally found south of New York State and their origin in the reservoir is unknown. Brown trout are also found in the reservoir, though in very limited numbers. They drop down from Butternut Creek, and a majority of them are taken close to the inlet of the creek. A few browns are also taken from the deep water near the dam. The special regulations that apply to Butternut Creek do not apply to the Jamesville Reservoir.

In recent years, the state has stocked tiger muskellunge here, with some success. This stocking policy was discontinued when walleye fingerlings became available. The reservoir is now stocked annually with 16,600 walleye fingerling, and it is hoped that this will establish a very good walleye fishery in the reservoir. If this doesn't occur, the state will probably revert back to stocking tiger muskies. On occasion, the Jamesville Reservoir is stocked with rainbow trout by Onondaga County.

NOTES: _____

_____

_____

ROUND LAKE

map coordinates.......... 43° 02' 52"   75° 58' 32"
USGS map(s)............. Manlius
location .... Green Lake State Park in Manlius township
access .... off Route 5 on Route 290

Physical Characteristics

area .... 38 acres
shoreline .... 0.9 miles
elevation .... 421 feet
maximum depth .... 180 feet
mean depth .... N.A.
bottom type .... marl, bedrock

Chemical Characteristics

water clarity .... extremely clear
pH....................... neutral
oxygen................... This lake is meromictic — see general information.

Plant Life

Rooted aquatic vegetation is extremely limited in this lake.

Species Information

rainbow trout............ common; put-and-take only

Boat Launch Sites

There are no launch sites on this lake.

General Information

Located adjacent to Green Lake, in Green Lake State Park, this lake, like Green Lake, is meromictic. The lower waters essentially never mix with the upper layers, and thus, there is no oxygen at the bottom of this lake. Formed as a glacial melt water plunge pool about 11,000 years ago, this deep, steep sided lake has been designated as a natural landmark because of its meromictic character and because of the unique nature of the mature mesophytic forests which surround it.

Fishing in Round Lake is limited to rainbow trout, which are stocked here annually by the County of Onondaga fish hatchery. The best action takes place in the spring (put-and-take only).

Green Lake State Park also provides hiking trails, a swimming beach, golf course, cabins and campgrounds.

Trout can be taken from Round Lake from April 1 to November 30, any size, 10 fish per day.

NOTES: _____

_____

_____

LABRADOR POND

map coordinates......... 42° 47' 12"   76° 03' 04"
USGS map(s)............. Tully
location .... township of Fabuis
access .... Cross Road off Markham Hollow Rd.

Physical Characteristics

area .... 102 acres
shoreline .... 1.6 miles
elevation .... 1,190 feet
maximum depth .... approximately 10 feet
mean of depth........... approximately 5 feet
bottom depth .... muck

Chemical Characteristics

water clarity .... brown stained
pH....................... acidic
oxygen................... oxygen depletion is a problem in the lake, especially in the winter.

Plant Life

Rooted aquatic plants are abundant in Labrador Pond, but not as much as would normally be expected in a body of water as shallow as this. This is probably due to the poor light penetration in the water.

Species Information

chain pickerel .... common; growth rate fair
largemouth bass .... common; growth rate fair
bullhead .... common; growth rate good
pumpkinseed .... common; growth rate poor
bluegill................... common; growth rate poor
yellow perch .... common; growth rate poor

Boat Launch Sites

Strictly speaking, there are no boat launch sites on this pond. Small boats (no motors) are allowed on the pond. They must be carried from the access point to the water, which is quite a distance.

General Information

Labrador Pond is located on the Onondaga/Cortland County line, in the Labrador Hollow Unique Area. The area covers approximately 1,300 acres of a glacial trough valley.

The steep sides of the valley are covered with a variety of hardwoods, while the lowland exhibit a mix of hemlock, pines, birch and alder. The pond itself is ringed by a bog where a number of unique plants grow (pitcher plants, sundew, etc.). To protect the plants from being trampled, shore fishing is prohibited.

The fish population in Labrador Pond is stressed. Chain pickerel and largemouth bass are the principle predators, but they are generally small. Occasionally a large 6 to 8 pound bass is taken here, but such fish are uncommon. This isn't a really good bass lake, because of the turbidity and problems with the pond's chemistry. The panfish are also stunted and the only species that seems to do well here are bullheads.

Aside from the fishing found here, the Labrador Hollow Unique Area is popular for bird watching and hiking, and a hang gliding site has been established northeast of the pond on the east scarp. A special use permit is required for hang gliding.

The area is administered by a lake committee. Regulations have been drawn up that prohibit camping, train biking, snowmobiling and motorized boats.

NOTES: _____

_____

_____

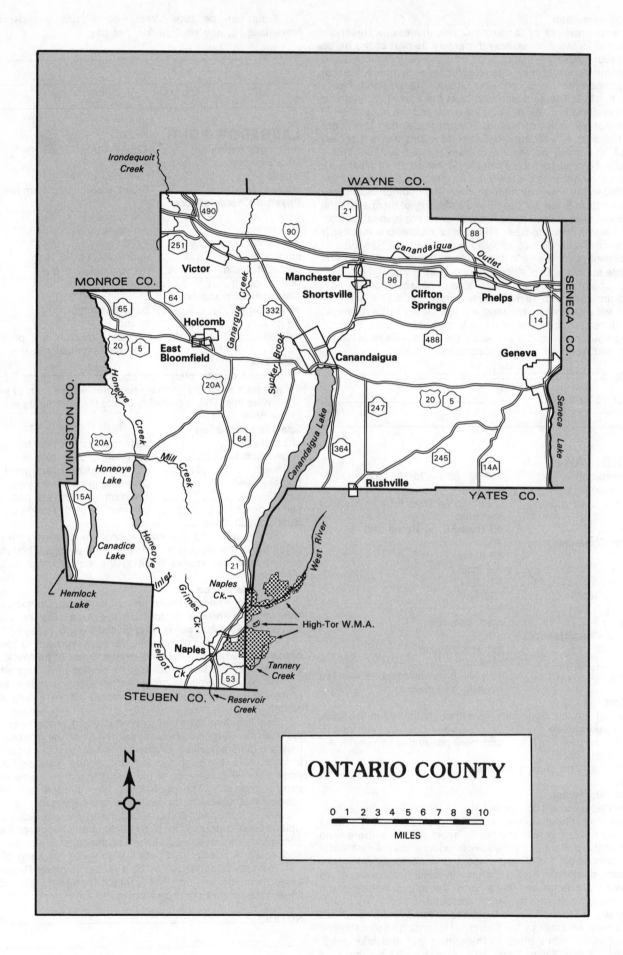

Irondequoit Creek

WAYNE CO.

490

251

21

90

Victor

Canandaigua Outlet

88

MONROE CO.

64

Manchester

96

Clifton Springs

Phelps

14

Shortsville

65

332

Ganargua Creek

488

Geneva

20

5

Holcomb

East Bloomfield

Sucker Brook

Canandaigua

247

20

5

20A

LIVINGSTON CO.

64

364

245

14A

20A

Mill Creek

Rushville

YATES CO.

15A

Honeoye Lake

Honeoye Creek

Canandaigua Lake

Seneca Lake

SENECA CO.

Canadice Lake

Honeoye Inlet

West River

Hemlock Lake

Grimes Ck.

21

Naples Ck.

High-Tor W.M.A.

Naples

53

Eelpot Ck.

Tannery Creek

STEUBEN CO.

Reservoir Creek

N

ONTARIO COUNTY

0 1 2 3 4 5 6 7 8 9 10

MILES

ONTARIO COUNTY STREAMS AND RIVERS

CANANDAIGUA LAKE OUTLET

map coordinates	43° 03' 41" 76° 59' 48"
USGS map(s)	Lyons, Newark, Geneva North, Phelps
location (township)	Lyons (Wayne County); Phelps, Manchester, Hopewell, Canandaigua (Ontario County)
access	roughly parallelled by Route 21 between Canandaigua and Manchester; parallelled by Outlet Road, off Route 21 east of Manchester; parallelled by Route 14 south of Lyons.
principle species	smallmouth bass, bullhead, chain pickerel

Canandaigua Lake Outlet is a major warmwater system averaging about 50 feet in width. Originating in Ontario County, it follows a circuitous route to the town of Lyons in Wayne County, where it enters the New York State Barge Canal.

A diverse waterway, its deep pools, slack-water areas and brisk rapids provide habitat for the major game species here, smallmouth bass. The bass are modest sized, but numerous. In the summer there are some very weedy pools that occasionally give up a chain pickerel, and the flat water in the upper reaches of the creek provide some fairly good bullhead fishing.

This stream offers one the opportunity to take a modest float trip in the summer. You can put in at Clifton Springs and take out at Phelps. Fly fishing for bass is superior here. An occasional trout will be taken in the upper reaches between Canandaigua and Clifton Springs.

There is limited public access to Canandaigua Lake Outlet, and most bank fishing is by permission only. But the quality of the bass fishing makes the effort worthwhile.

This stream is not stocked.

NOTES: _____

_____

_____

_____

GRIMES CREEK

map coordinates	42° 36' 35" 77° 24' 14"
USGS map(s)	Naples, Bristol Springs
location (township)	Naples
access	crossing at Route 21 — see below
principle species	rainbown trout (wild), brown trout (wild), brook trout (wild)

Grimes Creek is the largest most productive trout tributary of Naples Creek. This important stream can be divided into upper and lower sections by a bedrock falls, which is located about three quarters of a mile upstream of the confluence with Naples Creek.

The upstream section of Grimes Creek is a small, good quality brook and brown trout stream. Unfortunately, this reach is very heavily posted. Given the close proximity of so many other good quality trout streams that are open to the public, the upper reach of Grimes Creek can safely be ignored.

The lower reach of Grimes Creek is a real gem of a stream. Averaging 12 feet in width, this gravel and rubble bottomed stream has very few holding area for fish, such as pools and deep runs. In any one year you might expect to find two or three holes that hold any significant number of fish, with the exception of a large, deep (up to eight feet) pool at the base of the falls that holds

fish all season long. The water flow and quality of Grimes Creek are generally very good, though flows are reduced in the summer. Even in the summer, though, there are sections of the stream that are fishable.

In the spring Grimes Creek gets a good run of wild rainbows from Canandaigua Lake, via Naples Creek. This run is repeated, to a lesser degree, in the fall, if rainfall has been sufficient. Most of the rainbows taken in the fall will be two to four pound males. These will be supplemented to a small extent by runs of brown trout from the lake, and a few wild brook and brown trout that drop down from the upper reaches of the stream.

Like Naples Creek, Grimes Creek is most heavily fished in the spring, especially in the days just after the opening of trout season. Later in the spring, indeed into the summer, there are still fish to be caught here, and the crowds are decidedly thinner. Better yet, in the fall you can enjoy some fine rainbow trout and brown trout fishing, and have large sections of the stream to yourself.

An interesting side to the fishing on Grimes Creek is fish watching. Because of the clarity of the water, the general lack of hiding places and the large number of fish that run here in the spring, the spawning rainbows can be seen in the water very easily, especially when viewed through polorizing lenses. Many people come here just prior to the opening of trout season to do this, and it can be quite a rewarding experience for adults and children alike!

Due to the popularity of Grimes Creek, the state has obtained a total of .675 miles of public fishing easements on the stream, all located downstream of the lower falls.

Grimes Creek is not stocked.

NOTES: _____

_____

_____

_____

HONEOYE INLET

map coordinates	42° 43' 17" 77° 30' 43"
USGS map(s)	Springwater, Bristol Springs
location (township)	Canadice, South Bristol, Naples
access	parallelled by East Lake Road
principle species	brown trout (wild), black crappie

Upstream of the crossing of East Hill Road (County Road 36), Honeoye Inlet is a small gravel and rubble bottomed stream approximately ten feet in width. There is a substantial population of wild brown trout here, and this was augmented at one time by stocked browns. The stocking program was discontinued because of heavy posting. However, if you can get the landowners permission, the upper reaches of Honeoye Inlet should make your efforts worthwhile.

The lower portion of Honeoye Inlet could provide some fine black crappie fishing in the spring, but posting on the lower portions of the creek is even more prevalent than on the upper portions and landowner permission is not usually given.

The stream is not stocked.

NOTES: _____

_____

_____

_____

— 61 —

IRONDEQUOIT CREEK

NOTE: Although very little of Irondequoit Creek is in Ontario County, the importance of this creek to anglers in Central New York should not be underestimated, especially in light of the recent stockings of Atlantic Salmon. I'm taking this opportunity to revise and update my original article on this stream, which appeared in Sander's Fishing Guide to Western New York. - J.M.S.

map coordinates	43° 10' 39" 77° 31' 33"
USGS map(s)	Rochester East, Webster, Fairport, Pittsford
location (township)	Pennfield, Perinton, Mendon (Monroe County), Victor (Ontario County)
access	cartop and canoe access site off Route 404; Ellison Park, on Route 286 (Blossom Road); Penfield Linear Park, south of Route 441; Panorama Plaza; Powder Mill Park, off Route 96 (Pittsford-Victor Road); town access site, on Main Street in Fishers, north of Route 251.
principle species	rainbow trout (stocked), brown trout (stocked and wild), atlantic salmon, northern pike, bullhead, panfish

Not too long ago, Irondequoit Creek was a heavily polluted stream of little value to fishermen. In recent years, however, it has been returned to a relatively clean state. This turnaround has been accomplished by putting an end to the dumping of municipal sewage into the stream, with the result that today it ranks as one of the top rainbow trout (steelhead) streams in New York State.

Tremendous numbers of these big, hard fighting fish can be found in Irondequoit Creek from mid-fall until late spring. They will run at least as far up as the town of Fishers in Ontario County. If water levels are sufficiently high, steelhead will also be found in several tributary streams, most notably Allens Creek, north of Route 441. In the spring 24,000 steelhead are stocked in Irondequoit Creek.

At present Irondequoit Creek is not an important salmon stream. A few coho and chinook do stray into the lower creek in the fall, with a majority of these fish taken in the vicinity of Ellison Park. The quality of salmon fishing in this creek could improve in the very near future though, if experimental stockings of atlantic salmon prove successful. In the spring 18,000 atlantic salmon are stocked

here in the hope that this once native game fish can be reestablished. (Because of the need to protect the spawning atlantic salmon, Irondequoit Creek is closed to **all** fishing from October 1 to November 30; check the current New York State fishing regulations guide for current regulations).

Above Fairport Road, south of East Rochester, Irondequoit Creek is a good quality inland trout stream. Averaging ten to twenty feet in width, it is surrounded mainly by residential areas and park land, but does run through a wooded area near Bushnell Basin. This section of the stream is fishable all trout season. Wild browns can be found in fairly good numbers as far upstream as the mouth of Trout Brook, near Bloomfield Road in Mendon Township.

The County of Monroe maintains a hatchery at Powder Mills Park. This facility has always provided large numbers of brown trout for Irondequoit Creek. Recently, however, the hatchery has switched to stocking rainbow trout. At various times during the year, local sportsmens groups, in cooperation with the hatchery, hold fishing derbies for children and senior citizens in Powder Mills Park. Usually, the creek will be posted with "no fishing" signs a few days prior to the event and hatchery fish will be stocked specifically for the derby. A few breeder fish are added to the stocking to give the participants the opportunity to take a 6 lb. - 10 lb. brown trout.

In the spring, 1,300 brown trout yearlings are stocked in Irondequoit Creek, between the Barge Canal and the boundery of Powder Mills Park. An additional 300 brown trout yearlings are stocked between the Monroe/Ontario County line and the mouth of Trout Brook. In Ontario County, Irondequoit Creek is stocked in the spring from the county line upstream 0.8 miles to the hamlet of Fishers with 500 brown trout.

A number of warm water species are found in Irondequoit Creek, including northern pike, bullhead, rock bass and an occasional walleye. Northerns can be found in the very lowest reaches of the creek all year long. In the spring they run up Irondequoit Creek, at least as far as Allens Creek, to spawn. A limited run of suckers also takes place in the spring.

A major problem on Irondequoit Creek is access. It is very heavily posted, especially below the Barge Canal. There are tentative plans for the state to acquire public fishing rights on the creek. These plans, though, could be affected by the special regulations that are likely to be implemented if the atlantic salmon stocking program is successful. Be sure to check your current regulations guide when fishing this creek.

NOTES: _____

_____

_____

_____

Atlantic salmon were once native to Lake Ontario and provided a spectacular fishery. The salmon population in the lake was wiped out by the destruction of their spawning streams. Efforts are being made to re-establish a viable population of Atlantic salmon in Lake Ontario. Experimental stockings are presently being made in Irondequoit Creek, Lindsey Creek and Little Sandy Creek.

MILL CREEK

map coordinates . . . . 42° 47′ 20″ 77° 30′ 54″
USGS map(s) . . . . Honeoye, Bristol Center, Bristol
Springs
location (township) . . . . Richmond, Bristol, South Bristol
access . . . . crossed by County Road 33
(Egypt-Honeoye Road) approxi-
mately one-quarter mile west of
Egypt Road
principle species . . . . brown trout (wild)

Mill Creek is a small tributary of Honeoye Lake Outlet. A mediocre quality trout stream, it averages about fifteen feet in width, has a gravel and rubble bottom and a fair amount of bank cover. There are a number of good size pools in Mill Creek that could make stopping here worth your while if you are already in the area.

This creek is not stocked.

NOTES: _____

_____

_____

_____

NAPLES CREEK

map coordinates . . . . 42° 39′ 07″ 77° 21′ 31″
USGS map(s) . . . . Middlesex, Bristol Springs, Naples
location (township) . . . . Italy (Yates County), Naples (Ontario County)
access . . . . there is extensive public access
to this stream — see below
principle species . . . . rainbow trout (wild), brown trout
(stocked and wild), smelt

Naples Creek is truly a phenomenon. More than just a good trout stream (good is an understatement; Naples Creek is one of the most productive trout streams in New York State) it, like Catharine Creek and a very few other streams, has become intimately woven into the rights of spring for thousands of serious, and not so serious, trout fishermen. Every spring, when the stream is swollen by the cold runoff of the parting winter, anglers from all over the northeastern United States huddle elbow to elbow along Naples, waiting for that first exhilarating strike of the season. And the time spent in the cold, damp morning air is usually well rewarded. For Naples Creek gets one of the most spectacular runs of wild rainbows of any of the Finger Lakes tributaries. Literally thousands of sleek, hard-fighting rainbows can be found in the stream at any one time, ranging in weight from three to six pounds. Their lightning fast runs and high-flying acrobatics will cure even the most advanced cases of cabin fever.

Technically speaking, Naples Creek is formed by the confluence of Eelpot Creek and Grimes Creek. However, Eelpot Creek is usually considered to be nothing more than the upper reach of Naples Creek.

The main section of Naples Creek, from the crossing at Parish Road upstream to the mouth of Grimes Creek, averages 20 to 25 feet in width during a normal spring runoff. The bottom consists of gravel and rubble, and the surroundings are primarily farmlands and vineyards. The water is normally clear, but you might not think so in early April. It does not take a great deal of rain to make this stream turbid, and it usually takes about three days for it to completely clear up. Even if there has not been any rain for a week, though, the stream is usually muddied up by 10:00 a.m. during the opening days of trout season. This is accomplished by the hundreds of anglers wading in Naples Creek or its tributaries. When the water becomes too murky, either from the rains or from wading fishermen, the fishing can be adversely affected or shut right down. You do not want crystal clear water

when you are fishing with egg sacs, but you cannot fish in chocolate colored water either.

Fish begin moving into Naples Creek in large numbers as soon as there is a big runoff. This means that rainbows can be found here as early as February if conditions are right. By the time the season opens on this stream, the spawning runs are well underway, and rainbows are often stacked up like cordwood. Twenty years ago it was common to land fish up to 15 pounds. Now a fish of 6 or 7 pounds is about the limit. The reason for this, according to the D.E.C., is increasing angling pressure on Canandaigua Lake and the successful introduction of techniques, originally developed on the Great Lakes, for finding and landing adult rainbows in Canandaigua Lake. This effectively culls the larger rainbows from the population before they can enter the streams. Fortunately, this has not affected the numbers of fish that survive to spawn.

The most popular method for taking Naples Creek rainbows is drifting egg sacs, preferably brown trout eggs. Drifting worms is also a common and successful practice. Not many people fly fish this water, but most of the stream, from one-half mile below the bridge at Route 245 upstream to Grimes Creek, is sufficiently open to enable you to cast. One fisherman who has spent years fishing here suggested using small red and white or orange and white streamers tied on a #4 - #8 hook when nothing else seems to be working. He feels that someone who really knows how to fish a streamer properly could clean up on finicky, spawning rainbows.

While most people are familiar with Naples Creek as a spring fishery, few people, even among the locals, realize that there is summer fishing here as well. It's not fantastic, but it's not bad. The stream holds juvenile rainbows all year long, and they tend to congregate in the deeper runs and pools. The number of such holding areas has declined somewhat over the years as the D.E.C. constructs stream improvement structures that favor bank stabilization. There are still enough pool diggers and natural pools, especially between the old fair grounds and Grimes Creek,

A trophy rainbow from Naples Creek. Most rainbows taken here will weigh 3 to 6 pounds, but occasionally a real trophy of 10 pounds or better is recorded. Photo courtest of C. Scott Sampson.

to make a trip here worthwhile. By fishing small wet or dry flies, or very small spinners, juveniles up to 14 inches can be taken from the larger pools. And you won't have to worry about crowds. You will probably be the only person on the stream.

Another neglected aspect of Naples Creek is its fall run of not only rainbows, but brown trout. The D.E.C. stocks thousands of brown trout in Canandaigua Lake each year, and many of these fish find their way into Naples Creek in the late fall. Their numbers are augmented by a smaller, but significant run of wild rainbows. The stream gets very little fishing pressuring during this period (spring fishermen are often fall hunters), and you can have some outstanding trout fishing almost to yourself.

The upper reaches of Naples Creek, known as Eelpot Creek, is simply a smaller version of the lower sections. It runs between 6 and 12 feet in width, has a gravel bottom and is subject to the same turbidity problems as Naples Creek. The uppermost portion of Eelpot Creek flows through woodlands and has a lot of in-stream logs and brush piles, as well as numerous undercut banks, exposed tree roots, and difficult to fish pools, all of which hold fish. An overwhelming majority of the fish found in Eelpot Creek are spawning rainbows and browns, but the headwaters do have a small population of resident, wild brown trout.

Eelpot Creek is much too small and confined for fly fishing. This is typical drifting water. Worms or egg sacs drifted into a small pool or undercut bank will entice both rainbows and browns from their hiding places. In the lower most reach of Eelpot Creek, where there is enough room for a short cast, small spinner are also productive.

Twenty years ago Naples Creek was very heavily fished as late as May. Today many anglers are drawn to the waters of Lake Ontario, and consequently, pressure on this stream has diminished (this is generally true for all inland streams). Now the only time that you find the worst crowding on Naples Creek is during the first week or two of the season and a couple of the following weekends. Beyond that you can have much of this amazing stream to yourself.

To facilitate access to Naples Creek, the state has acquired 9.5 miles of public fishing easements on the stream as well as 5 developed parking areas and 3 foot path right-of-ways. The parking areas are located as follows: (1) On Route 21, about one-half mile upstream of the crossing at Parish Flat Road. (2) At the crossing of Route 245. (3) Off East Hill Road, near the mouth of Tannery Creek. (4) On Eelpot Road, 500 feet west of Cohocton Street (Route 21), (5) On Eelpot Road, between Dug Road and Tinney Road.

NOTES: _____

_____

_____

_____

RESERVOIR CREEK

map coordinates	42° 36′ 28″ 77° 24′ 44″
USGS map(s)	Naples
location (township)	Naples (Ontario County), Prattsburg (Steuben County)
access	crossing at Route 21 — see below
principle species	rainbow trout (wild), brook trout (wild)

Reservoir Creek is a small tributary of Naples Creek, which it joins just south of the town of Naples. The stream averages 10 feet in width, has a gravel and rubble bottom and has a good seasonal flow of water. It can get very low in the summer. Flowing through agricultural land and woodlands, Reservoir Creek is loaded with a lot of natural cover. Numerous log jams, pools, undercut banks and overhanging trees provide hiding areas for the wild rainbows that run here in the spring. This run of fish is very good and is repeated in the fall if the rains are sufficient. Reservoir Creek is such that it does not get fished out quickly in

the spring. There are so many places for the fish to hold over in that, if fished properly, the stream will be productive all spring. It is a little too small for fly fishing, but this is an ideal stream for drifting worms, egg sacs or very small spinners.

The upper reaches of Reservoir Creek, while very small, do provide some fishing for wild brook trout.

To guarantee public access to this stream, the state has purchased a total of .241 miles of public fishing easements on Reservoir Creek, near Route 21.

Reservoir Creek is not stocked.

NOTES: _____

_____

_____

_____

SUCKER BROOK

map coordinates	42° 52′ 25″ 77° 16′ 34″
USGS map(s)	Canandaigua, Canandaigua Lake
location (township)	Canandaigua
access	the New York State office of Parks and Recreation maintains a hard surface launch ramp on a Sucker Brook, off Routes 5 and 20, near the north end of Canandaigua Lake.
principle species	bullhead, crappie

In the spring of the year, the portion of Sucker Brook downstream of Routes 5 and 20 often provides good fishing for bullheads, and, on occasion, crappie. This is an otherwise unimportant fishery.

NOTES: _____

_____

_____

_____

TANNERY CREEK

map coordinates	42° 06′ 33″ 77° 24′ 17″
USGS map(s)	Naples, Prattsburg
location (township)	Naples (Ontario County), Italy (Yates County)
access	parallelled by East Hill Road — see below
principle species	rainbow trout (wild), brook trout (wild), brown trout (wild)

Tannery Creek is one of the more important tributaries of Naples Creek. Averaging twelve to fifteen feet in width, the stream has a gravel and rubble bottom, a lot of bank cover—it's too brushy to fly fish—and flows through steep-sided, shaded cut, so plan on doing some wading if you are going to fish here. It usually has a good flow of cold, clear water, though it does get a bit low in the summer. Even then, however, the stream holds fish.

There is a falls about three quarters of a mile above the confluence with Naples Creek, and it is this short lower reach that is really important as a fishery. Like other tributaries of Naples Creek, Tannery Creek gets a good run of wild adult rainbows each spring. This run is repeated, though to a lesser extent, in the fall if rainfall has been sufficient. Because of the general lack of pools, size of the rocks and shallow depth and clarity of the water, this stream can be very difficult to fish. Most of the rainbows will be found holding in the white water behind the larger rocks. The average fish taken from Tannery Creek is a bit smaller than those found in Grimes Creek or Naples Creek. Few if any fish in this stream will be over six pounds.

Above the falls, Tannery Creek has a good population of wild brown trout, and some wild brook trout can be found in the headwaters of the stream. As with the lower reach, the upper section of this stream is too brushy to fly fish, but is a good stream for drifting worms or salted minnows. Water levels get low in the summer, and the fish are easily spooked, but Tannery Creek is one of those streams that, if fished properly, can produce fish all season long.

Tannery Creek is very popular with fishermen in the spring. To assure access to the stream, the state has purchased .195 miles of public fishing easements on Tannery Creek, below the falls. A public parking area is located near the junction of Tannery Creek and Naples Creek.

Tannery Creek is not stocked.

NOTES: _____

_____

_____

_____

Opening day on Naples Creek. Some people might not consider this fishing, but the crowds and camaraderie of opening day have an almost religious significance for thousands of New York anglers. Photo courtesy of C. Scott Sampson.

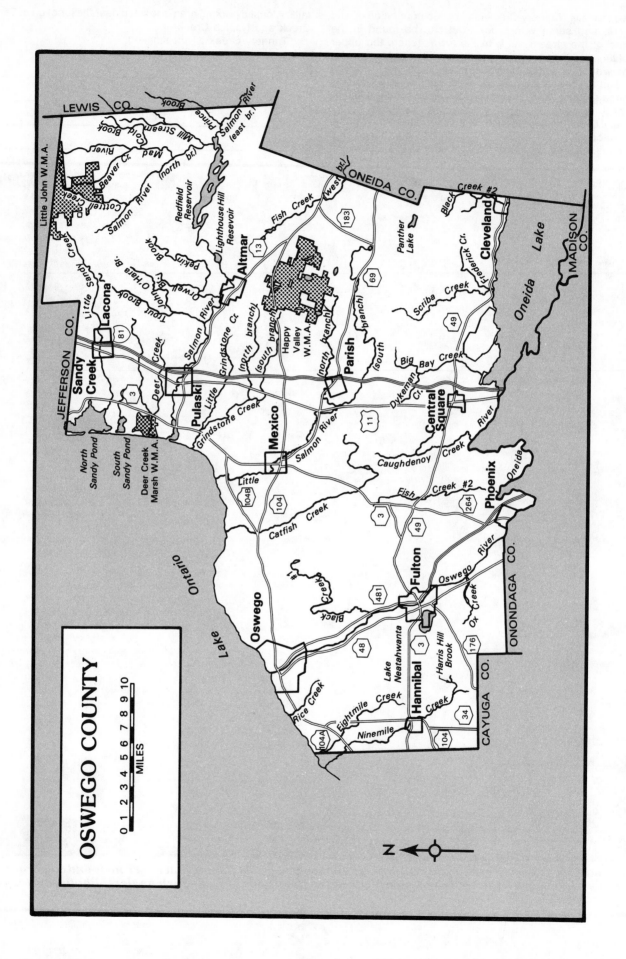

LEWIS CO.

Little John W.M.A.

Mill Stream
Old Stream Brook
Prince Brook

Salmon River
(east br.)

ONEIDA CO.

Creek #2

Beaver Cr.

Mad Cr.

Cottier Creek

Salmon River (north br.)

Redfield Resevoir

Lighthouse Hill Resevoir

Fish Creek

West br.

183

Panther Lake

Black Creek

Frederick Cr.

Cleveland

Oneida Lake

MADISON CO.

Salmon River

Little Sandy Creek

Lacona

pekin

Happy Valley W.M.A.

13

Altmar

(north branch)

(south branch)

O'Hara R.

Tight Brook

Orwell Brook

69

Parish

(north branch)

(south branch)

branch)

49

Scriba Creek

JEFFERSON CO.

Sandy Creek

81

Deer Creek

Little Grindstone Cr.

Pulaski

Grindstone Creek

Big Bay Creek

3

North Sandy Pond

South Sandy Pond

Deer Creek Marsh W.M.A.

Salmon River

Mexico

11

Dykeman Cr.

Central Square

River

Little

104B

104

Catfish Creek

Caughdenoy Creek

Fish Creek #2

Phoenix

Oneida

3

49

264

Lake Ontario

Oswego

Black Creek

Fulton

Oswego River

Ox Creek

ONONDAGA CO.

481

Lake Neatahwanta

48

Harris Hill Brook

3

176

Hannibal

Creek

Eightmile Creek

Rice Creek

34

104A

Ninemile

104

CAYUGA CO.

OSWEGO COUNTY

0 1 2 3 4 5 6 7 8 9 10
MILES

N

—66—

OSWEGO COUNTY STREAMS & RIVERS

NOTE: In several ways Oswego County is unique among the counties detailed in this book. The most distinguishing characteristic of the county, vis-a-vis the other counties, is its remote setting. This is especially true of the northeastern section of the county where many of the streams and rivers listed below flow through tracts of woodland that are not, for the most part, accessible by paved roads. Several of these streams are, in fact, so far from any road that they were used as roadways (see Cold Brook) by logging trucks. There are, however, innumerable tote roads, trails and paths used by the logging industry in the region. These can at least provide you with good foot access to some of the better inland streams and ponds of Oswego County. But be prepared for a long, leisurely hike through some beautiful scenery. These paths and trails were not designed specifically to provide fishermen with efficient stream access and often do not take you directly to the stream of your choice. If you plan on fishing a section of this county that you are not intimately familiar with, it would be a good idea to obtain **current** editions of topographical maps and aerial photographs of the area. Aerial photos, which are often the same scale as topos (1:24,000) can be obtained from the Soil Conservation Service. Many of the trails that do not show up on the topographical maps, do show up on the aerial photos. By combining the two you can save a great deal of time in locating the right trails.

Another basic difference between Oswego County and the others is the number and quality of its streams. The county boasts a total of 410 miles of trout streams, many of which do not even have names. It is safe to assume that almost every tributary of the streams listed below will have a resident population of brook trout. Again, this is especially true for the streams located in the northeastern portion of the county. The population and the fish might not be large in many cases, but some of the small rivulets that you encounter while fishing the major streams are definitely worth investigating. They are simply too numerous to list individually.

BEAVER CREEK

map coordinates.........	43° 37′ 03″ 75° 49′ 12″
USGS map(s).............	Redfield, Worth Center
location (township).......	Redfield
access..................	the upper reaches accessible from Little John Drive
principle species	brook trout (wild)

Beaver Creek is a small, high quality tributary of the Mad River. Averaging 15 to 20 feet in width, this stream has a good year round flow of cold water over a bottom of gravel and rubble. Flowing entirely through forests, there is a lot of tangled brush along the stream making fly fishing nearly impossible. Nearly all of the fish found here are wild brook trout. A few wild brown trout might be found in the lower reaches. The brookies are very numerous and fish up to 12 inches are common.

Access to Beaver Creek is difficult, due mainly to a general lack of nearby roads. The state has purchased some public fishing easements on the stream, but there is posting, so anglers should be careful to fish areas open to the public.

This stream is not stocked.

NOTES: _____

_____

_____

_____

Contrary to what many people think, you don't have to be able to cast a mile to be a good fly fisherman. Accurate casting of a fly 30 to 40 feet is usually adequate on most streams in New York State.

BIG BAY CREEK

map coordinates.........	43° 15′ 14″ 76° 06′ 47″
USGS map(s).............	Mallory
location (township).......	West Monroe, Parish
access..................	parallelled and crossed by County Road 37 — see below
principle species	brook trout (stocked & wild), brown trout (wild)

Big Bay Creek is a fair quality trout stream that empties into the Big Bay of Oneida Lake. Averaging 10 to 12 feet in width, this stream has a bottom of gravel and silt and is brush lined for most of its length. The surroundings consist primarily of farmlands giving way to marshland as you approach Oneida Lake. Much of the stream below the mouth of Dykeman Creek is posted, but the state has purchased six miles of public fishing easements on the upper sections of the stream. Access to the upper reaches of the stream is generally good, and there is little fishing pressure here. Big Bay Creek is too small for fly fishing, but it is an excellent stream for drifting worms or salted minnows into quiet pools or submerged brush piles.

In the spring Big Bay Creek is stocked with 300 brook trout yearlings in the one mile section of stream just above the village of Mallory.

NOTES: _____

_____

_____

_____

BLACK CREEK #1

map coordinates.........	43° 21′ 51″ 76° 25′ 51″
USGS map(s).............	Fulton, Oswego East
location (township).......	Scriba
access..................	crossings at Hall Road and O'Connor Road
principle species	brown trout (stocked), northern pike, largemouth bass

Black Creek is a small tributary of the Oswego River, which it joins north of Fulton. The stream can be divided into distinct cold and warm water environments. The upper reaches of Black Creek, between Crook's Pond and Mud Pond, is a fair quality trout stream. Averaging 15 feet in width, this section of the stream has a good year round flow of cool water over a bottom of gravel. The surroundings are a mix of farmlands and residential areas. The banks are very brushy for the most part, making fly fishing impractical. In the spring this 2.5 mile section of the stream is stocked with 1,100 brown trout yearlings. Downstream of Crook's Pond, Black Creek is a warm water stream. Although northern pike and largemouth bass are present, the small size of the stream limits the quality of the fishing for both species.

NOTES: _____

_____

_____

_____

BLACK CREEK #2

map coordinates.........	43° 13′ 55″ 75° 52′ 55″
USGS map(s).............	Cleveland, Jewell, Camden West, Panther Lake
location (township).......	Constantia
access..................	roughly parallelled by Center Street Road — see below
principle species	brown trout (stocked and wild)

Black Creek is a good quality brown trout stream that flows into Oneida Lake at Cleveland. Averaging 12 feet in width, the stream has a bottom of silt and gravel, extensive bank cover and flows through residential areas and farmland. There are a lot of small pools on Black Creek providing habitat for stocked browns. There is some carry over of fish in this stream, as well as a small population of wild brown trout. This is a good worm dunking stream, though you might have your patience tried by the large number of darter-like log perch that inhabit the lower end of Black Creek. Fly fishing should be possible on some sections, but with difficulty.

Black Creek is parallelled by Center Street Road. The stream can be accessed by taking the roads running east off Center Street Road, such as Tynan Road and Schraa Road. The state has obtained a total of 1.8 miles of public fishing easements on Black Creek and a tributary, Shinglemill Creek. Most of the easements are located downstream of Tynan Road, with a short section just upstream of that road.

In the spring Black Creek is stocked with 840 brown trout yearlings.

NOTES: _____
_____
_____
_____

CATFISH CREEK

map coordinates	43º 30' 47" 76º 19' 26"
USGS map(s)	Texas, New Haven, Pennellville, Mexico, Central Square
location (township)	New Haven, Palermo
access	crossing at Route 3
principle species	brook trout (wild), brown trout, rainbow trout, coho salmon, chinook salmon

The upper reaches of this stream has an intermittant population of wild brook trout, as do several of its tributaries. However, most of Catfish Creek is too warm to provide much habitat for trout. It is also heavily posted, and these factors combine to make this section of the stream of questionable value as a fishery.

At County Route 1 there is a dam, and from this dam downstream to Lake Ontario Catfish Creek has a good seasonal fishing for Lake Ontario rainbow trout, brown trout, coho salmon and chinook salmon. This lower reach is about 30 feet in width. Because it is heavily posted, the stream is best accessed by boat via Lake Ontario.

In the spring the state plans on stocking 10,000 Skamania steelhead in Catfish Creek.

NOTES: _____
_____
_____
_____

COLD BROOK

map coordinates	43º 36' 16" 75º 49' 08"
USGS map(s)	Redfield, Worth Center, Sears Pond
location (township)	Redfield
access	Otto Mills Road — see below
principle species	brook trout (wild)

Cold Brook is a small tributary of the Mad River, which it joins near Otto Mills Road. Averaging 15 feet in width, this stream has a gravel and rubble bottom and a good year round flow of cold, clear water. It meanders for the most part through picturesque stands of mature hardwoods.

In the not too distant past Cold Brook had been used as a logging road. This didn't ruin the stream, but it did tendb to uniformly scour the bottom. The result is a stream with very few pools of any significance. This fact notwithstanding, Cold Brook is a stream with very high water quality that has an excellent population of small wild brook trout.

Due to its remote setting, there is not very good road access to the sections of Cold Brook open to the public. The state has purchased extensive public fishing easements from the mouth of Cold Brook upstream to where it crosses the property line of the Mad River Club (posted), a distance of about 6 miles. It appears that the closest parking area to these easements is located on Otto Mills Road, about one mile west of the Mad River.

Cold Brook is not stocked.

NOTES: _____
_____
_____
_____

COTTRELL CREEK

map coordinates	43º 37' 00" 75º 53' 28"
USGS map(s)	Orwell, Boylston Center, Worth Center
location (township)	Redfield
access	crossing at County Road 17 — see below
principle species	brook trout (wild)

Cottrell Creek is a high quality brook trout stream, much of which flows through the Little John State Wildlife Management Area. The stream averages 15 feet in width, and it has a bottom of rubble and gravel. The surroundings are forestlands, and the stream is generally tree lined and brushy. There is an excellent population of wild brook trout in Cottrell Creek, and they can be taken on very small spinners or worms drifted into pools and log jams. Also, there are some stretches on this stream that are sufficiently open to make fly fishing feasible.

To increase public access to Cottrell Creek the state has purchased a total of .66 miles of public fishing easements on the stream and several of its tributaries (#17 & #18). These easements are located on the lowermost reach of the stream. The closest road access to this portion of Cottrell Creek appears to be the fishermans parking area located where Abes Road (formerly Yeardon Road) crosses the north branch of the Salmon River. This is about one-half mile downstream of the mouth of Cottrell Creek. Further upstream portions of the stream flow through the Little John State Wildlife Management Area.

Cottrell Creek is not stocked.

NOTES: _____
_____
_____
_____

DEER CREEK

map coordinates	43º 35' 17" 76º 12' 05"
USGS map(s)	Pulaski, Richland, Sandy Creek
location (township)	Richland, Sandy Creek
access	crossing at Route 3 (parking)
principle species	northern pike, bullhead, yellow perch, rock bass

This stream flows through the Deer Creek State Wildlife Management Area. A majority of the fishing takes place downstream of the crossing at Route 3. There is very good fishing in the spring here for bullhead and good fishing for northern pike in the summer. Deer Creek is multi-channeled in its lower

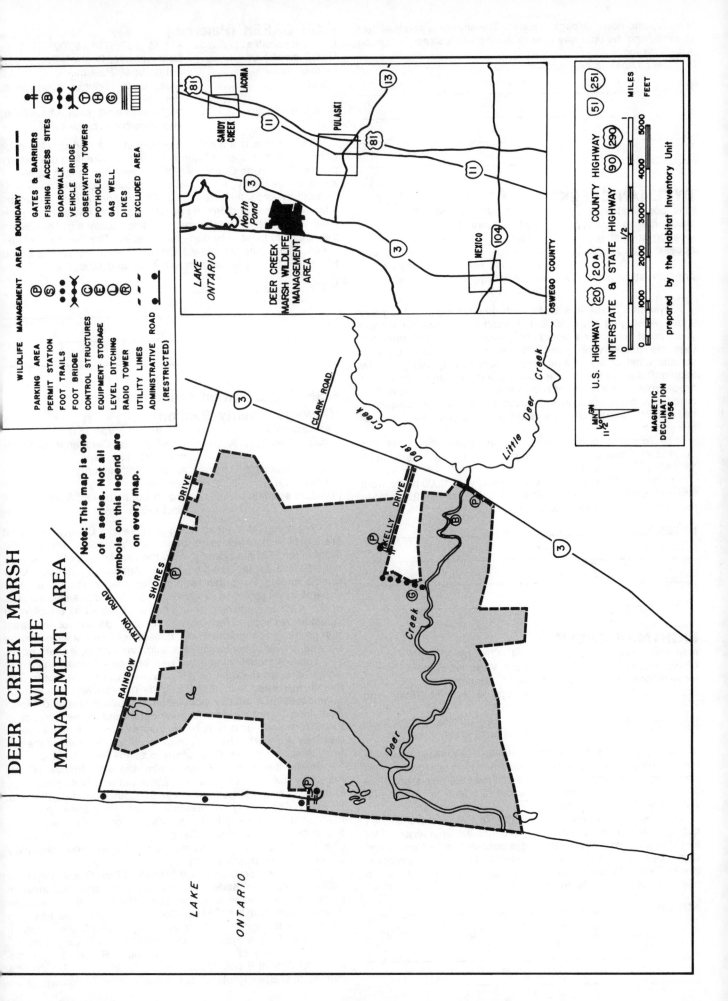

DEER CREEK MARSH WILDLIFE MANAGEMENT AREA

Note: This map is one of a series. Not all symbols on this legend are on every map.

WILDLIFE MANAGEMENT AREA BOUNDARY

⊕ GATES & BARRIERS		Ⓟ PARKING AREA	
⊛ FISHING ACCESS SITES		Ⓢ PERMIT STATION	●●● FOOT TRAILS
BOARDWALK		✕✕✕ FOOT BRIDGE	
VEHICLE BRIDGE		Ⓒ CONTROL STRUCTURES	
⊕ OBSERVATION TOWERS		Ⓔ EQUIPMENT STORAGE	
⊖ POTHOLES		Ⓛ LEVEL DITCHING	
Ⓖ GAS WELL		Ⓡ RADIO TOWER	
DIKES		UTILITY LINES	
EXCLUDED AREA		●—— ADMINISTRATIVE ROAD (RESTRICTED)	

LAKE ONTARIO

SANDY CREEK

LACONA

PULASKI

MEXICO

North Pond

DEER CREEK MARSH WILDLIFE MANAGEMENT AREA

OSWEGO COUNTY

U.S. HIGHWAY ⑳ ⑳Ⓐ   COUNTY HIGHWAY ㊾ ㉚

INTERSTATE & STATE HIGHWAY ㊿ ㉙Ⓖ   ⑤Ⓘ ㉕Ⓘ

MAGNETIC DECLINATION 1956

MILES   FEET

0   1000   2000   3000   4000   5000

prepared by the Habitat Inventory Unit

CLARK ROAD

Deer Creek

Little Deer Creek

SHORES DRIVE

TRYON ROAD

RAINBOW

KELLY DRIVE

Deer Creek

LAKE ONTARIO

reaches and flows through a marsh. The stream is about 40 feet in width, and the best way to access most of the stream would be with a canoe.

Deer Creek is not stocked.

NOTES: _____

_____

_____

_____

DYKEMAN CREEK

map coordinates......... 43° 19' 19"   76° 06' 43"
USGS map(s)............. Mallory, Central Square
location (township)....... Hastings
access.................. crossings at Wagoner Road and Hogsback Road — see below
principle species .... brook trout (stocked & wild) brown trout (wild)

Dykeman Creek is a small, high quality tributary of Big Bay Creek. Averaging about 10 feet in width, the stream has a good year round flow over a bottom of gravel and silt. The surroundings are primarily farmland. This is a typical worm dunking stream. Most of the stream side is very brushy, ruling out fly fishing. Dykeman Creek presently has a good population of wild brook trout, and a few wild brown trout up to 15" in length. This could change in the near future, though, due to the activities of beavers, which are having a detrimental effect on the quality of the stream.

To increase access to Dykeman Creek, the state has purchased a total of 1.01 miles of public fishing easements here, as well as a foot path right-of-way.

In the fall, Dykeman Creek is stocked with 1,300 brook trout fingerlings from the mouth of Shanty Creek upstream 2.5 miles to the crossing at Cornell Road.

NOTES: _____

_____

_____

_____

EIGHTMILE CREEK

map coordinates......... 43° 24' 47"   76° 37' 22"
USGS map(s)............. Oswego West, Hannibal
location (township)....... Oswego, Hannibal
access.................. crossings at Furniss Road and Route 104
principle species .... brown trout (stocked), rainbow trout, coho salmon, chinook salmon

A majority of the fishing on Eightmile Creek takes place blow the crossing at Route 104, where there are good seasonal runs of trout from Lake Ontario. A few stray salmon are also taken here on occasion. The stream is about 20 feet in width and predominently brush lined.

Upstream of Furniss Road, Eightmile Creek is a small, fair quality brown trout stream. Some sections are open enough for fly fishing, but small spinners and worms drifted into pools and under bank cuts will also work well. In the fall this stream is stocked with 700 brown trout fingerlings in the 2.6 mile section upstream of Furniss Road.

NOTES: _____

_____

_____

_____

FISH CREEK (Palermo)

map coordinates........ 43° 14' 22"   76° 16' 00"
USGS map(s)........... Baldwinsville, Pennellville
location (township)....... Schroeppel, Palermo
access................. crossed by County Road 54 a Pennellville
principle species .... brook trout (wild), brown trout (wild) largemouth bass, panfish

This stream is a mediocre fishery at best, and should not be confused with the west branch of the Fish Creek in the eastern portion of Oswego County, which is a very high quality stream. A sluggish generally low gradient bottomland stream flowing through swamps, the size of Fish Creek varies greatly. There are a few wild brook and brown trout in the stream, and as is often the case with streams of this type, they are usually big. The stream, though, is dominated by non-trout species. The lower end of Fish Creek, which empties into the Oneida River at Horseshoe Island has some fishing for largemouth bass and bluegills.

NOTES: _____

_____

_____

_____

FISH CREEK (west branch) — (Oswego County Section)

map coordinates......... 43° 16' 10"   75° 38' 00"
USGS map(s)............. Camden East, Camden West, Westdale, Williamstown
location (township)........ Amboy, Williamstown
access.................. see below
principle species .... brown trout (stocked & wild), brook trout (wild)

Beginning at Kasoag Lake in Oswego County, the west branch of Fish Creek skirts the southern slope of the Tug Hill Plateau for 33 miles before joining the east branch of Fish Creek, near Blossdale, in Oneida County. Meandering through fairly remote forests, this brush lined stream is larger than most other streams in the region. It averages 30 feet in width, and even in its upper reaches fly fishing, though difficult, would be possible on selected sections. The Oswego County portion of the west branch has a low gradient, and consequently it is a slow moving silt and gravel bottomed stream with many deep, languid pools.

The best trout fishing in the west branch is found in the 9 mile reach between the dam at Williamstown and Kasoag Lake. The stream is loaded with feisty, brightly colored wild brook trout, augmented by a smaller population of stocked and wild brown trout. Many, if not all, of the larger tributaries of the west branch of Fish Creek are high quality brook trout streams in their own right, and they are worth checking in to. In the spring many of the fish from these tributaries drop down in to the west branch.

Below the dam in Williamstown, the west branch is only marginal quality trout water. It widens out and is dominated by stunted, sublegal largemouth bass and other nondesirable fish. However, if you study the stream and can locate a few spring fed holes, you are likely to find some very substantial brown trout in this section of the stream. Canoeing would be an ideal way to check out these holes, but this reach of Fish Creek is usually canoeable only in the spring.

A large portion of the west branch of Fish Creek is open to public access. The state has purchased a total of 9.8 miles of public fishing easements on this stream, mainly between Williamstown and the Oneida County line. The state has also obtained 5 fisherman parking areas, 3 of which are currently developed. They are located as follows: (1) on County Road 17, about three-fifths of a mile south of State Route 13, near the mouth of Rowell Brook; (2) on County Road 17, three-fifths of a mile north of State Route 13, at the village of Williamstown; (3) on

Lovers Lane, off County Road 17.

In the spring a 6 mile section of the west branch of Fish Creek is stocked with 2,500 brown trout yearlings, from Oneida County line upstream to one mile above the crossing at Bare Bridge Road.

NOTES: _____

_____

_____

_____

FREDERICK CREEK

map coordinates . . . . 43º 15' 00" 75º 59' 54"
USGS map(s) . . . . Panther Lake
location (township) . . . . Constantia
access . . . . crossing at Kibbie Lake Road
principle species . . . . brook trout (stocked)

Frederick Creek is a small tributary of Scriba Creek, which it joins at Constantia. The stream averages about 10 feet in width, has a bottom of silt and gravel and flows through wooded and residential areas. In character Frederick Creek is typical of many brook trout streams-small, swampy and brush lined. It is too small and brushy for fly fishing. Drifting worms or salted minnows is the technique to use here. There would probably be a greater variety of species here if not for the dam that exists on Scriba Creek just below the mouth of Frederick Creek, which prevents the upstream migration of fish from Oneida Lake.

Access would be a problem on Frederick Creek. There are no public fishing easements on the stream, and sections are posted.

In the spring 800 brook trout yearlings are stocked on the stream, from Hatchery Road upstream 3.3 miles to the crossing at Kibbie Lake Road.

NOTES: _____

_____

_____

_____

Grindstone Creek has very good runs of rainbow trout and brown trout in the fall. Photo courtesy of Rick Kustich.

GRINDSTONE CREEK (main stream)

map coordinates . . . . 43º 33' 03" 76º 12' 53"
USGS map(s) . . . . Pulaski, Mexico
location (township) . . . . Richland
access . . . . parallelled by County Road 28 between the crossing at Route 3 and the hamlet of Fernwood — see below
principle species . . . . brown trout (stocked), rainbow trout (stocked), coho salmon, chinook salmon, northern pike, smallmouth bass, largemouth bass, bullhead, smelt

Grindstone Creek is a popular stream with local fishermen, offering a wide variety of angling opportunities. A fairly large stream, it averages at least 20 feet in width, and below the crossing at Route 3 it can easily accommodate small boats. Above Route 3, upstream to Fernwood, Grindstone Creek is almost uniformly fast-flowing, with a rocky bottom and a considerable amount of stream side cover.

The lower reaches of Grindstone Creek are adjacent to Selkirk Shores State Park. The stream widens out at this point into a long, pond-like estuary. In the spring there is a good run of smelt and bullhead here. Largemouth bass, smallmouth bass and northern pike are found in the lower reaches of the stream in the spring, summer and fall.

More important than the warm water fishing are the runs of trout and salmon that enter the stream from Lake Ontario. These fish can run as far up as the dam in Fernwood. There are good runs in the fall. The stream also has meager runs of coho and chinook salmon in the fall. Just off the creek mouth, in Lake Ontario, there is excellent fishing for brown trout, rainbow trout and pacific salmon. About 150 yards from the mouth of Grindstone Creek is a very popular fishing pier.

Due to its diversity and productivity, Grindstone Creek is very popular, though it does not get quite as much pressure as Sandy Creek or the Salmon River. To increase access to the stream, the state has recently purchased 3.6 miles of public fishing easements on the stream, between Fernwood and the crossing at Route 3, as well as three parking areas, none of which are as yet developed.

The main stream of Grindstone Creek is not stocked.

NOTES: _____

_____

_____

_____

GRINDSTONE CREEK (south branch)

map coordinates . . . . 43º 29' 31" 76º 09' 00"
USGS map(s) . . . . Mexico, Dugway
location (township) . . . . Richland, Albion
access . . . . can be fished from county land near the Tinker Tavern interchange of Route 81
principle species . . . . brook trout (stocked), brown trout (stocked), rainbow trout (stocked)

The south branch of Grindstone Creek is a small, good quality trout stream, averaging 15 feet in width. Flowing through farmlands, it has a good flow of slightly stained water over a bottom of gravel and rubble. The stream is very brushy in most sections, making fly fishing difficult, if not impossible. Most of the fish found here are stocked brook trout, but some anglers claim to have taken rainbows and browns as well.

The south branch of Grindstone Creek is popular with local anglers, and gets a moderate amount of fishing pressure. There are currently no public fishing easements on the stream, but good public access can be found near the Route 81 Tinker Tavern

LITTLEJOHN WILDLIFE MANAGEMENT AREA

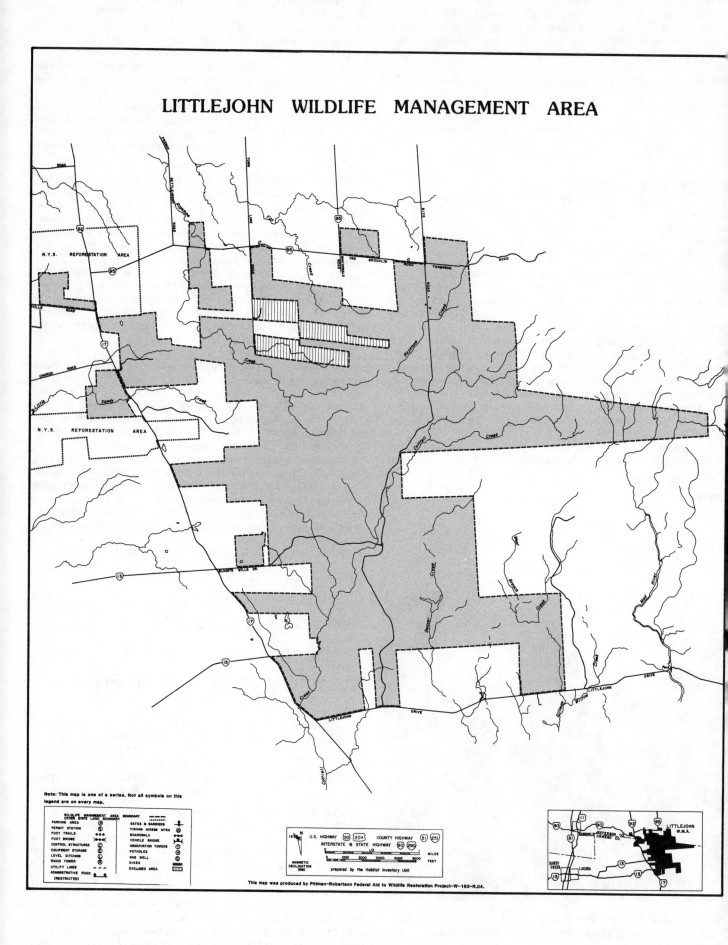

Interchange, where the stream flows across county property.

In the fall the south branch of Grindstone Creek is stocked with 3,600 brook trout fingerlings, from the stream mouth upstream 7.1 miles to County Road 22.

While fishing the south branch of Grindstone Creek, check out some of its larger tributaries. Some of them have good populations of wild brook trout. As is the case with most flatland brook trout, these fish are usually larger than the typical brook trout found in the classic wooded upland streams of the Adirondacks or Tug Hill Plateau.

NOTES: _____

_____

_____

_____

HARRIS HILL BROOK

map coordinates..........	43º 16' 41" 76º 32' 02"
USGS map(s).............	Hannibal
location (township)........	Hannibal
access...................	County Road 7
principle species.........	brown trout (wild)

Harris Hill Brook is an upper tributary of Ninemile Creek. Averaging 6 to 10 feet in width, this stream flows for the most part through a high canopied climax forest. It breaks out into abandoned fields in its lower end. Despite a fairly high gradient this stream has a bottom of silt and rubble. Harris Hill Brook has a good riffle/pool ratio and numerous little pockets provide holding areas for a fair population of wild brown trout.

The major problem on Harris Hill Brook is access. Road access is only fair at best, and the physical surroundings are a further impediment.

NOTES: _____

_____

_____

_____

JOHN O'HARA BROOK

map coordinates..........	43º 34' 20" 76º 02' 00"
USGS map(s).............	Richland
location (township)........	Richland, Orwell
access...................	Crossings at Jerry Look Road — see below
principle species.........	brown trout (wild), brook trout (wild) rainbow trout (wild), coho salmon, chinook salmon

John O'Hara Brook is the principle tributary of Trout Brook. A majority of the fishing on this stream takes place on the lower 2 mile reach. This section of John O'Hara Brook averages 15 feet in width, has a good year-round flow of cold water over a bottom of gravel and rubble and runs through woodlands. Much of the stream is brush lined, but even in its upper reaches there are stretches where the canopy is fairly high, so fly fishing is possible on parts of John O'Hara Brook.

This stream has been renowned for the quality of its fishing since before the turn of the century. Historically, John O'Hara Brook was known for its run of Atlantic salmon. Atlantic salmon no longer spawn here, but the stream does have excellent runs of wild rainbow trout (steelhead), coho salmon, chinook salmon, and brown trout. Unlike many streams that are tributary to Lake Ontario, the quality of John O'Hara Brook is such that these spawning runs are very successful, producing large numbers of wild steelhead and salmon. Needless to say, the seasonal fishing pressure on the lower reaches of this stream is extremely heavy.

John O'Hara Brook also has a good resident population of trout. The stream is dominated by juvenile Steelhead, but there are some large brown trout that hang in the stream all year long; mainly in the pools that can be found just above and below Jerry Look Road. Above Jerry Look Road the stream quickly narrows up and begins to look like a typical mountain brook trout stream, which it is.

Although it only averages 5 feet in width, the upper section of this stream is worth fishing, as it has a good population of wild brook trout.

Due to the popularity of John O'Hara Brook, the state has purchased a total of 2.82 miles of public fishing easements on the stream, which are acessible from the two crossings of Jerry Look Road. This stream is not stocked.

NOTES: _____

_____

_____

_____

LITTLE JOHN STATE WILDLIFE MANAGEMENT AREA

map coordinates..........	43º 42' 00" 76º 54' 00"
USGS map(s).............	Boylston Center, Worth Center
location (township)........	Boylston, Redfield (Oswego County); Worth, Lorraine (Jefferson County)
access...................	Little John Drive - see map
principle species.........	brook trout (wild)

The Little John State Wildlife Management Area is a remote tract of woodland straddling the Oswego/Jefferson County line. Encompassing approximately 8,000 acres the area is drained by numerous small streams, most of which have populations of wild brook trout. Included among these streams are the headwaters of Cottrell Creek, the Mad River and Beaver Creek. Access is a problem in many parts of Little John due to a general lack of good roads. However, there are tote roads and logging trails in the area. Read the special note at the beginning of this chapter for information on how these can be located. See also: Beaver Creek, Cottrell Creek and Mad River.

NOTES: _____

_____

_____

_____

LITTLE SALMON RIVER

map coordinates..........	43º 31' 27" 76º 15' 32"
USGS map(s).............	Texas, Pulaski, New Haven, Mexico
location.................	Mexico, Parish
access...................	Launch ramp at Mexico Point, 1 mile north of Route 104 B, on County Road 40
principle species.........	rainbow trout (stocked), brown trout (stocked), coho salmon, chinook salmon, smallmouth bass, largemouth bass, northern pike, bullhead, rock bass, crappies, yellow perch

Beginning at the confluence of the north and south branches of the Little Salmon River, near Parish, the main stream of the Little Salmon River flows north west, emptying into Lake Ontario at Mexico Point. This is a rather large stream. It averages about 40 feet in width, widening out to 200 feet below Texas. It has a good flow of water all year long, a bottom of bedrock and silt and, below Texas, a considerable amount of instream vegetation. The surroundings are mainly residential, but some sections flow through farmlands.

In the spring, the Little Salmon River gets a good run of stray domestic rainbow trout. Later, in the fall, there are good runs of rainbow trout, brown trout, coho salmon and chinook salmon. All of these fish can run as far upstream as the lower dam in Mexico.

Warm water species are also present in Little Salmon River. Between the mouth of the stream and the village of Texas there is good year round fishing for northern pike, bull head, largemouth bass and panfish. In the spring there is a very good run of smallmouth bass here, but these fish are usually out of the stream by the opening of bass season. There is also an excellent run of rock bass in the lower reaches of Little Salmon River late in the spring.

Above Mexico there is good fishing for smallmouth bass, crappies, bullhead and northern pike. The smallmouth are fairly common and unusually dark in color. They look as if they were taken from a lake or river in Quebec.

Access to the Little Salmon River is generally poor. Much of the stream is posted. Fortunately, there is a good launch ramp and parking area at Mexico Point and the section of stream below Texas can accommodate small boats. The best way to fish the stream above Mexico would be by canoe.

The Little Salmon River is not stocked.

NOTES: _____

_____

_____

_____

LITTLE SALMON RIVER (South Branch)
map coordinates.......... 43º 24' 07" 76º 09' 22"
USGS map(s) .... Mexico, Dugway, Mallory, Williams-town
location .... Mexico, Hasting, West Monroe, Parish
access .... Parallelled by Smith Road above Carleys Mill
principle species .... brook trout (wild)

The south branch of Little Salmon River is a small, fair quality brook trout stream. Averaging 12-15 feet in width, the stream has a bottom of sand and gravel and a good flow all year. The south branch is very brushy, too brushy for fly fishing. The stream gets very little attention, even from local anglers, and isn't worth a special trip.

Historically, the north branch of the Little Salmon River also held trout, but the construction of a pond on that stream destroyed much of their habitat, though a few trout will still be found there.

The south branch of the Little Salmon River is not stocked.

NOTES: _____

_____

_____

_____

LITTLE SANDY CREEK
map coordinates.......... 43º 38' 23" 76º 10' 10"
USGS map(s) .... Ellisburg, Sandy Creek, Boylston Center
location (township) .... Sandy Creek, Boylston
access .... Crossings at Norton Road — see below
principle species .... brown trout (wild), brook trout (wild) rainbow trout (wild), coho salmon (wild), chinook salmon (wild), Atlantic salmon, northern pike, smallmouth bass

Little Sandy Creek, often referred to simply as Sandy Creek, is one of the more important tributaries of Lake Ontario. The stream averages 20 feet in width and has a bottom of bedrock and rubble. The surroundings vary from residential to farmland to woodland. Sections of the stream are brush lined, but fly fishing is possible on much of the stream.

Little Sandy Creek gets an excellent run of wild rainbows (steelhead) in the late fall and early spring. To a lesser extent, coho and chinook salmon can be found in the lower section of the stream in the fall. There is some natural reproduction of chinook and coho salmon in this stream. In recent years, Atlantic salmon have been stocked in Little Sandy Creek, contributing to the run of fish here. However, in order to protect the spawning Atlantic salmon, Little Sandy Creek is closed to **all** fishing from October 1 to November 30, from the first bridge upstream to the first barrier impassable to fish (there are no really impassible barriers in this stream). Be sure to check for current regulations.

In addition to the seasonal fishing for migratory fish, Little Sandy Creek offers anglers the chance to take resident wild brown and brook trout. During the summer brook trout can be found in the upper reach of the stream as well as in most of its upper tributaries. Brown trout and juvenile steelhead are found throughout the stream. Rounding out the species found in this stream are the smallmouth bass, and northern pike, which are found in fair number in the very lowest reach of Little Sandy Creek.

The fishing pressure on Little Sandy Creek is very high in the spring and fall (minimal during the summer). To increase public access to the stream, the state has recently purchased a total of 2.6 miles of public fishing easements on Little Sandy Creek, most

TRADITIONAL SALMON FLIES

Jock Scott

Silver Rat

of which are located between Norton Road and Lacona.

In spring, Little Sandy Creek is stocked with 20,000 Atlantic salmon yearlings as part of an experimental program designed to re-establish atlantic salmon in Lake Ontario.

NOTES: _____

_____

_____

_____

MAD RIVER

map coordinates	43° 34′ 28″ 75° 49′ 52″
USGS map(s)	Redfield, Worth Center, Sears Pond
location (township)	Redfield
access	Crossings at Harvester Mill Road and Otto Mills Rd. — see below
principle species	brook trout (stocked and wild) brown trout (wild)

The Mad River is the principle tributary of the north branch of the Salmon River. Flowing through a remote, picturesque forest area, this river averages 40 feet in width, has a bottom of bedrock and rubble and a fairly high gradient. Most of the Mad River consists of fast moving, shallow runs and cascades. There are few pools of any consequence here.

Wild brook trout is the principle species found in the Mad River, and they can be found in all reaches of this tree lined stream. Fly fishing is certainly one way to take these elusive, brightly colored fish, but some anglers familiar with this river swear by small spinners. And drifted worms are always sure to give you some action.

Historically, brown trout were quite abundant in the Mad River. When the Redfield Reservoir was stocked with browns they would run into the Mad River, via the north branch of the Salmon River, as far upstream as the dam below Otto Mills Road. However, browns are no longer stocked in the reservoir and the runs naturally have stopped, but you may still be surprised by an occasional wild brown trout and they are apt to be very large.

The major problem with the Mad River is access. Much of the river flows through property leased by a private organization, the Mad River Club. All of the rivedr on their property is posted. In addition, much of the river that is open to public access (there are 6.71 miles of fishing easements on the Mad River above and below Otto Mills Road) is quite a distance from any road or trail — in some places well over a mile.

This is good if you like to fish in very isolated surroundings, but be prepared for a long walk before and after you fish. The closest parking area on Otto Mills Road is over 1 mile west of the river.

In the spring, the Mad River is stocked with 1,300 brook trout yearlings, from the mouth of the river upstream 1.5 miles to the crossing at Otto Mills Road.

NOTES: _____

_____

_____

_____

MILL STREAM

map coordinates	43° 32′ 29″ 75° 48′ 45″
USGS map(s)	Redfield, North Osceola, Worth Center, Sears Pond
location (township)	Redfield (Oswego County); Osceola (Lewis County)
access	The lower reaches are crossed by County Road 47 — see below
principle species	brook trout (wild)

Mill Stream is a very high quality brook trout stream. A tributary of the north branch of the Salmon River, which it joins near Redfield, this stream averages 20 feet in width, has a gravel and rubble bottom and is fishable all season. It flows through a rather remote reforestation area. Although some sections are a bit brushy, much of the stream is open enough for fly fishing.

Like many of the streams that flow through this region, some sections of Mill Stream are quit a distance from a road. If you're willing to take a bit of a hike through some very rugged and beautiful terrain though, Mill Stram and nearly all of its tributaries (some better tributaries are Willow Creek, Castor Brook, Boiling Spring and Grindstone Brook) offer some fine trout fishing in a setting that is as isolated and picturesque as any in the county.

To guarantee public access to Mill Stream and its tributaries, the state has purchased a total of 6.34 miles of public fishing easements on Mill Stream, 1 mile on Boiling Spring, 3.62 miles on Grindstone Brook and .232 miles on Castor Brook. The state has also obtained 3 fisherman parking areas on Mill Stream. These are located as follows: 1) on the trail that runs off Stedman Road (nearly all of the easements are downstream of this parking area); 2) off Trumbell Drive; 3) just south of the junction of Harvester Mill Road and Trumbell Drive, about 1 mile north of Redfield. A foot path right-of-way leads from the road to to the parking area, which is adjacent to the stream.

Mill Stream is not stocked.

NOTES: _____

_____

_____

NINEMILE CREEK

map coordinates	43° 24′ 29″ 76° 38′ 10″
USGS map(s)	West Ninemile Point, Oswego West, Hannibal, Cato
location (township)	Sterling (Cayuga County); Hannibal (Oswego County)
access	Crossings at Route 104A
principle species	brown trout (stocked), rainbow trout (stocked), coho salmon, chinook salmon, bullhead, smelt

This stream is a mediocre quality tributary of Lake Ontario. It is dominated by fish from the lake. In the spring there is a run of rainbow trout and, in the fall, stray coho, chinook, and brown trout can be found here. None of these runs are really noteworthy, and would only be of interest to local anglers. All of these fish can run quite far up Ninemile Creek. There is a damn in the village of Hannibal, in Oswego County, but it is in a bad state of disrepair and does not prevent the upward migration of fish. The dam is presently being rebuilt.

Unlike many tributaries of Lake Ontario, Ninemile Creek does not have a large estuary at its mouth and thus does not harbor such warm water species as northern pike and largemouth bass. It does get a run of smallmouth bass just before the opening of bass season, and bullhead and smelt can be taken near the stream mouth in the spring.

There is a very short section of Ninemile Creek, about 3/4 mile above Hannibal, that has fair quality fishing for brown trout. This part of the stream is gravel and silt bottomed, very brushy and full of snags. There aren't alot of trout here. A bait fisherman might catch 50 creek chubs to every trout hooked, but some of the browns are big. Again, this fishery would only be of interest to local anglers.

This stream is not currently being stocked.

NOTES: _____

_____

_____

ONEIDA RIVER

map coordinates . . . . 43º 12' 04" 76º 16' 50"
USGS map(s) . . . . Baldwinsville, Central Square, Brewerton
location (township) . . . . Hastings, Schroeppel
access . . . . Crossings at Route 11
principle species . . . . smallmouth bass, walleye, northern pike, channel catfish, bullhead, largemouth bass, pickerel, panfish

Fed by the waters of Oneida Lake, the Oneida River begins roughly at Route 11 and follows a remarkably circuitous course for 18 miles. It joins the Seneca River (at a place aptly named Three Rivers) to form the Oswego River. The river's short length belies its true size. It ranges up to 600 feet in width, has a depth generally over 12 feet, and many pools and runs over 20 feet deep.

Shortly after the turn of the century the Oneida River was incorporated into the New York State Barge Canal System. It was decided to shorten the river's course by 8 miles. This was accomplished by cutting channels across several of the river's loops, forming a number of man-made islands (Horsehead Island, Schroeppel Island, Glosky Island). The river thus takes on the character of a maze. To accommodate canal traffic, it was necessary to regulate the water level of the Oneida. This was accomplished by constructing water control gates at Caughdenoy and on the Anthony Cut.

These man-made changes have altered the character of the Oneida River in ways beneficial to the fishery (greater depth, increased shoreline), but some effects are also detrimental from the point of view of the fisherman. One of the obvious consequences of being a part of the barge canal system is the amount of boat traffic that one finds here. This river is very popular with boaters, especially on weekends, and this traffic can create problems for anyone fishing from a boat. Also, the partial impounding of the water by the control gates might be responsible for the potentially dangerous low levels of oxygen found in much of the river.

These problems notwithstanding, the Oneida River is a good quality, warm water fishery. Typical of many larger rivers the Oneida is deep, slow-moving and turbid. There are extensive weed beds, especially in the less heavily trafficed stretches that were by-passed by canal cuts. While there is good fishing throughout the river, a number of areas are especially good. Right at the start of the river there is good fishing (and access) for walleye, yellow perch and smallmouth bass, all of which can be taken from the deep (12-14 ft.) run beneath the Route 11 bridge. Further downstream, below the dam and locks at Caughdenoy, northern pike, smallmouth bass, yellow perch, walleye and channel catfish are taken on minnows, grubs and jigs. Caution should be exercised when fishing here due to the fast, deep water. At Horseshoe Island one will find good fishing for northern pike, smallmouth bass, walleye and channel catfish. The backwaters by-passed by the two major canal cuts (Big Bend cut and Anthony Cut) have a fair population of largemouth bass and the cuts themselves hold northern pike, walleye and largemouth bass. Panfish such as yellow perch, bullhead, bluegills and pumpkinseeds are found throughout the Oneida River.

Access to the Oneida River is good, both for shore anglers and boat fishermen. Most of the river is parallelled by all-weather roads and there are numerous bridge crossings. The only formal boat launch is at Pirates Cover Marina (hard surface ramp-fee) on Horsehoe Island Road in Clay. However, there are numerous launch sites available at the western end of Oneida Lake, giving boaters ready access to the river (see Oneida Lake Launch Sites).

NOTES: _____

_____

_____

ORWELL BROOK

map coordinates . . . . 43º 31' 28" 76º 01! 09"
USGS map(s) . . . . Richland, Orwell
location (township) . . . . Albion, Orwell
access . . . . Parking area on County Road 52 near the intersection of Tubbs Rd.
principle species . . . . rainbow trout (stocked & wild), brown trout (wild), coho salmon, chinook salmon, brook trout (wild)

Orwell Brook is one of the principle tributaries of the Salmon River below the reservoirs. Averaging 30-35 feet in width, the stream has a gravel bottom and excellent year-round flow. The surroundings consist primarily of active farmland, with some wooded sections well upstream of County Road 52. Even though much of the stream is brush lined, many sections can be fly fished, particularly the larger pools, of which there are a large number.

Orwell Brook is loaded with salmonids of every type found in the Salmon River system. The major species are wild rainbrow trout (steelhead) and naturalized pacific salmon, with lesser populations of brown trout and brook trout. The flow is not impeded by beaver dams and steelhead fry can be found even in the very upper-most reaches of the stream.

Needless to say, Orwell Brook gets alot of attention from fisherman during the spring and fall salmonid runs. To guarantee fisherman access to this stream, the state has purchased a total of 2.88 miles of public fishing easements on Orwell Creek. It has also obtained a fishermen parking area on County Road 52, near the intersection of Tubbs Road.

In the spring, Orwell Brook is stocked with 10,000 steelhead yearlings.

NOTES: _____

_____

_____

_____

OSWEGO RIVER

map coordinates . . . . 43º 27' 54" 76º 30' 51"
USGS map(s) . . . . Oswego East, Oswego West, Fulton, Pennellville, Baldwinsville
location (township) . . . . Oswego, Scriba, Minetto, Volney, Grandy, Schroeppel
access . . . . Parallelled for much of its length by Routes 48 and 57 — see below
principle species . . . . brown trout (stocked), rainbow trout (stocked), coho salmon, chinook salmon, smallmouth bass, largemouth bass, walleye, northern pike, channel catfish, panfish

The Oswego is one of the major rivers of Central New York. Formed by the joining of the Seneca and Oneida Rivers, appropriately at a place known as Three Rivers, the Oswego River flows north west for 19 miles before emptying in Lake Ontario, at the City of Oswego. Despite its short length, this is a large river. At several points it is over 600 feet wide. Incorporated into the New York State Barge Canal System in the last century, a navigation channel has been dredged to a depth of 12 feet, and there are sections of the river substantially deeper than this. No longer a free flowing waterway, the water levels are regulated in part by a series of locks (8) and dams (6) creating a largely sluggish, turbid river with numerous weed choked backwaters. The Oswego suffers from moderate algae blooms and some sections are possibly affected by oxygen depletion.

The Oswego River offers anglers the widest possible range of fishing opportunities. The lower reach of the river, below the dams in Oswego, has a good run of steelhead in the spring. The run is strongest in March and early April, but an early thaw and a

A wide, well watered stream, Orwell Brook has excellent fishing for trout and salmon. The quality of this stream is such that chinook and coho salmon both reproduce successfully here. Much of the stream is brush lined, but the larger pools can be a fly fisherman's paradise. Photo courtesy of J. Michael Kelly.

good amount of rain could bring the fish into the river as early as February. Lesser runs of steelhead take place in the late fall, and nearly year-round fishing for these silver sided torpedos is a possibility if the stocking of skamania steelhead is successful here.

By early September, chinook and coho salmon will begin to school up off the mouth of the Oswego River. When conditions are right, massive schools of salmon will run up the river, providing anglers with some of the fastest fishing anywhere on Lake Ontario. The lower Oswego is one of the few tributaries of Lake Ontario where salmon are consistently taken on plugs, egg sacs and spoons. The reason for this is the depth of the water in the lower river. At times it can reach 30 feet and, unlike the rest of the river, is fast moving. This offers sanctuary to the fish and keeps them from getting spooked. The runs of salmon will last until the end of November, and is followed by runs of steelhead and stray brown trout. Due to the depth of the river, browns and steelhead can hold over here all winter long, and the brown trout, in fact, will remain in the river until the end of May. Naturally, most of the fishing for trout and salmon takes place below the lower dam in Oswego. However, some salmonids are taken as far upstream as Phoenix. They can move upstream by passing through the system of locks on the river. The river has open water all winter long, at least in the lower reaches.

The fishing for warm water species is as good as it is for salmonids. Smallmouth bass are probably the most ubitquitous game species in the Oswego River, and they attain a good size. Taken on floating rapalas, river runts, and crayfish, these hard fighting fish can be found nearly everywhere. Check out the fast waters below the dams and lock spillway and the deeper holes of the river for the best smallmouth action.

Walleye are another prized game fish found in the river. Many walleye come into the river from Oswego Harbor. An even greater number of walleye drop down into the river from Oneida Lake. Many of the walleye caught here are lunkers weighing in at up to 10 pounds. By drifting worms or minnows or bouncing jigs along the bottom you can take walleye throughout most of the Oswego River, but your best bet would be to concentrate on the water around Battle Island (there is a real nice hole off the northwest end of the island), the stretch just downstream of Fulton, or the drop-off on the east side of Big Island.

Northern pike are also present here in good numbers. There are extensive slack-water areas and weed beds that provide habitat for these fish. Hot spots for northerns include the large estuary at the mouth of Ox Creek (Ox Creek itself is a good pike stream) and the waters around Battle Island, but most areas with weed bed associated with drop-offs will offer up these toothsome fighters.

Largemouth bass can be found in the same areas as northern pike. If you're looking to take the next state record bucketmouth, concentrate on the water around Battle Island and the mouth of Ox Creek. The fisheries people at the DEC suspect that the state record will be broken by a fish taken from the Oswego River and these are the two most productive areas. Don't be afraid to try other slack water areas though. Largemouth bass can be taken in many parts of the river.

In addition to the glamour fish, there are a large number of often overlooked species in the Oswego River that can provide some very fast action. In the lower reaches of the river there is very good fishing for white perch and white bass. Channel catfish, bullhead, white and black crappies and carp are found throughout the Oswego River. The channel cats especially can be an exciting species to stalk, given their size, range and relative abundance. Try fishing as close to the bottom as possible below the dams and spillways for good catfish action.

Foot access to the Oswego River is generally poor, but boat access, for large and small boats alike, is good. Small informal access sites for car top boats and canoes are found all along the river. These put-ins can be found at: 1) Three Rivers on the west side of Route 57; 2) at the north end of Lock #1 in Phoenix; 3) at the Great Bear Recreational Area, off Great Bear Road, between Hinminsville and Fulton; 4) The informal gravel launch site just

downstream of Big Island off Owens Rd.; 5) hard surface launch upstream of the bridge in Minetta (west side of river). Several marinas also service the Oswego River: Vacation Harbor, across from Battle Island State Park, off Route 57, has a good gravel ramp-fee; Wrights Landing, on West Lake Street in Oswego has 6 hard surface ramps-fee. The city of Fulton has a hard surface ramp in its town park, on the east side of the river (no charge) and the Oswego Municipal Landing, at Breitbeck Park, on the west side of the harbor, has a single concrete ramp (no charge). Additional shore access is available at the riverfront linear park, near the mouth of the river, and at Three Rivers Wildlife Management Area, off River Road near Baldwinsville.

The Oswego River is very heavily stocked. In the spring (these are 1986 figures) the river was stocked with 250,000 chinook salmon yearlings, 25,000 coho salmon yearlings, 15,000 steelhead yearlings, and 18,000 skamania strain steelhead yearlings.

NOTES: _____
_____
_____
_____

OX CREEK

map coordinates	43° 15' 08" 76° 22' 57"
USGS map(s)	Fulton, Lysander
location (township)	Granby
access	Bridge crossing at County Rd. 14
principle species	largemouth bass, northern pike, bullhead, carp

Joining the Oswego River 2 miles north of the hamlet of Hinmaneville, Ox Creek looks more like a major river than a small tributary. Originally, the stream was very small, but the artificially maintained water levels of the Oswego River have flooded the lower raches of Ox Creek as far upstream as the bridge crossing at County Route 14. The result is a flat, extremely slow moving expanse of relatively deep water measuring in places almost 1,000 feet across.

As you might expect, there are extensive weed beds in Ox Creek. Massive beds of floating aquatics are found about a mile upstream of the bridge crossing at Route 48 and these are replaced further upstream by emergant aquatic plants. These weed beds provide excellent habitat for largemouth bass, which can be found throughout most of Ox Creek below the Route 14 bridge crossing. Some of the bass taken here tip the scales at 4 to 6 pounds. Northern pike are also found in the stream in good numbers, especially in the spring and summer. In the spring, the lower reaches of Ox Creek are noted for good bullhead and carp fishing.

This stream is not stocked.

NOTES: _____
_____
_____
_____

PEKIN BROOK

map coordinates	43° 32' 41" 76° 00' 29"
USGS map(s)	Richland, Orwell
location (township)	Orwell
access	See below
principle species	rainbow trout (wild), brown trout (wild), brook trout (wild), coho salmon, chinook salmon

Pekin Brook is a major tributary of Orwell Brook, which it joins near County Road 52. Averaging 10-15 feet in width, this rush-lined stream supports runs of wild steelhead, brown trout, coho salmon and chinook salmon. There is a large beaver dam near the mouth of the stream. The steelhead that spawn in the spring can get over the dam and run up half the length of Pekin Brook. The fall spawning fish probably would not be able to get over the dam due to lower water levels and thus stack up like cordwood in the lower reach of the stream.

Historically, Pekin Brook was known as a high quality brook trout stream. While the stream still holds brook trout, their numbers are greatly reduced due to competition from other salmonids such as steelhead fry, and from habitat changes wrought by beavers. The beaver pool at the lower end of the stream probably still holds some nice brook trout.

During the seasonal salmonid runs, Pekin Brook is very heavily fished. The state has purchased a total of .42 miles of public fishing easements on the lower end of the stream, but access is still difficult due to the fact that there are no nearby roads. Probably the easiest access would be to park in the fisherman's parking area on County Road 52 and walk downstream on Orwell Brook to the mouth of Pekin Brook.

Pekin Brook is not stocked.

NOTES: _____

_____

_____

_____

PRINCE BROOK

map coordinates	43° 30' 42" 75° 45' 52"
USGS map(s)	Redfield, North Osceala
location (township)	Redfield (Oswego County), Osceola (Lewis County)
access	Crossing at Ryan Road
principle species	rainbow trout (wild), brook trout (wild)

Prince Brook is a very high quality rainbow trout stream. The stream is a tributary of the east branch of the Salmon River, which it joins near Ryan Road. Located primarily in Lewis County, Prince Brook averages 10 feet in width, has a cobble and gravel bottom, and a good year-round flow. A high gradient stream, it suffers somewhat from shifting gravel bars, erosion and is threaded (multi-channeled) in sections. The stream flows through remote, very picturesque woodlands and long abandoned farmland. Even though it is a small stream, most sections can be fly fished due to the lack of close stream side cover and the high canopy of the surrounding trees. There are a few pools of consequence just upstream of Ryan Road, but they are generally lacking on this stream. Most of Prince Brook consists of fast moving, shallow runs.

An overwhelming majority of the fish found in this stream are wild rainbow trout. Most of these resident fish, but occasionally you'll take a fish that has come up from the Redfield Reservoir. The reservoir is not good trout habitat, but its wild rainbow population has managed to hang on. The rainbows that have come up from the resevoir are easily distinguished from the resident fish of Prince Brook. The migrating rainbows are long and thin; an 18" fish will often weight less than 2 pounds.

Prince Brook is one of those amazing little streams where the fish will hit on almost anything. Fly fishing is extremely productive on this stream and you shouldn't have any problem taking enough fish before breakfast to satisfy your appetite.

This stream is not stocked.

NOTES: _____

_____

_____

RICE CREEK

map coordinates	43° 26' 37" 76° 34' 09"
USGS map(s)	Oswego West, Oswego East, Fulton
location (township)	Oswego, Minetto
access	Crossing at County Rds. 7 & 2
principle species	brown trout (stocked)

Rice Creek is a small tributary of Lake Ontario, which it empties into just west of Oswego. The only fishing readily available on the stream is for stocked and holdover brown trout. The stocked section runs between County Roads 7 and 2. This section of the stream averages 15 feet in width, has a good flow of cool, clear water over a bottom of gravel and is very brushy. The surroundings consist primarily of farmlands. Rice Creek is stocked in the spring with 700 brown trout yearlings.

Rice Creek does get a fair run of salmonids in the spring and fall. These fish can run as far upstream as a barrier just above Route 104. Unfortunately, this section of the stream has little or no real public access. For fishing near the mouth of this stream, see section on Lake Ontario.

NOTES: _____

_____

_____

_____

SALMON RIVER (mouth to lower resevoir)

map coordinates	43° 34' 32" 76° 12' 15"
USGS map(s)	Pulaski, Richland, Orwell, Redfield
location (township)	Richland, Albion, Orwell
access	See map and below
principle species	steelhead, rainbow trout, brown trout, chinook salmon, coho salmon, atlantic salmon, largemouth bass, smallmouth bass, northern pike, bullhead, panfish

The Salmon River is unquestionably the crown jewel of New York State's salmon and steelhead streams. Though diminutive when compared to waters such as the mighty Niagara River or Genesee River, the concentration of fish in the Salmon River is such that it is truly in a class by itself. For 16-½ miles, from its mouth at Lake Ontario upstream to the western end of the lower reservoir, this river offers anglers some of the top salmonid fishing in all of North America. (NOTE: fishing above the bridge crossing at Route 52 in Altmar is prohibited unless otherwise posted. Be sure to check for current regulations).

The major reason for the existence of this spectacular fishery is the Salmon River Fish Hatchery on Beaverdam Brook in Altmar. This facility supplies Lake Erie and Lake Ontario with million of trout and salmon each year. Hundreds of thousands of fish found in Lake Ontario are imprinted by being stocked first in the Salmon River. It is these fish returning to their natural stream that makes the Salmon River what it is today.

For most of its run below the lower reservoir the Salmon River is a typical bedrock and boulder stream. The river channel is very wide and is punctuated by numerous islands, chutes, and pools. The depth and width of the river fluctuate considerably. Slow run-off from the Tug Hill Plateau feeds the river and its tributaries, charging the system at times with tremendous amounts of water, especially in the spring. This water is regulated by a system of reservoirs which release water on an almost daily basis for the generation of hydro-electric power. However, flooding does occur at times, as happened in the winter of 1985, and this can radically alter the topography of the stream bottom. Information on when water will be released into the Salmon River can be obtained by calling (315) 298-6531.

Although the major cycles of trout and salmon runs do not usually begin until early September, the Salmon River does offer some fair fishing for brown trout and Atlantic salmon as early as

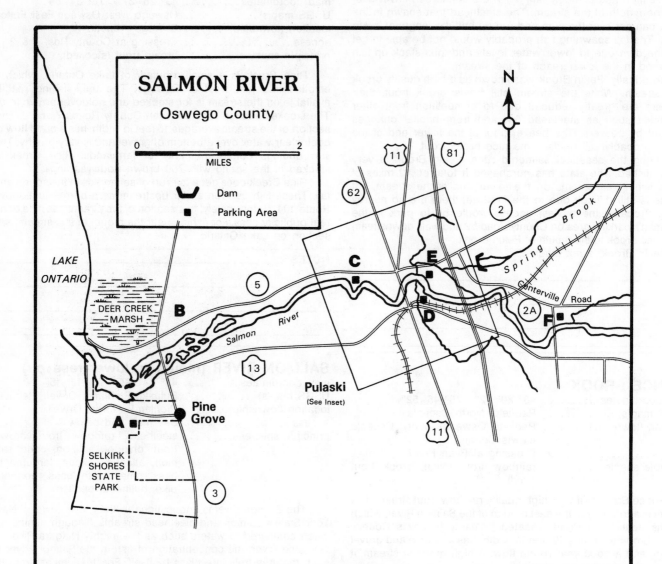

SALMON RIVER

Oswego County

0   1   2
MILES

⩗ Dam
■ Parking Area

LAKE
ONTARIO

DEER CREEK
MARSH

Salmon River

Pulaski
(See Inset)

Pine
Grove

A

B

C

D

E

F

SELKIRK
SHORES
STATE
PARK

Spring Brook

Centerville Road

A) Selkirk Shores State Park — There is presently a poor quality launch for small boats at the Pine Grove section of the park (small boats only-free). In the near future the Army Corps of Engineers is going to construct a break wall at the mouth of the river. High quality hard surface multiple ramps are also scheduled to be built at Pine Grove in the near future.

B) North side of estuary — there are several launch ramps on Route 5.

C) Parking area on Bridge Street, near Lake Street.

D) Parking area on Lewis Street, off Route 11.

E) Parking area at Haldane Community Center on Maple Avenue off Route 11.

F) Parking and drift boat take-out site on County Route 2A.

G) Parking area (presently being expanded) on Route 13.

H) Parking area (presently being expanded) and drift boat launch site (under construction) on Sheep Skin Road, off Route 48.

I) Parking area, via Route 13 at old railroad grade.

J) Parking area at Ellis Cove, on Route 52. Existing lots are being combined and expanded.

K) Parking area on School Street, via Route 52 or Route 13.

L) Altmar parking and access site, via Route 52 or School Street.

M) Parking area, on Route 52, north side of river in Altmar (under construction).

N) Parking area and drift boat launch site, on Bridge Street (County Route 52) in Altmar (under construction).

O) Parking areas on restricted section of Salmon River, on County Route 22, between the Route 52 bridge and the lower reservoir.

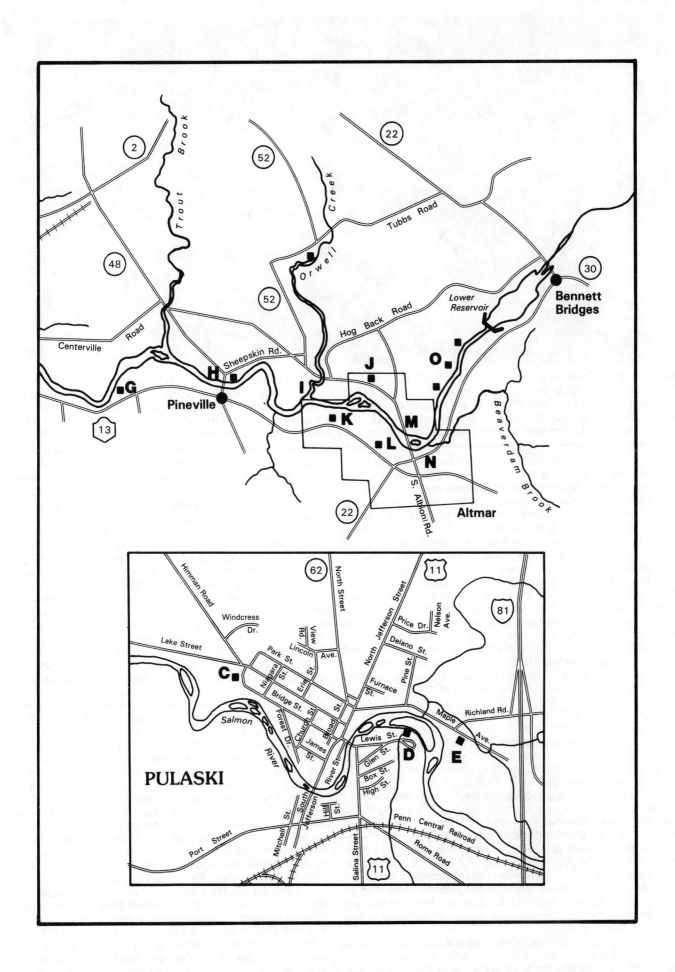

When the salmon are running in the fall, an army of anglers from all over North America converges on the Salmon River. This scene, photographed in Pulaski, is repeated up and down the river. It has been estimated by the DEC that up to 3,200 fishermen will crowd onto the 2½ mile stretch of the river between the bridges at Route 48 and Route 52 (the snagging section). All of this excitement is generated by a phenomenol stocking of over 800,000 salmonids in the Salmon River system each year. Photo courtesy of J. Michael Kelly.

mid-July. The DEC never recorded a run of brown trout here until browns that were raised in the Salmon River Hatchery and stocked in Lake Ontario matured. Why these brown trout returned to the Salmon River is understandable. Why they return in July isn't quite so clear. Whatever the reason, or reasons, they can be found here early and in good numbers. The relative importance of this run is increased when you take into consideration the fact that these are mostly, if not totally, mature browns, often weighing in at 10 to 15 pounds each. In early October a more typical run of stray brown trout takes place in the lower reaches of the Salmon River, but due to the great number of salmon in the river at that time, the browns do not contribute significantly to the fishery.

Coincidental with the July run of brown trout is a fair run of stray Atlantic salmon. These salmon, which are still relatively rare in Lake Ontario and its tributary system, are amongst the most sought after game fish in North America. Like the brown trout, they will range up to 15 pounds and are spectacular fighters. Their run is confined to the lower reaches of the Salmon River. Few Atlantic salmon will be found above Pulaski. The real excitement on the Salmon River begins around the first week of September. At this time the vast numbers of chinook and coho salmon that have been congregating off the mouth of the river in Mexico Bay begin to move into the river to spawn. These spawning runs last until the beginning of November and have to be seen to be believed!

Snagging (snatching) is by far the most popular method used to take spawning salmon in this river. Les Wedge, a biologist with the DEC, once estimated the number of fishermen on the river during a 2 hour period at 3,200. Most of these anglers were located on the short stretch of river between Route 48 bridge inPineville and the Route 52 bridge in Altmar, i.e. the section where snagging is allowed. Needless to say, crowding on this 2.5 mile section of the Salmon River is a real problem. If you plan on snagging salmon on this river be sure to check for current regulations regarding snagging here, which can be found in your fishing regulations guide.

Contrary to the opinion of many people, spawning salmon can be taken in a number of ways, not just by snagging. Because many of the pools of the Salmon River are quite deep, the salmon,

and trout for that matter, that hold in these pools are not easily spooked as fish in shallow water. Early in the morning, before the sheer number of fishermen on each pool make the fish line shy, salmon can at times be taken on lures or bait. Salmon do not actually feed during their spawning phase, but they can be enticed to chase or strike at baits such as shiners and egg sacs, lures such as Little Cleos or Hot Shots,or even brightly colored salmon or steelhead flies tied on sturdy #4 or #6 hooks. Later in the morning, when the hordes of fishermen have spooked all the fish into being tight-lipped cynics, snagging probably is your best bet. However, late in the morning rising water levels drive most anglers from the river and provide fish with an even greater amount of cover. It is then again possible to aggravate a salmon into striking a properly worked lure or bait.

Chinook and coho salmon are not the only species that draw anglers to the Salmon River in the fall. Domestic rainbow trout (as distinguished from steelhead) are often found here, usually in the later half of October. Unfortunately, fluctuations in the number of rainbows being stocked, as well as changes in the location of the stocking site, makes this run undependable. And even at its best, the run of rainbow trout is good, but certainly not spectacular.

Steelhead, on the other hand, often do make a good showing here in the fall. Although steelhead spawn in the spring, many of them choose to winter over in their natural streams. Traditionally, the best runs of steelhead occur in the Salmon River in the first 2 weeks of November, but a few fish can be found in the lower reaches of the river, if conditions are right, as early as September. Because they will not run up to the tributaries of the river to spawn until March, steelhead can be taken here all winter long, at least by shore fishermen. The steelhead fishing is very good here in the dead of winter, but conditions can be extremely trying. Make sure you dress for the occasion.

Come March, the melting snows swell the tributaries of the Salmon River. The steelhead, which have been holding in the river all winter then begin their spawning runs, which take place not in the river but in the tributaries such as Trout Brook, John O'Hara Brook, Orwell Brook and Pekin Brook (see individual entries for details on each stream). The fish do not all run at once, but in stages, so good steelhead fishing can be found in the river as well as in the above named tributaries as late as mid-May.

Warm water species also contribute significantly to the fishing in the Salmon River, at least below Pulaski. The smallmouth bass fishing is good everywhere below Pulaski, but the best catches are taken from the estuary at the mouth of the creek. Smallmouth from the lake often congregate here in the evening, looking to snatch up small fish, crustaceans, and insects washed down river by surges of water from the power plant. The lower 1½ miles of the river is a wide, slow moving reach. Northern pike and largemouth bass can be found in the weedier, backwater areas. This section of the river also has excellent fishing in the spring for bullhead, rock bass, many of which weight in at over a pound, and smelt. Unfortunately, due to vandalism and littering, some of the best areas to take smelt, which are found on the north side of the estuary, are   posted.

Each year the Salmon River is visited by fishermen from all over the United States. Because of its tremendous popularity, the state and local authorities have endeavored to create the best possible situation in terms of parking and access. The state has obtained approximately 5.1 miles of public fishing easements on the river, between Pulaski and the lower reservoir, and there are numerous parking areas and drift boat launch sites.

In the spring, the Salmon River is stocked with 120,000 steelhead yearlings, 90,000 coho yearlings, and an incredible 600,000 chinook fingerlings (note: these figures reflect all the stockings which generate runs into the Salmon River (i.e. tributary estuary and hatchery releases). These figures give a better idea of the magnitude of the runs in the Salmon River. The bulk of the Salmon River stockings are made at the hatchery smolt release pond to generate a run to the hatchery for egg production).

NOTES: _____

_____

_____

_____

SALMON RIVER (east branch — Oswego County Section)

map coordinates . . . . 43° 31' 50"   75° 47' 50"
USGS map(s) . . . . Redfield
location (township) . . . . Redfield
access . . . . Crossings at Ryan Road and Waterbury Road — See below
principle species . . . . rainbow trout (stocked & wild), brook trout (stocked & wild), brown trout (wild)

The east branch of the Salmon River is really just the main stream of the Salmon River above the reservoirs. Very little of the east branch flows through Oswego County, about 1.5 miles worth, but what is found here is a real gem of a stream. The section that is open to the public runs between Ryan Road and Waterbury Road. An excellent river for fly fishing, this section of the east branch averages 35 feet in width, has a bottom of gravel and rubble, and good year-round flow. The stream side cover consists of a mix of brush and mature hardwood. There is a large amount of instream shelter consisting of deep pools, cribbing and downed trees. Downstream of a large house known as "The Braes" you find a lot of undercut banks. This instream structure provides holding areas for excellent populations of rainbow, brown and brook trout. One angler that we talked to claims that every pool on the east branch holds a 4-8 lb. brown trout, and the relative ease with which brook trout and rainbow trout can be taken on flies attest to their abundance.

The east branch of the Salmon River gets a moderate amount of fishing pressure. To increase public access to the stream, the state has purchased extensive public fishing easements running from Waterbury Road to Ryan Road.

In the spring, the east branch is stocked with 1,000 brook trout yearlings and 1,100 rainbow trout yearlings.

NOTES: _____

_____

_____

SALMON RIVER (North Branch)

map coordinates . . . . 43° 31' 45"   75° 48' 45"
USGS map(s) . . . . Redfield, Orwell
location (township) . . . . Redfield, Boylston
access . . . . Abes Road — see below
principle species . . . . brook trout (stocked & wild), brown trout (wild), rainbow trout (wild)

The north branch of the Salmon River is the poor relations of this remarkable system. Though it does offer some good trout fishing on occasion, it is, for all intents and purposes, no great shakes.

The North branch of the Salmon River flows through a very isolated and picturesque region. The headwaters of the stream lie in the remote Little John State Wildlife Management Area. As you would expect, the upper reach of the north branch is small, running perhaps 10 feet in width. It often dries to pools in summer, but it has a substantial population of wild brook trout.

By the time the north branch joins the east branch of the Salmon River, near Redfield, it has grown to a stream of considerable proportions. Ranging up to 60 feet in width, much of the north branch is a rather deep, low gradient, meandering stream, with many large pools. Even though it is overhung by nature hardwoods, the stream is only marginally suitable for trout due to its relatively high water temperatures. The majority of the fish taken here are stocked brook trout. While there may be some carry over of fish, the amount is not significant, and this qualifies as a put and take fishery. There probably is a small number of wild rainbow trout in the lower reaches of the stream, straying up from the higher quality east branch, but they don't contribute much to the quality of fishing in the north branch.

The north branch of the Salmon River provides an excellent setting for fly fishing. In the spring, when the stream is heavily stocked, it gets a fair amount of attention from anglers, but it is large enough that you won't feel crowded. And what it lacks in terms of quality fishing is compensated, at least in part, by the beauty of the surroundings.

To guarantee public access to the north branch of the Salmon River, the state has purchased a total of 8.85 miles of public fishing easements on the stream, and 2.94 miles of easements on one of its upper tributaries, Pine Creek. The state has also obtained 8 fishermen parking areas, 4 of which are currently developed. They are located as follows: 1) On County Road 47 about 1 mile north of Redfield; 2) On Harvester Mill Road; 3) On Randall Road; 4) On Abes Road (formerly Yeardon Road).

In the spring, the north branch of the Salmon River is stocked with 8,600 brook trout yearlings, from stream mouth upstream 6.8 miles to the crossing at County Road 15.

NOTES: _____

_____

_____

SCRIBA CREEK

map coordinates . . . . 43° 14' 44"   75° 59' 42"
USGS map(s) . . . . Cleveland, Mallory, Panther Lake
location (township) . . . . Constantia
access . . . . Parallelled by County Rds. 23 & 23A
principle species . . . . brown trout (wild), brook trout (wild)

Emptying into Oneida Lake at Constantia, Scriba Creek is a long, fair quality trout stream. Averaging 20 feet in width, the

Polarized sunglasses enable you to see through glare on the water's surface, a definite advantage when scouting for fish or their lairs. Amber colored lenses are best for small streams. On shallow lakes, tan lenses are recommended, while grey lenses are best suited for deep water lakes.

stream has a good year-round flow of water over a bottom of gravel. The surroundings consist primarily of farmland and forestland and many sections are sufficiently open to make fly fishing possible. There are a number of large pools where the fishing is good, but the population of fish in the stream overall is relatively low. At one time Scriba Creek was stocked, but a local trout club requested that the DEC suspend the stocking, hoping that the stream would revert to a good quality trout stream. The stocking was suspended, but population of wild trout never reached the levels that were expected. Scriba Creek is not scheduled to be put back on to the stocking list. The stream thus remains less than adequate as a trout fishery.

To facilitate access to Scriba Creek and a tributary, Farrington Creek, the state has purchased a total of .69 miles of public fishing easements on these streams. Be sure to stay on sections open to public access, for much of Scriba Creek is posted.

Fishing is prohibited on Scriba Creek, from March 16 to the first Friday in May, between the stream mouth and the fish hatchery dam, to protect spawning walley. Check for current regulations.

NOTES: _____

_____

_____

_____

TROUT BROOK

map coordinates.........	43° 32′ 22″ 76° 02′ 54″
USGS map(s).............	Redfield, Orwell, Boylston Center
location (township)........	Albion, Richland, Sandy Creek, Orwell
access..................	Crossings at Centerville Road and County Road 22
principle species	rainbow trout (stocked & wild), brown trout (wild), brook trout, (wild), coho salmon, chinook salmon

Trout Brook is one of the major tributaries of the Salmon River below the reservoirs. Averaging 20 feet in width, this gravel and rubble bottomed stream has a good year-round flow of cold water. Most of Trout Brook is rimmed with tangled brush, but some sections flow through open woodland and can be fly fished.

Trout Brook benefits greatly from its relationship to the Salmon River. It has excellent runs of stocked and wild rainbows (steelhead), and lesser runs of naturalized coho salmon and chinook salmon. Brown trout and brook trout are also present in the stream, but they are losing ground due to predation by steelhead fry.

During the seasonal salmonid runs, this stream is very heavily fished. To increase public access to Trout Brook, the state has purchased a total of 5.3 miles of public fishing easements on the stream, and 1 foot path right-of-way. These easements are located downstream of Centerville Road and upstream of Wart Road.

In the spring, Trout Brook is stocked with 10,000 rainbow trout (steelhead) yearlings.

NOTES: _____

_____

_____

_____

Trout Brook is renowned for its runs of wild and stocked rainbow trout. Like other high quality tributaries of the Salmon River, it also has runs of naturalized chinook and coho salmon. Photo courtest of Rick Kustich

OSWEGO COUNTY LAKES & PONDS

HAPPY VALLEY WILDLIFE MANAGEMENT AREA

map coordinates......... 43° 26' 38" 75° 58' 29"
USGS map(s)............. Williamstown, Dugway
location (township)....... Albion, Amboy, Parish, Williamstown
access.................. see map
principle species .... largemouth bass, panfish

The Happy Valley Wildlife Management Area is a collection of 8,645 acres of generally flat woodlands in all stages of succession. The area has managed to provide habitat for a variety of upland wildlife including white tail deer, hare, squirrel, beaver, raccoon, mink, turkey, grouse and numerous types of waterfowl.

Fishing in the wildlife area centers around three ponds — Long Pond (76 acres), St. Mary's (25 acres) and Whitney Pond (96 acres) — all of which have populations of largemouth bass and panfish.

Long Pond: Occasionally this shallow pond has some very good bass fishing. Lily pads, weed beds and submerged stumps provide good habitat. Unfortunately, Long Pond has a serious winter kill of bass about every 6 to 7 years.

St. Mary's Pond: This small, weedy pond has a good population of pumpkinseed and bullhead. Largemouth bass were stocked here, but survival was poor and the stocking has stopped. Because of its swampy surroundings, St. Mary's Pond is very difficult to access.

Whitney Pond: As is the case with Long Pond, winter kills of largemouth bass occur here, but with less frequency. Occasionally, a bass up to 8 pounds is reported from this pond. The pond itself looks like good bass water. Numerous old stumps and partially submerged trees, patches of lily pads and dense shoreside brush provide cover for largemouth bass, pumpkinseed and bullhead.

Because of the dense brush surrounding these ponds, canoes or small cartop boats are recommended. All of these ponds are lightly fished, and despite problems with winterkill, can provide some fine fishing in a very remote setting.

Primitive camping (no water, sanitation or garbage facilities) is allowed on the Happy Valley Wildlife Management Area, by permit only.

For further information contact:

Regional Wildlife Manager, Region 7
N.Y.S. Department of Environmental Consevation
P.O. Box 1169, Fisher Avenue
Cortland, NY 13045

NOTES: _____

_____

_____

_____

LAKE NEATAHWANTA

map coordinates......... 43° 18' 32" 76° 26' 15"
USGS map(s)............. Fulton
location................. township of Granby, adjacent to city of Fulton
access.................. city of Fulton Park, at North Bay

Physical Characteristics

area .... 749 acres
shoreline................ 366 feet
elevation .... 366 feet
maximum depth .... approximately 11 feet
mean depth .... not available
bottom type .... muck, gravel

Chemical Characteristics

water clarity............. turbid
pH...................... alkaline
oxygen.................. Severe oxygen depletion occurs in this lake in the summer and in the winter.

Plant Life

This lake suffers from severe eutrophication resulting in an excess of aquatic vegetation. Algae blooms are also a problem here.

Species Information

largemouth bass.......... common, growth rate fair
northern pike............. common; growth rate fair
white perch.............. common; growth rate fair
black crappie............. common; growth rate fair
bowfin .... common; growth rate good
bullhead .... common; growth rate good
pumpkinseed .... common; growth rate fair
bluegills................. common; growth rate fair
tiger muskellunge........ uncommon; growth rate - not available
walleye .... rare; growth rate not available

Boat Launch Sites

1. There is a hard surface ramp available in the city of Fulton Park, located in the north   side of the lake.

General Information

Lake Neatahwanta is a shallow, weedy lake that is excessively productive, due in part to agricultural run-off. There are large populations of a number of species, almost all of which show poor growth rate. The only species that show healthy growth rates are bullhead and bowfin. The bowfin get to be quite large here (12 lbs. and up). These highly predatory fish compete heavily with the northern pike and largemouth bass in the lake, explaining to some extent their relatively poor growth rates. At one time walleye were stocked here, but the lake has rather poor walleye habitat and survival was poor. A few walleye are still found here, migrating in from the Oswego River. Tiger muskellunge have also been stocked here in an attempt to reduce the numbers of stunted fish. The success of this stocking program has been moderate at best.

NOTES: _____

_____

_____

LIGHTHOUSE HILL RESERVOIR

map coordinates......... 43° 31' 26" 75° 58' 15"
USGS map(s)............. Orwell
location .... township of Orwell
access.................. off Hog Back Road, or County Road 22 - see below

Physcial Characteristics

area .... 164 acres
shoreline................ 4.5 miles
elevation .... 651 feet
maximum depth .... approximately 22 feet
mean depth .... N.A.
bottom type .... gravel, sand

Chemical Characteristics

water clarity............. fair
pH...................... alkaline
oxygen.................. good due to flowage all year long

Plant Life

This reservoir does not have any significant amount of rooted aquatic vegetation.

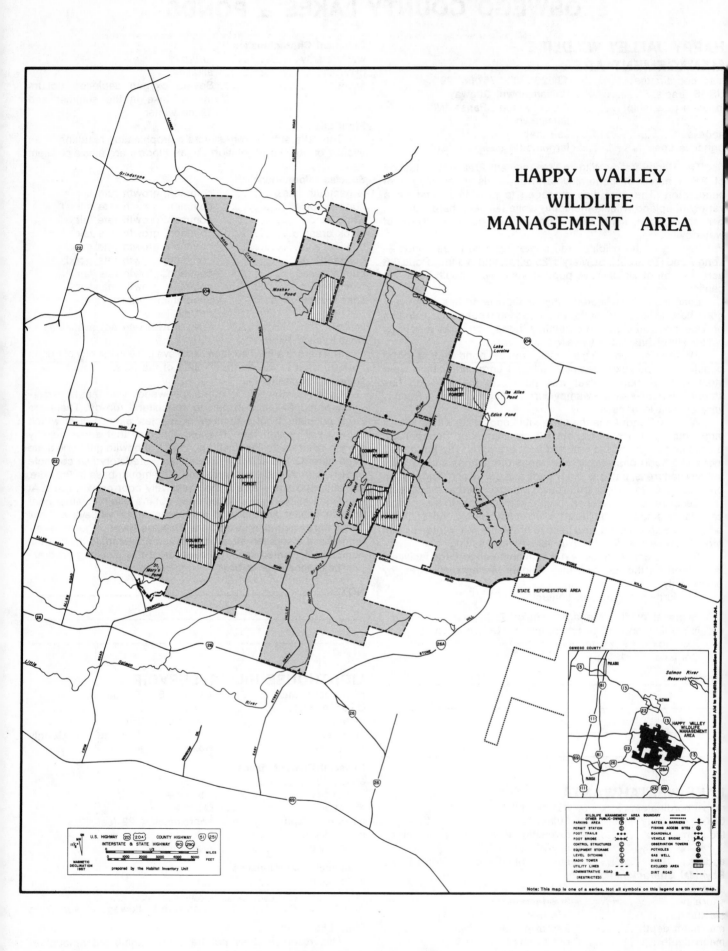

HAPPY VALLEY
WILDLIFE
MANAGEMENT AREA

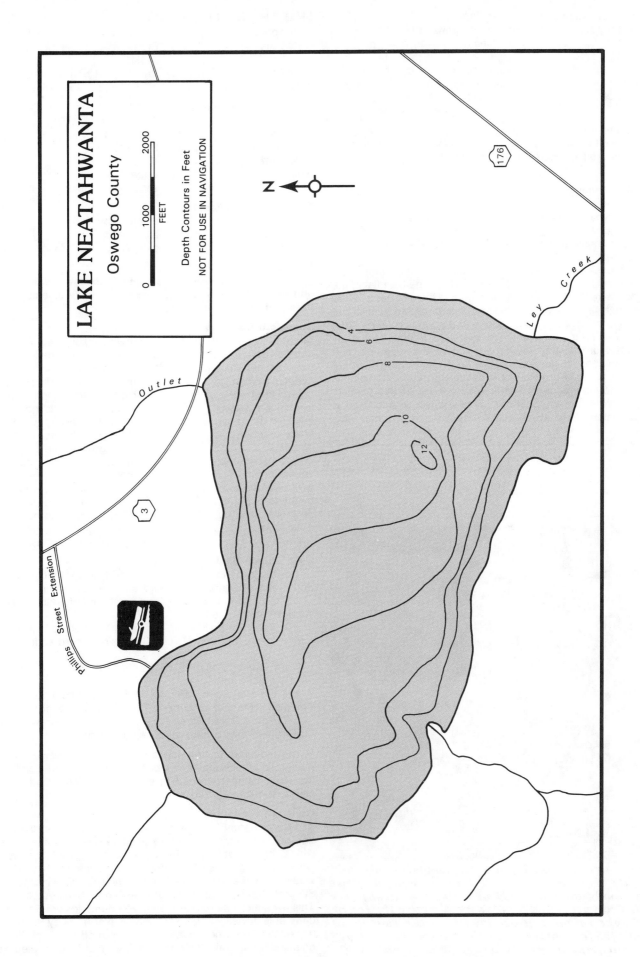

LAKE NEATAHWANTA

Oswego County

FEET

0   1000   2000

Depth Contours in Feet

NOT FOR USE IN NAVIGATION

N

176

Ley Creek

Outlet

3

Phillips Street Extension

4

6

8

10

12

Species Information

rainbow trout . . . . common; growth rate good
brown trout . . . . uncommon; growth rate good
largemouth bass . . . . common; growth rate fair
rock bass . . . . common; growth rate poor
bullhead . . . . common; growth rate fair to good
yellow perch . . . . common; growth rate poor
bluegills . . . . common; growth rate poor

Boat Launch Sites

1. Small boats and canoes can be hand launched from an informal pull-off on Hog Back Road on the north side of the reservoir.

General Information

This reservoir lies about 3 miles downstream of the Salmon River Reservoir, and is also referred to as the Lower Salmon River Reservoir. Like the larger impoundment, it is part of a hydro-electric generating station. It has a daily water level fluctuation of about 2 feet.

Lighthouse Hill Reservoir is typical of small, high flow impoundments in that it isn't very productive. The best fishing is for rainbow trout, which are stocked here in the amount of 4,300 yearling per year. Survival of these fish through the year is not good, but occasionaly a rainbow of 6 to 8 pounds is taken here. Large brown trout are taken here even less frequently. Large-mouth bass are a fairly recent invasion of this reservoir, first showing up about 15 years ago. They are found in good numbers throughout, but their growth rate is not very good. The remainder of the fish found in Lighhouse Hill Reservoir are stunted panfish, with the exception of bullhead. There is some pretty good bullhead fishing here at night in the spring and summer.

NOTES: _____

_____

_____

_____

A nice stringer of hand size pumpkinseeds and bluegills from North Sandy Pond. Found in most major ponds and lakes in New York State, these feisty sunfish can provide a lot of fast action to a fly rod or ultra light spinning gear. Pumpkinseeds can be differentiated from bluegills by the red spot on the tip of their gill flaps or by the irregular lines on the gill cover. Photo courtesy New York State DEC.

NORTH SANDY POND

map coordinates . . . . 43° 39′ 24″   76° 11′ 03″
USGS map(s) . . . . Ellisburg - see also N.O.A.A. chart
                                  #14803
location . . . . township of Sandy Creek
access . . . . off Route 3 - see below

Physical Characteristics

area . . . . 2400 acres
shoreline . . . . 13.4 miles
elevation . . . . 246 feet
maximum depth . . . . 13 feet
mean depth . . . . 8 feet
bottom type . . . . sand, rock, muck

Chemical Characteristics

water clarity . . . . some turbidity
pH . . . . alkaline
oxygen . . . . oxygen is good throughout the year

Plan Life

Extensive weed beds are found in shallow areas of this bay and near the mouths of major streams. Algae blooms do occur here, but they are not severe.

Species Information

rainbow trout . . . . common; seasonal (spring and fall)
chinook salmon . . . . common; seasonal (fall)
coho salmon . . . . common; seasonal (fall)
atlantic salmon . . . . common; seasonal (fall)
brown trout . . . . common; seasonal (spring and fall)
largemouth bass . . . . common; growth rate good
smallmouth bass . . . . common; growth rate good
black crappie . . . . common; growth rate good
bluegills . . . . common; growth rate good
pumpkinseeds . . . . common; growth rate good
yellow perch . . . . common; growth rate good
white perch . . . . common; growth rate good
bullhead . . . . common; growth rate good
northern pike . . . . common; growth rate good
rock bass . . . . common; growth rate good
walleye . . . . rare; growth rate not available

Boat Launch Sites

1. North Sandy Pond Marina and Campground, Route 2 on South end of pond; single hard surface ramp, parking - fee.
2. Jones Marine, Route 2 on south end of pond; single hard surface ramp - fee.
3. Seber Shore Marina, on Seber Shore Road between Little Sandy Creek and Blind Creek Cove; single hard surface ramp - fee.
4. Freeman's Marina, on Route 3 at Skinner Creek; single hard surface ramp - fee.
5. Greene Point Marina, off Route 3 (first left north of Freeman's Marina) at Greene Point, single gravel ramp - fee.
6. Noto's Green Acres Campground, on Renshaw Bay Road, off Route 3; single hard surface ramp - fee.

In addition to the launch sites listed above, there are numerous other support services available on North Sandy Pond, including campgrounds, bait and tackle shops, marine supply stores and charter services.

General Information

North Sandy Pond is a large protected bay on the eastern end of Lake Ontario. Due to its position relative to the prevailing winds, this bay changes physically rather quickly. Winds from the west constantly push sand from the lake into the bay, while the water from the tributaries (Little Sandy Creek, Lindsey Creek, Skinner Creek) are continuously flushing it back out to the lake. This dynamic situation results in everchanging contours, so extra caution is advised when navigating in North Sandy Pond. This is especially true when boating in or around the inlet. The inlet changes constantly. At one time the inlet was located at the channel that joins North and South Sandy Ponds. Now it is found

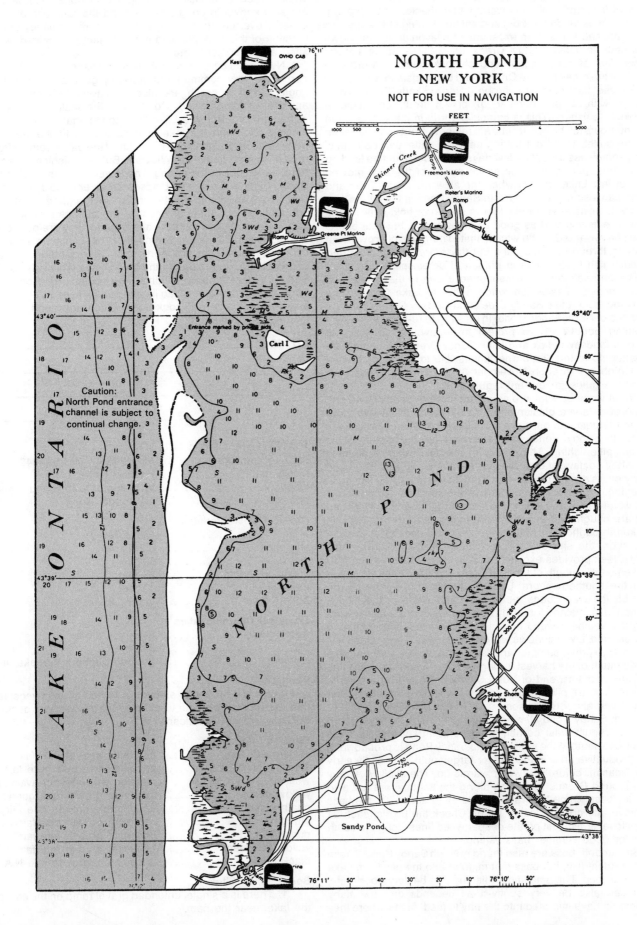

NORTH POND
NEW YORK
NOT FOR USE IN NAVIGATION

Caution:
North Pond entrance
channel is subject to
continual change.

LAKE ONTARIO

NORTH POND

Carl I

Entrance marked by private aids

Skinner Creek

Freeman's Marina

Reiter's Marina
Ramp

Greene Pt Marina
Ramp

Seber Shore
Marina

Lake Road

Sandy Pond

Ruins

43°40'

43°39'

43°38'

76°11'

due west of Carl Island. It can even change from day to day, so it's advisable not to blindly rely upon the buoy markers when entering or exiting North Sandy Pond.

North Sandy Pond has good to excellent fishing for a wide variety of fish, both cold and warm water species. In the spring, there are times when the trout and salmon fishing in the bay can be exceptional. There is an excellent population of wild rainbows (steelhead) in Little Sandy Creek as well as some natural reproduction of coho salmon and chinook salmon. In order to pass from the creek to Lake Ontario and back again to reproduce, all of these fish must go through North Sandy Pond. They, together with a fair number of brown trout, constitute a considerable fishery. This is particularly true in the spring when large numbers of brown trout and rainbow trout can be taken near the outlet. This trout fishing near the outlet can be erratic, lasting sometimes for only a few days. The trout might be feeding on alewives that concentrate at the mouth of the bay, moving back out into Lake Ontario when the alewives leave. Trout and salmon can also be taken in North Sandy Pond in the fall, as they head for their natal streams either to spawn or hold over for the winter. The fishing isn't as good as in the spring, but your efforts will still be rewarded. In the winter, limited numbers of brown trout are taken through the ice here, but these are for the most part incidental fish taken while in pursuit of other species.

The one salmonid not mentioned above is the landlocked atlantic salmon. These fish, once native to Lake Ontario, are being stocked in Little Sandy Creek and Lindsey Creek (both are tributaries of North Sandy Pond) in an effort to re-establish a self-sustaining population. To protect the spawning atlantics, all fishing in Lindsey Creek and Little Sandy Creek, including their tributaries up to the first barrier impassible to fish, is prohibited from October 1 through November 30. Be sure to check your regulations guide for current regulations.

Warm water species are abundant in North Sandy Pond and often provide some outstanding angling opportunities. Northern pike and largemouth bass are particularly common. Many years ago North Sandy Pond was renowned for the quality of its northern pike fishing. The quality of the pike fishing may have diminished somewhat over the years, but it is still very good and the bay offers some of the best and most consistent pike fishing in the region. The average northern pike taken from North Sandy Pond weighs in at about 8 pounds, and fish in the 12 to 15 pound class are caught with a fair amount of regularity. Northerns can be taken throughout this bay wherever weed beds exist. Early in the season, the shallow, weedy estuary at the mouth of Little Sandy Creek provides excellent pike fishing. Northerns can also be taken off the mouth of Lindsey Creek, in Blind Creek Cove and along the southern shore. Later in the season, northerns are taken off the weed beds along the south shore of the bay. A common local method for taking northerns is to drift with the wind along the southern weed lines, trailing Johnson spoons tipped with pork rind. Live minnows will also work well. This method will work in the spring, summer and fall. In the winter, northern pike provide much of the harvest through the ice. Again, the weed line along the southern end of North Sandy Pond will be a favorite haunt of northern pike. Blind Creek Cove and the waters around Green Point also provde some fine winter pike fishing.

North Sandy Pond also has excellent fishing for largemouth bass. The south-west corner, from the point known locally as Hog's Nose south to the inlet of South Sandy Pond is probably the most productive area in the bay for largemouth, especially early in the season, before the water warms up. The shallow weedy areas around Greene Point and along the south shore are also good for bass. Once the water warms up to about 70°, the bass will move into cooler, deeper water. Check the points, such as Hog's Nose, or fish just off the deeper weed lines along the south shore for good summer bass fishing.

Smallmouth bass are also found in North Sandy Pond. These aren't resident fish, but bass that migrate into the bay from Lake Ontario to feed. The smallmouth fishing can be very good here, but it can also be very spotty-it all depends on how many smallmouth have migrated into the bay to feed. Areas where they

are known to concentrate include the rocky shoreline just nor of Blind Creek Cove, the rock piles off the building on the sout shore known locally as "the lodge" (just west of Wigwam Bait an Tackle), around Carl Island and right at the outlet to the lake. The are also known to congregate around the rock pile off of Blin Creek Cove, but ther is currently some discrepancy about th location of this rock pile and it may in fact be covered wit sand at the present time.

Numerous panfish contribute to the fishery in this bay. Whit perch are very common, but currently generate little interest i anglers. Yellow perch are also common. They can be foun anywhere in North Sandy Pond but in the shallowest bays. Mos of the yellow perch are Lake Ontario fish that winter-over her moving back into the lake in the summer. In the winter, the provide excellent fishing, with much of the catch coming from th rock piles just west of the Wigwam. Bullhead fishing is very goo here, especially in the spring. The lower reaches of Little Sand Creek, Skinner Creek and Lindsey Creek and the shallows in th north-west and south-west corners provide good catch of thes fine tasting fish. Although most of the bullhead found in Nort Sandy Pond migrate in from Lake Ontario, they are perfectly saf to eat. The DEC has indicated that the contaminant levels i bullhead in the eastern portion of Lake Ontario are almos undetectable. Rounding out the panfish available in North Sand Pond are black crappie, which are very common in Renshaw Ba north of Greene Point, bluegills and pumpkinseeds, both of whic attain a good size and rock bass, which are found throughou much of the bay.

NOTES: _____

_____

_____

_____

PANTHER LAKE

map coordinates	43° 19' 35" 75° 54' 04"
USGS map(s)	Panther Lake
location	township of Amboy and Constanti
access	off County Road 17

Physical Characteristics

area	122 acres
shoreline	3.0 miles
elevation	600 feet
maximum depth	21 feet
mean depth	12 feet
bottom type	gravel, muck

Chemical Characteristics

water clarity	generally clear
pH	alkaline
oxygen	good throughout the lake all yea

Plant Life

There is a moderate amount of rooted aquatic vegetation i this lake, primarily on the west end. Algae blooms do occur here but they are not significant.

Species Information

largemouth bass	common; growth rate fair
smallmouth bass	uncommon; growth rate fair
walleye	rare; growth rate not available
yellow perch	common; growth rate good
chain pickerel	uncommon; growth rate fair
bluegills	common; growth rate fair
pumpkinseed	common; growth rate fair
yellow bullhead	common; growth rate fair
black crappie	uncommon; growth rate N.A.

Boat Launch Sites

1. There is a single, untended gravel ramp on the east end o the lake, near the dam.

General Information

Located 4 miles south-east of Amboy Center, this small impoundment offers fair to good fishing for many species of fish, most notably largemouth bass. The largemouth in this lake aren't large, but they are plentiful. Other predators are also found here (smallmouth bass, chain pickerel and walleye) but their numbers are relatively insignificant. There are many panfish in Panther Lake, including the recently introduced black crappie and the yellow bullhead, which is rather uncommon in small inland lakes of this region.

This lake has a heavily developed shoreline (cottages) and access is fairly limited. There is some access available at the east end of the lake by the dam.

NOTES: _____

_____

_____

_____

REDFIELD RESERVOIR

map coordinates	43° 32' 40" 75° 55' 11"
USGS map(s)	Orwell, Redfield
location	townships of Amboy and Constantia
access	off CCC Road and Jackson Road. The entire eastern end of the lake is posted.

Physical Characteristics

area	3,380 acres
shoreline	30.6 miles
elevation	937 feet
maximum depth	57 feet
mean depth	approximately 20 feet
bottom type	gravel, some rubble

Chemical Characteristics

water clarity	stained brown
pH	alkaline in summer; acidic in winter
oxygen	some oxygen depletion does occur in the deep channel near the dam, but it does not seem to affect fish.

Plant Life

There are significant patches of weeds in shallow areas, but rooted aquatics are not particularly abundant anywhere in this lake.

Species Information

largemouth bass	abundant; growth rate very good
brown trout	uncommon; growth rate good
rainbow trout	uncommon; growth rate fair
rock bass	common; growth rate fair
yellow perch	common; growth rate fair
bullhead	common; growth rate fair
pumpkinseed	common; growth rate fair

Boat Launch Sites

1. At Little America, on CCC Road, off the Orwell-Redfield Road, 1½ miles west of the hamlet of Redfield. Hand launch only — parking for 32 cars — no charge.

2. On Jackson Road, off the Orwell-Redfield Road 5½ miles west of hamlet of Redfield. Hand launch only — parking for 22 cars — no charge.

General Information

The Redfield Reservoir is also known as the Salmon River Reservoir. Constructed as a holding tank for hydro-electric stations, the reservoir is usually held at close to full pool level until May. It is then drawn down a total of 14 feet by October. Despite this serious fluctuation in water levels, there are some significant weed beds. These, combined with a lot of old stumps and submerged logs, provide habitat for an excellent population of largemouth bass. At first sight you wouldn't think that this lake, which sits in the heart of New York's trout and salmon fishery, could be a very good bass lake. But a lack of serious competition

from any other species and a population of crayfish that is nothing short of phenomenal help to keep the bass here numerous and well fed. Aside from the excellent bass fishing, the angling opportunities in Redfield Reservoir are rather limited. With the exception of the wild brown trout, which are not very common here, all of the other fish species found in the lake are stunted. There are some decent size wild rainbows, but, though they attain full adult length, they are pathetically skinny; so skinny in fact that even when they migrate into a tributary stream, they can be discerned from the streams population of resident rainbows.

A major problem on Redfield Reservoir is physical access. Small cartop boats or canoes can be launched fairly easily, but to put in with a full size bass boat at the 2 launch sites would probably require a four wheel drive truck and/or a winch.

NOTES: _____

_____

_____

_____

SOUTH SANDY POND

map coordinates	43° 37' 23" 76° 11' 15"
USGS map(s)	Ellisburg, Pulaski
location	township of Sandy Creek
access	The only access to South Sandy Pond is via the inlet to North Sandy Pond. There is no shore access or boat launch site here.

Physical Characteristics

area	301 acres
shoreline	4.4 miles
elevation	246 feet
maximum depth	25 feet
mean depth	approximately 14 feet
bottom type	muck

Chemical Characteristics

water clarity	clear
pH	alkaline
oxygen	Oxygen is adequate throughout South Sandy Pond all year.

Plant Life

Extensive weed beds are found in all of the bays and in most water under 10 feet deep. Algae blooms are not a problem here.

Species Information

largemouth bass	common; growth rate fair
northern pike	common; growth rate fair
white perch	very common; growth rate good
pumpkinseed	common; growth rate good
bluegills	common; growth rate good
black crappie	uncommon; growth rate fair
yellow perch	uncommon; growth rate poor
smallmouth bass	uncommon; growth rate fair
walleye	uncommon; growth rate not available
brown bullhead	common; growth rate good

Boat Launch Sites

There are no public boat launch sites on South Sandy Pond.

General Information

Although South Sandy Pond, known also as simply South Pond, is directly connected to North Sandy Pond (also known as North Pond) and indirectly to Lake Ontario, it is a relatively mediocre fishery. The only Lake Ontario species that migrates into South Sandy Pond in any great numbers are alewives and white perch. All of the resident species in this pond grow more slowly than in North Sandy Pond. There are healthy populations of largemouth bass and northern pike, but they generally run on the small side. Largemouth will most often be found in the shallow, weedy bays, while northerns can be taken by trolling along the edge of the weed beds. There is good fishing for

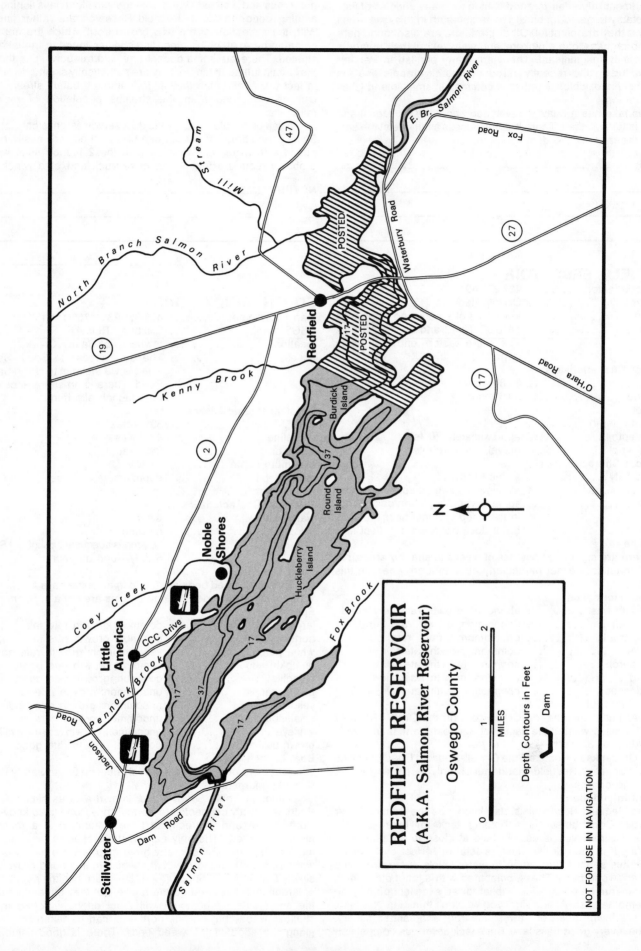

REDFIELD RESERVOIR
(A.K.A. Salmon River Reservoir)
Oswego County

MILES

0   1   2

Depth Contours in Feet

Dam

NOT FOR USE IN NAVIGATION

bluegills and pumpkinseeds in April, right after ice-out. Try the bay on the north-east section of the pond or the flats on the south-west corner. Because of their dark, almost black bottom, these areas warm up more quickly than the rest of the pond. This attracts the panfish in great numbers, who often feed ravenously in the spring. Large numbers of bullhead are also found in the north-east and south-west portions of South Sandy Pond in the spring. These bullheads aren't as large as those from Lake Ontario or North Sandy Pond, but they are plentiful and provide some fine fishing. The pond also has limited fishing for black crappie, walleye, smallmouth bass and yellow perch. At present, walleye are stocked here (720,000 fry per year), but survival is minimal and this stocking will most likely be stopped soon. The smallmouth bass population is limited by a lack of habitat. A

majority of the smallmouth are found around the point on the south side of the pond. The yellow perch population is kept in check by heavy predation by alewives or perch fry.

Ice fishing on South Sandy Pond is minimal. This is due to the almost complete lack of public access and to the fact that the ice-fishing in nearby North Sandy Pond is so much better.

NOTES: _____

_____

_____

_____

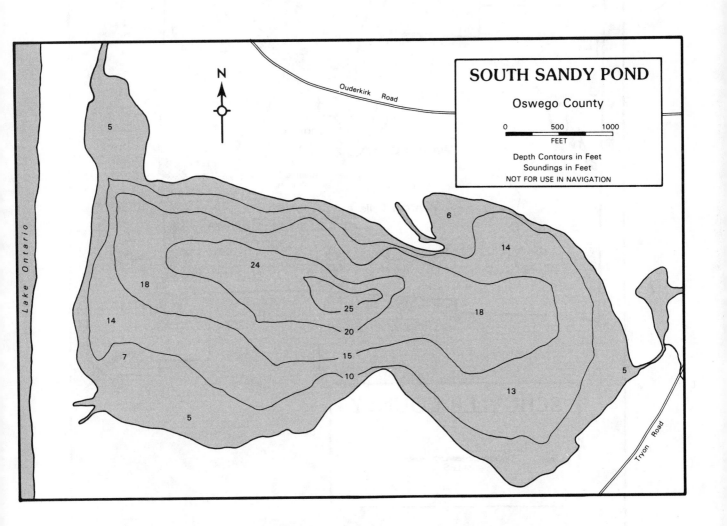

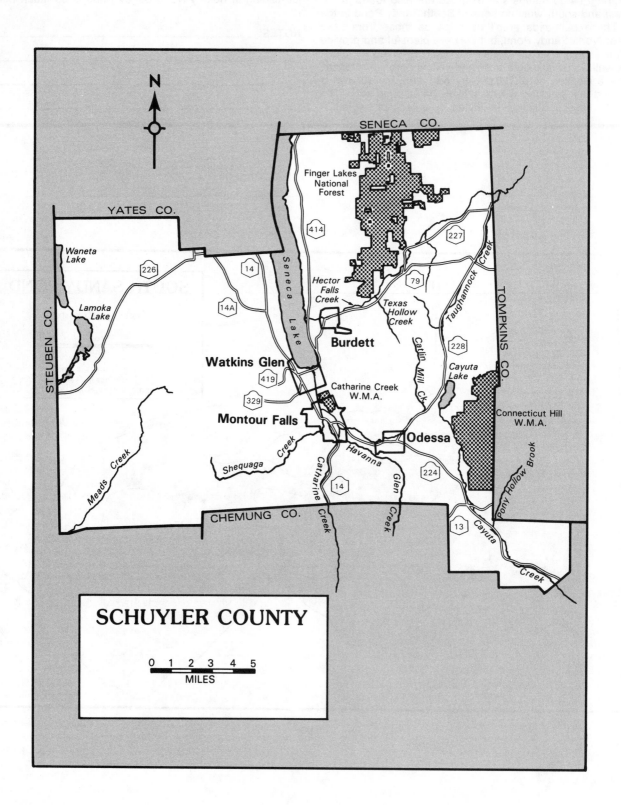

SCHUYLER COUNTY

```
0  1  2  3  4  5
        MILES
```

SCHUYLER COUNTY STREAMS & RIVERS

BIG STREAM — see Yates County Streams and Rivers

CATHARINE CREEK

map coordiantes.......... 42° 21' 05" 76° 51' 05"
USGS map(s)............. Horseheads, Montour Falls
location (township)....... Dix, Montour (Schuyler County); Veteran (Chemung County)
access.................. parallelled by Route 14 - see below
principle species........ rainbow trout (wild)

Catharine Creek is one of the streams that makes New York State a fisherman's delight. It has some of the finest runs of wild rainbow trout in the state, one of the best in fact, in the eastern United States. It's very name evokes images of anxious, shivering anglers standing shoulder-to-shoulder in the waning winter chill, partaking of a spring ritual that stretches back generations.

Catharine Creek has its origins in the hills of northern Chemung County. The stream is not as large as its reputation would have you think. From the hamlet of Pine Valley, the uppermost point of the stream that is classified as trout water, it flows north for 11 miles, emptying into Seneca Lake at Watkins Glen, via the old Seneca Canal. The stream averages perhaps 50 feet in width during periods of normal spring runoff. It has an excellent flow of high quality water over a bottom of gravel and rubble. Normally gin clear, Catharine Creek muddies quickly after a heavy rain or strong snow melt and takes several days to fully recover. Although the stream is closely parallelled by a major highway (Route 14) for much of its length, there are areas of extensive stream side vegetation. The overarching trees and short woody brush that crowds the waters edge foster a sense of isolation from the hustle and bustle of nearby traffic. On the other hand, some sections are as wide open as wide open can be.

As is the case with most streams that depend primarily on spawining rainbows for their fishing, the activity on Catharine Creek actually starts in the fall. Seneca Lake rainbows will begin to move into the stream as early as mid-October if there has been an adequate amount of rainfall. Though few anglers seem interested in this fall trout fishing, it can be truly impressive. Constant heavy rainfall will draw tremendous numbers of 2 to 3 pound jacks into the stream. The best action usually occurs from mid-November to early December. The season doesn't close here until December 31, (Finger Lakes tributary regulations apply throughout Catharine Creek) and good fishing can be had right to the season's end. This fall season sees none of the crowding that takes place on Catharine Creek come opening day. Rather, solitude is the order of the day, and the intrepid fisherman who braves the cold can have some of the finest fishing this stream has to offer, all to himself.

Catharine Creek's real moment of glory comes in the spring, April 1st to be exact, when trout season reopens. The stream that was so neglected by anglers the previous fall is suddenly something of interest to sportsmen (and women) from all over the country. Literally thousands of anglers make their way to Catharine Creek during the first week of the season, responding to an urge that is every bit as primal as that which draws Seneca Lake rainbows to the stream. The result is a cacophony of sights and sounds that resembles anything but a serious attempt at fishing. Standing elbow-to-elbow around a small pool with people you don't even know may not be your cup of tea. But many people find the camaraderie of opening day crowds a unique and valued element of their angling experience. It has become a ritual of almost religious significance.

Today's early season crowds, not just on Catharine Creek, but on Finger Lakes tributaries in general, are smaller than their predecessors of 10 or 20 years ago, and of less duration. The attraction of Lake Ontario, with its larger fish and year round season has drawn many people away. Rather than heading for Catharine Creek or Naples Creek, they're crowding on to such Lake Ontario tributaries as the Niagara River and the Salmon River, and the lake water both from shore and by boat.

Scott Miller pulled this rainbow from Catharine Creek, despite the competition from the crowd in the background. Photo courtesy C. Scott Sampson.

This has taken a great deal of pressure off the Finger Lakes tributaries, so that after the first week or two, some of these streams can be fished in near solitude, especially on weekdays. Good spring fishing will normally last to mid-May but can easily extend to June.

By a fortunate coincidence, Catharine Creek usually enjoys a good run of rainbows on or about the opening day of trout season. Several factors are involved in triggering a run of rainbows, but the major factor is a good flow of water at or near the critical temperature of 40 degrees. It is at this temperature that the females are stimulated to begin spawning, and a good hard rain at the right temperature can trigger a sudden and massive run of fish. On Catharine Creek these fish can run unhindered at least as far upstream as Pine Valley in Chemung County. The average size of these females will be 3 to 5 pounds, but every year some lucky angler stumbles across a pool or undercut bank that harbors a trophy rainbow up to 14 pounds.

A number of factors can effect the quality and duration of the spring rainbow runs. Temperature is a critical element. If the water temperature remains in the 50's for more than a few days, the actual spawning will take place quickly, primarily in the main stream. The fish will then begin to drop back down to the lake and the run will be over. Conversely, if excessively cold rainfall, or a strong sudden melting of the snow pack cooks the mainstream well below the 40 degree mark, many fish will seek refuge in the smaller streams where the water will be warmer and cleaner. Under such conditions it can be to your benefit to check out even the smallest rivulets that feed into Catharine Creek. In Chemung County, brooks as small as 3 feet in width and only a few inches deep can hold surprisingly large numbers of adult rainbows. Sleeper Creek is the most notable Catharine Creek tributary in Chemung County, but there are several small, unnamed brooks that get a good influx of fish under the right conditions. In

Stoneflies are common on many high quality streams that have a bottom consisting of small stones or cobbles (thus the name). A well tied stonefly nymph can be very effective on Catharine Creek when the rainbows resume feeding.

Schuyler County, check out such streams as Havana Glen Creek and Catlin Mill Creek.

Initially, as they move upstream to spawn, the rainbows will not be actively feeding, but they can be teased or angered into striking. Once the fish have spawned and begin moving back down to Seneca Lake, they resume active feeding. This explains why, in late April or early May when a majority of the fish have dropped back down to the lake, a persistent fisherman can enjoy some fine fishing, long after the run is supposedly over. Though there are relatively few fish holding in the deeper pools or under cut banks, what they lack in numbers they make up in their active feeding habits.

The bait most popular with Catharine Creek anglers is a small egg sac. Either salmon eggs or trout eggs will work well. Artificial egg sacs or sponge baits, soaked in scented oil or crushed trout eggs are regaining a degree of the popularity they once enjoyed when real trout and salmon eggs were illegal in the Finger Lakes tributaries. Garden worms are another popular choice for bait, and they can be extremely effective at times. When many of the fish have spawned and resumed their active feeding, artificials, particularly stonefly nymphs, and small single hook spinners will take their fair share of fish as well. Finger Lakes tributary regulations prohibit the use of more than one hook point and one line.

An important point to keep in mind when fishing on Catharine Creek, or any Finger Lakes rainbow trout tributary, for that matter, is that these fish are easily spooked. They have spent most of their lives roaming the depths of large, deep lakes, and the relatively shallow water of the stream gives them a very bad case of the jitters. This is especially true of the stream that is running gin clear. They have a tendency to be line shy and can be put off by the heavy monofilament they can see. By using a light line, 4 pound test is good, you'll avoid spooking a lot of fish. You will also enjoy greater sensitivity to detect a light hit.

If the water is running very clear, stealth will be one of the main ingredients of a successful trip. It is important that you locate the fish before it locates you.

Polarized glasses are a valuable tool, allowing you to see into the water to a much greater degree than you normally could. But, keep in mind that these rainbow are adept to finding cover, regardless of how clear the water is. Even polarized glasses won't let you see the bottom of the deepest pools, and undercut banks are even less amendable to visual inspection.

Due to Catharine's tremendous popularity, the state has purchased extensive public fishing easements. A total of 3.33 miles of easements have been purchased in Schuyler County, along with 3 fisherman parking areas, while 3.2 miles of easements and one parking area has been purchased in Chemung County. All of the parking areas in Schuyler County are located off Route 14. The Chemung County parking area is located just north of Pine Valley, on Clair Road.

Be sure to check your regulations guide for current Finger Lakes Tributary regulations that apply to Catharine Creek.

For information on the lower reach of Catharine Creek (the old Seneca Canal) see — Catharine Creek State Wildlife Management Area.

NOTES: _____

_____

_____

_____

CATHARINE CREEK WILDLIFE MANAGEMENT AREA

map coordinates.......... 42º 21' 50"   76º 51' 41"
USGS map(s)............. Burdett, Montour Falls
location (township)....... Dix, Montour
access................... Route 79
principle species .... largemouth bass, northern pike, bullhead, panfish

The Catharine Creek Wildlife Management Area is a large marsh drained by Seneca Lake Inlet and the lower end of Catharine Creek. The lower reach of Catharine Creek is a deep, dredged channel, part of the Barge Canal system. There is some fishing here for warm water species, most notably largemouth bass and northern pike. The quality of the fishing is only fair at best.But, Rainbow trout must migrate through the canal on their spawning runs to the headwaters of Catharine Creek. Few rainbows are taken in the canal, but due more to the lack of attention that the canal receives during the trout runs. Bank anglers at Clute Memorial Park where the canal enters the lake are often very successful.

Access to the wildlife area and the canal can be had off Route 14, in the village of Watkins Glen, where the state maintains a gravel launch ramp for small boats on the east side of the canal. Or, enter the canal at Clute Park on the south side of route 414.

NOTES: _____

_____

_____

_____

CATLIN MILL CREEK

map coordinates.......... 42º 20' 44"   76º 50' 15"
USGS map(s)............. Montour Falls, Burdett
location (township)....... Dix, Montour, Catharine
access................... parallelled by Route 224 west of the village of Odessa
principle species .... rainbow trout (wild), brown trout (wild)

Catlin Mill Creek is one of the more productive tributaries of Catharine Creek, at least in terms of its rainbow trout fishing. Approximately 7.5 miles of the stream are classified as trout water, and it can be divided into two distinct sections. The lower section of the stream runs from the stream mouth upstream ¼ mile to an impassible falls. This lower section is also referred to as Deckertown Creek, and joins Catharine Creek via the L'Hommedieu flood control channel.

Catlin Mill Creek gets very good runs of Seneca Lake rainbow trout. Rainbows can be found here as early as mid-November if rainfall is sufficient (Finger Lakes tributary regulations apply to this stream and fishing is permitted here to December 31). As with most other trout streams, Catlin Mill Creek gets little attention from anglers during the fall, and you can have some fine trout fishing all to yourself.

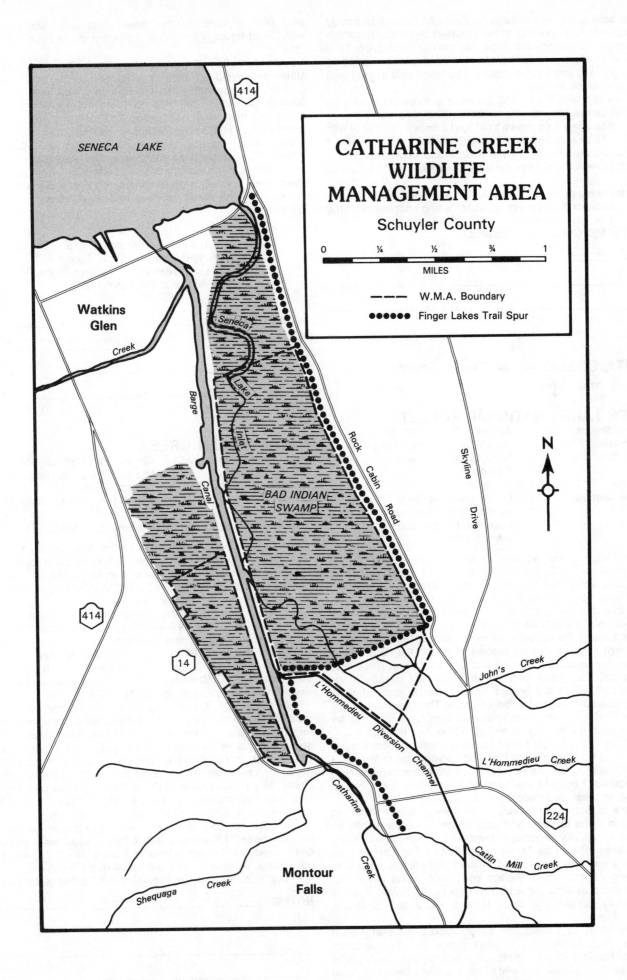

CATHARINE CREEK
WILDLIFE
MANAGEMENT AREA

Schuyler County

0   ¼   ½   ¾   1

MILES

– – – – – W.M.A. Boundary

●●●●●● Finger Lakes Trail Spur

SENECA LAKE

Watkins
Glen

Seneca Creek

Barge

Canal

Lake Inlet

BAD INDIAN
SWAMP

Rock Cabin Road

Skyline Drive

John's Creek

L'Hommedieu

Diversion Channel

L'Hommedieu Creek

Montour
Falls

Catharine Creek

Shequaga Creek

Catlin Mill Creek

414

14

414

224

N

The spring run of rainbows in Catlin Mill Creek generally coincides with the opening of trout season (April 1). These fish will average 3-5 pounds, but larger fish are not uncommon. All of the usual methods will be productive at this time, including drifting egg sacs and worms. Trout will be found here usually until the second week of May.

Above the falls, Catlin Mill Creek is a mediocre quality (at best) trout stream. The middle section, which runs along a state highway, has a few wild brown trout, and a limited number of wild brown trout can also be found in the headwaters of the stream. It could be worthwhile to fish the middle and upper reaches of Catlin Mill Creek if you're in the area, but it's not worth a special trip.

To increase public access to Catlin Mill Creek, the state has recently purchased .294 miles of public fishing easements on the lower part of the stream.

Catlin Mill Creek is not stocked.

NOTES: _____

_____

_____

_____

CAYUTA CREEK — see Tioga County streams and rivers

FINGER LAKES NATIONAL FOREST
map coordinates.......... 42° 29' 57" 76° 44' 54"
USGS map(s)............. Mecklenburg, Trumansburg
location (township)........ Schuyler and Seneca
                          Counties
access................... see map
principle species .... brown trout (stocked),
                          rainbow trout (stocked),
                          largemouth bass, bull-
                          head, panfish

The Finger Lakes National Forest, formerly known as the Hector Land Use Area, is a vast checkerboard expanse of more than 13,000 acres stradling the Seneca/Schuyler County line. Originally settled by the Iroquois Indian Confederacy, white settlers began moving into the area in 1779. Farming was the major activity of the inhabitants until the early 20th century, when the poor soils of the region were exhausted. In 1934 the federal government began acquiring parcels of land in the Hector Hills, the ridge that separates Cayuga and Seneca Lakes. Since then the emphasis has been to establish permanent pasture lands (5,000 acres) which are leased by a livestock association to support several thousand head of cattle. The remaining 8,000 acres of land have been developed as a multiple use area for activities such as hunting, camping, hiking and fishing.

Fishing in the Finger Lakes National Forest centers around the nearly 30 wildlife ponds (all marked on your map of the area.) Many of these ponds are nothing more than quarter-acre farm ponds that have outlived the farm, but they all hold fish. Don't let even the smallest pond escape your attention.

There is some remarkably good fishing for panfish and bullhead in some of them, and your efforts will occasionally be rewarded by a feisty largemouth bass. As an added bonus, three of the ponds (shown as Teeter Pond, Ballard Pond and Foster Pond on your map) are stocked by the U.S. Forest Service with brook and rainbow trout. Ballard and Teeter Pond are rather shallow and provide a put-and-take fishery, but Foster Pond is substantially deeper and does have a population of larger, holdover fish.

In addition to fishing, the Finger Lakes National Forest provides opportunities for a wide range of other outdoor activities. Hunting in the area is very popular and such game species as deer, grouse and wild turkey are found here. For those who like to keep on the move, there are numerous trails wandering through the forest, including the famous Interlocken Trail.

Camping and picnicking are allowed througout the area, either on developed sites or wherever strikes your fancy, but certain rules do apply, so be sure to check with the Forest Service personnel on duty for current regulations. Accommodations have even been made for those who wish to visit the forest on horseback. The Backbone Trailhead has been set up to provide all of the necessary facilities for up to 30 people and horses. Commercial trail rides were also available in 1987.

If you plan on visiting this remarkably beautiful and diverse forest area, you will want to contact the Forest Service for a full rundown on the area's facilities and regulations. Write or call:

District Ranger
U.S.D.A. — Forest Service
Finger Lakes National Forest
P.O. Box W, Odessa — Montour Highway
Montour Falls, NY 14868
607/594-2750

NOTES: _____

_____

_____

_____

HAVANA GLEN CREEK
map coordinates......... 42° 20' 10" 76° 49' 58"
USGS map(s)............. Montour Falls, Burdett
location (township)....... Montour, Catharine
access................... crossed by Route 14 in Montour
                          Falls
principle species .... rainbow trout (wild)

Havana Glen Creek, like Catlin Mill Creek, is a very productive tributary of Catharine Creek, which it joins west of Route 14 in Montour Falls. There is an impassible falls 0.6 miles upstream of the stream mouth, and it is only this short lower stretch that is important as a fishery.

If it has been a wet fall, rainbows will be found in Havana Glen Creek as early as mid-November (remember that, as a Finger Lakes tributary, this stream is open to trout fishing until December 31). These fall run fish will be smaller than those found here in the spring, averaging only 2-4 pounds, but few people fish the Finger Lakes tributaries in the fall, and you can have some excellent trout fishing all to yourself at this time.

In the spring, the melting snows will trigger runs of adult rainbows in Catharine Creek and these fish quickly find their way into streams such as Havana Glen. These spring runs can occur sporadically as early as mid-February. The major runs, however, occur later, in early spring. The opening day of trout (April 1) generally coincides with a good run of rainbows in Catharine Creek, and Havana Glen Creek certainly gets its share of these fish. These spring running rainbows will average 3-5 pounds, but rainbows over 10 pounds are taken at this time.

In order to guarantee public access to this stream, the state has purchased 0.15 miles of public fishing easements on Havana Glen Creek, but even where the state doesn't own fishing easements, access is reported to be good.

The stream has no appreciable fishing about the first falls.

NOTES: _____

_____

_____

_____

HECTOR FALLS CREEK

map coordinates	42° 25' 05" 76° 52' 09"
USGS map(s)	Burdett
location (township)	Hector
access	roughly parallelled by Route 79 east of Burdett
principle species	brown trout (wild)

Hector Falls Creek is one of the higher quality tributaries of Seneca Lake, which enters near the village of Burdett. There is an impassible falls just above the stream's mouth. Below the falls, the stream gets a fair run of Seneca Lake rainbows in the spring, but this stretch is too short to be of any real value, and is heavily posted, as well. It is above the falls that Hector Falls Creek earns its reputation as a high quality fishery. The stream averages 10-15 feet in width, has good stream side cover and a gravel and rubble bottom. There is a good ratio of riffles to pools here, providing excellent habitat for wild brown trout, which will be found right up into the headwaters of the stream. A tributary, Texas Hollow Creek (shown on the Burdett topographical map as Cranberry Creek) probably holds a few wild browns in its lower reaches. The stream is crossed by Route 79, ½ mile east of Bennettsburg.

Hector Falls Creek is not stocked.

NOTES: _____

_____

_____

_____

SHEQUAGA CREEK

map coordinates	42° 21' 02" 76° 50' 58"
USGS map(s)	Montour Falls, Beaver Dams
location (township)	Dix, Montour
access	parallelled by Coykendall Road and Route 414
principle species	brown trout (wild)

Shequaga Creek joins Catharine Creek in the town of Montour Falls. There is a large, scenic falls about ¼ mile upstream of the stream mouth.

Below the falls, the stream has been converted into a flood control channel. Although a few wild rainbows probably do stray into the channel, it is not really of value as a fishery.

Above the falls, slightly more than 8 miles of this stream is classified as trout water. The stream averages 25 feet in width, has a gravel and rubble bottom and a good stream side cover. Shequaga Creek has a very nice population of wild brown trout throughout its length, even to its headwaters. If you check this stream out on a topographical map, you will find that a major tributary enters Shequaga Creek about 3.5 miles above the falls. This is tributary #5, and it starts its flow in the vicinity of Beaver Dams. This tributary forms the major flow of Shequaga Creek above their junction, and is a good trout stream in its own right.

Shequaga Creek is not stocked.

NOTES: _____

_____

_____

_____

_____

MEADS CREEK — see Steuben County Streams and Rivers

PONY HOLLOW BROOK — See Tompkins County Streams and Rivers

TAUGHANNOCK CREEK — see Tompkins County Streams & Rivers

Many streams in the Finger Lakes region have picturesque waterfalls. This falls is on Shequaga Creek, in the town of Montour Falls.

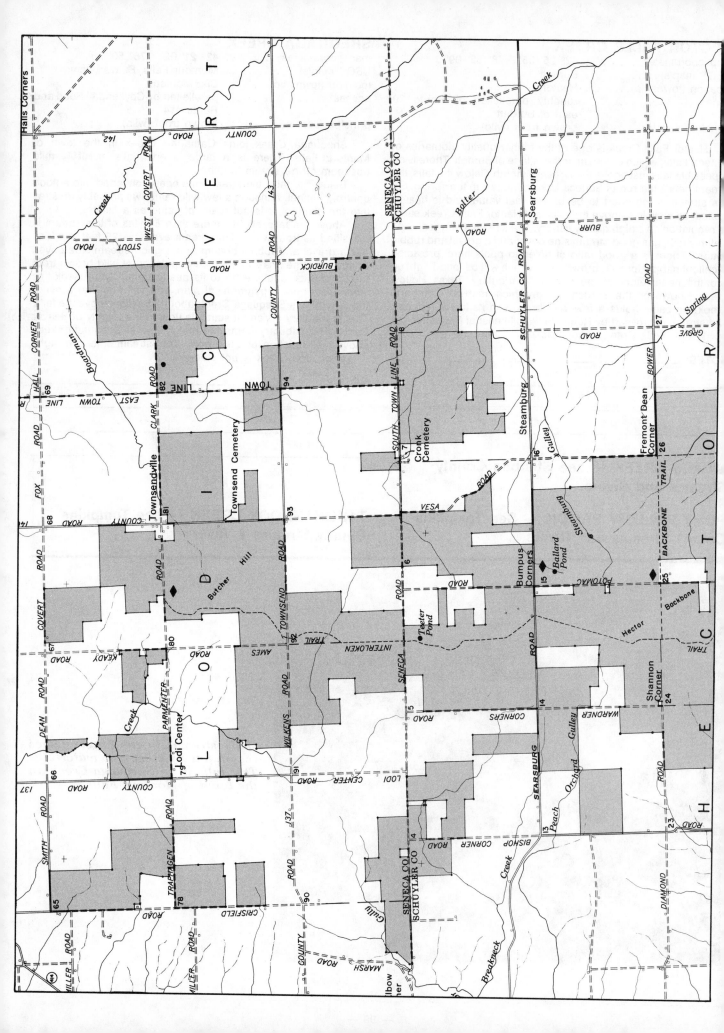

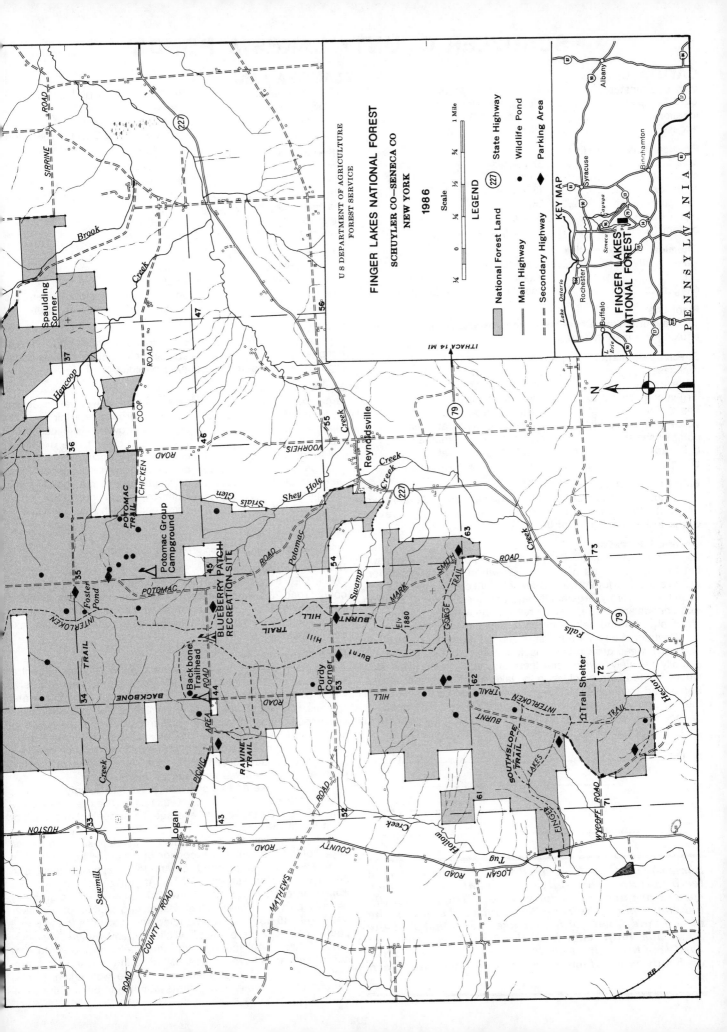

U S DEPARTMENT OF AGRICULTURE
FOREST SERVICE

FINGER LAKES NATIONAL FOREST
SCHUYLER CO—SENECA CO
NEW YORK

1986

Scale

¼   0   ¼   ½   ¾   1 Mile

LEGEND

National Forest Land

⟨227⟩ Main Highway

Secondary Highway

⟨227⟩ State Highway

● Wildlife Pond

◆ Parking Area

KEY MAP

FINGER LAKES
NATIONAL FOREST

PENNSYLVANIA

Albany
Syracuse
Binghamton
Rochester
Buffalo
L. Erie
Lake Ontario
Seneca
Cayuga

N

ITHACA 14 MI

SCHUYLER COUNTY LAKES & PONDS

CAYUTA LAKE

map coordinates......... 42º 21' 27" 76º 44' 34"
USGS map(s)............ Alpine, Mecklenburg
location .... township of Catharine
access .... off Route 228 - see below

Physical Characteristics

area .... 371 acres
shoreline .... 4 miles
elevation .... 1317 feet
maximum depth .... 26 feet
mean depth .... 14 feet
bottom type .... muck, gravel

Chemical Characteristics

water clarity .... some turbidity
pH...................... alkaline
oxygen.................. poor in deep water in the summer

Plant Life

Cayuta Lake suffers from very excessive weed growth, choking the lake in areas.

Species Information

rockbass .... common; growth rate fair
walleye .... uncommon; growth rate good
largemouth bass.......... common; growth rate good
chain pickerel .... common; growth rate good
yellow perch .... common; growth rate fair
pumpkinseeds .... common; growth rate fair
bullhead .... common; growth rate fair
bluegill.................. common; growth rate fair

Boat Launch Sites

There are no formal public boat launch sites on Cayuta Lake. Small car top boats or canoes could be launched on Cayuta Creek at the south end of the lake.

General Information

Traditionally, Cayuta Lake had a good population of walleye, but this has changed due to the growth of excess vegetation. Walleye are still found here, a few old lunkers, but the lake has been taken over by largemouth bass and chain pickerel. Bass up to 5 pounds are regularly taken here. In the winter, ice fishing for chain pickerel and yellow perch is popular and productive.

Cayuta Lake has a number of serious problems, particularly excessive weed growth and a lack of public access. The lake is actually privately owned, but there is a spot on the west side where Route 228 runs close to the lake, affording some access. Some land owners also allow fishermen to get to the lake from their property. Be sure to ask for permission. Small boats or canoes could probably be launched where the first county road off Route 228 south of the lake crosses Cayuta Creek.

NOTES: _____

_____

_____

_____

Some species, such as walleye, have cone shaped teeth that are sharp only at the point. Teeth of such species are not apt to cut your line. The pike family (northern pike, chain pickerel, muskellunge) on the other hand have teeth that are razor sharp at the point and knife edged on the side. These fish can easily cut through a light line, so its best to use a steel or heavy monofilament leader when pursuing such fish.

LAMOKA LAKE

map coordinates.......... 42º 24' 59" 77º 05' 10"
USGS map(s)............. Wayne
location .... township of Tyrone
access .... Waneta/Lamoka Channel-see below

Physical Characteristics

area .... 588 acres
shoreline .... 11.3 miles
elevation 1099
maximum depth .... 40 feet
mean depth .... 20 feet
bottom type .... muck, gravel

Chemical Characteristics

water clarity .... turbid
pH...................... alkaline
oxygen.................. poor in summer below 15 feet. This does not affect the fish at all.

Plant Life

Extensive rooted aquatics are found in water up to 20 feet deep, except along the north-east shoreline. Algae blooms occur regularly in the summer, causing turbidity.

Species Information

largemouth bass .... very common; growth rate excellent
smallmouth bass.......... common; growth rate fair
chain pickerel .... common; growth rate excellent
muskellunge.............. uncommon; growth rate excellent
yellow perch .... common; growth rate good
rock bass .... common; growth rate good
pumpkinseeds .... common; growth rate good
bluegills................. common; growth rate good
black crappie............ common; growth rate good
brown bullhead........... common; growth rate good
red bellied sunfish .... rare; growth rate good
white catfish .... rare; growth rate good

Boat Launch Sites

1. DEC fishing access site, on Waneta/Lamoka Channel, off county road 23, 2 miles west of Tyrone. This site has gravel ramps and parking and is suitable for small trailerable boats, car top boats and canoes. The channel provides access to Lamoka Lake and Waneta Lake.

General Information

Lamoka Lake is one of the most productive lakes in central New York, in terms of both its flora and fauna. Very extensive weed beds provide habitat for a wide variety of warm water species, the most important of which are largemouth bass, smallmouth bass, and chain pickerel. With the exception of smallmouth bass, all of the predator species in this lake have exceptional growth rates. This is due to the presence of a very large alewife (sawbelly) forage base. This is one of the few relatively shallow lakes with such a forage base.

Lamoka Lake and its sister lake, Waneta, supply water to a small hydro-electric station on Keuka Lake. The draw downs are minimal, about 2 feet on the average. This does not effect fish or plant life in the lake.

The predominant game species in Lamoka Lake is the largemouth bass. With the exception of the gravel beds along the north-east shore, largemouth can be found almost anywhere in the lake in water less than 20 feet. If you're looking to take a trophy largemouth in central New York, Lamoka would probably be your best bet. During electro-shocking studies of this lake, bass up to **10** pounds were handled and many fish in the 6 to 8 pound category were found. While largemouth are well distributed throughout the lake, the small bays on the south-east corner appear to have the best fishing, and it was from this area that the 10 pound bass mentioned above was taken. During periods of high water levels the swamplands behind the small

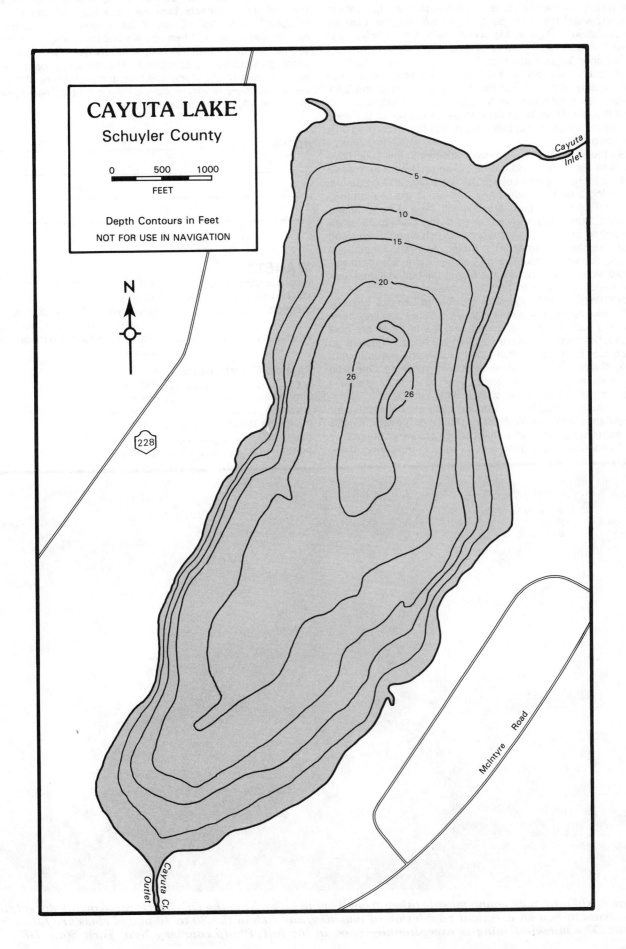

CAYUTA LAKE
Schuyler County

0   500   1000
FEET

Depth Contours in Feet
NOT FOR USE IN NAVIGATION

N

228

5

10

15

20

26

26

Cayuta
Inlet

McIntyre Road

Cayuta Cr.
Outlet

peninsula on the south-east corner fill with water, transforming the peninsula into an island. Bass and black crappie can be found in the lake proper as well as in the flooded swamps. Late in the summer, when the weed beds choke the lake, the Lamoka Lake Association brings in big weed harvesters to clear out navigational channels in the beds. These channels are excellent for late summer largemouth bass fishing and pickerel fishing.

Smallmouth bass are also common in Lamoka Lake, but account for only about 15% of the bass population in the lake. Their habitat is rather restricted. A majority of the smallmouth are found on the gravel beds on the north-east corner of the lake. Their numbers are good, but their size is only fair, averaging only 1 to 1½ pounds.

Chain pickerel are the third major species in this lake. They are very well distributed and can be taken anywhere that weed lines can be found. Lamoka Lake pickerel are big, up to 6 pounds, and averaging 3 to 4 pounds. Early and late in the season they can be taken on spinnerbaits dressed with hula skirts or Mister Twister tails. During the summer, deep diving crankbaits, silver flatfish, spoons or Texas-rigged worms, all fish along deep weed lines, will take chain pickerel. In the winter, ice fishing for pickerel is very popular and productive on Lamoka Lake. Standard tip-ups, baited with golden shiners (the bigger the better) fished over dormant weed beds should be productive.

At one time muskellunge were stocked in Lamoka Lake by the DEC. However, for some reason they never did very well here. The stocking has been discontinued, and few muskies are now found here. But those that have survived are huge. Monsters up to 46¼ pounds have been taken from this lake and several years ago a trio of fish in the 40 pound class were reported. One area that trophy hunting muskie fishermen seem to concentrate on is the drop off the outside edge of Red Bank Island.

As a group, the panfish in Lamoka Lake are impressive for their abundance and size. With the exception of the rare (for this region) redbellied sunfish, all of the panfish are very common or abundant and exhibit very good growth rates. In the spring, there

is excellent fishing for black crappies, especially in the shallow bays in the south-east corner of the lake and in the weedy channel that connects Lamoka Lake with Waneta Lake. The crappies will be forced out of these areas in the summer by excess weed growth. Then you will find them where ever you find submerged structure. The lake also has good fishing for yellow perch, pumpkinseeds, bluegills, bullhead and rockbass, making it an ideal lake to introduce children to the pleasure of fishing. In the winter there is very good ice fishing for big yellow perch off the outer edge of Red Bank Island.

NOTES: _____
_____
_____
_____

WANETA

map coordinates	42° 27' 56" 77° 06' 17"
USGS map(s)	Wayne
location	township of Tyrone (Schuyler County); Wayne (Steuben County)
access	Waneta/Lamoka Channel - see below

Physical Characteristics

area	813 acres
shoreline	6.8 miles
elevation	1099 feet
maximum depth	29 feet
mean depth	15 feet
bottom type	gravel, muck

Barb Kosowski with a 35 pound muskie taken from Waneta Lake. Note the DEC tag located on the dorsal fin of the fish. Waneta has an excellent population of muskies, and fish in the 30 to 40 pound class are taken here each year. The muskie fishing is exceptionally good in the fall. Photo courtesy New York State DEC.

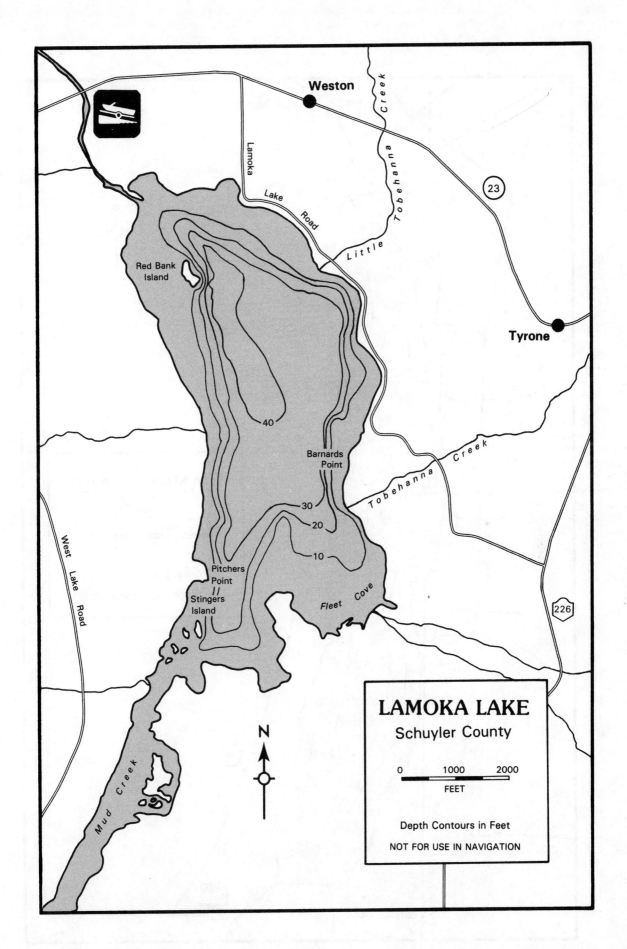

Weston

Lamoka Lake Road

Little

Tobehanna Creek

23

Tyrone

Red Bank Island

40

Barnards Point

30

20

10

Tobehanna Creek

West Lake Road

Pitchers Point

Stingers Island

Fleet Cove

226

Mud Creek

N

LAMOKA LAKE
Schuyler County

0   1000   2000
FEET

Depth Contours in Feet

NOT FOR USE IN NAVIGATION

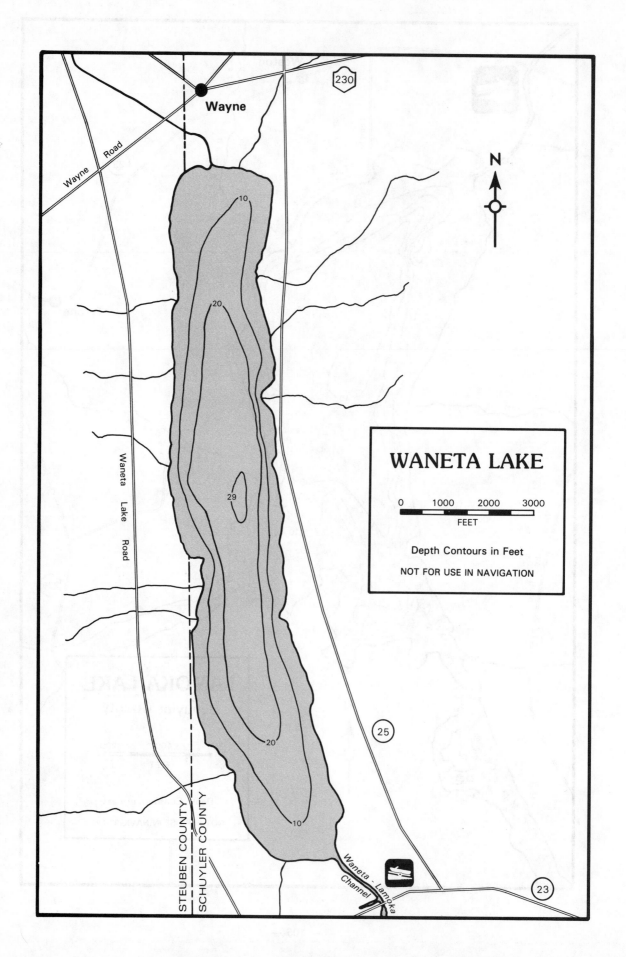

Wayne

230

N

Wayne Road

Waneta Lake Road

10

20

29

20

10

Waneta - Lamoka Channel

STEUBEN COUNTY
SCHUYLER COUNTY

WANETA LAKE

0   1000   2000   3000
FEET

Depth Contours in Feet

NOT FOR USE IN NAVIGATION

25

23

Chemical Characteristics

water clarity .... turbid
pH .... alkaline
oxygen .... poor below 20 feet in the summer; in the south end of the lake, oxygen is poor below 10 feet

Plant Life

Very extensive beds of rooted aquatic vegetation are found throughout much of this lake, up to depths of 20 feet. The only exception to this is along the east side of the lake where substantial gravel beds are found. Algae blooms occur on Waneta Lake, causing turbidity.

Species Information

largemouth bass .... common; growth rate excellent
smallmouth bass .... common; growth rate fair
muskellunge .... common; growth rate excellent
chain pickerel .... common; growth rate excellent
yellow perch .... common; growth rate good
black crappie............ common; growth rate good
rock bass .... common; growth rate good
pumpkinseeds .... common; growth rate good
bluegills .... common; growth rate good
brown bullhead .... common; growth rate good

Boat Launch Sites

1. DEC fishing access site, on Waneta/Lamoka Channel, off county road 23, 2 miles west of Tyrone. This site has gravel ramps and parking and is suitable for small trailerable boats, car top boats and canoes. The channel provides access to Waneta Lake and Lamoka Lake.

2. At the north end of the lake, in the town of Wayne, there is a rough road that leads down to the lake, where car top boats or canoes could be launched.

General Information

Waneta Lake, like Lamoka Lake, is a water supply reservoir for the hydro-electric plant on Keuka Lake. Water fluctuations due to draw downs are minimal, about 2 feet, and do not affect fish or plant species.

Waneta Lake is very similar to Lamoka Lake in many respects. It too has a good forage base, including a very large population of alewives, or sawbellies, enabling most predator species to grow to very respectable sizes. Two of the most sought after species in this lake are largemouth bass and smallmouth bass. Unlike Lamoka Lake their populations here are pretty evenly divided. Largemouth bass have more habitat. Generally speaking, they can be found anywhere in the lake in water shallower than 20 feet (deeper than that oxygen depletion is a problem) where weed beds exist. A few areas, however, do stand out. The Waneta/Lamoka Channel especially between the launch ramps and Waneta Lake proper, is excellent for bass all season. The DEC has electro-shocked largemouth close to **10** pounds in the channel. The south-east corner of the lake has a lot of fallen timber and brush piles and provides very good cover for bass. Near the northern end of the lake, several hundred yards south of the small park that sits on the north-west corner, is a small submerged rock filled crib. Approach the area with caution - a lot of boaters locate this structure with their props. The DEC shocked the waters around the wall and found good numbers of bass, including largemouth, smallmouth and black crappie.

The habitat available to smallmouth bass is a bit more limited, but the lake still offers some fine fishing for these scrappy fighters. As in Lamoka Lake, the smallmouth here are not trophy size, averaging only 1 to 1½ pounds. A majority of the fish are taken from the east side of the lake where much of the shallow water areas are gravel bottomed. Smallmouth are also found around many of the docks on the east side.

Unlike Lamoka, Waneta Lake has an excellent population of muskellunge and the DEC still stocks the lake with 4800 muskie fingerlings per year. They do very well here. Although no fish as large as the 46¼ pound specimen taken from Lamoka have been recorded here, 30 and 40 pound fish are taken from Waneta Lake each year. Anglers looking for trophy muskie often troll at a very fast speed along the outside edges of weed beds. Preferred lures include very big jointed perch imitations with an 8 ounce weight attached to the line about 2½ feet above the lure. This rig is very effective in October and November.

Chain pickerel is another species that can be found practically anywhere in this lake. Their size is impressive. The average pickerel taken from Waneta Lake weighs in at about 3 pounds and there are some real trophies weighing up to 6 pounds waiting to be taken. An exceptionally good pickerel area is in the lower end of the lake and up the east side to where the gravel beds start. Good numbers of pickerel are also taken from Waneta through the ice.

The panfish population in Waneta Lake is very healthy. Black crappie are the principle panfish and are found throughout the lake wherever you find submerged structure. The Waneta/Lamoka Channel offers excellent crappie fishing in the spring. Good crappie fishing can also be found among the brush piles and fallen timber in the south-east corner of the lake and around the submerged wall on the north-west corner. The lake also has excellent year round fishing for other panfish including big yellow perch, rock bass, bullhead and sunfish.

Waneta Lake (and Lamoka Lake) freezes early due to its shallow depth and altitude. There is good ice fishing for chain pickerel, yellow perch, and black crappie.

NOTES: _____

_____

_____

The largemouth bass in Waneta Lake are plentiful and big. The DEC has electro-shocked fish close to 10 pounds here. Photo courtesy New York State DEC.

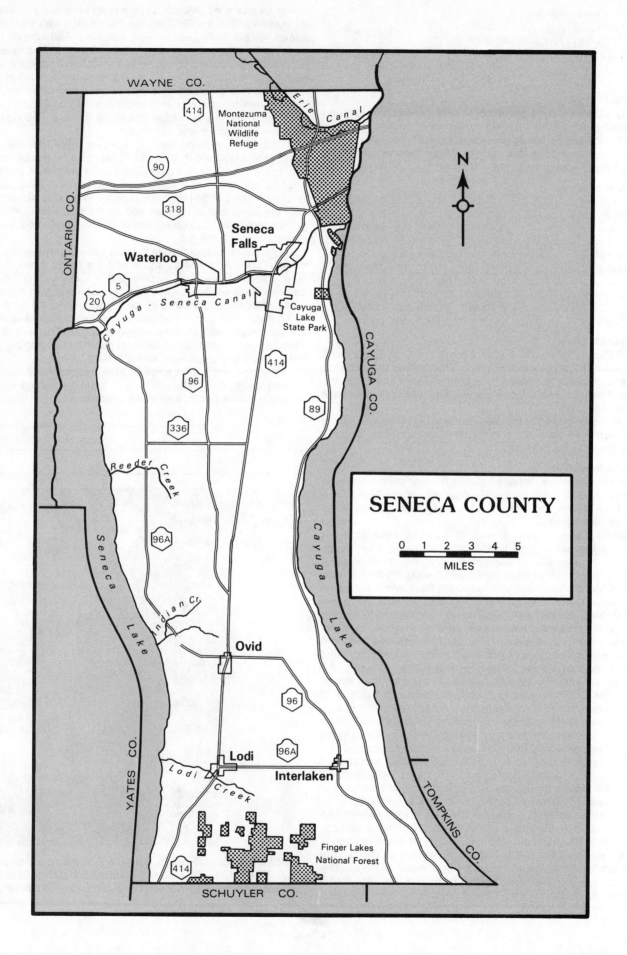

WAYNE CO.

ONTARIO CO.

414

Montezuma
National
Wildlife
Refuge

Erie Canal

90

318

Seneca
Falls

Waterloo

5

20

Cayuga - Seneca Canal

Cayuga
Lake
State Park

96

414

89

336

CAYUGA CO.

Reeder Creek

Seneca Lake

96A

Indian Cr.

Cayuga Lake

Ovid

96

YATES CO.

Lodi

96A

Lodi Creek

Interlaken

Finger Lakes
National Forest

414

TOMPKINS CO.

SCHUYLER CO.

N

SENECA COUNTY

0 1 2 3 4 5
MILES

SENECA COUNTY STREAMS & RIVERS

CAYUGA AND SENECA CANAL

map coordinates	42° 55′ 53″ 76° 46′ 08″
USGS map(s)	Seneca Falls, Geneva South, Geneva North, Cayuga
location (township)	Waterloo, Seneca Falls
access	parallelled by Route 5 and 20 — see below
principle species	largemouth bass, northern pike, bullheads, walleye, carp, channel catfish, panfish

The Cayuga and Seneca Canal is a manmade waterway connecting Cayuga Lake and Seneca Lake with the New York State Barge Canal. Constructed during the late 1820's, this 23 mile long canal was intended to link commercial traffic in the Finger Lakes with the rest of the state. However, commercial traffic died out in the 1960's, leaving the canal almost exclusively to pleasure boaters who now ply its waters to the tune of more than 9,000 trips per year.

Despite the fact that it is a short manmade body of water, the Cayuga and Seneca Canal is remarkably diverse, not just from end-to-end, but also from side-to-side. The central channel generally lacks bottom structure, and, because of the great amount of boat traffic between Memorial Day and Labor Day, it also lacks weed cover. Thus, fishing is essentially restricted to the weedy sides of the canal, with a few notable exceptions. These exceptions include the edges of many islands found along the canal, the mouths of major tributaries, especially Kendig Creek, at the fast water below the dams in Waterloo and Seneca Falls, and at a wide spot in Seneca Falls known as Van Cleef Lake.

There is very little fishing in the central portion of the canal, from Waterloo downstream to Van Cleef Lake, due primarily to pollution. What all of this boils down to is that there is some very good fishing to be found here, and it's usually in well defined areas.

Largemouth bass are the most important game fish found in the canal and their size and abundance draw local bass clubs to the canal each year. The best bass fishing is found in the extreme western section, between Seneca Lake State Park and the mouth of Kendig Creek. There are numerous docks and weed beds in this reach, providing excellent cover. Bass can be taken here all season long, but the best times are early in the season, and in the fall. Most fish head for Seneca Lake after spawning, but return when the warm surface waters of the lake are bled off into the canal to make room for spring runoff. The bass will follow the warm water back into the canal looking for warmth and food to fatten up on for the winter. It's during the fall period that you can expect some of the best bass fishing of the season.

Further downstream, there is very good bass fishing in the eastern portion of the canal that is bordered by the Montezuma National Wildlife Refuge and the Cayuga Wildlife Management Area. This area is a vast wetland, laced with numerous small channels, and open pockets as well as its main channel of the canal. (If you plan on investigating these side waters, use a shallow draft vessel, such as a canoe. Larger boats should stay within the well marked confines of the canal proper.) Bass can be found as far downstream as the junction with the Erie Canal, but downstream of lock #1, where the canal makes an abrupt turn north and heads straight through the Montezuma Refuge, cover can be hard to find.

Additional (though limited) bass fishing can be found in the fast waters below the dams in Waterloo and Seneca Falls and in Van Cleef Lake.

Northern pike are the second most important game fish found in the Cayuga and Seneca Canal. Far less abundant than largemouth bass, the pike here are known more for their size than for their quantity. The most productive areas are the extreme western end of the canal, the weed beds located adjacent to major islands, and the section downstream of lock #1. Pike here

usually run 6-8 pounds, but fish up to 20 pounds or better have been taken. The large pike are most often taken in the winter, but ice fishing is not always possible on the canal, and even when it is, it can be pretty risky business.

If you do plan on ice fishing on the canal, stay away from the main channel. Most of the fish will be found in the shallow bays and harbors, or the near shore areas of Seneca Lake and Cayuga Lake, and the moving water of the canal can cut away the ice cover from the bottom up, making seemingly solid ice very dangerous.

Bullhead and channel catfish are also found in this canal. Channel catfish are, for the most part, limited to the section of the canal between lock #1 and the junction with the Erie Canal. Try drifting a worm or stink bait along the bottom, in the fast water below the flood control dam, adjacent to lock #1 some summer night for the best catfish action. Bullhead are a lot more abundant here than catfish and can be found in many parts of the canal. In the spring there is excellent bullhead fishing at the head of the canal, at the mouth of Kendig Creek and just downstream of lock #1.

Rounding out the fishing found in the Cayuga and Seneca Canal is a limited number of walleye found downstream of lock #1, trout, which are found in the extreme western end of the canal at various times of the year, and panfish (yellow perch, rock bass, bluegills). Carp are also popular in this canal, due to the annual Cayuga Lake National Carp Derby each June. Both bowfishing and angling will produce trophies in excess of 25 pounds.

Access to the Cayuga and Seneca Canal is more than adequate. It is roughly parallelled by Routes 5 and 20 for much of its length and is serviced by a number of boat launch sites and full service marinas. Boats can be launched at the following locations:

1. Seneca Lake State Park — at Route 5, 20 near Route 96A. Hard surface ramp, pump out, parking — fee during park season.
2. Lakeland Marine — 773 Waterloo — Geneva Road, Waterloo. Single hard surface ramp, parking — fee.
3. Barrett Marine — 485 West River Road, Waterloo. Single hard surface ramp, parking — fee.
4. Finger Lakes Marina — 485 West River Road, Waterloo. Single hard surface ramp, parking — fee.
5. Village of Waterloo boat access site — north side of canal on city owned island just upstream of lock #4. Hard surface ramp, parking — no charge.
6. Cayuga Lake State Park — on Route 89, 3 miles east of village of Seneca Falls. Hard surface ramp, punp-out, parking — fee during park season.
7. Mud Lock Canal Park — off Route 90 on River Road, 3 miles north of village of Cayuga. Gravel ramp, restrooms, parking — no charge.
8. DEC Fishing Access Site — off Routes 5 & 20, on west side of canal adjacent to Montezuma National Wildlife Refuge. Hard surface ramp, parking - no charge.

For a highly detailed nautical chart of this and other sections of the New York State Barge Canal System, obtain NOAA chart #14786.

NOTES: _____

_____

_____

_____

CLYDE RIVER — see Wayne County Streams and Rivers

The Montezuma National Wildlife Refuge is a richly diversified environment. It serves primarily as habitat for waterfoul, but fishing is allowed on three designated sites. See the map on page 111 for the location of these sites.

INDIAN CREEK

map coordinates......... 42° 41' 01" 76° 53' 01"
USGS map(s) .... Dresden, Ovid
location (township)....... Romulus
access .... crossing at Route 96A
principle special .... rainbow trout (wild)

Indian Creek is known also at Risens Creek or Willard Creek. This small shale and gravel bottomed stream has excellent runs of wild rainbows in the spring. Fish up to 8 pounds are taken from the larger pools. The lower portions of the stream are posted, but permission to fish here can usually be obtained. The north and south branches run under Route 96A and anglers can generally gain access at these locations.

NOTES: _____
_____
_____
_____

LODI CREEK

map coordinates......... 42° 36' 52" 76° 52' 36"
USGS map(s) .... Dundee, Lodi
location (township)....... Lodi
access .... enters Seneca Lake at Lodi Point
                           State Park
principles species .... rainbow trout (wild)

Lodi Creek, known also as Mill Creek, is a small, short tributary of Seneca Lake that supports a fair spring run of adult wild rainbows. This isn't an especially productive stream, and some of it is posted. It can be worth trying if you're in the area, but it certainly isn't worth a special trip.

This stream is not stocked.

NOTES: _____
_____
_____

MONTEZUMA NATIONAL WILDLIFE REFUGE

map coordinates......... 42° 58' 56" 76° 45' 20"
USGS map(s) .... Seneca Falls, Cayuga, Savannah,
                         Montezuma
location (township)....... Tyre
access .... off Thruway exit 41 - see below
principle species .... northern pike, brown bullhead, walleye, carp

In the nineteenth century, the Montezuma Marsh was one of the largest and most important freshwater wetlands in North America. Unfortunately, its importance went unrecognized and all but 100 acres of the marsh were drained. In 1938 the Montezuma National Wildlife Refuge was established under the auspecies of the U.S. Fish and Wildlife Service. Its purpose was to restore much of the wetlands to its previous condition, and today the refuge encompasses 6820 acres of open wetlands, flooded woodland and upland woods and fields.

The primary purpose of the Montezuma Refuge is to provide waterfowl habitat. To insure that the wetlands are not unduly disturbed, fishing is restricted to three areas. The east shore of the Clyde River can be accessed off Armitage Road. The south shore of the New York State Barge Canal can be accessed at Mays Point, off Route 89. In addition, there is a DEC fishing access and boat launch site (hard surface ramp) on the Cayuga/Seneca Canal, off Routes 5 and 20 adjacent to the Montezuma Refuge.

For further information on what the Montezuma National Wildlife Refuge has to offer contact:

Refuge Manager
Montezuma National Wildlife Refuge
R.D. #1, Box 1411
Seneca Falls, NY 13148
(315) 568-5987

See also: Clyde River, New York State Barge Canal (Wayne County) and Cayuga/Seneca Canal (Seneca County).

NOTES: _____
_____
_____
_____

REEDER CREEK

map coordinates......... 42° 47' 09" 76° 55' 43"
USGS map(s) .... Geneva South, Romulus
location (township)....... Varick
access .... crossed by Route 96A (East Lake
                           Road)
principle species .... rainbow trout (wild)

Reeder Creek is a small tributary of Seneca Lake that supports a limited run of adult wild rainbow trout in the spring. Much of the stream is posted, and access can be difficult. It's worth trying if you're in the area, but not worth a special trip.

This stream is not stocked.

NOTES: _____
_____
_____
_____

NOTE: There are a number of small tributaries on the east side of Seneca Lake that offer limited fishing in the spring for rainbow trout and smelt. Most of these streams are posted. Some landowners will allow fishing. These streams are of local interest only.

MONTEZUMA NATIONAL WILDLIFE REFUGE
SENECA COUNTY, NEW YORK

UNITED STATES
DEPARTMENT OF THE INTERIOR

UNITED STATES
FISH AND WILDLIFE SERVICE

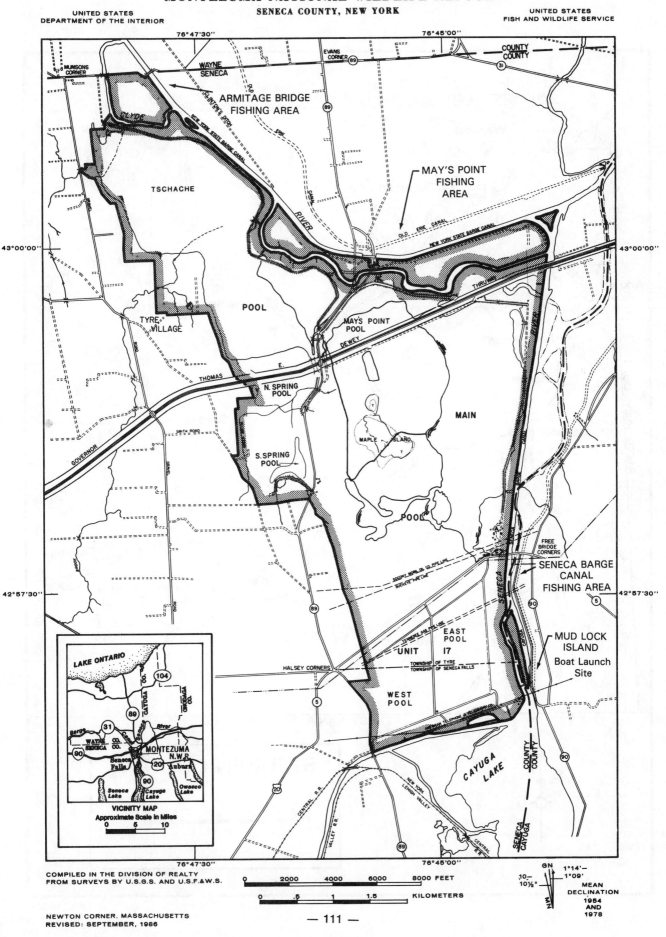

ARMITAGE BRIDGE
FISHING AREA

MAY'S POINT
FISHING
AREA

TSCHACHE

POOL

MAY'S POINT
POOL

TYRE
VILLAGE

N. SPRING
POOL

MAIN

MAPLE ISLAND

S. SPRING
POOL

POOL

FREE
BRIDGE
CORNERS

SENECA BARGE
CANAL
FISHING AREA

MUD LOCK
ISLAND
Boat Launch
Site

EAST
POOL
UNIT 17

WEST
POOL

HALSEY CORNERS

CAYUGA
LAKE

VICINITY MAP
Approximate Scale in Miles

LAKE ONTARIO

MONTEZUMA
N.W.R.

Seneca
Falls

Seneca
Lake

Cayuga
Lake

Owasco
Lake

COMPILED IN THE DIVISION OF REALTY
FROM SURVEYS BY U.S.G.S. AND U.S.F.&W.S.

2000   4000   6000   8000 FEET

0   .5   1   1.5   KILOMETERS

GN
1°14'-
1°09'

10'-
10½°

MEAN
DECLINATION
1954
AND
1978

NEWTON CORNER, MASSACHUSETTS
REVISED: SEPTEMBER, 1986

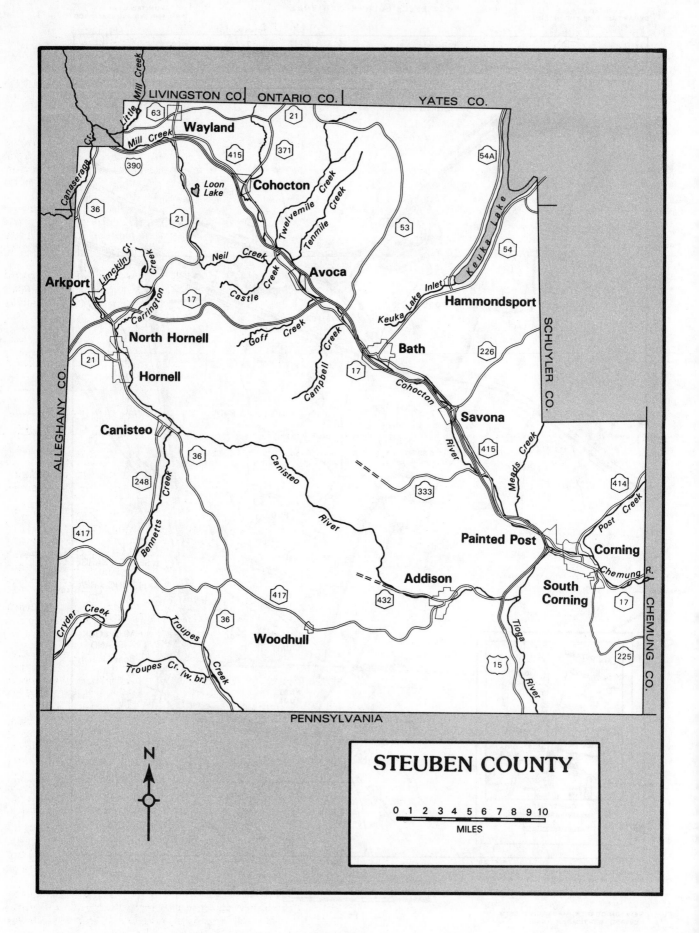

LIVINGSTON CO. ONTARIO CO. YATES CO.

Little Mill Creek

63

Wayland

21

Mill Creek

415

371

390

Canaseraga Cr.

Loon Lake

Cohocton

54A

36

Twelvemile Creek

Tenmile Creek

53

Keuka Lake

54

21

Neil Creek

Castle Creek

Avoca

Keuka Lake Inlet

Hammondsport

Limckiln Cr.

Creek

Carrington

17

Arkport

Goff Creek

SCHUYLER CO.

226

North Hornell

Bath

ALLEGHANY CO.

21

Campbell Creek

17

Cohocton

Hornell

Savona

River

415

Canisteo

36

Meads Creek

248

Bennetts Creek

Canisteo River

333

414

Post Creek

417

Painted Post

Corning

Cryder Creek

417

Addison

South Corning

Chemung R.

432

17

CHEMUNG CO.

Troupes Creek

36

Woodhull

Tioga River

15

225

Troupes Cr. (w. br.)

PENNSYLVANIA

N

STEUBEN COUNTY

0 1 2 3 4 5 6 7 8 9 10
MILES

STEUBEN COUNTY STREAMS & RIVERS

BENNETTS CREEK

map coordinates.......... 42 16' 02" 77° 35' 16"
USGS map(s)............. Canisteo, South Canisteo, Greenwood, Rexville
location (township)....... Canisteo, Greenwood, West Union
access.................. parallelled and crossed by Route 248 between Greenwood and Rexville; parallelled by County Road 98 above Rexville
principle species .... brown trout (stocked)

Bennetts Creek is a major tributary of the Canisteo River, which it joins in the town of Canisteo. The stream offers about 4.5 miles of fair quality trout fishing, roughly between the villages of Greenwood and Rexville. Downstream of Greenwood, Bennetts Creek quickly loses its value as a fishery. Averaging 15 to 20 feet in width, this stream has a good year round flow, a gravel and rubble bottom and good bank cover, especially in its uppermost reaches. The surroundings consist of farmland, pastureland and a small amount of woodland.

The fishing in Bennetts Creek is sustained by stocking. In the spring, the reach between Greenwood and Rexville is stocked with 900 brown trout yearlings. The only wild trout in this system are those found in the upper tributaries, such as O'Haran Creek, Fall Creek and Rock Creek, all of which flow into Bennetts Creek from the west, above Greenwood. All of these streams are small, rubble bottomed with intermittant bank cover. Rock Creek and Fall Creek are both stocked with brook trout each fall (300 fingerlings each) in their lower reaches. There is posting on these streams, so be sure to check with the land owners before fishing here. Fall Creek is parallelled by Fall Creek Road and empties into Bennets Creek just south of Carter Cemetary. Rock Creek is parallelled by Rock Creek Road and joins Bennetts Creek one mile north of Greenwood. O'Haran Creek joins Bennetts Creek near the intersection of Wileyville Road and Saltpeter Road and is roughly parallelled by Saltpeter Road.

NOTES: _____

_____

_____

_____

CAMPBELL CREEK

map coordinates.......... 42° 22' 02" 77° 21' 53"
USGS map(s)............. Bath, Towelsville, Canisteo
location (township)....... Bath, Howard
access.................. parallelled by Gulch Road
principle species .... brown trout (stocked)

Campbell Creek is a mediocre quality trout stream. A tributary of the Cohocton River, which it joins near the village of Kanona, this stream averages 15 feet in width, has a gravel and rubble bottom and a good year round flow of water. The surroundings consist primarily of farm lands and pastureland, and the stream has relatively poor bank cover. The stream was recently resurveyed by the DEC. It was found that the policy of stocking Campbell Creek with 1,000 brown trout fingerlings in the fall was not producing as well as desired. The policy was changed in 1987. This stream is now stocked with 800 brown trout yearlings in the spring in the three mile section immediately downstream of the crossing at Dublin Road.

NOTES: _____

_____

_____

CANASERAGA CREEK

map coordinates.......... 42° 45' 19" 77° 50' 27"
USGS map(s)............. Dansville
location (township)....... Dansville
access.................. roughly parallelied by Poags Hole Road
principle species .... brown trout (stocked & wild)

Only about 3 miles of Canaseraga Creek flow within the boundries of Steuben County. This section of the stream provides good fishing for stocked brown trout, augmented by a small population of wild browns. There is a good carry over of stocked fish here, so don't be overly surprised at the size of some of the trout taken from this water.

The stream averages 35 to 40 feet in width in the summer, has a bottom of gravel and rubble and generally good bank cover, though it is sufficiently open to allow for fly fishing. The one problem with this portion of Canaseraga Creek is its tendency to flood, especially in the spring.

The Steuben County portion of Canaseraga Creek is stocked in the spring with 5,800 brown trout yearlings. For a more complete description of Canaseraga Creek see Sander's Fishing Guide, Western New York edition.

NOTES: _____

_____

_____

_____

CANISTEO RIVER

map coordinates.......... 42° 06' 28" 77° 08' 09"
USGS map(s)............. Addison, Borden, Rathbone, Cameron, Towelsville, Canisteo, Hornell, Arkport
location (township)....... Erwin, Addison, Rathbone, Cameron, Canisteo, Hornell
access.................. parallelled between Addison and Rathbone by Route 432; parallelled between Rathbone and Canisteo by County Road 119 (Canisteo River Road)
principle species .... brown trout (stocked & wild), brook trout (wild), smallmouth bass, largemouth bass, walleye, panfish

The Canisteo River is a large, diverse waterway. The river can be divided into cold and warm water habitats at Hornell. Above Hornell the Canisteo is a good quality brown trout stream at least as far upstream as Arkport (5 miles). This section of the stream is very unlike other Steuben County trout streams. It averages 30 to 40 feet in width, and has a good flow of clear water over a bottom of gravel and rubble. However, the water is atypically slow moving and flat, looking more like the lower reaches of a river rather than the headwaters. The river is tree-lined and flows through a scenic region.

Nearly all of the trout taken from this reach of the Canisteo River are stocked fish. A few wild brook and brown trout are taken here occasionally, but it is probably safe to assume that these are fish that have dropped down from a tributary such as Carrington Creek. In the spring 1,900 brown trout yearlings are stocked in the Canisteo River, from the crossing at Routes 36 and 21 upstream 5 miles to the crossing at Bishopville Road in Arkport.

Below Hornell the Canisteo River is primarily a warm water fishery, but one of limited quality. It widens out to 60 to 70 feet in width and runs through a very picturesque, isolated valley. It was suggested at one time to give the Canisteo River official status as a scenic recreational waterway. The river, though, is more important to canoeing enthusiasts than to anglers, due to the poor quality of the fishing. As the following edited report, prepared by Gene Lane of the Region #8 office of the D.E.C. indicates, there are factors at work limiting the productivity of this river. The information in the report, which was collected in 1982 and 1983, is still current. The Hornell sewage treatment plant, while being updated, is still adversely affecting the river. I have included this report because this information indicates how easily a fishery can be ruined by seemingly small amounts of pollution. It also gives one an idea of how productive a river this could be once the pollution abates. Keep in mind that the comparison between the Canisteo River and the Cohocton River is qualified. Different shocking techniques and equipment were used on each river.

During the weeks of 8/9/82 and 8/22/83, the Region 8 Inland Fisheries unit conducted a baseline inventory survey of the Canisteo River commencing near its confluence with the Tioga River near the Hamlet of Erwin, New York, and proceeding upstream to just below the point where the river becomes classified as a trout stream near Hornell, New York. Survey emphasis was on fish sampling by electro-fishing.

Comparison of fish populations in the Canisteo and lower Cohocton Rivers suggests that some form of environmental stress is at work in the Canisteo that is **strongly** inhibiting fishery quality. Densities of all fish are lower than observed in the Cohocton, except that extraordinarily high densities of minnows of a number of species were encountered at the uppermost station of this survey—the only station sampled upstream from the City of Hornell's sewage treatment plant (STP) outfall.

As a qualified comparison of the density of smallmouth bass encountered in the Canisteo versus the Cohocton, the one Cohocton station that it was possible to electrofish with the boat shocker yielded 31.3 smallmouth per 1,000 lineal feet of river channel. The catches in the Canisteo for the seven stations sampled with the boat shocker ranged from 0.8 to 15 smallmouth per 1,000 feet of river channel. No obvious, physical deficiencies were noted in the Canisteo that would explain its relative dearth of fish.

Coincidentally, the lowest smallmouth bass catch rates encountered in the Canisteo's seven boat shocker stations were in the two stations most immediately downstream from the Hornell STP. Accordingly, the STP is strongly suspected as being the source of whatever is limiting the Canisteo's fishery.

Other sportfish species encountered in the Canisteo during this survey include walleye, largemouth bass and chain pickerel. Comments concerning their status in the river are as follows:

Walleye — Three adult specimens were captured; one at Rathbone in '82 (16"), one just below Trib. 29 in '83 (18.7"), one in the vicinity Canisteo Center in '83 (20"), and another was seen but not captured at this last location. No juveniles were captured or observed. Area anglers report limited success for this species, mainly during the mid-summer months. The river appears to offer physical potential for this species to increase in abundance.

Chain Pickerel — Two adults were captured in '83; one at Adrian (15"), and another (15.5") just below Trib. 29. No juveniles were taken or observed. This species is sparse in the Canisteo and offers little angling opportunity. Occasional individuals are found in large pools and stillwaters and these areas appear to offer some potential for this species to increase in number. The apparent absence of juveniles in weed beds of still water areas may be a significant symptom of the water quality problem discussed earlier.

Largemouth Bass — One (8") specimen was taken at Addison in '82 and two (4", 4.5") juveniles were taken vicinity Canisteo Center in '83. An area angler reported that he takes quite a few of this species in large pools near Addison. As with the pickerel, there may be some potential for this species to increase in abundance in stillwater habitats.

Additionally, the **rock bass** is worthy of mention as a component of the Canisteo's fishery. It is fairly abundant in pools and stillwaters where underwater shelter is present, and achieve acceptable "pan" size.

NOTES: _____
_____
_____
_____

CARRINGTON CREEK

map coordinates . . . .   42° 24' 00"   77° 37' 09"
USGS map(s) . . . .   Haskinville
location (township) . . . .   Freemont
access . . . .   crossed by Route 21 just north
                                       Hornell Reservoir #2
principle species . . . .   brook trout (wild)

In the 1.5 mile section above Hornell Reservoir #3, Carringto Creek is a high quality trout stream. Averaging 8 to 10 feet i width, the stream has a gravel and rubble bottom, good flow an a nice ratio of riffle to pools. Carrington Creek flows through a isolated, wooded valley (access can be a problem) and has a l of bank cover. Some sections of the stream are posted, so be su to talk with the landowners before fishing here.

This stream is not stocked.

NOTES: _____
_____
_____
_____

CASTLE CREEK

map coordinates . . . .   42° 26' 18"   77° 27' 09"
USGS map(s) . . . .   Avoca, Haskinville
location (township) . . . .   Avoca, Howard
access . . . .   roughly parallelled by Wessels H
                                       Road
principle species . . . .   brook trout (wild), brown trout (wil

Castle Creek is a high quality tributary of Neil Creek, which joins about one-half mile southwest of Bloomerville. Much of th stream flows through picturesque woodlands. It is a small strea averaging only 8 to 10 feet in width and has a good amount alder bank cover, making fly fishing difficult or impossible in mo sections. The bottom consists of gravel and rubble, and the flo of water on this creek is adequate all year, making fishin possible all season long. While investigating Castle Creek, yo might want to try some of the tributaries that flow into it. Many these tiny streams hold populations of wild brook and brow trout, but nothing like Castle Creek itself, which in terms of quali and productivity versus size is almost like a fish hatchery strea

Though much of Castle Creek is posted, the state ha recently obtained .22 miles of public fishing easements on th stream and is confident that more can be purchased. Thes easements are all located on the lower reaches of the strea

Castle Creek is not stocked.

NOTES: _____
_____
_____

Monofilament lines and leaders eventually develop nicks and cracks that can result in line breakage Before needlessly losing a fish, check for lin damage by rubbing it with a cotton ball. Cotton fiber will catch in damaged areas, indicating whether o not the line should be replaced.

COHOCTON RIVER

map coordinates......... 42° 09' 07" 77° 05' 26"
USGS map(s)........... Corning, Campbell, Savona, Bath, Rheims, Avoca, Haskinville, Wayland, Naples, Springwater
location (township)....... Erwin, Campbell, Bath, Avoca, Cohocton (Steuben County), Springwater (Livingston County)
access................. parallelled by Route 415 between Painted Post and the town of Cohocton; parallelled and crossed by Tabors Corners Road in Livingston County — see below
principle species .... brook trout (wild), brown trout (stocked & wild), rainbow trout (wild), smallmouth bass

Rated as one of the finest inland trout streams in New York State, the Cohocton River slices diagonally across the entire county of Steuben. It provides anglers with over thirty miles of high quality trout fishing, as well as a fair amount of angling for smallmouth bass. The name Cohocton is derived from an Indian word meaning trees in the water, a reference to the alder swamps that the river meanders through above and below the village of Atlanta.

Below the town of Bath, the Cohocton is a fair quality river for smallmouth bass. A recent stream survey by the D.E.C. indicates that the river sustains a substantial population of smallmouth bass in this lower reach, and recorded a density of 31.3 bass per 1,000 lineal feet of river channel. Unfortunately, these fish are generally small, averaging less than 10 inches in length. The reason for this is probably the physical nature of the lower Cohocton River. Downstream of Bath the river is a wide, shallow waterway with relatively few holes deep enough to provide habitat for larger fish. Some smallmouth up to 13.9 inches were recorded, indicating that where there is good habitat, larger fish

will be found. Until something can be done to improve the number and quality of pools in the lower Cohocton, it will remain a mediocre fishery at best.

From Bath upstream to its headwaters, in Livingston County, the Cohocton River is classified as trout water. Generally speaking the river is similar to some of the larger trout streams found in eastern New York and the Adirondacks. This is especially true for the section between Bath and the town of Atlanta. This reach of the river runs between 20 and 40 feet in width, has a gravel bottom and a good year round flow of cold, clear water. Unlike the lower reaches, there are many deep pools throughout this part of the river, as well as undercut banks, submerged tree roots, and numerous runs and riffles, everything you would expect to find in a stream of this quality. The surroundings range from residential and agricultural to stands of mature hardwoods and alder swamps.

The upper reaches of the Cohocton River, from west of Atlanta upstream to the headwaters near Tabors Corners, is more typical of the smaller trout streams found in western New York. Averaging about 10 feet in width, this portion of the Cohocton has a gravel and rubble bottom, an excellent flow of cold, clear water and a great deal of bank cover. Fly fishing is not really feasible above the Steuben/Livingston County line. The Livingston County portion of the Cohocton is not stocked, but is managed as a wild trout stream. The very uppermost headwaters contain large numbers of wild brook trout. Brown trout begin to predominate below Scribner Road. There are many deep, productive pools on the upper Cohocton, and the partially effective brown trout barrier dam near the county line qualifies as a genuine hot spot.

The Steuben County section of the river is stocked in the spring with a total of 10,200 brown trout yearlings, from the mouth of Goff Creek, just below Avoca, upstream 18.7 miles to the mouth of Spring Brook, near the town of Cohocton (the 1.75 mile long special regulation section is not stocked). In Steuben County trout can be taken from the Cohocton River all year, with a 9 inch minimum size limit, 5 per day except in the following areas: (1)

The Cohocton River, just north of Bath. Rated as one of the top trout streams in the state, the Cohocton River provides anglers with over 30 miles of high quality trout water. Be sure to consult your state regulations guide before fishing here, as special regulations apply to some sections of the river.

The MARCH BROWN, a common mayfly hatch from late May to early June.

From the north boundry of the village of Avoca upstream to the mouth of Neil Creek. In these sections trout can be taken all year, with a 12 inch minimum size limit, 3 fish per day, using artificial lures only. Besure to check for current regulations.

Access to the Cohocton River is excellent. Parallelled by major roadways for most of its length, there are numerous bridge crossings. The state has purchased a total of 20 miles of public fishing easements on the trout section, and there are several well marked fisherman parking areas and foot path right-of-ways.

The following article, written by members of Trout Unlimited, gives a good first hand impression of this remarkable river.

"John Monin (W.N.Y. Trout Unlimited) has provided me with a wealth of information about the Cohocton River, a good trout stream about 50 miles east of the Wiscoy, which starts in the town of Springwater in Livingston County and flows southeast to Painted Post where it joins the Chemung River. Route 15 parallels the stream from Cohocton south.

"John mentions a number of good sections, from the V.A. Hospital in Bath upstream to its source. An artificials only section beginning at the hospital and running upstream to Knights Brook holds some real nice brown trout. From Avoca upstream 1.75 miles is another artificial lures only section, and this, along with a section in the town of Wallace, are the most popular sections of the river, both heavily stocked and heavily fished. From Wallace upstream to the town of Cohocton the fishing is spotty, with the road and rail bridges the best bets for the man who fishes salted minnows and night crawlers.

"The section between Cohocton and Atlanta runs through mostly swampy ground, and John advises the use of a boat or a canoe. He usually starts at the railroad bridge about halfway between the two towns and works upstream to Atlanta with spinners, which John feels are probably too deadly and should be outlawed (guess what I'm going to use when I fish the Cohocton?). Once in Atlanta, the section behind the old church is good with nymphs, especially the March Brown; and the section between River Street bridge and Beecher Road bridge is very good with night crawlers along the undercut banks. Both sections hold native brookies and stocked browns which will rise late in the day to a Royal Coachman or a #14 Light or Dark Cahill. There are also many native brook trout in the section upstream from Parks Road who like nothing more than a salted minnow, but will settle for a small Coachman streamer or size 14 Picket Pin fished slow and deep.

"The next section John recommends is further upstream at the town of Springwater. To get there from Atlanta, go west on Route 21 from Parks Road. At the bridge where Route 21 crosses the Cohocton, turn right on county road 37 and go upstream about one mile to a sign saying "Welcome to Springwater." There is a white house on the left, then a chicken yard where you can park. Although the stream is public fishing, access is limited by posting, so you can only get to the stream by means of the ditch by the chicken yard. It's worth the trouble, says John, who promises to be at this spot on opening day to catch one of those

20 inchers this section produces early in the season. There is a fish trap built here to keep trash fish out of the upstream brook trout spawning grounds. Fish just below the trap and the first bend above it, for though the stream is small here, these are two very good pools.

"Further upstream at Scribner Road there is more public fishing. The stream is small but the holes are productive — the D.E.C. electroshocking has produced a 24 inch brown here. And if you like tasty brook trout, here's where to get them, especially at the cemetary upstream and the old beaver dam.

"Though best as a bait stream, the Cohocton does produce with flies in the evening when the sun is off the water. Try a Blue Dun wet in the swamp section, or a dry Royal Coachman at Beecher Road bridge and at the burned down lumber yard in the south end of Atlanta. A Cahill also works well in the dusk between sunset and dark."

NOTES: _____

_____

_____

_____

CRYDER CREEK

map coordinates . . . . 41° 59' 53"   77° 52' 12"
USGS map(s) . . . . Whitesville, Rexville
location (township) . . . . West Union
access . . . . parallelled by Route 248 — see below
principle species . . . . brook trout (stocked)

The Steuben County portion of Cryder Creek, which is known locally as Marsh Creek, is a typical brook trout stream. Flowing along a valley bottom, it is a silt and gravel bottomed, alder lined stream averaging 15 to 20 feet in width. This reach of the stream is much flatter and slower moving than the Allegany County section, and there are some very substantial beaver ponds here. Fishing on this part of Cryder Creek is sustained by stocking, although a few wild trout might be found near some of the larger tributaries, such as Wileyville Creek. In the spring 600 brook trout yearlings are stocked in the 3 mile section above the mouth of Wileyville Creek.

NOTE: On current topographical maps (Rexville) the stream parallelled by Route 248 is shown as Marsh Creek. The D.E.C. considers this to be the main stream of Cryder Creek, not the stream that is parallelled by County Road 124, which is south of Marsh Creek. The information here refers to the stream marked as Marsh Creek.

See also: Sander's Fishing Guide - Western New York edition.

NOTES: _____

_____

_____

_____

GOFF CREEK

map coordinates . . . . 42° 23' 34"   77° 24' 20"
USGS map(s) . . . . Avoca, Towelsville, Canisteo
location (township) . . . . Avoca, Howard
access . . . . parallelled by Routes 17 (Southern Tier Expressway) and 70A
principle species . . . . brown trout (stocked & wild), brook trout (wild)

Goff Creek is a good quality tributary of the Cohocton River, which it joins about one-half mile south of Avoca. This is the stream that you see parallelling the Southern Tier Expressway between Cohocton Valley and Hornell. The entire stream is classified as trout water (8.5 miles) and provides good angling, primarily for stocked browns. Goff Creek averages 20 to 25 feet in width, has a gravel and rubble bottom and a very good flow of water all year long. There are a lot of open sections, with most of the surroundings consisting of pastureland. About one-third of the stream flows through heavily vegetated areas of woodlands and alders, but the rest is sufficiently open to make fly fishing a viable option. The very upper reach of Goff Creek has a limited fishery for wild brook trout, and the remainder of the stream supports a small population of wild brown trout.

In the fall, the lower 4.6 miles of Goff Creek are stocked with 3,100 brown trout fingerlings. There is a good amount of carry over of these stocked fish so don't be surprised at the size of some of the browns taken here.

NOTES: _____

_____

_____

_____

KEUKA LAKE INLET (a.k.a. Cold Brook)

map coordinates.......... 42° 22' 40" 77° 16' 46"
USGS map(s)............. Hammondsport, Rheims, Bath
location (township)....... Urbana, Bath
access.................. parallelled by the old Hammonds-
                         port Road and a railroad grade —
                         see below
principle species .... rainbow trout (wild), brown trout
                         (wild), atlantic salmon, bullhead,
                         smelt

As far as I can tell, the actual name of this stream is Keuka Lake Inlet, though most people will recognize it by the name Cold Brook. However you wish to call it, this stream ranks as one of the finest stretches of seasonal trout water in New York State. Running a mere 4.5 miles between Hammondsport and Bath, Keuka Lake Inlet is considered to be the best nursery stream for spawning wild rainbows in the state. The water quality of this cold, spring fed stream is superlative — better than either Naples Creek or Catharine Creek! For this reason the state has located one of its principle fish hatcheries on the headwaters of the stream, in Bath.

A very pretty stream, Kueka Lake Inlet averages about 12 feet in width, has a bottom of gravel and rubble and flows primarily through woodlands and grape vineyards. Although fairly narrow, much of this stream could be fly fished if you do not get too extravagant with your casting.

In the spring, the inlet gets a tremendous run of adult wild rainbows. While the entire stream will hold some fish, a vast majority will be found in the lower 3.5 miles of the stream. The uppermost reach is a bit too confining for these fish. There used to be a dam at Pleasant Valley, but it is now washed out, and the fish can run up the stream unhindered. Due to the great concentration of fish here in the spring, practically any piece of this stream will be productive. However, if you want to give yourself an edge, locate one of several diggers that the state has constructed on Keuka Lake Inlet. Installed primarily to prevent erosion, they also serve to provide holding areas to large numbers of spawning rainbows.

The resident population of fish in Keuka Lake Inlet is minimal. Due to this fact, there is little or no fishing here after the spring spawning runs have ended. That is to say, not until the fall. As soon as the leaves begin to turn color and cool autumn rains begin to swell the creeks, rainbows, brown trout and atlantic salmon will all be found in this stream. Unlike the spring runs, these fall fish are generally overlooked. Many people are either out hunting or simply do not realize the quality of the fall runs. With regard to rainbows, their numbers are less than in spring, but nevertheless abundant. Atlantic salmon will also make a good

Keuka Lake Inlet, or Cold Brook as it is more commonly known. Some of the best runs of trout in the region occur here in the spring and fall.

showing in the fall, especially if there has been a lot of run-off. It is the brown trout, however, that can really give you a case of fishing fever, for some of the browns that spawn here in the fall are monsters! This should not surprise anyone if you remember that **two** state record browns were taken from Keuka Lake, the home waters of these fish. Imagine pitting your skills against a 20 pound brown in a stream only 12 feet wide. It's enough to make even the most confident angler shiver with excitement. And all of this can be had in relative solitude, for very few people partake of this fall bonanza.

In addition to the fine trout fishing in Keuka Lake Inlet, the very lower reaches of the stream also offer a limited spring fishery for smelt and very good fishing for bullhead. The state has set aside a marked area at the lower end of the stream where bullhead fishing is permitted, prior to the opening of trout season.

Access to the inlet is generally excellent. Just below the Bath hatchery is a posted section, but below this the stream is usually open to fishing. The state has purchased 3.5 miles of public fishing easements, which are spaced intermittently along the stream, as well as one foot path right-of-way. When fishing here, be sure to check with landowners first, and be familiar with current regulations that apply to Finger Lakes tributaries.

This stream is not stocked.

NOTES: _____

_____

_____

_____

LIMEKILN CREEK

map coordinates	42º 23' 29" 77º 41' 53"
USGS map(s)	Arkport
location (township)	Hornellsville, Dansville, Fremont
access	crossed by Arkport-Fremont Road
principle species	brook trout (wild)

This is a small, medium quality brook trout stream, similar in characteristics to Carrington Creek. Averaging 6 to 10 feet in width, it flows for 3.8 miles through a very isolated, wooded area known as Reddy Hollow. This stream has a considerable amount of bank cover, a gravel bottom and a good mix of riffles and pools. The brook trout are generally small in Limekiln Creek. A 12 inch fish would be exceptional. While most of the stream above the Arkport-Fremont Road is fishable, access is poor in the upper reaches due to a lack of nearby roads.

Limekiln Creek is not stocked.

NOTES: _____

_____

_____

_____

LITTLE MILL CREEK

map coordinates	42º 32' 48" 77º 40' 57"
USGS map(s)	Dansville, Conesus
location (township)	North Dansville, Sparta (Livingston County), Wayland (Steuben County)
access	crossing at County Line Road or Mendoleine Road
principle species	brook trout (wild), brown trout (wild)

Little Mill Creek is a small, good quality tributary of Mill Creek, which it enters about one-half mile southeast of Dansville. Though most of the stream is in Livingston County, it is of sufficient quality and uniqueness to merit mention here. Averaging 8 to 10 feet in width, the stream has a gravel bottom, good water quality and lots of bank cover. Surrounded by woodlands, there are several very pretty bedrock waterfalls on the stream.

Above the Dansville Reservoir the stream is primarily a brook trout fishery, with a smaller population of brown trout. What makes this stream unique is the presence of naturally occurring tiger trout, a hybrid mix of brook and brown trout that is quite rare. They are not abundant, but if you are fortunate enough to hook one, you will know it. They are extremely aggressive fighters.

Below the Dansville Reservoir brown trout predominate and the fishing can be very good all season long.

The major problem with Little Mill Creek is access. Most of the stream is posted and difficult to access due to a lack of nearby roads. This stream is, however, well worth getting a landowners permission to fish.

Little Mill Creek is not stocked.

NOTES: _____

_____

_____

_____

MEADS CREEK

map coordinates	42º 10' 22" 77º 07' 12"
USGS map(s)	Corning, Campbell, Bradford
location (township)	Erwin, Campbell, Orange
access	parallelled by County Road 26 (Meads Creek Road)
principle species	brown trout (stocked), smallmouth bass

Meads Creek is a large tributary of the Cohocton River, which it joins just west of Painted Post. Averaging approximately 25 feet in width, it has a rock and rubble bottom, a number of large, deep pools and a good year round flow. About half of the stream flows through woodlands. Much of the remainder runs through trailer parks, and residential developments.

Most of Meads Creek is mediocre quality trout water. The lower one-mile section has a fair population of smallmouth bass. Above this section the stream offers about 7 miles of fair quality fishing for stocked brown trout, and there is a small amount of carry over here. The headwaters of Meads Creek, in Schuyler County, are not worth fishing.

In the spring Meads Creek is stocked with 2,100 brown trout yearlings, from one mile above the stream mouth upstream 8.6 miles to the junction of Corbett Hollow Road and Meads Creek Road. Several of the tributaries of Meads Creek, most notably Dry Run, have small populations of wild brook trout.

NOTES: _____

_____

_____

_____

MILL CREEK

map coordinates	42º 33' 10" 77º 42' 23"
USGS map(s)	Dansville, Wayland
location (township)	North Dansville (Livingston County), Wayland (Steuben County)
access	crossed by Schwarzenback Highway in Patchinville and parallelled by Michigan Road near Perkinsville see below
principle species	brook trout (wild), brown trout (wild)

Mill Creek is a little known, very underutilized trout stream in the northwest corner of Steuben County and southern Livingston County. This relative anonymity is ironic, for Mill Creek is unquestionably one of the finest wild trout streams in the region, if not the state. Given its size, there are few streams more productive than Mill. During a recent survey, an electro-shocking of a 500 foot section of the stream produced an incredible 300 trout. Not bad for a stream that only averages 10 to 15 feet in width.

The uppermost reaches of Mill Creek, above the hamlet of Patchinville, is a small, wild brook trout stream flowing through remote, picturesque woodlands. This section averages only 4 to 6 feet in width, but there is a very good year round flow of cold water, enough to sustain quite a good population of trout. The bottom consists primarily of gravel. The stream is thickly hedged by alders, making any type of fishing difficult, but a little persistence will almost certainly pay off. There are very few dace or chubs in Mill Creek, so the old fashioned method of drifting a worm or very small spinner into the numerous pools or submerged root tangles will prove to be very productive for trout.

Below Patchinville you start picking up wild brown trout, and they quickly come to dominate the stream. The reach of Mill Creek between Patchinville and Perkinsville is similar in characteristics to the upper reaches of the stream. However, there are some important differences. There is some siltation in the stream where it runs along the old railroad grade. Also, close to Perkinsville Mill Creek is influenced by the Marlbed Ponds, warm water impoundments that drain into the stream, resulting in the presence of some carp and suckers. This in no way affects the trout fishing, though.

The middle reach of the stream is a bit more open than the headwaters, averaging perhaps 10 feet in width. It is still too restricted for fly fishing, but some sections below the crossing of Route 390 should be sufficiently open to allow for short casts of a small spinner. However, much of the fishing will still involve drifting a small spinner or worm, and this will put you into some of the best trout fishing around. As in the headwaters, there are plenty of deep pools, submerged roots and trout. Lots of trout. So many, in fact, that they generally run a little on the small size, 8 to 10 inches (this is the reason there are no size restrictions on trout in Mill Creek). Some fish, though, do get up to a respectable 16 to 18 inches.

By the time the stream enters Perkinsville, it is exclusively brown trout water. In Perkinsville Mill Creek goes over a small falls. The pool below this falls holds some nice browns. Fish up to 5 pounds have been taken there.

Below Perkinsville the fishing is a bit easier, at least in terms of the mechanics. Mill Creek begins to widen out at this point, and although still heavily rimmed by alders and willows, there is some encroachment of the stream by farmland. It is probably not open enough for fly fishing, but you would toss a spinner a short distance. This lower section of Mill Creek, from Perkinsville to its confluence with Canaseraga Creek in Dansville, is the least productive part of the stream. There is a lot of siltation in this reach and gravel areas, pools and other fish holding areas are less frequent. This is not to say that there are not trout here, but the massive density of fish found above Perkinsville does not exist in this reach. The browns do run much larger here, so there is some compensation, and they can be found right down to the mouth of the stream.

To facilitate access to this remarkable stream, the state has obtained 1.42 miles of public fishing easement along the stream, on the section just above Perkinsville, where it runs along Michigan Road.

Mill Creek is not stocked, but is managed as a wild trout stream. Trout can be taken from this stream all year, any size, 10 fish per day. Be sure to check for current regulations.

NOTES: _____

_____

_____

_____

NEILS CREEK

map coordinates	42° 26′ 18″ 77° 27′ 09″
USGS map(s)	Avoca, Haskinville
location (township)	Avoca, Howard, Fremont, Wayland
access	parallelled by Neils Creek Road below Haskinville. Parallelled by Route 21, above Haskinville — see below
principle species	brown trout (wild) brook trout (wild)

Neils Creek is the principle nursery stream for Cohocton River brown trout and is a superb trout fishery in its own right. Providing fishermen with over 10 miles of high quality trout water, this stream originates just south of Loon Lake and empties into the Cohocton River at Wallace.

The lower reach of the stream, from Haskinville downstream to Wallace, averages 15 to 20 feet in width, though some sections are considerably wider and washed out by seasonal flooding and bank erosion. The bottom consists of rock and rubble, and bank cover is only intermittant. This is due to the encroachment of dairy farms, which become quite prevalent the further downstream you go. The state has planted willow trees along the banks of Neils Creek, in the public fishing sections, to provide additional cover for the fish and to keep the cows away from the stream. This section of Neils Creek is loaded with wild brown trout. While it may not be nearly as productive as Mill Creek, the lower half of Neils Creek certainly rates a special trip by anyone's standards.

The upper section averages 6 to 8 feet in width, has a gravel and rubble bottom and a lot of bank cover. It is very picturesque in this reach, flowing through isolated stands of woodland. There is a good ratio of riffles to pools, providing habitat for a good population of wild brown trout. In the very uppermost reaches you will find a modest population of wild brook trout.

Neils Creek is a very popular stream with local anglers, and to insure access to the stream, the state has purchased a total of

The BLACK NOSE DACE, an imitation of a common dace minnow found in many streams in Central New York.

4.5 miles of public fishing easements here, as well as one developed fisherman's parking area on County Road #6, just east of Clymo Road.

This stream is not stocked.

NOTES: _____

_____

_____

_____

POST CREEK

map coordinates	42° 08′ 48″ 77° 02′ 15″
USGS map(s)	Corning, Big Flats, Beaver Dam
location (township)	Corning, Hornby (Steuben County), Catlin (Chemung County)
access	parallelled by Route 414 — see also below
principle species	brown trout (stocked & wild)

Originating in northwest Chemung County, Post Creek enters the Chemung River in the City of Corning. Very popular with local anglers, this stream offers some fine fishing for wild and stocked brown trout. Averaging 15 to 20 feet in width, it has a gravel and rubble bottom, numerous riffle/pool situations and a lot of bank cover. The following guest article, written by Chuck Annis of Elmira, will give you a first hand impression of what Post Creek is like.

"Post Creek offers some fairly good wild brown trout fishing. Wild browns are fairly well spread out in Post Creek, and there are some larger browns in the 20 inch range. Heavy bank cover along most of the stream discourages most fishermen. While primarily a bait fishing stream, small spinners, dry flies and streamers will also catch fish. Muddler minnows and black-nose dace work well.

"Access to Post Creek is easily obtained by following the railroad bed which pretty much parallels the stream. There is some posting, but most landowners will give you permission to fish if you ask. Areas around the bridges over Post Creek get fished fairly hard. If you are willing to put up with thick mosquitoes and brush, get off the beaten path, and you will find some good wild brown trout fishing. Post Creek is stocked annually with 1,110 brown trout in Chemung County and 950 brown trout in Steuben County."

NOTES: _____

_____

_____

_____

TEN MILE CREEK

map coordinates......... 42º 25' 32" 77º 26' 13"
USGS map(s)............. Avoca, Rheims, Prattsburg
location (township)....... Avoca, Wheeler, Prattsburg
access.................. crossings at Lynn Road (shown as West Creek Road and Spaulding Road on some maps) i.e. County Road #7
principle species .... brown trout (wild)

This small stream enters the Cohocton River midway between Wallace and Avoca. Ten Mile Creek is a mediocre quality stream that you might want to consider if you are in the area, but it is certainly not worth a special trip. Averaging just 6 feet in width, it has a rocky/rubble bottom, alder bank cover and a tendency to go nearly dry in sections during the summer. A small tributary of Ten Mile Creek, known as West Creek, enters the stream near the crossing of Lynn Road. Essentially a nursery stream, there are some decent wild brown trout in its lowermost reaches.

Ten Mile Creek is not stocked.

NOTES: _____

_____

_____

_____

TROUPS CREEK (west branch)

map coordinates......... 42º 02' 17" 77º 32' 31"
USGS map(s)............. Troupsburg, Rexville
location (township)....... Troupsburg
access.................. parallelled at a distance by Brown Road
principle species .... brook trout (wild)

This stream is a very isolated, mediocre quality brook trout stream. It is only being mentioned here because it is one of the few, if not the only fishable trout stream in this section of Steuben County. Averaging 6 to 8 feet in width, the stream has a gravel and rubble bottom, a fair flow of water year round and a lot of bank cover. The fishable portion of the stream consists of a scant 2 mile section immediately above the settlement of Young Hickory. It flows through a valley known as Young Hickory Hollow which is dotted with stands of mature hardwoods and old,

overgrown pasturelands. All of the lands along the stream is private, so be sure to check with landowners before fishing here.

The west branch of Troups Creek is not stocked.

NOTES: _____

_____

_____

_____

TWELVE MILE CREEK

map coordinates......... 42º 26' 19" 77º 27' 38"
USGS map(s)............. Avoca, Naples
location (township)....... Avoca, Wheeler, Cohocton
access.................. parallelled (usually at a distance) by County Road 9 (Twelve Mile Creek Road)
principle species .... brown trout (wild)

A fairly lengthly tributary of the Cohocton River, which it empties into at Wallace, Twelve Mile Creek provides about 8.5 miles of good wild brown trout water. Originally, this was not a trout stream. Farms had denuded its banks to the point where it was too warm. As the farms disappeared the bank cover returned, water temperatures went down and now Twelve Mile Creek rates as a good quality trout stream. Averaging 15 to 20 feet in width, the stream has a gravel and rubble bottom, good year round water flow and has generally wooded embankments. This is a good stream to try if you don't like crowds.

An upper tributary of this stream, Lyons Hollow Creek, joins Twelve Mile Creek near the junction of Lyon Hollow Road and Twelve Mile Creek Road. This is a fair quality wild brook trout stream, averaging 10 to 12 feet in width. Surrounded by a wooded, isolated valley, Lyon Hollow Creek is accessible from a dirt road that runs off of Lyon Hollow Road. Be sure to check with landowners before fishing here.

Twelve Mile Creek and Lyon Hollow Creek are not stocked.

NOTES: _____

_____

_____

_____

Neils Creek is a major tributary of the Cohocton River, and serves as a nursery stream for many of the trout found in the Cohocton. A high quality trout stream in its own right, wild brown trout can be found nearly the full length of the stream.

STEUBEN COUNTY LAKES & PONDS

LOON LAKE

map coordinates......... 42º 29' 35'' 77º 34' 02''
USGS map(s)............. Haskinville
location................. township of Wayland
access.................. off Route 21

Physical Characteristics

area..................... 141 acres
shoreline................ 3.1 miles
elevation................ 1698 feet
maximum depth......... 45 feet
mean depth............. approximately 20 feet
bottom type............. muck, some gravel

Chemical Characteristics

water clarity............. generally clear
pH....................... alkaline
oxygen.................. oxygen is poor below 20 feet in the summer.

Plant Life

Extensive weed beds are found along the shallow western and southern portions of the lake. Smaller weed beds are found in the bay at the northern end of the lake in water to 15 feet.

Species Informtion

chain pickerel............. common; growth rate good
smallmouth bass.......... common, growth rate good
tiger muskellunge......... common; growth rate good
yellow perch............. abundant; growth rate poor
bullhead................. common; growth rate good
bluegills................. common; growth rate fair
pumpkinseed............. common; growth rate fair
rock bass................ common; growth **rate fair**
black crappie............. common; growth rate fair
walleye.................. rare; growth rate good

Boat Launch Sites

The only current access available to the public is via the Laff-A-Lot business on the north-west corner of the lake. Small boats can be launched from the private ramp there, but permission must be obtained first. The DEC is currently trying to obtain public access on the lake.

General Information

At an elevation of 1698 feet, Loon Lake is the highest of any lake in this region. Accordingly it freezes earlier than most lakes (it can often be ice-fished by Thanksgiving Day) and thaws last. Ice fishing is very popular here. The majority of fish taken here through the ice are small yellow perch and chain pickerel.

Panfish are overly abundant in Loon Lake. In an effort to decrease their numbers and improve the overall quality of fishing here, the DEC stocked 1,000 tiger muskellunge here in 1982, 1984, 1985 and 1986. They have done very well in Loon Lake and fish up to 15 pounds have been taken.

The one major problem on Loon Lake is access. The lake is heavily ringed with cottages and there is no formal public access. The Laff-A-Lot business often allows fishermen access but this is strictly private property. The DEC is trying to obtain formal public access sites.

NOTES: _____

_____

_____

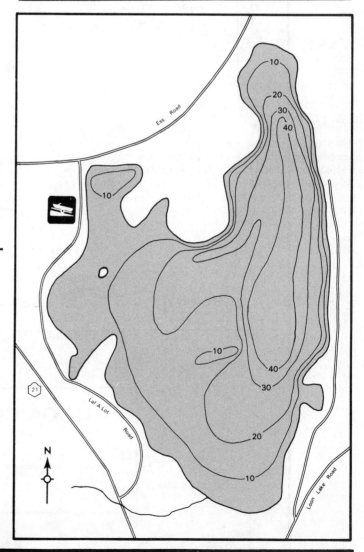

LOON LAKE

Steuben County

0 _____ 1/8

MILES

Depth Contours in Feet

NOT FOR USE IN NAVIGATION

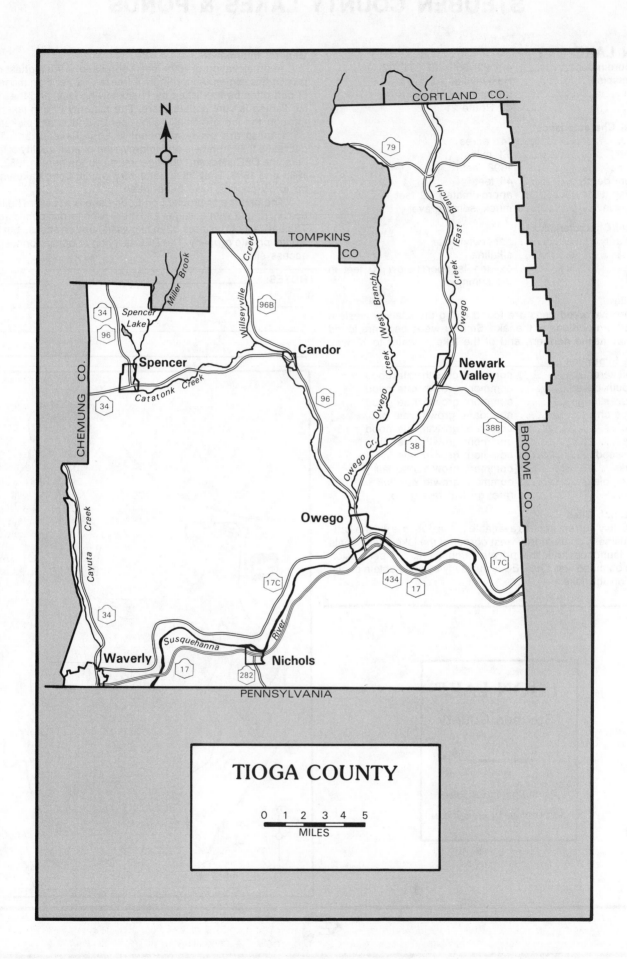

N

CORTLAND CO.

79

TOMPKINS CO

CHEMUNG CO.

BROOME CO.

PENNSYLVANIA

34
96
Spencer Lake
Miller Brook
Willseyville Creek
96B
Candor
96
Spencer
34
Catatonk Creek
34

Owego Creek (West Branch)
Owego Creek (East Branch)

Newark Valley

38B
38
Owego Cr.

Owego
17C
434 17
17C

Cayuta Creek
34
Susquehanna
River
17
Waverly
282
Nichols

TIOGA COUNTY

0 1 2 3 4 5
MILES

TIOGA COUNTY STREAMS & RIVERS

CATATONK CREEK

map coordinates	42° 07' 28" 76° 16' 41"
USGS map(s)	Owego, Candor, Spencer
location (township)	Owego, Tioga, Candor, Spencer
access	parallelled by Route 96 between Owego and Spencer
principle species	smallmouth bass, largemouth bass, walleye, pickerel, bullhead, panfish

Catatonk Creek is a major tributary of Owego Creek, which it joins just north of the town of Owego. The stream is fairly large; 21.6 miles in length, it averages 90 feet in width. It has a good constant flow of warm water and is a bit sluggish. In a lot of ways Catatonk Creek looks like an oversize trout stream. Its clear waters flow over a bottom of gravel and rubble, and it has a nice combination of long runs, well defined pools (some of which are up to 15 feet deep) and riffles.

Contrary to appearances, Catatonk Creek is a medium quality warm water stream, though a few brown trout are occasionally encountered (they drop down from the cold water tributaries). There is fair to good fishing for the species listed above and the stream gets quite a bit of use. Much of the value of Catatonk Creek lies in its surroundings and accessibility. Surrounded by woodlands and farmlands for most of its length, the stream is popular with campers and picnickers and, in the spring, canoeing enthusiasts.

Catatonk Creek is now experimentally stocked with brown trout.

NOTES: _____

_____

_____

_____

CAYUTA CREEK

map coordinates	41° 59' 00" 76° 30' 25"
USGS map(s)	Sayre, Waverly, Van Etten, Erin, Alpine
location (township)	Barton (Tioga County), Van Etten (Chemung County), Cayuta, Catherine (Schuyler County)
access	parallelled by Route 34 between Waverly and Van Etten; parallelled by Route 224 between Van Etten and the hamlet of Alpine — see below
principle species	brown trout (stocked & wild), smallmouth bass, chain pickerel, panfish

Originating at Cayuta Lake in Schuyler County, this stream follows a meandering route south and east for approximately 30 miles before emptying into the Susquehanna River just south of Waverly. Known also as Sheppard's Creek, the stream can be divided into cold and warm water habitats at the hamlet of Reniff. Above Reniff, Cayuta Creek is a good brown trout stream and averages roughly 30 feet in width. It has a good year-round flow of cold, clear water over a bottom of gravel and rubble. Surrounded by farmlands and woodlands, there is usually a good amount of bank cover here, except where it flows through pastureland. This section of Cayuta Creek can be fished all trout season, though the quality drops in the summer. There are some wild trout in the uppermost reaches, but the trout fishing is sustained primarily by stocked fish.

Below Reniff Cayuta Creek rapidly grades into a warm water stream of mediocre quality, although brown trout will occasionally be taken. This section of the stream averages 60 feet in width, has a

bottom of gravel and rubble and a good year-round flow. There are numerous pools, some of which are up to six feet deep, providing habitat for smallmouth bass, chain pickerel and panfish, but nothing to really go out of your way for.

Because of its setting and accessibility, this is a popular stream for picnicking and camping, as well as fishing. The state has purchased 2.98 miles of public fishing rights on the Schuyler County section and access to the lower section is more than adequate.

In the spring a 20.4 mile section of Cayuta Creek, from the hamlet of Reniff in Tioga County upstream to the mouth of Jackson Creek in Schuyler County, is stocked with a total of 15,900 brown trout yearlings.

NOTES: _____

_____

_____

_____

MILLER BROOK

map coordinates	42° 14' 02" 76° 29' 20"
USGS map(s)	Spencer, Willseyville
location (township)	Spencer
access	crossing at Fisher Settlement (Miller Creek) Road
principle species	brown trout (stocked & wild)

Miller Brook is a small, occasionally good quality tributary of Catatonk Creek. Short in length (6 miles) and averaging 12 feet in width, it has a constant flow of cold water over a bottom of gravel and rubble. It has a considerable amount of bank cover and is surrounded by woodlands for much of its length. Ithaca College maintains a camp on the Tompkins County portion, and access is generally poor due to posting.

In the fall 800 brown trout fingerlings are stocked in Miller Brook, from its junction with Catatonk Creek, up stream to the mouth of tributary #3, a distance of 2.5 miles.

NOTES: _____

_____

_____

_____

OWEGO CREEK (main stream)

map coordinates	42° 05' 42" 76° 16' 22"
USGS map(s)	Owego, Candor
location (township)	Tioga, Owego, Candor
access	crossed and parallelled above Owego by Park Settlement Road
principle species	brown trout (stocked), smallmouth bass, walleye, brook trout (stocked), panfish

The main stream of Owego Creek flows south for 6 miles between the junction of the east and west branches at Flemingsville and its own junction with the Susquehanna River in Owego. More of a river than a stream, Owego Creek averages 100 feet in width, 4 feet in depth with pools up to 8 feet deep. It has a constant, sluggish flow of warm to cool water over a bottom of gravel and rubble.

Although short in length, Owego Creek can be divided into distinct cold and warm water sections. Above the town of Owego the stream is essentially a put and take brown trout fishery. However, near the mouth of the west branch there is an influx of cold spring water. Consequently, for a short distance there is some very good fishing, not only for large carry over brown trout, but for brook trout as well (they drop down from the west branch). The trout section of Owego Creek is certainly fly fishable and can be productive all season long, but the stream gets little attention after the first few weeks of trout season.

Below the crossing at Route 96, Owego Creek is dominated by warm water species. There is fair fishing for smallmouth bass and walleye throughout this section, and the fishing for these species can be quite good right at the stream mouth.

In the spring, Owego Creek is stocked with 2,800 brown trout yearlings, from the crossing at Route 96 upstream 4.3 miles to the junction of the east and west branches of Owego Creek.

NOTES: _____

_____

_____

_____

OWEGO CREEK (east branch)

map coordinates	42° 10′ 05″ 76° 15′ 04″
USGS map(s)	Candor, Newark Valley, Richford, Harford
location (township)	Owego, Newark Valley, Berkshire, Richford, (Tioga County), Harford (Cortland County)
access	parallelled by Route 38 — see below
principle species	brown trout (stocked & wild), brook trout (wild), smallmouth bass

The east branch of Owego Creek is a long, diverse stream nearly 30 miles in length. The lower reaches, from its junction with the west branch of Owego Creek upstream to the town of Newark Valley, is a mediocre quality brown trout stream. The stream averages 45 feet in width in this section and has a good flow of marginally warm water over a bottom of gravel and rubble. Flowing through woodlands and farmlands, there is a good amount of bank cover, but this section of the stream could be fly fished.

From Newark Valley upstream to Berkshire, the east branch of Owego Creek suffers from low flows in the summer, severe flooding in the spring and high temperatures. As a result, there is little trout fishing in this reach. The dominant species of interest to anglers is smallmouth bass, but even they are few in number.

Above Berkshire the stream averages about 20 feet in width (6 feet in Cortland County), and has a good, constant flow of cold water over a bottom of gravel and rubble. It takes a very heavy rain to muddy this stream. Trout are again the predominant species, beginning with brown trout and shading to brook trout as you move upstream to the Cortland County line. This upper section is excellent trout habitat. There are several deep pools, all of which hold big browns and stream improvement structures have been installed (pool diggers and deflectors). There is a fair amount of bank cover in the upper reaches, making fly fishing difficult in areas, but bait fishing is very productive. In the uppermost reaches in Cortland County, brook trout are abundant and range up to 12 inches. The most productive brook trout fishing is found in the sections that flow through state reforestation lands. A small tributary of the east branch, Roods Creek, which enters the stream at Harford Mills also provides some fishing for stocked brook trout.

The east branch of Owego Creek is popular with local anglers all season long. To facilitate access the state has purchased 1.1 miles of public fishing rights on this stream in Cortland County and 4.2 miles in Tioga County. One of the parking areas is developed and is located on the east side of Route 38, one mile north of Route 79.

In the spring the lower end of this stream is stocked with 4,000 brown trout yearlings, from the crossing of Route 38, north of Flemingsville, upstream 4.5 miles to the Bridge Street crossing

The upper sections of Cayuta Creek provide good season long fishing for stocked brown trout. Wild trout can be found in the uppermost reaches of the stream. Photo courtesy New York State DEC.

near Newark Valley. Further upstream 4,300 brown trout yearlings are stocked each spring from the crossing of Route 38, 1.5 miles north of Berkshire, upstream 6.3 miles to the mouth of tributary #15 located one mile south of Harford Mills. In Cortland County the stream gets a fall stocking of 800 brown trout in the one mile section between the county line and Harford Mills. The lower three miles of Roods Creek is stocked each fall with 600 brook trout fingerlings.

NOTES: _____

_____

_____

_____

OWEGO CREEK (west branch)

map coordinates	42° 10′ 05″ 76° 15′ 04″
USGS map(s)	Candor, Newark Valley, Richford, Speedsville, Dryden
location (township)	Tioga, Candor, Newark Valley, Berkshire, Richford (Tioga County), Caroline (Tompkins County)
access	parallelled by West Creek Road in Tioga County; parallelled by Route 79 in Tompkins County — see below
principle species	brook trout (stocked & wild), brown trout (wild)

This stream is predominantly a good quality brook trout stream. Most of the trout water is located above the village of Speedsville. Below Speedsville there are isolated stretches of trout water where wild browns and brookies can be found. Just below Speedsville there are several large pools, some of which hold large wild brook trout, and right at the mouth of the west branch there is a strong influx of cold water water providing habitat for wild brook trout. For the most part, however, the west branch of Owego Creek below Speedsville is too warm for trout.

Above Speedsville this stream runs along the Tioga/Tompkins County border. The upper section averages 15 feet in width, has a gravel and rubble bottom and a good, constant flow of cold, clear water year-round. There is a slight problem with unstable gravel bars due to seasonal flooding. The stream flows through farmland and woodlands and generally has a good amount of bank cover. Sufficient sections are open, especially in the upper reaches in Tompkins County, to make fly fishing possible. Except for its lack of deep pools, the upper reaches of the west branch provide very good habitat for wild and stocked brook trout and wild browns. Brown trout predominate just above Speedsville but quickly shade to brook trout further upstream. To offset the lack of pools and stabilize the shifting gravel bars, the D.E.C. has worked with the Tioga County Soil and Water Conservation District to install stream improvement structures.

Fishing pressure on the west branch of Owego Creek is moderate to heavy all season long. To increase access to the stream, the state has purchased 1.4 miles of public fishing rights in Tioga County and 1.6 miles in Tompkins County. In addition, the state has acquired 2 fishermen parking areas and 2 foot path right-of-ways in Tioga County (all developed) and 3 foot path right-of-ways in Tompkins County (undeveloped).

In the spring the west branch of Owego Creek is stocked with 5,600 brook trout yearlings, from one mile below Jenksville upstream 9 miles to the hamlet of Caroline. A further spring stocking of 700 brook trout yearlings is made in the 2.3 mile reach above Caroline.

NOTES: _____

_____

_____

_____

SUSQUEHANNA RIVER
(Tioga County section only)

map coordinates . . . .
USGS map(s) . . . . Waverly, Barton, Owego, Apala-
                                       chin, Endicott
location (township) . . . . Owego, Tioga, Nichols, Barton
access . . . . parallelled by Route 17 (South-
                                       ern Tier Expressway) and
                                       Route 17C — see below
principle species . . . . smallmouth bass, tiger muskel-
                                       lunge, walleye, muskellunge,
                                       panfish

The 33 mile portion of the Susquehanna River in Tioga County ranges from 250 to 1,000 feet in width and has numerous pools up to 25 feet deep. The river has a good constant flow of warm water and is subject to seasonal flooding. It has a high pollution load, which is most evident in the vicinity of Owego and the Broome County line, but this certainly does not seem to detract from the fishing.

This river is known for its abundance of warm water species. Smallmouth bass are the most evenly distributed fish in the river — there is a chance of taking these hard fighting fish almost anywhere in the Susquehanna. Especially productive areas for smallmouth include the stretch between Smithboro and Barton (the bass here are big), and the area between Owego and Hiawatha Island (this island is located 3 miles upstream of Owego).

Walleye, while not nearly as ubitquitous as smallmouth bass, are found in most of the deep pools scattered throughout the river. The best pools are found near Hiawatha Island, Owego, in the big bend off the state ramp at Nichols, at Cannon Ball pool near Barton and at the Pennsylvania border. While productive all season long, the 3 miles of generally slack water between Owego and Hiawatha Island offers exceptionally good walleye fishing in the fall, especially just off the island.

The third major species found in this portion of the Susquehanna River is the muskellunge. Both the natural strain and the hybrid tiger muskellunge are found in relatively good numbers. Concentrate on the waters around Hiawatha Island, the big bend near Nichols and the large, deep pools between Barton and the state line if your looking to test your angling skills against possibly trophy size muskellunge. 8,600 tiger muskie are stocked throughout the Tioga County portion of the river each year.

Rounding out the fishing opportunities present in this river are good populations of rock bass, yellow perch, crappies, channel catfish and bullhead, all of which can be found throughout the Susquehanna.

Access to the Susquehanna River is excellent. There are several bridge crossings off Route 17 and 17C and many areas where informal approaches to the river can be found. There are 4 public boat launch sites located as follows:

1. at Hickory Park, town of Oswego, one-half mile east of Owego on Route 17C — hard surface ramp.

2. on East River Drive, just upstream of Nichols — hard surface ramp.

3. on West River Drive, 4 miles west of Nichols — hand launch only.

4. at the village of Barton, one-quarter mile south of Route 17C — hard launch only.

NOTES: _____

_____

_____

_____

WILLSEYVILLE CREEK

map coordinates . . . . 42° 14' 27"   76° 22' 09"
USGS map(s) . . . . Candor, Spencer, Speedsville,
                                   Willseyville
location (township) . . . . Candor, Caroline, Danby
access . . . . roughly parallelled and crossed
                                   by Route 96B
principle species . . . . chain pickerel, panfish

This is a small, warm water tributary of Catatonk Creek, which it enters near the town of Candor. Averaging 25 feet in width, this is a slow moving, brush lined stream. Silt bottomed, it has a great deal of submerged aquatic vegetation, which provides habitat for a remarkably large population of chain pickerel. Most of these fish are sub-legal in size, but can still be a lot of fun to fight. The best fishing is found in the lower 2.5 miles of the stream. Willseyville Creek is not stocked.

NOTES: _____

_____

_____

_____

The Light Cahill is a traditional wet fly used for trout, very effective in June.

TIOGA COUNTY LAKES & PONDS

SPENCER LAKE

map coordinates..........	42° 14' 35" 76° 29' 43"
USGS map(s).............	Van Etten, Spencer, West Danby
location.................	northwestern Tioga County (Spencer township)
access..................	located off Routes 34 and 96

Physical Characteristics

area	77 acres
shoreline................	2.10 miles
elevation	1,014 feet
maximum depth	45 feet
mean depth	approximately 12 feet
bottom type	muck, gravel

Chemical Characteristics

water clarity.............	slightly turbid
pH......................	alkaline
oxygen..................	oxygen depletion occurs in deepest water in summer

Plant Life

Extensive weed beds (rooted aquatics and lily pads) exist where the water depth is 8 feet or less.

Species Information

chain pickerel	common; growth rate good
largemouth bass	abundant; growth rate good
bluegills.................	common; growth rate good
pumpkinseeds	common; growth rate good
bullhead	common; growth rate good
yellow perch	common; growth rate fair

Boat Launch Sites

The only real access to this privately owned lake is via the campground located on the lake. There is a boat launch ramp at the campground and boat rentals are available. The campground is located near the dam.

General Information

Spencer Lake consists of three separate basins. The original basin (the south basin) is reputed to be up to 45 feet deep. The lake was dammed, raising the water level 6 feet, flooding the 2 north basins.

Spencer Lake offers some very good fishing for largemouth bass and chain pickerel. Although heavily fished by campers, most seem to concentrate on the panfish, which are very plentiful here. Other uses of the lake include swimming, boating and camping. Water skiers are not a problem on the lake.

NOTES: _____

_____

_____

_____

Top to bottom: chain pickerel, northern pike, tiger muskellunge. Members of the pike family can be distinguished by their unique markings.

Central New York has more to offer than just good fishing. Much of the scenery is breathtakingly beautiful. Waterfalls like these abound in the region.

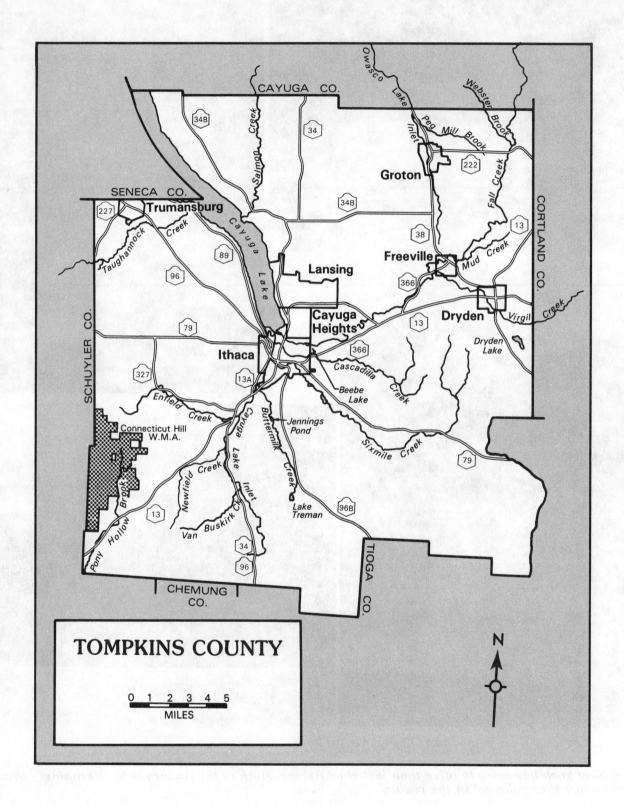

TOMPKINS COUNTY

```
0  1  2  3  4  5
       MILES
```

N

—128—

TOMPKINS COUNTY STREAMS & RIVERS

BUTTERMILK CREEK

map coordinates......... 42° 25' 05"   76° 31' 35"
USGS map(s)............. Ithaca West, Ithaca East, Willseyville
location (township)....... Ithaca
access.................. Buttermilk Falls State Park
principle species .... brown trout (stocked), rainbow trout
(wild)

Buttermilk Creek is a major tributary of Cayuga Inlet. Averaging 25 feet in width, the stream has a bottom of gravel and rubble, a moderate gradient and a fairly constant flow all year long. Below Buttermilk Falls, Buttermilk Creek is a typical secondary tributary of Cayuga Lake. In the short section of the stream below the falls (.2 miles) there is an intensive spring fishery for wild lake-run rainbows. There is no significant run of fish here in the fall. Above the falls, Buttermilk Creek is a brush lined trout stream of mediocre quality, offering limited put-and-take fishing for stocked brown trout.

In the spring, the state park section of Buttermilk Creek is stocked with 200 brown trout yearlings.

NOTES: _____

_____

_____

_____

CASCADILLA CREEK

map coordinates......... 42° 27' 06"   76° 30' 36"
USGS map(s)............. Ithaca West, Ithaca East
location (township)....... Ithaca, Dryden
access.................. crossings at Genung Road and
Ellis Hollow Road
principle species .... brown trout (stocked & wild), brook
trout (wild)

Cascadilla Creek is a tributary of Cayuga Inlet, which it joins in the City of Ithaca. It has a gorge section at its mouth, preceeded by a series of falls and cascades (hence the name), but there is no significant fishery in this section. Above the falls the stream flows through the property of Cornell University and abandoned farmland. From the edge of Cornell's property to its headwaters, the stream is a good quality trout stream. Wild brown trout predominate, but wild brook trout can be found in the headwaters.

Cascadilla Creek averages 20 to 30 feet in width, has a bottom of gravel and rubble and a good year round flow. The stream runs through mature hardwoods for the most part and has adequate streamside cover. Fly fishing, though difficult, should be possible on much of the stream. There is a good ratio of riffles to pools on the middle and upper sections of Cascadilla Creek, providing holding areas for some good size brown trout.

In the fall a 2.4 mile section of Cascadilla Creek is stocked with 600 fingerling brown trout, from the crossing at Genung Road upstream to .5 miles above the crossing at Ellis Hollow Road.

Well over 50% of Cascadilla Creek is either on Cornell University property or is posted. Be sure to check with the University or local landowners before fishing this stream.

NOTES: _____

_____

_____

New York State has a lot more to offer is than just great fishing. An excellent source of information on what the state has to offer the Department of Environmental Conservation (DEC). Contact your local DEC office for pamphlets on hunting, hiking, camping, and cross country skiing, as well as fishing.

CAYUGA LAKE INLET

map coordinates......... 42° 27' 34"   76° 30' 45"
USGS map(s)............. Ithaca West, West Danby
location (township)....... Ithaca, Newfield, Danby
access.................. crossed and parallelled by Routes 34
and 96 — see below
principle species .... rainbow trout (wild), landlocked
salmon (stocked), smallmouth bass,
northern pike, panfish, bullhead

This stream is the major tributary, in terms of fisheries, of Cayuga Lake. One mile upstream from the stream mouth is a flood control dam. Below the dam Cayuga Inlet is a straight, dredged, turbid channel. The city of Ithaca owns the property along the flood control channel. This section provides anglers with fair to good fishing for smallmouth bass, northern pike, bullhead and panfish. Few trout are taken here, even though large numbers of them must pass through the channel as they migrate into the upper reaches of Cayuga Inlet. However this is due to a lack of fishing pressure, for trout fishing in the first two weeks of April and in the fall (mid-October to mid-November) can be excellent here.

Above the flood control dam, Cayuga Inlet averages 40 feet in width, has a bottom of gravel, rubble and clay, and flows through stands of hardwoods and brush. Stream side cover is generally good, and there are a considerable number of stream improvement projects here, providing holding areas for migrating trout and salmon. Cayuga Inlet gets the bulk of the wild rainbow trout that leave Cayuga Lake in the spring to spawn, resulting in what is truly excellent fishing. The spring rainbows average about two pounds, but rainbows up to eight pounds are not all that uncommon. There is also a moderate run of rainbows here in the fall, beginning in mid-October and lasting to mid-December. These fish are generally smaller than those taken in the spring,

A majority of the wild rainbows in Cayuga Lake spawn in Cayuga Lake Inlet, resulting in some truly fine fishing.

averaging one to one and one-half pounds, but some fish as large as five pounds will be taken on occasion. In addition to the fall rainbow runs, landlocked salmon, which are stocked above the fishway also run here. These salmon generally weigh in at 4 to 10 pounds. These fish generally weigh four to ten pounds.

Due to its popularity with fishermen, the state has purchased a total of 7.28 miles of public fishing easements on Cayuga Inlet. These easements are located between the mouth of Buttermilk Creek and West Danby. It has also obtained two fishermen parking areas, located near the junction of Newfield-Depot Road and Routes 96 and 34 and off Brown Road near Routes 96 and 34.

In the spring Cayuga Inlet is stocked with 5,000 rainbow trout yearlings.

NOTE: Cayuga Inlet, Salmon Creek and Cayuga Lake are all "stocked" with fish designated Finger Lakes wild. These fish are wild strains of rainbows and have been temporarily reared in a hatchery situation. They are wild fish themselves.

NOTES: _____

_____

_____

_____

ENFIELD CREEK

map coordinates	42° 24' 03" 76° 32' 30"
USGS map(s)	Mecklenburg, Ithaca West
location	Enfield
access	Robert Treman State Park — see below
principle species	brown trout (stocked), rainbow trout (wild), landlocked salmon

Enfield Creek is a major tributary of Cayuga Inlet. The stream can be divided into three distinct sections. The first section, below the impassible falls in Robert Treman State Park, is very similar to Cayuga Inlet. This 0.8 mile reach of Enfield Creek is relatively poor trout habitat, consisting of a shifting stream bed of gravel and rubble. It gets a major run of wild, Cayuga Lake rainbows, via Cayuga Inlet, in the spring and the fishing at this time is quite good. However, aside from this run, the only other fishery of significance in the reach is a minor run of stray land locked salmon in the fall.

Above the falls, the park section of Enfield Creek is a good quality brown trout stream. This middle reach is a high gradient, shale bottom stream flowing through a gorge and is characterized by cataracts and deep plunge pools. Some of these pools are fairly large, and they provide a majority of the habitat for the trout found in the park. Fly fishing is a definite possibility here.

The third section of Enfield Creek, above the state park, is a moderate gradient stream. Averaging 20 to 30 feet in width, this reach flows through abandoned farmland and residential areas. There are some fairly deep stretches here that provide habitat for carry-over brown trout. Bank cover is good along much of this section, and fly fishing is limited to selected spots.

Fishing pressure is intense on the lower reach of Enfield Creek, at least in the spring, light in the park section, and light to moderate on the upper section. To increase public access to the stream, the state has purchased a total of .34 miles of public fishing easements, which are located between the mouth or the stream and Treman State Park.

Many fishermen believe that your hands should be wet before handling a fish, to prevent the protective mucus from being removed. Unfortunately, you must hold the fish more tightly with wet hands, because your grip is so slippery. Studies have shown that more fish are killed by being tightly held then by having some of their mucus removed, which is secreted almost continuously.

In the spring a 1.3 mile section of Enfield Creek is stocked with 1,100 brown trout yearlings, in the area just above the falls in Robert Treman State Park. In the fall the upper section of the creek is stocked with 1,000 fall fingerlings, from the crossings at Hines Road upstream two miles to the mouth of tributary #15, which is three-quarters of a mile above the village of Enfield (this section can be accessed from road crossings at Bostwick Road and Enfield Center Road). Tributary #4, which comes into Enfield Creek just upstream of the crossing at Hines Road, is stocked in the spring with 100 brown trout yearlings in its lower reaches.

NOTES: _____

_____

_____

_____

FALL CREEK

map coordinates	42° 27' 36" 76° 30' 37"
USGS map(s)	Ithaca West, Ithaca East, Dryden, Groton, Sempronius
location (township)	Ithaca, Dryden, Groton (Tompkins County), Summerhill (Cayuga County)
access	crossings at Route 222 and Davis Road — see below
principle species	brook trout (stocked & wild), brown trout (stocked), rainbow trout (wild), landlocked salmon, smallmouth bass, bullhead, smelt, panfish

Fall Creek is a very long, diverse stream, offering anglers an enormous variety of fishing opportunities. The stream empties into Cayuga Lake in the City of Ithaca. Less than one mile from the mouth of the stream there is an impassible falls. Below the falls, Fall Creek is a typical Cayuga Lake tributary. It gets a big run of wild Cayuga Lake rainbows in the spring and a smaller, but still significant, run of rainbows in the fall. One of Fall Creek's biggest drawing cards are the runs of landlocked salmon that take place here. Fall Creek is, in fact, the principle spawning stream for Cayuga Lake salmon. What is especially unique, and from the anglers point of view, very fortunate, is the fact that Fall Creek gets a very respectable run of salmon in the spring as well as in the fall. Why the salmon are running in the spring is not fully understood by the fisheries biologists in the D.E.C. (they think this run is due to warm water temperatures and the presence of smelt in the stream), but they are found here in good numbers in April and early May.

The lower reach of Fall Creek is a large stream, ranging from 50 to 100 feet in width. There are few pools in this part of the stream, but it is large and deep enough to provide holding areas for large numbers of trout and salmon.

In addition to trout and salmon fishing, the lower section of Fall Creek has an excellent run of smelt, from late March to early May (the run here is second only to that of Salmon Creek), and fair to good fishing for smallmouth bass, bullhead and panfish. The best time to take bass in Fall Creek is in June and July. This section of the creek can be accessed via the City of Ithaca Park off Lake Street.

Immediately above the falls, Fall Creek runs through property owned by Cornell University, and just a little upstream is a small instream lake known as Beebe Lake. This short stretch of Fall Creek is an unremarkable piece of water. It is full of very small smallmouth bass, especially in the upper end of Beebe Lake. Brown trout are only occasionally taken from this part of the stream. These are not resident fish, but trout that have dropped down from the upper reaches of Fall Creek.

Above Beebe Lake upstream to Freeville, Fall Creek is a fairly productive warm water stream. Averaging about 50 feet in width, the stream flows over a bottom of bedrock and rubble. Though much of the stream has extensive bank cover, it is open enough for fly fishing. This would be a great place to practice your fly

Fall Creek, upstream of Freeville, is a good quality brown trout and brook trout stream.

ishing techniques for bass. Smallmouth are abundant in this each of the stream, and while not quite lunkers, some fish do achieve a respectable size. For the trout fisherman, armed as much with patience as tackle, there are a number of large, deep pools on this mid-section of Fall Creek that hold a few large brown trout, even though this is not really trout quality water.

Fall Creek is recognized as trout water from its junction with Virgil Creek, near Freeville, upstream to its source near Lake Como in Cayuga County. The reach of the stream between the mouth of Virgil Creek and Groton City is a fair quality brown trout stream, relying primarily on stocked trout for its fishery. This section of the stream averages 40 feet in width, has a bottom of gravel and rubble and a good year round flow. It flows through active farmlands, and the stream banks are subjected to extensive grazing. Thus, there is little bank cover along this section except where it runs through areas of mature woodlands. There are almost no wild trout in this part of Fall Creek. Stocked brown trout are the predominant species, but you do begin to pick up a few brook trout as you approach the hamlet of Groton City. Most of the brookies are also stocked, but there is a small population of wild brook trout here.

The fishing pressure on this middle reach of Fall Creek is extremely high in the early part of trout season, especially on the sections that have public fishing easements, but tapers off very quickly. To increase public access to this part of the stream, the state has purchased a total of 5.7 miles of public fishing easements between the village of McLean and the county line.

In the spring a 5.0 mile section of Fall Creek, from McLean upstream to Groton City, is stocked with a total of 6,300 brown trout yearlings.

The following special regulations apply to Fall Creek: (1) from Ithaca Falls upstream to the county line largemouth and smallmouth bass may be taken from April 1 to November 30, any

size, limit five per day; (2) from the Route 38 bridge at Freeville upstream to the bridge at Groton City, trout may be taken from April 1 to November 30, any size, limit ten per day.

Above Groton City (not to be confused with the Village of Groton) Fall Creek is a small, high quality brook trout stream. Most of the stream averages about 25 feet in width, has a good flow of clear, cool water over a bottom of gravel and rubble and is heavily cloaked by tag alders. The only exception to these circumstances is the middle portion of this reach, where the stream flows through a swamp. This part of Fall Creek is a slow moving, muck bottomed, typical swamp stream, flowing through stands of dead hardwoods. Aside from this swampy section, the stream flows through abandoned farmland.

Brook trout are the dominant species in the upper section of Fall Creek. Wild brook trout predominate above Creech Road while stocked brookies are found below. Few brown trout are found here. A tributary of Fall Creek, known as Eaton Brook, enters the stream just below the crossing at Route 41A. Eaton Brook is a small, very high quality brook trout stream. There are few fish over ten inches in the stream, but they are abundant. In fact, many of the small tributaries of the upper end of Fall Creek are good trout streams in their own right. Check them out while fishing Fall Creek.

The upper reach of Fall Creek is heavily fished in the early weeks of trout season, but the crowds taper off thereafter.

To increase public access to Fall Creek, the state has purchased a total of 5.71 miles of public fishing easements on Fall Creek, and they are located above Creech Road and below Route 90.

Both sections have fisherman parking areas. One is located on Route 90, one-quarter mile east of Lake Como Road. The other is on Lake Como Road, one-quarter mile north of Peth Road. The state has also obtained .47 miles of public fishing easements on Eaton Brook.

In the spring, a 2.5 mile section of Fall Creek is stocked with 1,800 brook trout yearlings, from Groton City upstream to the mouth of Lake Como Outlet.

NOTES: _____

_____

_____

_____

MUD CREEK

map coordinates . . . . 42° 30' 58"   76° 19' 50"
USGS map(s) . . . . Groton
location (township) . . . . Dryden
access . . . . crossings at Dryden Road and Mott Road
principle species . . . . brown trout (wild), brook trout (stocked)

Mud Creek, in its lower section, is a good quality brook trout stream. A tributary of Fall Creek, this stream averages ten feet in width, has a silt bottom, with some pockets of gravel, and flows through abandoned farmland. Mud Creek is densely covered with tag alders, making much of the stream difficult to fish (it's a good place to drift worms or salted minnows). This stream gets very little fishing pressure.

There are a few wild brown trout in Mud Creek, but a majority of the fish taken here are stocked brown trout. In the fall, Mud Creek is stocked in its lower two mile reach with 400 brook trout fingerlings.

NOTES: _____

_____

_____

_____

One factor often overlooked when deciding what tackle to use is the choice of hook. Hooks come in many different sizes, styles, and shank lengths. Be sure to match your bait, techniques and conditions with the right type of hook.

NEWFIELD CREEK

map coordinates	42° 22' 30" 76° 33' 18"
USGS map(s)	West Danby, Alpine
location (township)	Newfield
access	crossing at County Road 130
principle species	rainbow trout (wild), brown trout (stocked)

Newfield Creek is also known as the west branch of Cayuga Inlet (old timers might know it as Greenville Creek). There is an impassible falls about 3/8 to 1/2 mile above the mouth of Newfield Creek, and below the falls it is typical of Cayuga Lake tributaries. It averages 20 feet in width below the falls, and has a number of good size pools that provide habitat for wild rainbows that migrate up this stream from Cayuga Lake. The spring run of rainbows is very good, but the fall run is only fair.

Above the falls, Newfield Creek is a mediocre brown trout stream, averaging 12 feet in width.

In the fall a 1.3 mile section of Newfield Creek is stocked with 600 brown trout fingerlings, from the falls upstram to the Village of Newfield.

There is a short section of public fishing easements on the stream below the falls.

NOTES: _____

_____

_____

_____

OWASCO INLET - See Cayuga County Streams & Rivers

PEG MILL BROOK

map coordinates	42° 36' 45" 76° 23' 30"
USGS map(s)	West Groton
location (township)	Groton
access	crossing at Route 38, about one-half mile south of county line
principle species	brown trout (wild), brook trout (wild), rainbow trout (wild)

Peg Mill Brook is a good quality tributary of Owasco Inlet, which it joins downstream of Groton. Averaging 6 to 8 feet in width, the stream has a very good year round flow of cool, clear water over a bottom of gravel. It flows through abandoned farmland and residential areas and has good cover in most sections. There are a number of good size pools providing habitat for wild brown trout, and a small population of wild brook trout inhabits the headwaters, but the stream is dominated by wild rainbow trout. Peg Mill Brook gets a fairly heavy run of adult wild rainbows from Owasco Lake, via Owasco Lake Inlet, in the spring, and it is the source of the juvenile rainbows that dominate the stream. There is also a small population of resident rainbows in the upper section of the stream.

Peg Mill Brook is not stocked.

NOTES: _____

_____

_____

_____

PONY HOLLOW CREEK

map coordinates	42° 16' 34" 76° 41' 37"
USGS map(s)	Alpine
location (township)	Cayuta (Schuyler County), Newfield (Tompkins County)
access	crossing at Route 13 and Route 224
principle species	brown trout (stocked), pickerel

Pony Hollow Creek is a mediocre quality tributary of Cayuta Creek, which it joins near the hamlet of Cayuta in Schuyler County. The stream is fairly long, but the combined trout sections in Schuyler and Tompkins Counties only amount to about 2.2 miles. Pony Hollow Creek averages 20 feet in width, has a gravel and rubble bottom and only fair stream side cover. In dry summers the flow of water is greatly reduced, but it does not dry to pools. When fishing this stream, do not wander too far from the crossing at Route 13. The best trout fishing is found in short, intermittant stretches above and below this road, with the exception of a short section near Cayuta. There are a number of isolated pools near Route 13 that hold some very nice carry over brown trout, some as large as two pounds. Some of these pools could be fly fished. There are a few wild (very few) brook trout in Pony Hollow Creek, and wild brook trout can also be found in several of the tributaries to this stream. As a bonus, there is fair fishing for pickerel near the mouth of Pony Hollow Creek. The fishing pressure on this stream is light to moderate.

In the fall the lower .8 miles of Pony Hollow Creek is stocked with 300 brown trout fingerlings.

NOTES: _____

_____

_____

_____

SALMON CREEK

map coordinates	42° 32' 17" 76° 33' 02"
USGS map(s)	Ludlowville, Genoa
location (township)	Lansing (Tompkins County), Genoa (Cayuga County)
access	parallelled and crossed by Salmon Creek Road - see below
principle species	brown trout (stocked), rainbow trout (wild), brook trout (wild), smallmouth bass, smelt, landlocked salmon

Known also as Big Salmon Creek, this stream is a major tributary of Cayuga Lake. As is the case with many of the tributaries of the Finger Lakes, Salmon Creek has an impassible falls a short way upstream of its mouth, in the Village of Ludlowville. Below the falls the stream is about 80 feet in width, has a bottom of rubble and bedrock and flows through a gorge. It is dominated by runs of fish from Cayuga Lake. In the spring there are excellent runs of wild rainbows and smelt (this is the best smelt run on Cayuga Lake) and both runs are intensively fished by local, and not so local anglers. Landlocked salmon are also taken here on occasion in the spring, and there is usually a good run of smallmouth bass in Salmon Creek just about the time that bass season opens. In the fall, there is only a fair run of wild rainbow trout in lower Salmon Creek, and this is augmented by a minor run of landlocked salmon. At times, when there has been a long period of heavy fall rains, lake trout will also be found in the stream in fair numbers. The lower reach of Salmon Creek certainly could be fly fished, but the concentration of fishermen here, especially in the spring, would make this difficult.

To increase access to Salmon Creek the state has purchased a total of 1.01 miles of public fishing easements along the lower reach of the stream. It has also obtained and developed three fisherman parking areas located as follows: 1) off County Road 159 where it crosses the lower most reach of the stream, about 600 feet upstream of the railroad tracks; 2) on Ludlowville Road, three-fifths of a mile north of Route 34B; 3) from the southern end of Salmon Creek Road go right one-quarter mile. Parking area is at end of road.

Above the falls, Salmon Creek is a long, medium quality brown trout stream. Averaging about 35 feet in width, the stream has a bottom of gravel, with sections of bedrock, generally good stream side cover and flows through farmlands. In the summer the flow is greatly reduced, but it does not dry to pools. Stocked brown trout predominate in this stream, both in Cayuga County and Tompkins County, but part of Salmon Creek is used by the D.E.C. as a rearing area for rainbow trout and salmon (these fish do not really contribute to the fishery in the upper creek). There are several long, still pools on this stream, very amenable to fly fishing, where browns over 20 inches can be taken.

In the spring, Salmon Creek is stocked in Tompkins County with 2,100 brown trout yearlings, in the 5.9 mile reach above Ludlowville. The Cayuga County portion of the stream is stocked in the spring with 2,200 brown trout yearlings, from the county line upstream 6.1 miles to the crossing at Meyers road.

NOTES: _____
_____
_____
_____

SIX MILE CREEK

map coordinates . . . . 42° 26' 47"   76° 30' 44"
USGS map(s) . . . . Ithaca West, Ithaca East, Dryden
location (township) . . . . Ithaca, Dryden, Caroline
access . . . . crossings at Route 79, Midline Road and Irish Settlement Road
principle species . . . . brown trout (stocked & wild), brook trout (wild), rainbow trout (wild)

Six Mile Creek is a major tributary of Cayuga Inlet, which it joins in the City of Ithaca. There is an impassible falls about six-tenths of a mile upstream of the stream mouth. Unlike most other similar tributaries of Cayuga Inlet, Six Mile Creek does not get a substantial run of fish from Cayuga Lake. There are a few wild rainbows found in this section of the stream in the spring, but not enough to warrant a special trip.

Above the falls are a series of reservoirs. There is no fishing in the reservoirs or the stream sections that connect them. The fishable portion of Six Mile Creek begins at the hamlet of Brooktondale. There are about 6 miles of trout water between Brooktondale and Slaterville Springs. This section of the stream averages 25 feet in width, has a bottom of unstable gravel bars and silt and generally good stream side cover. The surroundings consist primarily of abandoned farmlands and light residential areas. Most, if not all, of the fish taken here are stocked brown trout. They provide only a fair quality fishery, and this reach of the stream gets only moderate attention from local anglers.

One mile above Slaterville Springs is an area known locally as "The 600". From "The 600" upstream to Irish Settlement Road the characteristics of Six Mile Creek change considerably. This reach of the stream averages 12 feet in width, has a high gradient rubble bottom and flows through remote stands of hardwoods. Much of the property above "The 600" is owned by Cornell University and the state. Though this property is open to the public, access is difficult due to a lack of nearby roads. The population of fish picks up considerably in this section. Most fish are wild brown trout, but wild brook trout begin to turn up as you move upstream. For those willing to put in the time and energy to find it, there is a real gem of a pool on Six Mile Creek, several miles below the crossing at Irish Settlement Road. Located at the base of a remote 30 foot falls, this pool is huge, something on the order of one-fifth of an acre. It is easily large enough for fly fishing and holds a nice mix of wild brook and brown trout. A major tributary of Six Mile Creek, Duzenberry Hollow Brook, comes into the stream just above the falls and provides good fishing for wild brown trout as far upstream as County Road 162. Unfortunately,

much of this stream is posted.

Above the falls, Six Mile Creek is a small, gravel bottomed stream that is fishable at least as far upstream as the crossing at Irish Settlement Road. Wild brook trout are found here in good numbers, and wild brown trout are also taken on occasion. Hugged by alders and stands of hardwoods, this section of the stream averages only 10 feet in width and is best fished by drifting worms or salted minnows through brush piles or small pools.

In the spring, Six Mile Creek is stocked with 2,800 brown trout yearlings, from the crossing at Banks Road upstream 5.4 miles to the crossing of Route 79 at Slaterville Springs.

NOTES: _____
_____
_____
_____

TAUGHANNOCK CREEK

map coordinates . . . . 42° 32' 56"   76° 35' 58"
USGS map(s) . . . . Ludlowville, Trumensburg, Mecklenburg
location (township) . . . . Ulysses
access . . . . Taughannock Falls State Park
principle species . . . . rainbow trout (wild), brown trout (wild), smallmouth bass, smelt

Originating in Schuyler County south of the village of Mecklenburg, Taughnannock Creek is a very long, mediocre quality tributary of Cayuga Lake. It empties into the lake at Taughannock Creek State Park. There are a series of falls in the park. From the mouth of the stream upstream to the first impassible falls, the fishing is very limited, with the exception of the spring smelt run which is extremely good. There are a few wild rainbow trout and smallmouth bass in this lowermost reach of Taughannock Creek, but they do not really amount to much of a fishery.

From the lower falls to Taughannock Falls there are essentially no fishable sections, with the possible exception of the large pool at the base of Taughannock Falls where the D.E.C. has found brown trout. This pool, however, is not open to public access.

Above Taughannock Falls this stream is a fair quality wild brown trout stream, though it does hold some fish of very respectable size. Averaging 30 feet in width, the stream has a bottom of bedrock and rubble, intermittant bank cover and flows through farmland and abandoned farmland. Most of the stream suffers from marginally high water temperatures, resulting in generally poor trout habitat. The trout population, at least in Tompkins County is intermittant, but there are some sections worth fishing, and fly fishing is possible.

In Schuyler County the stream is a bit higher in quality. There is some good fishing for wild brown trout in the section above Mecklenburg. This reach of the stream averages about 20 feet in width, has a gravel and rubble bottom and flows through stands of woodlands that shade the stream and keep the temperature down. Two of the uppermost tributaries, Smith Valley Creek and Reynoldsville Creek, provide good fishing for wild brook and brown trout.

There are no public fishing easements on Taughannock Creek, but there is also little posting.

This stream is not stocked.

NOTES: _____
_____
_____
_____

VAN BUSKIRK CREEK

map coordinates	42° 20' 48" 76° 32' 32"
USGS map(s)	West Danby
location (township)	Danby, Newfield
access	parking area at Brown Road and Routes 34 & 96
principles species	rainbow trout (wild)

Van Buskirk Creek is a small tributary of Cayuga Inlet, which it joins near Stratton. The only fishable section of the stream is the .8 mile reach of Van Buskirk Creek between the mouth of the stream and an impassible falls. This stream is only about 15 feet in width, has a bottom of gravel and rubble and flows through a stand of mature hardwoods. It gets a very good run of wild rainbows in the spring and is heavily fished at that time. There is no appreciable run of fish here in the fall.

Van Buskirk Creek is not stocked.

NOTES: _____

_____

_____

_____

VIRGIL CREEK

map coordinates	42° 30' 17" 76° 21' 34"
USGS map(s)	Groton, Dryden, Harford, Cortland
location (township)	Dryden (Tompkins County), Harford, Virgil (Cortland County)
access	crossings at George Road and West Meeting House Road
principle species	brown trout (stocked & wild), brook trout (wild)

Virgil Creek is well known for its excellent trout fishing, and deservedly so. And yet, for much of its length, it is a mediocre quality trout stream. The lower most reach of this stream, from its junction with Fall Creek, near Freeville, upstream to Dryden, is deep, turbid and slow moving. Flowing through old pastureland it has a bottom of silt and gravel, high silt banks and marginally warm temperatures that support a large population of chubs and panfish. The trout fishing in this section is wholly sustained by stocking, and there is little, if any, carry-over of fish. In the spring this reach of Virgil Creek is stocked with 1,600 brown trout yearlings.

At Dryden there is a short stretch of Virgil Creek where the quality picks up. This section has a higher gradient, gravel bottom and is overhung by large black willows. The fishing is noticably better here than it is downstream, but it still does not rate a special trip.

From Dryden upstream to West Meeting House Road in Cortland County, Virgil Creek is a wide, turbid stream, with occasional deep pools. Flowing through active pastureland, the banks are very exposed due to extensive grazing. This reach is sustained primarily by stocked fish, but wild trout begin to contribute to the fishery, especially as you move upstream of the Cortland County line. There are a number of large, deep holes between the Cortland County line and West Meeting House Road that harbor some big brown trout. In the fall Virgil Creek is stocked with 1,700 brown trout fingerlings, in the 5.8 mile section between Dryden and West Meeting House Road.

Virgil Creek's reputation as a superlative trout stream rests on the quality of the fishing found in the upper reach of the stream, above West Meeting House Road. It is one of the very few small streams in the region that holds fish up to 6 pounds, and such fish are by no means rare.

Averaging 15 to 20 feet in width, the upper reach of Virgil Creek is actually a series of large deep pools connected by narrow riffs. Flowing through farmlands, swamps and stands of hardwoods, this brush lined section of the stream has a bottom that ranges from silt and gravel to rubble. It is subject to mild seasonal flooding in the spring and suffers from reduced flows in

Above Dryden, Virgil Creek has numerous large pools that hold big carryover browns. A popular local technique for taking these trout is to cast downstream with a K.C. nymph. Twitch the nymph back slowly, but periodically allow it to drift back downstream for a short distance.

the summer. Though normally clear, the water is quickly muddied by even a moderate amount of rain, due to the clay content of the stream banks.

Most of the stream between West Meeting House Road and the village of Virgil meanders through a swampy area. There is a strong infusion of spring water in this reach creating habitat suitable for wild trout. Browns predominate in this section, but brook trout are not uncommon.

Above Virgil, Virgil Creek is very small, but you still find some good size pools that hold large numbers of wild brook trout. Due to the cooling influence of a spring fed tributary that enters the stream above Virgil, this reach of Virgil Creek can be fished through the summer. Don't get your hopes up though. The flow, while cool, is very reduced in summer, and the fish are very easily spooked. Stealth, patience and luck are required tackle when fishing these headwaters. A fly rod could probably be used on some of the stream above Virgil, as well as near Meeting House Road, but most of the upper reach of Virgil Creek is more suited to drifting worms or short casts of small spinners.

The Cortland County section of Virgil Creek is not stocked above West Meeting House Road.

NOTES: _____

_____

_____

_____

WEBSTER BROOK

map coordinates . . . . 42º 35' 50" 76º 17' 06"
USGS map(s) . . . . Groton, Sempronius
location (township) . . . . Groton
access . . . . crossings at Champlain Road and
                               Oldstage Road
principle species . . . . brook trout (stocked & wild)

Webster Brook is a fair quality brook trout stream, tributary to Fall Creek. Averaging 15 feet in width, this stream has a gravel bottom, poor bank cover in its lower sections (due to heavy grazing) but good in other sections and a year round flow of water. In dry summers, the flow is very reduced, and the stream could dry to pools. The surroundings range from active farmlands to abandoned farmlands and swampland. Much of the stream is too small and brushy for fly fishing, but it could be done on some sections. This stream gets a minimal amount of fishing pressure.

There are wild trout in Webster Brook, but most of the fish taken here are stocked trout. The stream is stocked in the fall with 400 brook trout fingerlings in the two mile section immediately above the crossing at Champlin Road.

Some areas of this stream are heavily posted.

NOTES: _____

_____

_____

_____

The Finger Lakes Region has more to offer than just great fishing. It also has some of the most picturesque scenery in the country. An example of what the area has to offer can be seen at Taughannock Falls, pictured at left.

TOMPKINS COUNTY LAKES AND PONDS

BEEBE LAKE

map coordinates	42° 27' 03" 76° 28' 30"
USGS map(s)	Ithaca East
location	on Fall Creek in city of Ithaca
access	via Campus of Cornell University

Physcial Characteristics

area	19 acres
shoreline	0.8 miles
elevation	782 feet
maximum depth	not available
mean depth	not available
bottom type	silt, bedrock

Chemical Characteristics

water clarity	some turbidity
pH	alkaline
oxygen	good

Plant Life

The Lake has a moderate amount of submerged aquatic vegetation.

Species Information

smallmouth bass	very common; growth rate fair
bullhead	common; growth rate good
pumpkinseed	common; growth rate good

Boat Launch Sites

1. None

General Information

Beebe Lake is a small impoundment of Fall Creek (see Tompkins County Streams and Rivers) on the campus of Cornell University, which as long been known for its picturesque setting. Surrounded by mature hardwoods, Beebe Lake offers good fishing for smallmouth bass. The bass in the lake are usually very small, but smallmouth and largemouth bass can be taken from Fall Creek (including Beebe Lake) anywhere above Ithaca Falls, any size, 5 fish per day, from April 1 to November 30.

NOTES: _____

_____

_____

_____

CONNECTICUT HILL STATE WILDLIFE MANAGEMENT AREA

map coordinates	42° 20' 52" 76° 41' 18"
USGS map(s)	Alpine, Mecklenburg
location (township)	Newfield, Enfield (Tompkins County); Catharine, Cayuta (Schuyler County)
access	Carter Creek Road, off Route 13
principle species	largemouth bass

Located 16 miles southwest of Ithaca, the Connecticut Hill Wildlife Management Area is the largest of its kind in the state, totalling 11,610 acres. A part of the Appalachian highlands, the Hill provides a scenic view of much of the surrounding countryside. The area is covered by sub-climax forests of beech, birch, maple and hemlock interspersed with open fields and meadows. A section of the Finger Lakes Trail system winds through Connecticut Hill, as does a shorter DEC Conservation Trail.

For a comprehensive guide to nearly 200 lakes and streams in Western New York obtain a copy of Sander's Fishing Guide - Western New York edition.

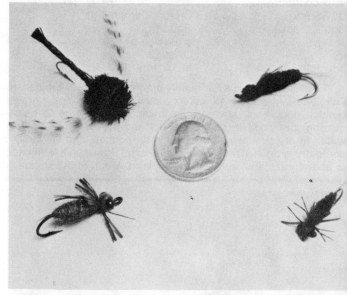

In many small ponds, such as Beebe Lake, the bass are numerous but small. To get the maximum spot out of fishing for them, try using a fly rod. The dragonfly imitations pictured above (adult and nymphs), combirted with a 6 weight fly rod, would be ideal. Also effective are small poppers, Dahlberg Divers and various types of stonefly imitations.

Home to a wide variety of flora and fauna, Connecticut Hill offers a wide variety of outdoor recreational pursuits, including hunting, primitive camping (by permit only), picnicking and cross country skiing. Limited fishing for largemouth bass is available at the pond nearest the refuge headquarters. The other ponds only hold stunted bullheads and few, if any, of the streams in the wildlife area are fishable.

NOTES: _____

_____

_____

DRYDEN LAKE

map coordinates	42° 27' 43" 76° 16' 20"
USGS map(s)	Dryden
location	township of Dryden
access	West Lake Road

Physical Characteristics

area	100 acres
shoreline	2.1 miles
elevation	1156 feet
maximum depth	12 feet
mean depth	approximately 5 feet
bottom type	muck, some gravel

Chemical Characteristics

water clarity	poor
pH	alkaline
oxygen	There is some oxygen depletion of the bottom of Dryden Lake, but it does not affect the fishing.

Plant Life

This lake is extremely weedy throughout. In the summer, Dryden Lake is often choked by weeds. Algae blooms do occur here and affect water clarity.

CONNECTICUT HILL
WILDLIFE
MANAGEMENT
AREA

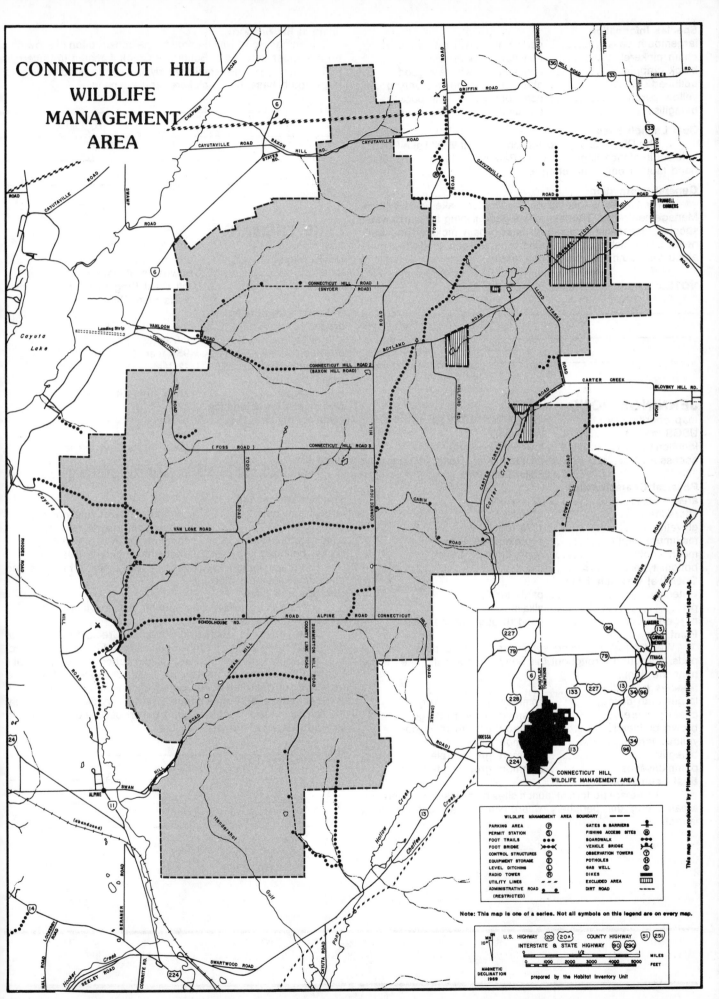

WILDLIFE MANAGEMENT AREA BOUNDARY

PARKING AREA	Ⓟ	GATES & BARRIERS
PERMIT STATION	Ⓢ	FISHING ACCESS SITES Ⓡ
FOOT TRAILS		BOARDWALK
FOOT BRIDGE		VEHICLE BRIDGE
CONTROL STRUCTURES	Ⓒ	OBSERVATION TOWERS Ⓣ
EQUIPMENT STORAGE	Ⓔ	POTHOLES
LEVEL DITCHING		GAS WELL
RADIO TOWER	Ⓡ	DIKES
UTILITY LINES		EXCLUDED AREA
ADMINISTRATIVE ROAD		DIRT ROAD
(RESTRICTED)		

Note: This map is one of a series. Not all symbols on this legend are on every map.

CONNECTICUT HILL, WILDLIFE MANAGEMENT AREA

This map was produced by Pitman-Robertson Federal Aid to Wildlife Restoration Project-W-163-R.04.

U.S. HIGHWAY	⑳ ⑳Ⓐ	COUNTY HIGHWAY ㉛ ㉛ⓘ
INTERSTATE & STATE HIGHWAY	⑨⓪ ②⑨⓪	

MAGNETIC DECLINATION 1969

0 1000 2000 3000 4000 5000   MILES   FEET

prepared by the Habitat Inventory Unit

Species Information

largemouth bass	common; growth rate good
chain pickerel	common; growth rate fair
black crappie.............	common; growth rate good
bullhead	abundant; growth rate very good
yellow perch	common; growth rate poor
bluegills..................	common; growth rate poor

Boat Launch Sites

1. The DEC has a gravel launch ramp off West Lake Road, 1 mile south of the village of Dryden. Parking for 10 cars; no motors; hand launch only - no charge.

General Information

Dryden Lake is located on the Dryden Lake State Wildlife Management Area. The lake offers good fishing for warm water species, especially largemouth bass, chain pickerel and bullhead. Shore fishing is facilitated by a railroad grade that runs along the southwest side of the lake.

NOTES: _____

_____

_____

_____

JENNINGS POND

map coordinates..........	42° 20' 40" 76° 29' 15"
USGS map(s)	Willseyville
location	township of Danby
access	off West King Road, in Buttermilk Falls State Park

Physical Characteristics

area	32 acres
shoreline	1.0 mile
elevation	1278 feet
maximum depth	approximately 8 feet
mean depth	approximately 4 feet
bottom type	muck

Chemical Characteristics

water clarity	partly turbid
pH.......................	alkaline
oxygen...................	good throughout the lake

Plant Life

Weed beds, including submerged aquatic plants and lily pads, are found throughout this pond, except in the deep water near the dam.

Species Informtion

largemouth bass	common; growth rate good
chain pickerel	common; growth rate good
brown bullhead...........	common; growth rate good
yellow perch	common; growth rate poor
bluegills..................	common; growth rate poor
pumpkinseeds	common; growth rate poor

Boat Launch Sites

1. There are no formal launch sites on this lake, but there are areas along the periphery where small boats can be hand launched.

General Information

Jennings Pond was created by the construction of a low dam on the upper reaches of Buttermilk Creek. Located in Buttermilk Falls State Park, this small, weedy pond has good fishing for largemouth bass, chain pickerel and bullhead.

NOTES: _____

_____

_____

_____

LAKE TREMAN

map coordinates..........	42° 24' 02" 76° 30' 47"
USGS map(s)	Ithaca West
location	township of Danby
access	off West King Road, in Buttermilk Falls State Park

Physical Characteristics

area	6.4 acres
shoreline	0.6 miles
elevation	957 feet
maximum depth	12 feet
mean depth	N.A.
bottom type	shale and silt

Chemical Characteristics

water clarity	clear
pH.......................	alkaline
oxygen...................	good throughout the lake

Plant Life

There are some patches of rooted aquatics in the shallower parts of this pond.

Species Information

largemouth bass	common; growth rate good
chain pickerel	uncommon; growth rate poor
smallmouth bass..........	common; growth rate good
brown bullhead...........	uncommon; growth rate fair

There are limited populations of yellow perch, bluegills and pumpkinseeds here also.

Boat Launch Sites

There are no formal boat launch sites on this pond.

General Information

Lake Treman is located on Buttermilk Creek, downstream of Jennings Pond. It has all of the species found in Jennings Pond, but the only species of any significance to anglers are largemouth bass and smallmouth bass. Because of the shale cliffs that surround the pond, shore fishing would be difficult. This pond is best fished from a canoe. Set in a very picturesque area, the fishing in Lake Treman is good, but probably wouldn't be able to handle a lot of fishing pressure.

NOTES: _____

_____

_____

_____

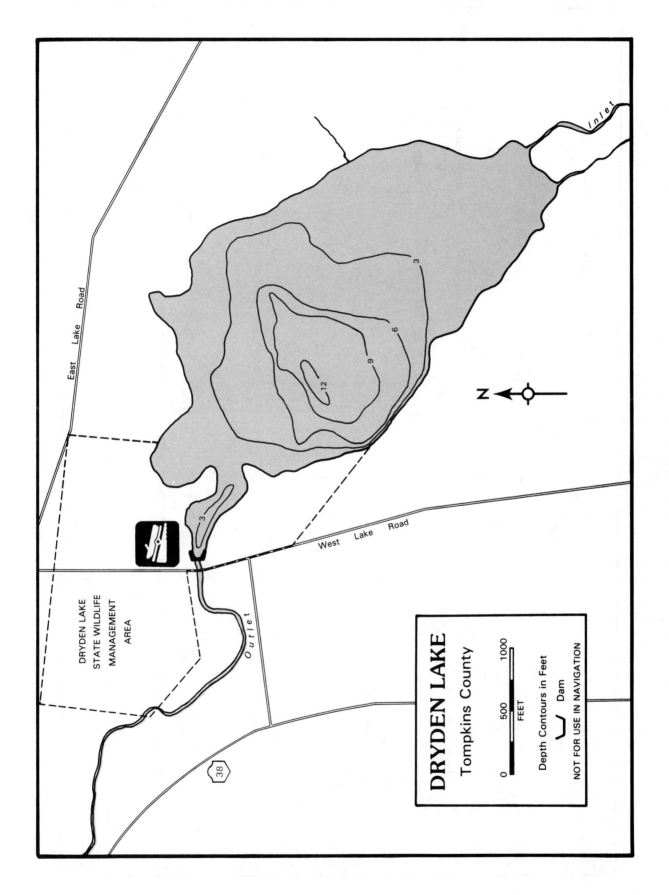

Inlet

East Lake Road

DRYDEN LAKE
STATE WILDLIFE
MANAGEMENT
AREA

3

6

9

12

3

West Lake Road

Outlet

38

N

DRYDEN LAKE
Tompkins County

0   500   1000
FEET

Depth Contours in Feet

Dam

NOT FOR USE IN NAVIGATION

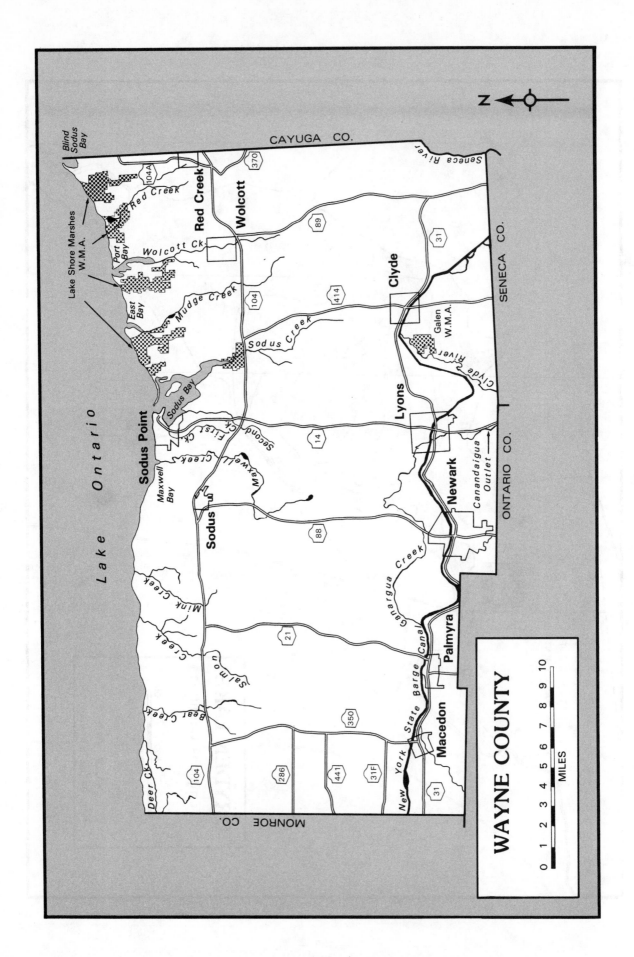

WAYNE COUNTY

0 1 2 3 4 5 6 7 8 9 10
MILES

WAYNE COUNTY STREAMS AND RIVERS

BEAR CREEK

map coordinates . . . . 43º 16' 39'' 77º 16' 36''
USGS map(s) . . . . Furnaceville, Ontario
location (township) . . . . Ontario
access . . . . town of Ontario ramp (open to public during derbies; otherwise open to town residents only) at Bear Creek Harbor off Lake Road in town of Ontario
principle species . . . . brown trout (stocked), rainbow trout (stocked), coho, chinook

The majority of the fishing on Bear Creek takes place in the very lower reaches where the creek mouth widens out to form a small harbor. In the fall there is an unexpectedly good run of brown trout, augmented by limited numbers of rainbow trout, coho salmon and chinook salmon. Trout and salmon fishing here in the spring is only marginal. In its upper reaches this small, gravel bottomed stream has a limited fishery for wild rainbows, but access is restricted by heavy posting. There is no significant warm water fishery in Bear Creek.

Bear Creek is not stocked.

NOTES: _____

_____

_____

_____

CANANDAIGUA OUTLET - see Ontario County Streams and Rivers.

CLYDE RIVER

map coordinates . . . . 42º 59' 58'' 76º 43' 52''
USGS map(s) . . . . Cayuga, Seneca Falls, Savannah, Lyons
location (township) . . . . Galen (Wayne County), Tyre (Seneca County)
access . . . . public access and parking is provided on the section of the river fronted by the Galen Wildlife Management Area off River Road, 2 miles southwest of the village of Clyde. Cartop boats and canoes can be launched here, as well as at lock #27 of the New York State Barge Canal on Lock Road. See also: Montezuma Wildlife Refuge-Seneca County.
principle species . . . . northern pike, largemouth bass, walleye, bullhead, panfish

Meandering through the towns of Tyre and Galen, the Clyde River is a murky, slow moving stream about seventy-five feet in width. Described by one writer as New York's version of a southery bayou, its banks are cloaked by vine draped trees. Numerous partially submerged stumps and brush piles provide habitat for largemouth bass, northern pike and turtles (lots of turtles). In addition, the Clyde River has many deep holes that give up an occassional walleye. Joining, then leaving, the Barge Canal several times, this river is easily accessed and provides a unique setting for fishing, canoeing and nature watching.

This stream is not stocked.

NOTES: _____

_____

_____

DEER CREEK

map coordinates . . . . 43º 16' 33'' 77º 18' 39''
USGS map(s) . . . . Furnaceville, Ninemile Point, Ontario
location (township) . . . . Ontario
access . . . . by permission only - roughly parallelled by Lake Road (Route 18) between Lakeside Road and Ontario Center
principle species . . . . rainbow trout (stocked)

This small gravel bottomed stream should be checked periodically in the spring and fall for lake-run rainbows. It is often closed off by a recurring sand bar at its mouth, but when open it usually gets a respectable run of fish. This lightly fished stream also gets a fair number of stray salmon.

There is no significant warm water fishery in Deer Creek. Deer Creek is not stocked.

NOTES: _____

_____

_____

_____

FIRST CREEK

map coordinates . . . . 43º 15' 44'' 76º 59' 36''
USGS map(s) . . . . Sodus Point, Salmon Creek, Rome, Sodus
location (township) . . . . Sodus
access . . . . bank access by permission only; boat access via Sodus Bay. See Sodus Bay.
principle species . . . . rainbow trout (stocked), brown trout (stocked), coho, chinook, bullhead, panfish

This small tributary of Sodus Bay enters the bay from the west, near Arney's Marine. There's a good run of rainbows in the lower reaches in the spring, with equally good runs of rainbows, brown trout, coho salmon and chinook salmon occurring in the fall. At the mouth of First Creek there is good fishing for brown bullhead and panfish.

First Creek is not stocked.

NOTES: _____

_____

_____

_____

GANARGUA CREEK

map coordinates . . . . 43º 03' 48'' 77º 00' 12''
USGS map(s) . . . . Newark, Palmyra, Macedon, Canandaigua
location (township . . . . Lyons, Arcadia, Palmyra, Macedon (Wayne County); Farmington, Victor (Ontario County)
access . . . . access to this stream can be found at Swift Landing Park, 2 miles east of Palmyra off Hogback Road on north side of canal -hard surface ramp; and at Abbey Park, ¼ mile west of canal lock #27, off Water Street on north side of canal - hard surface ramp.
principle species . . . . smallmouth bass, walleye, bullhead

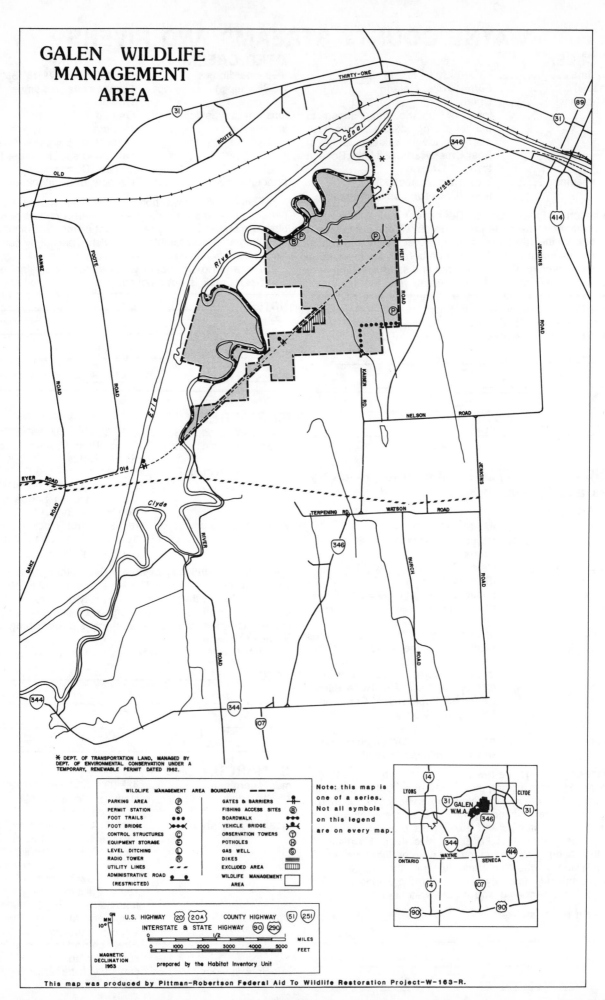

GALEN WILDLIFE MANAGEMENT AREA

※ DEPT. OF TRANSPORTATION LAND, MANAGED BY
DEPT. OF ENVIRONMENTAL CONSERVATION UNDER A
TEMPORARY, RENEWABLE PERMIT DATED 1962.

WILDLIFE MANAGEMENT AREA BOUNDARY	– – – –
PARKING AREA	Ⓟ
PERMIT STATION	Ⓢ
FOOT TRAILS	● ● ●
FOOT BRIDGE	⟩●⟨
CONTROL STRUCTURES	Ⓒ
EQUIPMENT STORAGE	Ⓔ
LEVEL DITCHING	Ⓛ
RADIO TOWER	Ⓡ
UTILITY LINES	–··–··–
ADMINISTRATIVE ROAD	● ●
(RESTRICTED)	
GATES & BARRIERS	
FISHING ACCESS SITES	Ⓑ
BOARDWALK	
VEHICLE BRIDGE	
OBSERVATION TOWERS	Ⓣ
POTHOLES	Ⓗ
GAS WELL	Ⓖ
DIKES	
EXCLUDED AREA	
WILDLIFE MANAGEMENT AREA	

Note: this map is
one of a series.
Not all symbols
on this legend
are on every map.

GN
MN
10°
U.S. HIGHWAY ⟨20⟩ ⟨20A⟩   COUNTY HIGHWAY ⟨51⟩ ⟨251⟩
INTERSTATE & STATE HIGHWAY ⟨90⟩ ⟨290⟩

0   1/2
                              MILES
0   1000 2000 3000 4000 5000
                              FEET

MAGNETIC
DECLINATION
1953
prepared by the Habitat Inventory Unit

This map was produced by Pittman-Robertson Federal Aid To Wildlife Restoration Project-W-163-R.

A long and complicated system, Ganargua Creek originates in Ontario County, where is is known as Mud Creek. Flowing north and east, it momentarily merges with the Barge Canal at Palmyra. It then branches off, wanders east and empties into the canal at Lyons. The portion of the creek associated with the canal system is a well watered, fast moving turbid stream averaging about seventy-five feet in width. Its' banks are overhung by an amazing array of trees, nearly forming a canopy in places. Its muck and rubble bottom is strewn with brush piles and other forms of debris, and there are intermittant weed beds.

The principle game fish in Ganargua Creek are smallmouth bass, and they can be found throughout its length. With the exception of readily available access points, such as bridge crossings in larger towns, this creek is very lightly fished. Biologists at the DEC feel that Ganargua Creek could be a real sleeper in terms of the quality of its bass fishing. You might be pleasantly surprised at the number of "bronzebacks" that can be taken in the more remote sections of this creek.

In addition to smallmouth bass, there is a fair walleye fishery in this stream, especially in the vicinity of Palmyra. There are also several fairly deep sections in the lower portions of Garnargua Creek that could hold walleyes. Limited numbers of northern pike, bullhead, suckers and panfish round out the angling opportunities of this stream.

NOTES: _____
_____
_____
_____

GALEN WILDLIFE MANAGEMENT AREA

map coordinates.......... 43° 05' 00"   76° 55' 00"
USGS map(s)............. Lyons
location (township)....... Galen
access.................. River Road north of Route 344
principle species........ largemouth bass, northern pike, walleye, bullhead, panfish

The Galen Wildlife Management Area was purchased by the state in 1980. Consisting of two parcels of land totaling 741 acres, the area is a mixture of swamps, marshes, wooded flood plains, agricultural plots and wooded uplands. The larger parcel is known as the Ezra and Kate Heit Marsh Unit, is accessible from River Road. the smaller tract, known as Creager Island, is best reached by boat or canoe from either the Clyde River or the Erie Canal.

The area has long been popular with fishermen, hunters and trappers, due to its diverse environment. With extensive frontage on the Clyde River and the nearby Erie Barge Canal, The Galen WMA offer anglers a wide range of fishing opportunities, under a variety of settings. The reach of the Clyde River adjacent to Galen is a slow-moving, murky river, filled with submerged stumps, snags and overhung by vine draped trees. It has a good population of largemouth bass, bullhead, northern pike and panfish, and every so often a lucky angler will take a walleye from one of the deeper holes found along the river. In addition to the fish, the river and surrounding marshlands have excellent populations of turtles. Shore fishing is possible, but the best fishing will be had by drifting a small boat or canoe down the river or canal. there is a hand launch site for car top boats and canoes off River Road.

See also - Clyde River

NOTES: _____
_____
_____
_____

LAKE SHORE MARSHES
Wildlife Management Area

map coordinates......... 43° 20' 00"   76° 55' 00"
USGS map(s)............ Rose, North Wolcott, Sodus Point, Fair Haven
location (township)....... Wolcott, Huron, Rose
access.................. see map for access to individual units
principle species........ rainbow trout, brown trout, lake trout, chinook salmon, coho salmon, smallmouth bass, largemouth bass, northern pike, bullhead, panfish

The Lake Shore Marshes Wildlife Management area is a wetlands complex composed of several units totalling approximately 6,200 areas. Located in northeastern Wayne County, the area exhibits a wide range of natural environments. Within its boundries are lake frontage, bays, marshes and glacial drumlins. Every unit of this wildlife area has some type of aquatic enviornment, giving anglers a remarkably wide choice of species to choose from, with an equally wide choice of settings.

In addition to fishing, Lake Shore Marshes offers the outdoors enthusiast such activities as canoeing, hiking, bird watching and hunting. Hunters will find an abundance of such quarry as squirels, rabbits, woodcocks, pheasants, deer, and water fowl, including black ducks, mallards, wood ducks and teal. On open water areas are found a wide variety of diving ducks. Numerous muskrat and mink provide trapping recreation.

Interim development of the area has included the construction of small water impoundments, parking areas, trails and several boat access sites.

For information on the great fishing to be found in the Lake Shores Wildlife Management Area see: Mudge Creek, Red Creek, Wolcott Creek, Sodus Bay, East Bay, Port Bay, and Lake Ontario.

NOTES: _____
_____
_____
_____

MAXWELL CREEK

map coordinates.......... 43° 15' 16"   77° 01' 33"
USGS map(s)............. Salmon Creek, Sodus, Williamson
location (township)........ Sodus, Marion
access.................. there is a state owned parking and access area on the east side of Maxwell Bay, off Lake Road, between Pultneyville and Sodus Point
principle species.......... rainbow trout (stocked), brown trout (stocked), coho salmon, chinook salmon, bullhead, smelt

The correct name of this stream is Salmon Creek, but it is referred to locally as Maxwell Creek to differentiate it from the Salmon Creek in the township of Williamson.

Because of some as-of-yet unidentified attractant, this creek gets an unusually large run of fish in the spring and fall, and as a result, is probably the most heavily fished stream in Wayne County. A majority of the angling takes place in the lower reaches of the creek, where the mouth forms Maxwell Bay. In late winter and early spring, significant number of lake-run rainbows can be found in Maxwell Creek and rainbows, browns and some stray salmon are found here in the fall. These fish can run upstream about a half-mile to an impassable barrier and land owners in this area usually allow fishing from their property (public fishing rights on this stream are being pursued by the state).

Weekday fishing is more productive on this stream because of angler pressure in the spring and fall. Lake fishing for brown trout just off the creek mouth with floating spawn sacks in February and March is a shore anglers best chance for big fish here.

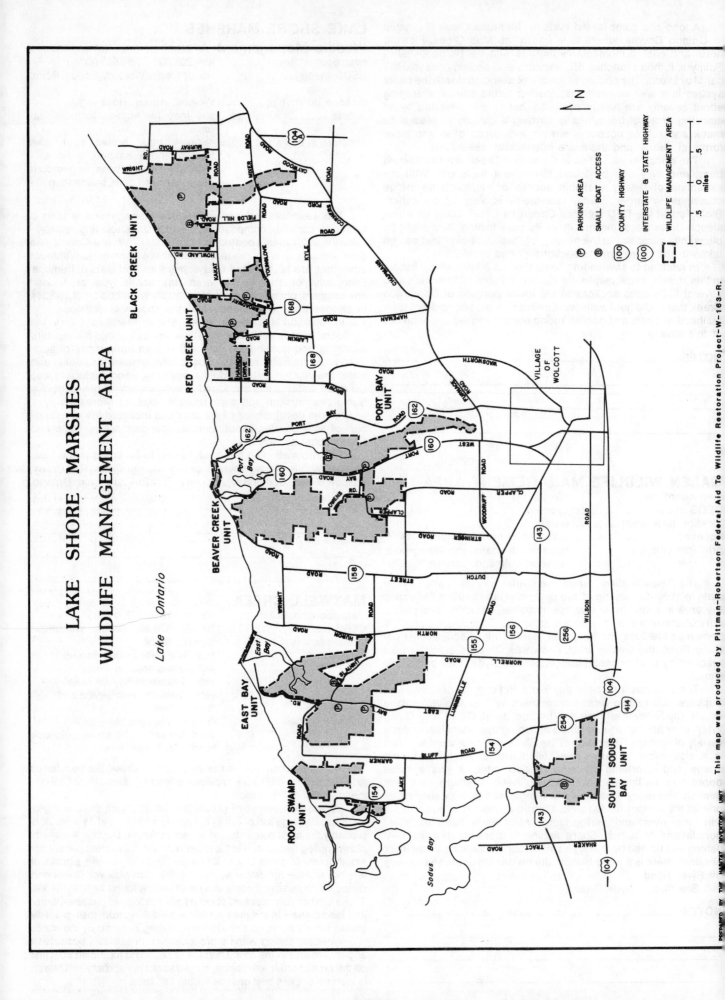

LAKE SHORE MARSHES
WILDLIFE MANAGEMENT AREA

Lake Ontario

PARKING AREA

SMALL BOAT ACCESS

COUNTY HIGHWAY

INTERSTATE & STATE HIGHWAY

WILDLIFE MANAGEMENT AREA

miles

PREPARED BY THE HABITAT INVENTORY UNIT   This map was produced by Pittman-Robertson Federal Aid To Wildlife Restoration Project—W-163-R.

In the spring, there is usually a good run of bullhead and smelt in Maxwell Creek, and an occassional northern pike is taken in the bay.

In the spring of 1986 Maxwell Creek was scheduled to receive 8,000 skamania steelhead.

NOTES: _____

_____

_____

_____

MINK CREEK

map coordinates . . . . 43° 17' 09"   77° 08' 15"
USGS map(s) . . . . Pultneyville, Williamson
location (township) . . . . Williamson
access . . . . Route 18 bridge crossing, 2 miles east of Pultneyville, near Townline Road
principle species . . . . rainbow trout (stocked), brown trout (stocked), coho salmon, chinook salmon

This small, lightly fished tributary of Lake Ontario is often closed off by a recurring sand bar at its mouth, especially when there is a prolonged north wind. However, heavy rains in the spring and fall can open the creek mouth, and bring in good runs of rainbow trout. Some stray pacific salmon and brown trout are also taken here in the fall.

There is no appreciable warm water fishery in this creek. Mink Creek is not stocked.

NOTES: _____

_____

_____

MUDGE CREEK

map coordinates . . . . 43° 16' 52"   76° 53' 48"
USGS map(s) . . . . Sodus Point, North Wolcott, Wolcott
location (township) . . . . Huron, Rose, Butler
access . . . . the lower section of this stream can be accessed at the bridge crossing on North Huron Road near Slaught Road, or via East Bay - see East Bay. The stocked section (above Route 104) is crossed by Salter Road. Permission to fish is usually given by area land owners.
principle species . . . . brook trout (stocked), northern pike, channel catfish, largemouth bass, black crappie, bullhead, white perch

Mudge Creek, a major tributary of East Bay, is presently the only inland stream in Wayne County that is stocked with brook trout. This may change soon, though, as Mudge Creek is scheduled for a quality survey that will probably result in its being dropped from the stocking program. At present, however, this 10 to 15 foot wide, gravel bottomed stream is stocked with between 300 and 400 brook trout, roughly from the road crossing on Route 104 upstream to the streams source.

The extreme lower section of Mudge Creek is a slow moving, muck and rubble bottomed stream feeding into East Bay. Some of the species found in the bay can at times be taken in the stream, but these fish don't generally run very far up the creek.

NOTES: _____

_____

_____

NEW YORK STATE BARGE CANAL

(Wayne County Section)

map coordinates . . . .
USGS map(s) . . . . Motezuma, Cayuga, Seneca Falls, Savannah, Lyons, Newark, Palmyra, Macedon
location (township) . . . . Calen, Lyons, Arcadia, Palmyra, Macedon
access . . . . roughly, parallelled by Route 31 - see below
principle species . . . . northern pike, largemouth bass, walleye, smallmouth bass, bullhead, channel catfish, panfish

From the town of Macedon, near the Monroe County line, eastward to its junction with the Seneca River near the Howland Asland Wildlife Management Area, the New York State Barge Canal serves as a multi-purpose recreational waterway.

For the fisherman, the canal offers a wide variety of warm water species. There are good populations of largemouth and smallmouth bass, northern pike, channel catfish, bullhead and panfish (yellow perch, white perch, rock bass, silver bass, sunfish, crappie). Walleye, while not nearly as common as the bass, are taken occasionally, especially where such large streams as Garnargua Creek and the Clyde River come into the canal. The most productive areas of the canal are the two large wide water sections. One wide water area is located 2 miles west of Macedon, while the other is just west of Newark. These wide water areas are not completely dewatered in the fall and winter, as much of the western portion of the canal is, and this results in less of an impact on the fish and aquatic vegetation found in the canal. Limit catches of largemouth and smallmouth bass are not at all uncommon from these areas, and they are very underutilized.

Boating is another popular activity on the barge canal, and is allowed from May to November. Nearly 90,000 lock passages are recorded on the canal each year. Use of this waterway is toll free and requires no special permits. There are no restrictions on the size of boats or motors, but the maximum speed on the canal is 10 mph. Be sure to check with the New York State Department of Transportation for a complete list of regulations.

Shore access to the barge canal is facilitated by an extensive system of parks and trails. The main section of the trails runs from the Monroe County line east ward to the Newark Canal Park.

Boat Launch Sites (going west to east)

1. Palmyra-Macedon Aqueduck Park - off Route 31, in village of Palmyra. Hard surface ramp on south side of canal - no charge.

2. Swift's Landing Park - off Hogback Road, between Palmyra and Newark. Hard surface ramp on north side of canal - no charge.

3. Wide Water's Park - off Route 31, west of Newark. Hard surface ramp, on south side of canal - no charge.

4. Abbey Park - off Water Street in village of Lyons. Hard surface ramp on south side of canal - no charge.

For more information on the New York State Barge Canal System, write to:

New York State Department of Transportaion
Waterways Maintenance Division
1220 Washington Avenue
Albany, New York 12232

For a complete navigational chart of the canal system (available only for sections of the canal east of Lyons) obtain NOAA Chart #14786.

For a comprehensive guide to nearly 200 lakes and streams in Western New York obtain a copy of Sander's Fishing Guide - Western New York edition.

See also - Clyde River, Ganargua Creek, Cayuga-Seneca Canal, Montezuma Wildlife Management Area, Galen Wildlife Management Area, Howland Island Wildlife Management Area.

NOTES: _____

_____

_____

RED CREEK
map coordinates.......... 43° 18' 30'' 76° 47' 53''
USGS map(s)............. North Wolcott, Fair Haven, Victory
location (township)....... Wolcott (Wayne County); Victory (Cayuga County).
access................. runs through the Red Creek unit of the Lake Shore Marshes Wildlife Management Area. Parking is available on Broadway Road and Larkin Road.
principle species .... rainbow trout (stocked), brown trout (stocked), coho, chinook.

Red creek is one of those small lake Ontario tributaries that can be surprisingly good if conditions are right. Often impounded by a recurrent sand bar at its mouth, this creek, when open, often has good runs of trout in the spring and trout and salmon in the fall. There is no significant warm water fishing here. Like most small tributaries of Lake Ontario, Red Creek is only lightly fished.

NOTES: _____

_____

_____

SALMON CREEK
map coordinates.......... 43° 17' 00'' 77° 11' 07''
USGS map(s)............. Pultneyville, Williamson, Ontario
location (township)....... Williamson
access................. Cornwall's Pultneyville Yacht Club - end of Hamilton Street, off Lake Road (Route 18). Single ramp, no fee. Users are encouraged to park on knoll behind ramp. Also parallelled by Salmon Creek Road.
principle species .... rainbow trout (stocked), brown trout (stocked), coho salmon, chinook salmon

Emptying into Lake Ontario at Pultneyville, Salmon Creek has no problem with recurrent sand bars due to the harbor at its mouth; it is therefore open all year long. The extreme lower portion of Salmon Creek gets a good run of trout and salmon in the spring and fall, but few fish are taken very far up from the harbor area.

NOTES: _____

_____

_____

SECOND CREEK
map coordinates.......... 43° 14' 50'' 76° 58' 29''
USGS map(s)............. Rose
location (township)....... Sodus
access................. heavily posted - must get permission. parallelled by Shaker Road
principle species .... rainbow trout (stocked)

Second Creek is a small tributary of Sodus Bay. There is no problem with sand bars here, and the flow is open all year. The

only significant fishing here if for lake-run rainbow trout in the late fall and spring. These fish can only run a short way upstream to an impassible barrier. This stream is heavily posted, so permission must be gotten from the land owners.

Second Creek is not stocked.

NOTES: _____

_____

_____

SODUS CREEK
map coordinates.......... 43° 13' 00'' 76° 55' 36''
USGS map(s)............. Rose, Wolcott, Savannah
location (township)....... Huron, Rose
access................. runs through the south Sodus Bay unit of the Lake Shore Marshes Wildlife Management Area, accessible via Route 104, 3/5 miles west of Route 414. Small boat access available- see Sodus Bay
principle species .... rainbow trout (stocked), brown trout (stocked), chinook salmon

Also known as Glenmark Creek, an overwhelming majority of the angling on this stream is for lake-run trout and salmon in the spring and fall. A significant number of the chinook salmon stocked in Sodus Bay find their way into this creek, and a recent D.E.C. electroshocking, made in December, near Glenmark Road, produced large numbers of rainbows. It was noted at the time that fishing pressure on Sodus Creek at the time of the shocking was very light.

Snagging is allowed on Sodus Creek, from Ridge Road upstream to an impassible bedrock barrier at Glenmark Road.

In addition to lake-run salmonids, there is a limited fishery for inland brown trout. These fish (1,300) are stocked in a five-mile section of the stream above and below the barrier at Glenmark. There is a good possibility that water quality problems will result in Sodus Creek being dropped from the stocking program in the near future.

A small tributary of this creek, Little Glenmark Creek, enters Sodus Creek near Glenmark Road, and is known to have a small population of wild brook trout. This is at best a very limited fishery, however.

NOTES: _____

_____

_____

WOLCOTT CREEK
map coordinates.......... 43° 16' 21'' 76° 49' 43''
USGS map(s)............. North Wolcott, Wolcott
location (township)....... Wolcott
access................. there is a D.E.C. access site, with parking and gravel ramp, of West Port Bay Road on Port Bay.
principle species .... rainbow trout (stocked), coho salmon, chinook salmon

Wolcott Creek is one of those streams that should be checked periodically in the spring and fall for water conditions. If water levels are sufficient, Wolcott Creek can get runs of trout in the spring and trout and pacific salmon in the fall. There is an impassible barrier on this stream in the town of Wolcott.

This stream is not stocked.

NOTES: _____

_____

_____

WAYNE COUNTY LAKES & PONDS

BLIND SODUS BAY

map coordinates	43° 20' 20" 76° 43' 41"
USGS map(s)	Fair Haven
location	township of Wolcott
access	Blind Sodus Bay Road

Physical Characteristics

area	approximately 250 acres
shoreline	2.3 miles
elevation	246 feet
maximum depth	approximately 15 feet
mean depth	approximately 8 feet
bottom type	rock, rubble, silt

Chemical Characteristics

water clarity	turbid in summer due to algae blooms
pH	alkaline
oxygen	There are no apparent problems with oxygen depletion in this bay.

Plant Life

Weed beds exist along much of the periphery of this bay, outside of the inshore gravel beds. Algae blooms occur here in the summer.

Species Information

walleye	uncommon; growth rate not available
northern pike	common; growth rate good
largemouth bass	common; growth rate good
yellow perch	common; growth rate good

Boat Launch Sites

1. Holiday Harbor Resort, 9415 Blind Sodus Bay Road; single ramp — fee.

General Information

Blind Sodus Bay is one of the smaller of the closed bays that lie along the south shore of Lake Ontario. It has a well balanced population of warm water species and provides good fishing for largemouth bass and northern pike. Historically, this bay had very good fishing for walleye. Until the late 1950's it's extensive gravel beds were a major spawning ground for Lake Ontario walleye. Today, walleye are still found here, but in greatly reduced numbers. Yellow perch are also found in Blind Sodus Bay. As is the case with walleye, their numbers are dependant upon the size of their population in Lake Ontario, which is currently depressed. When the perch population is up, ice fishing for yellow perch is very popular on Blind Sodus Bay.

Interaction of Blind Sodus Bay with Lake Ontario is often restricted due to a recurrent gravel bar at the mouth of the bay. It does break open at times, and the DEC has issued permits to local land owners to open it.

In general, this lightly fished embayment offers fair to good fishing for a wide variety of warm water species. But it isn't really worth driving any great distance for, considering its lack of formal access and the availability of superior fishing sites nearby.

NOTES: _____

_____

_____

_____

EAST BAY

map coordinates	43° 17' 28" 76° 53' 28"
USGS map(s)	Sodus Point
location	township of Huron
access	off Slaght Road, just east of East Bay Road

Physical Characteristics

area	150 acres
shoreline	2 miles
elevation	246 feet
maximum depth	not available
mean depth	10 feet
bottom type	rock, rubble, silt

Chemical Characteristics

water clarity	turbid in summer
pH	alkaline
oxygen	There are no apparent problems with oxygen depletion in this bay.

Plant Life

Extensive weed beds are found throughout this shallow bay. In the summer, it is subject to severe algae blooms.

Species Information

northern pike	common; growth rate good
largemouth bass	common; growth rate good
black crappie	common; growth rate good
channel catfish	uncommon; growth rate good
bullhead	common; growth rate good
yellow perch	common; growth rate good
bluegills	common; growth rate fair
pumpkinseed	common; growth rate fair

Boat Launch Sites

1. There is an unimproved DEC access site suitable for launching cartop boats and canoes off Slaght Road, just east of East Bay Road.

General Information

East Bay is a small, shallow embayment adjacent to a parcel of the Lake Shore Marshes Wildlife Management Area. Very weedy and subject to algae blooms, it has a fair resident population of warm water species. A barrier bar at the mouth of East Bay often closes it off from Lake Ontario. The DEC has

Wayne County has numerous bays and estuaries along the Lake Ontario shore line. These provide much of the lake's warm water habitat.

issued permits to the East Bay Association to open the bar in the summer.

A major problem with East Bay is its lack of good shoreline fishing. Although it is adjacent to state land, the perimeter of the bay is extremely swampy, making it necessary to utilize a boat when fishing here.

East Bay is a good body of water to fish if you're already in the area, but it certainly isn't worth a long drive, especially considering the high quality fishing found in nearby water, such as Sodus Bay.

NOTES: _____

_____

_____

_____

An aerial view of the outlet at Port Bay. Some of the best fishing for smallmouth bass on Lake Ontario is found in the waters just off Port Bay. Photo courtesy New York State DEC.

PORT BAY

map coordinates.........	43⁰ 17' 54" 76⁰ 49' 52"
USGS map(s).............	North Wolcott — see also NOAA Chart #14804
location.................	townships of Huron and Wolcott
access..................	West Port Bay Road

Physical Characteristics

area.....................	approximately 750 acres
shoreline................	10 miles
elevation................	246 feet
maximum depth..........	35 feet
mean depth.............	18 feet
bottom type.............	rock, rubble, silt

Chemical Characteristics

water clarity.............	turbid in summer due to algae blooms
pH......................	alkaline
oxygen..................	There are no apparent problems with oxygen depletion in this bay.

Plant Life

Extensive weed beds are found in water up to 15 feet deep. The smaller bays and the lower end of Port Bay are weed choked. In the summer this bay suffers from algae blooms.

Species Information

chinook salmon..........	seasonal (fall)
brown trout.............	seasonal (spring and fall)
rainbow trout............	seasonal (spring and fall)
largemouth bass.........	common; growth rate very good
smallmouth bass.........	seasonal (spring)
rock bass...............	seasonal (spring)
northern pike............	common; growth rate good
yellow perch............	seasonal (spring and fall)
bluegills................	common; growth rate fair
pumpkinseed............	common; growth rate fair
walleye.................	rare; growth rate not available
crappie.................	seasonal (spring)

Boat Launch Sites

1. DEC fishing access site, off West Port Bay Road at southern end of the bay. Single gravel ramp, parking, hand launching only — no charge.

2. Pier One Marina, West Port Bay Road, just south of Loon Point. Double hard surface ramp, dockage, fuel, bait, — fee.

3. DEC fishing access site, on west barrier bar, off West Port Bay Road. Double ramp, parking for about 20 cars — no charge. **Note!** This launch site can be rendered unusable during periods of high water on Lake Ontario.

4. McCoy's Port Bay Marina, East Port Bay Road, Wolcott. Single hard surface ramp, docks, fuel, parking, lodging — fee.

Note: When the road on the west barrier bar is serviceable, you can access the concrete groin at the end of the bar, which was designed to accommodate handicapped anglers.

General Information

Port Bay offers anglers good to excellent fishing for a wide variety of warm water species and seasonal fishing for trout and salmon.

In the spring, large numbers of brown trout will be found in the bay if the forage fish, alewives and smelt, come in to spawn. This doesn't appear to happen every year, but when it does the brown trout fishing in Port Bay can be very good. Limited numbers of rainbow trout will also follow the forage fish into the bay. Most of the trout are taken by trolling with flat lines, but shore bound anglers can be successful fishing from docks or from the barrier bar at the north end of the bay. The trout will remain in the bay until the alewives and smelt leave, usually in early June.

In the fall, tremendous numbers of trout and salmon will concentrate along the shore of Lake Ontario in the Port Bay area. (The same concentration of trout and salmon occurs in the spring as well). The bay lies between two of the most heavily stocked sections of Lake Ontario, Sodus Bay and Little Sodus Bay. Port Bay, though it's not stocked, benefits from this near shore concentration of salmonids. Beginning shortly after Labor Day fishing from the barrier bar for both trout and salmon picks up. By mid-October the salmon, almost exclusively chinook, will move into the bay to spawn, followed in November by brown trout and rainbow trout. Although the bay only gets an influx of stray salmonids, the quality of these spawning runs are surprisingly good. These fish quickly find their way into the southern end of the bay and Wolcott Creek, and the fishing can be extremely good.

The end of the spawning runs doesn't necessarily mean the end of trout fishing in Port Bay. Significant numbers of brown trout and rainbow trout winter over in this bay providing some fast action through the ice.

Trout aren't the only Lake Ontario species to migrate into Port Bay. In the spring, smallmouth bass come into the bay to spawn and significant numbers of them will still be available to fishermen when bass season opens. Early in the season the channel at the mouth of the bay will often have spectacular bass fishing. In the bay itself, check out any point jutting out into deep water. Most of the smallmouth bass will be out of Port Bay by the first of July. But you don't have to travel far to find them. The shoals just off the mouth of Port Bay provide some of the best bass fishing on all of Lake Ontario (see the section on Lake Ontario for more information on this exciting and underutilized fishery).

Rockbass also move into the bay in the spring, often in tremendous numbers. They average ½ to 1 pound in size and

— 148 —

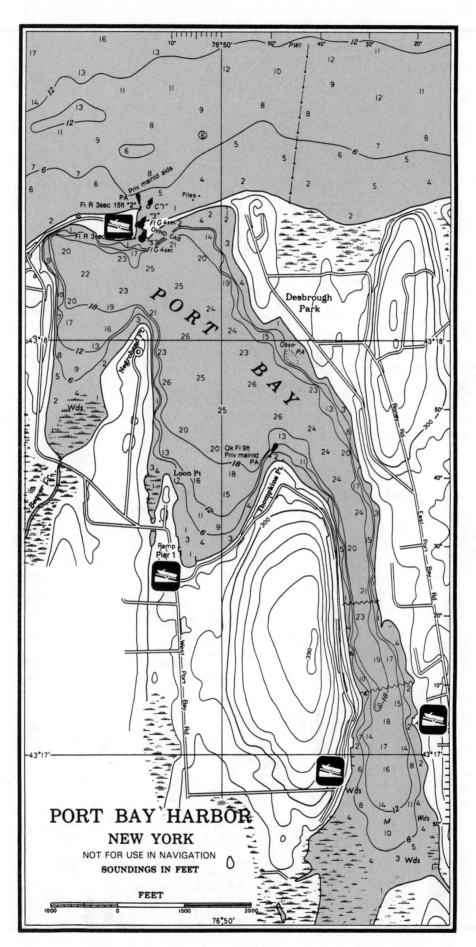

PORT BAY

Desbrough
Park

PORT BAY HARBOR
NEW YORK
NOT FOR USE IN NAVIGATION
SOUNDINGS IN FEET

FEET

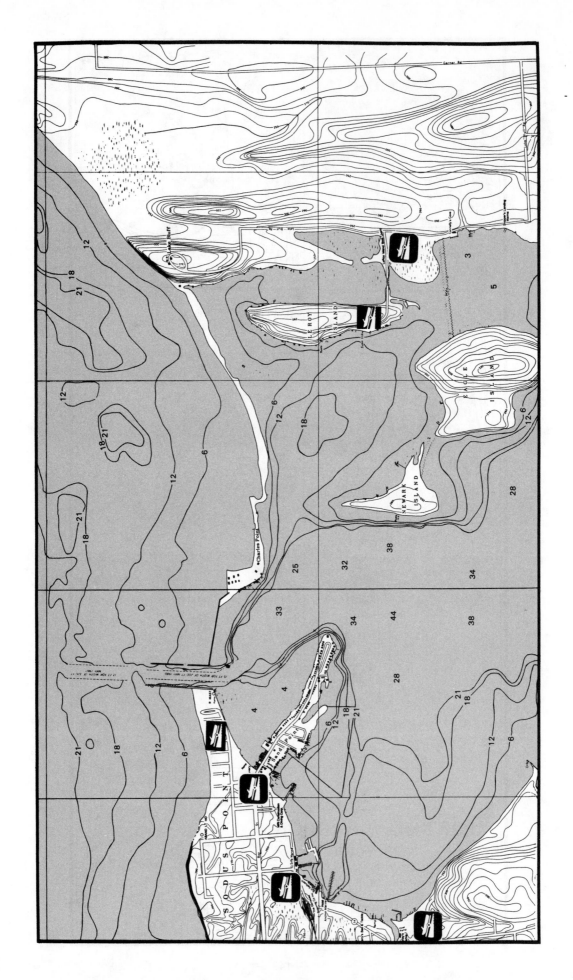

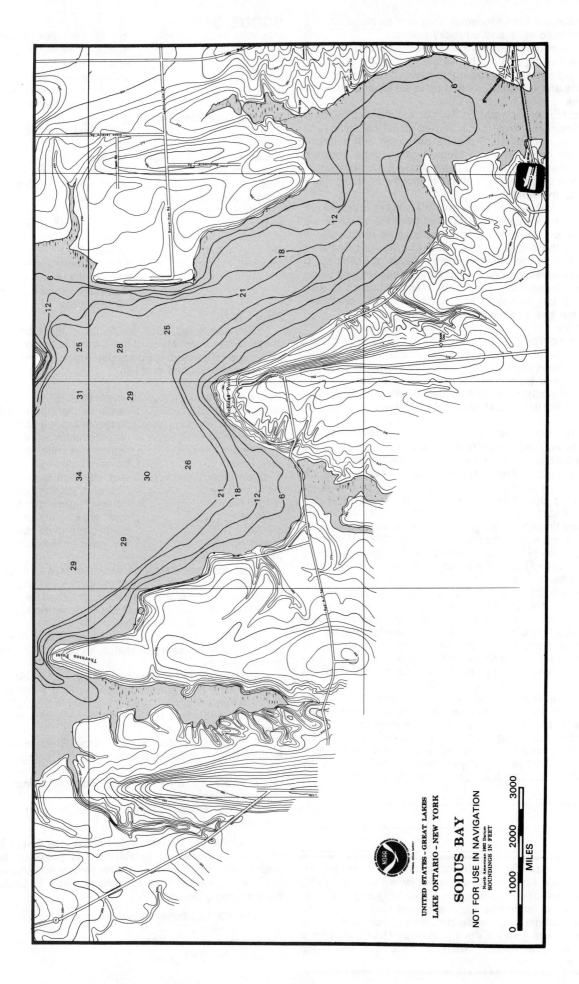

UNITED STATES - GREAT LAKES
LAKE ONTARIO - NEW YORK

SODUS BAY

NOT FOR USE IN NAVIGATION

North American 1982 Datum
SOUNDINGS IN FEET

MILES

0   1000   2000   3000

much larger fish are not uncommon. They can be found around docks, along weed lines and off rocky points.

Most of the crappie found in Port Bay are also migratory fish from the lake, moving into the bay in the spring (just about the time that apple trees are blossoming) to spawn. They are found in good numbers around the docks and up in the lower reaches of Wolcott Creek.

In the not too distant past Port Bay had excellent spring runs of big Lake Ontario bullhead. Local anglers report that these runs are now greatly diminished. But that's not to say that bullhead can't be taken here. The bay does have a good resident population of these tasty fish. You can still take good numbers of brown bullhead fishing at night off creek mouths or along shore lines roiled by the wind.

Yellow perch are still an important fishery in this area, though their numbers are considerably reduced from the levels of the early 1980's. From early May to late June big lake-run perch will be found near the shore of Lake Ontario in the Port Bay area (Some local anglers take large numbers of perch by sneaking up on them with an electric motor while they're concentrated along the shore and fishing with small jigs). Many of these fish also move into the bay to spawn and will be found in shallower sections of the bay and near creek mouths.

Early in the summer the yellow perch move out of the bay into Lake Ontario. They return again in the fall and can be caught in deeper parts of Port Bay and on points and drop-offs. Significant numbers of yellow perch will winter over here and still provide some good ice fishing. The winter perch fishing seems to be the best just after the bay freezes (usually late December) and just before ice-out (March). Most perch will be taken in at least 20 feet of water.

In the summer, most of the fishing in Port Bay is for largemouth bass. They can be found nearly anywhere along the perimeter of the bay in water up to 15 feet. The bass here average about 1½ pounds, but several fish over 7 pounds have been taken from these waters over the years. Concentrate your efforts on deep weed lines, downed trees and around docks. For an added advantage, check out the bay about one week after weed harvesters are brought in (the harvesters are scheduled to clean out sections of the bay for the first time this year (1987). Very often the channels these machines make through large weed beds serve as ambushing sites for predatory fish, such as largemouth bass and northern pike.

Port Bay also has excellent fishing for northern pike. As with largemouth bass, they can be found all along the perimeter of the bay, as well as in the lower reaches of Wolcott Creek and under docks. The best time of the year to take northerns is in September and October, but a few old timers still fish for these toothsome predators in June, July and August using flat lines, and they usually do fairly well. Many pike are also taken here through the ice.

At one time, Port Bay had excellent seasonal fishing for walleye, but with the collapse of the Lake Ontario walleye fishery this came to an end. If the bay still holds a few old remnant fish, they are either not being caught or not being reported. This dismal situation could come to an end in the near future, however, if a walleye rearing project, being carried out jointly by Sea Grant, the DEC and local private groups, is successful.

NOTES: _____

_____

_____

A log book can be an invaluable addition to an angler's tackle box, be he a novice or an expert. Like any other endeavor, fishing is a learning experience. Properly used, written logs can not only help you figure out what you're doing right, but more importantly, what you're doing wrong, thus turning a bad day on the water into a valuable learning experience.

SODUS BAY

map coordinates	43° 15' 26" 76° 58' 01"
USGS map(s)	Sodus Point, Rose — see NOAA chart #14814
location	townships of Huron and Sodus
access	Route 14 or Ridge Road — see launch sites below

Physical Characteristics

area	approximately 3000 acres
shoreline	not available
elevation	246 feet
maximum depth	44 feet
mean depth	approximately 20 feet
bottom type	rock, rubble, silt

Chemical Characteristics

water clarity	slightly turbid in summer due to algae
pH	alkaline
oxygen	There is thermal stratification in this bay in the summer, and oxygen depletion occurs in water over 25 feet deep.

Plant Life

Extensive weed beds are found in most areas of the bay under 12 feet deep. Many of the smaller bays are weed choked, as is the southern end of Sodus Bay. Algae blooms do occur here but are not a serious problem.

Species Information

chinook salmon	seasonal (fall)
rainbow trout	seasonal (spring and fall)
brown trout	seasonal (spring and fall)
largemouth bass	very common; growth rate good
smallmouth bass	seasonal (spring)
rock bass	seasonal (spring)
northern pike	very common; growth rate good
black crappie	common; growth rate good
yellow perch	common; growth rate good
walleye	rare; growth rate good
bluegill	common; growth rate good
brown bullhead	common; growth rate good

Boat Launch Sites

1. Sodus Point Park - on Wickham Blvd - adjacent to Coast Guard Station. Double hard surface ramps, parking — no charge. Ramps closed Memorial Day through Labor Day.

2. Krenzer Marine - on Greig Street in Sodus Point. Single ramp, fuel, marine sales — fee.

3. Haher's Sodus Point Bait Shop - Greig Street in Sodus Point. Multiple hard surface ramps, fuel, bait, tackle, boat rentals, dockage — fee.

4. Town of Sodus Municiple ramp - off Route 14 in Sodus Point. Double hard surface ramps, parking — no charge.

5. Arney's Marina - 7254 Route 14N in Sodus Point. Double hard surface ramps, fuel, parking, marine repairs, marine sales — fee.

6. Bay Bridge Sport Shop - Ridge Road (west end of Bay Bridge). Double ramps, fuel, boat and motor rentals, bait, tackle — fee.

7. Fowler's Marina - Leroy Island. Single ramp, fuel, marine repairs, marine sales — fee.

8. Cove Marina - Leroy Island. Single ramp, fuel, dockage, bait, tackle — fee.

In addition to the sites listed above, the Sodus Bay area is serviced by numerous establishments providing bait, tackle, marine services and supplies, boat rentals and charter services. For a complete listing of services available in Sodus Bay and Wayne County contact:

The Wayne County Public Information Office
Department J87
Lyons, New York 14487
(315) 946-6191

General Information

Sodus Bay offers anglers some of the best fishing on all of Lake Ontario. Combining excellent year round fishing for warm water species with massive seasonal influxes of salmonids, the bay is one of the most versatile and productive bodies of water in New York State. Conveniently situated mid-way between Rochester and Syracuse, the bay offers anglers a safe haven to fish when inclement weather makes Lake Ontario too rough for boating. Because of its size and central location, the bay also serves as the main port for charter boats that ply Lake Ontario (a listing of charter services can be obtained from the address listed above).

Pleasure boating is very popular here, and because of this fishing in the congested north-western section of Sodus Bay is best when done early in the morning or at night. On weekends sail boat races are held in the central portion of the bay, limiting fishing in that area. Aside from these minor restrictions, Sodus Bay is wide open to the fisherman.

Principle species in the bay include:

Chinook Salmon: Approximately 200,000 chinook salmon are stocked in Sodus Bay annually, and when they return to their natal waters to spawn the concentrations of salmon in this area is incredible. Shortly after Labor Day anglers will begin to pick up chinook from the pier and from near shore areas of Lake Ontario. When conditions are right the salmon begin to move into the bay itself, providing some of the best salmon fishing on all of Lake Ontario. When the salmon come in to the bay, most of them will head for shallow water. Many anglers will have success simply fishing from docks or from the Bay Bridge at the southern end of the bay. Some local fishermen recommend using a small (14 foot) boat equippped with an electric motor or oars. The electric motor or oars are less likely to spook the fish and will allow you to get close enough to cast to them. Contrary to what many people believe, chinook will hit a lure during their spawining phase, either out of anger or sheer orneriness. Often you can see the fish on the surface of the water. Cast ahead of them as you would for bass, using nearly any type of spoon, spinner or plug - Donnie Davenport, of Davenport and Son Boat Livery, took a 43 pound chinook on a bass plug several years ago while fishing off Grassy Point. Remember that you're not necessarily trying to match a food pattern, just trying to entice the salmon to strike.

Chinook salmon will be found all along the shore line of the bay in the fall. Eventually a great many of them will find their way into Sodus Creek (known locally as Glenmark Creek) at the southern end of the bay. Snagging is permitted in Sodus Creek, between Ridge Road (the Bay Bridge) upstream to the impassible falls at Glenmark Road, from August 15 through November 15. Be sure to check your state regulations guide for current regulations.

Brown Trout: Brown trout are not stocked in Sodus Bay, but they do contribute to the fishery here. In the spring, large numbers of brown trout move into the channel and the bay (May). They move into this area for a number of reasons. The temperature of the water in the channel is in the mid 50's at this time, ideal for browns. They also come into the bay to feed. Massive numbers of forage fish, primarily alewives, move into the bay in early May to spawn and the trout follow them in and gorge themselves. Usually, so many alewives are in Sodus Bay at this time that it can make fishing rather difficult. Most browns are taken from the west pier or by trolling in the central portion of the bay. Many anglers prefer to troll in thirty feet of water in a circle roughly bound by Eagle Island, Sand Point and the mouth of Second Creek. Trolling with flat lines (at least 150 feet), using spoons or rapalas is very effective.

While the brown trout will usually be found in the deeper parts of the bay, they do occasionally concentrate in shallower water (12 to 15 feet) between Thornton Point and Nichols Point.

If the areas mentioned above are unproductive, try fishing off Newark Island. The sharp drop-off on the west side of the island usually holds good numbers of browns in the spring. This trout fishery lasts until about the first week in June, when they move back out into the lake. The only other time when browns will be found here is in the winter, when very limited numbers are taken through the ice.

The author with a hefty smallmouth taken from the channel at Sodus Bay. Smallmouth often foray into the bay from the lake to feed.

Rainbow Trout: Rainbow trout are stocked near the mouth of Sodus Bay (20,000 yearlings per year). These fish tend to home in on the bay in October and this results in a very productive fishery. Good numbers of rainbows are taken from the west pier by anglers using egg sacs. The pier can get pretty crowded, but there are plenty of fish for everyone. Eventually these rainbows will move into tributaries of Sodus Bay to spawn (primarily First, Second and Third Creeks). There is little fishing for these rainbows when they run into the streams due to heavy posting. There are some open areas on Third Creek. A few fish will be taken through the ice in the winter.

Largemouth Bass: In the summer, largemouth bass constitute the primary fishery in Sodus Bay. The average bucketmouth taken from this bay weighs in at about 2½ pounds, but fish up to 7 pounds are caught on occasion. The fishing is good all season long, but as in the case with other largemouth waters, the best fishing occurs in the late summer and fall. Essentially any shallow water area in Sodus Bay will hold at least a few bass, but some areas are decidedly better than others. Some of the prime largemouth locations include: above and below Grassy point (this is one of the best bass hang-outs on the bay); the shallows around Leroy Island; the shallows between Eagle Island and the east shore of the bay; the shallows from the mouth of Clark's Creek down to the east side of the Bay Bridge; the weed line that runs from Nichols Point down to the mouth of Third Creek and up to Thornton Point; the weed beds just off the mouth of Second Creek; the sunken pier on the west side of Newark Island and the shallows off the east side of the island; and the shallow weed beds off the north side of Eagle Island. Concentrate your efforts on weed lines, docks and other submerged structure, using standard bass hardware (crankbaits, large spinnerbaits, rubber worms, etc.). Your chances of taking a limit of largemouth bass is good, even if you're only a beginner. The quality of the bass fishing here is so good that it draws bass clubs from all over the state and there are those who argue that Sodus Bay has the best largemouth fishing in the state.

Smallmouth Bass: In the spring, great numbers of smallmouth bass move into Sodus Bay to spawn. While a majority of these fish will have moved back into Lake Ontario when bass season opens, enough of them will be left to provide a few weeks of good fishing. A few fish will be found in shallow water (less than 15 feet) in the bay, but most of smallmouth will be taken by anglers fishing from the piers or trolling in the channel. Locals favor crankbaits, hair jigs and soft shell crabs. As the season progress, essentially all of the smallmouth will move out into the lake. By the end of July or early August, smallmouth bass will again be found in good numbers off the Sodus Bay Piers and in the channel, feeding on bait fish. The bass fishing at this time can be quite good.

Rock Bass: In the spring, tremendous numbers of rock bass migrate into Sodus Bay from Lake Ontario to spawn. These are big fish, many weighing in well over a pound. The fishing is excellent until about the second week of June. Literally tons of these scrappy fighters (and tasty table fare) are harvested between ice-out and their exodus to the lake. Small worms, spinners, surface poppers, wet flies and leeches are all highly effective for rock bass. One of the best rockbass hotspots in the bay is the sunken pier off the west side of Newark Island — the action here can be fantastic! Other productive areas include: the west side of Leroy Island; the north side of Sand Point; the shore line between Thornton Point and the mouth of First Creek; and the rip-rap along the foot of the west pier.

Northern Pike: Sodus Bay has some truly excellent fishing for northern pike. The average pike here runs 6 to 8 pounds, but fish up to 16 pounds are taken on occasion.

Early in the season try still fishing with live bait (large chubs, shiners, etc.) close to the bottom. Concentrate your efforts around the edges of weed beds, rock piles and drop-offs. Later in the spring switch to spinnerbaits, spinners (Panther Martins, Mepps Aglia, etc.) or live baits fished with a bobber.

In the summer and fall northern pike are found in basically the same areas as largemouth bass. Traditionally, flat lining with copper wire, trailing spoons, was the method most commonly used to take pike during this period. Few people use this method now, although it certainly would work, as would regular trolling, using spoons, large spinners or jointed plugs. A very productive troll, especially in the fall, follows the outer weed line that runs in 10 to 15 feet of water from Thornton Point to just south of Grassy Point and back up the east shore of the bay to the southern end of the area known as the "Pork Barrel." The troll then continues along the southern shore of Eagle Island; and Newark Island and back to Thornton Point. Other areas that are extremely productive include: The "Pork Barrel" (this area is excellent all season long); the drop-offs on the west side of Newark Island and the south west side of Eagle Island.

In the winter, Sodus Bay has some of the best ice fishing in the state for northern pike. Usually, the first section of the bay to freeze up is Connelly's Cove (east of Eagle Island) and the southern end of the bay, both of which have excellent pike fishing. When the entire bay freezes safely, northerns will be found around the islands, off points and in shallow, weedy areas. Standard tip-ups baited with large chubs or shiners should produce some very exciting action.

Black Crappie: A majority of the crappie (known locally as strawberry bass) in Sodus Bay are fish migrating in from Lake Ontario to spawn. Good numbers of these tasty fish start showing up on stringers around the middle of April and provide some good fishing until the bay warms up in late spring. Nearly the entire shoreline of the bay will be productive. Use ultra light tackle when fishing for crappie and set your drag lightly. They have very soft mouths and the hook can easily be pulled out. Small live minnows are a top bait when fished with a bobber, but small spinners, jigs dressed with Mister Twister tails or small red worms will also work well.

Yellow Perch: The perch fishing in Sodus Bay is mainly dependant upon the stock of fish in Lake Ontario. At present, the population of yellow perch in the lake is depressed, due primarily to predation on perch fry by alewives. Nevertheless, enough perch do come into Sodus Bay to make for a fairly good fishery. They begin moving into the bay around the middle of November.

The walleye population in Lake Ontario has collapsed, but there are a few caught in the shallower portions of the lake and in the bays each year. These are generally old and large fish. Bill Abraham, pictured above is responsible for managing the region #8 portion of Lake Ontario. Photo courtesy New York DEC.

A majority of the perch caught in the fall are taken from the deep central portion of Sodus Bay, off Newark Island and Eagle Island. Good numbers are also taken from the deep hole between Charles Point and Sand Point. Minnows fished close to the bottom will be very effective during this period. Using perch rig (spreaders) will increase your catch considerably.

In the winter, ice-fishing is very popular on Sodus Bay and yellow perch are a principle quarry. A lot of fish will be taken from the deep water areas, but a number of other sites begin to produce, as well. The drop-off at the northern end of Thronton Point is a prime area for taking perch through the ice. The same is true for the shallows just south of Newark Island, off the mouth of Third Creek and in the southern end of the bay, south of Nichols Point. The ice fishing will be good all winter, with especially good fishing coming just after ice-up (early January) and just prior to ice-out (March).

Yellow perch spawn in the spring. Shortly after ice-out they will be found in very shallow areas in very impressive numbers. While many areas along the shoreline of the bay will hold perch, some areas are known to be especially productive. The shallows along the breakwall, between the east pier and Charles Point, is always a spring hotspot. The shoreline above and below the mouth of Clark's Creek, the bay off Second Creek and Third Creek and the weed beds above and below Grassy Point also produce well. Nichols Point also has good spring perch fishing but because of its exposure to the wind, it's a difficult area to fish on anything but a calm day. Fishing from the Bay Bridge can also be productive. Local anglers find minnows and jigs to be the best baits for spring time perch. Fish the jig near the bottom, with the minnow rigged about a foot above it.

After spawning, a majority of the yellow perch vacate Sodus Bay. There is a fair population of small resident perch in the bay but most of these are only taken incidentally while fishing in smallmouth bass territory.

Brown Bullhead: Sodus Bay has some of the very best bullhead fishing in Central New York. The bay has a good population of resident bullhead, and gets a very good run of lake-run fish in the spring. These Lake Ontario Bullhead are big (1 pound and up) and essentially free of contaminants.

The best bullhead fishing takes place in the spring (late March through early April). The evening after the first heavy rainstorm after ice is off the bay is always an exceptionally productive period. Bullhead prefer muddy, roiled water. Check out the mouth of streams discharging muddy water into the bay, marshy shorelines stirred up by carp or shorelines roiled by the wind. Some of the more productive areas in the bay include: off the Bay Bridge; the marshland oppositive the east side of Leroy Island; the mouths of all major streams, especially off the mouth of Third Creek. The bullhead fishing will be good for about four weeks.

Bluegill: Bluegills are a popular quarry on Sodus Bay. The chances of taking a mess of big (½ pound and bigger) tasty bluegills bring scores of fishermen to the bay. They can be found almost anywhere in the bay in water 2 to 15 feet deep, all year long. Especially productive bluegill fishing occurs just as soon as Sodus Bay freezes. The water between Eagle Island and Connelly's Cove, and the south end of the bay near the Bay Bridge often produce excellent catches of fish at this time. In the spring, soon after ice-out, bluegills can be taken in good numbers off the west side of Leroy Island, from the Bay Bridge and from the weed beds above and below Grassy point.

NOTES: _____

_____

_____

_____

An aerial view of Sodus Bay, showing Leroy Island and Eagle Island. This section of Sodus Bay has outstanding fishing for northern pike, largemouth bass and panfish. Photo courtesy New York State DEC.

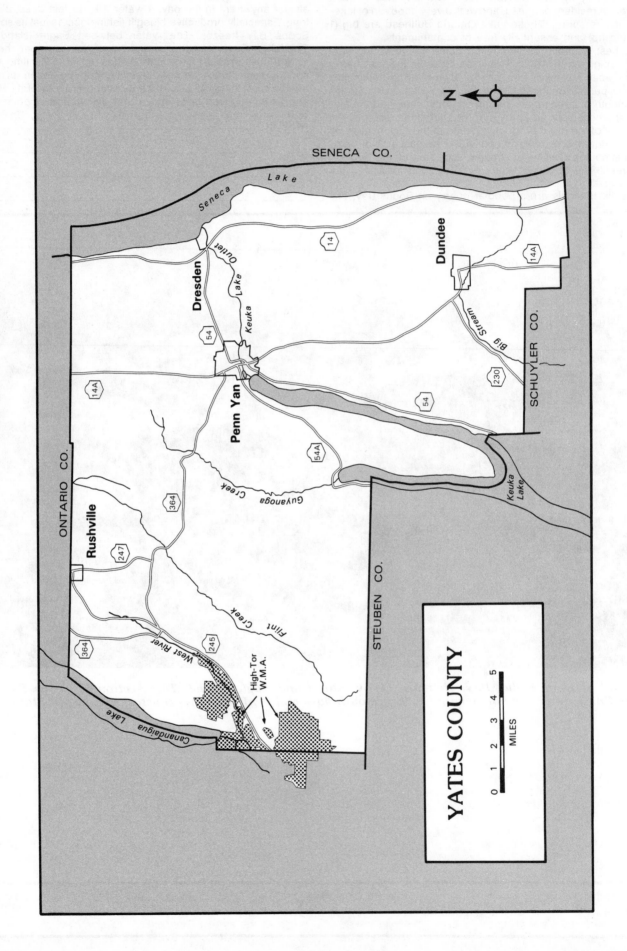

SENECA CO.

Seneca Lake

Seneca

Dundee

14

14A

Dresden

Lake Keuka Outlet

54

Big Stream

SCHUYLER CO.

Penn Yan

14A

230

54

54A

Keuka Lake

ONTARIO CO.

Guyanoga Creek

Rushville

364

247

Flint Creek

STEUBEN CO.

364

245

West River

High-Tor
W.M.A.

Canandaigua Lake

YATES COUNTY

0 1 2 3 4 5

MILES

N

YATES COUNTY STREAMS & RIVERS

BIG STREAM

map coordinates . . . . 42° 29' 24" 76° 54' 42"
USGS map(s) . . . . Reading Center, Dundee, Keuka
                                    Park, Wayne
location (township) . . . . Starkey, Barrington
access . . . . crossed by Charles VanGorden
                                    Road
principle species . . . . brown trout (wild)

As the name implies, Big Stream is a sizeable tributary, at least in terms of its length. Unfortunately, very little of the stream supports a viable fishery. The section that is fishable runs from the Schuyler/Yates County line downstream (north) ½ mile to the mouth of tributary #7. This section is roughly parallelled by Crystal Spring Road. Averaging about 15 feet in width this portion of Big Stream is lined with alders, has a gravel and rubble bottom and flows through a sparsely settled valley. Fishable all trout season, this reach has a good flow of cold, spring-fed water and supports a nice population of wild brown trout. Due to its short length, Big Stream probably isn't worth a special trip, especially considering the wealth of trout streams in the region. But if you're in the neighborhood, the spring-fed section of Big Stream can be well worth investigating.

NOTES: _____

_____

_____

_____

The upper reaches of Flint Creek are generally very brushy. But some sections, such as that pictured above, are wide open and lined with rip-rap. The rip-rap is there to stabilize the stream's banks during periods of high water flow. A unique aspect of this stream is the non-migratory strain of rainbow trout found in its head waters. Photo courtesy New York State DEC.

FLINT CREEK (Yates County Section)

map coordinates . . . . 42° 57' 39" 77° 02' 59"
USGS map(s) . . . . Phelps, Stanley, Rushville, Potter,
                                    Pulteney, Prattsburg
location (township) . . . . Potter, Italy
access . . . . parallelled and crossed by Italy
                                    Valley Road (County Road 18)
principle species . . . . rainbow trout (wild), brown trout
                                    (stocked)

Flint Creek is an extremely long stream, rising out of the hills of northern Steuben County and emptying into Canandaigua outlet in northern Ontario County. Most of the stream, however, flows through a vast muckland, is dredged and is entirely uninviting. The fishable portion of the stream runs from just above (south) of the Steuben/Yates County line downstream 6.5 miles, or about 3 miles downstream of the hamlet of Italy.

This upper reach of Flint Creek is known locally as Italy Valley Creek. A good quality trout stream, it averages, depending on rainfall, 15 to 30 feet in width, has a gravel and rubble bottom and is fishable all season. It has a moderate gradient, a good riffle/pool ratio and streamside cover consists of woody vegetation and mature, overhanging trees. The sections where the stream could be fly fished are very limited.

In the very uppermost reach of Flint Creek there is a resident (i.e. non-migratory) population of wild rainbow trout, which is quite unique in this region. Few of these fish will be larger than 7 or 8 inches, but their numbers are significant and they do consistitute a viable fishery.

As you move downstream to the hamlet of Italy, Flint Creek grades to a stocked brown trout stream, and remains so to the most downstream crossing of Italy Valley Road.

There is a lot of posting on the trout section of Flint Creek, but most land owners will grant permission to fish the stream if asked. In the spring, Flint Creek is stocked with 400 brown trout yearlings, from the hamlet of Italy downstream 3 miles to the most downstream crossing of Italy Valley Road.

NOTES: _____

_____

_____

_____

GUYANOGA CREEK

map coordinates . . . . 42° 35' 49" 77° 08' 53"
USGS map(s) . . . . Pulteney, Penn Yan, Potter
location (township) . . . . Jerusalem, Potter
access . . . . crossed by Route 54A near Branch-
                                    port - see below
principle species . . . . rainbow trout (wild), bullhead

Known locally as Sugar Creek, Guyanoga Creek is a major tributary of the western branch of Keuka Lake, which it enters near Branchport. This is a decidedly seasonal stream. In the spring or fall, if there has been a lot of rain, the stream will average about 25 feet in width. Flowing through farmlands and pastureland, much of the stream is devoid of cover, but there are intermittent areas where the stream is overhung by mature willows. The upper reach of the stream has a high gradient and consequently a good riffle/pool ratio. The lower reach of Guyanoga Creek is a sluggish, flatwater stream, broken up by several beaver dams.

In the spring, Guyanoga Creek gets a very good run of wild, Keuka Lake rainbow trout. If water levels are sufficiently high, these fish will be able to breech the beaver dams and run the full length of the stream. This run isn't as impressive as those of Naples Creek, Catharine Creek, or Cold Brook, but it certainly is

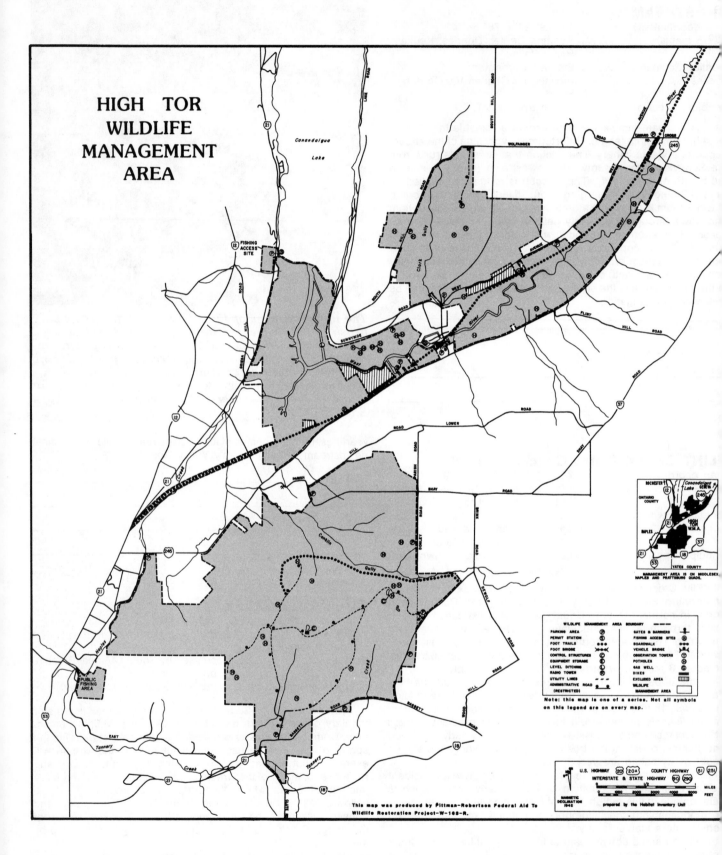

HIGH TOR
WILDLIFE
MANAGEMENT
AREA

Canandaigua Lake

FISHING ACCESS SITE

PUBLIC FISHING AREA

MANAGEMENT AREA IS ON MIDDLESEX, NAPLES AND PRATTSBURG QUADS.

WILDLIFE MANAGEMENT AREA BOUNDARY

PARKING AREA
PERMIT STATION
FOOT TRAILS
FOOT BRIDGE
CONTROL STRUCTURES
EQUIPMENT STORAGE
LEVEL DITCHING
RADIO TOWER
UTILITY LINES
ADMINISTRATIVE ROAD (RESTRICTED)

GATES & BARRIERS
FISHING ACCESS SITES
BOARDWALK
VEHICLE BRIDGE
OBSERVATION TOWERS
POTHOLES
GAS WELL
DIKES
EXCLUDED AREA
WILDLIFE MANAGEMENT AREA

Note: this map is one of a series. Not all symbols on this legend are on every map.

U.S. HIGHWAY
INTERSTATE & STATE HIGHWAY
COUNTY HIGHWAY

MILES
FEET

MAGNETIC DECLINATION 1942

prepared by the Habitat Inventory Unit

This map was produced by Pittman-Robertson Federal Aid To Wildlife Restoration Project-W-168-R.

— 158 —

worth fishing. The stream can be a bit on the crowded side during the first week or two of trout season, but the good fishing will outlast the crowds. This stream is also known for its excellent spring bullhead fishing, which is found in the lower reach of Guyanoga Creek.

As with many other streams, Guyanoga Creek often has a good, but highly underutilized fall run of rainbows. The quality of this run depends on the amount of rainfall. If the rainfall has been sufficient, large numbers of 2 to 4 pound, primarily male rainbows, will enter the stream by the middle of November. Occassionally, this stream also gets a fall migration of landlocked salmon. Keep in mind that special Finger Lakes tributary regulations apply to this stream, but only as far upstream as the road crossing at Route 54A. General statewide regulations apply further upstream. Thus, only a small section of the stream can be fished in the fall, but the crowds are minimal and the fishing can be quite good.

To guarantee public access to Guyanoga Creek, the state has purchased a total of 1.63 miles of public fishing easements on the stream, which are located intermittently between the stream mouth and the crossing at Route 364.

This stream is not stocked.

NOTES: _____

_____

_____

_____

HIGH TOR STATE WILDLIFE MANAGEMENT AREA

map coordinates	42° 36' 47" 77° 21' 29"
USGS map(s)	Prattsburg, Naples, Middlesex
location (township	Italy, Middlesex (Yates County), Naples (Ontario County)
access	main enterance on County Road 21 - see map
principle species	largemouth bass, black crappie, chain pickerel, bullhead, brook trout (stocked), rainbow trout (stocked & wild), panfish

The High Tor Wildlife Management Area consists of 5,728 acres straddling the Yates/Ontario County line. The area is composed of three separate units or areas, all clustered around the southern end of Canandaigua Lake. High Tor exhibits a remarkable degree of ecological diversity. The word Tor means craggy hill or peak, and refers to the largest of the three units, which is adjacent to the village of Naples. This section of the wildlife area consists primarily of scenic, steep wooded terrain, studded with several isolated ponds. Most of these small ponds offer good fishing for largemouth bass and panfish, but one of them is stocked with brook trout, and one with rainbow trout (300 and 200 fall fingerlings, respectively are stocked annually).

To the immediate north of the largest unit lies a smaller (1,000 acre) unit composed primarily of marshland. This marshland is drained by the West River (see below) and was once known for its productive stands of wild rice. This unit of High Tor offers good fishing for largemouth bass, chain pickerel, bullhead and black crappie. For information on fishing opportunities and boat launch sites, see the articles on West River (Yates County) and Canandaigua Lake (Finger Lakes section).

The third and smallest unit of High Tor lies due east of the southern end of Canandaigua Lake. This unit is also drained by the West River, but this upper reach of the river doesn't seem to support much of a fishery.

Because of this regions diversified environments, High Tor has a wide variety of wildlife including deer, grouse, cotton tail rabbits, grey squirrels, muskrat, raccoon, mink, woodchuck and several species of waterfowl. It has also been the summer home of several immature bald eagles originally hatched at the Montezuma National Wildlife Refuge.

The area is open to various activities, such as fishing, boating, hunting, bird watching, picnicking and camping for organized groups with permits and hiking. A spur of the Finger Lakes Trail system runs through High Tor and is designated by signs where it enters the area.

NOTES: _____

_____

_____

_____

KEUKA LAKE OUTLET

map coordinates	42° 41' 02" 76° 56' 52"
USGS map(s)	Dresden, Penn Yan
location (township)	Torrey, Milo
access	crossed by County Road #9 - see below
principle species	smallmouth bass, largemouth bass, bullhead, smelt, brown trout (stocked), rainbow trout (wild), catfish

Exiting the eastern arm of Keuka Lake at Penn Yan, the waters of this stream flow for approximately 8 miles before emptying into Seneca Lake at Dresden. Meandering through an especially scenic valley, the surroundings of Keuka Lake Outlet consist primarily of meadows and pastureland. The stream has an especially high gradient, resulting in numerous small falls, plunge pools and scour pools. Most of the stream is wide open and fly fishing is certainly a possibility here.

The only major problem on Keuka Lake Outlet concerns its waterflow. The outlet is used to control the level of Keuka Lake. If

An aerial view of the High-Tor Wildlife Management Area at the southern end of Canandaigua Lake. The West River and the duck channel are clearly visable. The fishing is this area is exceptionally good, particularly for largemouth bass. The increasing popularity of bass fishing has resulted in very high boat traffic in the West River in recent years, but this doesn't seem to have hurt the quality of the fishing. This section of High-Tor also has good fishing for chain pickerel, black crappie, bluegills and bullheads. Photo courtesy New York State DEC.

the level is too low, the gates at the head of the stream are closed, thus reducing the flow of water in the stream. In recent years the summer outflow has been severely reduced and this is probably affecting the quality of the summer fishing throughout Keuka Lake Outlet. Conversely, there are periods when the pool level of the lake is too high. The gates are then opened to allow the lake level to go down, and the resulting flush of water through the stream is so great that the fishing can be difficult at best. This usually takes place in the fall, but it can occur in the spring, as well. The only beneficial aspect of this situation is that Keuka Lake Outlet is not heavily impacted by such circumstances,and deep pools tend to protect the fishery in periods of both high and low water.

The lower 3.5 miles of Keuka Lake Outlet, that is, below Cascade Mills, supports a fair run of wild Seneca Lake rainbow trout (they cannot run up further than an impassible barrier at Cascade Mills) and this run is repeated to a lesser extent in the fall,depending on water conditions. Smallmouth bass also spawn in the lower reach of the stream, and many of these fish will often remain in the stream well past the opening of bass season.

There is a fossil fuel electric generating plant with a strong warm water discharge located just upstream of the mouth of Keuka Lake Outlet. This warm water serves as a strong attractant to such species as smallmouth bass, largemouth bass, bullhead and yellow perch. Brown trout, rainbow trout,and lake trout will also be found in the estuary of the stream when even the lake waters are below their preferred temperatures. This warm water discharge doesn't seem to attract salmonids in the same concentrations as other discharges, such as that at Nine Mile Point, east of Oswego on Lake Ontario,but it is still worth investigating.

Rounding out the current fishing opportunities found in the lower end of this stream is an excellent spring smelt fishery. In the future, there might also be a fishing here for landlocked salmon. This species is expected to be stocked in Seneca Lake in 1990. In addition, salmon are stocked in Keuka Lake and enter the outlet occasionally. They eventually find their way down to Seneca Lake. If sufficient numbers of these fish survive to sexual maturity, there could be a run of salmon in the lower end of Keuka Lake Outlet.

Above Cascade Mills, Keuka Lake Outlet is a fair to good fishery for stocked brown trout and in some years splake,a trout hybrid. Because of the generally low water levels in the summer, most of the stocked browns will not survive. Consequently, there are special regulations that apply to this stream. Above Cascade Mills, trout can be taken all year, any size, limit 10 per day. Be sure to check for current regulations.

Public access to Keuka Lake Outlet is very good. The state has not purchased any public fishing easements, but a public agency has bought the old railroad bed that runs along the stream for almost its entire length. The railroad bed is operated as a public trail system and it provides extensive access to the stream.

In the spring, Keuka Lake Outlet is stocked with 4,000 brown trout yearlings, from 0.3 miles above the stream mouth upstream 6 miles to the mouth of tributary #10.

NOTES: _____
_____
_____
_____

WEST RIVER

map coordinates	42° 39′ 59″ 77° 21′ 29″
USGS map(s)	Middlesex, Canandaigua Lake Rushville
location (township)	Italy
access	see below
principle species	largemouth bass, bullhead, chain pickerel, panfish

The West River is a large warm water stream that empties into the south end of Canandaigua Lake. The majority of the fishing that is available here is found downstream of the crossing at South Hill Road, which runs off Route 245. This fishable reach is about 2.5 miles long. Averaging about 100 feet in width in the summer, the West River is heavily encrouched upon by trees, weeds and snags, but is nevertheless navigable by full size bass boats. The only area where there might be a navigation problem is at the junction with Naples Creek, where there is excess sedimentation.

Largemouth bass are the most important species found in the West River, and the fishing for them can be extremely good. There are extensive weed beds along the river, scattered patches of lily pads and numerous snags, providing prime bass habitat. Bass can also be found in a cut known as "The Duck Channel," which is a short, 40 foot wide channel that starts near Canandaigua Lake and runs southeast. Originally constructed as a waterfowl habitat, this navigable channel has some fine fishing for largemouth bass.

Chain pickerel can also be found in the West River, but their numbers are considerably less than those of the largemouth. Also available are panfish, particularly crappie, which can be found here in good numbers in the spring. A proven hot spot for spring crappie is at the old marina, now owned by the DEC, off Route 245. Shore fishermen can fish either the waters of the marina itself, or the access channel that leads to the river. Both have very good spring crappie fishing. Bullhead are also found throughout the river, especially in the spring.

The entire West River is open to public fishing, as the fishable reach flows through the High Tor Wildlife Management Area. Boat access is provided by three state owned launch sites.

1. The DEC fishing access and boat launch site, along Route 21 on Canandaigua Lake, at Woodville. Hard surface ramp — no charge.
2. The old marina, off Route 245, downstream of South Hill Road. This property is now owned by the DEC and boats can be launched from a dirt ramp — no charge.
3. The DEC fishing access and boat launch site, just off Route 245 on South Hill Road. Hand launch site for cartop and canoes — no charge.

The West River is not stocked.
See also — High Tor Wildlife Management Area.

NOTES: _____
_____
_____
_____

Invest in the future of your sport. Take a kid fishing. The rewards can last a lifetime.

— 160 —

PART II
MAJOR LAKES

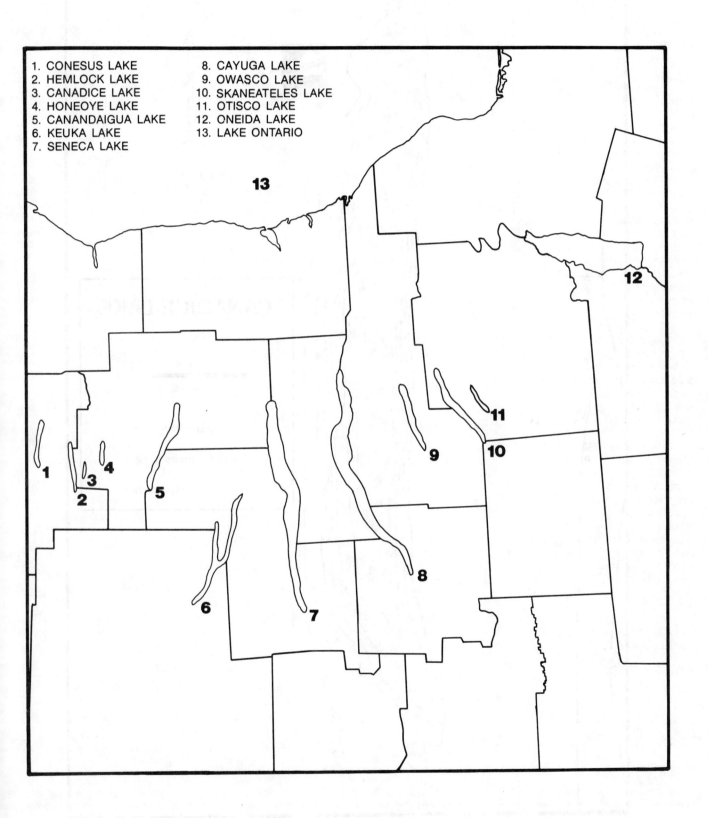

1. CONESUS LAKE
2. HEMLOCK LAKE
3. CANADICE LAKE
4. HONEOYE LAKE
5. CANANDAIGUA LAKE
6. KEUKA LAKE
7. SENECA LAKE
8. CAYUGA LAKE
9. OWASCO LAKE
10. SKANEATELES LAKE
11. OTISCO LAKE
12. ONEIDA LAKE
13. LAKE ONTARIO

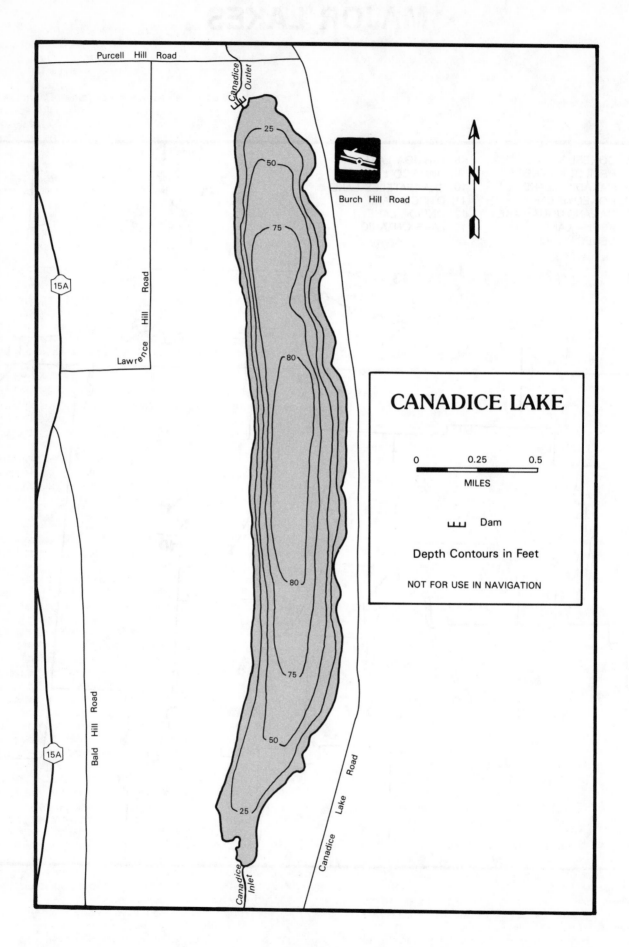

Purcell Hill Road

Canadice Outlet

25

50

75

Burch Hill Road

N

Lawrence Hill Road

80

CANADICE LAKE

15A

0   0.25   0.5

MILES

⊔⊔⊔   Dam

Depth Contours in Feet

NOT FOR USE IN NAVIGATION

80

Bald Hill Road

75

50

Canadice Lake Road

15A

25

Canadice Inlet

CANADICE LAKE

ap coordinates......... 42° 43' 08" 77° 34' 08"
SGS map(s)............. Springwater
cation................. Western Ontario County
ccess................. Extensive informal access is available off Canadice Lake Road.

hysical Characteristics
rea.................... 649 acres
horeline............... 7.1 miles
lecation............... 1096 feet
aximum depth.......... 83 feet
ean depth............. 54 feet
ottom type............ gravel, cobblestone, muck
ean thermocline depth.. 25 feet

Chemical Characteristics
vater clarity.............. very clear
H...................... alkaline
xygen.................. generally good. There is a problem with oxygen depletion in the deepest parts of the lake during the latter stages of summer stagnation. This currently has no detrimental effect on cold or warm water species.

Plant Life

Because the lake is so steep sided, major weedbeds are imited to the north and south ends of the lake. There are about 50 acres of weedbeds located at the southern end, 20 acres at the northern end and small, but significant, patches located in the arger coves, primarily on the east side of the lake, in water up to 15 feet in depth.

Boat Launch Sites

The city of Rochester provides an unimproved gravel ramp near the northeast corner of the lake, off Canadice Lake Road, near the intersection of Birch Hill Road. Informal shore assess is available all along the east side of the lake for shore fishing, and here are several sites along the east side where small cartop poats or canoes could be put in.

pecies information

Rock Bass............... abundant; growth rate good

Rock bass are almost certainly the most important warm vater species in Canadice Lake, far outnumbering their larger cousins, the largemouth and smallmouth bass. The rock bass are pig here, nearly as big as those taken from Sodus Bay, and they are abundant. A catch of 40 to 50 10 inch rock bass in a days outing is common on this lake from mid-May to mid-June.

The best rock bass fishing is found along the west side of the ake, which is rockier then the east side. There are also several arge gravel (cobblestone) bars and numerous fallen, partially submerged trees on the west side of Canadice Lake that provide habitat for rock bass. For rock bass fishing on the east side of the ake, look for points that are rocky, not composed of pea gravel. The best rock bass fishing on the east side is found along the 1/4 mile of shoreline immediately south of the boat launch site.

Late spring is the most productive period for rock bass ishing, but good numbers of fish will be taken in the summer and all. You usually have to fish deeper in the summer, but if you're not having any luck, go back to shallow water. On some days rock bass will be found in 15 feet of water, on some days they will move into shallow habitat.

Night crawlers, crayfish and leeches are popular and productive natural baits for rock bass. Small spinners, small black poppers, and 1/16 to 1/32 oz. dark colored jigs will also take fish. Taken on ultralight tackle, rock bass are scrappy fighters and provide excellent table fare.

largemouth bass.......... uncommon; growth rate good

There is limited habitat in Canadice Lake for largemouth bass and consequently, limited fishing for largemouth bass.

Early in the season, depending on how late the spawning season is running, the northwest corner of the lake will often provide some bass fishing. More dependable, however, is the southwest corner of the lake. Occassionally, largemouth bass will be taken from along the southeast corner, where there are numerous tree stumps, or from the larger weed beds found along the east side of the lake.

Largemouth bass are really a bonus fish in Canadice Lake. This isn't a lake that you would go to in order to fish specifically for largemouth. Because of their rather small numbers, this would be a good lake to practice a catch and release policy for largemouth bass.

Smallmouth Bass......... common; growth rate good

Canadice Lake offers good fishing for smallmouth bass. Most smallmouth are taken from the same areas where rock bass are found, that is, from the central section of the western shore, and from the 1/4 mile stretch of water immediately south of the boat launch site. Early in the season, they can also be found along the large point on the northeast side of the lake (the point off Birch Hill Road).

In late June and early July, smallmouth bass will be found in shallow water. These fish are fairly easy to catch on top surface lures, spinners and dry flies. Later, as the water warms up, the fish will move into deeper water. When this occurs small jigs and deep diving crank baits will be highly effective. Anglers report that the smallmouth bass in Canadice Lake prefer chartreuse, yellow and white jigs. Brown bucktail jigs will also work well here. For the fly fisherman, crayfish patterns, leech patterns and small streamers, all size 6 and under, can be very effective when fished along deep weed lines, rocky ledges or over deep, rocky points (10-25 feet). Fan casting for bass is more productive on Canadice Lake than trolling. Most of the fish are located on isolated gravel bars and rocky points. Trolling will waste a lot of time over non-smallmouth habitat.

The smallmouth bass in this lake average 12 to 14 inches, but many fish 18 to 20 inches are taken here each year. Finger Lakes regulations allow smallmouth and largemouth bass to be taken from Canadice Lake from the third Saturday in June through March 15.

Chain Pickerel............ common; growth rate good

Chain pickerel can be found in good numbers almost anywhere in Canadice Lake where weeds exist, and provide good fishing all season long.

Spinnerbaits dressed with twister tails or hula skirts seem to be the most effective lures for chain pickerel on this lake, especially in the spring and fall. Deep driving crankbaits, Texas-rigged worms, silver flatfish and spoons, such as the red and white Daredevle, all fished along deep weed lines, will also be effective through the summer and fall.

Chain pickerel often strike from the side, taking line, lure and leader into their mouth. Because their teeth are so sharp, they can often cut through a 30 lb. tippet, so a tippet of 50 lb. or a wire leader is recommended when fishing for chain pickerel. When using Texas-rigged worms, a wire rig should be used.

Due to its small size, Canadice Lake is usually frozen over by the middle of January. This gives ice fishermen a long season for taking pickerel through the ice. The weed beds at the south end of the lake are very productive in the winter. Standard tip-ups, baited with big shiners, will take the most fish, but chubs and suckers can also be used. Chain pickerel are the major species taken through the ice here, and limit catches are not uncommon.

Trout...................... common, growth rate good

Canadice Lake has healthy populations of lake trout, rainbow trout and brown trout. Lake trout are the dominant predator species, and their numbers are maintained mainly by natural reproduction. Rainbow trout and brown trout populations are maintained solely by stocking. There are no adequately large tributaries in which these fish can spawn.

In the spring and early summer, all species of trout will be found near shore in relatively shallow water. They will be seeking out their preferred temperature ranges and forage fish, mainly smelt and alwives. While they are in shallow water, trout are fairly easy to take. Shore fishermen will be successful using live smelt or alewives, fished on the bottom, with a slip sinker. Egg sacks are also a good spring bait. Real eggs, fished in a cluster about the size of a dime, are the best, but artificial egg sacks soaked in crushed trout eggs or scented oil are also effective. For the boat fishermen, flat lining is a productive method for taking early season brown trout and rainbow trout. Jointed Rapalas, big silver or blue flatfish, Sutton spoons or any other lure that imitates a smelt or alewive will be productive.

As the water temperatures rise the trout begins to move out of the shallows and into deeper water. Canadice Lake seems to warm up a little more slowly than other nearby lakes, possibly due to its higher altitude. Local anglers routinely take rainbow trout from shallow water as late as mid-July here. But by the middle of summer the most consistent trout fishing will be in the deeper parts of the lake.

One aspect of Canadice Lake that will be of interest to summertime trout fishermen involves the oxygen deficit in the deepest parts of the lake. Although the lack of oxygen doesn't directly threaten the survival of trout species, it often forces them into a very narrow band of water, compressed between oxygen poor water on the bottom and excessively warm water on the top. Because their vertical range is so restricted in the late summer, they are very easy to take once the proper depth has been found. Traditional deep water techniques, such as still fishing, downrigging and copper line fishing can be extremely effective at such times. For a detailed explanation of these techniques see C. Scott Sampson's article on Seneca Lake, keeping in mind that Canadice is a much shallower lake than Seneca, and your techniques should be adjusted accordingly.

There are times during the summer when temperature tolerent rainbows can be found near the surface of the lake, feeding on bait fish. This usually occurs very early in the morning. If you are in such an area where this feeding is taking place, try casting to the fish. Often times they will hit on dry flies, nymphs, small floating Rapalas or surface spoons.

As the summer wanes, Canadice Lake begins to cool down and trout begin to move back into shallow water. Lake trout move into the shallows to spawn, seeking out areas of loose gravel and rubble. Rainbows and browns will be seeking out prefered temperatures. The same tecniques that worked in the spring time will again work in the fall.

At 1096 feet, Canadice Lake is the highest of all the Finger Lakes. Its also the smallest, and these two factors combine to make this one of the earliest lakes in the area to freeze over. Usually, the lake is frozen over by mid-January. Trout are commonly taken through the ice using tip-ups baited with minnows, but swedish pimples, small jigging Rapalas and trout flies will all take trout through the ice.

Other Species

Aside from the species of fish listed above, Canadice also has lesser populations of smelt, cisco, yellow perch, pumpkinseed, bluegill, brown bullhead, white suckers and carp. Though, as a

Canadice Lake offers good trout fishing in a remote setting. Rainbows, browns and lakers are common here.

group, they constitute a considerable fishery, none of them are present in sufficient numbers to be important individually.

General Information

Canadice Lake is the smallest of the Finger Lakes and the highest in altitude. Nestled in a near pristine wilderness 31 miles south of the city of Rochester, it serves as a important source of drinking water for that city. Water levels are maintained artificially by a dam at the northern end of the lake, but fluctuations average only 4.3 feet per year. This does not appear to have any detrimental effect on the flora or fauna of the lake.

The habitat of Canadice Lake is well suited to the needs of salmonids, but due to the lakes lack of any sizeable tributaries the populations of rainbow trout and brown trout must be maintained by stocking. In the spring, 2,500 brown trout yearlings 2,500 rainbow trout yearlings and 2,300 lake trout yearlings are stocked here. In the fall, an additional 4,500 lake trout fingerlings are put in the lake. Most of the lake trout in Canadice are however, wild.

In order to maintain the pure quality of the water in this lake the city of Rochester has banned activities such as bathing swimming and water skiing on Canadice. Boats are restricted 16 feet in length and outboard motors to 10 horsepower. To fish on Canadice Lake a free permit must be obtained from the city of

A Michigan Wiggler. This nymph is commonly used for taking rainbow trout or steelhead, but is also very effective on smallmouth bass. Photo courtesy Mike Keller.

Rochester. This permit can be obtained by sending a stamped self-addressed envelope to:

City of Rochester
Watershed Permit
7412 Rix Hill Road
Hemlock, NY 14466

Be sure to check for current Finger Lakes regulations.

NOTES: _____

_____

_____

_____

Fly fishing is an effective way to take brown trout when they are in shallow water. The two most productive periods are dusk and dawn.

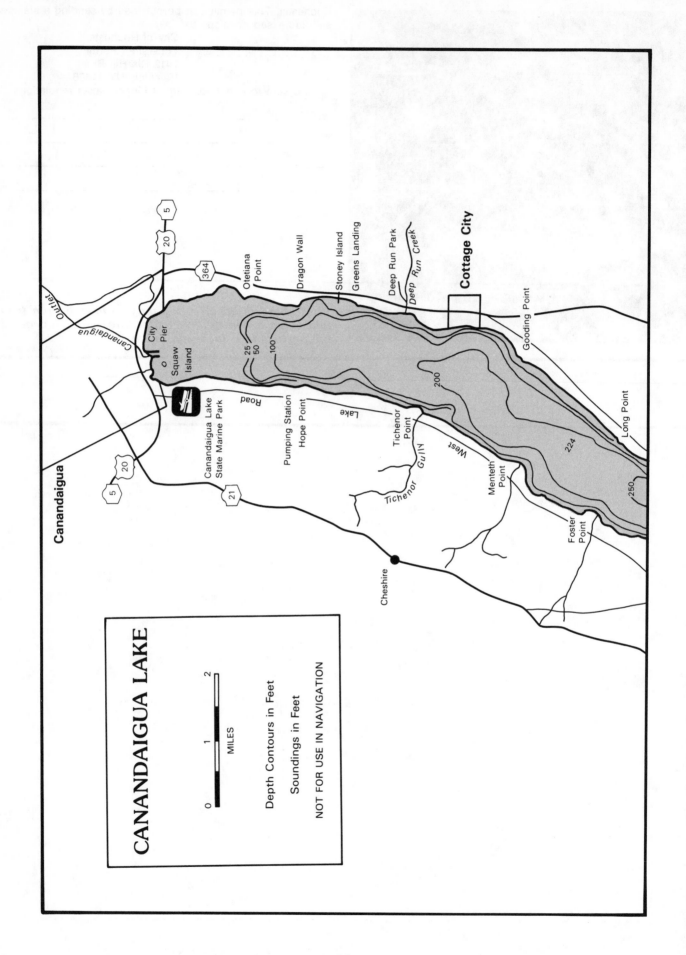

CANANDAIGUA LAKE

MILES

0   1   2

Depth Contours in Feet

Soundings in Feet

NOT FOR USE IN NAVIGATION

Canandaigua

Canandaigua Outlet

City Pier

Squaw Island

Canandaigua Lake State Marine Park

Lake Road

Pumping Station

Hope Point

Otetiana Point

Dragon Wall

Stoney Island

Greens Landing

Deep Run Park

Deep Run Creek

Cottage City

Gooding Point

Long Point

Tichenor Point

Tichenor Gully

West

Menteth Point

Foster Point

Cheshire

25
50
100
200
224
250

5
20
364
5
20
21

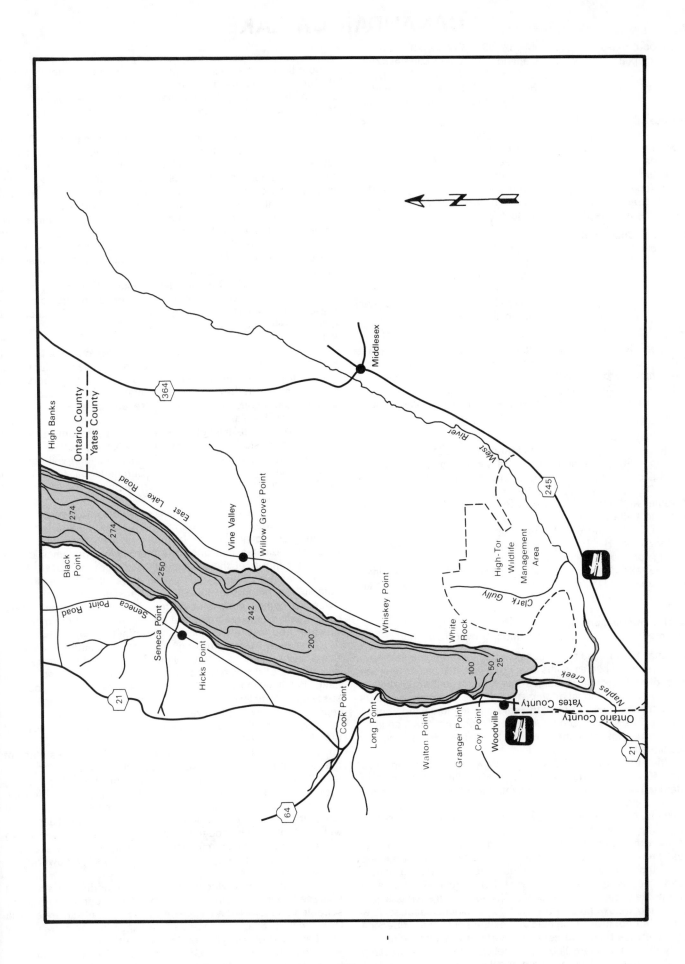

High Banks

Ontario County
Yates County

364

Middlesex

West River

245

274

274

250

East Lake Road

Black
Point

Vine Valley

Willow Grove Point

242

200

Seneca Point Road

Seneca Point

Whiskey Point

High-Tor
Wildlife
Management
Area

Clark Gully

21

Hicks Point

White
Rock

100

50

25

Creek

Naples

Cook Point

Long Point

Ontario County
Yates County

Woodville

64

Walton Point

Granger Point

Coy Point

21

CANANDAIGUA LAKE

map coordinates . . . . 42° 52' 30"   77° 16' 20"
USGS map(s) . . . . Canandaigua Lake, Middlesex
location . . . . Ontario County, Yates County
access . . . . Routes 5 & 20 at north end of lake; Route 21 at south end of lake.

Physical Characteristics

area . . . . 10,558 acres
shoreline . . . . 35.9 miles
elevation . . . . 688 feet
maximum depth . . . . 278 feet
mean depth . . . . 129 feet
bottom type . . . . gravel, rubble, muck
mean thermocline depth . . 49 feet

Chemical Characteristics

water clarity . . . . clear
pH . . . . alkaline
oxygen . . . . oxygen levels are good throughout the lake all year long. There is no serious oxygen depletion even during the summer.

Plant Life

Extensive weed beds are found at the south end of the lake (256 acres) and at the north end (960 acres). A narrow, intermittant band of weeds is found along both sides of the lake in water up to 15 feet deep. Small but significant weed beds are found in many of the large coves, and on either side of major points.

Boat Launch Sites

1. Canandaigua Lake State Marine Park - off Routes 5 and 20 in the City of Canandaigua. Hard surface ramps, pump-out, parking for 110 cars and trailers - no charge.
2. DEC Fishing Access Site - on Route 21, three miles north of Naples at Woodville. Hard surface ramps, parking for about 60 cars and trailers - no charge.
3. DEC Fishing Access Site - on West River, just off Route 245 on South Hill Road near trail park. Hand launching only, parking for 5 cars - no charge.

The lake is also serviced by a number of private marinas, located mainly at the north and south ends, providing bait, tackle, rentals and marine supplies.

Species Information

Smallmouth Bass . . . . common; growth rate good

Smallmouth bass are unquestionably the predominant warm water predator species in this lake. For a lake that has an average depth of 129 feet, Canandaigua has an excellent population of smallmouth. Some local anglers, though, feel that their numbers have declined over the past 15 years due to increasing angling pressure. The smallmouth here generally run from 1 to 3 pounds, but exceptional specimens of 6 to 7 pounds are caught occasionally.

Prior to spawning the smallmouth will be located in deep water (40 to 60 feet) near structure. In early June, as near shore water temperatures begin to climb into the 50° to 55° F range, the fish will start moving into the shallows in anticipation of spawning. As they move shoreward, the bass tend to congregate along major drop offs in 15 to 20 feet of water, moving into very shallow water (3 to 10 feet) only during the actual act of spawning. Areas known to harbor large numbers of smallmouth bass in the late spring and early summer include: the water around Squaw Island; the rocky ledges south of Long Point (this area is appropriately called "High Banks" by locals); the waters just above and below the "White Rock" (so called because it is usually, but not always, painted white); the south side of Seneca Point; the rock bottomed cove just north of Otetiana Point; and nearly the entire shore line from Otetiana Point down to Deep Run Park, particularly around the shoal known as Stoney Island,

which lies between Greens Landing and Turner Road. Undoubtedly, other areas of the lake also hold smallmouth during this period. Canandaigua Lake has numerous shallow rocky flats and ledges adjacent to deep water. Concentrate your efforts in these areas early in the season and you should have no problem taking limits of fish.

All of the fishermen that contributed information on Canandaigua Lake were unanimous on at least one point. For taking late spring/early summer smallmouth they all recommended jigs, especially small deer hair jigs in natural colors. Also recommended were small, shallow running crankbaits, or live bait (worms, small crayfish or minnows) fished with a bobber.

After spawning, smallmouth bass will begin to move into somewhat deeper water and can be taken on deep diving crankbaits, larger deer hair jigs or lead head jigs dressed with Mister Twister tails. This phase of smallmouth fishing, where the bass are found in moderately deep water just out from their spawning areas, lasts for about two weeks on Canandaigua Lake, though some fish will continue to be picked up sporadically in these waters all summer long. After this period Canandaigua gives up relatively few smallmouth until the late summer or early fall.

Many a frustrated fisherman has wondered how a lake that has such good spring and fall bass fishing can be so reluctant to give up fish in the summer, especially during daylight hours. This summer hiatus in the harvesting of smallmouth bass occurs not only on Canandaigua Lake, but on several other Finger Lakes, most notably Keuka. In the section on smallmouth bass fishing on Keuka Lake I wrote at length on how to take bass from that lake at night. The basic gist of that section can also be applied successfully to Canandaigua Lake. In this section I will concentrate on taking smallmouth from Canandaigua Lake in the daytime. The major points of this information will apply with equal validity to Keuka Lake.

The movement of the smallmouth bass into deeper water, and their sudden "disappearance," coincides with the setting up of the thermocline on the lake. All of the information that I received indicates that once the thermocline becomes established a majority of the smallmouth disperse just above it and range over the entire lake in search of bait fish. There isn't any data in the records of the DEC to back up this theory. Hard evidence comes from rainbow trout fishermen who often take smallmouth suspended over the thermocline in 200 or more feet of water and from those anglers who practice "woodchucking."

The term "woodchucking" refers to a method used by a handful of anglers to take smallmouth early in the summer. I've only heard of it being used on Canandaigua Lake and Keuka Lake, but it would probably work on any lake where you find suspended smallmouth. The technique is very simple, and reportedly highly productive.

Just as the thermocline is setting up the bass will move off the sides of the lake and suspend just above the thermal break. Initially, this will put the smallmouth fairly close to the surface of the lake and makes them susceptible to "woodchucking." The technique involves trolling at a relatively high speed (5 to 7 knots) with white streamers equipped with tandem hooks. When the termocline is at its shallowest these streamers are trolled just under the surface. As it gradually sinks, drawing the bass down with it, weight can be added to the line to get the streamers down to the fish. When the thermocline goes really deep, however, you are more likely to pick up these deep water bass on downriggers or Seth Green rigs.

One reason that "woodchucking" is so productive is the fact that the smallmouth that are suspended are normally tightly schooled up close to bait fish. The schools of bait fish are easy to locate with a sonar and once it's determined that bass are nearby you can concentrate your efforts in one area.

When the smallmouth bass go too deep for "woodchucking" to be effective, other techniques can be utilized. There are a few anglers who routinely take bass on spoons and plugs using downriggers or Seth Green rigs. One very successful local fisherman, Barton Butts, prefers to hover over suspended bass, moving when necessary to stay over the fish. Once he locates a school of fish he uses a jigging or slab spoon to entice numerous strikes. One of the advantages to using a jigging spoon is that it can be put right in the thick of the bass and worked there until a fish either strikes out of hunger or out of anger.

Not all of the smallmouth in Canandaigua Lake (or Keuka Lake) suspend over the thermocline in summer. A few can still be taken in the daytime in what would be considered "traditional" summer smallmouth habitats, such as deep weed lines, underwater points or rocky ledges. Two areas that seem to be especially productive in the summer are the rocky ledges between Otetiana Point and Deep Run Park, and the outer edge of the weed beds at the south end of the lake. Both of these locations hold bass all summer long, though the best fishing is to be had early in the season.

On both Canandaigua and Keuka smallmouth bass seem to associate strongly with the top of the termocline, at least during the day, until late September or early October, at which time they return to the sides of the lakes and orient around physical structures. Because a scientific study has never been done to determine what triggers this change in their behavior, it's hard to say just why the bass leave the deep open water. At least one angler who has made a serious study of Canandaigua Lake believes that it occurs when the thermocline intersects the side of the lake at a depth of 45 to 50 feet. He could be right, but I'm inclined to disagree. Numerous fishermen have reported taking smallmouth bass in water as deep as 70 feet in August and September on Canandaigua Lake and Keuka Lake. Because bass will not venture below the top of the thermocline much less enter the cold hypolimnion, it stands to reason that in certain areas the thermocline will be as deep as 70 feet well before late September. And it goes this deep without triggering a reorientation in the bass. I think a more likely explanation involves the turning over of the lake in the fall. This involves a redistribution of bait fish and oxygen in the lake, as well as a restructuring of the thermal regime. That this happens at about the same time that the smallmouth return to the sides of the lake would seem to be more than just a coincidence.

When the bass do begin relating to structure they will initially be found in 35 to 40 feet of water. For a short period their exact positions and patterns of movement will be unpredictable, probably due to the unsettled state of the lake after the disintegration of the thermocline. This can be compounded by the fact that early in the fall warm rains or extended warm spells can draw the bass up into shallow water (6 to 8 feet) for days at a time. It's not too long, however, before the fish are forced into water 60 to 90 feet deep in order to find amenable temperatures. This migration to deep water occurs roughly between Halloween and Thanksgiving Day. But this is not an all encompassing movement of bass. A few fish will continue to hold in water as shallow as 20 feet. And, depending upon conditions, many smallmouth will make excursion up and down the face of the lake. For the most part, though, fall smallmouth fishing means working water over 50 feet deep.

The areas that hold smallmouth bass in the fall are similar in structure to spring holding areas. They are in fact, one and the same, for the bass will remain on these sites until just prior to spawning in the spring. Generally speaking, most of the deep water points and ledges will hold smallmouth in the fall, particularly those that have an abundance of rocky structure, as opposed to sand or shale. The ledges along High Banks, the White Rock area, the south side of Seneca Point, and the points between Granger Point and Cook Point are all known to harbor large numbers of bass in the fall. Other areas worth investigating would be small points where streams have washed big pockets of rocks out into the lake.

The most popular method for taking smallmouth here in the fall is jig fishing. Some anglers recommend using small bucktail jigs, while others suggest using larger jigs to match the growth

pattern of the bait fish. Jigging with 1 to 1½ inch slab spoons is also a very productive method once a school of bass has been located. On Keuka Lake our sources often used these on fairly shallow points. On Canandaigua Lake slab spoons are used to take deep, bottom oriented bass.

As is the case on Keuka Lake, the winter smallmouth fishery on Canandaigua is really just an extension of the fall fishery. The bass tend to be a bit deeper, and often lethargic, but the locations and techniques are basically the same as in the fall. One very noticable difference is that the fish caught in the winter are usually larger than those taken in the fall. From discussions with anglers on Canandaigua and Keuka, it seems that three factors are responsible for this. The first is the fact that the bass appear to school up according to size as the lake cools down. When bass fishermen start catching small fish, they move on, preferring to expend their effort on pockets of larger bass. Secondly, studies have shown that as water temperatures go down, the smallmouth becomes increasingly structure oriented and that this affects the smaller fish first. Apparently, many of the smaller bass retreat into cracks and crevices in the cold weather months and are simply not accessible to fishermen. Thirdly, it has been shown that a major feeding response is triggered in big female **largemouth** bass by the initiation of sexual changes in the fish, and that this occurs in January or February. This sexually triggered feeding response might also occur in the closely related smallmouth bass. This would explain why, when you can get out on the lake the best fishing for big smallmouth also occurs in January or February.

Few people fish for smallmouth on Canandaigua Lake in the winter, and there isn't enough information to generate a clear picture of any idiosyncrasies of this fishery. It's probably safe to assume that it is very similar in nature to the winter fishery on the other large Finger Lakes (Keuka, Cayuga and Seneca). For a detailed explanation of methods used to take smallmouth bass in the winter on these lakes, see Keuka Lake.

Lake Trout . . . . common; growth rate fair

Lake trout are the primary coldwater game fish in Canandaigua Lake, and the species most sought after by the lake's fishermen. The population of lake trout here would probably be considered abundant when compared to the size of populations of lakers in the other Finger Lakes. Their numbers are maintained almost solely by the planting of hatchery fish (95%). They are stocked here to the tune of 13,400 yearlings and 26,800 fingerlings annually. Initially, their growth rates are very slow, possibly the slowest in the Finger Lakes. This is due to competition for food from other salmonids and each other. At age 6 years they are only approaching 20 inches in length. But, once they reach this size, they grow very rapidly, feeding on the large alewives that then become available to them as forage. The average weight of the lake trout caught on Canandaigua Lake is about 3 pounds, but fish over 10 pounds are taken here regularly.

Ice-out on Canandaigua usually occurs around the third week in March. Immediately after this event, the best fishing for lake trout will be in close to shore, usually in water less than 40 feet deep. The trout will be drawn in to the shallow water by bait fish, primarily smelt, which are schooling up in these water prior to spawning. The smelt will be found off the mouths of many of the lake's tributaries, but only those that have an appreciable amount of flowing water. A lot of the smaller streams are still ice-choked in late March if there has been a severe winter, or have no flow due to a lack of meltwater. Some of the more reliable outflows occur at Seneca Point, Menteth Point, Tichenor Point and Willow Grove Point. The large bay just south of Willow Grove Point also holds a good number of lake trout in the spring and is seldom heavily fished. After the smelt have spawned the lakers will be found throughout the shallows of the lake until late June.

All of the traditional methods are used here to take lake trout early in the spring. Probably the most productive technique is still fishing with live smelt. Frozen sawbellies can also be used. The bait is threaded on an English style hook and fished on the bottom, using a slip sinker. Unimpeded by the sinker, the action of

Night fishing is very productive for lake trout. The light from a lantern attracts bait fish, which in turn draw in trout. On some lakes, such as Keuka, many anglers prefer to drift or troll. On Canandaigue Lake many anglers anchor their boats in 100 to 120 feet of water and fish 50 to 70 feet down.

the wounded live bait can be very enticing to trout foraging in the area. Even dead bait can appear to be pretty lively when fished in the currents found off the mouths of streams or in wind generated currents of the lake. Still fishing can be done from a boat or from shore.

Flatlining with copper wire is another method used in the spring, but it's very seldom used on Canandaigua anymore. Though very productive, it takes a bit of time, patience and muscle and just doesn't seem to appeal to today's modern angler. For those willing to give it a try, use Sutton spoons (sizes 44 or 71 in hammered brass or silver), Miller spoons or natural bait rigged on a Miller Hemlock spinner.

The source for much of our information on trout fishing on Canandaigua Lake was Captain Bill Kelley, a highly regarded charter boat captain who has fished this lake for fun and profit for several decades. One of the points that Bill stresses is that in the spring, as long as the lake trout are in shallow water, the wind can play an important role in determining where they are going to be. For example, if you're not finding lakers in their normal haunts off Menteth Point, and the wind is blowing from the west, check the shallows on the opposite side of the lake, between Long Point and Gooding Point. The west wind tends to push the warmer surface waters away from the west side of the lake, causing it to stack up along the east shore. When this occurs the lake trout will often be found in water as shallow as 10 feet and very close to the east shore line. Similar situations can occur around the lake, depending upon the direction of the wind and the topography of the land. At times the wind will affect not only the surface of the lake, but deeper levels of the water column as well, setting up remarkably strong currents in the lake. This happens on all of the large Finger Lakes (Cayuga, Seneca, Keuka and Canandaigua) and plays an important role in determining where and how you fish.

One area of Canandaigua Lake that often has a pronounced current in the spring is the open water between the pump station,

north of Hope Point, and the structure known locally as the Dragon Wall on the opposite side of the lake. Anglers will line themselves up between the pump station and the Dragon Wall and fish the current for lake trout using Seth Green rigs in April, May and early June.

In the spring, Bill Kelley goes after lake trout using a two pronged attack. He begins by still fishing with live bait in water less than 40 feet deep. The areas where he concentrates his efforts usually have three characteristics: a significant amount of bottom structure; at least some bait fish; and the presence of a temperature differential. A temperature differential can be caused by the relatively warm outflow of a stream or by an underwater spring. Bill says that there are a number of such springs seeping into the lake. They can be located with a sonar (the bubbles show up on your graph) and the springs that Bill has checked read a constant 41° F. They are almost always good locations for lake trout in the spring. He fishes these areas from 6:00 am to 9:30 am. If he's picking up fish he naturally stays in the area, but if the fishing has been slow he'll move out into deeper water and troll with Seth Green rigs. Working water 75 to 80 feet deep, he uses a sounding lead of 24 to 26 ounces and no more than 5 leaders per rig. The leaders are rigged with bait fish or flutter spoons and the bottom rig is trolled close to the bottom. Bill thinks that very light flutter spoons designed for slow trolling (1 - 1½ mph) work best for spring lake trout in deep water. If you're marking fish on the graph but aren't picking any up on your lures, try a slightly faster troll. If that doesn't get a response, change the size or color of your spoons.

Fishing for lake trout is very popular on Canandaigua Lake, and there is always the temptation to follow the crowd and fish the traditional areas, such as Tichenor Point or the pump house. But many a honey hole has been found by the angler who breaks away from the pack and does a little surveying. One such hole was found by Bill Kelley just out from White Rock, far from where most people fish for lakers in the spring. Other such sites are just waiting to be discovered.

Lake trout can be taken from the shallows until the near shore water temperatures begin climbing into the low 50's. This usually occurs around the middle of June. Just as the thermocline starts to set up the fishing for lake trout tapers off for a period of about 3 weeks. The fish are constantly moving during this transition period, searching for favorable temperatures. Once the lake stratifies however, lakers will almost always be found in or very near the thermocline. The mean depth of the thermocline on Canandaigua Lake is 49 feet according to the DEC, but its actual location can fluctuate greatly as it raises and falls in response to the effects of wind.

Lake trout are usually rather particular about what temperatures they are willing to forage in (they prefer hypolimnial water about 49°F), but there are times of the year when they can be found in unexpectedly warm water for short periods. Bill relates that during the transition period between the lake's spring and summer thermal regimes he has caught lake trout very close to the surface in water that registered 65° to 68° F! He says that this usually occurs off some of the points just south of Vine Valley. The trout feed on bait fish that are schooled up near the surface of the lake. They only feed for a short while, comming to the surface at sunrise and retreating to deeper water about an hour later. These fish can be taken on Mepps spinners or Panther Martins. Fly fishermen should be able to pick them up on streamers.

Once the thermocline has set up on the lake, fishing for lake trout is a pretty straightforward affair. They are almost always in or just under the thermocline. This is especially true of the larger fish. Locate the thermocline (it can be anywhere from 40 to over 100 feet down) and work it with downriggers or Seth Green rigs. The deep central portion of the lake has traditionally been the most productive area for lakers from early July through early September.

Today, most anglers employ standard deep water trolling techniques to catch lake trout. Years ago, though, a unique and highly productive method of night fishing was practiced on several of the Finger Lakes, including Canandaigua. It wasn't at all uncommon on some of the lakes to see over 100 boats out after dark, each illuminated by the warm glow of a lantern, and the collective lot of them looking like a small village. Not nearly as many boats are seen on the water at night these days, but the method is still extremely productive and there are indications that it's popularity is increasing with some of the younger anglers who are rediscovering its potential.

Though slight, but often important, variations developed on individual lakes, the basic method of night fishing for lake trout was always the same. It's really very simple. A light source is suspended over the water to attract bait fish. The bait fish in turn attract lake trout. The best light to use is a low heat 25 watt bulb, powered from a car or boat battery. They throw sufficient light and, because they don't get very hot, won't break if they get wet. Be sure to use a shade to reflect the maximum amount of light down to the water and to protect your eyes from glare. Coleman lanterns, especially those with a wide shade, can also be used.

The rig used for night fishing usually consists of 6 or 8 ounces of lead attached to a main line with three, 42 inch leaders spaced at least 6 feet apart. The leaders can be baited with either smelt or sawbellies. Most anglers use English style hooks, but Scott Sampson, a genuine authority on Finger Lakes techniques, recommends using black O'Shaughnesy hooks in size 3/0. The bait would then be hooked through the back, just under the dorsal fin.

The rig is fished 50 to 70 feet below the surface, regardless of how deep the water is. One some lakes, such as Keuka, the general practice is to drift with the wind or use an electric motor and slowly troll. On Canandaigua the rule is to anchor in 100 to 120 feet of water. Probably any area in the central portion of the lake will produce lake trout at night, but local anglers seem to prefer the west shore, between Black Point and Tichenor Point. Anchoring securely along the steep sides of this lake can be a real challenge. Anchors can easily loose their hold, particularly if the wind is pushing you out toward deeper water. Some of the more successful night fishermen use bow and stern anchors to get a better grip on the bottom and to prevent the boat from swinging.

If you're using more than one rig it's a good idea to fish one of them shallow, and the other deep until you find the exact depth at which the larger fish are holding. The smaller lake trout will leave the thermocline to feed on the bait fish gathering under the light near the surface. They don't generally enter the zone of light penetration, preferring to feed just below it. The really big lake trout are even more wary of the light. They usually gather under the light but stay in or near the thermocline.

When a fish strikes don't set the hook immediately. Let him run with it. Some anglers suggest letting the trout run with the bait until it stops. They don't advise setting the hook until the fish starts to run again. With a little practice you should be able to boat at least a few good size lakers in an outing. Night fishing of this sort is effective from about 11 pm to sunrise through July, August and early September. Toward the end of this period bait fish might be hard to come by. Spoons can then be used.

The lake trout in Canandaigua enter their spawning phase in late September and for a period of about a month they turn off to feeding. They are rarely caught here during this period.

Once their spawning phase has been completed lake trout quickly become vulnerable to angling. After October this means fishing in very deep water (100-150 feet). The DEC reports that excellent catches of big lake trout are taken from Canandaigua Lake in December and January, or until skim ice prevents the launching of boats. These big trout are taken by slowly trolling with spoons very close to the bottom. Ice fishing for lake trout is only possible during severe winters. Safe ice usually doesn't form over deep water on this lake.

Brown Trout . . . . common; growth rate good

When compared to the fishery for lake trout in Canandaigua, brown trout rank as a species of only secondary importance.

The brown trout in Canandaigua Lake average 2½ pounds, but big fish are relatively common. This brown trout weighed in at 11 pounds 12 ounces.

Their existence in this lake is supported solely by an annual stocking of 8,000 yearling. The average brown here weighs about 2½ pounds, but fish of 6 to 8 pounds are relatively common.

The only time that brown trout are a significant part of the fishery on this lake is in the spring and winter. From early May to late June browns can be taken by trolling near shore in shallow water. Hemlock spinners baited with either a smelt or sawbelly and fished 35 to 40 feet behind the boat can be deadly when the trout are in shallow. Another very effective method is to troll hammered brass or silver Sutton 88's 100 to 150 feet behind the boat in 25 to 30 feet of water. This method is most effective from just after sunrise to just before the sun crests over the hills on the east shore. Bill Kelley has found this to be a good technique for catching the big browns that are often found between White Rock and Whiskey Point. Shore fishermen can also take brown trout from Canandaigua in the spring by fishing with live bait.

In the late spring, just as the thermocline is beginning to set up, brown trout can be taken off the south bar at the southern end of the lake, where the outer weed line drops off to a depth of 80 to 90 feet. These fish can be taken with a variety of methods. Early in the morning try trolling out from, and parallel to, the weed line with spoons or spinners. Bobber fishing with live bait (minnows or night crawlers) right off the drop off will also take trout. Fish the bait 6 to 8 feet below the surface and let the bobber drift freely. On calm, fair weather mornings fly fishermen can take trout along the drop off using large streamers.

In the summer, the brown trout in Canandaigua Lake are fairly difficult to catch. They become very partial to areas where water in their preferred temperature range (58°-60° F) intersects the bottom of the lake, especially a bottom with large rocks or other structure to hold bait fish. The most productive way to catch these browns is to fish with live bait right on the bottom, using slip sinkers. Unfortunately, the areas where this temperature zone intersects the bottom is often a very steep-sided drop off, making it difficult to hold your position. If you're not picking up browns along the side of the lake, try trolling in open waters. Some brown trout will range out over very deep water, cruising above the thermocline in much the same water as the rainbows. For the most part, though, brown trout are only caught here incidentally in the summer.

By the middle of August the brown trout begin to enter their spawning phase and they turn off to feeding. The catch rate for these fish drops accordingly. They don't become vulnerable to angling again until late October or early November. When they do resume feeding they must replace the nutrients that were lost over the previous two months. They often go on a post-spawn feeding binge in the late fall to accomplish this. Surprisingly, not many browns are caught during this period. This is due to the fact that the bulk of the trout fishermen are gearing up for the excellent late fall/early winter lake trout fishing.

In the winter, if safe ice has formed over the north and south ends of the lake, brown trout are commonly caught on tip-ups baited with large minnows. The minnows are fished 2 to 4 feet below the ice, regardless of water depth. In years when a significant amount of ice fishing takes place here, brown trout are usually the most commonly caught salmonid. For the really hardy angler, excellent catches of brown trout can be had just prior to ice-out by trolling very close to shore, especially near docks, using large tandem hook streamers, Rapalas or silver spoons.

Largemouth Bass .... common; growth rate good

Unquestionably, the popularity of bass fishing has increased on Canandaigua Lake over the past 10 to 15 years. This is especially true with regard to largemouth bass. All of my sources for information on this lake confirmed (lamented) this fact, and it is obvious to anyone familiar with the south end of the lake or the West River that the number of bass boats on the water has risen dramatically over the past decade.

Although some fishermen feel that this increasing fishing pressure has diminished the overall quality of the bass fishery, the population of largemouth in Canandaigua is still quite healthy. The fish average about 1½ pounds in size and lunkers up to 6 pounds are still found here. A majority of the bass are found in or near the large, dense weed beds at the south end of the lake. Lesser populations are found in the weed beds of larger sheltered bays (Vine Valley, Cottage City), at the north end of the lake or along some sections of the weed line that runs intermittantly along the sides of the lake. The north end of the lake doesn't hold nearly as many largemouth as you might at first expect. The beds are scattered and not nearly as dense as those found at the south end of the lake, and the bottom consists primarily of an almost uninterrupted plain of sand and gravel. This is not the best habitat for largemouth bass.

The weed lines along the periphery of the lake can be tricky to fish successfully. Unlike the weed beds at the south end of the lake, these weeds probably don't have permanent populations of bass. They are too sparse and too removed from suitable spawning areas. Most likely, they only hold fish in the summer, after they have developed to their maximum extend and after the bass have had a chance to move out of the larger beds and migrate along the sides of the lake. Because these peripheral weed lines are not continuous, isolated stretches surrounded by habitat unsuitable to largemouth bass might not hold any bass at all.

In the late spring and early summer, largemouth bass are going to be found in shallow water along developing weed lines or adjacent to a structure, such as a boulder or piling. The latter is particularly true on sunny days. The sun warms objects that are exposed, and they in turn warm the water around them, which serves as a strong attractant to the bass. Extremely good fishing for largemouth can be had in the shallower portions of the south end of the lake or the West River at this time. They can be taken with spinners, safety pin type spinnerbaits, plastic worms or shallow running crankbaits.

Two of my sources for bass fishing on Canandaigua Lake, John McGough and Barton Butts, both successful tournament anglers, were unable to agree on what size baits to use early in the season. John prefers smaller baits (⅛ ounce) while Barton goes with larger sizes (½ ounce). Both men catch fish, however. I mention this disagreement because it illustrates the fact that fishing is not a strictly formula sport. Once you get the basics down one of the most important elements of angling success is having confidence in your techniques and tackle. Studies have actually shown that the ability of a lure to catch fish is due in part to the fisherman's belief that it will. Naturally, you can't throw just anything at the fish, but if you find something that works for you stick with it, even if it goes against conventional wisdom.

One element of bass fishing that John and Barton both agreed on was being able to put your bait or lure in the right spot. This is critical. Being off in your placement by as little as 2 feet can mean the difference between catching a fish or coming up empty-handed. The techniques of pitching, skipping and flipping

a lure are indispensable to the tournament fisherman, and should be a part of your repertoire if you're serious about fishing for largemouth bass. They're not the easiest skills to master, requiring a lot of practice, but they pay off when it comes to taking fish.

In the summer, bass fishing typically centers around working weed lines and, where available, docks. If fished properly, docks can be amazingly productive. Again, accuracy is the key here. You must be able to put your lure well under the dock, not just next to it. Often it's the smaller, more aggressive fish that you pick up first. Be persistant. Barton Butts has picked up as many as 10 to 15 good size bass from under a single dock! Jigs dressed with Mister Twister tails, plastic worms or crankbaits are highly effective around docks, particularly at dusk and dawn. Weed lines can be worked using jigs, spinnerbaits, and deep diving crankbaits, while top water spoons, weedless worms and buzzbaits can be worked over the top of weedbeds.

There isn't much location change with largemouth bass in the fall. They simply move out into slightly deeper water, orienting off the deepest weed lines available. If you get an extended cold spell and then sunny weather, they often will be found relating to adjacent rocky points. If warm weather persists, the fish will usually return to summer haunts. When the largemouth go deep, you should consider going to smaller lures and slightly slower retrieves. Spinnerbaits are highly effective in the fall, as are deep diving crankbaits. The fish are usually very aggressive in the fall, at least until the water temperatures drop into the mid-50's. This is due to their going on a feeding binge in late September and October. When the water temperature approaches 55° F, the bass become lethargic, but can still be taken on small jigs dressed with minnows or pork rind. Work these jigs slowly along deep weed lines.

Rainbow Trout .... common; growth rate good

The rainbow trout fishery in Canandaigua Lake is supported entirely by natural reproduction, nearly all of which occurs in the lake's principle tributary, the famed Naples Creek. The rainbows here average 3 to 6 pounds, and a few lucky anglers manage to creel fish up to 10 pounds each year. This is down a little from previous years, when rainbows in excess of 15 pounds were found here.

Needless to say, the fishing for rainbow trout starts here on April 1 with the tremendous runs of fish in Naples Creek (see Ontario County Streams and Rivers). Of course, not every single rainbow in Canandaigua Lake is going to run up this stream at the same time, and sexually immature fish won't enter the stream at all. Areas in the lake proper that will hold rainbows early in the spring include the outflows of several tributaries (check those at Menteth Point, Tichenor Point, Walton Point, Cook Point and Seneca Point) and shallow rocky points. If the wind is calm and the water gin clear you can see these trout in the early morning chasing bait fish. They can be taken on light spinning gear using small Rebels, Rapalas or Mepps spinners. If you prefer using a fly rod, they can be taken on streamers.

Beginning around the middle of May, when live bait becomes available, night fishing for rainbows becomes a popular and productive method. Anchor your boat in about 140 feet of water, off points adjacent to deep water, such as Menteth Point or Seneca Point. Bill Kelley recommends using an eight foot rod equipped with roller guides or very large eyelets and a heavy duty reel, such as the Penn 350 or Penn 209. He uses a 4 to 6 ounce weight attached to the main line. At 10 foot intervals above the weight he attaches 3 leaders, each 4 feet in length and each terminating in an English hook baited with a sawbelly or alewife. The leaders are attached to the main line with branch swivels. The rig is fish so that the bottom leader is between 35 and 60 feet below the surface, depending on what depth you're marking fish at. This method of taking rainbows is used as early as the first weeks of May, but is especially productive from mid-June to late August. The trout will hit on this rig from sundown to sunrise. Once the sun comes up the fishing slows to a crawl.

In the late spring and early summer rainbow trout can be taken close to the surface, just off the south bar. The methods are identical to those used for taking brown trout in this area and the two species are often caught together.

In the summer rainbows become pelagic, scattering just above the thermocline in search of bait fish. They can be caught with standard downrigging techniques, Seth Green rigs and dipsey-diver rigs. The trout will be found suspended 60 to 70 feet down throughout the deeper portions of the lake. An especially productive area is the deep water between Long Point and Cottage City.

Rainbow trout can also be taken by trolling in the fall, but depths and locations are different than in the summer. If you're using downriggers, troll with your lures 25 to 40 feet down, and 35 to 40 feet behind the boat. With Seth Green rigs, your bottom leader should be no more than 60 feet down. Of course, the wind and other factors can seriously affect the depth at which the trout will be found, but generally speaking 40 feet is a good depth to start looking for rainbows in the fall. Unlike the summer fishery, the best success is had on the west side of the lake, between Menteth Point and Black Point. It seems that the warm run-off from streams in this area draws the trout in.

In October, the sexually mature rainbows in Canandaigua Lake begin moving into Naples Creek to winter over and spawn, a phase which lasts until May. An overwhelming majority of the rainbows that move into the creek in the fall and early winter are small males averaging about 2 pounds. The fishing can be excellent at this time and the crowds are minimal.

Rainbows can be taken through the ice here, primarily at the south end. Good catches of rainbows can also be had by trolling as close to shore as possible in the winter month, using the same hardware as in the spring. Troll at a slightly slower pace.

Additional Species

Canandaigua Lake has good but localized fishing for a number of species. The most important game species under this category is chain pickerel. Traditionally, this lake has had good pickerel fishing in the weed beds of the south end. They are limited to this area by their invariant need to orient adjacent to, or in, dense vegetation. The weeds along the sides of the lake or at the north end simply aren't adequate to their needs. The pickerel here reach a healthy 4 to 5 pounds. Observations by some bass fishermen suggest that as the population of largemouth bass decreases due to angling pressure, the number of pickerel in the lake increases. There is no empirical evidence to back this up, but it would make sense, since these two species coexist in the same habitat, compete for the same food and the pickerel have a faster growth rate than the bass. In the summer, they can be taken on surface plugs, spinners (Mepps #2 and #3), spinnerbaits and worms. In the fall, troll along weed lines with minnow imitations, such as a jointed Rapala. During the winter these toothsome predators are caught through the ice at the south end in good numbers.

Canandaigua Lake has never been known for its yellow perch fishing, but the DEC says that this fishery has really improved over the past few years. The perch in this lake are big, nearly as big as those in Keuka or Seneca. Areas noted for perch include the waters around Squaw Island and Stoney Island, and off High Banks and Butler Road. The fishing is especially good in September and October.

Immediately after ice-out (usually mid-March) excellent pan fishing can be had at the south end of the lake. Seek out shallow, black bottomed coves for bluegills and pumpkinseeds. Such coves can be as much as 8° to 10° F warmer than surrounding waters, attracting tremendous numbers of fish. Bullhead can also be found in these warm shallow areas, as well as in the mouths of Sucker Brook and the West River. In early April Black Crappie begin to spawn in the very southern end of the lake, and through out the West River. Good fishing for these tasty fish lasts until mid-May. For good catches, work the numerous blow downs, brush piles and stumps with small (1/32 ounce) jigs dressed with

The white spot in the center of this photo is the landmark known as "White Rock". It's usually, but not always, painted white.

Mister Twister tails (white and chartreuse are popular) or fish with small minnows and a bobber.

Rounding out the species found in Canandaigua Lake are rock bass, smelt, channel catfish, whitefish (rare), cisco (rare), walleye (rare), American eel (rare), carp, white suckers, northern pike (rare) and burbot (rare).

General Information

Canandaigua is the fourth largest of the Finger Lakes, surpassed only by Keuka, Seneca and Cayuga Lakes.

The only major population center on the lake is the City of Canandaigua, which lies at the north end. Fishing pressure on this lake is very high, however, probably higher than on any other Finger Lake. This is due to the excellence of the fishing for cold and warm water species, the scenic beauty of the area surrounding the lake, and its proximity to the City of Rochester.

Public access to Canandaigua Lake, though better than on most of the other lakes, is inadequate. Approximately 83% of the shoreline is taken up by residential or commercial sites. Public access to the shore is limited to the following areas: the DEC fishing access and launch site on Route 21 at Woodville; the High Tor Wildlife Management Area at the south end of the lake (limited by swampy terrain); Kershaw Park in the City of Canandaigua; the Canandaigua City Pier; and the Canandaigua Lake State Marine Park at the mouth of Sucker Brook. Limited shoreline access can also be found at the county operated park at Deep Run, though this is primarily a swimming beach.

In the winter, ice fishing is usually limited to the extreme north and south ends of the lake. On rare occasions the lake does freeze completely. Safe ice is normally available by early February on the south end, but caution is advised when fishing near the mouth of the West River. The relatively warm outflow can make the ice in that area risky.

Because Canandaigua is in a developed region, it has much more to offer vactioners than just great fishing. In close proximity to the lake are such attractions as the world famous Sonnenberg Gardens, the Finger Lakes Race Track, Bristol Mountain Ski Area, and the Mormon Pageant at Hill Cumorah.

NOTES: _____

_____

_____

_____

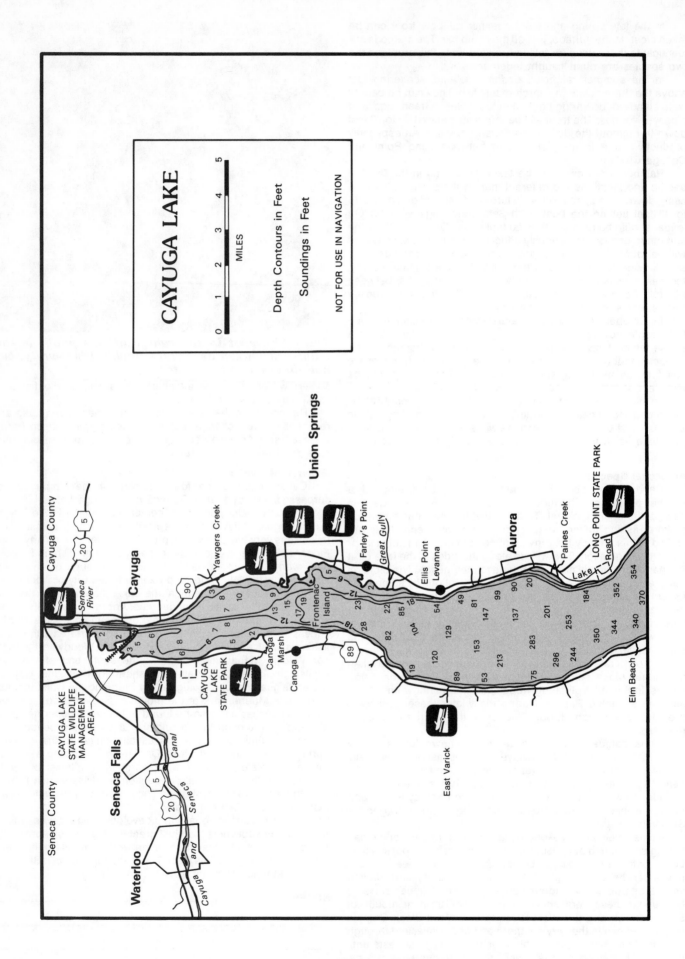

CAYUGA LAKE

MILES

Depth Contours in Feet

Soundings in Feet

NOT FOR USE IN NAVIGATION

Cayuga County

Seneca County

CAYUGA LAKE WILDLIFE MANAGEMENT AREA

Waterloo

Seneca Falls

Canal

Seneca and Cayuga

Cayuga

Seneca River

CAYUGA LAKE STATE PARK

Canoga Marsh

Canoga

Yawgers Creek

Union Springs

Frontenac Island

Farley's Point

Great Gully

Ellis Point

Levanna

Aurora

Paines Creek

LONG POINT STATE PARK

Road

Lake

Elm Beach

East Varick

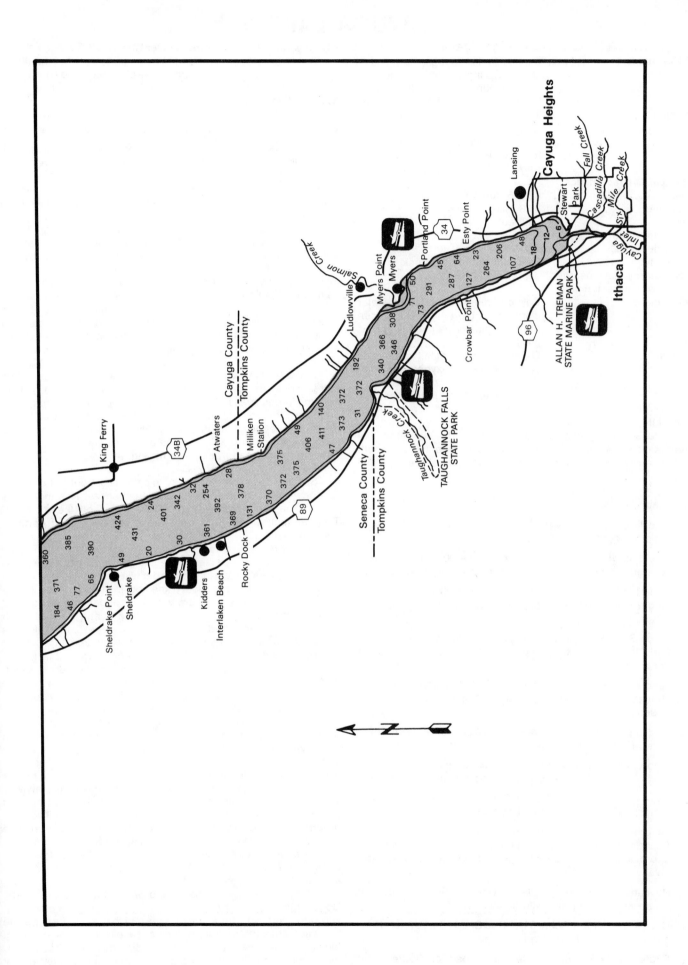

CAYUGA LAKE

map coordinates . . . . 42° 56' 50"   76° 44' 09"

USGS map(s) . . . . Seneca Falls, Cayuga, Romulus, Union Springs, Ovid, Sheldrake, Trumansburg, Ludlowville, Ithaca West (see also N.O.A.A. chart 14791)

location . . . . Tompkins, Cayuga and Seneca Counties

access . . . . The west side of the lake is paral-lelled by Route 89; the east side is parallelled by Route 90.

Physical Characteristics

area . . . . 42,956 acres
shoreline . . . . 84.8 miles
elevation . . . . 382 feet
maximum depth . . . . 435 feet
mean depth . . . . 181 feet
bottom type . . . . sand, silt, rubble, bedrock
mean thermocline depth . . approximately 70 feet

Chemical Characteristics

water clarity . . . . Cayuga Lake has the lowest water clarity of all the Finger Lakes, due to phytoplankton (algae).

pH . . . . alkaline

oxygen . . . . Oxygen is good at all depths all year long. Some oxygen depletion does occur in the deepest waters, it is not severe enough to affect fish species.

Plant Life

Extensive weed beds are found at the north end of the lake (approximately 4,000 acres) and to a lesser extent at the south end. A narrow fringe of weeds also runs along the shoreline of the lake.

Boat Launch Sites

1. Mud Lock - at Lock #1 of Seneca River off Rt. 90/ Single ramp for boats less than 20 feet.

2. Troy's Marina - Backus Road, off Route 90, north of Union Springs. Hard surface ramp, marine supplies - fee.

3. Hibuscus Harbor - Harbor Drive, off Route 90, Union Springs. Single hard surface ramp, pump out, marine supplies, gas, repairs - fee.

4. Union Springs Municipal Launch - off Route 90 at Frontenac Park. Will handle boats up to 25 feet. Multiple, concrete ramps- no charge.

5. Long Point State Park - off Route 90. Will handle boats up to 20 feet. Not protected in a south or west wind. Park user fee in season.

6. Lansing Town Marine Park Minicipal Launch - Myers Point Road. Entrance fee in season. Hard surface ramp.

7. Finger Lakes Marine Service - 44 Marina Road, Myers. Single hard surface ramp, gas, marine supplies, repairs - fee.

8. Allan H. Treman State Marine Park, Ithaca - Route 89. Four ramps, temporary dockage. Entrance fee in season.

9. Taughannock Falls State Park - Route 89. Double launch. Boats must pass under a foot bridge before lake. Bridge has approximately an 8 foot clearance depending on the water level.

10. Haviland Bait Shop - Kidders - Deerlick Springs Road off Route 89. Single ramp with limited access. Fee.

11. Cecil's Bait Shop - Route 89, at Red Creek, East Varick. Hard surface ramp, fishing supplies - fee.

12. Pirates Cove Marina - Lower Lake Road, off Route 89, in Seneca Falls. Double gravel ramp. Marine supplies - fee.

13. Cayuga Lake State Park - Lower Lake Road, Seneca Falls off Route 89. Double launch for boats up to 25 feet depending on the water level. Entrance fee charged in season.

Species Information

Lake Trout . . . . common; growth rate good

Historically, Cayuga Lake had a modest size population of native lake trout. However, by the late 1920's lakers were rare in the lake, probably due to destruction (i.e. siltation) of their main spawning areas. Today, the population is maintained solely by stocking. Cayuga Lake is stocked annually with 72,000 lake trout fingerlings and 36,000 yearlings.

Lake Trout fishing on Cayuga Lake starts in early April. The best fishing is usually centered on the shoreline between Canoga and Sheldrake Point. Traditionally, the fish were taken by still fishing using live smelt, frozen sawbellies or dead sculpin, known locally as tonies or stone cats, for bait. Always kill sculpin before using them as bait or they will swim under a rock. Still fishing is still the preferred method, but now dead smelt are used. Rig the smelt on an English hook, cast out into 10 to 20 feet of water and set the rod down with the bail left open. Wait for the laker to finish his first run before setting the hook. Flat line trolling can also be used.

In the past few years the number of lake trout in Cayuga has increased to the point where a number of other areas have become productive in the spring. Very popular and productive areas are the waters off the railroad track just north of Myers Point. Of secondary importance is the southeast corner of the lake. There is a pull-off on Route 34 near Esty Point that leads down to the railroad tracks. The fishing here is good, but not as good as at the above areas.

Still fishing isn't the only way to catch lake trout in the spring. They can also be taken by casting from shore. This method is popular on the north side of Myers Point, off the mouth of Taughannock Creek, and from the small points just north of Milliken Station.

Lake trout will also be taken very early in the spring by trolling. Before the alewives move into the shallows, they will be in deep (100+feet) water and the trout will be down there feeding on them. The most productive method for taking these fish is trolling with cowbells and alewives. Downriggers are being used with increasing frequency for these deep spring trout, but with less success than traditional methods. (See Earl Holdren's articles on how to fish with traditional techniques, and C. Scott Sampson's article on how to use downriggers in the Finger Lakes). The best spring deep trolling area is off Sheldrake Point in April and May. A lot of lake trout are also taken by flat line trolling in shallow water along the drop-offs north of Myers Point and along the shoreline of Taughannock State Park.

In late May, as the lake begins to warm up, alewives begin to move into the shallows. They concentrate on the central portion of the west shore of the lake, especially the area around Rocky Dock, south of Sheldrake Point. This region has a lot of shelves, and great concentrations of lake trout will be found there just as they begin to move out of the deep water to feed on the alewives. Typically, anglers will troll in 30 feet of water, roughly from Elm Beach down to Rocky Dock, from late May to mid-June. The most productive techniques here are the traditional ones. Wire line trolling with single hook spoons, such as the Sutton 66, Pflueger 4 or Baracuda, is extremely effective. Some people also troll smelt behind cowbell rigs or flasher rigs. This is also a productive method.

At the same time you can use downriggers for these lakers. Downrigging reportedly isn't as effective as the older method, but you will catch fish. The problem is the fact that you have to get the lure very close to the bottom to take these lake trout. Aside from feeding on alewives, they are also feeding heavily on sculpins at this time of year, which are a bottom oriented bait (the red-dot Twin-Minnows that are so popular on Cayuga Lake are sculpin imitations). There is bedrock in this area, especially as you get south of Rocky Dock, so you must be very careful not to hang up your downrigger. Popular spoons to troll with downriggers here are Sutton series, such as the 44's and 31's but don't overlook some of the newer spoons, such as the Stinger and Evil Eye.

Generally speaking, the lake trout in Cayuga Lake move in a clockwise pattern from early spring through fall. In the spring, the greatest concentrations are going to be centered around Sheldrake Point. After the lake stratifies, the fishing will be centered on the east side of the lake, off Long Point. By late summer they will have moved down to King Ferry. In the fall, they again move across the lake, heading for their spawning grounds in the Taughannock area. Presumably, there is a winter movement of fish back up toward Sheldrake Point.

By late June the lake will have stratified or developed a thermocline. Initially the best lake trout fishing will be centered off Long Point, but as the summer progresses the King Ferry area will become more prominent. Lake trout can be taken, though, with varying degrees of success anywhere in the deep central region of the lake in summer, roughly from Long Point down to Myers Point. Trolling with copper lines is an effective method in the summer, but instead of using sawbellies on English hooks, most anglers now switch to single hook spoons.

Downriggers become very effective in the summer. They are easier to use in the warm weather months than in the spring because the lake trout become more temperature oriented than structure oriented and thus are up off the bottom.They will be found in and just below the thermocline.

While lake trout can certainly be taken on copper lines or with downriggers in the summer, many people, including some of the fisheries personnel from the DEC and some charter boat captains, feel that the most effective way to take these fish is on Seth Green rigs. They aren't the easiest thing to use, and it can take years to really master the art of taking fish with one, but in the hands of an expert they are unsurpassed in their ability to harvest fish.

By late August or early September the lake trout begin homing in on their principle spawning grounds, and will be found in great numbers from Taughannock Falls State Park down to Crowbar. For the most part these fish turn off to feeding. But a few lakers can still be taken by trolling in 70 to 100 feet of water. Copper line should be used, as opposed to downriggers, because the lake trout become bottom oriented in the fall, and there is some bedrock in this area.

In the winter, lake trout are most commonly taken on Cayuga Lake by casting from shore with spoons and spinners or by fishing shiners under a bobber. The traditional method of still fishing with frozen smelt from shore or boat is also very productive. Popular areas include the shore along Taughannock Park, the thermal discharge at Milliken Station, and the small points north of Myers Point. On Seneca Lake winter trolling for lakers in deep water is very productive, and there is no reason that it wouldn't be just as good on Cayuga Lake. The launch at Taughannock State Park is now being bubbled so that it can be used in the winter.

Landlocked Salmon . . . . common; growth rate good

Originally, the true Atlantic strain of salmon were native to Cayuga Lake, but the building of mill dams in the 1800's destroyed their spawning habitat. Today, the salmon population of the lake is maintained by an annual stocking of 15,000 yearling salmon. These fish are a strain of true landlocked salmon, which do have morphological characteristics and developmental patterns somewhat different from true Atlantic salmon.

Early in the spring, landlocked salmon will be concentrated in the southern end of the lake. The best fishing will be found off the mouths of Cayuga Inlet and Fall Creek, and as far up the east side of the lake as Esty Point. Occasionally, they can be found as far north as Portland Point. Flat lining with Rapalas, small silver spoons or Alpena Diamonds is the method commonly used in these areas. If you prefer using downriggers, run them shallow, trailing Sutton Spoons — 05's, 08's, 61's, 44's etc., but troll them

Scott Sampson and son with a mixed bag of Cayuga Lake trout. Scott was the source of much of the information contained in this article. Photo courtesy C. Scott Sampson.

faster for salmon than you would for other salmonids. Stickbaits in size 07 also work well. Effective color patterns include blue and silver, black and silver, and gold with a florescent red back. When fishing in the 6 to 8 foot shallows of the very south end of the lake, try plain gold baits. The water is often murky in that area and gold is a good color to use in such cases.

Landlocked salmon can also be taken by casting from shore in the spring. This is very popular off Esty Point and Myers Point.Anglers frequently wade to get added distance when shore fishing in these areas. Popular lures include small Mepps spinners, Little Cleos and Rooster Tails.

By mid-May the salmon will usually have moved out of the above areas. The greatest numbers of fish will then be found off Sheldrake Point, Myers Point and Long Point. A few salmon will also be found near the discharge at Milliken Station, left over from the previous winter concentration there. In the latter half of May the salmon will still be close to the surface suspended in 50 to 60 degree water. They begin to drop down in the water column in June, until they are located about 20 to 35 feet down. Flat lining is especially productive for these shallow running fish. Flat line techniques are commonly used from the second week of May until the third week of June, with the waters between Myers Point and Milliken Station producing the best catches.

In late June, Cayuga Lake stratifies. Once this occurs, salmon will be found practically everywhere. There are a few areas that produce more fish than others, but these concentrations are much less distinct than in the spring. The waters off Taughannock Falls State Park, Myers Point, Milliken Station, Long Point and Sheldrake Point all reportedly produce the best fishing, but it really isn't much better than anywhere else. The best fishing occurs on windy days on the four points mentioned above. On choppy days the salmon congregate off these points in 25 to 30 feet of water. Otherwise, the salmon will be spread out over the lake, orienting above the thermocline. This situation persists until mid to late September.

In late September, the salmon are on the move again. The most productive area of the lake will be the waters south of Taughannock Point. Good salmon fishing can be had by trolling back and forth in front of the stack on the southwest side of the lake or off Taughannock Point. Run parallel to and just off the drop-off in that area, and run your lures shallow. Landlocked salmon orient close to the surface in the late fall.

Cayuga Lake does have a winter salmon fishery. It is centered on the warm water discharge at Milliken Station. Fishing from shore at Milliken is very popular and very productive. Some anglers feel that the most consistantly successful lure for winter salmon is a white or chartreuse Rooster Tail, but Little Cleos, Rapalas, worms, minnows and even egg sacs all work well here. One problem with fishing this area is a lack of adequate parking. There is also a relatively dangerous current that can sweep an angler off his feet. A number of fisherman have lost their lives here and extreme caution should be exercised when wading in this area.

Brown Trout.............. common; growth rate good

The impact of sea lamprey on Cayuga Lake was nowhere more devastating than on the lake's brown trout population. Prior to lamprey control, nearly all of the brown trout in this lake had succumbed to the effects of lamprey attacks by their second year. A few fish did manage to survive, attaining a weight of 6 to 8 pounds, but they are rare fish. The average brown trout caught here was a mere 1½ pounds. This situation is changing. A lamprey control program went into effect in 1986, and the results are already beginning to appear. Anglers are catching more and larger brown trout.

The bulk of the brown trout fishing currently takes place in the spring at the south end of the lake. It begins in late March and lasts until the first or second week of May. The browns seek out the warmest water available, and will be found close to shore from Cayuga Inlet up to Esty Point. These fish averaged about 14 inches before lamprey controls were initiated but should reach a weight of 8 to 10 pounds within the next couple of years. They can be taken with flat lines or shallow running downriggers. Use

the same lures as you would for spring salmon. There is also some limited spring fishing for brown trout in the Myers Point area. Concentrate your efforts on the north side of the point in front of Salmon Creek.

No one knows how this fishery is going to shape up but the DEC did have this to say. Their information indicates that from mid-June until the lake is strongly stratified the browns are not being caught in any great numbers.Once the thermocline is set, however, this lake has or will have typical summer brown trout fishing. In the fall the DEC expects to find a majority of the fish concentrating off the small point just south of Myers Point where they were stocked.It's too early to tell whether or not these browns will be vulnerable to angling during their spawning phase.

Cayuga Lake is stocked annually with 15,000 brown trout .
Rainbow Trout............ uncommon; growth rate fair

Rainbow trout constitute a fishery of secondary importance on Cayuga Lake. The rainbows found here may be considered wild fish. There is a self-sustaining population from stockings made in the mid-1950's. The tributary system of the lake provides for a significant amount of natural reproduction. Supplemental stocking is used periodically.

The sea lamprey don't predate as heavily on the rainbow trout as they do on the browns, but they do a considerable amount of damage, nevertheless. Most rainbows here are 16 to 18 inches, and few will reach 6 pounds.

In the spring, rainbows can be caught at the south end of the lake in shallow water, from Cayuga Inlet up to Esty Point, and in most estuaries such as off Salmon Creek. Common techniques include using flat lines, still fishing with smelt or drifting salmon eggs out into the lake with the stream current. They are also taken at Esty Point from shore by casting small Mepps spinners, Little Cleos and Rooster Tails. The fishing for rainbow trout in both of these areas is only fair.

When the lake stratifies in late June the area most likely to have consistent fishing for rainbows are the waters around

J. Michael Kelly with a Cayuga Lake rainbow taken during its spawning run in Salmon Creek. Notice the lamprey scar on the fish. Photo courtesy of J. Michael Kelly.

Milliken Station. An area of secondary importance would be the bay between Myers Point and Portland Point. A few rainbows area also taken in the summer off Sheldrake Point, but not enough to constitute a real fishery. Fish all of these areas in 25 to 50 feet of water, using silver spoons dressed with chartreuse or red tape, Alpena Diamonds, or Sutton 44's. Rainbows can be found in the above areas until mid-September.

In the early fall, the best rainbow trout fishing on the lake will be found along the shores south of Taughannock Falls State Park. You can follow the shore to the shallow south basin that begins at the stack on the southwest side of the lake. Later in the fall (October-early November) the troll from Cayuga Inlet up to Esty Point will again hold fish.

There is relatively little fishing for rainbow trout here in the winter. A few fish are caught at Milliken Station and off the mouth of Taughannock Creek, but these are usually small fish. Very few big rainbows are caught in Cayuga Lake in the winter.

Smallmouth Bass .... common, growth rate good

Cayuga Lake has a very healthy population of smallmouth bass. The average smallmouth here runs 12 to 14 inches, but fish 15 to 18 inches are not at all uncommon, especially in the winter.

The bulk of the smallmouth in this lake are found along the east and west shorelines. Smaller populations are also found where the shallows at the north end drop off into the deep central basin of the lake, and at the south end. The DEC feels that the bass population at the south end of the lake is really rather sparse, but it gets a lot of attention from local anglers.

In the spring tremendous numbers of smallmouth bass move into the shallows along the sides of the lake to spawn. On the west side of the lake concentrate your efforts on the shelves between East Varick and Taughannock Point. On the east side of the bass will be found in good numbers from Frontenac Island down to Milliken Station (Frontenanc Island is just off shore of Union Springs).

When fishing for Cayuga Lake smallmouth in late spring and early summer work the weed lines and any narrow flats. In the early part of the season the shore side of the weed beds are the most productive, especially when there is a steep rocky drop-off between the shore and weeds. Exceptionally good early season smallmouth fishing can be had by working these areas with small deer hair jigs, Mister Twisters and small white spinnerbaits. This early season fishing is often most productive in the stretch between Levanna and Frontenac Island, but anywhere along the shoreline between the points mentioned above will hold small-mouth.

Because of the configuration of the weedlines running parallel to the shore, it's tempting to anchor between the weeds and the shore and cast along parallel to the weed line. Jay Nelson, a top bass fisherman from Dundee, New York doesn't recommend this. He feels that these fish are pretty skittish at this time of year and can be easily spooked by seeing you or your boat or by the sounds you inevitably make. Jay's method for taking these bass is to anchor on the deep side of the weed line and cast over it toward shore with small spinnerbaits. He says that the weeds act as an effective barrier between you and the fish and this can make a big difference in the number of fish caught.

By mid-July, the bass will be moving out of the shallows. From this point until early October the bass fishing is very typical. Fish will be found on the deep side of the ribbon of weeds that runs parallel to much of the shore line. They can be taken by working the weed lines with deep diving crankbaits, deer hair jigs or jigs dressed with Twister tails. Jay Nelson has had considerable luck taking these smallmouth with Jig 'n Pigs. He employes a stop-and-go retrieve, with the bass usually hitting the offering while it is resting on the bottom.

Be sure not to neglect the rocky points on the lake in the summer. Smallmouth bass are found on practically every point on both sides of the lake between East Varick and Taughannock Point. Especially good is the whole shore line ½ mile north and south of Milliken Point. Sheldrake Point is another very

productive site. Just north of Sheldrake Point is a deep hole. Many anglers are very successful fish with large crayfish or minnows where the bottom drops off here.

There are few hard and fast rules for taking smallmouth bass from Cayuga or any other lake. One angler I spoke to who fishes this lake regulary feels that the best fishing is found in water less than 20 feet deep. He's very successful taking bass close to the surface on flat lines. Other anglers strongly recommended working the sides of the lake in 40 to 60 feet of water. So don't approach this lake with inflexible attitudes on how to fish it. Be willing to adjust your techniques to fit conditions that are constantly changing. There are always bass hitting somewhere on Cayuga Lake.

Beginning around the middle of September a lot of bass fishermen start picking up smallmouth in very shallow water, often as shallow as three feet. This probably occurs along the shore of the lake where shallow flats provide adequate forage adjacent to deep water retreats, but the hottest area is usually the stretch of shoreline between Sheldrake Point and Taughannock Point. On a calm day you can stand up in your boat, and with polarized glasses see the bass cruising these flats. Surface plugs and vibrating plugs work well on these fish. This lasts until the shoreward water temperatures drop in to the mid 50's. The bass then retreat to deeper, warmer waters.

One of the principle reasons that the fishing is so good between Sheldrake Point and Taughannock Point in the fall is the fact that beginning in late September or early October a large portion of the bass population in Cayuga Lake is migrating southward toward the area known as Flat Rock, which lies just south of Taughannock Point. Flat Rock is the major winter concentration for smallmouth on Cayuga Lake. They start showing up here in early October and Cliff Creech of the DEC office in Cortland has estimated the number of fish that gather into this small area at several thousand! The same type of winter bass fishing takes place here as on the Bluff at Keuka Lake. Many anglers on Cayuga Lake use minnows to take these bass, but a jig fisherman could really clean up here. The one problem with fishing this area later in the year is that the closest launch ramp,

The bass in Cayuga Lake are big. Darren Dalton with two fish taken from Cayuga Lake and Seneca Lake. Photo courtesy of C. Scott Sampson.

at Taughannock State Park, is often locked in ice during the winter.

Largemouth Bass . . . . common; growth rate good

Largemouth bass are of primary importance in Cayuga Lake. In the weedy north end of the lake they are abundant, and attain a very respectable 4 to 6 pounds. The large size and abundance of this species attracted no less than 38 professional bass tournaments to this water in 1987.

The bulk of the largemouth in Cayuga Lake are found north of Aurora on the east side and north of East Varick on the west side, right up to the outlet of the lake at lock #1 on the Seneca River.

In the late spring and early summer, the fishing is especially good in the shallow, weedy waters north of Union Springs. Shallow weed lines will be very productive when fished with spinnerbaits, Jig n' Pigs, and other conventional bass hardware.

Work the shallowest areas until mid-July. From that point on the largemouth will seek out deeper weed lines. An exceptionally good area to fish would be the edges of the navigation channel that runs from the twin buoys at Union Springs to the outlet. This channel is dredged to a depth of about 14 feet. Working ⅜ ounce jigs dressed with black or purple Mister Twister tails very slowly along the edge of this channel is very effective. Texas-rigged nightcrawlers will also work well. During daylight hours many largemouth will be found along the edges of openings in the weed beds south of the railroad causeway. At dusk and dawn, however, fish move back into the shallow near-shore waters that were so productive in the early summer to feed on minnows. Working small jigs or spinnerbaits along the inside of weed lines during these low light periods is very productive. Small poppers fished with a fly rod will also take bass at these times, and fighting a 4 pound largemouth on a limber fly rod will be an experience you're not soon to forget!

In the fall, the bass will tend to orient off the deepest weed lines and points available to them, though extended warm spells will cause them to move back into shallower areas. This movement to deep water isn't so noticable in the areas north of Union Springs because there isn't much deep water to move to. It is noticable in the populations of largemouth found along the lake sides south of Union Springs and Canoga.

Cayuga Lake has excellent fishing for largemouth bass in the winter. These winter bass, which are usually taken incidentally by perch and crappie fishermen in 8 to 10 feet of water, average 14 to 16 inches. They can be taken anywhere on the northern end where safe ice has formed. The best area for bass alone is off Canoga. Jigging Rapalas, Swedish Pimples, or minnows will catch largemouth in the winter. The best fishing often occurs in February when sexual changes in female bass trigger a feeding binge.

Northern Pike . . . . common; growth rate very good

Cayuga Lake has a good northern pike fishery, most of which is found at the shallow northern end of the lake, from Union Springs to the outlet. Smaller populations are also found at Milliken Station, Rocky Dock, Taughannock Park, the north side of Myers Point and at the extreme south end of the lake.

When the season first opens northerns can be taken by fishing with large chubs or shiners. They are usually bottom oriented for a short period after spawning, so use a small sinker to keep your bait near the bottom. By the end of May the fish become more aggressive and mobile, so bringing your bait up off the bottom with a big bobber is recommended. Late spring is also the time when lures become effective. Red and white Daredevle spoons, and spinners, such as the Mepps Aglia, Panther Martin or Vibrex will take a lot of northerns in the late spring and summer.

Northern pike are structure oriented in the summer, and there is a lot of it in the north end to work over. There are the remains of old duck blinds north of the causeway that provide good pike habitat. Row into this area unless you carry a spare prop. Blind supports cut off by the ice are just under the surface

A 23 pound northern pike taken off Canoga Marsh. Photo courtesy of C. Scott Sampson.

of the water. In the latter half of the summer mechanical weed cutters are brough in to cut navigation channels. The edges of these channels also hold good numbers of fish. These fish can be taken with traditional pike harvesting techniques. If you're looking strictly for the really big pike, fish with big baits. A foot long sucker hooked through the upper lip with a #2 short shank hook and fished under a slip-bobber should do the trick. Bait this large usually only attracts the larger northern pike, and so you won't have to contend with any hungry largemouth bass that might be in the area.

In the fall, big jigs become especially effective for northern pike. Half ounce and one ounce jigs dressed with bucktails, 5 to 7 inch waterdogs or 4 to 6 inch Mister Twister tails all work well when fished along deep weed lines. Deep diving minnow imitations, such as a large jointed Rapala, are also a favorite pike bait.

Although the northern end of Cayuga Lake has a very healthy pike population, fewer fish are caught here in the summer and fall than you would expect. The truly great northern pike fishing takes place in the winter, when great numbers of fish are taken through the ice. Standard ice-fishing techniques are used. Tip-ups baited with a large sucker or shiner hooked through the back will do the trick. There is also an open water fishery for northerns on this lake. Good numbers of fish are caught by shore fishermen casting big yellow jigs or flashy spoons. This commonly takes place at Milliken Station, just north of Myers Point and at the yacht club at Glenwood.

Additional Species

In addition to the species mentioned above, Cayuga Lake has fair to good fishing for a number of fish of secondary importance. Yellow perch are prominent among this group. Historically, this lake has had good, but not great, perch fishing. Since the early 1980's, however, the perch fishing has improved significantly and the DEC feels that this could be the beginning of a long term trend. In May and early June there is good perch fishing on almost every point on the lake. These fish are easily caught from shore using small jigs or minnows. The area from Sheldrake Point down to Taughannock Point is especially productive. In the fall, great perch fishing is found at the southern end of the lake anywhere south of the stack on the southwest shore. Ice fishing for perch is very productive at the north end of the lake. On good ice start working the channel north from the twin buoys.

Chain pickerel are found in the northern end of Cayuga Lake in fairly good numbers, especially in the waters of Canoga Marsh. They are commonly taken there in the summer months using the same techniques used to catch northerns. Reportedly, few pickerel are taken here in the winter, just the opposite situation you have with northern pike.

Smelt are very important to locals as a fishery. Salmon Creek, Taughannock Creek, Great Gully Creek, Paines Creek, Yawgers Creek and Fall Creek usually have good runs of smelt in April and access is good on each. Over the past few years, though, the quality of these runs has been on the decline. Unlike Lake Ontario, there is a limit to the amount of smelt that can be taken on any of the Finger Lakes. Current regulation limit your daily harvest to 8 quarts of smelt per day. You may also find dipping hours posted at the request of the landowners.

The pan fishing in Cayuga Lake is excellent almost anywhere north of Union Springs. The spring crappie fishing is excellent and these tasty fish average a good 10 inches here, and some get up to 12 to 14 inches. Crappie aren't the only pan fish that grow big in Cayuga Lake. Bluegills the size of a man's hand are commonly taken from these waters. For a mixed big of fish try ice fishing right on the edge of the navigation channel north of the causeway with minnows or small jigs. The action can be fast!

Also found in Cayuga Lake are rock bass, white bass, white perch, pumpkinseeds, channel catfish, white suckers, carp, brown bullhead, gar, bowfin and American eels.

General Information

Cayuga Lake, at 42,956 acreas, is the largest of the Finger Lakes, surpassing its neighbor, Seneca Lake, by a scant 325 acres. Centrally located in the heart of the Finger Lakes Region, Cayuga Lake lies within easy driving distance (40 miles) for 1,500,000 people. The lake is heavily utilized, not just for fishing, but for nearly every water related activity you can think of.

To facilitate use of the lake the state has created four lakeside parks. They are Cayuga Lake State Park on the northwest shore, Taughannock Falls State Park on the southwest shore, Allen H. Treman Marine Park at the south end and Long Point State Park on the east shore. These are all full facility parks and all but Treman Marine Park have facilities for camping. Additional shoreline access is provided at Stewart Park on the southeast corner of the lake, Lansing Village Park at Myers Point, the Myers Point state land parcel and the Lehigh Valley railroad grade that runs north and south of Salmon Creek. Unfortunately, public access to the central portion of the lake is severly limited. Excessively long travel distances effectively exclude small boats from some of the best fishing on the lake, not just because of travel time, but because of the potential dangers in the event of sudden, severe storms. The areas most in need of additional public access are the Sheldrake Point-East Varick section on the west shore and the Lake Ridge-King Ferry section on the east shore.

Another problem that has plagued Cayuga Lake until recently was the damage to the fishery caused by sea lamprey. Most heavily impacted were the brown trout, few of which survived past their second year. The lake trout and rainbow trout populations were also affected, but not nearly as severely as the browns. The reason the brown trout were so heavily affected is that each spring they gather at the south end of the lake off the mouth of Cayuga Inlet just as the young sea lamprey are leaving the stream to take up residence in the lake. In 1986 a sea lamprey control project was initiated for the lake and the results should be an almost immediate improvement in the quality of the trout and salmon fishing in the lake.

The following article, written by noted outdoor writer C. Scott Sampson, gives a detailed first hand impression of the great fishing on Cayuga Lake.

CAYUGA LAKE
by C. Scott Sampson

In less time than it takes to tell you about it, two silver plated Sutton spoons and Sampo swivels were on the bottom of Cayuga Lake. The loss of nearly $8 worth of tackle had me grinning from ear to ear.

All four downriggers releases had tripped at once. From the antics and directions the fish went, combined with the identification of the two fish that remained, they were all landlocked or Atlantic salmon. The two fish that were lost had crossed the downrigger cables and sawed the 8-pound test line in two.

That was the third time that had happened to me and I am still looking to land all four fish. In fact, the best I have ever done is three, and that was more a matter of luck.

In the fall and spring of the year the salmonid populations of the lake, especially the rainbow and salmon, are concentrated off Cayuga's tributaries. Taughannock and Salmon Creeks are my personal favorites.

The fish on the average are not huge, normally about 2 pounds. But, there is always the chance that you will lock into a real trophy. Landlocks have been taken up to 14 pounds both in the lake and in the tributaries during the fall months such as below the falls on Fall Creek in the City of Ithaca. Salmon Creek has produced a steady run of fall salmon when rains have brought a steady supply of water coming over the rapids. Working the pools with a flyrod and streamers could provide an unforgetable moment.

Cayuga Inlet will also produce the opportunity for both fall and spring runs of trout and salmon but the environment is not as picturesque. Spring angling for rainbow is much more predictable and consistent than the fall runs of salmon. You also need to keep in mind that angling does not open in the tributaries until April 1 for those spawning rainbow trophies.

Both Cayuga Inlet and Salmon Creek are important natural nurseries for rainbow trout and salmon. While both these species are also stocked, there is general agreement among biologists that these fish have established at least limited natural reproduction.

There is no question that stocking is the backbone of the cold water fishery in Cayuga Lake. Early fisheries studies conducted by Cornell University proved that there is virtually no natural reproduction of lake trout that remains in the lake from this once native specie. Currently the state stocks more that 100,000 lake trout annually in Cayuga; nearly 40,000 yearlings and almost double that in fingerlings.

Rainbows are stocked at the rate of 25,000; 15,000 brown trout and 43,000 landlocked salmon make up the rest of the nearly 200,000 fish that annually enter the lake to support a fishery valued at nearly $4 million annualy to the local economy.

It is not so much the economy and stocking figures that interest the angler, it is what is in his fish box or how many fish he has had the opportunity to play and release. Opportunity is there and in the 38 miles of lake you should be able to fill your most ferocious angler appetite. Bass, yellow perch, pickerel, northern pike, lake trout, brown, rainbow, Atlantic salmon, smelt and bullheads are just some of the 53 species of freshwater fish found here.

The lake, for angling purposes, can be divided into sections. The northern six miles, the southernmost two miles and selected shoreline areas make up 26 percent of the angling surface of the

An aerial view of the north end of Cayuga Lake. The railroad causeway that cuts across the top of the lake is seen at left. Photo courtesy New York State DEC.

lake that are relatively shallow weed-filled areas. These regions, with an average depth of less than 20 feet are ideal for warm water species.

Talk to any professional bass angler and the name Cayuga starts the imagination working as much as the term Beaverkill inspires the fly fisherman. To give you a better idea of the quality of the bass fishing all you need to do is look at the history of the professional BASS tournament that, in 1983, was headquartered in Watkins Glen on Seneca Lake. The majority of those professional anglers elected to run nearly 40 miles of open water, 10 miles of canal and three locks to reach the Cayuga Lake honey holes.

History also says they did not win, but only because a storm came up on the final day and not one of the traveling anglers could make it back down Seneca Lake in the 8 foot plus waves.

I wouldn't tell you that all the bass that you catch will be over five pounds but you should be able to bring in a limit where the fish average 2 pounds. Work the holes in the weed cover or along some of the channels that edge the railroad dike which crosses the north end of the lake. The edges of the main navigation channel that marks the weed free lane that traverses the lake from the Barge Canal on the north to the twin bouy markers, just north of Union Springs is also excellent. This is also the prime ice fishing area when this northern shallow is covered over. Always proceed with caution in ice fishing as the rest of the lake is open water and wind and wave action can destroy ice overnight.

The "twin markers", by the way, are not twins as the name might suggest but they are the red and the white channel markers that are opposite each other and mark the beginning of the channel or the open water depending on your direction of travel.

Access to this area can be had at the Cayuga Lake State Park in Seneca Falls. The ramp has recently been expanded to four lanes and the area dredged so that you no longer have to wade the waters to pull your boat free of the trailer.

Adjacent to Mud Lock or Lock Number 1 off Rt. 90, is a DEC ramp that enters the water at the very northern edge of the lake.

Access to the southern portions of the lake, which is more noted for smallmouth bass, is best obtained at Allen H. Treman State Marine Park off Route 89.

Between the two shallow extremes are the deep cold waters that the Finger Lakes are best known for. With depths of up to 435 feet and an overal average of 181 feet there is significant habitat in Cayuga Lake for trout and salmon.

The location of the downrigger releases, described in the beginning, was just off Taughannock State Park which has a small but efficient launch and harbor. It can handle boats in the 20 foot range providing they do not have a high cabin structure. You gain access to the lake under a walk bridge that has approximately an 8 foot clearance depending on the water level.

For larger boats, use the Treman Marine Park in Ithaca and motor back the seven miles or if you are on the east side of the lake, use the Meyers Point facility launch at Lansing off Route 34B or the Long Point State Park area off Route 90. Long Point Park has recently been improved to include the addition of restroom facilities.

While the lake is serviced by another dozen private facilities, few of these offer the quality launch and small boat services that you would expect. Many of the private areas, especially in the Ithaca and Union Springs areas cater to cruisers and sailboats. Boat rentals are currently available on the lake in the Seneca Falls area.

From Long Point to Salmon Creek you will find some of the best deep water angling anywhere in the Finger Lakes. Sheldrake Point area has consistently produced mixed creels of all the salmonid species with Atlantics up to 12 pounds, brown trout in the 8 pound class, lake trout at 10 pounds plus and rainbows in the 8 pound range.

If you do not find success immediately, you may need to move toward Long Point or south toward Milliken Station, a coal fired electric plant that uses lake water to cool its turbines and discharges the warm water back into the lake. The warm water flume is an important location for winter, late fall and early spring fishing.

In summer fishing, you will generally find a thermocline established at about 90 feet. Browns, salmon and rainbows will be in the 30 to 60 foot range and in some cases on the thermocline but, lake trout will be in the thermocline or slightly below it.

Multi-leader thermocline rings or Seth Green Rigs are used on Cayuga Lake but perhaps not as much now as the modern downrigger for deep trolling. Terminal tackle is more often than not silver spoons such as the Suttons but the colored salmon selections are moving in from the west coast and the Great Lakes with exceptional success.

The Alpina Diamond in chartreuse with firedots, Joe Riefer's Pirate 44 with green or chartreuse tape, Fire Plugs, Hot Shots and of course the Rebel and Rapala plugs are all being used for salmonids. Little Cleo is the number one favorite for shore fishing or top line trolling in the spring and fall.

When Bill Haessner, a professional guide on the Finger Lakes attempted to set the light line world record for landlocked salmon, he did so with a chartreuse Hot Shot on his 1-pound test line. He was not successful but he is committed to continuing his search in the early spring and the late fall when the salmon are concentrated near the surface and when the gossimer line can be used effectively on the 12 foot custom rods built by Dick Swan.

That record is currently only 4½ pounds and well within the fishery of Cayuga Lake.

Bait, such as alewives and smelt, are also used in the traditional Finger Lakes fashions. The bait may be still fished off an English hook, using an egg or barrel sinker to take it to the bottom or it may be fished on a gang hook harness behind a flasher system or lake troll.

Cayuga Lake's average lake trout in the last ten years has ranged from 3.7 to 5.1 pounds according to DEC diary statistics. The landlocked salmon ran from 2 to 4½ pounds and rainbows and browns have been quite consistant at the 2 pound class for 'bows and 1½ pounds for brown trout.

Those sizes will increase drastically in the immediate future. After years of sportsmen pressure followed by nearly a half-dozen more years of environmental impact statements and public hearings on chemical treatment of lamprey, control became a reality in the fall of 1986. Anglers will see immediate results in both increased sizes and the number of trout and salmon available.

The sea lamprey, the same parasite that killed the Great Lakes, attaches itself to and kills thousands of salmonids or at best stunts their growth. Brown trout were and are especially susceptible to attack and seldom lived past the two pound size even though they are the same strain or stock that, in Lake Ontario, reach record proportions.

The same chemical control treatment on Cayuga's sister lake, Seneca, begun in 1980, has brought results never experienced by anglers in the Finger Lakes. The fragile brown trout fishery, for example, is now producing browns that average 4 pounds when taken by anglers, and browns in the 7 and 8 pounds class will no longer make the local newspapers.

On Cayuga Lake, you can expect similar results but with the added bonus of the Atlantic salmon. The salmon action and the beauty of the fish is nothing short of spectacular, expecially when it is caught in the fall of the year at the hight of the color changes in the forests that line the steep hillsides to the lake. They may also be caught at that time on a flat line or shallow set downrigger lines that allows the freedom for the fish to perform at its best.

While I have illustrated Taughannock Point as a major trout and salmon area, I must tell you that the steep underwater structure next to shore is also smallmouth bass habitat. I remember one day when I struggled to produce one trout while trolling, a young man landed a limit of bass by using a jig cast from shore. He simply threw out the bait and then crawled the lure up the sloping ledge toward shore.

It is the fast drop-offs that concentrate the smallmouth within easy reach of shore in the central portions of the lake. At one area near Frontenac Point, just ten feet from shore you are in 90 feet of water.

Taughannock Creek offers the best but not the only smelt runs of the lake in early and mid-April. When the stream water hits 48 degrees the little fish move from the depths of the lake to the gravel riffles to follow the urge of nature. An 8-quart limit is more than enough smelt to clean.

If northern pike and pickerel are your goal, I would concentrate my search in the northern sections. The area of Canoga Marsh is excellent and with a local name like Pickerel Cove, the northeast corner of the lake south of the railroad dike is another ideal place. North of the railroad are areas of old structure, left over from previous permanent duck blinds that were cut off at the waterline by ice, which hold bass and pike. You must use extreme caution, however, if you go in with anything more than paddle power.

Traditional baits and lures are used and pay particular attention to working your offering parallel to any weed lines or cuts. Mechanical weed cutting is done throughout the north end of the lake to allow better boating access. It is along these edges that mid-summer and fall fishing is the best. Each year pike of 20 plus pounds are taken from these waters.

Both yellow perch and panfish are found throughout the lake along the shoreline habitat. Crappie are concentrated in the spring of the year at the Cayuga Lake Park and along the railroad dike. Small fathead minnows are the favorite baits and catching a pail full is not out of the question.

Cayuga is another lake for all seasons. It only requires you to say, "Let's go fishing".

Angling services on the lake have gone through a number of major changes in recent months. The most consistent information and assistance may be obtained at the Hook Line and Sinker Bait and Tackle Shop in Canoga on Route 89 south of Seneca Falls or call (315) 549-8386. The Ithaca area is presently without an anglers full-service center. This situation is expected to change rapidly as the results of lamprey control bring quality angling back to Cayuga Lake.

NOTES: _____
_____
_____
_____

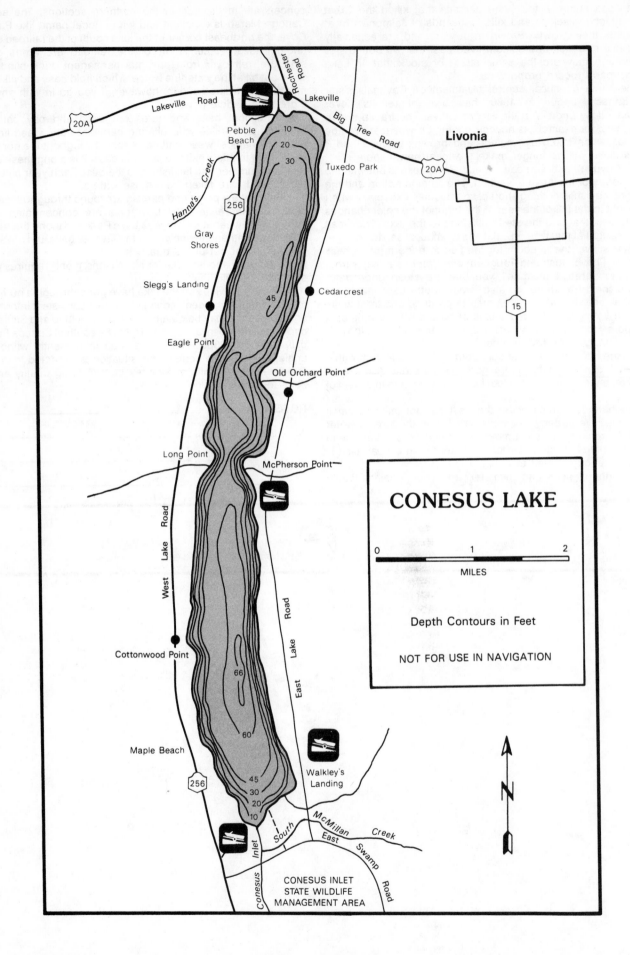

Lakeville Road

20A

Rochester Road

Lakeville

Big Tree Road

Livonia

20A

Pebble
Beach

10

20

30

Tuxedo Park

Hanna's Creek

256

15

Gray
Shores

Slegg's Landing

45

Cedarcrest

Eagle Point

Old Orchard Point

Long Point

McPherson Point

West Lake Road

East Lake Road

Cottonwood Point

66

60

Maple Beach

45

30

20

10

Walkley's
Landing

256

Conesus Inlet

South

East
Swamp
Road

McMillan Creek

CONESUS INLET
STATE WILDLIFE
MANAGEMENT AREA

N

CONESUS LAKE

0   1   2
MILES

Depth Contours in Feet

NOT FOR USE IN NAVIGATION

CONESUS LAKE

Map coordinates......... 42° 47' 12" 77° 43' 00"
USGS map(s)............. Livonia, Conesus
Location................. Central Livingston County
Access.................. parallelled by East
Lake Road (County Road #8) and
West Lake Road (route 256)

Physical Characteristics
Area..................... 3420 acres
Shoreline................. 18.47 miles
Elevation................. 818 feet
Maximum depth.......... 69 feet
Mean depth.............. 38 feet
Bottom type............. muck, gravel and sand
Mean thermocline depth .. 36 feet

Chemical Characteristics
Water clarity............. clear
pH...................... alkaline
Oxygen.................. good throughout the lake except
during the summer at depths greater
than 36 feet

Plant Life
There are significant weed beds in the northern end of the lake to a depth of about 15 feet. Weed beds are also present in the southern end of the lake to 15 feet. There are sporadic patches of weed in all of the major bays and coves. There is a slight problem with algae blooms here in the late summer.

Species Information

Note: In the early 1980's, alewives were introduced into Conesus Lake. Shortly thereafter, their population exploded, and they are now the dominant fish species in the lake. Their dominance of the lake has resulted in a number of significant changes. First and foremost is the affect this has had on the yellow perch population. Until recently, Conesus was one of the top yellow perch lakes in the state. The winter harvest alone was estimated to be in excess of 175,000 fish per year. The alewives wiped out an important forage base for the perch, a large crustacean known as *Daphnia Pulex*. The immediate effect of this has been to greatly slow down the growth rate of the yellow perch. Most of the perch taken here now are emaciated. In addition, although it is not known for sure, there is a very good possibility that the alewives are feeding on the perch fry, reducing the actual numbers of yellow perch that survive to enter the fishery (it was just such a situation that so greatly depressed the perch fishing in Lake Ontario).

Another result of the presence of alewives in Conesus Lake concerns the abundance of plankton. Before the alewives took over, the population of plankton was kept in check by the large population of *Daphnia Pulex*. Now that these crustaceans have been eliminated, Conesus Lake is generally less clear than in previous years (to see how this factor can affect your choice of tackle see the sections on smallmouth bass and largemouth bass), and it is experiencing slightly more significant algae blooms in the late summer. This hasn't greatly affected the fishing here yet, but it could if the situation gets much worse. The abundance of alewives in Conesus Lake is so great that they have actually impacted on the composition of terrestrial wildlife around the lake. Recently, the DEC has received reports of large numbers of gulls on the lake, feeding on dead alewives. This is indicative of the far reaching effects that a non-native species can have on a lake. It is hoped that a point of equilibrium will be reached, whereby the alewives will be kept in check by predation from such species as northern pike, largemouth and smallmouth bass and walleye. Until such a state occurs, the only definate thing that can be said about Conesus Lake is that its species structure is in a state of severe flux. Keep this in mind when reading the following information, which was collected in 1987.

Yellow Perch............. abundant; growth rate fair

Until the invasion of alewives in the early 1980's, yellow perch were arguably the most popular fish found in Conesus Lake. Despite its relatively small size, this lake was consistently one of the top perch producing lakes in the state.

Early in the year, right after ice-out, many anglers concentrate their perch fishing efforts on the deep narrows between Long Point and McPherson Point. This natural bottleneck has good perch habitat and serves to concentrate the schools of perch as they migrate around the lake. Another spring hot spot, is the cove between McPherson Point and Old Orchard Point. This cove, in fact, is one of the most productive areas for perch on Conesus Lake, from ice-up until late June. The waters off Maple Bay also provide some early spring perch action. Later in the spring, yellow perch are known to concentrate on the outside edges of the weed beds off Walkley's Landing, along the weed beds off Eagle Point, and along the weed beds between McPherson Point and Old Orchard Point.

A popular and productive method for taking springtime perch is to anchor along the edges of dormant weed beds and stillfish with worms, grubs or minnows. The use of perch rigs (spreaders) will increase your catch considerably.

Later in the year, as the summer's sun warms the waters of Conesus Lake, the schools of perch become much more migratory and decidedly hard to find. They will most ofter be found over hard rocky bottoms and near structure associated with deep water. For the most part, yellow perch are taken incidentally in the summer, while you're fishing for smallmouth bass with small spinners of jigs. If you're really serious about fishing for perch in the summer, check out the points, especially on the southwest side of the lake.

Between Long Point and Maple Beach, there are several points running into deep water. Stillfish the points with small crayfish or minnows, or use small jigs tipped with minnows. Keep moving until you find some action.

In the fall, the perch fishing picks up considerably. Yellow perch begin to move into very deep water by mid-October, and there is relatively little really deep water in Conesus Lake. Very productive areas will include the hole directly across from Cottonwood Point, the narrows between McPherson Point and Long Point, and the deep water off Eagle Point. Minnows fished close to the bottom would probably be your best bet. Again, use spreaders to take full advantage of the multitudinous perch just waiting for something to hit on.

It is in the winter that Conesus Lake earns its reputation as one of the top yellow perch lakes in the state. Standard tip-ups will work well on this lake, but the most popular method here for taking buckets full of perch is jigging. The most popular jig is the classic "Conesus Jig" either in silver or copper. These are available from local tackle shops. Other standard ice fishing jigs, such as the red or white russian jig, or the swedish pimple are also effective. Tipping the jig with a mousey grub, an oak leaf grub or a perch eye will increase your chances of success. Keep moving and changing jigs until you locate a school and then get ready for some real action.

Initially, perch will be found in the shallow portions of the lake in 10-20 feet of water. On Conesus Lake that means most of the early ice fishing will take place near the northern end of the lake. (The south end of the lake does have shallow water, but the relatively warm water from the inlet keeps that end ice-free longer than the north end. Even when it does freeze up, the south end can be treacherous to venture out on.) As the ice and snow pack thicken, the plants in the northern end are cut off from sunlight and the oxygen levels diminish. This will force the yellow perch to move into progressively deeper water, i.e. southward.

Once the perch begin this migration, the only way to find out where they're hitting is to check with local tackle shops (Bob's Bait & Tackle at the north end of the lake on U.S. 20 is a good source of information) or to follow the crowds on the ice.

There are three major access points on Conesus Lake for winter anglers. There is popular, but informal, access via the water authority property on the northwest side of the lake, between Slegg's Landing and Gray Shores. There is a DEC parking and access site at the south end of the lake, off route 256. There is also the public boat launch and access site south of McPherson Point. This site is the most popular because it has plenty of parking and provides good access to the bottleneck that concentrates the perch as they migrate southward.

Smallmouth Bass .... common; growth rate good

There are a lot of smallmouth bass in Conesus Lake, but their habitat is surprisingly limited. Therefore, if you know how to read the lake and familiarize yourself with some of the bass hangouts, you're likely to find some good and consistent fishing for smallmouth bass.

When the bass season opens, most of the female smallmouth will be spawned out. A majority of the females will disperse throughout various habitats in the lake, exhibiting no tendency to concentrate in particular areas. However, adult males will linger in the shallows, protecting nest and fry from predators. Because they aggressively protect their nests, they can be taken very easily early in the season. It really makes sense to avoid taking smallmouth bass until the water temperature in the shallows warms up into the low 60's. For every adult harvested from the nesting area, hundreds of unprotected bass fry will perish due to predation.

Once the 60 degree mark is reached, adult smallmouth will switch from paternal chores to active feeding habits. Adult fish will begin to be found in deeper water (10-25 feet) near deep weed lines, rocky ledges and off submerged points. They can be taken on small jigs (1/8 to 1/4 oz.), such as bucktails or Mister Twisters.

Grape, chartreuse and yellow are productive colors on this lake. Crank baits, such as Hot'n Tot's or Bagley's Killer B's will also be effective. For the fly fisherman, leech patterns, in claret or white, or crayfish patterns can be deadly effective. In the early morning (6 am to 9 am) small spinners and bluegill poppers will take bass as they feed near shore in shallow water. The same is true in the evening (7 pm to dark). You want to keep your hardware as small as possible in this lake. Because the water is so clear, the bass get a good chance to give it a visual inspection and they're less likely to be put off by a small jig or popper. Natural baits will also work well. Crayfish or minnows fished close to the bottom over rocky points or other structure near deep water will usually produce fish.

A majority of the smallmouth habitat is found in the lower end of Conesus Lake and it is almost exclusively on the western side of the lake. All of the points between Long Point and Maple Beach

hold smallmouth bass and some are better than others, so you'll have to do some investigating. The south side of Long Point is exceptionally good. Good fishing can also be found just south of Eagle Point, off Old Orchard Point, and on the north side of McPherson Point. There is some fishing for smallmouth between Gray Shores and Pebble Beach and off the point at Cedarcrest but its rather sporadic.

Conesus Lake is fairly regular in shape. It doesn't have a lot of exaggerated points or coves, and this makes for fairly simple trolling. You can hit a lot of smallmouth water while trolling, and you certainly will catch fish, but fan casting from an anchored boat does have some advantages. It doesn't waste time (a lot of the water you'll cover while trolling this lake won't have smallmouth habitat) and it allows you to familiarize yourself completely with specific points, drop-offs and weed lines.

Although some smallmouth bass will continue to be taken in the shallows during periods of low light, there is a general tendency for them to move into increasingly by deeper water beginning around the end of August. Begin to oncentrate your efforts on the rocky points, fishing with crabs or minnows in 20-40 feet of water, or trolling deep diving crankbaits. In October and early November, smallmouth bass often go on a pre-winter feeding binge. Live bait or small jigs fished over deep bottom structure can be incredibly effective.

Northern Pike .... common; growth rate good

Northern pike are well distributed throughout Conesus Lake and exhibit good growth rates. Conesus northerns average 25-30 inches, but fish considerably larger have been taken, particularly from the weed beds just above and below Cottonwood Point. While they can be found nearly everywhere in the lake where beds exist, there are four areas of particular importance: 1) the extreme northern end; 2) the extreme southern end; 3) the cove between McPherson Point and Old Orchard Point, and 4) the stretch of shoreline between Long Point and the south side of Cottonwood Point.

At the southern end of Conesus Lake is the Conesus Lake Wildlife Management Area. This marshy tract is drained by Conesus Inlet and was obtained by the DEC to serve as a spawning ground for northern pike. Because a majority of the northern in this lake spawn here, the lower end of Conesus is the place to concentrate your early season efforts.

Shortly after spawning, most northern pike will seek out adjacent flats in 10-20 feet of water, relating to rock piles, small patches of weeds or small drop-offs. For the best early season pike action, try still fishing with live bait, preferable large shiners (8-12 inches). Large chubs and suckers will also work well. These baits can also be used while backtrolling or drifting very slowly over the flats. During the first few weeks of the season, northern

Ice fishing is still very popular on Conesus Lake, despite problems caused by the introduction of ale-wives. Standard ice fishing gear includes an auger, a short jigging rod or tip-up, and a warm place to sit. Photo courtesy New York State DEC.

Dahlberg Divers & Sliders. These are very effective top water bass bugs. Fly fishing is one of the most exciting and productive ways to fish for bass.

will tend to be close to the bottom. To keep your bait near the bottom, be sure to use a sinker. However, by the end of May the northerns will have sufficiently recuperated from their spawning rituals to become more active and aggressive. Then you'll want to fish without a sinker, using a bobber to keep your bait off the bottom and out from the cover of emerging weeds. The late spring is also a good time to begin using spinners, such as the Mepps Aglia, Panther Martin or Vibrax. Safety pin type spinners, tipped with a minnow, will also produce fish in the late spring and early sunner. Although they will catch fish later in the summer, they're definitely more effective in the late spring/early summer period.

In the summer, northerns can be taken using a number of methods. Conesus Lake has very well defined structure, making it an easy lake to troll. Troll the inside, then the outside weedlines, using large spinnerbaits tipped with a minnow (i.e. 4-6 inch shiners, chubs or suckers), large silver flatfish, crankbaits, or large spoons, such as the classic red and white Dardevle. Play with the trolling depth as you work the weedlines, but keep in mind most northern are taken from this lake in less the 30 feet of water.

If trolling isn't to your liking, fan casting can also be productive, and it allows you to learn the structure of a particular area very quickly. All of the above hardware will work, but for a little variety, try using salt water flies. Several local anglers use large (5-15 inch) flies here with considerable success. Whether trolling or casting, be sure to use a short wire leader or 20-30 pound shock tippet. Northern pike have teeth as sharp as razor blades and your going to lose a lot of fish and a lot of tackle if you don't.

Most of the really big northern pike seem to come from the weed beds just north and south of Cottonwood Point. This may be due to the close juxtaposition of shallow weedlines and relatively deep, cool water, a situation generally favored by large northern pike. If you're looking to fish exclusively for large pike, this would be the area in which to concentrate your efforts. The trick to fishing for these trophy size northerns is to use large baits. Try using a 12 inch sucker, hooked through the upper lip with a #2 short shank hook, fished from a slip-bobber. A bait this size will usually only attract the attention of the large northern pike, and at the same time you won't be bothered by any pesky largemouth bass that hold in the same areas.

In the fall, another method is added to your angling arsenal, namely jigs. The variety of jigs that will work in the fall is very wide, but they all have something in common - they are big. Half ounce and one ounce jigs, dressed with a bucktail, a plastic

waterdog (5-7 inch size) or a 4-6 inch Mister Twister tail will all take pike from this lake. The fall is also a good time to use large (5-15 inch) minnow imitations, such as a jointed Rapala.

One of the most productive pike harvesting times on Conesus Lake, or any other lake for that matter, is the winter, immediately after the lake freezes. A majority of the northern pike will be found in shallow water, 5-15 feet deep, primarily in the weedy bays, or at the north and south ends of the lake. As the season progresses, however, they have a tendency to follow the bait fish, such as the yellow perch, into increasingly deeper water. Later still, their spawning urge awakens and a majority of the pike will head for the south end of the lake to be near their spawning grounds.

Standard ice fishing techniques are used on Conesus Lake. A tip-up, baited with a large sucker or shiner hooked through the back is about a fancy as you have to get. Size 2 or 4 hooks are the most commonly used, and most veteran pike fishermen prefer braided nylon line terminating in either a short wire leader or heavy duty (40-60 lbs.) monofilament shock tippet. A short handled gaff is good to have around too. A lot of pike, especially the big ones, are lost at the hole, while they're being landed. A gaff will eliminate this problem.

Keep in mind that the water from the inlet is warmer than the lake and can make the ice on the south end of the lake less safe than ice on other parts of the lake.

While fishing for northern pike, don't be surprised if after close inspection, some of the smaller northerns you catch turn out to be chain pickerel. Pickerel are present in Conesus Lake, though in far fewer numbers than northerns. Closely related to northerns, they are similar in appearance, inhabit much of the same habitat and can be caught with the same techniques.

Largemouth Bass . . . . common; growth rate good

There is a wide variety of habitat for largemouth bass in this lake, from the slowly tapering flats at the north end of the lake to the deeper weed lines at the outer edges of the larger bays.

Early in the season, before the lake reaches its maximum average temperature, spinners will usually be the most effective here. This is expecially true in the first few weeks after the opening of the season. Start out with smaller spinners, (such as an 1/8 to 1/16 ounce Panther Martin), and fish the shallow weedy coves.

The shallow water at the extreme southern end of the lake and the tapering flats at the northern end should also be good. Gradually switch to slightly larger spinners, safety pin type spinnerbaits, top surface baits and small, shallow running crankbaits. Plastic worms, worked very slowly through weed

The southern end of Conesus Lake is the primary spawning area for the lake's northern pike. Photo courtesy New York State DEC.

beds will also produce well.

In July, August and September, largemouth bass can be taken from 5-15 feet of water, depending on conditions. The bay between McPherson Point and Old Orchard Point, the shallow water just south of McPherson Point, and the small cove on the southwest side of the lake are all consistent producers. Random populations of largemouth bass are also found between Tuxedo Park and Old Orchard Point and from the state boat launch site, near McPherson Point, half way down the Walkley's Landing.

Because many of the areas where largemouth bass are likely to be found are well defined but intermittent weed beds, fan casting is probably the best way to go on Conesus Lake. Trolling would, however, be a more appropriate way to fish in the areas where bass are randomly and thinly distributed.

Conesus Lake is a very clear lake, usually, and because of this, many local anglers prefer to use smaller than usual tackle. During the summer, ⅛ to ¼ ounce jigs, dressed with a 1½ inch Mister Twister tail, are highly effective. Small spinnerbaits, while not nearly as effective later on as they were early in the season, will still take fish. For really fast action, try fishing with small jigs or spinnerbaits along the inside edge of weed beds or around docks just at daybreak. Later, work the outer edge with jigs or deep diving crankbaits. For areas with extensive shallow weed growth, buzzbaits worked over the weeks just after daybreak and just at sunset will product a lot of action. Dusk, dawn and overcast periods are also a good time to try plastic worms, frog (real or imitation) and top water spoons.

In the fall, largemouth bass tend to orient more off drop-offs and deep weed lines, though some fish can still be taken in the shallows during extended warm spells. Spinnerbaits, again become top bass producers, followed by deep diving crankbaits and buzzbaits. When the water cools below 55 degrees, small jigs, dressed with a minnow or pork rind, will take fish if worked very slowly. Remember, as the water cools down, the metabolism and reactions of fish slow down, necessitating a slower retrieve. When the water is almost ready to freeze over, largemouth bass will still be feeding, but not very aggressively.

Stationary fishing with live baits, such as small minnows on a bobber, or with jigs are about the most effective methods for taking these lethargic largemouth bass. Both largemouth and smallmouth bass may be taken in this lake from the third Saturday in June through March 15th.

Walleye . . . . uncommon; growth rate good

In the late 1960's the DEC estimated the adult walleye population of Conesus Lake at 12,000. By 1986, this estimate had dropped to 2,000 adult walleye. The reason(s) for this precipitous drop is not known. About all that can be said for the walleye fishing in this lake is that there are some real lunkers in Conesus, but they are few and far between, and most walleye are taken incidentally by bass fishermen.

Even then, very few walleye are currently being caught. They are feeding on alewives, which invaded the lake in the early 1980's, and show little interest in traditional walleye lures presented in traditional ways. If you're really intent upon taking one of the huge walleye still left in the lake, it might be a good idea to adopt the downrigger strategies used successfully by Lake Erie fishermen for suspended walleyes.

The walleye fishing in Conesus Lake might be down, but it could rebound explosively. If some of the important limiting factors, which are currently unknown, are suddenly removed, the walleye fishing could return to its former glory very quickly. Conesus Lake has generally good walleye habitat and the state has put the lake on the top of its walleye stocking list. In 1985, 60,000 walleye fingerlings were stocked here. In 1986 and 1987 85,000 were stocked here. This is in addition to an annual stocking of 15,900,000 walleye fry.

Additional Species

In addition to the species listed above, Conesus Lake also has populations of chain pickerel (see northern pike), carp, white suckers, brown bullhead, rock bass, bluegill, and pumpkinseeds.

Boat Launch Sites

1. Bob's Bait and Tackle - at Lakeville Road and route 15, private launch for small boats rented at Bob's Bait and Tackle.

2. New York State launch site - off East Lake Road, just south of McPherson Point. Hard surface launch ramps, 2 floating docks and parking for 70 cars and trailers. This is the principle launch site on the lake - no charge.

A typical catch of Conesus Lake panfish. One effect of the explosion of the alewife population in Conesus has been to slow the growth rate of many of the lake's original species.

Leisure Time Marina - 2365 East Lake Road, Conesus. Private trailer launch ramp, marine supplies, boat rentals, gas - fee.

New York State fishermen access site - off route 256 at southern end of the lake. Hand launching for cartop boats and canoes, parking for 40 cars - no charge.

A state launch site for cartop boats and canoes is presently under construction at Pebble Beach.

General Information

Conesus Lake is the most westerly of the Finger Lakes. Relatively small and shallow, it is nevertheless, one of the most productive and popular lakes in New York State. Recent studies by the DEC indicate that most of the game species in the lake are in good shape in terms of population and growth rate. The notable exceptions are walleye, which have been in decline for over a decade, and yellow perch, which are being severly impacted by alewives. What effect the dominance of alewives in this lake will have on other species is not known.

The habitat exists in Conesus Lake for a cold water fishery, and attempts were made in the 1960's and 1970's to establish a trout population in the lake. Unfortunately, low survival of the trout yearlings, probably due to predation by northern pike, doomed the experiment to failure.

A major problem on Conesus Lake is lack of public access. Almost the entire perimeter of the lake is privately owned. The best access is limited to two parcels of land owned by the state, just south of McPherson Point and at the southern end of the lake.

NOTES: _____

_____

_____

_____

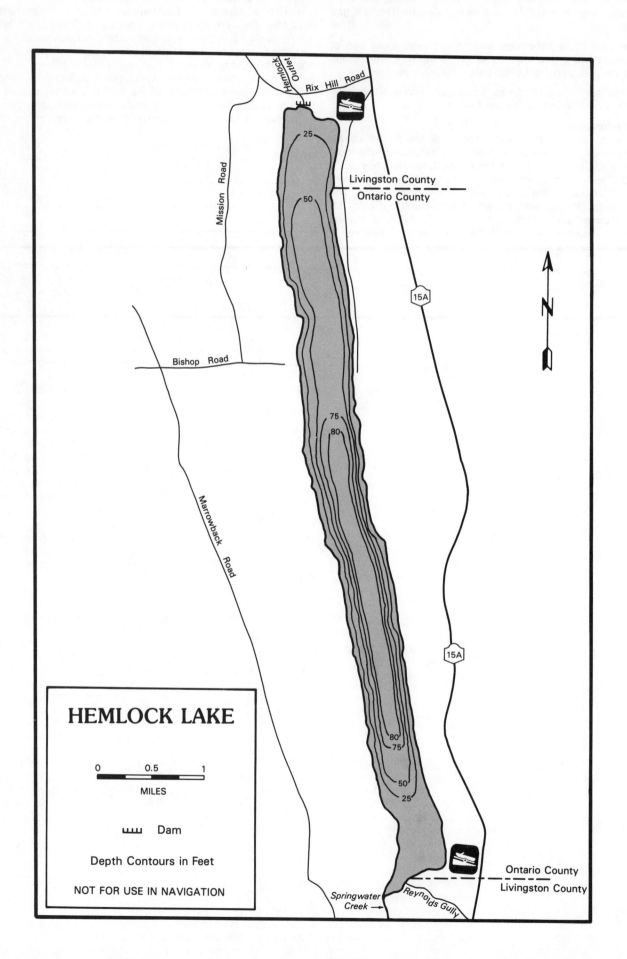

HEMLOCK LAKE

Hemlock Outlet

Rix Hill Road

Mission Road

Livingston County

Ontario County

15A

Bishop Road

25

50

75

80

Marrowback Road

15A

80
75

50

25

Ontario County

Livingston County

Springwater Creek

Reynolds Gully

0   0.5   1

MILES

ᴎᴜᴜ   Dam

Depth Contours in Feet

NOT FOR USE IN NAVIGATION

N

HEMLOCK LAKE

map coordinates	42° 42' 39" 77° 36' 28"
USGS map(s)	Springwater, Honeoye
location (township)	Eastern Livingston County and Western Ontario County
access	parallelled by Route 15A

Physical Characteristics

area	1800 acres
shoreline	17.10 miles
elevation	905 feet
maximum depth	91 feet
mean depth	45 feet
bottom type	muck, rock, clay
mean thermocline depth	28 feet

Chemical Characteristics

water clarity	clear
pH	alkaline
oxygen	Always good throughout the shallow areas of the lake. Oxygen depletion occurs in water below 60 feet during the summer. This does not jeapardize the survival of any species. It does affect how salmonid should be fished. It confines them to a narrow stratum in the water column.

Plant Life

Extensive weed beds (primarily water milfoil) occur at the southern end of the lake. Intermittent weed beds are found along the eastern and western sides of the lake. Weeds are also present at the northern end of Hemlock Lake, but to a much lesser extent than in the south end. Algae blooms are not a severe problem on this lake, but do occur.

Boat Launch Sites

1. The City of Rochester has an unimproved access point and gravel ramp off the town road along the northeast corner of the lake, off Rix Hill Road.

2. An unimproved access site and gravel ramp is also found at the southeast corner of the lake, off Route 15A.

Species Information

trout and salmon .... common; very good

Hemlock Lake has very good populations of lake trout, rainbow trout and brown trout. A lesser population of atlantic salmon is found here, as are a small, and soon to be eliminated, number of brook trout.

Studies by the DEC indicate that lake trout are the dominant predator in this lake, and that the lakers found here are possibly the fastest growing of their kind in the entire north eastern US. A 5 to 6 year old lake trout from Hemlock Lake averages close to 10 pounds, and the DEC has handled several fish from 14 to over 20 pounds. Unfortunately, creel census figures indicate that the harvest of lake trout is extremely low here, although the population is very healthy. State fisheries biologists aren't sure why this is so, but hypothesize that they might be feeding so heavily on forage fish, which are abundant here, that lures go unnoticed.

Rainbow trout were established in Hemlock Lake in the late 1940's, and have been an important tributary fishery since that time. With the development of modern techniques for deep water salmonid fishing in the late 1970's and 1980's, a very significant lake fishery has developed here for rainbows. At present, the population of rainbow trout in Hemlock Lake is considered to be at an optimum level by fisheries management personnel. Unlike lake trout, of which 85% or better are stocked fish, all of the rainbow trout in this lake are wild, having been bred in the high quality waters of the Springwater Creek system. The average rainbow taken from Hemlock Lake is a 3 to 4 year old fish weighing less than 2 pounds. However, older fish weighing over

Hemlock Lake has a good population of lake trout. These fish grow rapidly here and the average fish weighs close to 10 pounds! Photo courtesy New York State DEC.

10 pounds are taken occasionally in the lake and from Springwater Creek.

Over the past few years, the DEC has managed to establish a fair fishery for landlocked Atlantic salmon. One of the most highly prized game fish in North America, these hard fighting fish are currently sustained solely by stocking and it is not expected that a naturally self-sustaining population will develop. The first really good year for salmon fishing on this lake is expected to be 1987.

Brown trout have also been established in this lake recently and provide some very good angling. Their numbers are maintained solely by stocking. Though they grow well here, indicating that they are feeding heavily on the abundant forage fish, browns are taken fairly easily from Hemlock Lake. This is in sharp contrast to the poor harvest of lake trout, which is thought to be due to a dense forage base.

Soon after ice-out, trout will be found in shallow areas of Hemlock Lake. Trolling with long lines or planer boards, using Little Cleos, Rapalas or Rebels is a very productive method for spring time trout. Slow drifting along the shore, slowly working a very small jig tipped with a minnow along the bottom, is also highly effective for brown trout and rainbow trout. Be sure to use a light line (4 lb. test) in the spring, as access is available, try fishing with cut smelt for lake trout. Cast out, using a slip sinker to take the bait to the bottom. Many trout fishermen feel that it is necessary to use a slip sinker and to leave the reel bail open to avoid spooking the fish. Close the bail and set the hook after the second run has started to ensure that the trout has the whole bait in its mouth.

While you're at Hemlock Lake in the spring, don't neglect the excellent run of rainbows that takes place in Springwater Creek. For information on Springwater Creek, obtain a copy of Sander's Fishing Guide to Western New York.

In the summer, deep water fishing techniques are necessary to take trout and salmon from Hemlock Lake. These techniques include still fishing, thermoclining, copper line fishing and downrigging. For details on these methods see Scott Sampson's excellent article on Seneca Lake. Keep in mind that the thermocline sets up at a different depth on this lake than on Seneca Lake. By adjusting for such differences, the methods will be every bit productive as on Seneca Lake.

Beginning in the late summer or early fall, salmonids start to move back into shallow waters, some to feed, others to spawn. All of the techniques and tackle that worked in the spring will also work well in the fall.

Finger Lakes fishing regulations allow trout to be taken from Hemlock Lake all year long, which means ice-fishing for trout is legal here. The lake usually freezes over entirely, but the north and south ends are accessible first. A majority of the ice-fishing takes place at the south end of the lake, but there is nothing to indicate that the north end is any less productive then the south, at least in terms of trout. (Note: The city of Rochester prohibits ice fishing at the very north end of Hemlock Lake where the water intake is located.) Tip-ups baited with minnows are productive, as are various jigging lures, like the swedish pimple, Russian jig or the Rapala jigging minnow. Certain cold weather fly patterns can also be used, such as the lead wing Coachman or any shrimp imitation.

Hemlock Lake is currently stocked annually with 3,600 lake trout yearlings, 7,300 lake trout fingerlings, 5,000 brown trout yearlings, and 4,100 landlocked atlantic salmon yearlings. Brook trout, which have been stocked here in recent years, are being discontinued in 1987.

chain pickerel . . . . common; growth rate very good

Chain pickerel are commonly found anywhere in Hemlock Lake where weed beds exist. They aren't nearly as popular with fishermen as smallmouth bass and lake trout, but they do provide some very good angling. The pickerel in Hemlock Lake are larger than those found in Honeoye. Pickerel taken from this lake usually run 18 to 24 inches.

Chain pickerel are found throughout more of this lake than you would initially thick. The weed filled southern end is undoubtedly the most productive for these toothy predators, but the thick weed beds of the northern end also hold pickerel, as do the intermittent weeds along the periphery of the lake.

Early in the season, spinners, such as the Mepps Aglia or Panther Martin, are effective pickerel lures. Spoons, like Little Cleos or Daredevles, also work well early on, particularly if fished slowly to in part a fluttering motion rather than a fast spin.

In June, July and August pickerel can be taken with a variety of lures. The larger pickerel are often taken by trolling the outside weed lines with deep diving crank baits, silver and blue flatfish and spoons. For fishing in the weed beds at the southern end of Hemlock Lake, use weedless lures, such as Johnson's Silver Minnow, Texas-rigged worms or the Mean Mister Twister.

In the fall, live baits, including small suckers, shiners and minnows are top pickerel producers. The same hardware that worked throughout the summer months can also be used in the fall, but spinnerbaits are often better, returning to the level of effectiveness that they displayed in the spring.

Chain pickerel ar a popular quarry through the ice on Hemlock Lake. An overwhelming majority of the ice fishing takes place on the southern end of the lake, and the weed beds located there provide some good winter pickerel fishing. Tip-ups baited with live minnows, chubs or small suckers are always good when used over shallow weedbeds (10 feet or less), and cut smelt, so

popular with northern pike fishermen, should also work fo pickerel.

largemouth bass . . . . common; growth rate very good

Despite the fact that their overall habitat is rather restricted in this lake, largemouth bass are present in significant numbers and have a better then average growth rate. Local anglers estimate that the average Hemlock Lake largemouth is a solid 2 pounds and that 4 to 5 pound fish are taken each year.

Largemouth bass are limited to areas of the lake that exhibit significant weed growth. The lower end of the lake has extensive weed beds and accounts for a majority of the largemouth taken in the lake. While nearly the entire lower end of Hemlock Lake has a good habitat, an especially productive feature is the old submerged creek bed. When the lake was first dammed up at the north end, the south end was premanantly flooded, but the creek bed is still discernable. Deep diving crankbaits, plastic worms bucktail jigs and jigs dressed with Mister Twister tails are all effective for working the creek bed, weed lines or the naturally occuring openings in the weed beds. For working the tops of submerged weed beds use a top water plug or surface spoons.

Largemouth bass are also found at the north end of the lake along the west side of the lake, between the gaging station and Mission Point (the point, in fact, is pretty good), and along the east side as far south as the launch site. Scattered populations of largemouth can also be found elsewhere in Hemlock Lake wherever weed beds exist.

smallmouth bass . . . . common; growth rate good

According to DEC surveys, smallmouth bass are currently the single most sought often warm water quarry in Hemlock Lake. They are randomly distributed along the east and west sides of the lake, favoring rocky points and drop-offs. The points on the northwest side of the lake are considered by the anglers we interviewed to be about the most productive on the lake for smallmouth. But nearly any rocky point or steep rocky ledge on this lake should hold a few smallmouth. One suggestion for locating probable smallmouth habitat is to check out the mouths of the numerous streams that feed Hemlock Lake. Where a stream empties into the lake there is often an out-wash of rubble. Smallmouth will often be found on or near these small gravel beds. Once a likely area has been found, drift over the site casting ⅛ to ¼ oz. bucktail jigs or jigs dressed with black, yellow or white Mister Twister Tails. Deep diving crankbaits like the Ho N' Tot Wiggle Wart or Mann's Deep Hog and Deep Pig can also be used.

Other Species

Hemlock Lake hosts a number of species of secondary importance. Rock bass are abundant in the lake, but get very little attention from area anglers. They are well distributed along the periphery of the lake, inhabiting much the same water as smallmouth bass. Smelt, so important to the maintenance of the

The DEC has recently es-tablished a fishery for Atlantic salmon in Hemlock Lake. They are spectacular fighters and good table fare. Photo courtesy New York State DEC.

ke's trout and salmon population, are abundant, but contribute
tle to the fishery in terms of overall harvest. Some smelt are
ken through the ice, but the vast majority are taken during their
pawning run in two small tributaries on the northwest corner of
e lake (smelt apparently never run in the lakes main tributary,
oringwater Creek). There is short-lived, but popular fishing for
own bullhead in the spring of the year. Yellow perch can be
und in many parts of the lake. Their numbers are only fair at
est, but this lake's perch are usually big. The trick to taking them
eems to be fishing in deep water (but above the level of oxygen
epletion) as close to the steep sides of the lake as possible.
ounding out the available species in Hemlock Lake are
uegills, pumpkinseeds, white suckers and carp, the last of
hich are often taken by lake trout fishermen in the lake's
ypolimion, the cold layer of water below the thermocline.
istorically, whitefish and walleye were important species in
emlock Lake, but their population have suffered an all but total
ollapse.

eneral Information

Hemlock Lake lies 25 miles south of the city of Rochester. It
erves as a principle source of water for that city. To insure the
urity of the lake's water, the lake and the surrounding
ountryside have been maintained in a nearly pristine state.
here is almost no development on the lake's periphery,
roviding fishermen a unique wilderness setting close to a major
netropolitan area.

The major problem on Hemlock Lake is the lack of adequate
ccess. The two unimproved launch sites are capable of
andling the small boats allowed on the lake, but they are located
t either end of this 7 mile long body of water. This means that a
ong boat ride faces anyone who wishes to fish the central
ortion of Hemlock Lake. Shore access is even worse. Almost the
ntire shoreline of the lake is open to public access, but, with the
xception of the north and south ends of the lake, there are no
earby roads, greatly restricting the areas of the lake available to
hore fishing. This problem is compounded in the winter by the
act that the access road at the south end of the lake, where a
najority of the ice fishing takes place, is not plowed. If you don't
se a snowmobile, its a long, cold walk from Route 15A to the ice
shing areas.

If you plan on fishing Hemlock Lake, be aware that special
egulations apply here. Boats are permitted on the lake, but are
estricted to a maximum of 16 feet. Motors are restricted to 10

Hemlock Lake offers good fishing in a wilderness setting. There is no developement along the shores of this lake. Photo courtesy New York State DEC.

horsepower. Fishing is by permit only which can be obtained (free) by sending a stamped, self-addresses envelope to:

City of Rochester
Watershed Permit
7412 Rix Hill Road
Hemlock, NY 14466
(716) 367-3250

NOTES: _____

_____

_____

_____

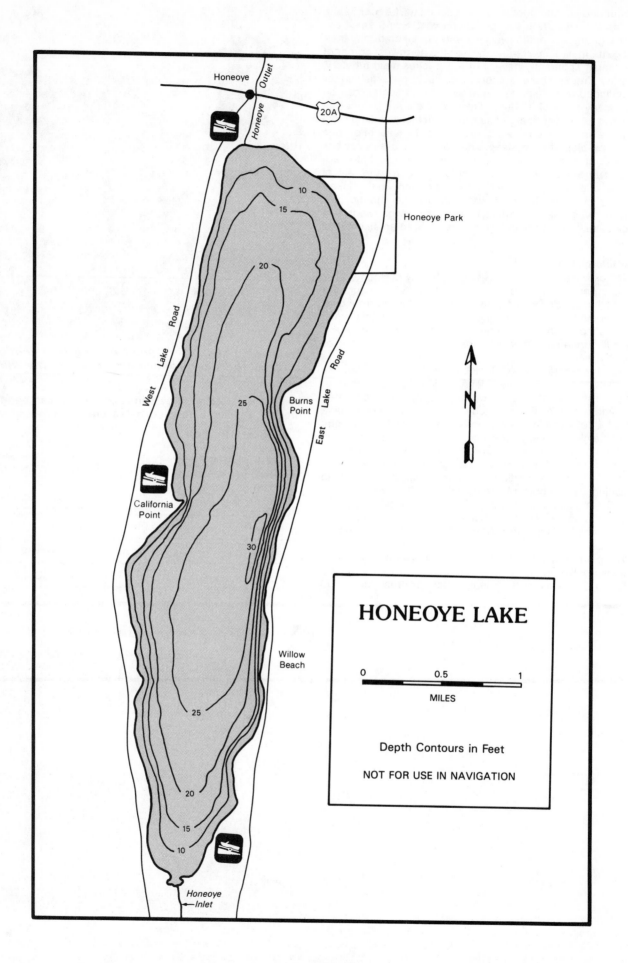

Honeoye

Honeoye Outlet

20A

Honeoye Park

10

15

West Lake Road

20

East Lake Road

Burns Point

25

N

California Point

30

Willow Beach

25

HONEOYE LAKE

0   0.5   1

MILES

Depth Contours in Feet

NOT FOR USE IN NAVIGATION

20

15

10

Honeoye
Inlet

HONEOYE LAKE

Map coordinates.......... 42° 47' 00" 77° 30' 42"
USGS map(s)............... Honeoye, Bristol Center
Location.................. Western Ontario County
Access.................... closely parallelled by West Lake Road and East Lake Road off Route 20A

Physical Characteristics

Area..................... 1772 acres
Shoreline................ 10.8 miles
Elevation................ 804 feet
Maximum depth........... 31 feet
Mean depth.............. 16 feet
Bottom type............. primarily soft bottomed, limited areas of gravel
Mean thermcline depth.... lake does not stratify — too shallow

Chemical Characteristics

Water clarity............. turbid
pH....................... alkaline
Oxygen................... The waters at the bottom of the lake are not completely oxygenated, but this does not seem to affect fish in that area. Limited fish kills periodically take place in shallow bays due to localized nocturnal oxygen depletion. Otherwise, there are no problems with oxygen here.

Plant Life

With the exception of the central region of the lake, weeds are found throughout Honeoye Lake in significant amounts in water up to 15 feet deep. These beds provide excellent habitat for bass, pickerel and perch. Honeoye does suffer somewhat from algae blooms, causing turbidity and localized fish kills.

Boat Launch Sites

1. The principle launch site on this lake is the state maintained site, off East Lake Road, approximately 1 mile from the south end of the lake. Double hard surface ramp, parking for 35 cars — no charge.

2. There is an informal launch site for cartop boats and canoes, off Sandy Bottom Road, at north end of lake.

3. California Ranch, off West Lake Road. Private, gravel launch ramp — fee.

Species Information

Largemouth Bass .... common; growth rate very good

Despite its relatively small size, Honeoye Lake has a great deal of habitat suitable for largemouth bass. With few exceptions, largemouth bass can be found (depending upon the time of year and time of day) in all areas of the lake up to 15 feet deep. Exceptions to this would be the gravel bottomed areas off Pickerel Point, and Log Cabin Point, the area just south of California Ranch, and the gravel bar north of the state launch ramps. These are prime smallmouth bass areas.

Early in the season, many largemouth bass will be found in shallow water, 6 feet or less, especially if there has been a late spring. The fish will be close to their spawning beds, but because so much of the lake is a potential spawning area, the fish will be fairly scattered. This is one of the times when trolling can give you an edge, enabling you to cover an area completely. In the morning, troll along the near-shore weedline, using spinnerbaits, floating Rapalas or shallow running crankbaits. Later in the day, work the outer weedlines, using Texas-rigged plastic worms, deep diving crankbaits, and bucktail jigs. As the season wears on and weedbeds become more developed, trolling becomes difficult except along the outer weedlines.

In the summer, largemouth bass will be found throughout Honeoye Lake wherever weeds are found, but several areas seem to be the most productive. Local anglers indicated that most

of the western side of the lake south of California Ranch produces well, as does the water directly across from Trident Marine. On the eastern side of the lake, the waters directly north of the state boach launch site were recommended. Crankbaits, top water plugs, surface spoons worked over submerged vegetation will be effective. Texas-rigged worms, in purple or red, and bucktail jigs, or jigs dressed with a Mister Twister tail will take bass if fished in the weeds or in the naturally occurring openings that are often found in the more congested weed beds.

Later in the season, as the weeds begin to decay, spinnerbaits will again be effective. The metabolic rate of bass also begins to slow down in the fall, so use a slower retrieve than you would during the summer. Slowly worked crankbaits and jigs will also take largemouth bass in the fall. Fish along whatever weedlines still remain in the shallows on a warm day. When the water temperature falls below 55 degrees, largemouth bass quickly become lethargic. Live minnows fished with a bobber or very slowly worked jigs will then be your best bet to take fish.

Smallmouth Bass .... common; growth rate very good

The smallmouth bass habitat in Honeoye Lake is fairly restricted when compared to that available for largemouth bass, but it supports a very good population of fish, in terms of numbers as well as size. Eighteen inch smallmouth are not uncommon in this lake, and fish in the 4 to 5 pound class are taken each year.

Early in the season, female smallmouth are usually dispersed in deep water, recuperating from the rigors of spawning. They are very difficult to find at this time, and just as difficult to catch. Males, however, will be found in the spawning beds, protecting the newly hatched fry. Male smallmouth are very susceptible to being caught by fishermen during this period. Be a sportsman and don't bother the male fish while they are on the beds. For every adult fish taken from the spawning beds, hundreds of fry are jeopardized.

By the time surface waters of Honeoye Lake approach 70 degrees, smallmouth bass will have settled into their normal summer feeding habits. Early in the morning (6 am to 9 am) many fish will be found feeding in shallow water. Spinnerbaits and surface lures, such as floating Rapalas and small bluegill poppers, are all effective early morning smallmouth lures. As the sun rises higher in the sky, smallmouth bass move into deeper water, often locating near deep weedlines, rocky outcroppings or submerged structure. If they are holding in areas of excessive weed growth, small floating Rapalas worked slowly over the tops of submerged weeds will often take fish. A twitch-and-wait type

Although the lake is very weedy, Honeoye has a good population of smallmouth bass and they have a better than average growth rate. Big fish are not uncommon.

An aerial view of the south end of Honeoye Lake. Shallow and weedy, this lake offers fishermen some fine angling opportunities for a wide variety of warm water species. Photo courtesy New York State DEC.

of retrieve works best. If the smallmouth bass are close to the bottom, deep diving crankbaits, jigs or natural baits (worms, leeches, crayfish, minnows) are your best choices. Local anglers often use a jig dressed with a long, black Mister Twister tail, but brown bucktail jigs, or small ¼ to ⅛ ounce jigs dressed with small white, yellow or black Mister Twister tails work as well. Some area anglers also suggest using chartreuse tails on bright sunny days, and claret colored tails on overcast days. Later in the day, roughly from 7 pm to dusk, some smallmouth will return to the shallows to feed.

The same shallow water tackle and techniques that worked in the morning will also be effective in the evening. After dark, noisy top water lures and spinnerbaits are called for.

In the fall, there is a general tendency for smallmouth bass to disperse into increasingly deeper water. Live baits are very productive in the fall season. Chubs, shiners and small waterdogs fished slowly along remaining deep weedlines or along the edges of gravel beds will often result in some excellent late season fishing. Slow back trolling or controlled drifting will cover a lot of area and give the bait sufficient movement to attract increasingly slugglish smallmouth bass.

Walleye .... common; growth rate very good

Studies by the DEC indicate that Honeoye Lake has a very good population of walleye. For some reason, however, few anglers seem to do very well here when fishing for walleye, although it does seem to be picking up a little in recent years. We don't get many reports from anglers who regularly catch walleye. The walleye may be feeding heavily on the lake's large yellow perch population, ignoring offerings from fishermen. Information from local anglers indicates that only two areas are known to consistently hold walleyes, i.e. the water just south of Log Cabin Point and the south end of the lake, in 15 to 25 feet of water. Normally, you would think of using deep diving crankbaits and jigs, fished close to the bottom, for walleye, but comments from area fishermen and personnel from the DEC seem to indicate that the walleye in Honeoye Lake may be more suspended than usual. One fisherman who has luck taking walleye from this lake trolls the central portion of the south end. He uses a floating Rapala, weighted to get it down 8 to 10 feet, with two trolling flies tied above it. A majority of his walleye are taken on the flies. Perhaps

all that is needed on this lake is a change in techniques for it to b recognized as a good walleye fishery.

Chain Pickerel .... common; growth rate fair

Chain pickerel are widely distributed throughout Honeoy Lake. Pickerel run small here. A larger fish might go 20 to 2 inches, but the average pickerel is closer to 15 inches. This fac plus recent angler surveys, would indicate that chain pickerel ar an underutilized fishery in this lake.

Chain pickerel inhabit the same type of areas as largemout bass, which means that they can be found in about 60% c Honeoye Lake. Generally speaking, they will be found more ofte in the flats and in the back sides of bays, rather than in more ope water. The southern end of the lake is substantially mor productive than the north end.

Early in the season, spinners are highly effective for takin pickerel in shallow water. Mepps Aglia (size 2 or 3), Panthe Martins and Vibrax spinners are all good spring pickerel lures Spoons also work well, if retrieved slowly, to give them a flutterin motion as opposed to a rapid spin. If fly fishing is your game, larg streamers, muddler minnows, white wooly buggers, leec patterns and surface poppers are the recommended patterns.

As the lake begins to warm up and the extensive weedbed of this lake become established, pickerel become more widel distributed. The fishing can be good at this time, but usually it pretty random. Many local anglers prefer a large shiner fishe with a bobber, but floating Rapalas, silver flatfish or red and whit Daredevils are all good when fished along weedlines or over th tops of weedbeds. Keep in mind that chain pickerel are found i weedbeds as well as adjacent to them. Weedless lures, such a the Johnson Silver Minnow or Texas-rigged worms, worke through the weeds, will entice fish that other lures can't get nea Be sure to use wire leaders or a very strong shock tippet or you'r going to lose a lot of tackle.

Pickerel are commonly taken through the ice on Honeoy Lake. Standard tip-ups, baited with live shiners or minnows, o fresh cut bait are about as fancy as you have to get. The water off Califonria Ranch and Trident Marine are known to produce lot of pickerel in the winter, but there are so many pickerel in thi lake and there is so much available habitat for them that they ca turn up almost anywhere.

Yellow Perch .... abundant; growth rate good

Yellow perch are probably the most sought after fish i Honeoye Lake. The excellent population of perch here justifie Honeoye's reputation as a top year-round producer of thes piscatorial delicacies.

In the spring, yellow perch will often be found off the edges c dormant weed beds in anticipation of their spawning rituals. productive method for taking yellow perch at this time is t anchor along the edge of weed beds and still fish with worms grubs or minnows. You can increase your catch considerably b employing the use of perch rigs (spreaders). Fishing with sma brown jigs is also effective.

As the lake warms up, yellow perch become more difficult t find, spending much of their time in the open waters of the lake The anglers we talked to indicated that the best summer perc fishing was found in the central portion of the lake. Other areas t concentrate on would be the drop off at California Point and th gravel beds off Log Cabin Point. Yellow perch can also be take at various points or along deep weed lines in the southern end o the lake, but the perch in the southern end seem to be decidedl smaller than those found in the northern half of Honeoye Lake Many of the perch taken in the summer are taken incidentally while bass fishing or pike fishing. They will hit worms, small cray fish, minnows or small jigs tipped with minnows.

In the fall, yellow perch usually seek out the deepest portion of a lake where suitable habitat is available. Still fishing very clos to, or right on the bottom with minnows is your best bet. As in th spring, using spreaders will increase your catch substantially The deep water directly across from California Point would be a ood area to concentrate on in the fall, as would the gravel beds off Log Cabin Point.

As with many lakes that have a good perch population, Honeoye shines most brightly in the winter. Tremendous numbers of yellow perch are harvested through the ice here. Ice fishing is especially productive in the first few weeks after the lake freezes over. The most popular area early on seems to be the waters just off Log Cabin Point. Large schools of perch congregate there because of the refuge afforded by the submerged structure. Fewer, though larger, perch are reportedly taken off California Point. Standard ice fishing jigs (red or white Russian jigs or Swedish pimples) or the Conesus jig in silver or copper will be effective. Tipping the jigs with mousey grubs, perch eyes or oak leaf grubs will increase your chances of success. If the perch don't seem to be biting, move on until you get some action.

Other Species

In addition to species listed above, Honeoye Lake also has populations of rock bass, pumpkinseed, bluegill, black crappie, brown bullhead, white suckers and carp. Probably the most significant of these are the black crappie. In the spring (April-May) there is very good fishing for crappie at the south end of the lake. Using very small Mister Twisters (1/32 oz.), in black, yellow or white, work the shallow weedbeds and brush piles. Or fish a salted minnow, using a pencil bobber. The action is not as good as at Chautauqua Lake, but its not bad.

General Information

Located 28 miles directly south of the City of Rochester, Honeoye Lake is the second smallest of the Finger Lakes (Canadice is the smallest). Its small size, however, belies this lake's importance as a fisheries resource. When compared to other state waters, Honeoye Lake ranks highly in the production of yellow perch, largemouth bass, panfish, bullhead and walleye.

The one major problem on Honeoye Lake is shoreline access. Much of the shoreline is privately owned and developed. There is a lack of adequate safe parking on the perimeter roads in the winter and additional parking and access is severely needed.

In an effort to improve catches of walleye in Honeoye Lake, the DEC stocks it yearly with 8,670,000 walleye fry and 33,400 walleye fingerlings.

For up-to-date information on what is hitting at Honeoye Lake, stop in at one of the local tackle shops. Cratsley's Bait and Tackle is located on West Lake Road. Batzel's Bait and Tackle is located at California Point, next to the California Ranch Restaurant.

NOTES: _____

_____

_____

_____

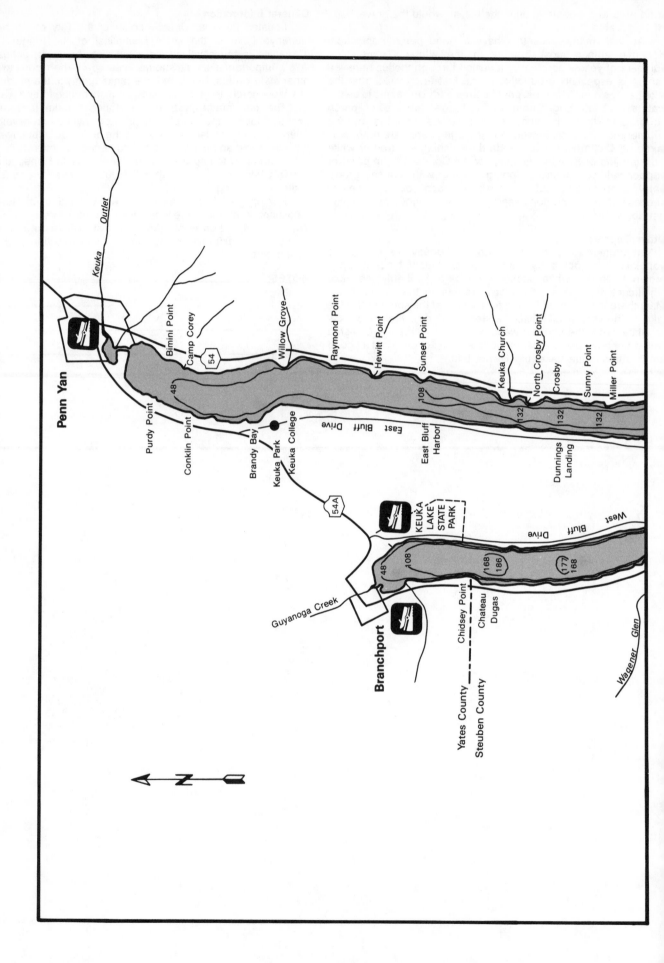

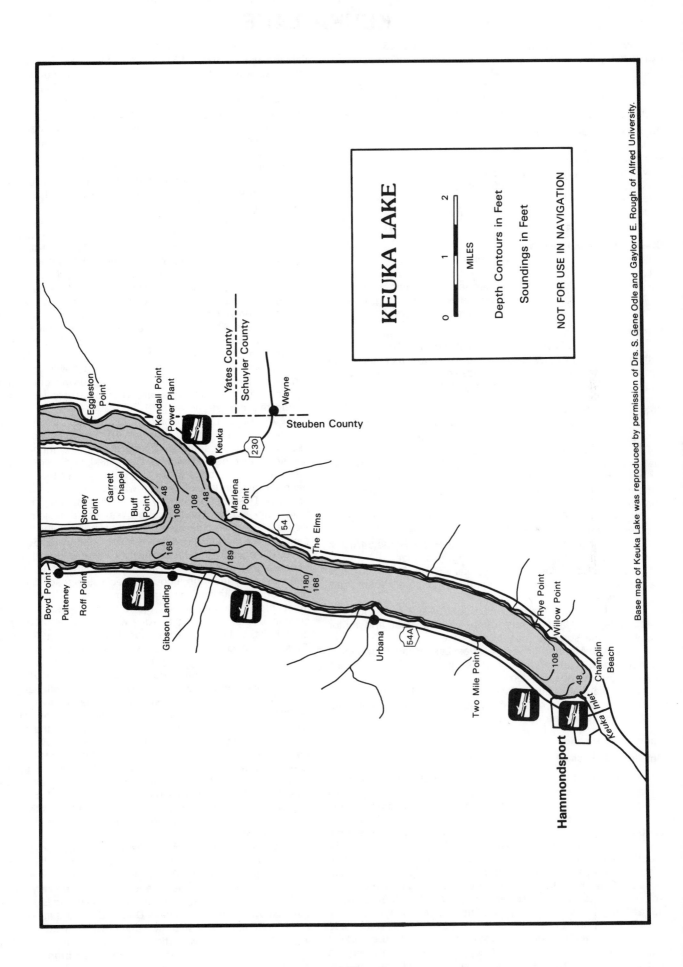

KEUKA LAKE

MILES

0　1　2

Depth Contours in Feet

Soundings in Feet

NOT FOR USE IN NAVIGATION

Eggleston Point

Kendall Point

Power Plant

Yates County

Schuyler County

Wayne

Keuka

Steuben County

230

Garrett Chapel

Stoney Point

Bluff Point

Marlena Point

48

108

108

108

48

54

The Elms

168

189

180

168

Boyd Point

Pulteney

Roff Point

Gibson Landing

Urbana

54A

Two Mile Point

Rye Point

Willow Point

108

Champlin Beach

48

Keuka Inlet

Hammondsport

Base map of Keuka Lake was reproduced by permission of Drs. S. Gene Odle and Gaylord E. Rough of Alfred University.

KEUKA LAKE

map coordinates.......... 42° 33' 47" 77° 05' 55"
USGS map(s) .... Keuka Park, Hammondsport, Wayne
                                 Pulteney, Penn Yan
location .... northeastern Steuben County,
                                 southern Yates County
access .... parallelled by Route 54 and 54A

Physical Characteristics

area .... 11,730 acres
shoreline .... 58.4 miles
elevation .... 715 feet
maximum depth .... 186 feet
mean depth .... 101 feet
bottom type .... gravel, rubble, muck
mean thermocline depth .. 33 feet

Chemical Characteristics

water clarity .... very clear
pH...................... alkaline
oxygen.................. oxygen levels are high throughout
                                 Keuka Lake all year long, even in
                                 in the deepest waters.

Plant Life

Extensive weedbeds are found at the north end of the lake, in both the Branchport and Penn Yan arms, as well as in the south end near Hammondsport. Smaller beds are found off major points and deltas. Algae blooms are not a problem here.

Boat Launch Sites

1. Village of Penn Yan - off Route 14A in Penn Yan. Multiple hard surface ramps, docks, parking - no charge.

2. Town of Wayne - this is on small gravel ramp owned by the town, off Route 54 near the Switzerland Inn. It is only suitable for small boats. Limited parking is available on Route 54. The ramp is only open between the hours of 7 a.m. and 10 p.m. - no charge.

3. Hammondsport Motel - on Water Street in Hammondsport. Hard surface ramp, parking, motel service - fee.

4. Clark's Boat Livery - on West Lake Road (Route 54A) just north of Hammondsport. Ramp, parking, gas - fee.

5. Jake's Boat Livery - 666 West Lake Road, 6 miles north of Hammondsport. Hard surface ramp, boat and motor rentals, bait, tackle, gas - fee.

6. Harbor Lights Marina - on Route 54A, 7 miles north of Hammondsport. Hard surface ramp, parking, boat and motor rentals, marine supplies, gas, tackle - fee.

7. Jensen Marine Service - 47 West Lake Road, Branchport. Launch ramps, boat and motor rentals, marine supplies, gas, bait, tackle, storage, repairs - fee.

8. Keuka Lake State Park -on Route 54A, just east of Branchport. Concrete ramps, pumpout, parking for 50 cars and trailors. Park user fee after 9 a.m.

Species Information

Smallmouth Bass .... common; growth rate very good

Keuka Lake has an excellent population of smallmouth bass. A majority of these fish are 12 to 14 inches, but lunkers weighing 3 to 5 pounds are reported here each year. The DEC considers this to be an underutilized fishery, even though smallmouth are the second most sought after specie on the lake, behind lake trout.

Beginning around mid-June, tremendous numbers of smallmouth bass will be found in the shallow portions of the lake, ready to spawn. Depending on weather conditions and water temperatures, these fish will be in their spawning phase or post-spawning phase when bass season opens the third Saturday in June. If they are still on the spawn, they will be found in about 12 feet of water, unless they are actually spawning, in which case they will be found in water as shallow as 3 feet. Many areas of the lake will hold smallmouth during this period, but several areas are outstanding for early season bass, and they all have several

characteristics in common. They consist of wide, boulder strewn flats that extend 100 to 150 yards into the lake before dropping off into deep water. The most productive flats are found on the east side of the Penn Yan arm of the lake, between Camp Corey and Willow Grove. Good fishing can also be found on the flats that run for a mile or so just south of Keuka College on the west side of the Penn Yan arm, or on the flats above and below Marlena Point, near the center of the lake. These favorable conditions are also present to some extent in several of the bays along the lake, most notably in those found between Conklin Point and Brandy Bay. Early season smallmouth can be found in numerous locations around Keuka Lake, but the best fishing will be from the areas listed above.

When smallmouth bass are on the flats they are very susceptible to small jigs and shallow running crankbaits. Quarter ounce jigs dressed with three inch Mister Twister Tails in natural colors are very effective, as are deer hair jigs.

As long as the fish are on the flats, the fishing can be fantastically productive. Catches of 30 or 40 smallmouth are common during this period. However, if weather conditions are right, this spawning phase will be just about over by the time bass season opens. The bass will then be found in somewhat deeper water. For about 10 days after they are through spawning, smallmouth will move out to the deeper parts of the flats. These post-spawn fish can still be taken, but not with the ease and regularity of spawning phase fish. Deep diving crankbaits and jigs, both in natural colors, are your best bets for taking fish during this period.

Early season bass fishing normally ends on Keuka Lake by the second week of July. Relatively few smallmouth will be caught here in the summer, at least during daylight hours. By the middle of July the lake will have stratified, and there is evidence that many of the bass will move out just over the thermocline, often foraging in the deep open waters of the lake for schools of bait fish. This phenomenon, which also occurs on several other Finger Lakes (see Canandaigua Lake) would explain why many Keuka Lake bass fishermen feel that most of the smallmouth caught here during the day are taken from water 50 to 60 feet deep. Biologically they are drawn to these waters by amenable temperatures and bait fish. But they are also forced to retreat to deep water by the high amount of recreational activity that takes place on the lake during warm summer day. (Keuka is one of the most highly populated of the Finger Lakes.) Most of the smallmouth taken during the day will be caught on deep diving crankbaits, or large deer hair jigs dressed with a 2 inch Mister Twister tail and fished very slowly. The few productive daytime areas include the ledges on the south and west sides and Bluff Point, off Chateau Dugas, and from Camp Corey to Willow Grove. The last mentioned area is usually good only until early August, while the others will hold fish through the summer.

While Keuka Lake has the reputation of being reluctant to give up many smallmouth bass during the day, the situation is markedly different at night. Many of those who know the lake feel that some of the best bass fishing in the region is to be had here after sundown. Beginning around 9:30 PM, bass that had been holding in deep water start moving onto adjacent shallow water flats to feed on Keuka's excellent population of crayfish. The anglers that we interviewed felt that the most productive period at night was from 10 PM to midnight, preferably on nights with little or no moonlight.

The areas where night fishing will be productive are numerous. Just look for areas where the water drops off abruptly from 15 feet down to 35 or 40 feet. The west side of the Hammondsport arm of the lake is reported to be very productive for smallmouth at night, as are the shelves around Bluff Point, and the shallows in front of Chateau Dugas. But nighttime bass can be taken from nearly any shallow water cove or flat adjacent to deep water. The one shallow portion of the lake where this isn't always the case is in the north end of the Penn Yan branch of the lake. After the middle of August few smallmouth will be taken north of

The smallmouth bass fishing on several of the Finger Lakes is outstanding in the winter. Keuka, Seneca and Cayuga Lakes all produce fine catches like the one shown above. These fish were taken from Seneca Lake in the month of January. Photo courtesy Craig Nelson.

Willow Grove or Keuka College, due to a lack of deep water juxtaposed to shallow water flats.

Some of the same methods used to take smallmouth during the day can be used to take them at night as well. Crankbaits worked along the edge of a drop off or large jigs slowly worked across the flats will take fish. But possibly the most productive method uses a top water lure. A classic piece of hardware for this type of fishing is Heddon's Zara Spook. This stickbait is made to be "dog walked" on the surface of the water. It is designed in such a way that, when you lift your rod tip, it starts first to the left and then to the right. Slowly retrieved over the flats in this matter it is very effective for taking the big smallmouth that inhabit this lake. Jitterbugs are another effective lure at night. These are cast tight up against the bank and retrieved perpendicular to the shoreline. Small plastic worms are another good choice at night, especially the so-called "Do Nothing Worm," a prerigged four inch worm with a weight attached about three feet ahead of it. Cast up against the bank and very slowly retrieved with short sudden jerks, this worm rig can be highly productive on this lake. And they say it's even better on Cayuga Lake. Another proven bass catcher is a small black flatfish trolled very close to shore. And if all else fails, don't forget what is drawing the bass to the shallows in the first place. Live crayfish, or suitable imitations, should take limits of smallmouth.

The night fishing for smallmouth bass begins to taper off on Keuka Lake by early September. Their general tendency at this time will be to move out into increasingly deeper water (80 to 90 feet), but there are sporadic periods when smallmouth bass can be found around shallow points and bluffs in the fall. The shallow water methods mentioned above can be used in the fall, but many local anglers prefer to use small slab spoons on these points.

By the end of October Keuka Lake will have turned over, and for a short period the bass will be found in 35 to 40 feet of water.

Initially, their movements will be unpredictable, but it's not too long before they make a noticable move into deep water (60 to 90 feet), orienting off ledges and points. Many bass fishermen hang up their gear right around this time. Many of them are under the impression that the fishing is too slow and arduous once the weather turns cold. They're half right - it can be arduous. But, armed with a little know-how, the period from October 15 to the close of the season (March 15 on this lake) can be the most productive period of the year for smallmouth. This is the little known and seldom utilized winter bass fishery.

Undoubtedly, much of what follows will go against what most fishermen have been taught, namely, that bass, especially smallmouth, are at best difficult to catch in the cold weather months. All that is really needed, though is a change in techniques.

As mentioned above, this fishery lasts from mid-October to March 15. The peak month is February, but often a build up of ice around the edge of the lake, and particularly around launch ramps, makes access to the open water areas of the lake impossible by this time. When this happens, the dozen or so hardy anglers who partake of this sport run over to Seneca Lake. There is a winter bass fishery on Seneca, just as on Keuka, and some of the launch ares on Seneca never freeze up (reportedly, this fishery also exists on Cayuga Lake at Flat Rock, but is seldom utilized). The worst enemy of the winter bass angler, aside from the ice and cold the wind, which makes it difficult to hold over a particular bass haunt. Keep in mind that even a small change in postion can result in a drastic change in the depth of water your fishing in. Look for days with little or no wind for the best cold weather bass fishing on Keuka or Seneca.

One of the extraordinary aspects of Keuka's winter bass fishing are the size of the fish that are caught. My source for much of the information contained in this article was Jay Nelson of

Dundee, New York, a very successful tournament fishermen. In one contentst, on Keuka Lake, held in the middle of November, Jay brought in five smallmouth whose cumulative weight was a very impressive 26 lbs. 4 oz. Jay needed every one of those pounds. The angler who placed right after him had five bass whose total weight was 25 lbs. 1 oz. Needless to say, big smallmouth are not a fluke in the winter. Fish up to 7 pounds are certainly waiting to be pulled from this lake.

A number of things can be used to take smallmouth in the winter. Live minnows fished close to the bottom are known to be highly effective on some lakes, such as Conesus, and some fishermen do take bass during this period using various types of slab spoons, but each of these have serious drawbacks. Live minnows are productive when you've located a large concentration of bass, but they don't allow you to investigate large areas quickly. Slab spoons can be very effective and do allow you to cover a lot of water fairly fast, but they are expensive and you're likely to lose a few on the rocky ledges where the smallmouth are invariably going to be found. By far the most popular lure used by the few fishermen who partake of this sport are naturally colored deer hair jigs or leadhead jigs dressed with a Mister Twister tail. They are relatively inexpensive, especially if you make your own. If you're fishing properly you are going to lose 20 or 30 jigs in a day's outing. This won't hurt the pocket book nearly as much if you keep your tackle simple and inexpensive.

As for other equipment, use the stiffest 5 to 5½ foot spinning rod you can get your hands on. A strong rod is necessary because you're going to be fishing in water at least 20 feet deep, and will often be in water 60 to 90 feet deep. And unless the water is unusually cloudy, stay with lines that test 4 to 6 pounds. These fish seem to be a bit line shy.

By far the most productive area of the lake for bass during this period centers around Bluff Point, roughly from Stoney Point on the west side of the bluff to Garrett Memorial Chapel on the east side. The recommended launch site to use when fishing this area in the winter is the ramp at the Hammondsport Hotel, on the south end of the lake.

If conditions are right, some smallmouth will be found schooled up in as little as 20 feet of water. The cold weather anglers we talked to indicated that essentially all of the smallmouth will be in tightly packed schools and that all of the bass in a school will be approximately the same size.

The normal pattern for this type of fishing is to begin fishing early in the morning (7 AM) in about 20 feet of water. Just off the face of Bluff Point is a drop off that quickly runs down from 22 feet to 32 feet, and this is the shallowest area in which you can expect to find big bass schooled up. When fishing this relatively shallow water ¼ ounce jigs are recommended. Work your way up to 9/16 ounce jigs as you move out to deeper water later in the day. If you don't catch fish from this drop off, or you only pick up small fish, move out to the next deepest drop off. Keep prospecting until you land a bass worth bragging about, then work the area thoroughly. There probably are a lot more big fish close by.

One of the most important things to keep in mind if you plan on taking smallmouth in the winter is that they behave very differently than they do in the warmer months. These fish are very lethargic and will not chase your bait or lure. You must run it right under their nose and hope they notice it. And when they do hit, it is anything but an aggressive strike. The smallmouth will simply close their mouth on the offering as it goes by and then just sit there. Jay Nelson refers to this as "assuming the bait." Because there is no action on the end of your line to indicate a strike, you must set the hook whenever the movement of the jig is impeded. It could be caught on a weed or hung up on rocks, but very often it will be a fish.

On account of the depths where winter smallmouth will usually be found, slight modifications to standard jigging techniques are necessary. Typically, jigs are cast shoreward into shallow water and worked down the slope of the lake's bottom into deeper water. The usual retrieval method is to lift the jig up off the bottom with the rod tip, and letting it fall back to the bottom while the slack in the line is reeled in. To detect a strike on a falling jig is a real talent, but most people can master this skill if they are fishing in shallow water where drop offs might only run

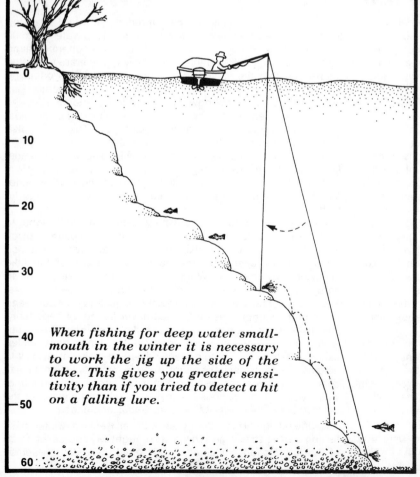

When fishing for deep water smallmouth in the winter it is necessary to work the jig up the side of the lake. This gives you greater sensitivity than if you tried to detect a hit on a falling lure.

When you have located a stair step ledge, don't pull the jig all the way over the top. Let is fall back down repeatedly. In the winter, bass often locate at the base of these ledges.

from 12 down to 20 feet. But when the bass move out into deep water this becomes extremely difficult. You have very little feel for a falling jig in shallow water, almost none in water that can range up to 90 feet deep. And this is further exacerbated by the passive strikes of the bass. What you must do is change your technique in such a way that you gain added sensitivity. To do this you must retrieve the jig **up** the side of the lake. Determine what depth you want to fish in, move shoreward of this and cast into the deeper water. Your retrieval method is the same as before, but you are getting much more feedback from the business end of your line. You feel the action of the jig as it works its way up inclines or ledges. You are going to lose a lot of jigs with this method, but it's about the only way to take big smallmouth in great numbers in the winter.

Very often the smallmouth will be very tightly schooled up on a small ledge or a larger drop off. If you've located such a ledge, don't retreive the jig over the top of the vertical face of the ledge (Imagine yourself standing at the top of a stairway and the fish are all located on one step. You don't want to bring your jig over the top of the step because it won't be able to fall back down to the fish). Instead, lift the jig up a short distance and then let it fall back down to the base of the ledge. When you no longer feel the jig drop back to the bottom, set the hook. Unless you unwittingly pulled the jig over the top of the ledge, a bass has come to "assume" it.

These methods are very rough on your line and this can cause you to lose fish unnecessarily. Replace the last 8 to 10 feet of your line very half hour or so to avoid this problem.

While the bluff is the most productive area for big winter smallmouth, a few other areas of the lake will also produce bass at this time. In the Branchport arm of the lake, the drop offs on the east side of the arm, directly across from Chateau Dugas are good, as are the waters between Boyd Point and Stone Point on the west side. In the Penn Yan arm, check out the small bays that lie just north of Miller's Point, Crosby Point, and Keuka Church. There is little or no winter bass fishing in the lake south of Bluff Point.

Yellow Perch.............. common; growth rate, excellent

Keuka Lake has very good fishing for yellow perch, but the lake's reputation as a perch fishery has always been over-shadowed by the excellent perch fishing on Seneca Lake. The perch in Keuka are nearly as large as those in Seneca, though they aren't quite as abundant. It takes about thirty 15 inch perch to fill a 5 gallon pail, and it's not overly difficult to fill a pail at certain times of the year here.

One of the most productive periods for yellow perch is the springtime, when these piscatorial delicacies move into shallow water to spawn. Until the middle of April there are many areas on Keuka Lake that are every bit as productive for yellow perch as Seneca Lake. Generally speaking, perch are going to seek out shallow flats adjacent to deep water where there is at least some submerged vegetation. They will also be looking for water in the 45^0 to 50^0 F range. There are many areas of the lake that will exhibit these conditions, but by far the best spring perch fishing takes place in the Penn Yan arm. Excellent catches are reported each year from the mile or so of flats immediately south of Keuka College. Perch are also found off of Camp Iroquois and just north of Willow Grove. But these aren't the only areas where big spring perch can be found. They can be taken wherever suitable spawning grounds are found.

In the spring, perch can be taken on a wide variety of offerings including worms, minnows (use a spreader for real effectiveness), and small deer hair jigs. A popular and productive Keuka perch rig consists of three 1/32 ounce jigs dressed with small Mister Twister tails. These are attached to a single line (use short leaders) at the bottom of which is a one ounce sinker. This rig is cast out over the flats and slowly retrieved. If perch are in the area it's not uncommon to pick up two or three fish at a time with this setup.

After their spawning period, yellow perch begin to migrate into deeper water in very loosely associated schools. As in the case on many lakes, perch are difficult to catch on Keuka in the period between the end of their spawning and the fall. A majority of the perch taken in the day during the late spring and summer are probably incidental fish taken by fisherman working deep water ledges and points for smallmouth bass. For the die-hard perch fisherman, some local anglers suggest fishing at night, using the same type of lights that trout fisherman have traditionally used on this lake. Check out the areas where smallmouth bass are taken at night (the west side of the Hammondsport arm, off Chateau Dugas and the shelves around Bluff Point, etc.). The odds are that you'll pick up at least a few perch from these waters.

In the fall, yellow perch will again be found in more concentrated schools. They also begin to migrate into deeper water (40 to 60 feet). The areas where the perch will be found in the fall are often on or close to the spawning grounds of lake trout. More than one angler on Keuka has noticed that as soon as the lake trout spawn you start picking up good catches of perch in the same general area. When these fish are brough up from the depths, they often lose the contents of their stomachs, which very often consist of lake trout eggs.

For good catches of yellow perch in the fall, it would be a good idea to stick close to areas where lake trout spawn. They will be found on almost every major point on the lake, but two areas in particular are noted for big concentrations of lakers. The shelves around Bluff Point are probably the principle spawning area for lake trout in the entire lake, and will certainly attract large numbers of perch. The second area to consider are the small points that run between "The Elms" and Willow Point, on the east side of the Hammondsport arm of the lake.

In the fall, yellow perch can be taken on small crayfish, and minnows, both fished close to the bottom, as well as on small slab spoons or jigs. Small deer hair jigs tipped with oak leaf grubs are highly affective when slowly worked along the bottom.

When the weather really turns cold perch can be taken on Keuka Lake either from open water or through the ice.

As far as open water fishing is concerned, perch will be found in the same general area as smallmouth bass in the winter. Generally, though, they will be in water a little shallower than the bass. If you're picking up smallmouth in 40 feet of water, move inshore and fish in 25 to 30 feet for yellow perch.

In the winter, the perch in this lake love to hit on small minnows fished close to the bottom directly under the boat. While live minnows will account for most of the fish taken from open water in the winter, the same jigs that are used on other Finger Lakes will also work well here, such as a red or white Russian jig, Swedish Pimple or a small jigging Rapala.

When you start picking up perch, don't settle for just any size fish. If you catch more than a couple perch under 10 inches, you're probably onto a school of small fish. They school up by size in the winter, and there is no sense wasting your time on these small fish. You might have to move only 20 or 30 yards to find a school of perch in the 15 to 16 inch class.

Some local anglers on Keuka Lake refer to schools of yellow perch as "tunnels." Their experience tells them that these fish move through the water in a pattern similar to a rotating funnel, like a wide tornado. Because the school is slowly, but constantly, moving, it's difficult to maintain your position over it. You can be into excellent fishing one minute and out of it the next. To mark the position of a "tunnel" local fisherman employe a technique known as "ballooning." Once several large perch have been landed, establishing the fact that the anglers are on to a school of large fish, the next perch to be firmly hooked is not reeled in. Instead, the line is cut and a small balloon is blown up and tied to the end of it. The balloon is then sent adrift. If the fish hasn't been badly injured by being hooked, it will stay with the school, marking its position as it moves by the balloon on the surface. If the perch was seriously injured, it will almost always move away from the school. You can tell that this has happened when a fish that was hooked directly under the boat suddenly moves 30 or 40 feet away when the balloon is released. That fish has probably left the school. Ignore the balloon, or better yet, cut it off the line and use it again. Also, if the balloon suddenly lays on its side it's a sign that the perch is no longer hooked. Again, retrieve the balloon.

Except during the very coldest winters, not much of Keuka Lake freezes to safe ice. Consequently, ice fishing is usually limited to the shallow portions of the lake. Most of the ice fishing for yellow perch takes place on the Penn Yan arm north of Eggleston Point. The fishing can be excellent anywhere along the east or west sides of this arm, but the best fishing over all seems to be in the north end. Concentrate your efforts on shelves in 15 to 18 feet of water. Standard ice fishing jigs and live minnows will work well here. Remember that the perch school by size under the ice, just as in open water. Keep moving until you're over big fish. With a little effort, you should have no problem filling a 5 gallon pail with big tasty perch.

Largemouth Bass . . . . common; growth rate good

Compared to smallmouth bass, largemouth are of secondary importance on Keuka Lake. However, they are plentiful in several areas of the lake and are an important, if localized, fishery.

An overwhelming majority of the largemouth caught in this lake are taken from the large weedbeds found in the northern ends of the Branchport and Penn Yan arms of the lake. Lesser populations are found in the weedbeds at the south end of the lake off Champlin Beach, in Brandy Bay, and between Marlena Point and Kendall Point. Occasionally, largemouth are also taken from the narrow band of weeds that ring this lake. Finally, skipping jig 'n pigs under the approximately 2,300 boat docks on Keuka Lake will more than likely turn up more than a few bass.

One of the keys to successful largemouth fishing here is being on the water at the right time. Nearly all of the good habitat for largemouth is found in close proximity to the major population centers on the lake. These areas are very popular with locals and tourist for sailing and water skiing. Between Memorial Day and Labor Day your angling efforts will be more productive if you fish early in the morning, late in the evening or at night.

Probably the best area overall for largemouth is the northern portion of the Penn Yan arm, north of Keuka College and Willow Grove. Very early in the season, bass can be found in Keuka Lake Outlet, especially in the wide, lake-like reach between the lake and Route 14A. By early July, however, most of these fish will have moved back into Keuka Lake, finding shelter in the 2500 acres of weeds that blanket the shallows in this area.

The weed beds near Branchport also hold a lot of largemouth, but they don't seem to be nearly as productive as the beds near Penn Yan. The least productive of the major largemouth bass haunts are the shallows just off Champlin Beach. Bass are found there in the spring and fall, but relatively few are taken between July and October.

Early in the season, before water temperatures maximize, small spinners will often be the most effective offering for largemouth. Panther Martins (1/16 oz. to 1/8 oz.) are a good example of a spinner that works well early on. As water temperatures increase, switch to larger spinners, saftey pin type spinnerbaits, top surface baits and shallow running crankbaits.

In July, August and September largemouth bass will often be found waiting in ambush at the edge of the weed cover. Any sizable break in the cover is a good spot to work. Large purple or chartreuse plastic worms are very productive when fished along these breaks, as are large spinnerbaits. Just out from Holiday Harbor, near Branchport, a sand bar runs across the top of the lake and is marked by buoys. This water can easily be read from the high seat of a bass boat and it's not hard to pick out the open water pockets in the weed growth where bass are laying in wait.

In the fall, largemouth tend to move into somewhat deeper water, orienting off drop-offs and deeper weedlines. They will return to shallow water during extended warm spells. Deep diving crankbaits and large spinnerbaits are effective for getting down to these fish. As the water cools below 55° F the bass become less aggressive and lures that can be worked slowly become necessary. Try using small jigs dressed with a minnow or pork rind for these deep, lethargic fish.

In the winter, it appears that most of the largemouth return to shallow water about the time that these areas freeze up Surprisingly good numbers of largemouth are taken through the ice on Keuka Lake. In the Penn yan branch, largemouth constitute a considerable percentage of fish taken through the ice. The shallow bay at Branchport is also very good for taking largemouth in the winter. Occasionally, a largemouth will be taken in the winter by smallmouth bass fishermen working deep water, but this happens only rarely.

Chain Pickerel . . . . common; growth rate good

Chain pickerel are a predator of secondary importance in Keuka Lake. Although they are found in all of the major weedbeds of the lake and grow to respectable size, relatively few anglers actively pursue them here. In a 1970 DEC survey of angler preferences on Keuka, chain pickerel weren't even mentioned to any significant degree. And yet, at times the fishing for these toothsome predators can be good.

During the warm weather months most of the pickerel are going to be found in the major weedbeds off Branchport, Penn Yan, Champlin Beach, Marlena Point and in Brandy Bay. Keep in mind the fact that pickerel will locate directly in the weeds, as well as adjacent to them, much more so than their close cousin the northern pike. Early in the season they are going to be found most often in shallow water and can be taken on spinners, such as the Mepps Aglia or Panther Martin, or on slowly retrieved spoons. Later, as the shallow portions of the lake approach their maximum temperature, pickerel become more dispersed, but still orient in or near weeds. On other Finger Lakes fishermen often use large shiners to take pickerel in the summer, but floating Rapalas, flatfish and DareDevles are also effective when fished along weed lines. To get to fish located directly in the weeds use Johnson Silver Minnows or weedless plastic worms. No one that we interviewed for Keuka Lake mentioned it, but I strongly suspect that by trolling along the narrow band of weeds that rings this lake you would more than likely pick up a few pickerel, as well as some largemouth bass.

The most productive period for taking pickerel on Keuka is the winter, after the shallow portions of the lake have iced up. Most of the ice fishing here seems to be centered on the Penn Yan arm, and pickerel make up a sizeable portion of the fish landed through the ice in the area. They are also taken from the shallow bay at Branchport. Standard tip-ups baited with live shiners or fresh cut bait should do the trick.

Lake Trout . . . . abundant; growth rate good

Lake trout are the primary predator in Keuka Lake and, according to DEC surveys, the fish that is most popular with anglers on the lake. All of the lakers here are wild fish, and the abundance of small 7 to 12 inch fish indicates that natural reproduction of lake trout is still very successful in Keuka. Not all of the lakers taken here are small, though. The trout creeled in recent years have averaged close to 3½ pounds and some real lunkers are known to be in these waters.

The fishing for lake trout begins on Keuka Lake in early April. Traditionally, the best early season fishing will be found at the south end of the lake, near Hammondsport, and in the waters of "The Basin", which is located just off Keuka Lake State Park. They will also be found in good numbers off Willow Grove. The trout will be feeding on alewives, which will be found in waters closest to 39° F, or on smelt, which will be close to the shore in the spring during their spawning phase. As the season progresses, the lakers move toward the central part of the lake off Bluff Point.

Years ago, fishermen used to take most of the lake trout at night, using the traditional Keuka Lake method of fishing under a suspended light. Today, however, most people fish in the daytime. Alewives (sawbellies as they are known locally) and smelt fished on a Seth Green rig are both very productive baits. They can be found in local tackle shops in the spring. When the trout begin to follow the bait fish in to shallow water later in the spring stillfishing with live bait will take fish, and there is no reason that long lining with copper wire won't be as effective here as on other Finger Lakes.

Wild lake trout from Keuka Lake, gorged on sawbellies. Photo courtesy New York State DEC.

By mid to late June the bait fish will have moved back out into deep water, drawing the lake trout with them. From then until early October the most productive area for lake trout will be the deep central portion of the lake, roughly bounded by Urbana on the South, Roff Point on the west and Eggleston Point on the east. Especially good is the water between Bluff Point and Marlena Point. Other areas of the lake known to hold lakers in the summer include the deep hole off Chateau Dugas and the deep central section of the Penn Yan arm of the lake. With regard to the latter area, the lake trout here seem to run smaller than in other parts of the lake. This is offset, however, by the fact that the east arm of the lake isn't as heavily fished for lake trout as are other areas.

Standard downrigging techiniques and Seth Green rigs work well on this lake. They are especially productive when using live bait, but if this isn't available spoons will suffice. Another way effective technique, especially for a novice who is not familiar with or equipped for the above methods, is copper line fishing. Many of the tackle shops in the area sell copper wire. Buy about 600 feet of wire and something to wind it up on, and a spoon made for trolling on the bottom, such as Sutton spoons (made in Hammondsport), flatfish or Twin Minnows. Attach the spoon to the copper line with a swivel. Trolling at a low speed (2½ mph) feed out the line until you can feel the spoon tap the bottom. You might get a bit more sensitivity if, instead of attaching the spoon directly to the swivel, you tie 18 inches of 20 pound monofilament to the swivel and attach the spoon to that. This method works best in 40 to 70 feet of water. One of the keys to copper line fishing is not trying to roll the copper back on the holder when landing a fish. Simply hand haul the line back into the boat and put it next to you. As long as you don't move the pile of wire it should go back out just as easily as it came in.

Another simple and productive way to take trout is to still fish using sawbellies. Secure an egg sinker on your line with a snap swivel. Attach a small split-shop sinker between the egg sinker and the swivel to keep the sinker from beating on the knot. Then thread a sawbelly with an English style hook and attach that to the snap swivel. Throw the rig as far out as you can and let it go all the way to the bottom. Reel in most of the slack. Leaving your bail open, secure your line to the cork handle of your rod with a rubber band. Set the rod down and set up another rod the same way. When a lake trout takes the bait he will swallow it and run off. When he stops running close the bail. When he starts to run again set the hook. This method is also used in water 40 to 70 feet deep.

Regardless of the method you plan on using, keep in mind that in the summer lake trout will usually be found below the thermocline in water between 45° and 55° F. In Keuka Lake this means that they will be found 40 to 70 feet down, regardless of how deep the water is.

Unlike other Finger Lakes, where lake trout spawn in mid-October, the lakers in Keuka spawn in mid to late November. Also, unlike some lakes, these fish do not completely stop feeding. For a period of 7 to 10 weeks they can be taken in the spawning areas. The fishermen we talked to claimed catches of 20 or 30 fish per day were common using white and gold slab spoons. Jigs, which are so productive on Skaneateles for fall lake trout, might also work well here.

During the spawning period, lake trout will be found in large numbers on nearly all of the major points on the lake in 30 to 40 feet of water. This is especially true of the points on the southern arm of the lake, between The Elms and Willow Point. Exceptional catches can also be had from the waters around Bluff Point.

In the cold weather months lake trout can be taken from open water or through the ice, primarily in the Hammondsport arm of the lake. After spawning the trout return to following the alewives, which means that they again will be found in deep water. Until the shore areas are so frozen over that you can't get a boat out (usually this occurs shortly after Christmas) lake trout can be taken on Seth Green rigs and copper lines. Once the ice starts to form, however, you are presented with a dilemma. It prevents you from getting a boat out, but very often safe ice doesn't extend out far enough to cover the deep water where lakers will be found. When the ice over deep water is safe, the fishing can be excellent, but this rarely occurs.

Brown Trout . . . . common; growth rate excellent

Keuka Lake is renowned for the size of the brown trout that it produces. In 1979 and 1983 state record browns were caught here, weighing 22¼ pounds and 23¾ pounds respectably. Both of these fish were taken near the buoy at the mouth of Keuka Inlet. Most of the browns caught in this lake weigh 2 to 3 pounds, but fish of 16 to 18 pounds are reported each year.

Until recently, all of the brown trout in this lake were fish that escaped from the Bath State Fish Hatchery on Keuka Inlet (Cold Brook). They weren't stocked here, nor did they reproduce in any of the lake's tributaries. Today, however, the population of browns in Keuka is augmented each year with a stocking of 9,400 brown trout yearlings.

The brown trout fishery in Keuka Lake is essentially a spring and fall affair. Browns will be found in the Branchport arm of the lake and part way up the Penn Yan arm, but the bulk of the brown trout come from the Hammondsport arm. In the spring, they can be taken almost anywhere in the Hammondsport area where you have deep water close to shore.

In the spring and early summer brown trout will be found cruising the shore line, especially in the Hammondsport area. The most productive method for taking these fish is trolling as tight up against the shore as possible. Effective lures include large tandem hook streamers, brightly colored Rebels and Rapalas, and large silver or white spoons. Browns can also be taken early in the spring on jigs, worms or minnows fished in the relatively warm outflow of some of the lakes tributaries, most notably Keuka Inlet. The outflow of the power generating station near Kendall Point is good, not just for browns, but for rainbows, lake trout and landlocked salmon as well.

By early summer brown trout will begin to move out into deeper waters, seeking out their preferred temperature range of 50^0 to 60^0 F. Because of their relatively low population density and tendency not to concentrate in any one area, few brown trout are taken here in the summer. Most of those that are landed are taken by lake trout fishermen.

In the fall, brown trout are again drawn into near shore waters, partly by the urge to spawn. As in the spring, most of the browns will be found in the lower end of the lake, close to Hammondsport. It might also be worth your while to check out the waters just off Eggleston Point and Lakeside Park. Browns are stocked in those areas in the spring and they might become imprinted by these waters, just as the browns in Owasco Lake are imprinted by the waters off Ensenore.

The technique favored for taking browns in the fall (i.e. early November through early December) is the same one as in the spring. Troll in 30 to 60 feet of water, with your lure running 16 to 30 inches below the surface.

Bobber fishing from the shore with golder shiners is another popular and productive method for taking brown trout from Keuka in the fall. The shiner should be hooked 18 inches below the bobber with an English hook. Position yourself on shore so that you can cast the shiner into water that is 30 to 60 feet deep. After casting set your rod on a forked stick leaving the bail open. When a trout hits, let it run, just as you would still fishing for lake trout. When it stops close the bail, and when it starts to run again set the hook. This is a very popular method with anglers who fish from the wall in Hammondsport and it will catch browns there all winter long.

Keuka Lake seldom freezes over completely, and the ice that does form isn't always safe. When safe ice does form on the south end of the lake, the ice fishing for trout and salmon can be exceptionally good. Brown trout can be taken on jigging Rapalas, Swedish Pimples or Russian jigs. They also hit well on shiners fished 12 to 18 inches below the surface.

Rainbow Trout . . . . common; growth rate good

Rainbow trout were first introduced into Keuka Lake in 1897 when a Pacific coast strain of steelhead was stocked here. The stocking policy was discontinued and now all of the rainbows found in the lake are wild descendants of these fish. The population is maintained by natural reproduction in Keuka Lake Inlet and Guyanoga Creek. The population of this species normally cycles up and down. Currently (1988) the population of rainbows in Keuka Lake is depressed.

Compared to the number of lake trout or smallmouth bass found in Keuka, rainbow trout are less than common. But during the spring and fall, when rainbows are concentrated in certain areas of the lake, the fishing can be surprisingly good.

In the early spring, rainbow trout are usually taken with the same methods used for brown trout, and they are frequently found in the same areas. Most of the rainbows will be found in the south end of the lake and can be taken by trolling Rapalas, Rebels and silver spoons. They can also be caught using live bait (worms and minnows) or jigs fished in the warm (relatively speaking) outflow of feeder creeks. Of course, many of these rainbows are going to be found increasingly close to the mouths of Keuka Lake Inlet and Guyanoga (Suger) Creek. They run up these streams in early April, at which time the fishing, especially in Keuka Lake Inlet, is excellent. The warm water outlet of the power plant south of Kendall Point is also a hot spot for rainbow trout all during the spring.

In the summer, rainbow trout disperse throughout the deeper portions of the lake, but the DEC feels that most of those caught are taken from the deep water between Hammondsport and The Bluff. This could be due to the high concentration of lake trout fishermen in that area. Many of the rainbow trout taken in the summer are caught incidentally by lake trout fishermen using downriggers or Seth Green rigs.

Not all of the rainbows taken on Keuka Lake in the summer are caught accidentally. There is a small group of anglers from the Branchport area that have developed a technique for taking big rainbows in July and August. The method is simple. Trolling parallel to shore at the slowest possible speed, giant streamers are cast with nine foot fly rods tight up against the bank. The streamers aren't retrived, but are slowly pulled away from shore by the boat. Used very early in the morning, this technique doesn't produce a lot of fish, but a good number of those caught are in the 4 to 5 pound range. The excitement of fighting a 5 pound rainbow on a 9 foot fly rod more than makes up for the paucity of fish that are caught. The anglers that use this method usually concentrate their efforts on the stretch of shore line between Branchport and Chateau Dugas. There is no reason, however, that this technique wouldn't work on other parts of the lake that are similar in structure to the aforementioned area.

By the middle of September, rainbow trout will again begin to concentrate close to shore, orienting off points, especially in the south end of the lake. The same techniques that produced fish in the spring will again be productive in the fall. And don't neglect the fall run of rainbows, particularly in Keuka Inlet. It isn't as spectacular as the spring run, but it certainly is deserving of attention.

Relatively few rainbow trout are taken from Keuka Lake in the winter. Most of the rainbows winter over in the south end of the lake, and that area seldom freezes sufficiently to be safe. As late as early January you can usually get a boat out onto the lake, but after that the periphery of the south end freezes up, making launching difficult or impossible. When you are able to launch a boat, use the same trolling techniques as in the spring and fall, but troll a bit slower. Trolling can be a numbing experience in the winter, but it can pay off handsomely. Some of the few fishermen who work the south end of the lake in the winter keep diaries for the DEC. If their records are any indication, there is a veritable fishing bonanza that is going unutilized here in the winter. This is true not only for rainbows, but for brown trout and landlocked salmon as well.

In the few years when the south end does freeze enough to allow ice fishing, rainbows can be taken in good numbers on tip-ups baited with live smelt or golden shiners or on standard ice fishing jigs.

Landlocked Salmon . . . . common; growth rate good

Landlocked Atlantic Salmon are a relatively recent introduction to Keuka Lake. They were first stocked in this lake as fingerlings in 1976. The policy of stocking fingerlings was not successful, and was changed to the present policy of stocking 24,000 yearlings annually. The vast majority of the salmon caught in this lake are 15 to 20 inch fish, but occasionally a 10 pound salmon is reported. The reason most of these fish are small is due to their vulnerability to angling techniques, resulting in most of the salmon being culled from the population as soon as they reach legal size.

Landlocked salmon strongly prefer smelt over alewives, and their spring movements are determined accordingly. Shortly after ice-out, landlocked salmon will be found off the mouths of any stream that has a significant flow into Keuka Lake. They are drawn to these areas by the smelt that congregate there prior to running up the streams to spawn. Particularly large numbers of salmon are found off the mouth of Keuka Inlet at this time. Attention should also be paid to the warm water discharge of the power plant south of Kendall Point.

Odd as it might seem, landlocked salmon are also drawn to the outflow of water at Keuka Outlet, near Penn Yan. In their natural state these salmon tend to move downstream, seeking to find the Atlantic Ocean. They still have this strong migrating instinct, and a significant percentage of the salmon stocked in euka Lake find their way into Senaca Lake.

When the salmon are in close to shore in the spring they are easy to catch using a number of methods. Many are caught by anglers fishing with live bait from the wall in Hammondsport. Smelt can be used for this, but golden shiners last a lot longer on hook. They can also be taken on 1/8 to 1/4 ounce lead head jigs. This method is similar to that used for taking brown trout in the spring except that, instead of casting toward shore from your boat, you cast away from shore into 20 to 30 feet of water. Let the jig sink to the bottom and slowly work it back to the boat. Occasionally the jig won't even make it to the bottom. Landlocked salmon are notorious for comming up to the surface to take an offering.

On calm spring (or fall) days you will often see landlocked salmon dimpling the surface of the water in the same manner as rainbow trout. This occurs throughout Keuka, but it's more commonly seen in the Hammondsport arm of the lake. When the salmon are on the surface they can be taken on small silver or gold spinners or tandem hook smelt imitation streamers, both fished just below the surface.

In the summer, many of the landlocked salmon are taken incidentally by lake trout fishermen on downriggers or Seth Green rigs. They can be caught with some consistancy, however, by any technique that keeps you at or very near the thermocline, in water that is 56° to 58° F. Downriggers, Seth Green rigs, diving planes or copper lines can all be used to take salmon once the proper temperatures have been located. Productive lures include Alpena Diamonds, small Sutton spoons, and Rapalas in blue and white, or gold with a flourescent red back. They will be found throughout the deeper portions of the lake in July, August and early September.

In September, landlocked salmon begin moving back into shallower waters. Unlike lakes such as Owasco or Skaneateles, the salmon here don't generally run in the feeder strams of the lakes in the fall, thought a few are taken in Keuka Inlet. Most of the salmon will be located off the mouths of larger streams searching for bait fish. All of the methods used in the spring will catch salmon in the fall, including those used when the fish are dimpling the surface.

Winter fishing for landlocked salmon involves the same problems as those found in winter fishing for brown trout and rainbow trout. There is either not enough ice, or too little ice. As long as you can safely get a boat out onto the lake, salmon can be caught with the same techniques used in the fall. As an alternative, you could try fishing with live bait from the wall at Hammondsport, using the same method as that described for taking brown trout. During those exceptional periods when safe ice does form on the south end of the lake, landlocked salmon can be taken on live bait or jigs. Occasionally they are also taken through the ice near Penn Yan.

Additional Species

Keuka Lake has a number of species that individually are of minor significance, but taken as a whole are an important part of this fishery.

Northern pike are probably the most important game species in this category. The number of northerns in Keuka is small, but they can be taken in good numbers if you're persistent and know where to look. One angler we talked to claimed to have caught seven pike on one late summer day. Most of the northern pike are found in the weed beds near Branchport and Penn Yan, with smaller populations being found at Brandy Bay and in the weeds just north of Marlena Point. For a seasonal run down on techniques for taking northern pike see the section for pike fishing on Conesus Lake.

For some very fast action, you might consider taking pumpkinseeds and bluegills on a fly rod. These panfish usually aren't very big in Keuka Lake, but they are numerous and can be a lot of fun. Early in the morning and late in the evening they love to hit on top water lures. Fish the smallest poppers available or small dry flies on weed beds to take almost limitless numbers of sunfish.

Brown bullhead are a popular quarry on Keuka Lake in the early spring. They run up into the lower reaches of Keuka Inlet and Guyanoga Creek in good numbers, but can be found off the mouths of nearly every tributary of the lake. The marshy area at Penn Yan is also a productive area for bullhead, as is the discharge south of the power station at Kendall Point.

Smelt are abundant in Keuka Lake, but are much more important as a forage base than as a fishery. They do run in Keuka Inlet and Guyanoga Creek, providing some fishing.

Rounding out the species found in this lake are rock bass, black crappie (rare), whitefish (rare) cisco, carp and white suckers.

General Information

Nestled in the rolling, vine covered hills of New York's wine country, Keuka Lake has long been known as one of the state's premier fisheries. Indeed, as far back as 1881 the legendary Seth Green wrote of Keuka as follows:

"I think it (Keuka) unsurpassed by any waters in America as a fishing resort. On August 28 last I took with hook and line, 19 salmon trout (lake trout) weighing 113 pounds, and on October 1, 1880, 33 black bass weighing 106 pounds."

Hopefully, creel limits prevent such excessive harvesting of fish, but it's nice to know that the potential for such numbers still exists.

Remembered as the "Father of American Fish Culture," and a one time U.S. Fish Commissioner, Seth Green set the stage for many of our "modern" fishing techniques when he developed, at Keuka Landing, his famous Seth Green rig. Now referred to by some as a thermocline rig, this multi-leader harvester revolutionized deep water fishing on the Finger Lakes. The Seth Green rig of course was the precursor of today's downrigger, which have been so instrumental in the development of New York's spectacular trout and salmon fisheries.

The population in the vicinity of Keuka Lake is large and shoreline development is extensive. Recreational activity on the lake is very high. An indication of this is the fact that there are nearly 4,000 boat docks and boat lifts on Keuka. While some congestion does occur, there isn't as much conflict between the various recreational activities (water skiing, swimming, boating, fishing) as you might expect.

Ecologically, Keuka Lake is in good shape. Water level fluctuations are kept to a minimum and presently pose no threat to the narrow littoral zone of the lake. Water quality is very high, and the lake serves as a source of water for several municipalities. The discharge of municipal or domestic waste into the lake is minimal and contaminant levels in the fish are very low when present at all.

As might be expected on a lake as developed as Keuka is, access, particularly shoreline access, is poor. The only significant access points for shore bound anglers is found at Keuka Lake State Park on the northeast side of the Branchport arm of the lake, and at the mouth of Keuka Inlet at the south end of the lake. Boat launch sites, while adequate at the extremities of the lake, are almost non-existant elsewhere. The state is currently attempting to purchase a site for a launch ramp at the south end of the lake at Hammondsport.

Notes: _____

_____

_____

_____

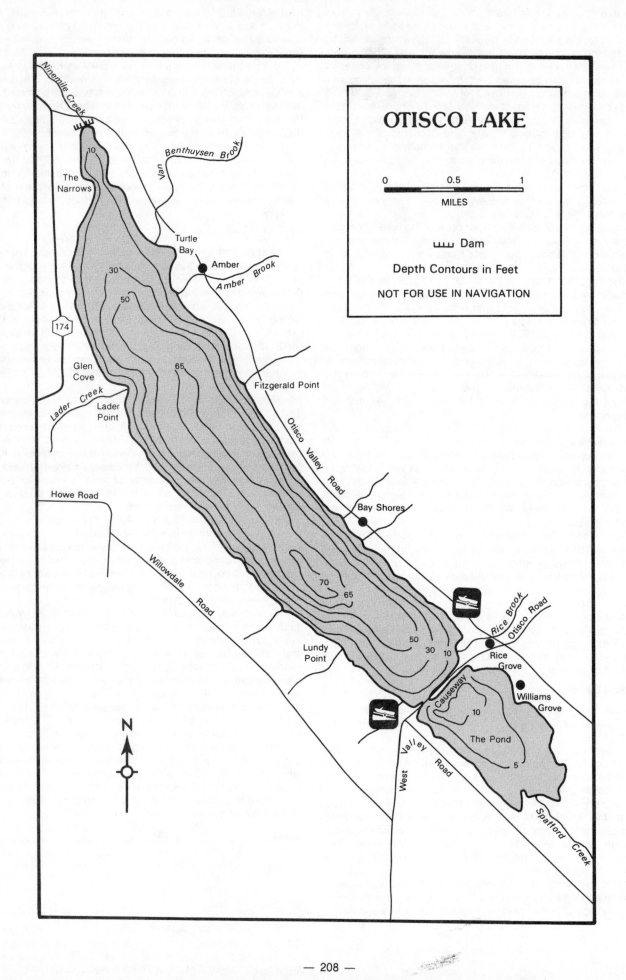

OTISCO LAKE

0   0.5   1
MILES

‿‿‿ Dam

Depth Contours in Feet

NOT FOR USE IN NAVIGATION

Ninemile Creek

The Narrows

10

Van Benthuysen Brook

Turtle Bay

Amber

Amber Brook

30

50

174

Glen Cove

Lader Creek

Lader Point

65

Fitzgerald Point

Howe Road

Otisco Valley Road

Bay Shores

Willowdale Road

70

65

Rice Brook

Otisco Road

50

30

10

Rice Grove

Lundy Point

Williams Grove

Causeway

10

West Valley Road

The Pond

5

Spafford Creek

N

OTISCO LAKE

map coordinates . . . . 42° 54' 16" 76° 18' 48"
USGS map(s) . . . . Marcellus, Otisco Valley, Spafford
location . . . . southwestern Onondaga County
access . . . . The north east shore is parallelled by Otisco Valley Rd. (Amber-Preble) Road; The south east end of the lake is reached via West Valley Road; The northwest corner is off Route 174.

Physical Characteristics

area . . . . 2,214.4 acres
shore line . . . . 13.4 miles
elevation . . . . 788 feet
mean depth . . . . 34 feet
maximun depth . . . . 76 feet
bottom type . . . . muck, rubble, clay, gravel
mean thermocline depth . . 33 feet

Chemical Characteristics

water clarity . . . . The larger basin of this lake is generally clear, though transparency is reduced at times by algae blooms; the lower basin is turbid with transparency generally less than 3 feet.
pH . . . . alkaline
oxygen . . . . The high fertility of this lake, in combination with its slow flushing rate results in oxygen depletion in waters deeper than 40 feet in the summer. In some years all waters deeper than 32 feet have severely limited amounts of oxygen.

Plant Life

Rooted aquatic vegetation is limited in this lake, even though the littoral zone (water under 20 feet deep) comprises 51% of the lake. This is due to water level fluctuations. Some weeds are found at the north end, at Turtle Bay and along the cause way. Algae blooms do occur, but are not a serious problem.

Boat Launch Sites

1. Otisco Lake Marina — on Amber-Preble Road (Otisco Valley Rd.). Two hard surface ramps, full service marine facilities, open all year — fee.
2. There is an informal launch site on the west side of the causeway on West Valley Road. Hand launch only, parking for about 10 cars.
3. A launch site has been proposed for the northeast side of the lake. The DEC says that this launch will be constructed within the next 10 years.

Species Information

Walleye . . . . uncommon; growth rate good

The population of walleye in Otisco Lake tends to fluctuate considerably as a result of the stressed environmental condition of the lake. In the yearly 1970's walleye were abundant here, but the last strong year class from that period has virtually disappeared. There was a minorly successful spawning in 1977, but for the most part the walleye that survive in Otisco Lake are very old. And very big. Walleye over 10 pounds are caught here almost every year.

The walleye population collapsed because the abundant alewives outcompete walleye fry for the limited zooplankton forage base.

The lunkers that are left in Otisco didn't get to be old or big by being easy to catch. This lake is notoriously difficult to fish successfully for any species, including walleye. This isn't because they are hard to find; most of their haunts are well known. It's just that there is so much for them to eat that they are usually well fed, and a walleye with a full stomach is a very uncooperative animal when it comes to fishing.

The most consistent method for catching Otisco Lake walleyes is trolling at night as tight up against the shore as possible. If you're using side planers be careful not to get tangled up in the floats that are often set out on the lake. Black and silver Rapalas work very well at night here. The entire west shore, from Lader Point down to Lundy Point, is productive, especially on all of the small points in between. Walleye are also taken at night along the causeway and along the rip-rap north of Otisco Lake Marina. You might only pick up two or three walleye in a night's trolling, but they are all going to be fish in the 6 to 8 pound category.

A productive way to fish the causeway is to cast with jigs or Rapalas at night. Be very quiet. The fish will be cruising the shallows close to the edge of the causeway. Cast the lure parallel to the rocks and only a foot or two out and slowly work it back. This is particularly effective on the west end of the causeway.

The DEC has shown that walleye are present in the smaller basin of the lake. They were taken by electro-shocking the shoal areas on the northeast side of that basin. However, not many walleye are taken from the southern part of the lake using traditional angling techniques. A few are caught each year by anglers trolling along the causeway on that side, but it's not really productive.

Walleyes can also be taken during the day on Otisco Lake. In mid-summer these fish spend the daylight hours suspended about 30 feet down. Slow trolling with black and silver Rapalas or large black or silver flat fish is an effective method for taking these fish.

When it comes to fishing this lake successfully for walleye in the fall there is a real dearth of information. It seems that very few people pursue walleye here in the fall, and I wasn't able to identify anyone who was doing so with consistent success. So what follows are a few speculative recommendations on where to find them.

There are two likely scenarios. One is that the fish are going to be typical, gravitating toward the areas where they will spawn in the spring. If this is the case the walleye will be in shallow water. The areas to check on the north end of the lake would be just off the mouth of Van Benthuysen Brook, along the weeds in Turtle Bay, all around Lader Point and along the small points just to the south of Lader Point. On the south end the waters off the mouths of Rice Brook and Spafford Brook would be your best bets in the fall.

The second possibility, and the one that gets my vote, is that the movements of the walleye in Otisco Lake are determined largely by the movements of the alewives. If this is true then the walleye are going to spend the fall and winter months in the deep parts of the lake, and you'll have to adjust your tactics accordingly.

Very few walleyes are taken from Otisco Lake through the ice. The abundant forage base becomes an even greater impediment to angling success in the winter because of the reduced area that can be thoroughly covered by fishing through the ice.

Otisco Lake has the ability to be an exceptionally good walleye lake. When the state walleye hatchery begins producing large numbers of walleye fingerlings, as opposed to fry, the quality of the walleye fishing in this lake could turn around dramatically. Until then, the lake remains a good choice for pursuing trophy walleye only.

Tiger Muskellunge . . . . common; growth rate very good

Tiger muskies were first introduced into Otisco Lake in 1977 in an attempt to bring the bait fish population under control. They have thrived to such an extent that now jit is almost a certainty that the state record tiger muskie resides here.

Sean Kelly took this Otisco Lake smallmouth while fishing off the causeway. Photo courtesy of J. Michael Kelly.

They first start catching tigers here in early May. The highest concentrations of fish are probably at the north end of the lake in the area known as "the narrows." This area has the most luxuriant weed growth in the whole lake, a situation generally favored by this species. But the majority of the muskies are caught along the causeway at the south end, particularly on the side bordering the main basin. This is probably due to the fact that there is better access on the causeway and it is a much easier area to fish because it's not nearly as weedy. They are also found in good numbers in Turtle Bay, and to a lesser extend in the smaller basin, known locally as "The Pond." The west shore of the Pond is the most productive.

There are many ways to catch tiger muskies, but in Otisco Lake the most productive method is to cast with #2 Mepps Aglia spinners. Perhaps these mimic white perch, which the muskie feed heavily on. Muskies are also caught by still fishing from shore with minnows, with or without a bobber. Some people also troll with traditional muskie hardware, such as big Daredevles and big jointed stickbaits, but this doesn't seem to be nearly as effective as it is on other lakes.

Until 1987 you didn't hear of many muskies being taken on Otisco during the summer months. A few were picked up sporadically, but it wasn't a very exciting fishery. That appears to have changed in 1987. During the summer of that year quite a few muskies were taken. The reason or reasons for this is unknown.

On most lakes that have a good muskie population the fishing is best in the fall. A good fall fishery hasn't developed here, however, but this could be due to a lack of fishing pressure. There is no reason to expect that the muskie fishing wouldn't be good here if you're willing to give it a try.

A few tiger muskie are taken through the ice at the north end of the lake, but Otisco Lake doesn't have a significant winter fishery for this species.

The state currently stocks 13,200 tiger muskie fingerlings in Otisco Lake each year.

Smallmouth Bass .... common; growth rate very good

Otisco Lake has a well-deserved reputation for having a lot of big smallmouth. Unfortunately, it also has a well-deserved reputation for not giving very many of them up. There are a couple of reasons for this. First, these fish are very well fed, feeding at leisure on this lake's massive alewife population. And when bass aren't hungry they aren't nearly as likely to chase your offerings. Secondly, many people probably fish for smallmouth in the wrong parts of the lake. Otisco is a unique lake in that the smallmouth here are pelagic during the summer, ranging out over the thermocline to feed on schools of bait fish. This is the same phenonenon that occurs to a lesser extent on Keuka, Canandaigua and Seneca Lakes.

The smallmouth bass in Otisco Lake are big. The average fish is a good 14 inches, and many of them reach 18 inches.

Just as the season opens there is some pretty good bass fishing along both sides of the causeway, off Lundy Point, off the rip-rap just north of Otisco Lake Marina, and along the west shore between Lader Point and Forest Home restaurant. The gravel shoals on the north east side of the smaller basin is also productive early in the season.

The most productive method for taking Otisco Lake smallmouth early in the season is to troll the above areas in 10 to 20 feet of water using Rapalas, silver flatfish and other lures that imitate alewives. The most productive times appear to be dusk and dawn, but few anglers troll here at night.

By the middle of July the fishing for smallmouth bass slows down here. The areas known to hold good numbers of fish include the Onondaga County Water Authority pipe line that runs out into the lake from the north west shore (this pipe line is easily found with a good depth sounder), the entire east shore of the lake, and causeway. A popular technique in the summer is to drift fish with nightcrawlers or Dixie spinners and worm combos down the steep rocky sides of the lake. They also backtroll along drop-offs and deeper weed lines with night crawlers. On the OCWA pipeline jigs are very effective, as are drifted minnows and small spinners. At night there is fair fishing along the causeway. Worms fished with a slip sinker are productive. Some bass will also be taken at night casting Rapalas and big black jigs tipped with a minnow.

As I noted earlier, it is known that many of the smallmouth in this lake suspend just over the thermocline in the summer. I've never heard of any one trying it, but fishing with downriggers might be the way to go on this lake. There is precendent for this. Smallmouth bass are taken on Seth Green rigs on Keuka and Canandaigua Lakes by anglers pursuing rainbow trout.

In the fall, after the lake has turned over, the smallmouth will orient off rocky points and ledges in water 20 to 30 feet deep. Drifting with crayfish will take fish, especially in the area just off the causeway.

Largemouth Bass . . . . common; growth rate very good

The population of largemouth bass in this lake isn't nearly as big as the smallmouth population, but they are here in good numbers are are available all season long. Their growth rate is above average due to the abundant forage and fish in excess of 7 pounds have been caught here.

At one time largemouth bass were abundant in Otisco Lake and could be found practically everywhere. Today, their numbers are reduced, but they can still be found in many of the typical bass holding areas. Early in the season the fish are going to be in shallow water. They are found in good numbers along the causeway, especially on the turbid side early on, and in the stump field just south east of the narrows. They also tend to be found under the overhanging black willows that are found around the lake, especially on the south basin. These early season bass can be caught on shallow running crankbaits and spinnerbaits.

The DEC reports that a unique aspect of this fishery is that the largemouth in Otisco Lake are often found in water deeper than normal for this species by mid-summer. It's not uncommon to find them in 20 to 30 feet of water here, although some fish will continue to be caught in water less than 10 feet through the season. When they move into this relatively deep water they are often caught along the OCWA pipeline and are taken on jigs or plastic worms. But that's not to say you can't fish in more typical water. At dawn and dusk largemouth are caught on crankbaits and spinnerbaits under docks and overhanging willows. Later in the day these baits will take fish from weed lines in areas such as the narrows, Turtle Bay, along the causeway and off the rip-rap north of the marina.

Brown Trout . . . . uncommon; growth rate excellent

From 1969 through 1972 the brown trout fishing in Otisco Lake was superb. By the mid-1970's the fishery had all but collapsed, although stocking has continued to the present.

They start fishing for brown trout here in April. It's popular to troll with flat lines or planer boards on this lake from Lundy Point north to about ¼ miles south of Lader Point, or along the clear side of the causeway. Commonly used lures include Alpena Diamonds, Little Cleos and various jointed stickbaits. Most people limit themselves to size 9 or 11 stickbaits, but it wouldn't be unreasonable to try something as large as size 13. The alewives in Otisco are exceptionally big and it would take a big lure to match them. This spring fishery is only moderately productive.

When Otisco Lake stratifies in the late spring or early summer the brown trout leave the shallows and spread out over the thermocline. Brown trout have a strong preference for areas where 58 to 60° water intersects the bottom. This occurs at the north end of the lake in 30 to 35 feet of water (the thermocline sets up here at about 33 feet), providing the only summertime

concentration of brown trout. Typical downrigger methods are used to take these fish.

In the fall there is moderately productive fishing for brown trout in the shallows from late October to early December. The same techniques used in the spring will also work in the fall. Locations are also the same as in the spring.

Brown trout are taken here through the ice, but not in very good numbers. The best ice fishing seems to be at the north end of the lake in the narrows.

Additional Species

Otisco Lake has a number of species other than those listed above. Because of the unbalanced prey/predator situation in the lake the individual status of these species vis-a-vis the overall fishery tends to fluctuate. At present, only brown bullhead are important to the fisherman. They are caught in good numbers in the spring from the causeway. In some years black crappie are also taken in good numbers from the causeway, but this can change on an almost yearly basis. In the early 1950's chain pickerel were the dominant predator in the lake. At present they are almost rare. White perch are abundant, so much so that they are stunted and serve only as a nuisance to anglers fishing for other species. Yellow perch are uncommon and show poor growth rates. Also present are rock bass, bluegill, pumkinseeds, suckers, and carp.

General Information

Otisco is a lake with a lot of problems and a lot of potential. Seemingly always in a state of flux, a number of factors contribute to the lakes unsettled condition. Probably the most significant of these was the introduction of alewives and white perch. Explosively prolific, these species quickly came to dominate the lake after they were first put here in the 1960's. A boon as well as a bane, they are the forage base for the trophy size game fish found in Otisco Lake, but make fishing for them difficult and seriously affect the ability of these species to reproduce.

Another problem facing Otisco Lake is the severity of the draw dawns that occur here each year. The lake is an importence source of water for the City of Syracuse and the average annual water level fluctuation of about 4 feet greatly inhibits the production of rooted aquatic vegetation. This limits the habitat available to such species as largemouth bass and chain pickerel.

These problems are not insurmountable and the state feels that, if properly managed, this lake could be exceptionally good for such game species as walleye and tiger muskellunge. At present, however, Otisco is a lake best fished for trophy walleye, smallmouth bass, brown trout and tigers, but not for big numbers of fish.

In the following article, J. Michael Kelly, outdoor writer and avid fisherman from Marcellus, New York, gives his impression of this frustrating and enticing lake.

OTISCO LAKE
by J. Michael Kelly

Otisco Lake has long been noted for its big but hard to catch bass, walleyes and brown trout. In the past few seasons, it has also earned a reputation as perhaps the premier spot in the state for trophy norlunge, or tiger muskies.

The easternmost body of water in the Finger Lakes formation, Otisco is governed as a public drinking water supply by the Onondaga County Water Authority. Its depth has been known to fluctuate as much as 100 inches in a year during severe drought periods, but in normal years, depths are sufficient for good fishing even in late summer.

Syracuse area bass fisherman know Otisco as a haven for many 2 to 3 pound smallmouths and some 4 to 6 pound largemouth bass. The lake attained national prominence for its trout fishing in the early 1970's, when stocked growns grew at an incredible rate by feasting on a newly-introduced forage base of alewives. It produces a few 10-12 pound walleyes each year, and has yielded norlunge up to 23 pounds.

A view of the causeway, a popular fishing site on Otisco Lake. Most of the species found in the lake can be caught off this old road bed.

Yet most Otisco fishermen are frustrated by the lake most of the time. Ardent bass anglers, for instance, leave the water shaking their heads after encountering schools of big fish on their sonar screens, but fishing for hours without a strike.

Much of the blame for this situation belongs to whoever introduced alewives and white perch in Otisco, according to D.E.C. senior aquatic biologist Tom Chiotti. The alewives, apparently dumped from a fisherman's bait bucket in the mid-60's, proliferated rapidly in the next few years and accounted for phenomenal growth in the browns that were stocked in the lake from 1969-72. However, when the alewife population nose-dived temporarily after that, so did the browns.

Today, alewives are actually too abundant, and keep Otisco's large trout, bass and walleyes so well fed that they are seldom tempted to strike a fisherman's lure.

Worse, the competition by alewives for zooplankton, the principal food of walleye fry, is so great that the future of Otisco walleyes is very much in doubt. The native walleyes have not produced a strong year class since 1975, as far as the biologists can determine.

White perch, introduced to the lake by unknown means in the late 60's, have also harmed walleye fishing. Although the perch seldom attain a size of more than 6 inches, they are very abundant, and believed to feed heavily on pike fry. The white perch may also be a factor in the mysterious failure of recent brown trout stockings in Otisco, Chiotti feels. Few of the 10,000 browns planted annually in the past few years have survived, although a few 4 to 8 pound trophies are caught each year. It could be that the small stocked fish simply can't compete for food with the greedy white perch.

The sterile norlunge grow to trophy size by feasting an alewives, suckers and other fish, but will never be present in numbers sufficient to reduce the alewife or white perch populations, Chioti explained.

The D.E.C.'s long-range hope is that Otisco's walleye population can be restored through the stocking of fingerlings, rather than fry, after a proposed new state hatchery is built. The fingerlings would survive on insects and fry of other fish, instead of competing with alewives for the limited supply of zooplankton. Eventually, as adult walleyes become more plentiful, numbers of both alewives and white perch might be reduced by predation, and brown trout stockings then would stand a better chance of being successful.

Otisco should not be written off until these problems are solved, of course.

Patient anglers have a decent chance of picking up a large brown or two in April, just after ice-out, by trolling medium size Little Cleos or similar silver finish spoons in 3 to 10 foot depths along both shores. Lader's Point and the small points opposite the Marina are two hotspots at this time.

Smallmouth fishing is sometimes phenomenal in May, a month before the season opens. You can catch a dozen or more good smallies on a good day, trolling small spoons or casting green or white Mr. Twisters up against the rocky western shore at this time of year. Just remember to put them back.

In the summer, smallmouths averaging 14 inches or better can be caught on black jigs, spinner baits or assorted plugs worked in 10-20 foot depths. One of the best spots is along the water authority's intake pipeline, which pokes through the lake bottom about halfway between the shore in front of the Forest Home restaurant.

Otisco smallmouths go on a feeding spree in late October and early November. They can readily be caught then on live crayfish, chartreuse Twisters or slowly-trolled black and silver Rapalas. The Marina, Fitzgerald Point and west shore drop-offs are good autumn areas.

Largemouths aren't as abundant as smallmouths here, but skilled anglers take some lunkers throughout the season around the weedy bays. Black spinner baits and plastic worms the color of motor oil are among the favored lures.

Most of the big walleyes captured in Otisco fall to Rapalas or other plugs cast from shore at night, but one friend of mine nabs a couple each spring by trolling a floating rapala, held near bottom with a large split shot, in water less than 10 feet deep. The big bay in front of Forest Home and the rocky shoreline just north of the Marina are among the hotspots for walleyes.

Norlunge seem to haunt the causeway, which is an old road bed that cuts across the lake near its south end, as well as the weedy shallows near the dam. Although the lake's norlunge can be expected to move into deeper water in the heat of summer, they never stray far from the weeds. Norlunge anglers have had some success with trolled, magnum-size plugs or spinner baits worked over and through the weed beds. Large shiners fished beneath a bobber can be effective, and my uncle, Tom Kelly, has caught several Tigers through the ice, fishing near the lake narrows.

Anglers should keep two oddities about this lake in mind when they map their plans of attack.

First, the causeway acts as a natural trap for sediments washed into the lake from Spafford Creek, Otisco's largest tributary. Consequently, the south end of the lake is exceedingly silty and shallow, with average depths of only four or five feet. It produces some bullhead fishing in April and May, and has fair numbers of carp, but is generally lacking in gamefish.

Second, the depths of the lake below 35 feet have low oxygen levels, and aren't worth fishing. However, large pike and trout may be suspended at 25 to 35 feet over such spots.

NOTES: _____

_____

_____

_____

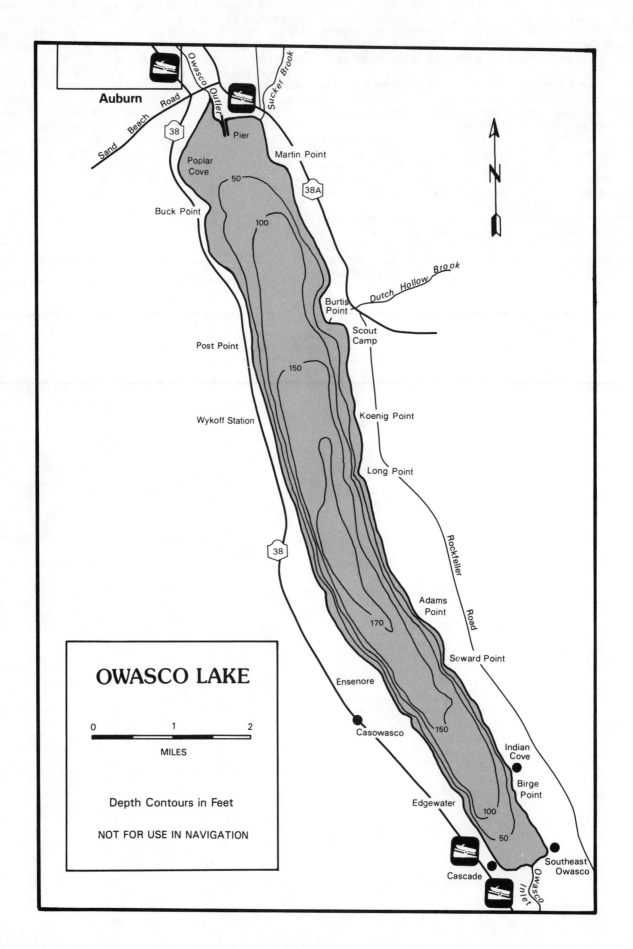

OWASCO LAKE

0   1   2

MILES

Depth Contours in Feet

NOT FOR USE IN NAVIGATION

Auburn

Sand Beach Road

Owasco Outlet

Sucker Brook

Pier

Poplar Cove

Martin Point

Buck Point

Post Point

Wykoff Station

Dutch Hollow Brook

Burtis Point

Scout Camp

Koenig Point

Long Point

Rockfeller Road

Adams Point

Seward Point

Ensenore

Casowasco

Edgewater

Indian Cove

Birge Point

Cascade

Southeast Owasco

Owasco Inlet

50

100

150

170

150

100

50

38

38A

38

N

OWASCO LAKE

map coordinates......... 42° 54' 05" 76° 32' 18"
USGS map(s)............ Auburn, Scipio Center
location.................. Central Cayuga County
access.................. Parallelled by Route 38 and Route
                        38A (Rockefeller Road)

Physical Characteristics

area..................... 6665 acres
shoreline................ 24.7 miles
elevation................ 711 feet
maximum depth......... 180 feet
mean depth............. 97 feet
bottom type............. gravel, rubble, muck
mean thermocline depth .. 37 feet

Chemical Characteristics

water clarity............. fair; some turbidity
pH...................... alkaline
oxygen.................. high levels of oxygen exist through-
                        out the lake, even in the deepest
                        waters, all year long.

Plant Life

The only part of the lake where weed beds are significant is at the very southern end, in water up to 20 feet deep. The lake does not have any problems with algae blooms.

Boat Launch Sites

1. Owasco Marine - 377 Owasco Road, Auburn, about ¾ mi. down Owasco Outlet. Single ramp, gas, marine supplies, repairs - fee.

2. Cayuga County launch site - at Emerson Park on north end of lake - no charge.

3. May's Landing - on southwest side of lake. Single hard surface ramp (a bit steep) - fee.

4. Scotty's Boat Yard - on southwest corner of lake near inlet. Single hard surface ramp, gas, marine supplies, repairs - fee.

Species Information

Lake Trout .... abundant; growth rate good

Lake trout are probably the predominant predator in Owasco Lake. As in most of the other Finger Lakes, lakers here grow at a rate that makes them vulnerable to angling in their fourth year. The average Owasco Lake lake trout weighs in at about 3½ pounds, but a significant part of the catch is made up of fish weighing 6 to 8 pounds. Trophy size fish tipping the scales at 18 pounds have been confirmed, and occasionally a 20 pound laker is reported.

Just as the ice is leaving Owasco Lake, the lake trout will be located in deep water (90 - 100 ft.), feeding on alewives. Fishermen normally start picking up these deep water lakers at the north end of the lake. The most successful techniques used during this period include: running downriggers as close to the bottom as possible, trailing large silver lures (ex. Sutton 88's) or large stick baits (ex. Rapalas); very slow trolling with single hook spoons or plugs on long wire flat lines; and still fishing with live alewives, known regionally as sawbellies.

By the middle of April, anglers start to pick up lake trout along much of the eastern shore of Owasco Lake. This could be in response to movements of alewives. Whatever the cause, the lake trout will usually show up in the greatest concentration off the Boy Scout Camp north to Burtis Point, and off the point at Indian cove, near the south end of the lake. A concentration of secondary importance is usually found off Burtis Point. These fish are usually taken in approximately 70 feet of water. However, there are some areas where lake trout can be taken in fairly shallow water. What draws these fish in close are schools of smelt staging off stream mouths just prior to spawning. Although they are abundant in Owasco Lake, smelt are only of secondary importance as a forage base for lake trout, and only a small fraction of the lakers will follow them inshore. The principle areas where lake trout will move inshore include off the mouths of the streams at Ensenore and Indian Cove. A secondary concentration of fish occurs off the mouth of Dutch Hollow Brook, at Burtis Point.

By the first of May fisherman really start hammering the lake trout using live bait. The most effective rig employs English hooks and a slip sinker. Normally, the bait is fished in about 70 feet of water, but as the month progresses the lakers move into shallower water. This movement is triggered by the shoreward migration of alewives, which begins by about the third week in May. Once the trout are located in fairly shallow water (35 to 50 feet) another technique is added to the angler's arsenal - flat lining with copper wire. Although fishermen can use this method when the fish are deeper, it's during this period that it earns its reputation as a highly effective technique, especially for taking really big lake trout. The wire line functions in the manner of a fast sinking fly line, taking the lure quickly to the bottom. Traditional lures include black or silver flatfish, twin minnows and a wide variety of single hook spoons. Much of the near shore waters of Owasco Lake will produce lake trout, using the above mentioned methods, until the alewives move back into deeper water. The most productive areas seem to be the northeast corner of the lake, off Casowasco, off Burtis Point, from Ensenore around the south end of the lake to Indian Cove and along the east shore from Seward Point to Long Point.

By late June the alewives will have moved back into the deeper portions of the lake, and a majority of the lake trout will follow them out. But due to usually favorable water temperatures, some lakers will remain behind until the end of June.

By late June, and lasting until mid-September, lake trout will generally be found in deep water (90 - 150 feet). Very often the same deep water techniques that are used on Lake Ontario are employed here, but with much less success. Why they are less effective on Owasco Lake isn't really known. The one downrigger technique that has proven to be effective here involves attaching a series of flashers (3 or more) to the downrigger weight and running a plug or spoon 6 to 8 feet behind the flashers. Be sure to set your line at least 12 inches about the flashers, or the spinning blades will cut the line.

Another method that consistently takes lake trout here in the summer is copper line fishing, but very few people use this method during the summer on Owasco.

Unquestionably, a majority of the lakers landed on this lake between June and September are brought in on Seth Green rigs. Employing as many as 15 trailing lines per rig, this precursor of the downrigger can cover a lot of water, vertically speaking, and it's almost certain that one of those lines is going to be at the same depth as the trout. A common practice on this lake is to jug the Seth Green rigs (suspend them from a floating jug some distance from the boat). Some boats will have as many as 4 or 5 jugged rigs in tow. Most of the jugging is done over deep water between Burtis Point and Ensenore, but some lake trout can be taken as far south as Casowasco, or even Indian Cove.

The summer lake trout fishery lasts until about the middle of September. Lakers then enter their spawning phase and don't generally feed. It isn't as extreme as on Lake Ontario, where the lake trout cease feeding entirely, but the fishing does slow to crawl. A few lakers are taken by fishermen seeking out smallmouth bass. They can be taken if you can locate their spawning grounds, where they will congregate in shallow water (1 - 8 feet), even at mid-day. Lake trout spawn in unusually shallow water here. The trouble with this is the fact that, out of 25 miles of shoreline, only about 3½ miles of it are suitable for spawning. The fall simply isn't a good season to be fishing for lake trout on Owasco Lake. There is fairly successful fall lake trout fishing on nearby Skaneateles Lake.

By the time winter has set in lake trout will again be feeding. Though brown trout and landlocked salmon comprise a majority of the salmonids taken through the ice on Owasco, the ice fishing for lake trout is good and can be excellent.

In the winter, lake trout won't range much, choosing instead to locate in the same waters as the alewives (in lakes where alewives aren't present lakers can be found at almost every depth, from 2 to 200 feet). This means that you'll be looking for water temperatures of 39.4 degrees and depths of at least 70 feet.

The areas where ice fishing is productive are somewhat limited. Although the entire lake usually freezes over entirely by mid-February, safe ice over deep water is of short duration. The lower end of the lake, south of Ensenore, is generally frozen over and safe by mid-January. The ice fishing in this area is very good. The only other area where deep water ice fishing can be practiced safely is along the western shore, between Buck Point and Wykoff Station, with the best catches coming from the waters between Wykoff Station and Post Point. South of Wykoff, the ice over deep water is very questionable.

The vast majority of the lake trout taken through the ice here are taken on large minnows, such as big golden shiners or buckeyes. If you could get your hands on some live alewives they would work very well. Cut smelt aren't often used here, but there's no reason that they wouldn't be as productive as on other lakes. To increase their chances of fishing at the right depth, many anglers use a rig similar to a Seth Green rig. This enables them to fish with several minnows at different depths.

In the spring, 10,300 lake trout yearlings are stocked at the south end of the lake. In the fall, an additional 20,700 lake trout fingerlings are stocked off Ensenore.

Brown Trout . . . . common; growth rate excellent

Brown trout are probably the most sought after fish in Owasco Lake, and with good reason. Browns weighing 10 pounds are regularly taken here, and fish up to 16 pounds have been reported.

Information from the DEC and local anglers indicates that the spring brown trout fishing on this lake is somewhat erratic in most areas. The only near-shore waters that are consistently productive in the spring are located in the northeast corner of the lake and just south of Buck Point. Flat line fishing is very productive in these areas when the browns move in to feed on alewives and smelt. Another area that can be productive, but often isn't, is the stretch of shoreline between Ensenore and Casowasco.

By late spring, when the lake begins to stratify, brown trout will be found dispersed along most of the western shore of the lake with few areas of concentration and in less numbers than you would expect, given the numbers of browns in this lake. The one area that often does produce a lot of browns at this time is between Wykoff Station and Polish Home. Large plugs or spoons fished on Seth Green rigs or flat lines in 30 to 60 feet of water are often highly effective here.

The brown trout come into the near-shore waters, lured by combination of favorable temperatures and available forage fish (alewives). Around the middle of June the alewives will have finished spawning and shallow water temperatures will be rising above those preferred by brown trout. At this time, most of the browns will break out into the open waters of the lake. When this happens, the fishing for brown trout drops off considerably, for they show little tendency to concentrate in any great numbers or in any one area, with the possible exception of the waters just off Ensenore. Some fish are taken using traditional deep water techniques, but until the middle of September, when they begin schooling off the mouths of larger tributaries, the fishing for brown will only be fair at best.

In the fall, great concentrations of brown trout will be found just off Ensenore. Brown trout are stocked off Ensenore in the spring, and the fish imprint here just as if it was their natal stream. The DEC reports that, unlike most brown trout, these fish often continue to feed prior to and during their spawning phase, making them much easier to catch. While the major concentration of fish will be found near Ensenore, good fall brown trout fishing will be found throughout the south end of the lake in about 60 feet of water, roughly from Rocky Point, just north of Ensenore, around to Indian Cove. Be sure not to neglect the fine brown trout

fishing in Owasco Inlet when these fish finally make their spawning runs.

In the winter, brown trout can be taken through the ice along the entire western shore line, but the best fishing is concentrated in two areas of Owasco Lake: the south end, where ice fishing usually begins by mid-January and between Wykoff Station and Buck Point, which is usually frozen over by mid-February. With regard to the latter area, the waters just off Post Point are probably the most productive. The techniques are very similar to those used for taking lake trout in the winter, except that the bait is fished close to the surface, about 1 to 2 feet below the ice.

In the spring, a total of 10,000 brown trout yearlings are stocked in Owasco Lake, just off Ensenore.

Landlocked Salmon . . . . uncommon; growth rate good

Landlocked salmon were first introduced into Owasco Lake in 1978. They have not been able to establish themselves as any more than a put-and-take fishery of secondary importance. Most are taken incidentally by anglers fishing for brown trout or lake trout. From our information it appears that the only time during which landlocked salmon can be taken with any consistency is in the winter, when they constitute a significant part of the salmonid catch. They are taken through the ice at the south end and along much of the western shore of the lake. Aside from this, however, there simply isn't enough data to generate a clear picture of the movements of these salmon or what techniques are best suited for taking them. Probably your best chance to land one of these hard fighting salmon would be to concentrate your efforts on Dutch Hollow Brook and Owasco Inlet, both of which have significant runs of landlocked salmon in the fall. You might also consider trying the pool below the dam on Owasco outlet, as some trout and salmon do manage to escape through the dam system.

In the spring, the south end of Owasco Lake is stocked with 12,000 landlocked salmon yearlings.

Rainbow Trout . . . . common; growth rate fair

Although Owasco Lake itself generally has excellent habitat for rainbow trout, a number of factors combine here to prevent the development of a really good rainbow fishery. The two most important factors are poor fry survival due to excessive competition from alewives and yellow perch generally poor spawning and nursery areas in the lake's tributaries.

Rainbow trout are taken through out the deeper portions of the lake in the summer, primarily by fishermen with their sights set on lake trout. The only consistent rainbow trout fishery in the lake proper is in the spring at the southern end, when many of the rainbows congregate just off the mouth of Owasco Inlet, prior to spawning. The fishermen we talked to concentrated their efforts in 20 to 30 feet of water, from Edgewater around to Indian Cove. Using small spoons on downriggers they claim to have great success, though most of the fish are only 12 to 16 inches. Aside from this, it seems that most of the wild Owasco Lake rainbow trout are taken in the lake's tributaries, in the spring and, to a lesser extent, in the fall. Rainbow trout do not contribute significantly to the ice fishing on this lake.

In June, the DEC stocks Owasco Lake at the south end with 5,000 rainbows. These are a wild strain of trout, not your typical stocked strain.

Northern Pike . . . . common; growth rate good

Owasco Lake has a good, if localized, population of northern pike. The typical northern from this lake runs 4 to 6 pounds, but fish up to 20 pounds have been reported. They are found almost exclusively in the weedy southern end of the lake, south of Indian Cove. On the opening day of their season, northern pike will be found in the lower half mile of Owasco Inlet, or very close to the inlet of the lake. They will remain heavily concentrated near the mouth of the inlet during the early part of the season. The traditional method for taking spring pike is still fishing with large shiners (8 - 12 inches) chubs or suckers. Early on in the season you will want to keep your bait close to the bottom. Later on however, using a bobber to keep your bait off the bottom is important. Spinners are also effective for northerns in the spring. Especially good northern pike fishing can be had by taking a small boat or canoe out in to the swampy areas on the south end and casting large white salt water streamers with a fly rod. This method is very effective in the spring, not just on Owasco Lake, but on many of the Finger Lakes.

Later in the season, northerns will move out into weedy areas of the lake and can be taken on a wide variety of tackle, including large silver flatfish, crankbaits and spoons. The same large salt water streamers that worked in the spring will also produce well in the summer. For really large pike, try using a big (10 to 12 inch) sucker fished with a slip bobber. This lake isn't known for the size of its northern pike, but there are a few trophy size northerns to be had here.

In the fall, jigs are effective pike baits. Large bucktail jigs, and yellow jigs tipped with a minnow or Mister Twister tail are very effective.

Some of the best northern pike fishing on Owasco Lake takes place after the lake freezes. The shallow southern end of Owasco Lake freezes over earlier then nearby Skaneateles Lake. Ice fishing is usually possible here by the middle of January (the rest of the lake doesn't freeze up until February). A tip-up, baited with a sucker or shiner hooked through the back with a size 2 or 4 hook, is a time honored method and usually works well. Most experienced pike fishermen prefer a braided nylon line in the winter, terminating in a short wire leader or a heavy duty (40 - 60 lbs.) monofilament shock tippet. To prevent losing a fish right at the hole, it's good to have a short handled gaff within reach.

Smallmouth Bass .... common; growth rate good

Owasco Lake is not widely known for its smallmouth bass fishing, but it is good here and has a faithful following among some local anglers. Smallmouth bass are generally distributed through out the shallow areas of the lake. The best smallmouth fishing seems to be off Martin Point and around the submerged water intakes at the north end of the lake. The intakes are located due south of the pumphouse pier, in 30 feet of water. Early in the season, a lot of the old timers use small brown jigs with considerable success. They drift slowly over submerged structure, cranking the jig very slowly, but giving it a lot of action with the rod tip. Black, yellow and yellow and brown jigs will also work well here. A 3/8 ounce deer hair jig will not only take smallmouth, but rock bass and yellow perch will hit on it as well.

Later in the season, live baits (minnows, leeches, crabs) slowly drifted over the bottom can be very productive. This is true not only for the area around the water intakes and off Martin Point, but probably every rocky point of the lake. Deep diving crankbaits worked as close to the bottom as possible will take smallmouth bass from shallow, rocky areas during periods of low light, from June through August, and all day long in the late fall. This method is especially effective when used over rocky points, such as Martins Point and the point at Casowasco.

In the fall, smallmouth bass go on a feeding binge in preparation for the winter months. Minnows drifted in 15 to 30 feet of water can be incredibly effective at this time. Again, the areas around the pumphouse intakes and Martins Point are going to supply much of the action, but don't neglect the point at Casowasco, Indian Cove or other significant points.

Yellow Perch .... abundant; growth rate fair to good

Owasco Lake has an abundant population of yellow perch, but the lake is not usually regarded as a good perch fishery. This is due to the fact that most of the perch here are too small to be of interest to fishermen. However, big perch can be found in this lake. There are a few perch specialist on Owasco who consistently locate and take good catches of 10 to 12 inch perch.

The best perch fishing occurs in the spring (late April through May) when these larger fish are schooled up by size or year class fairly close to shore. The majority of the large perch are taken along the east shore of the lake, with the most consistent catches coming from the waters just north of the mouth of Dutch Hollow Brook, at Burtis Point. Owasco's spring perch fishing certainly isn't as good as on Seneca Lake or Skaneateles Lake, but with a little luck it can be very good.

Most of the good perch fishermen on Owasco seem to prefer using jigs in the spring. Although there is no reason to argue with their success, I see no reason that other traditional methods would be any less successful. Still fishing with minnows or grubs on perch rigs should take fish here in the spring.

Toward the beginning of June, as the lake's waters begin to warm up, yellow perch become more migratory, and decidedly harder to find. This is especially true of the larger perch. As they spread out over the lake their early spring concentration becomes diluted by the overwhelming numbers of smaller perch. A knowledgeable and persistent perch specialist should still be able to manage a good catch of large perch, but the action would be considered erratic at best.

Yellow perch don't contribute much to the fishing on Owasco Lake in the fall. But in the winter, after the lower end of the lake has frozen over, they can be taken through the ice. The very southern end of the lake is the place to concentrate your efforts. Again, the fishing isn't spectacular, but it can be good.

Additional Species

In addition to those listed above, there are a number of species in Owasco Lake that, as an aggregate, contribute to the fishing here. Pan fish (rock bass, blue gills, pumpkinseeds) are found in fair numbers, but are restricted to shallow, near-shore waters. Brown bullhead are found in the lower reaches of Owasco Inlet, as well as in the southern end of the lake and the bullhead fishing in these areas in the spring can be very good. At one time walleye were the principle game species in this lake. Their population collapsed after 1948. Walleye are still found in Owasco Lake, but they are very rare. Cisco were also a major species in this lake in the 1940's and 1950's. Often taken by fly fishermen on early summer evenings, cisco were so popular here that a cisco derby was held on the lake, but the population collapsed by the early 1970's. They are now very rare, if indeed they still exist here. Rounding out species available here are limited populations of largemouth bass and chain pickerel, both of which are found primarily at the south end, white suckers, longnose suckers and carp.

General Information

Owasco Lake is intermediate in size compared to other Finger Lakes. Five of the lakes are larger (Seneca, Cayuga, Keuka, Canandaigua and Skaneateles) and five are smaller (Conesus, Hemlock, Canadice, Honeoye and Otisco).

Located in central Cayuga County, the major population center on the lake is the city of Auburn, which lies on the lake's northern shore. A total of 1.02 million people live within a distance of 40 miles of the lake. Currently, Owasco Lake is heavily utilized by anglers in this region. Historically, however, fishing pressure was only moderate compared to other finger lakes. This changed in 1978 with the advent of a strong newly developed lake trout fishery that regularly produces trophy size fish.

As with many other lakes in the region, access is a major problem on Owasco Lake, particularly shore access. The lake shore is closely parallelled by Route 38 on the west and Rockefeller Road on the east, but two thirds of the shoreline is developed for residential or commercial purposes and most of the remainder is brush lined or forested. For all practical purposes the only access available to shore bound fishermen is via the pumphouse pier at the north end of the lake in Auburn.

NOTES: _____
_____
_____
_____

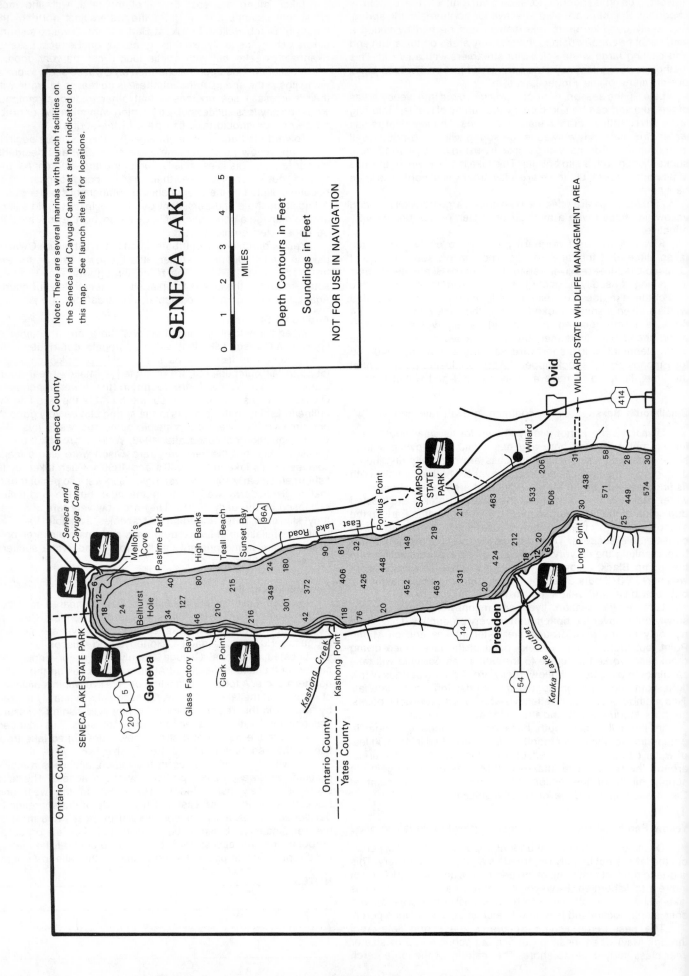

SENECA LAKE

MILES
0 1 2 3 4 5

Depth Contours in Feet

Soundings in Feet

NOT FOR USE IN NAVIGATION

Note: There are several marinas with launch facilities on the Seneca and Cayuga Canal that are not indicated on this map. See launch site list for locations.

Seneca County

Ontario County

Seneca and Cayuga Canal

SENECA LAKE STATE PARK

Geneva

20
5

Ontario County
Yates County

Glass Factory Bay

Clark Point

Kashong Creek

Kashong Point

Mellon's Cove

Pastime Park

High Banks

Teall Beach

Sunset Bay

96A

East Lake Road

Pontius Point

SAMPSON STATE PARK

Willard

Ovid

WILLARD STATE WILDLIFE MANAGEMENT AREA

414

Dresden

14

54

Keuka Lake Outlet

Long Point

Belhurst Hole

12
18
6
24
34
40
80
127
46
210
215
216
349
180
24
301
42
372
90
61
32
406
426
448
149
219
452
463
331
118
76
20
20
8
12
6
20
212
424
463
30
533
206
506
571
449
574
25
31
58
28
30
21
438

— 218 —

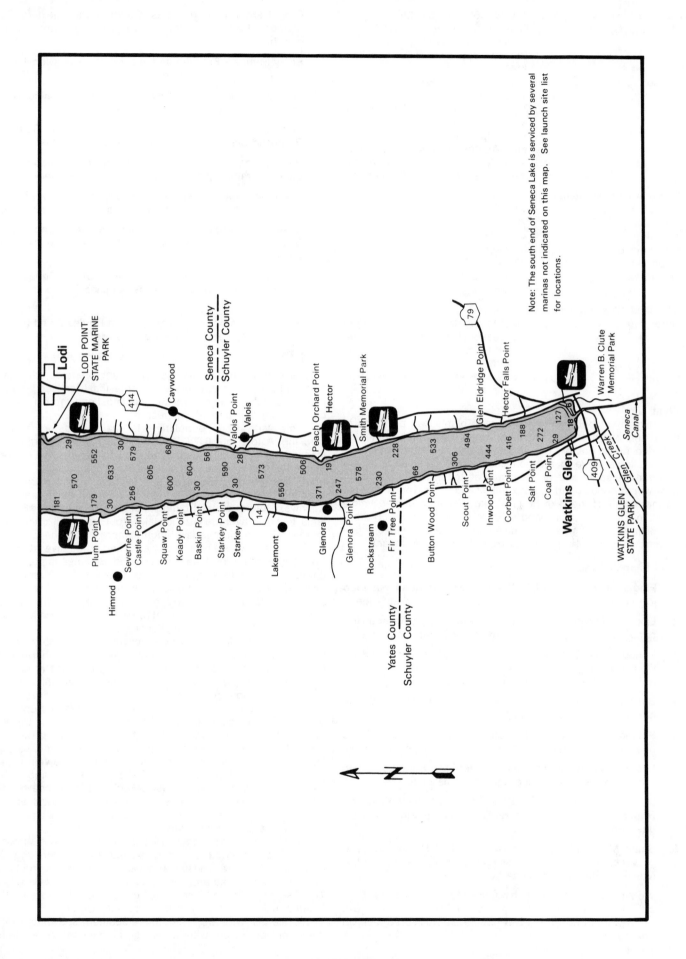

Lodi

LODI POINT
STATE MARINE
PARK

Caywood

414

Seneca County
Schuyler County

Valois Point
Valois

Peach Orchard Point
Hector

Smith Memorial Park

Glen Eldridge Point

Hector Falls Point

79

Warren B. Clute
Memorial Park

Watkins Glen

409

WATKINS GLEN -
STATE PARK

Seneca Canal

Glen Creek

Himrod

Plum Point

Severne Point
Castle Point

Squaw Point
Keady Point
Baskin Point
Starkey Point
Starkey

14

Lakemont

Glenora

Glenora Point

Rockstream

Fir Tree Point

Button Wood Point

Scout Point
Inwood Point
Corbett Point
Salt Point
Coal Point

Yates County
Schuyler County

181
570
179
30
552
633
29
256
30
579
600
605
68
30
604
56
590
30
28
573
506
19
550
371
247
578
230
66
228
533
306
494
444
416
188
272
29
127
18
6
230

Note: The south end of Seneca Lake is serviced by several
marinas not indicated on this map. See launch site list
for locations.

N

— 219 —

SENECA LAKE

map coordinates . . . . 42° 38' 45" 76° 52' 25"
USGS map(s) . . . . Geneva South, Dresden, Ovid, Dundee, Lodi, Reading Center, Burdett. See also N.O.A.A. Chart #14791
location . . . . Seneca, Ontario, Schuyler and Yates Counties
access . . . . The west shore of the lake is parallelled by Route 14; the north shore is reached via Routes 5 and 20; the east shore is paralelled by Routes 96A and 414; the south shore is also off Route 144.

Physical Characteristics

area . . . . 43,281 acres
shore line . . . . 75.4 miles
elevation . . . . 445 feet
maximum depth . . . . 618 feet
mean depth . . . . 291 feet
bottom type . . . . rock, sand, muck
mean thermocline depth . . 88 feet

Chemical Characteristics

water clarity . . . . clear to slightly cloudy, depending on seasonal variations in algae content and wind.
pH . . . . alkaline
oxygen . . . . oxygen levels are adequate at all depths all year long.

Plant Life

Significant beds of rooted aquatic plants can be found in most shallow areas of the lake. Major beds are located at Dresden, Glass Factory Bay, at the extreme north end of the lake and Mellon's Cove in the northeast corner. Smaller beds are found at the south end, at Valois and at Peach Orchard Point. A nearly continuous band of water milfoil and pond weeds rims the northern half of the lake, from Starkey Point around to Valois Point. In some areas this band is 300 to 900 feet in width. There is very little rooted vegetation in the souther third of the lake. Algae blooms do occur on Seneca Lake, but have little impact.

Boat Launch Sites

1. Finger Lakes Marina - 634 Waterloo-Geneva Road, Waterloo (on canel). Single concrete ramp, marine supplies - fee.

2. Lakeland Marina - 773 Waterloo-Geneva Road, Waterloo (on canal). Single ramp, rentals, marine supplies, gas - fee.

3. Seneca Lake State Park and Marina - off Routes 5 and 20. Double ramps and temporary dockage that will handle any trailerable craft. Park entrance fee in season.

4. Barrett Marine - 485 West River Road, Waterloo. Single concrete ramp, marine supplies, gas - fee.

5. Sampson State Park - off Route 96A. Four ramps for all size boats and temporary dockage. Park entrance fee in season.

6. Lodi Point State Marine Park - Lower Lake Road Lodi. Twin ramps and temporary dockage for boats under 25 feet.

7. Dunham's Boat Livery - Peach Orchard Point Road, off Route 414, Hector. Single ramp, rentals, marine supplies, gas, repairs - fee.

8. Smith Memorial Park - off Route 414 at Hector. Dirt and gravel launch with dirt access road over some steep grades. Not recommended for large boats - fee.

9. Watkins Glen - state launch adjacent to Clute Memorial Park off Route 414 on the canal portion of Catharine Creek. Dirt ramp without docks but can handle craft up to 20 feet. No charge.

10. Glen Harbor Marine - East Fourth Street, next to Clute Memorial Park. Gravel launch area, rentals, marine supplies, gas, bait, tackle - fee.

11. Ervay Marine - Franklin on the canal, Watkins Glen. Launch ramps, marine supplies, gas - fee.

12. Village Marina - on Seneca Harbor, Watkins Glen. Single hard surface ramp, marine supplies - fee.

13. Severne Point - on Severne Point Road off Route 14. Proposed state launch expected to be completed by 1989.

14. Baker's Boat Livery - RD #1, at Plum Point, Himrod. Single concrete ramp, gas, marine supplies, rentals, tackle - fee.

15. The Gold Coast - Plum Point Road, off Route 14, Himrod. Single gravel ramp for small trailerable boats only - fee.

16. Dresden - There is a small private launch facility on Dresden Bay, just north of Keuka Lake Outlet in the village of Dresden - fee.

17. Roy's Marina - Route 14, four miles south of Geneva. Two concrete ramps, rentals, marine supplies, gas, bait, tackle - fee.

18. Geneva Chamber of Commerce - on Routes 5 and 20. Free launch ramps and temporary dockage.

Lake Trout . . . . abundant, growth rate very good

Lake trout are by far the dominant predator species in Seneca Lake. Their numbers are so great that it isn't too far off the mark to say that they can be caught almost anywhere in Seneca Lake during any part of the year.

This lake trout population is maintained primarily by stocking. A total of 36,000 yearlings and 72,000 fingerlings are stocked here annually. In addition, the DEC reports that between 5% and 20% of any one year class of fish is composed of wild lake trout. The lakers in Seneca Lake average 4 to 5 pounds, but specimens up to 14 to 18 pounds are caught each year. Dave Kosowski, senior aquatic biologist at the DEC's region #8 office, feels that the average size of lake trout here will continue to increase. All in all, this is a mighty impressive fishery.

Seneca Lake is a remarkably easy and productive lake to fish from shore when the lake isn't stratified. Because the lake is so cold and deep it doesn't even start to stratify until late June, and it turns over by late September. Thus, from late September until late June of the following year lake trout can be taken from shore, and this holds true for almost the entire lake, though there are some areas that at times are exceptionally productive.

Most of the lake trout here spawn in late September and October, which coincides with the break up of the thermocline. From this point on, shore fishing will be productive around the lake. Lake trout are commonly caught here in water 60 to 90 feet during their spawning phase. The most productive areas naturally will be on the major spawning grounds. In September and October concentrate your efforts on the shore line between Valois and Peach Orchard point on the east side of the lake, and from Starkey Point down to Glenora on the west side. Later, in November and December, another round of spawning takes place in the northern end of the lake, off the pier and wall in Geneva and in the area of Glass Factory Bay. These are fish spawning in shallow water, usually less than 20 feet deep. The DEC thinks lake trout might also be spawning at this time on the reefs off Sampson State Park.

The DEC collects eggs from the lake trout that spawn at Peach Orchard Point, and they tag these fish before they are returned to the lake. These fish appear to make a beeline for the north end of the lake and will be found off the wall at Geneva by Thanksgiving. This indicates that the bulk of the lake trout will be located in the north end of the lake after October.

While the trout are still on there southern spawning rounds they can be taken with a variety of methods. I've already mentioned shore fishing. Casting out a sawbelly threaded with an English hook and weighted down with a slip sinker is easy and productive almost anywhere from shore. Because the lake is essentially homothermal in the fall, lake trout can be found in deep as well as shallow levels of the water column. Many anglers do very well trolling with downriggers, copper lines or Seth Green rigs and take lake trout in 50 to 100 feet of water.

At the north end of the lake, the same techniques will be productive. On the wall at Geneva they also take a lot of lake trout in the late fall by casting silver spoons and yellow Roostertail spinners and retrieving them very slowly along the bottom.

The one hot spot for lake trout I haven't mentioned yet is the "Belhurst Hole," which lies just off the Belhurst Castle on Route 14, just south of Geneva. This narrow trench isn't very big, but they catch inordinate numbers of lakers here, and a lot of them are bigger than average fish. They are taken either by still fishing with a live sawbelly or by trolling spoons very close to the bottom often as terminal bait off flashers or cowbells. This is one of the hottest spots on the lake in January, February and March, but due to the weather not very many people take advantage of this fishing opportunity.

In April smelt move into shallow areas and streams to spawn. This causes the lake trout to concentrate off the mouths of streams that get smelt runs. Many of the tributaries of the lake get runs of smelt, including the lower reaches of Catharine Creek. Every once in a while some astonished angler pulls a lake trout out of Catharine Creek. Sometimes these fish get a little carried away in their pursuit of food). When the lakers are concentrated off the streams they are commonly taken by trolling with Rapalas. Run the lure just below the surface. They can also be taken by casting from shore or by still fishing with live bait.

On Memorial Day weekend the Geneva Chamber of Commerce becomes the headquarters of the National Lake Trout Derby. This popular derby draws in several thousand participants annually. They catch a mess of fish during this tournement, but it hardly puts a dent in the lake trout population. If it has been a late spring you will have no trouble taking trout from shore during the derby. But if it has been a warm spring, you'll probably have to go to fishing from a boat, as the fish begin to move off shore as the water warms.

Seneca Lake begins to strongly stratify in late June and by early July the thermocline is usually set up. With a few exceptions, this signals the end of shore fishing for lake trout. The lakers are temperature oriented and spread out over the lake in search of 48° F waters. Again, practically the entire lake will have fishing for lake trout wherever their preferred temperatures are found. Downriggers, Seth Green or thermocline rigs as they are also called and copper lines are all used on Seneca Lake in the summer.

If you're looking for big lakers you might want to concentrate your efforts on the steep contour between Hector Falls and Glen Eldridge Point. The DEC often sets sampling nets in that area in the summer and they consistently take good numbers of 8 to 10 pound lake trout in 100 to 150 feet of water. The areas of Lodi, Sampson and Kashong also hold good numbers of trout in deep water.

Rainbow Trout .... common; growth rate good

Rainbow trout are the second most abundant salmonid in Seneca Lake. Most of the rainbows found here are wild fish, many of which are spawned in the high quality waters of Catharine Creek. There are a number of smaller good quality tributaries all around the lake that also produce rainbow trout. In addition, the state annually stocks 25,000 rainbow trout yearlings in Seneca Lake. These are a wild strain of fish that have been raised in a hatchery situation.

Because Seneca Lake's rainbow population is heavily dependent upon natural reproduction for its survival, the size of the population can fluctuate considerably over the span of a couple years. Environmental factors, such as low rainfall during spawning periods or excessively warm temperatures in natal streams can result in low recruitment in one or more year classes.

Two veteran anglers with a nice catch of trout from Seneca Lake. Photo courtesy C. Scott Sampson.

Some of the best fishing for rainbow trout in the state takes place at the south end of Seneca Lake in the spring when great numbers of fish run up Catharine Creek to spawn. The opening day of trout season (April 1) often corresponds to a good run of fish in the stream. For a complete run down on the spring fishing in Catharines Creek and other Seneca Lake tributaries see Seneca, Schuyler and Yates County sections.

Not all of the rainbows in this lake run up the streams to spawn in the spring. Rainbows will run these tributaries from late fall to May and before the run will stage in the lake off the creek mouths. Aside from Catharine Creek, rainbows are known to gather off Keuka Lake Outlet, Hector Falls Creek, Indian Creek, Lodi Creek and Reeder Creek. A lot of fish also gather on the shoreward side of the breakwalls off Watkins Glen.

When the rainbows are in close to shore they can be taken with a wide variety of methods. Trolling tight up against the shore or as close to docks or walls as possible with double tanden streamers is very effective. So is trolling with Rapalas on shallow running downriggers. Keep in mind that rainbow trout require a significantly faster trolling speed than brown trout or lake trout. When fishing in the mouths of streams rainbows can also be taken on live bait (worms or minnows) or egg sacs.

In the summer months rainbows disperse throughout the lake, orienting above the thermocline, searching for bait fish and their preferred temperatures (55°-60° F). They can be taken using downriggers and Seth Green rigs, but as on other Finger Lakes, the summer time is not usually a very productive period for rainbow trout. Most are caught as incidental fish by lake trout fishermen. Perhaps given this lakes great size, there may not be enough rainbows in it to generate a really consistent summer fishery.

Beginning in mid-September rainbows again begin orienting off the mouths of streams. The same areas that were productive in the spring will also hold fish in the fall. By the end of October many of these fish will again start running in the streams. These fall runs of rainbows aren't quite as good as the spring runs, but they do provide some very fine fishing. Usually you can have a large section of these streams all to yourself in the fall. The season in the tributaries closes on December 31.Check for other special tributary regulations in your state license and regulations guide.

Brown Trout .... common; growth rate good

The brown trout fishery in Seneca Lake is wholly dependent on stocking. The state annually stocks 10,800 yearlings and 65,000 fingerlings here. The DEC plans on discontinuing the stocking of fingerlings in the next few years due to poor survival, and increasing the number of yearlings.

Until lamprey controls were instituted for Seneca Lake in 1982 few browns here got over 3 pounds or lived longer than 2 years. It wasn't uncommon to see a 1½ pound brown with 6 or 7 lamprey scars on it. Now that the sea lamprey have been brought under control, Seneca Lake brown trout have been known to weigh 10 to 12 pounds and live up to 5 years.

Beginning in early April and lasting through May brown trout can be found in good numbers at the south end of the lake. Shore fishermen often do very well fishing from shore at Clute Memorial Park using live bait. Usually the fishing is pretty good in this area, but for some reason there are years when the bait fish just don't come in close to the southern shore of the lake. If you find that the spring fishing for brown trout isn't very good off the park, move up to one of the tributaries that enters the lake from the east or west sides. That's where you'll find the bait fish and the brown trout. Brown trout can also be taken by trolling close to shore lines or docks in the spring. Try using Hemlock spinners baited with a sawbelly or smelt. Trolled 35 to 40 feet behind the boat they can be deadly for shallow water browns. Also, don't overlook flutter spoons and other Lake Ontario techniques.What you really want to do is present your lure in the warmest possible water you can find.

Another spot you might want to consider, not just for brown trout but also for rainbows is the warm water outflow at Dresden. This outflow doesn't attract nearly as many salmonids as do other power plant discharges, but it could be worth investigating if your already in that area.

By late May or early June brown trout begin moving off shore, seeking temperatures of 50° to 60° F. They strongly prefer areas where 58° water intersects the bottom. This situation occurs at the north end where the shallows drop off into deep water and along the sides of the lake at the south end. Few people seem to pursue brown trout on Seneca Lake in the summer, but those that do so successfully are taking them close to the bottom, using modern downrigging techniques, copper lines or Seth Green rigs.

The summer brown trout fishing tapers off by the middle of August, when the browns enter their spawning phase. They don't become readily available again until late October or early November. When they do become vulnerable to angling they will be found in shallow water, usually close to the area where they were stocked (Severne Point, Lodi and Sampson). They will remain in these areas through the late fall and winter and can be taken by trolling as close to shore as possible with Rebel or Rapala type minnow imitations.

Smallmouth Bass .... abundant; growth rate good

NOTE: While gathering material for the Finger Lakes many different sources were used. For the most part the information dovetailed quite nicely, but there was one exception. It was difficult to piece together a precise picture of the movements of smallmouth bass in several of the Finger Lakes during the summer months. Some local experts strongly recommended fishing for smallmouth in deep water after the post-spawn period, while others were equally convinced that fishing in shallow water was

Wayne Brewer with a typical Seneca Lake brown trout. This fish showed no sign of lamprey attacks Photo courtesy C. Scott Sampson.

the surest route to success. As it turns out, both schools of though are probably correct. There are several distinct populations of bass in many of these lakes, each apparently favoring somewha different conditions.

Regardless of whether they favored shallow water or deep however, almost all of these fishermen were conveying information about fairly conventional smallmouth bass fishing That is to say, they were talking about angling for structure oriented fish. What will be hard for many bass fishermen to accep is the third school of thought regarding the movements of bass on five of the lakes: Canandaigua, Cayuga, Keuka, Otisco and Seneca. These anglers, all better than average bass fisherme who have made a serious study of these lakes, are convinced tha many of the smallmouth bass in these lakes are essentially pelagic moving out over the thermocline during at least part of the day to forage on bait fish. To support this theory they cited several facts 1.) It is not unheard of for trout fishermen to pick up smallmouth on the top leader of a thermocline rig; 2.) These fishermen routinel take bass by looking for them in open water; 3.) netting studie done in the mid-1950's on Cayuga Lake in fact showed that larg numbers of smallmouth were pelagic during the summer. Thes anglers were even able to detect differences in the way the fis suspend on different lakes. For example, on Canandaigua Lak the smallmouth are lossely schooled up and wander the entir length and breadth of the lake. On Seneca Lake, the fish ar randomly dispersed, but seldom move out more than 100 yard form the deepest weed lines. Even this puts them out over 100 plu feet of water, so they are still truly suspended. All of the biologists spoke to in the DEC admitted that suspended smallmouth are a least a possibility on these lakes, and were unable to come up with

A fine catch of Seneca Lake smallmouth bass taken on opening day. In the early part of the season the bass fishing is exceptionally good, particularly in the north end of the lake. Photo courtesy C. Scott Sampson.

a reason why they couldn't be suspended.

So, if you're looking for a way to increase your catch of smallmouth bass, you might want to consider looking for them in deep water suspended in the upper levels of the water column. You can temper your skepticism about this by remembering that it took a major bass tournament in the 1970's to prove that there was a potentially good largemouth bass fishery in the Thousand Islands, although these fish had always been there. It was simply a matter of anglers not finding what wasn't being looked for. J.M.S.

Seneca Lake has an excellent smallmouth fishery, and except for a few months during the summer they are quite easy to catch.

In the spring and first half of summer the best smallmouth fishing is centered on the northern end of the lake, north of Kashong Point on the west side and Sunset Bay on the east side.

One of the principle spawning areas for smallmouth bass in this lake is along a stretch of bluffs between Sunset Bay and Teal Beach known locally as High Banks. A shallow water shelf runs along the shoreline here, and from late April usually until early July you can drift along these flats and see bass spawning beds. A similar area lies between Sampson and Willard. While the fish are in this fairly shallow water they are readily taken on crankbaits, ¼ ounce deer hair jigs and lead head jigs dressed with Mister Twister tails. A popular and productive lure used by some locals is a small white spinnerbait. Live bait also works well, especially softshell crabs.

Getting your lure into the rock and rubble habitat which can be found almost anywhere along the east and west shores will produce smallmouth. Look for navigation markers along the shore for a clue to these locations.

By early July the bass are moving out of these shallow water regions into deeper water habitats. Immediately after this happens many of the rocky points in the north end will be the most productive. Deep diving crankbaits and large deer hair jigs will be needed to take these fish. The fishing can be good, but it's not as productive as it was earlier in the season.

At the north end of the lake, off Seneca Lake State Park, is an area of scattered rock piles. Some local anglers have borrowed a technique commonly used on Lake Ontario to fish this area. They drift fish, dragging on undersize anchor or cinder block. The anchor turns over rocks, dislodging crayfish and churning up the bottom. The smallmouth are attracted to all this commotion and are caught by anglers drifting crayfish just behind the anchor.

As happens on many of the larger Finger Lakes, the quality of the bass fishing drops considerably on Seneca Lake by mid-July.

The exact reasons for this are unclear. Jay Nelson, a highly regarded tournament angler who fishes the lake hard and often, feels that two events take place that make the fishing difficult. First, he believes that the smallmouth begin a slow southward migration once they have finished spawning. This puts the bass on the move, making it more difficult to locate big concentrations of fish. The DEC doesn't have any empirical data to back this contention, at least that I've seen, but Jay's experience and that of other bass fishermen point to such a migration. To further reinforce this theory are the results of a tagging study a few anglers conducted several years ago (don't do this yourself — the DEC frowns on it). They tagged fish caught at the south end of the lake in the winter and caught many of the same fish the following spring at the north end of the lake. This indicates a seasonal migration of fish from one end of the lake to the other.

The second event to put a damper on the fishing is the movement of at least some of the fish out over the thermocline, especially during the daylight hours. Again, the DEC doesn't have any real scientific data to substantiate this claim, but there are anglers I spoke to who looked for and found significant numbers of bass suspended out over deep water on this lake. (See note at top of heading)

This isn't to say that smallmouth can't be caught in Seneca Lake in the summer. They can. You just have to be at the right place at the right time.

This lake doesn't get a great deal of pressure from smallmouth fishermen in the summer, but there are a few anglers who are successful during the dog days of the year. Beginning in late July they fish the shoreline early in the morning and in the evening. The productive areas are from Kashong Point to Long Point on the west side, and from Sunset Bay to Lodi Point on the east shore. Scattered boulder fields are found in the shallows of these waters and act as holding areas for smallmouth at dusk and dawn. Drift fishing these boulder fields with nightcrawlers, deer hair jigs or lead head jigs dressed with Mister Twister tails is the technique most commonly used.

The smallmouth bass fishing really picks up on Seneca Lake in the fall. By this time the bulk of the smallmouth will have moved into the southern half of the lake. The most consistent fishing will be found between Baskin Point and Fir Tree Point on the west side, and from Lodi Point down to Hector Falls on the east side of the lake. Good bass fishing will be found on all of the points and ledges in these areas.

In the southern third of the lake there is very little shallow water. Forty feet from shore in some areas the water can be as deep as 70 feet. These steep drop-offs act as holding areas for the bass through the fall and winter months, much as the ledges off the Bluff do on Keuka Lake.

Initially, when the bass move into these southern haunts they are fairly well distributed between the points mentioned above. As the year wanes fish will continue to be taken all along the ledges south of Baskin Point and Lodie Point, but the best fishing will be found from Valois down to Hector Falls.

Seneca Lake's fall and winter bass fishing is very similar to that on Keuka Lake and Cayuga Lake. A days fishing normally starts around 7 AM. At first the bass are going to be found in fairly shallow water (15 to 20 feet). As the day progresses you must continuously move into deeper water. By late afternoon you should be fishing in water at least 50 to 70 feet deep. In fact, you often have to go as deep as 120 feet to locate these fish.

Just before sunset the fishing in deep water usually shuts down rather abruptly. This signals that the bass have left the area to move into the narrow shallow ledges near shore to feed on minnows. Casting back into the shallows with deer hair jigs can be highly productive.

The one major way that Seneca Lake's fall and winter bass fishery differs from that of Keuka Lake is that on Seneca Lake the fish don't appear to school up nearly as much as they do on Keuka. On Keuka Lake you have to search for areas where smallmouth are concentrated and then work the area thoroughly. On Seneca the bass are more evenly distributed. For a rundown on the techniques used to catch smallmouth in the winter see the chapter on Keuka Lake.

Largemouth Bass .... uncommon; growth rate good

Compared to the population of smallmouth bass in Seneca Lake, largemouth would have to be considered uncommon. But in a few localized areas they are readily available and thus constitute an important aspect of the lake's overall fishery. A 1½ to 2 pound fish is typical, but on occasion a 4 to 5 pound lunker is landed here.

As you would expect, the largemouth are found in relatively shallow water that has a significant amount of vegetation interspersed with breaks of open water. In the lake proper the best largemouth fishing is found in the several hundred acres of weeds in Dresden Bay. The warm water discharge there doesn't draw in the great numbers of trout that you would normally expect, but it does set up conditions generally favorable to the bass.

The northern end of the lake is another area where largemouth out rank smallmouth in abundance. A shallow water shelf extends for several hundred yards off Seneca Lake State Park and intermittent weed beds offer some good fishing opportunities. Glass Factory Bay also has a fair population of bass.

There are scattered populations of largemouth in other areas of the lake, but they are really insignificant. A few are caught each year at the southern end of the lake, but to catch two largemouth bass there in a single day is a notable event. You might think that the band of weeds that extends almost continuously around the northern half of the lake, from Starkey Point on the west side to Valois Point on the lake's east side would hold a fair number of bass, but it doesn't. Certainly a few largemouth will be taken in this ribbon of vegetation, which is several hundred feet wide in spots. But the bass population is kept rigidly in check by the large population of northern pike that are in residence almost everywhere in the perimeter weed beds.

If you're really intent on pursuing largemouth while on this lake you should consider fishing the canal at the south end. They are taken in good numbers there all season long. At the north end of the lake, the Cayuga/Seneca Canal also offers some better than average bass fishing opportunities.

The techniques used to catch largemouth bass on Seneca Lake are pretty standard. Early in the season, before the lake temperatures maximize, small spinners and spinnerbaits will be very effective when fished in shallow water along developing weed lines.

On warm sunny mornings, the bass are often found under some of Seneca Lake's more than 1700 boat docks. This is especially true in the early summer when the fish can be seen huddled next to pilings that are warmed by exposure to the sun. Later in the summer they will move well under the docks looking for shade and points of ambush. Accurate casting with shallow running crankbaits and jigs dressed with Mister Twister tails or plastic worms can be highly productive under these docks at dusk and dawn.

Throughout the summer, largemouth can be taken by working the edges of weed lines with crankbaits, spinnerbaits and jigs. Weedless worms, buzzbaits and top water spoons are effective when worked over submerged weeds.

In the fall, the largemouth will move into slightly deeper water, orienting off the deepest weed lines available. If you get on extended cold spell followed by mild sunny weather you'll often find them on very rocky points. During extended warm spells the fish will usually be drawn back into their summer haunts.

When the largemouth drop down to the edges of deep weed lines try using smaller baits and slower retrieves. Spinnerbaits are highly effective, as are deep diving crankbaits. The fish will feed aggressively until the water temperatures drop into the mid 50's. Below that temperature the bass become lethargic, but can still be taken on small jigs dressed with minnows or pork rind. Work these jigs very slowly along deep weed lines.

Largemouth bass can be taken in Seneca Lake through the winter. They are occasionally taken by perch fishermen through the ice at the northern end of the lake. Jigging Rapalas, Swedish Pimples and minnows are all effective on cold weather largemouth.

Northern Pike .... common; growth rate very good

In the 1970's the population of northern pike in Seneca Lake increased dramatically, probably due to subtle changes in the lake's habitat. It appears that this expansion coincided with a similar increase in the amount of the aquatic plant Myriophyllum (water milfoil). Since that time the lake has enjoyed a reputation as a top northern pike lake.

The northerns in Seneca Lake are big. You don't see the monsters that they pull out of Sacandaga Reservoir, but a fish 20 to 25 pounds is possible. On the average the pike here run 8 to 12 pounds.

Dave Kosowski, the DEC biologist responsible for managing the lake, feels that the best pike fishing is in the weed beds at Dresden Bay. But pike can be taken in practically every weed bed in the lake. A large population is found at Glass Factory Bay and in the vegetation at the extreme northern end of the lake. The wide band of weeds that rims the northern half of the lake, also holds a healthy population of fish. The section of this weed band from Plum Point north to Long Point is especially noted for its pike fishing. South of Plum Point the weed band starts to break up, but there are isolated populations of pike at least as far south as Starkey Point. On the east side of the lake northerns are found along the perimeter weed band, in the small weedy bay just north of Valois and in the bay at Peach Orchard Point. The area from Pontious Point to Wilson Creek is an excellent pike producing area as are the weed lines off Willard.

Northern pike aren't found in any significant numbers at the extreme southern end of Seneca Lake during most times of the year, but in the spring they move into the southeast corner in great numbers. Full of old pilings and scattered weed beds, this area is one of the principle pike spawning areas. For a short period immediately after the season opens the fishing here can be exceptionally good. Northern pike can also be taken in the spring in other shallow weedy areas, but initially the best fishing will be in the southeast corner.

Just after spawning northerns tend to be bottom oriented. Still fishing with large shiners, chubs or 8 to 12 inch suckers is very effective. Use a slip sinker to keep your bait close to the buttom but with some freedom of movement. A few weeks after the season opens the pike will have recuperated from the rigors of spawning. They then move off the bottom, becoming more active and aggressive. Live bait can still be used, but instead of fishing on the bottom a bobber is used to keep the bait up. The late spring is also a good time to employe such traditional terminal tackle as Rapala and Rebel type minnow plugs. Spinners, such as the Mepps Aglia or Panther Martin and spinnerbaits tipped with a minnow will also catch fish in the spring and summer.

In the summer months northern pike will be found in all of the weed beds of the lake except for those at the extreme southern end. They move out of that area shortly after spawning. There are a number of ways to take northern pike in the summer months. Troll along weed lines with spinnerbaits tipped with a 4 to 6 inch shiner or chub. Work the inside weed lines early in the day and the deeper weed lines later in the afternoon. For really big pike still fish with big baits. Hook a 12 inch sucker through the upper lip with a #2 short shank hook. Using a slip-bobber fish the bait along the outer edges of weed lines and over submerged weed beds. Large spoons, such as the classic red and white Daredevle, crankbaits and large silver flatfish will also catch fish.

Some anglers here feel that a lot of northern pike won't hit even a well placed offering because they are easily spooked. To reduce this factor they cast big spoons with 8 foot rods so far away from their boat you have to squint to see the splash. Reportedly, it pays off.

Most of the pike fishing in Seneca Lake is pretty conventional, but in the fall a unique twist is put into this fishery. In the early fall, the lake turns over, resulting in relatively little temperature difference up and down the water column. When this happens it's not uncommon for lake trout fishermen to pick up a northern pike in deep water (70 to 90 feet)! More traditional methods include working deep decaying weed lines with Rebel and Rapala type minnow plugs, or with half ounce and one ounce jigs. Dressed with 4 to 6 inch Twister tails or 5 to 7 inch plastic waterdogs, jigs are highly effective in the fall. Scott Sampson recommends verticle spoon jigging off weed lines in 20 to 40 feet of water. Let your casting spoon drop straight down in a fluttering action.Then reel it up 10 or more feet and let it drop back.

Northern pike fishing in the winter is both popular and productive. All of the areas that were productive in the summer months will produce in the winter, but a majority of the fish seem to be caught either at the extreme northern end of the lake through the ice, or by anglers casting from shore on the central portion of the lake. On the west side of the lake the shore line from Starkey Point north to Kashong is popular, while on the eastern shore they concentrate on the waters between Valois Point and Pontius Point.

The ice fishermen do well with tip-ups baited with chubs or small suckers. The DEC relates that there are good winter concentrations of northerns in the northwest and northeast corners of the lake. Occasionally, pike are also taken through the ice in the marina at Sampson State Park. Open water is normally avaible off the marina seawall and is a favorite area for anglers.

Shore fishermen also do very well here in the winter. Working the shore lines mentioned above, some anglers fish with big shiners suspended 2 to 3 feet under a large bobber. They cast their rigs out to deep weed lines where the pike are waiting to ambush bait fish.

There is also a group of anglers who use a tanden streamer known in the Finger Lakes region as a "woodchuck." This is the same streamer that fishermen on Canandaigua Lake us to take smallmouth bass. On Seneca Lake these anglers use woodchucks in areas where the perimeter weed band comes up against a point. Casting out along the inside weed edge, they retrieve the streamer in such a way as to give it an erratic swimming motion. These are very effective, catching a lot of northerns in the 10 to 14 pound class.

Yellow Perch . . . . abundant; growth rate excellent

Seneca Lake is renowned as one of New York State's premier yellow perch fisheries. Abundant in many parts of the lake, these tasty fish average 1 to 1½ pounds and occasionally a whopper tipping the scales at 3 pounds is boated.

The perch action starts in March when the fish move into the shallows to spawn. Good fishing can be found along many of the weed lines in the northern end of the lake. Especially productive areas include: the weed beds of Glass Factory Bay, the weed lines between Glass Factory Bay and Kashong Point, the shallows from Dresden Bay down to Long Point, and the shelves off High Banks.

To catch these fish you first have to pin point their location. That can be done by noticing where the locals are going. Many people in this area fish for perch on an almost daily basis in the spring, keeping tabs on their movements. Or check with Roy's Marina, 3 miles south of Geneva on Route 14.

The techniques used to take yellow perch here are pretty standard. Anchor your boat in 15 to 20 feet of water just off the outside weed lines. Using ultra-light tackle fish directly under the boat with small (1/16 to 1/8 oz.) deer hair jigs or plain jigs tipped with minnows, oat leaf grubs, meely worms or spikes. Some anglers use larger jigs in an attempt to discourage the smaller fish, but it's amazing what a 6 inch yellow perch will attempt to ingest. Also, minnows fished on a perch rig or spreader below a bobber works well. With a little luck it's possible to fill a 5 gallon pail in a day's outing on Seneca Lake.

This spring fishery is good through March and April. The perch then become less concentrated. But they can usually be

Franz Wohlegemuth caught this 20 pound 9 ounce northern pike while perch fishing at the north end of the lake. Seneca Lake has long been known for the size of its pike. Photo courtesy C. Scott Sampson.

taken with some degree of success until early July in areas north of Starkey Point or Valois. Concentrate your efforts on coves or on long points that gradually taper into deep water.

By mid to late July yellow perch become difficult to find on many lakes, and Seneca is no exception. They are taken occasionnaly by bass fishermen, but there really isn't much of a perch fishery here from mid-July to mid-September.

Starting around the middle of September yellow perch again begin concentrating in the shallows where they were found in the spring. They tend to congregate on points and other areas where shallow water is readily accessible from deep water, such as at Glass Factory Bay and Dresden. The fish will move back and forth from deep to shallow water and are most readily taken when in shallow at dusk and dawn. The fish will hold in these areas until late in the fall. It's not unusual to see scores of boats in areas like Dresden Bay at Thanksgiving, all of them catching perch like mad.

In the winter a lot of the yellow perch in this lake head south. They will be found in good numbers in all of the areas where smallmouth bass are found in the winter, but in slightly shallower water. Using jigs tipped with minnows, oak leaf grubs or mousy grubs you might fill a 5 gallon pail with perch in about 2 hours.

Additional Species

A number of lesser fisheries also contribute to the great fishing on Seneca Lake. Prominent among these are bullhead and smelt. Exceptionally good bullhead fishing is found at Dresden Bay near the mouth of Keuka Lake Outlet in March. They are also found at the south end of the lake,and at the entrance to the Seneca-Cayuga Canal.Bullheads are best fished for right after a heavy rain when the water turns to a light cholcolate color.

The smelt fishing (dipping) is popular and productive. They can be found running practically every tributary of the lake in mid-April. Smelt don't often run up the canal at the south end in any great numbers, though most years they do concentrate off the mouth of the canal. Be sure to consult your fishing regulations guide before taking smelt in any of the Finger Lakes.

A small number of landlocked salmon are also found in Seneca Lake. These are fish that were stocked in Keuka Lake and escaped via Keuka Lake Outlet into Seneca. Landlocked salmon are notorious for moving as far downstream in a watershed as possible, a trait held over from their days when, as true Atlantic salmon, they naturally tried to reach the ocean. They are only a bonus fish at present, but anglers manage to land a few 10 pounders here each year. To increase the number of salmon in Seneca Lake the state plans on initiating a stocking policy for this species in the near future.

Channel catfish are on other bonus fish in this lake. The most productive area for these often large fish is at Dresden Bay. They seem to be attracted by the warm outflow of the power plant there. They can also be found in the canals at the north and south ends of the lake.

Also found in Seneca Lake are good populations of rock bass, bluegill, pumpkinseed, white suckers, and carp.

General Information

Seneca Lake is the second largest of the Finger Lakes, and with a maximum depth of 618 feet, the deepest. Because of its great depth the lake rarely freezes. In fact, Seneca Lake has only frozen over completely once in the past century. This fact explains in part why Seneca lake has such good fishing for yellow perch. The perch population isn't hammered during the winter by ice fishermen.

For a long time one of the major problems on Seneca Lake was the abundance of sea lamprey. These parasitic fish were spawned in great numbers in Catharine Creek and Keuka Lake Outlet and their respective estuaries.. When they dropped down into the lake they wrecked havoc with Seneca salmonid species, particularly the brown trout. In 1982 a lamprey control program was initiated, and the results were swift and dramatic. The brown trout are fast becoming a significant part of the overall fishery and healthier populations of lake trout and rainbow trout have also been achieved. The lamprey haven't been totally eradicated, but they are under control.

A problem that persists to this day on Seneca Lake is access. Though access for boaters and shore fishermen is good in many areas, there are sections of the lake where it is wholly inadequate. Boats often must travel several miles to reach the prime fishing grounds, which can effectively eliminate the small boat owner due to the time involved or the potential dangers of travelling these distances in the event of a storm. Additional access is especially needed between Kashong Point and Glenora. A state launch is planned for Severne Point and is only awaiting funding.

Private ownership and steep shore lines, especially on the south end, combine to limit the available shore fishing on the lake. There are sites where shore fishing is available, and are found in the following areas: at the City of Geneva Chamber of Commerce Park, Seneca Lake State Park, Sampson State Park, Lodi Point Marine Park and at Clute Memorial Park on the lake's south east corner. The Village of Watkins Glen recently built a fishing pier and in the next few years it will be connected to a new breakwall providing a lot of new access to the waters of the south end of the lake.

A first hand impression of Seneca Lake is given by local

Seneca Lake is renowned for the size of the yellow perch taken here. Many of these fish weigh 2½ to 3 lbs. just prior to spawning. Photo courtesy New York State DEC.

utdoor writer C. Scott Sampson in the following article. Scott is n accomplished angler who has fished Sneeca Lake for over 40 ears.

SENECA LAKE
by C. Scott Sampson

The first time an angler faces the prospects of fishing Seneca ake, the 66.6 square miles of surface water spread out over a istance of approximately 38 miles of length and an average width f just under two miles staggers his imagination.

Seneca's reputation of being a difficult water also helps to hatter confidence but as with any large body of water you can reak it down into seasons and species and claim immediate uccess.

The National Lake Trout Derby was started on Seneca in 1964 nd continues to this day over Memorial weekends, providing a eputation to the resource as a cold water fishery. If you read the esults of the Genesee Fishing Contest, however, your eye will be aught by the listings of giant yellow perch which are consistently ntered from this water. Catharine Creek attracts spring rainbow out runs from the lake and anglers from across the state as well s many non-residents to taste the excitement of a 10 pound plus out on light tackle in stream conditions.

IN 1986 three northern pike were caught during the same veek in May in excess of 20 pounds. Brown trout are just eginning to become a serious challenge to anglers and browns of to 8 pounds are becoming common place with potential of near ecords in future years.

Bass fishing at times is overlooked but only because of the uality of the other fisheries. The Bass Angler Sportsman's Society 3ASS) was impressed enough with Seneca Lake to hold a ational tournament on the water in 1983.

In short, Seneca is a lake for all seasons , including an winter pen water trout fishery that is second to none.

Before getting into particulars, allow me to give you some brief eography lessons as they relate to anglers. At the north end of the ake is Geneva, the major shoreside community with an bundance of services for food, lodging, bait and tackle and aunch access to the lake. To the south is Watkins Glen, again ffering a wide variety of services but with slightly less efficient and vell designed access to the lake. The east and west shorelines are n large measure steep hillsides with limited access. There are xceptions to this. On the east shore is Sampson State Park pproximately 14 miles south of Geneva off Rt. 96A. This facility as the best lake access of all the launch sites, a state marina with easonal and transit slips and a full-service campground.

Lodi Point State Marine Park at a mid-lake point and again on he east shore, provides quality boater access and docks but no amping facilities.

The west side of the lake has very limited access with Roy's Marina near Geneva the only major access for this shore. Severne Point is scheduled for development by the Department of Environmental Conservation as an angler access site but the roject is not expected to be finished before 1988 and may be delayed.

At the southern end of the lake, Clute Memorial Park has a each style launch on Catharine Creek. At the northern shore, Seneca Lake State Park has an acceptable launch and the City of Geneva offers a free launch site at the Chamber of Commerce area. Private marinas on the Seneca-Cayuga Canal also offer aunch facilities as well as boater services.

In very simple terms the ends of the lake offer habitat for bass, pike and perch. It is relatively shallow water with good weed cover. However, smaller weed lines run the east and west sides of the ake and it was at the area of Dresden off Keuka Outlet where Paul Elias won the BASS tournament. He used crank baits on the smallmouth bass that he found pocketed in 12 to 18 feet of water in the weed openings.

The principle black bass of the lake is the smallmouth, with the exception of the northern area where the largemouth is king.

Traditional angling techniques for bass are the standard and while you may take bass up to 4 pounds, a 1½ to 2 pound is the rule.

The same areas that are bass producers hold the giant yellow perch and norther pike. When anglers are fishing for any particular species, the chances are excellent of taking a mixed creel. Franz Wohlegemuth of South Otselic was fishing ultra light tackle with a fathead minnow for bait when he connected with a 20 pound, 9 ounce northern in May. He was expecting perch that were schooled at the north end of the lake.

Of course if you are fishing exclusively for pike you will normally be using large spoons, spinners or golden shinners for bait and not often attract the smaller species. A trick that is used on Seneca Lake is to use a slip bobber which will allow you to drift bait over the weeds and yet adjust the depth of the bait as you go by letting out more line or taking it in. The bobbers are home made of balsa wood shaped like a dollar cigar with a plastic tube in the center running the full length of the cylinder. They remain on the line and can be cast as easily as a lure.

Perch anglers are also concentrating their efforts on weed lines with brown jigs, fathead minnows or softshell crabs in season. The areas of Dresden, Glass Factory Bay and Mellons Cove are the most consistent areas for these yellow trophies which may weigh up to 3 pounds.

While the warm water fish inhabit the shorelines, the trout may be found in nearly any area of the lake and will be at times on shore cruising under docks in the spring and fall of the year, or they may be at the other extreme, suspended over the depths in the center of the lake. The secret to finding them is water temperature. Lake trout prefer 48 degree water, rainbows 60 and browns 55 degree water. When those particular temperatures are not available they will generally seek the warmest water available.

Both the lake trout and the browns are bottom oriented. That is to say they will, when possible, look to area where their preferred water temperature meets structure. Fortunately for the lake trout the 48 degree temperature is also the preferred temperature of the rainbow smelt, a principle forage fish for the trout along with the alewife which is locally known as a sawbelly. The alewife prefers 50 degree water temperature but all trout will move out of temperature to feed on these minnows.

Smelt runs in the spring of the year are in and of themselves a fishery on Seneca, especially on the small tributaries that ring the lake. It is in this mid-April time frame when shallow water trout are relatively easy to catch. Both live smelt used as bait or the drifting of trout or salmon eggs in the lake estuaries is productive. Anglers should be aware that while you may not buy or sell rainbow trout eggs you may use them for bait in the Finger Lakes.

As bait and trout move to deeper water special angling techniques are needed for success. Deep water angling in Seneca can be broken out into still fishing, thermoclining, copper and downrigging.

Still fishing is easy and effective but the technique is not like dunking a worm. Live smelt, sawbellies or frozen baits of either specie are used. They are fished off a spinning rod and reel using an English bait hook and a barrel sinker as the terminal bait. The English style hook is sewed under the back skin of the bait with a baiting needle along the dorsal fin. The double hook lies along the head of the bait with points facing the tail. The hook snell is attached with a small snap swivel to the main line which not only allows you to change hooks rapidly but it holds the barrel or egg sinker away from the bait.

In the Spring of the year shallow water bait fishing in 20 to 30 feet of water is successful and as summer arrives anglers will find the 90 to 100 foot depths more productive. The bait is left on the lake bottom and the reel bail left open. That open reel is critical. Some anglers will double their line back and lightly place it under a rubber band on the rod but just to hold it in place and to signal a hit. When the trout picks up the bait and moves off, it is normally carrying the food crossways in its mouth and it must not feel resistance or it will drop the bait. The trout will stop, turn the bait in its mouth and swallow it head first. When the second run starts close the bail and strike.

Should you catch a lake trout under the legal 15 inch size limit

The quality of the trout fishing in Seneca Lake is maintained by the annual stocking of over 100,000 trout here by the DEC. Since the initiation of the lamprey control program in 1982 the quality of the trout fishing has improved tremendously. Photo courtesy C. Scott Sampson.

the Finger Lakes with this method, cut the hook snell as close to the mouth as possible and release it. Nature and the stomach acids of the fish will take care of the hook.

In years past you could tell a local copper angler just by shaking hands. His index finger would be heavily calloused and a groove would be worn in the center of the thick skin. Copper line either braided or single strand was used to troll at the great depths where the lake trout live. Silver plated Pflueger spoons in number 4 or 5 with a large single hook was the traiditional bait. Today that combination is still a most effective method and while the original Pfluegers are no longer available, anglers may find some copies or use a Baracuda spoon, Twin Minnow plug generally in black and white or they may pull a troll or flasher rig as it is commonly called in the Finger Lakes.

The idea with copper is to tunk or bounce the lure on the bottom, raising clouds of sand like a feeding minnow or alewife. The line is played by hand to feel the proper control. When hand lining a trout to the boat the slack copper is most often reeled in on an electric reel, which is commercially available, or on a Victrola box. The box is a homemade system that uses the old phonograph spring motor and a movie reel on which to coil the line. In the early days, anglers most often used hand reels in the form of an H with handles to hold their line but when a fish was coming in they would coil large loops on the bottom of the boat and then hope they could play it back out without kinking and breaking the copper. When trout are bottom feeding this is a most productive method.

Seth Green, the father of American hatcheries and fish culture, was one of the more effective anglers of the Finger Lakes area. While he may have been best known for starting the Caledonia Hatchery, he was also a commercial fisherman in the 1830's. He designed a form of tackle called the Seth Green rig which has now been modernized to be called a thermocline rig that is used by sports and modern day guides alike in the Finger Lakes when they are meat fishing. It is a multi-leader trolling system that covers a broad depth of water and is capable of reaching depths where the trout may be schooled from just below the surface to on or near the bottom. It is most useful when the trout are suspended over waters of the middle of the lake.

The thermocline rig is able to cover a wide area of water on either side of a thermocline, that layer of water that separates the oxygen rich surface water from the colder bottom layers, and is fished off a heavy boat rod with roller guides and a large salt water reel. Often the main line is monel steel to assist in getting deeper, although monofilament line may be used. Three, five or seven leaders are attache main line and the terminal weight of lead may be 24 to 36 ounces.

How the thermocline rig is setup is up to the individual angler but the common way calls for a main line of at least 30 pound test monofilament. The weight is attached directly to the main line with a snap swivel. The bottom leader and those above are normally 15 to 20 pound test. That way, if one line gets hung up, hopefully you will not lose everything. Leaders of 20 feet hold the trolling spoon or terminal bait. Often a silver plated Sutton 44, 35 or 77 is used but so are Hemlock spinners with live bait. Each leader is attached to the main line or main leader with a snap swivel at a barrel swivel in the main. Space between leaders is generally 25 feet or just longer than the length of the leader. A five leader rig is most common.

As the angler sets his rig he has to attach each leader as the main line feeds off the reel and likewise when he gets a fish he reels, stopping to take off each leader as the barrel swivel comes to the rod tip. Styrofoam blocks are most often used to hold the leaders from tangling.

At times it is difficult to tell if you have a small fish on the Seth Green rig but it is not uncommon to have two and three fish at a time.

Randy Snyder, now a professional guide on Lake Ontario started by fishing the Finger Lakes. His nickname was Super Rig and Snyder and his family would often set seven, seven leader thermocline rigs out of an 18 foot boat. He was pulling a school of 49 lures at one time. Anglers pulling more than two rigs will often use a plastic bottle to hold up the main line and drift it a hundred yards or so behind the boat. The weight and the leaders then work down to the depths beginning at the jug. Rigs without jugs are run between the boat and the jug. The action of the floating jug will tell you if you have a fish.

Downriggers are used successfully on Seneca and those who catch the most lake trout are bouncing the downrigger weight on the bottom. You take some risk of losing the weight but the method takes fish. The secret is to use a release that can swivel on the cable in order to maintain an untangled fishing line.

While tradition gives priority to silver plated spoons on Seneca, the same tackle being used on Lake Ontario trout and salmon will work in the Finger Lakes. Evil Eye, Ontario Flasher and Stinger spoons are just some of the examples that will produce lake trout, browns and rainbows. Chartreuse is a favorite color as are blues and reds in these flutter spoon baits. Apparently light reflection, as first thought with the use of silver plating, is not as important at great depths as the size and action of the bait. Don't be afraid to experiment. Some anglers are even finding success with dodgers and lures such as squids, a popular salmon bait on the Great Lakes.

Brown trout fishing in Seneca is improving with each passing year since the beginning of lamprey control in 1982. The southern portion of the lake seems to have better early spring brown trout angling especially along the salt flats near Watkins, but actually any of the shallow waters will produce browns if you fish for them. The use of planer boards or surface lines with baits such as Rapala or Rebel or even the popular Little Cleo will produce browns in the 5 pound plus class.

Rainbows are more unpredictable with the exception of the months of March and April when they stage off tributaries preparing for spawning runs. The rest of the year they will be found suspended in the upper 40 feet of water in almost any area of the lake.

The great depth of Seneca, over 600 feet, is ideal for salmonids and the fact that it has only frozen over one in the past century gives you an opportunity for open water winter angling. The Belhurst hole is the traditional spot for winter lake trout and presently Roy's Marina is the only open port and launch for the months of January and February. It is also within a ½ mile of the hole and anglers using small boats with small engines that can be quickly drained when removed from the water have been taking advantage of the year around trout season. It is not uncommon to take a limit of three lake trout in the 6 to 8 pound class in less than three hours. Copper line with flashers or trolls and terminal spoons is the traditional tackle for this angling.

Seneca Lake is truly a water for all seasons. It has a reputation of being difficult water to fish but if you follow the simple techniques of angling and concentrate your efforts on one specie at a time you will discover success.

For current information a telephone call to these facilities will be of assistance: Roy's Marina (315) 789-3094; Fisherman's Friend (315) 539-3847; or Fred's Place (607) 535-6690.

Seneca Lake receives an annual stocking of trout in excess of 100,000 fish per year. Anglers can expect to average a legal trout for just over 2 hours of angling time. That is one of the best rates for angler effort in the state.

NOTES: _____

_____

_____

_____

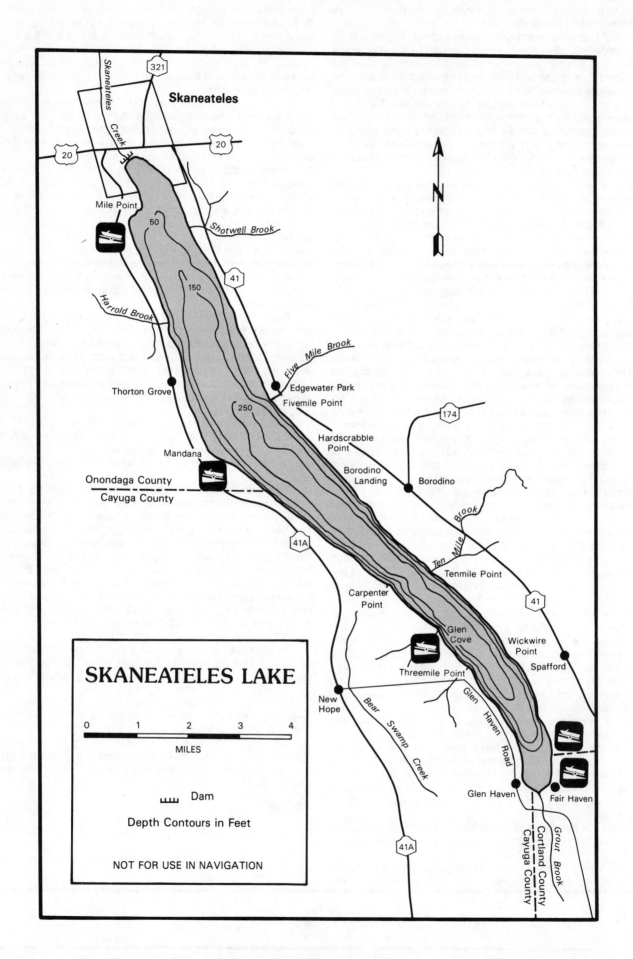

SKANEATELES LAKE

0   1   2   3   4

MILES

⊥⊥⊥ Dam

Depth Contours in Feet

NOT FOR USE IN NAVIGATION

Skaneateles

321

20

20

Mile Point

Skaneateles Creek

50

Shotwell Brook

41

150

Harrold Brook

Five Mile Brook

Thorton Grove

250

Edgewater Park

Fivemile Point

174

Hardscrabble Point

Mandana

Borodino Landing

Onondaga County

Cayuga County

Borodino

Ten Mile Brook

41A

Tenmile Point

41

Carpenter Point

Glen Cove

Wickwire Point

Spafford

Threemile Point

Glen Haven Road

New Hope

Bear Swamp Creek

Glen Haven

Fair Haven

41A

Cortland County

Cayuga County

Grout Brook

— 230 —

SKANEATELES LAKE

map coordinates . . . . 42° 56' 43" 76° 25' 48"

USGS map(s) . . . . Skaneateles, Spafford, Owasco

location . . . . southeastern Cayuga County and southwestern Onondaga County parallelled by Route 41 and Rt. 41A

Physical Characteristics

area . . . . 8960 acres

shoreline . . . . 32.8 miles

elevation . . . . 863 feet

mean depth . . . . 145 feet

maximum depth . . . . 315 feet

bottom type . . . . gravel, rubble, muck

mean thermocline depth . . 35 feet

Chemical Characteristics

water clarity . . . . very clear

pH . . . . alkaline

oxygen . . . . high levels of oxygen exist through out the lake, even in the deepest waters, all year long

Plant Life

There is very limited rooted aquatic vegetation in this lake, and most of it is located at the south end of the lake. Small weedbeds are located on some points and along some coves. Dense algae blooms do not occur here.

Boat Launch Sites

1. DEC launch site - on Route 41A, 2 miles south of the Village of Skaneateles. Multiple hard surface launch ramps - no charge.

2. Village launch site - on Route 41A, adjacent to Marina On Skaneateles Lake, Inc. - no charge. Gas, marine supplies, boat rentals are available at the marina.

3. Mau's Marineland - foot of Glen Cove Road (west side of Lake). Single gravel ramp, parking, gas, marine supplies, storage, repairs - fee.

4. Glen Haven Hotel - on southeast corner of lake, off Route 41. Hard surface ramp - fee. This ramp is not useable when water levels are low.

5. There is a single gravel ramp at the general store just north of Glen Haven Hotel.

Species Information

Lake Trout . . . . common; growth rate fair

Because this lake lacks a major forage base, such as alewives or smelt, many of the game species, lake trout included, have relatively slow growth rates. The angler success rate for lakers is almost certainly higher here than anywhere else in the Finger Lakes, due to the fact that a fisherman's bait or lure is going to get very little competition from bait fish in the lake. These lake trout are always hungry, and respond to anglers offerings accordingly.

The lake trout in this lake, all of which are wild, are decidedly on the small side. In fact, many of the lakers taken here will be sub-legal in size (minimum size - 15 inches). But a few 20 to 25 pound fish are occasionally reported, and they are invariably taken from the waters north of Mandana, off the mouth of Harrold Brook.

Unlike the pattern in lakes with a large alewife forage base, the lake trout in Skaneateles Lake aren't forced to follow their food base into deep water in the winter and early spring. Thus, until the lake begins to stratify (mid-June) lakers will be found in shallow water (30 feet or less) and they will be oriented close to the bottom.

Fishermen usually start picking up lake trout consistently on Skaneateles in early May. Still fishing with large live minnows,

employing a slip sinker and English style hook is a very productive method during this period. Another good springtime technique, though one that is not commonly used here, is flat line trolling with copper wire. Aside from being found in shallow water, these spring time lakers show little tendency to concentrate in any particular area, but with a little persistence you should be able to catch them consistently.

This is possibly the only Finger Lake where they still fish with big suckers for large lake trout. The method is similar to the one used on Saranac Lake or Lake Placid. A three way swivel is attached to the main line. Two lines, each equiped with a treble hook are then tied to the swivel and the hooks are embedded in the sucker, one in the nape of the neck and one near the tail. Only large lake trout are going to be taken by this method, and on Skaneateles that means that you can go for days without a hit. This method is usually only used in early June, before the thermocline sets up, in waters 20 to 25 feet deep.

In the spring, lake trout fishing can be very good on this lake, but most anglers don't pursue lakers here until late June when the lake has stratified. After the thermocline has set up the lake trout will generally be found in water 70 to 140 feet deep. A few individuals will still use wire lines for these deep water fish, but the majority of anglers use Seth Green rigs or downriggers. And with good reason. These fish are very susceptible to this technique, especially during the first three weeks of June. The productivity of this late spring/early summer fishing seems to be tied to the migration of juvenile yellow perch to the deep central portion of the lake. Due to the lack of an alewife/smelt forage base, the lake trout here must feed primarily on yellow perch. When the juvenile perch move out and suspend in deep open water, the trout are drawn out also. The perch are fairly concentrated for a period of about three weeks. When they disperse the lakers also disperse, becoming much more difficult to locate.

While the lake trout are concentrated, an extremely effective lure is a small silver spoon. Fished 15 to 30 feet below the surface on weighted monofilament line or downriggers, they account for many of the lake trout taken during this period. Spoons, in fact, are effective all summer long.

Later in the summer, lake trout will be dispersed the length and width of the lake, in search of favorable temperatures and forage. They are commonly taken by trolling up and down the central portion of the lake with downriggers or Seth Green rigs. Commonly used hardware usually consists of small silver spoons, such as the Sutton (size 22, 25, or 44) or Miller (size 22). Don't neglect some of the shallower portions of this lake. Because Skaneateles Lake is so cold, lake trout can often be found in water as shallow as 65 feet, right on the bottom.

Unlike many other lakes, lakers can be taken here in the fall (they probably can't afford to pass up a potential meal). This fishery usually begins right after the first killing frost, when the trout have begun to move in shore to spawn. It is centered along the shale cliffs on the southeast shore of the lake, between Ten Mile Point and Wickwire Point, in water 5 feet to 25 feet deep. At times this can be a very productive fishery. By working the various points in this area it isn't uncommon to pick up 20 or 30 lakers in a day. Traditionally, the lures of choice were jigs. These were cast right up against the cliffs and slowly worked down to the bottom. This technique doesn't seem to be very popular nowadays, but there is no reason that it shouldn't still be effective.

In the winter very little of Skaneateles Lake freezes over. Safe ice does usually form over a small portion of the south end, but his only lasts for 3 to 6 weeks, beginning in late January. The lake trout will be found in 15 to 40 feet of water and can be taken with tip-ups baited with live minnows or with medium size Jigging Rapalas, or Swedish Pimples. In open water areas where anglers have shore access, such as on the wall at the north end of the lake, anglers should try using jigs, spoons or other hardware for lake trout. Although this isn't commonly done, some of the anglers that we talked to in the DEC felt that plenty of lake trout could be taken in this manner.

Landlocked Salmon....... common; growth rate fair

Landlocked salmon are a relatively new introduction to Skaneateles Lake, having been stocked since 1980. They have only done moderately well here, and their growth rate leaves something to be desired. Until late summer, many of the salmon caught here will be sub-legal in size (minimum length - 15 inches). They eventually get up to 15 to 18 inches, with a very few fish attaining 20 inches. The stocking of landlocked salmon in this lake could be discontinued if the demand for them in lakes where they are move successful increases. At present, however, they do provide an additional fishery on this lake.

From early May to early July, landlocks will be found close to the surface, and can be taken by shallow trolling with small Sutton spoons, Alpena Diamonds or blue and silver Rapalas. Many of the salmon caught at this time are taken by trolling just out from Five Mile Point.

Later in the season, when the lake has fully stratified, landlocked salmon will usually be found at or above the thermocline, suspended 20 to 35 feet down. They are very vulnerable at this time to any technique that keeps you in this narrow stratum (downrigging, Seth Green rigs, diveing planes, etc.). The same lures that were productive earlier on will still be effective right through the summer. While the salmon can be found through out much of this lake in the summer, a number of areas are especially good. In the north end, the waters just off the state launch ramp are producitve, as is the area around Five Mile Point. This fishery peaks, however, in the southern third of the lake during the first two weeks of August. Trolling with downriggers, using small spoons or spinner/worm combinations can be very effective until the salmon enter their spawning phase.

There isn't much of a fishery for salmon here in the fall. They do run in Grout Brook, providing some opportunities, but they are of secondary importance. They are only rarely found in Bear Swamp Creek.

Landlocked salmon can be taken here in the winter, through the ice on the south end. They bite well in the winter and many are caught on tip-ups baited with live minnows. They will most often be found in 15 to 20 feet of water.

In the spring, Skaneateles Lake is stocked with 8960 landlocked salmon yearlings.

Rainbow Trout .... common; growth rate good

Skaneateles Lake provides very good fishing for rainbow trout. Based on angler diaries the rainbows caught here average 13 to 15 inches, which is roughly comparable to rainbows taken from other Finger Lakes. But few rainbows over 20 inches are found here.

Anglers start picking up rainbows on Skaneateles Lake in early April. Most of them are located in the top 10 feet of the water column, and can be found suspended over deep water or close to shore. Initially, jigs are the most commonly used hardware for these trout. Yellow, yellow and brown, or yellow and green, in sizes ranging from ¼ oz. are popular and effective jigs. This jig fishing, which only lasts for the first couple weeks in April is most productive off the points on the southeast side of the lake. A few rainbows are taken on flatlines at this time, but flatlining doesn't really become productive until late April or early May.

One very effective technique to use in the spring is trolling the surface with streamers. This method involves trolling at a fairly good pace (3 to 4 knots) with double hook tandem streamers. Special patterns have developed on this lake over the years. Popular patterns include plain fuchsia feather streamers, orange deer hair streamers or Mickey Finns. An alternative to streamers are #7 gold and red Rapalas. Streamers and Rapalas are both highly effective when fished on wind slicks (flat shiny areas on the lake surface) or along debris lines. Most streamer fishing takes place at the south end of the lake, but there is no reason that it wouldn't be productive elsewhere, off Five Mile Point, for example.

Starting around the end of June Skaneateles Lake experiences some of the best hatches of burrowing mayflies seen on any of the Finger Lakes. These hatches are found on many parts of the lake, but appear to be most abundant at the north end. Rainbow trout feed heavily on these mayflies and are very vulnerable to dryflies at this time.

Once the lake has stratified, rainbow trout are most often found above the thermocline, suspended 25 to 30 feet down. In July and August they show little tendency to concentrate in any particular area. They are often taken by trolling with small Rapalas, Little Cleos or Sutton spoons. A common local technique involves trolling with a rig very similar to the Dixie spinners used on Lake Erie for walleye. These are baited with a whole night crawler and are very productive.

Fishing for Skaneateles rainbows really comes into its own in the late summer or early fall. On rare occasions anglers start picking up rainbows from shore as early as the last week in August, but usually shore fishing doesn't start until the third week of September. Many of the same techniques that were used in the spring can also be used in the fall, including streamer fishing in the south end, trolling just under the surface with small Rapalas and jig fishing. Fall jig fishing takes place off the points on the southeast side of the lake, starting right after the first killing frost.

A fairly unique method for taking fall rainbow trout has developed on Skaneateles Lake over the year - night fishing with marshmellows and worms. This fishery is centered along the east shore of the lake, south of Borodino, but some anglers are successful using this technique as far north as the wall in Skaneateles. Nearly anywhere that you can obtain shore access south of Borodino will be productive. A very popular, albeit private, access site is found at Lourdes Camp at Ten Mile Point. The public can access the shore of the lake here, but keep in mind that this is private property and should be treated accordingly. This night fishery peaks in late September and October, but lasts until late December. Some anglers claim to take as many as 100 rainbows during this period. This method of taking rainbows is also used in the spring.

For some reasons, very few rainbow trout are taken through the ice in the winter. A limited number of rainbows are taken by shore anglers through out the cold season.

In the spring, Skaneateles Lake is stocked with a total of 20,000 rainbow trout yearlings.

Smallmouth Bass .... common; growth rate fair

Skaneateles Lake has a good population of smallmouth bass. Well distributed throughout the shallow portions of the lake, smallmouth here generally run ½ to 1 pound in size. There are very few big bass in this lake, thus the reduced size limit imposed on bass taken from this lake.

Due to the fact that Skaneateles Lake warms up so slowly, smallmouth bass are almost always on their spawning grounds when the season opens. On other lakes I've recommended waiting until their parental duties are over before fishing for bass, but that probably isn't necessary here. The lake has a large population of bass and it is basically untapped by anglers. Their heavy infestation by parasites and small size would seem to indicate that their population could stand some culling.

A majority of the bass are taken from the narrow band of shallow water that rings the lake, primarily south of Mandana on the west side and south of Five Mile Point on the east side. The only real concentration of bass in the north end is found just off of Mile Point.

Smallmouth bass can be found almost anywhere along the shoreline of the central and southern portions of the lake, all season long, though the best fishing appears to be in June and July. They are readily taken on jigs (⅛ oz. to ¼ oz.) dressed with bucktails or Mister Twisters. Crankbaits are also highly effective.

In the south end there is very good bass fishing along the shale cliffs between Ten Mile Point and Wickwire Point. Jigs, cast toward shore and slowly worked down to the base of the cliffs, are very productive.

One technique that works very well from late July onward in

The DEC fishing access site on Route 41A is the principle boat launch facility on Skaneateles Lake.

he south end, off Wickwire Point, is drifting with large (2 inch) minnows in 20 to 30 feet of water. This not only produces good catches of smallmouth, but usually lands some big yellow perch as well.

ellow Perch . . . . common; growth rate very good

Skaneateles Lake has a moderately productive fishery for yellow perch. They run large in this lake, averaging about 10 inches.

Jigging for perch starts earlier here than on most other lakes, beginning around the first week of March. This takes place at the north end and south end in 15 to 25 feet of water. Popular jig colors include green, brown and yellow in various combinations. Still fishing with minnows on perch rigs will also take good numbers of perch in the spring.

Starting in early July many anglers on this lake take perch by drifting minnows. The minnows are hooked on a drifting rig and fished in 20 to 30 feet by water. This method is very productive at the north and south ends of the lake and on the shelf that runs between the state launch ramp and the yacht club.

In the fall, just after the first killing frost, excellent catches of yellow perch can be had along the shale cliffs on the south east side of the lake. This fishery coincides with the spawning of lake trout in the area, and the perch are probably drawn in to feed on the trout eggs. A popular local method to catch these perch is to anchor about 75 feet off shore and cast jigs close to the cliffs, retrieving slowly.

Ice fishing for yellow perch is not very productive on Skaneateles Lake, due at least in part to a lack of adequate ice. The south end always freezes, but the ice doesn't extend over very deep water. A typical catch in the winter consists of 6 to 12 perch. Most of these are taken early in the morning or late in the evening on tip-ups baited with minnows.

Additional Species

A large number of other species are also found in Skaneateles Lake. A very fast growing strain of cisco, believed introduced from Lake Erie, are found here. They are very numerous, but are only rarely caught by anglers. Panfish, consisting of rock bass, pumpkinseeds and bluegills, are found through out the shallow portions of the lake. The rock bass are

especially ubiquitous and good catches of these scrappy fighters can be taken from any rocky point along the lake using small jigs, leeches or crayfish. In the south end of the lake, where significant shallow water weedbeds exist, there are very limited populations of chain pickerel and largemouth bass. The pickerel have been known to exist here for several decades and are most commonly taken through the ice. They average 18 to 20 inches in length. Largemouth were first reported from this lake in the early 1970's and are only rarely taken. Also found in the south end are brown bullhead. The bullhead fishing is very good in late April when they concentrate near the mouth of Grout Brook. The state owns property at the south end of the lake providing fishermen good access to this fishery. Rounding out the available species in Skaneateles Lake are whitefish (rare), walleye (rare or possibly no longer found here), carp, suckers, brown trout and brook trout. Brown trout are only stocked here when supplies of landlocked salmon are low, and they contribute little to the fishery. Brook trout have been stocked here experimentally for the past few years. The hope is that a population of brookies can be established. With this lake's shallow thermocline, it's possible that they can survive in Skaneateles Lake and the DEC feels that 20 inch brook trout could be found here in the not to distant future.

General Information

Skaneateles Lake is a very strange lake, indeed. The fish caught here are, on the average, smaller than in any other Finger Lake, and their relative abundance is certainly below the norm for these lakes. And yet, according to DEC surveys, the anglers here are more satisfied with their lake than are anglers on any other Finger Lake. The reason is obvious to anyone who has been on Skaneateles Lake. In terms of sheer beauty, there are few lakes in New York State to compare with it. Its crystal clear waters, nestled in a setting of rolling hills and hundred foot high cliffs, have a pristine quality and aura of tranquility not seen on any of the other Finger Lakes, with the possible exceptions of Hemlock Lake and Candice Lake.

Skaneateles Lake has the cleanest water of any of the Finger Lakes, and is used as a source of water for nearby Syracuse. That city also regulates the lake level by the use of sluice gates. The average lake level fluctuation is approximately 3 feet and this could adversely affect the reproduction of lake trout. Lake levels are lowest from November through December, possibly exposing recently deposited trout eggs to dessication, freezing or abrasion by ice. It could also affect the overall productivity of the lake's narrow littoral.

The major obstacle to increasing the productivity of the fishery here is the inability of the lake to support alewives or smelt. The current forage base consists of young ciscos, yellow perch, golden shiners and sculpins. This forage base is inadequate for most of the salmonids (rainbow trout can feed on mayflies and plankton), limiting their numbers and resulting in slow growth rates.

Access is a major problem on Skaneateles Lake. Private marinas are located at the south end of the lake and on the west shore. A state launch ramp is located on the north west side of the lake and a village site is found at the north end, but use is restricted to Skaneateles village residents. There are no launch facilities at all on the east side of this lake. Shore access is even more limited. The north end of the lake can be accessed at the village of Skaneateles. At the south end, the state owns about 100 yards of shore line. This area gets some use, but expanding facilities is unlikely since it is located in a wetland. That is the limit of public shore access. There is currently limited shore access on the east shore, via private property, but this could be rescinded spontaneously.

Excerpts from FISHING NEW YORK STATE LAKES FOR FABULOUS TROUT AND SALMON

by
Earl B. ("Maverick") Holdren

Earl Holdren

Shortly before this book was completed I had the distinct pleasure of meeting Earl (Maverick) Holdren. He is the author of a remarkable little book entitled "Fishing New York State Lakes for Fabulous Trout & Salmon". The book is a comprehensive study of the successful angling techniques that have evolved over the years for taking trout and salmon in the Finger Lakes.

Initially, I only wanted to talk to Mr. Holdren about his book and his fishing experiences. I'm constantly trying to develope new sources of information, and though it was late in the writing of this book when I met him, I was sure that he could still have some valuable input. When he told me that he was going to let his book go out of print, I was dismayed, for it would be difficult to duplicate the information contained therein. It was the result of a great deal of research, interviews with master anglers, and a tremendous amount of Earl's own personal experience.

It then occurred to me that one way to keep this valuable information available to the angling public would be to reprint various chapters as an appendix to this book's section on the Finger Lakes. I approached Mr. Holdren with the idea and he agreed to give me permission to reproduce the following chapters and illustrations. Because of time constraints, I wasn't able to update some of the information on the tackle that is presently used on the lakes, but I'm sure that you will find the basic techniques described here highly productive for taking trout and salmon from the Finger Lakes.

To obtain a complete copy of Mr. Holdren's book you can contact him by writing to:

Earl Holdren
Box 20, RD #1
Stanley, New York 14561

CHAPTER 3

THE EIGHT MOST IMPORTANT FACTORS IN LOCATING TROUT, AND SELECTING THE MOST EFFECTIVE FISHING METHOD, TACKLE RIG AND LURES

1. KNOW THE LAKE YOU ARE FISHING LIKE THE BACK OF YOUR HAND!

(By studying maps of the Finger Lakes) you can get a general idea of the characteristics these lakes have in common, and why they are such good trout lakes. Large areas of shallow water may be found at the south and north ends of the lakes where the inlets and outlets flow, and at the points where feeder streams enter. Also the lakes are lined on both sides with strips of shelves or "tables" which drop precipitously into great depths. These plant-covered areas are important to the rich production of food fish for the trout. During the months of May and early June these shelves and shallow areas usually become the "dining tables" where the trout gorge themselves on sawbellies to fatten up after their winter "nap."

Some of these flat areas are cut into deep valleys and holes. (Out of many of these holes flow great springs of ice cold, clear water.) Rocky ridges and piles of glacial gravel intersperse them. Suddenly the edge of the shelf drops off into a sheer cliff, often undercut, that may go 200 feet or more before hitting the bottom level or next shelf.

The "deeps" of these lakes, (Cayuga, Seneca, Keuka, Canandaigua), which range from 186 feet to over 618 feet, are usually gravel and rock, free of plant life. Since there is no rotting vegetation in many areas to burn up oxygen, these lakes remain high in dissolved oxygen at all depths all year long. The "hypolimnion" is not a stagnant and dead area. Also, there is no "winter-kill" of any of the various species of fish.

In most of these lakes too, these "deeps" are crossed by tremendous gravel bars or shoals, which break up the deeps into separate inner lakes. Some of the best fishing for all trout species may be had by trolling "criss-cross" these shoals, when the wind and current are right.

In the Fall, during the month of October, the lake trout migrate to, and school up on, the gravel bars about 100 to 125 feet deep, where they spawn. After the spawning is completed, many trout usually remain on the spawning beds, and these bars become real hot spots for catching lakers up to 20 lbs. or more.

Now! Here is one of the most unique characteristics of these lakes, which few fishermen fully understand, and which unlocks the secret of successful trout fishing all season long! The Finger Lakes are bordered by rolling hills and valleys to the west and east, which on most lakes keep getting bigger toward the south, changing into high "mountainous" ridges, palisade cliffs, and eep-cut canyons of breath-taking, rugged beauty. This topography produces rapidly changing air turbulence...variable strong wind currents...which in turn affect the flow of water in the lakes, thus creating strong "tides" or currents of amazing velocity. These currents induce the ebb and flow of vast areas of cold or warm water, up through the valleys of the lake floor, over the bars and shoals, and into the holes! And the trout and their food fish move with these currents.

These tides are stronger in Seneca Lake than in the others due to Seneca's great depth...but these currents exist in all four lakes when sustained turbulence and wind velocity develops.

(Warning! This same turbulence, of course, is the reason why these placid blue-green waters can become, in a matter of a few minutes, violent, roily, choppy seas, that soak you to the skin and jar your teeth loose as your boat crashes into the deep troughs. You are advised to fish only out of sound, seaworthy boats with ample freeboard. Do not venture more than several miles from your base unless you are in a boat of at least 17 feet equipped with a powerful motor. These waters are tricky and dangerous, and must be respected. Even experienced ocean boatsmen often get into serious trouble on the Finger Lakes.)

So, the shallow flats, rocky shoals and bars, holes, springs, deeps, and strong currents combine to make these four Finger Lakes like great rivers. Think of them constantly as rivers or streams. Actually, this is exactly what they were...great rivers flowing south to north...flowing into the vast pre-glacial St. Lawrence Basin...until the Great Glacier blocked their flow.

2. TROUT FOOD

All of the salmonids in the Finger Lakes feed on essentially the same food fish. The principal food item is the "sawbelly" or alewife. To these silvery, oil-laden, little fish goes the credit for the high production of trout in these lakes. This "landlocked" form of alewife (a member of the herring family) is only 4 to 5 inches in length when mature. They move in large schools, and occur in tremendous numbers. The second-rated food fish is the sculpin (or northern muddler), sometimes called a "stone cat" by fishermen. They are a mottled dark brown or grayish, lighter on the underbelly. They have large flat heads, bulbous eyes and taper down quickly toward the tail. Trout also eat sculpin eggs, large (1/8" diameter) pearlescent pink eggs laid in clusters under rocks. Probably the third food fish is the smelt, found in Canandaigua, Seneca, and Cayuga Lakes(now also found in Keuka-J.S.) These smelt are a smaller version than their Great Lakes brothers, and are eaten by the trout only in the spring when they are in shallow water.

Other food fish eaten in small quantities include the odd trout-perch, cisco, whitefish and sucker chubs. In addition, of course, the brown trout, rainbows, and salmon will feed on worms, insects, simulated trout eggs and soft shell crabs. In May and early June, when the spring rains spread warmer water over the lake flats at the creek outlets, even the dry fly fisherman can have a real ball, fly casting for all the trout species in early morning or late evening. During the summer, bass fishermen frequently get the surprise of their lives when a fighting rainbow of 5 pounds or more swallows their soft shell crab, and proceeds to peal off the fishing line as he speeds down the lake!

As this suggests, trout change their diet as the season progresses, water temperatures change, available food supply changes, and they move into deper water. It is essential that the fisherman change his selection of baits and lures accordingly. How does one do this? Mainly by opening the stomachs of trout caught on each trip to study the contents and check their current food supply. Little variations are important. For example, you will usually find sawbellies in the trout 60% of the time. But, the sawbellies change in size as the season moves ahead. In early spring the trout are usually feeding on all large mature sawbellies of 5 inches. You should match these with spoons and plugs of a similar size. Later they may be feeding on the smaller immature sawbellies. At this time your smaller spoons and plugs will produce best results. At certain times you may suddenly start finding a good percentage of sculpin in their diet. This is a signal

to fish one of the plugs imitating this fish, such as a Flatfish, or a Lutz "Tabu." It is also a warning to fish right on the bottom where the sculpin are found.

And, just to make it more puzzling and challenging, to you...frequently trout won't hit their usual food at all.

So, once again....change, change, experiment, if you don't get hits, until you find what they want. Don't just sit and do nothing.

3. DEPTHS OF FEEDING

There is a marked difference between the feeding depths of the lake trout and the brown trout, rainbows and the Atlantic salmon.

The controlling factor is water temperature. Lake trout will never be found feeding in any appreciable numbers in water above 50° or below 40°. The usual temperature plateau at which they are found in greatest numbers is 48°. Lake trout, contrary to popular opinion, do not like the "ice cold" deep waters of 39°. When ever-changing winds and currents raise the temperature plateau of 48° upward into shallower depths...the lake trout move up too.

Rainbows, Atlantic salmon, and brown trout will be found in greatest numbers in the Finger Lakes where the temperature plateau hits 65°. They will often be picked up in the same lower temperature ranges of the lake trout, but these species prefer warmer temperatures if the food is there, and can be "at home" in temperatures up to 70°. Atlantic salmon, particularly, can withstand warmer temperatures than both the rainbows and brown trout...a fact that has been scientifically verified only recently.

The popular concept that trout feed in the shallow water in the spring, deep water in the summer, and return to shallow water to feed in the fall is absolutely untrue.

Let me repeat...water temperature plateaus determine trout feeding depths at all times.

In April, when shallow water temperatures are 36°, you will find few trout there. Trout do not enter shallow water for Spring feeding forays until the shallow water raches 45° to 48°. On April 1, you may have to go down to 150 feet to find 38° to 40° ...and that's where your semi-dormant trout will be.

In August, when the top water layer is warm, wind and current may carry a plateau of 48° water upward to a 40 foot depth. If it does, brother, you'd better fish for trout in 40 feet of water...not 100 feet!

These same temperature-depth feeding rules apply whether you are fishing the bottom, or in the middle of a lake in 500 feet of water. Fishermen trolling Seth Green rigs in the "deeps" during the summer months frequently fish way too deep to find the trout.

The two important facts to remember about Finger Lakes water depth temperatures are:

(a) There is a gradual warming of top water during spring and summer...a gradual cooling off during fall and winter...but water temperatures vary widely at different depths during these periods due to wind and currents.

(b) There are no gradual temperature changes in these lake waters from top to bottom. Temperature changes occur abruptly in "plateaus," forming stratified "layers" of temperature ranges at various levels. Sometimes these temperature "layers" are thick or deep; sometimes they are fairly thin layers of only 3 or 4 feet deep. Sometimes they are deep on the west side of the lake, and very thin on the east side, or vice versa.

4. TROUT FEEDING LOCATIONS AND HABITAT

All trout are "wild" game fish. They seek maximum protection at all times, and usually forage for food only when conditions afford protection. The exceptions to this are when they are "excited" into feeding, and when they are gorging recklessly in a feeding spree. They like to lie just under or over the currents, on the edge of currents, and on the edge of temperature changes.

They much prefer to lie close to the bottom, at the edge of ridges, drop-offs and bars, or in holes (Figure 1).

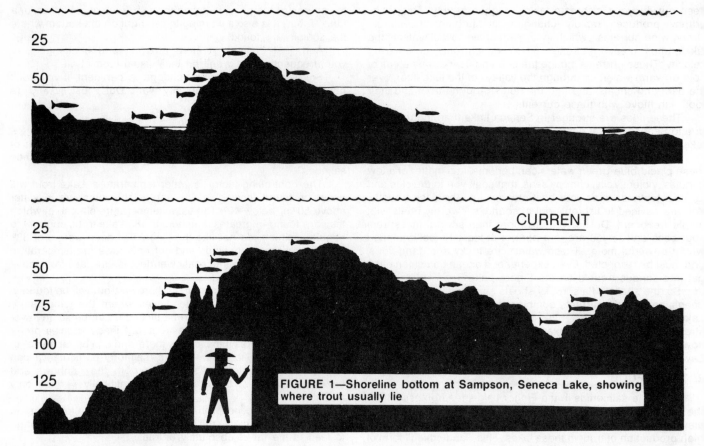

CURRENT

25

50

75

100

125

FIGURE 1—Shoreline bottom at Sampson, Seneca Lake, showing where trout usually lie

Here they can lie with a minimum of motion and effort, and strike out at food fish going by. This is true whether they are in shallow water in the spring, or in deeper water in lake summer and fall. This is also true whether the species is lake trout, rainbows, browns, or Atlantic salmon.

Lake trout are known essentially as "bottom feeders" because of this. But, schools of big lunker lake trout frequently move out in the "deeps" following schools of "sawbellies," and remain there for long periods of time. They feel secure in the deeper water, and want to stay close to their food supply. Although most lake trout will usually be found on the bottom at the highest level at which they can find 48⁰, a trout fisherman should always be trying the "deeps" for schooled-up lunkers, making sure his lure is at the 48⁰ depth.

Rainbows, browns, and Atlantic salmon, liking higher temperatures, will consequently be found on the bottom in shallower water. However, during much of the day, this shallower water (unless it is rough) doesn't afford the protection and freedom from disturbance they prefer, so they move out into the "deeps" or along the edges of the drop-offs. Because they are caught in deeper water so often, many fishermen develop the mistaken opinion that these three species have deep water preferences. Just ask any Finger Lakes expert on rainbows, browns, or salmon where he gets most fish! He'll tell you, "In the shallows at dawn and late evening."

One of the most important factors in locating trout in the Finger Lakes is the "annual gradual trout migration," caused primarily by spawning habits, and secondarily by temperature changes. Most of the great gravel spawning beds of the lake trout are located adjacent to the "deep", generally about 2/3 of the way toward the south end of the lakes. As October approaches and the 48⁰ water "plateau" reaches a level of 85 to 150 feet, the mature, spawning trout move into these gravel beds. It is estimated that over 50% of the lake trout move to the south, with the balance scattered over various smaller spawning beds near the deeps in other sections. When water temperatures begin to change in early spring, these trout migrate northward again...but large schools of them may not appear in the northern sections until May.

This migration works differently in Keuka Lake, which has its deepest areas and spawning beds at the north end of the West Fork near Branchport, and off Marlena Point, 2/3 of the way toward the south end of the lake.

Rainbow trout migrations for spawning purposes follow a different pattern. Rainbows begin to spawn in November, schooling up around the outlets to the many different spawning streams. Spawning reaches a peak in March and usually is completed in May. By far, the bulk of rainbow spawning occurs in Cayuga Inlet at Ithaca by Cayuga Lake, Catherine Creek at Watkins Glen and Montour Falls by Seneca Lake, Cold Brook at Hammondsport by Keuka Lake, and Naples Creek at Woodville and Naples by Canandaigua Lake. After spawning the rainbows leave the streams, school up around the creek outlets for a month or so, then migrate throughout the lakes.

Brown trout and Atlantic salmon follow the same pattern, except that they spawn in October and November in the same streams used by the rainbows. Browns and salmon may be found schooling in the lake areas at the mouths of the spawning streams in September.

While we are discussing feeder streams, let me emphasize their importance to trout fishing in the spring. Trout rarely "school up" when the "plateau" of 47⁰ expands into a broad area covering the entire lake from the top of the water down to 60 to 70 feet. The sawbellies and the trout are scattered everywhere! Many trout fishermen "go nuts" at this time trying to get their limit. This is when you really have to fish both a top and bottom line to get fish. But this is the time smart fishermen concentrate heavy fishing action around the mouths of the feeder streams. Warm rains wash rich food into the lakes for both the bait fish and the trout. Frequently, you can locate lakers, rainbows, browns, and salmon lurking in great numbers at the edge of the clouded water, enjoying the "feast."

This is the period when all species of trout cruise just under the surface of water everywhere, rolling on the surface, and leaping clear out of the water, as they hit the schools of sawbellies and minnows. When you first see trout rolling on the surface, get out your top-line light tackle rigs, and keep them out until the trout go down. It is the most exciting, thrilling time of the year, as it is the only time you can get big lunker lake trout on the surface.

5. HOW AND WHEN TROUT FEED

This subject is probably one of the most controversial in trout fishing. Every expert fisherman, guide, and ichthyologist has his own opinions based upon personal observations. There is no dependable scientific data, because no scientist is going to live in the bottom of a lake all year to get it. Nor can you interview the fish! Various studies made of trout feeding behavior in tanks are inconclusive and misleading. To obtain accurate, reliable data, fish must be observed in their natural, normal environment. This is possible to do to some extent in trout streams.

After having spent many years studying trout behavior in streams, and comparing this data with trout behavior in the Finger Lakes, I have concluded that trout react essentially the same in the Finger Lakes as they do in streams.

They respond with killing and feeding action out of hunger, fear, excitement and competitive aggressiveness. About 60% of the time you catch trout you'll find only two to four sawbellies, or other food fish in their stomachs in various states of digestion. This is apparently normal daily feeding action. About 30% of the time they'll have absolutely nothing in their stomachs. Only about 10% of the time do you find trout gorging themselves...chock-full of sawbellies...with some still sticking out of their gullets while they hit your bait!

Digestive action is much slower and hunger less frequent at the temperature ranges salmonids prefer. Browns, rainbows, and Atlantic salmon, however, have somewhat faster digestion than lake trout when they are cruising the warmer waters, and consequently feed more often.

Observations by fishermen and scientists over long periods of time seem to substantiate the following data on trout feeding in the Finger Lakes:

(a) The biggest percentage of trout do their heaviest feeding of the year from May 1 to July 1. (This may vary a little, earlier or later, depending upon weather and bait factors.)

(b) There is usually another smaller peak of feeding which occurs from August 15 through to October. (NOTE: This is not true of spawning fish-J.S.)

(c) During May and early June, trout do most of their heaviest feeding at night or just at dawn.

(d) When the moon is nearly full, either new or on the wane, trout feed heavier late in the morning, around noon, and in the two hours before dark. This seems to be true any month during the full season from April 1 to November 30.

(e) Unless it is cloudy and dark, or the water is rough, trout generally do most of their feeding during the day in the hours of early morning and late evening when the sun is at an angle.

(f) Trout do extremely little feeding during these conditions:
*Long, sustained periods of "sameness" in the weather... either continued excessive roughness and storming; or day-after-day calmness.

*The early stages of the first formation of the thermocline lower temperature "plateau." (Usually sometime in July or early August.)

*A heavy "die-off" of millions of sawbellies, due probably to population cycles. This often occurs in late June or early July, accompanied by either long periods of high temperature, or extended periods of rain and coolness.

*"Milky" clouded water conditions due to excessive algae, plankton, insect life, silt, and the like.

(g) Rainbows, Atlantic salmon, and browns hit in a curving arc coming down on the bait or lure from the top fast and hard. They kill and suck in the bait at the same time. They must be struck and hooked immediately.

(h) Lake trout hit in a curving arc coming up on the bait or lure from below. They kill the bait first, then swallow. When trolling, they usually hook themselves when "killing" the bait, or will come back and try to swallow the "killed" moving bait if they don't feel the hook. Don't try to strike a lake trout when you are trolling...you'll pull the lure away from him and miss him! While

he's hitting, FEED HIM LINE! This gives the trout time to "mouth" the bait and get hooked. When still fishing for lake trout you must usually let them "run" with the bait until they stop and swallow it...then strike them hard. If the trout run and drop the bait...you know they are just "killing out of excitement and you must take a chance on striking them before they stop.

(i) During periods of maximum "hunger" feeding, all trout hit hard and fast, with the rainbows, salmon and browns hitting much harder and faster than the lakers. During slack feeding periods they usually hit slow and soft, playing with or mouthing, the bait or lure.

(j) All trout utilize the senses of sight, taste, smell, touch, and hearing (vibration) in their feeding and killing action. Keep this in mind!

(k) All trout respond with killing action out of hunger, fear (protectiveness), excitement, and competitive aggressiveness. Keep this in mind!

6. WATER CONDITIONS

As mentioned a number of times previously, water conditions are the most important influence on where the trout are, and how they feed. They also are a strong influence on your selection of fishing methods and lures. Water conditions must be observed just as carefully by the trout fisherman on a lake as on a stream. The velocity and direction of wind, velocity and direction of top water and submarine currents, clarity or cloudiness of the water (visibility), temperature plateaus, and oxygen content (and your skill in meeting these problems)...can make or break your fishing success.

Let's take wind velocity and direction first. If the wind is too strong to roll or drift with your conventional tackle rig, you may have to add more weight to get your lures at the right depth, use sea anchors to slow you up, or get out 300 feet of anchor rope, a heavy anchor, and still fish. But if you are moving too fast, or can't keep your lures where they belong, either still fish or quit fishing. Don't kid yourself into wearing yourself out for nothing.

Wind direction sometimes helps you catch more trout... sometimes hinders you. There's an old saying, "Fishing's best when the wind is in the West." There's also an old saying on the Finger Lakes, "Fishing's best when the wind is out of the South." Both statements are completely cockeyed. It all depends on which area you are fishing. At Seneca, for example, fishing is usually always best on the Belhurst bar at the north end of the lake, when the wind is out of the north, either north, northeast, or northwest. Conversely, fishing at the Sampson or Pontius areas at Seneca is usually best when the wind is out of the south. Why is this true? Nobody seems to know. But my theory based upon observations at the Finger Lakes and in trout streams is this: trout always lie facing into the submarine currents; food fish also swim against these currents; and when wind direction enables you to present your lures to them in the most natural manner in that particular area, you get more fish. I've noticed that the key point seems to be the relationship of wind to currents. When the currents switch direction at Sampson you can often get more fish when the wind is out of the west.

Wind direction and prevailing currents must be observed each time you fish, and you should decide what your trolling direction has to be to take your lures across the current, or against the current. When you have to troll against the wind to accomplish this, and you can't control your boat lures...stop trolling and go still fishing, or climb back in the sack!

Incidentally, when two persons are fishing trolling rigs out of one boat, and you suddenly find yourselves trolling in the same direction as the submarine current...you'll get your rigs so fouled up you think you'll never get the mess untangled!

Wind and roughness act together too, to either help you or plague you. When the wind and roughness continue unabated for several days you might just as well play golf or do some other "horrible" thing. This stirs up the bottom, loads the water with silt and debris, and puts the fish into a state of inactivity. Not only that, but if you go out in a 3 or 4-day Finger Lakes "blow," you'll come back so exhausted, beaten and bloody, you'll need a transfusion and first aid at the local Red Cross Chapter!

Wind and roughness, rising and falling, in a moderate way, are a great boon to fishing for all the trout...and particularly rainbows, salmon and browns. These three are likely to be closer to the surface, but are more skitterish than the lakers. The rough water does several things. First, it creates a constantly changing pattern of light and shadow, which gives the fish concealment while in motion. Secondly, it seems to provide more oxygen, stimulating more action by both the food fish and the predators. Proof of this is the fact that when the wind is blowing out of the west, fishing action is nearly always better on the east side of the lakes, where it is rough. The protected, tranquil waters of the west side are much less productive. Another thing, trout are more likely to move into shallow water when it is moderately rough, so move in close when you have a chop.

The prevailing winds in the Finger Lakes are from the west, blowing chiefly in shifting directions from southwest to northwest. This results in stronger currents, greater water turbulence, greater concentrations of food, and scouring along the eastern shorelines. Could this be the reason why fishing experience indicates greater populations of trout on the eastern shores?

The degree of clarity, cloudiness, or the degree of visibility available to the fish, also affects your fishing success, and choice of fishing method, lures and bait. Water silted or clouded by storm debris, or "milky" with plankton and algae, means visibility of the trout is reduced to a few feet or less. During these periods trout feeding is greatly reduced. Trout are forced to forage around the bottom looking for food or have (vibration-sensitivity) to find food. To the exceptionally talented trout fisherman, this calls for use of the brightest, shiniest lures, added brilliant attractors, special "sonic" or "audio" blades, and even special odiferous additives, whose stench would make you dive overboard. You'll hear more about these techniques later. But make a note right here: Don't stick to standard rigs and lures with the water is cloudy or milky. Change!

An abundant supply of dissolved oxygen is found at all depths tested in the Finger Lakes (maximum depth tested I believe was 435 ft.) In research work conducted, trout have been caught in nets down to about 300 feet. So you can forget about the oxygen problem as it affects many other lakes. I repeat here, there is no stagnant, dead area in the hypolimnion. However, the amount of oxygen increases or decreases due to many different factors such as oxygen-producing plants, oxygen-burning plant decomposition, and action of the wind, waves, and currents. As oxygen supply increases fish become more active and feed. Conversely, a decrease of oxygen makes the fish sluggish and kills their appetites. Wind and waves tend to increase oxygen, hence make trout more active and the fishing better. When you sense the fish are sluggish and the oxygen supply low, there isn't much you can do about it but try to find a strong submarine current where there will be more oxygen, and troll or drift very, very slowly, using attractors and teasers as suggested in Chapter Eight.

7. WEATHER CONDITIONS

I have already covered the marked effect of wind velocity, wave action, and the aftermath of storms, on trout fishing. Also, I have suggested that too much "sameness" of either calm weather, or stormy weather lessens chances for fishing success.

Here I should like to add that dark, cloudy, rainy days...yes, even snow storms...definitely increase the number of strikes you get. Sometimes heavy fog will do the same. But, decreased atmospheric visibility seems to improve fishing only when the water itself is "gin-clear." This is probably due to the fact that trout can see your lure action or bait clearly, but are not scared by bright sunlight above....

Another weather condition that is almost always a sure sign of trout activity is an abrupt, quick weather change and corresponding rise or fall of the barometer. If the day has been reasonably decent, and suddenly changes into a new weather front with winds and clouds...such as an approaching storm... jump in your boat and go after them. In case it's a summer

thunder shower...and you have guts enough to face the dangers...keep right on fishing until the storm really gets bad!1 If you don't get struck by lightning you may get "struck" by the biggest trout you ever caught.

This same principle also applies if we have had a 3 or 4 day "blow," which suddenly stops, and the day turns out clear and bright.

Since sunlight, and angle of the sun, are a part of our weather (and time) I would like to stress the importance of varying your lures as the direct vertical rays of the sun hit the water. During morning and evening hours, you may find spoons and lures of brightest reflectivity, such as bright silver, hammered, pearl, or swirl-finished spoons, very productive. But in late morning on sunny bright days, switch to duller lures, such as the plain chrome or satin fished spoons, or darker plugs, and keep them on until the sun begins to move towad the western horizon.

8. SEASONAL VARIATIONS WITH THE THERMOCLINE CHANGE

This point, too, has been covered under trout habitat and feeding discussions....But for emphasis let me repeat here: "Water temperature plateaus determine trout feeding depths at all times."

CHAPTER 5

STILL FISHING, DRIFTING, AND SPINNING WITH LIGHT TACKLE RIGS, USING LIVE OR DEAD BAIT, OR SPOONS

YOU CAN TROUT FISH WITH LIGHT TACKLE ALL SEASON!

Just mention trout fishing the Finger Lakes to the average fisherman! He'll instantly respond with a long dissertation on why he doesn't think there is much sport in bouncing heavy tackle off the bottom, and dragging in a half-dead "log" that happens to strike. When you get this reaction, you can be sure you're talking to a novice who has had little or no experience in the sport.

First of all, deep fishing with heavy tackle has its own special kind of skill and thrills, and can be one of the most thrilling fishing sports you can find. This is covered fully in Chapter Seven.

Secondly, for those who are light tackle fishermen exclusively...You can fish for trout in the Finger Lakes all season long, shallow or deep, with light spinning tackle and fly rods. And, even in summer, when you may have to fish in 85 to 100 feet of water, your trout will fight all the way to the net. All you have to do is still fish, or slow-drift, with the correct hook-up and live or dead sawbellies, or minnows. In the late spring, when trout are in shallow water, you can also catch them by spin casting light spoons or casting flies or streamers with your fly rod. Deep water spin-casting of light spoons, sometimes called "jigspinning," popular and effective in many Canadian trout lakes, doesn't seem to be very successful in the Finger Lakes in late summer or fall.

To enjoy your still fishing or slow-drifting with light spinning and fly rods in deep water during summer and fall, the only additional equipment you must have is an anchor rope at least 300 feet long, and a good heavy, holding anchor, preferably the Danforth type....By using a temperature probe you sometimes find springs, or currents of cold water at amazingly shallow depths, enabling you to fish for trout in 30 to 40 feet of water in July or August.

In light tackle fishing, as in all lake fishing for trout, you follow the temperature plateaus, and you follow the trout. In April, chances are you'll have to start deep, then move in shallow as the sun and feeder streams warm up the water and the bait moves in. First places to light-tackle fish in shallow water are at the mouths of she feeder streams. You may be able to pick up all species of trout at these "flats" by still fishing, drifting, or casting spoons and streamers. Many fishermen fish right from shore at these spots, casting their bait from shore; or by wading out with chest-high waders, and casting flies or spoons; or by taking bait out with a boat, dropping it at the dropoffs and stripping line off as they come back to shore with their rods and reels.

As soon as all the top water warms up sufficiently, you can find hot-spots almost everywhere up and down the shore at flats, rock piles, drop-offs, holes, and even by fishing shallow in deep water. This usually occurs in May and might last through the first weeks of June. This is the big, exciting peak of light tackle trout thrills, when the big lunker trout have fully migrated from their winter haunts, are ravenously hungry, and full of fighting energy. Night fishing gets in full swing, with hundreds of bright, bobbing lanterns, scattered over the hot spots up and down the lakes.

This is the time when you find your rainbows, browns, Atlantic salmon, and lake trout in the same areas and depths. I've fished for many species in the streams, rivers, lakes, and ocean. There is only one fishing sport that can beat this Finger Lakes trout fishing at this time...and that's Atlantic salmon or steelhead fishing in the rivers of the west and north when they are running. You not only get trout in fantastic numbers, but you seem to get the bigger ones then. Trout from 15 to 20 pounds or more are taken often. Trout from 9 to 12 lbs. are found in catches almost every day! Have you ever had a 11½ lb. lake trout on a spinning rod, and a 6 lb. rainbow on a fly rod at the same time? Man, that's living! And it's right in our own "backyard."

In late June and early July, when the trout begin to move out, you still fish or slow-drift the same way, but you don't do it in deeper water where the trout lie. For rainbows, salmon, and browns, you still might only have to go down 15 to 35 feet or so to hit their temperature range, but the lakes might be 70 to 80 feet deep. Later, you can still fish the same way, using your long anchor rope and anchor in water 85 to 150 feet deep.

HOW TO RIG UP FOR STILL FISHING WITH BAIT

The accompaning diagrams in Figure 2 illustrate the most popular, most successful method for rigging up terminal tackle, and hooking your sawbelly, live or dead. This same method applies, whether you are using a bait casting level wind reel and rod, spinning outfit, or a fly rod. I would like to stress several very, very important factors about your reel, rod, line, and terminal tackle that will help you get maximum catches:

a. Your reel must be adjustable to permit holding your tackle in the water with least possible drag! Any excessive resistance felt by the trout may make him drop the bait after he hits. Spinning reels seem to be best for obtaining minimum drag resistance. Don't be misled by the fact that trout will, when they are feeding hungrily, strike hard and not only run against heavy resistance, but pull your whole outfit right in the lake! Most of the time they are cautious and scary. One day I was catching all m;y trout on one spinning rod. On the fly rod I had a heavy salmon-type fly reel that had a fairly heavy "click" drag. I pulled this line in, substituted a free running fly reel, rerigged it, and threw the bait back in. Within a short time, I was catching trout on both rods! That taught me a lesson I shall never forget.

b. Use monofilament line on all your reels, preferably nothing heavier than 8 lb. test, in the smallest diameter you can get. ...If you are using level wind bait casting reels, or fly reels where your personal skill in playing the fish off the rod has to substitute for setting precision reel drag, you might feel safer using a 10 lb. test line. If you do, get the smallest diameter you can find.

c. Use the very small, light snap swivel No. 12 at the end of your line. Larger sizes are too heavy and conspicuous.

d. Whether you hook your sawbelly or minnow through the lips, under the dorsal fin, or sew snelled English gorge hooks through the back skin, use the very small size 8 hooks. If the trout feels the hook to soon, he'll spit out the bait. Bigger, heavier hooks also interfere with bait action.

e. Some fishermen attach a 3 to 5 foot leader to the end of the line at the swivel, then snap their hook to the end of the leader, so the sawbelly can swim or float up off the bottom. The big disadvantage of this rig is your sawbelly gets fouled up in your line while sinking to the bottom. I find it better to simply feed out 4 or 5 feet of line to the sawbelly after the sinker is laying on bottom. This permits the sawbelly freedom to swim up off the bottom. Also, this extra line gives him more swimming action. Often just before a trout hits him, he'll burst off with s sudden bolting action, causing an extra vibration of your rod tip, signaling you that you're about to get a hit. When you see this, feed a little extra line, and let the trout hit him on the run.

f. Keep your reel filled to capacity with line. Many spinning reels have a capacity of just 80 yards of 8 lb. test monofilament. This is barely enough for lake trout, and not nearly enough to play a rainbow, brown, or Atlantic salmon, which may take very long runs. Reels having a capacity of 175 yards or more are preferable. I see many a trout fisherman every year stand helpless, while a trout of 10 to 15 lbs. runs off his whole line, breaks it off the reel, and keeps right on going! You can't turn these heavy fish, until

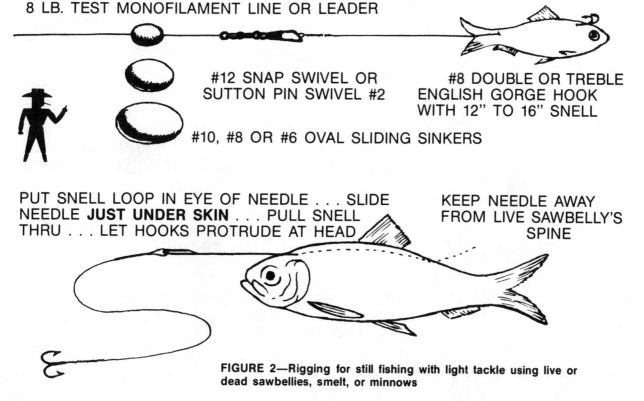

8 LB. TEST MONOFILAMENT LINE OR LEADER

#12 SNAP SWIVEL OR
SUTTON PIN SWIVEL #2

#8 DOUBLE OR TREBLE
ENGLISH GORGE HOOK
WITH 12" TO 16" SNELL

#10, #8 OR #6 OVAL SLIDING SINKERS

PUT SNELL LOOP IN EYE OF NEEDLE . . . SLIDE
NEEDLE **JUST UNDER SKIN** . . . PULL SNELL
THRU . . . LET HOOKS PROTRUDE AT HEAD

KEEP NEEDLE AWAY
FROM LIVE SAWBELLY'S
SPINE

FIGURE 2—Rigging for still fishing with light tackle using live or dead sawbellies, smelt, or minnows

they are ready, without breaking your line. The only answer is to fish with maximum length of line.

g. Keep at least three sizes of slip barrel sinkers in your tackle box. I use the heavy size 6 on very rough days and when currents are exceptionally strong. The medium size 8 is used on moderately rough days and in moderate currents. In flat calms and where current is no problem the lighter size 10 is used. Never use a sliding sinker any larger than you have to.

So, the general rule is...use the lightest line, terminal tackle, and smallest hooks you can at all times. Just slide your barrel sinker on your line; attach your snap swivel; sew your live or dead sawbelly, or minnow on your snelled gorge hook, with the hook at the top of his head; attach the hook leader eye to your snap swivel; cast it out gently down wind or down current; set your drag to hold your line with minimum drag; set your rod at an angle where your tip can work (and it won't fall over the side); and you're set for action.

HOW TO RIG UP FOR SLOW DRIFTING WITH LIGHT TACKLE AND BAIT

This method usually works best in shallow waters up to about 40 feet deep, and requires very slow drifting in moderate winds, or slow occasional rowing. Rigs for slow drifting, and jigging with hand lines and heavier tackle (one of the most popular Finger Lakes methods among "old timers") in deeper water will be covered in Chapter Seven.

There are several ways of rigging up your light tackle and attaching your sinkers and bait as indicated in Figure 3. If currents and winds are not running strong, you can rig up for very, very slow drifting or rowing just the same as for still fishing as shown in Figure 2. Too much current or motion, as you can see, would drag your sawbelly or minnow backwards, when it is sewed on a gorge hook, and sideways when hooked through the dorsal fin.

Many trout fishermen use larger hooks, about size 3, hooking the sawbelly through the lips. They "jig" the bait slowly up and down occasionally. With these larger hooks, they have to strike hard instantly, when the trout first hits the bait, in an attempt to hook the fish through the lips or fore part of the mouth.

When you use the smaller hooks through the sawbelly's lips and the sliding sinker rig, you can let the trout run as in still fishing, and hook him when he stops to swallow the bait.

The same general rules of using light tackle, especially lightest possible sinkers, applies in rigging for slow drifting. If you use the larger hooks, requiring hard, fast striking, you might find a 10 lb. test line more practical.

TIPS ON HOOKING AND LANDING MORE TROUT STILL FISHING AND SLOW DRIFTING

a. Know your strikes—as mentioned several times previously, a lake trout usually hits the bait deliberately, with moderate speed. There are three to five dips of the rod tip, then a strong steady pull as he starts his run with the bait. You get your rod in your hands, feed him line freely with the rod tip down or level. He'll normally run from 50 to 150 feet, then stop to swallow the bait. This is a critical moment! Don't strike him until he moves again! You might pull the bait right out of his mouth. Ath the moment he moves again or you feel him tug strike hard instantly several times.

It is often difficult to tell the difference between a lake trout hit and a hit from a rainbow, Atlantic salmon, or a brown trout. This is especially true when the lakers are feeding ravenously, and hitting harder than usual. But, normally, when you get an unusually hard single smash, your rod tip bends sharply, the line starts reeling off with terrific speed, and the fish keeps going on a long run without slowing down or stopping...strike hard instantly...don't wait for him to stop.

b. soft, slow strikes—Many times while still fishing, the trout will "tick, tick, tick" at the bait, carry it for a short distance, and drop it. When this happens, strike the trout as soon as he starts to move. You'll miss some of them, but you'll miss them all if you wait for them to stop. They usually have no intention of swallowing the bait anyway, and you have to try to hook them in the mouth while they're carrying it.

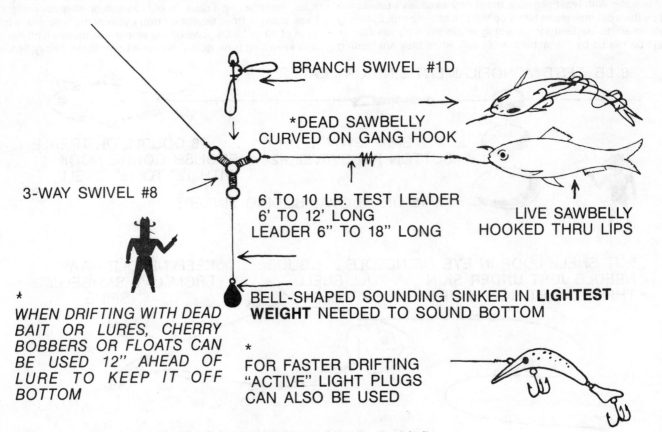

BRANCH SWIVEL #1D

*DEAD SAWBELLY CURVED ON GANG HOOK

3-WAY SWIVEL #8

6 TO 10 LB. TEST LEADER
6' TO 12' LONG
LEADER 6" TO 18" LONG

LIVE SAWBELLY HOOKED THRU LIPS

BELL-SHAPED SOUNDING SINKER IN **LIGHTEST WEIGHT** NEEDED TO SOUND BOTTOM

*
WHEN DRIFTING WITH DEAD BAIT OR LURES, CHERRY BOBBERS OR FLOATS CAN BE USED 12" AHEAD OF LURE TO KEEP IT OFF BOTTOM

*
FOR FASTER DRIFTING "ACTIVE" LIGHT PLUGS CAN ALSO BE USED

FIGURE 3—Rigging for drift fishing with light tackle using live or dead bait

c. Off-bottom, and top feeding—is a problem many still fishermen never think about. They rig one way, and fish one way...and that's it. If I don't get hits on the bottom...I do two things. First, I take the sinker off one line completely, cast the sawbelly out, and let him swim around right on or just under the surface. Secondly, I keep casting, and reeling in the other sawbelly very slowly. Many times I'll get hits when this sawbelly is half-way up.

d. Poor bait action—When fishing half-dead or dead sawbellies, and you're not getting hits, try "jigging" one bait slowly up and down. While you're doing this, reach over and reel in your other bait, just a few feet at a time.

e. Play your trout right—Far too many trout fishermen, and good men too, lose their fish while playing them to net by horsing them. When a good, strong trout decides to run, let him run. When you work him up to the boat, and get set to put the net under him, don't hold your line in your fingers, or set the reel so he can't run. This is the critical point where a lot of fishermen lose fish. Almost any fish will put up one last mighty flurry, or run, just as you get him close to the boat, or he sees the net. When he does, let him go, and play him back in.

Another "danger" factor is your anchor rope. As you are playing trout they will frequently make runs around the boat, swimming under the anchor rope, and sometimes swim around it, in a deliberate effort to snag the line and break free. Each time he goes under the rope...you must climb up on the bow and pass your rod under the rope to the other side! One day, while playing a 10½ lb. trout on a light fly rod, I had to do this five times. The fishermen around me were hysterical with laughter...hoping no doubt, I would fall in the lake.

Remember too, when fishing with reels having adjustable drag, to set up the drag just under your line pound test as soon as you strike your fish. Some guys forget to do this, and wonder why they can't tire and bring in a big trout!

f. Don't still fish closer than 150 feet from an other boat. If somebody pulls up closer than this to you, raise "hell" with him if he starts to anchor! If you see another boat pulling them in, line up with him, but don't get too close. You'll both get your lines tangled, or lose your fish in each other's anchor ropes. Why ruin the fishing for everybody?

If you are trolling past boats still fishing, don't cross in front of them closer than 100 feet. You'll just get your rig caught on their anchor rope. Don't cross their lines either. You can usually judge from the direction of their lines about where their bait lies.

Trolling fishermen sometimes take a "burn" when still fishermen anchor in a hot spot and block them. This is ridiculous. There's plenty of hot fishing water for everybody. Be a good sportsman on the water.

g. Net your trout right—don't let people kid you about having a maximum size trout net. Anybody who fishes for big lakers, rainbows, salmon, or browns with a "bass" size net should have his head examined by a "head shrinker." Use a big trout net, come up on the trout from behind and under him. You'd be surprised how many fish are lost because some "yo-yo" knocks them off the hook by coming down on top of them, or tries to net a 10 lb. trout in a bass net.

h. Keep your live sawbellies alive and peppy—As the bait dealers say, live sawbellies are "fragile." You can't crowd too many in one container, because they need a lot of oxygen. Neither can they stand water that has warmed up, or bouncing up and down against a minnow bucket that has been hung over the side of the boat. I discovered...a good way to keep them alive and peppy all day, even in hottest weather. Just keep them in a styrofoam insulated ice cooler, or "Coca-Cola" insulated cooler with plenty of water. Add a few cubes of ice now and then, or change the water often. Keep the cover on tight, removing it only when you need bait.

SPIN-CASTING FOR TROUT AND SALMON

As indicated previously, spinning for trout in the Finger Lakes with small, spinning weight spoons, is most successful during May and early June when the trout are in shallow water. After the lakers go deep and the rainbows, browns and salmon go down to 50 or 60 foot depths, this sport seems to drop off. Just why this is I really don't know yet. I hope to find out. Perhaps it's because not enough fishermen keep trying it. I know that anglers like Frank Luellen, George Poirier, Jack Peckham and many of the top spin fishermen from Rochester, who fish 31-Mile Lake at the Gatineau Club in Canada, have very successful deep trout fishing with this method. This technique is to cast out a West River, Daredevil Imp, or some other effective spoon, let it sink clear to the bottom, in water several hundred feet deep, then reel in with a jerky kind of jigging motion. On the way up they get hits from whitefish and lake trout. This is really the same action you use when spinning in shallow water.

One reason why this method might be unsuccessful in Finger Lakes deep water is because the "plateaus" of water temperature later in the season are usually quite limited in their depth area, and a spoon goes through this narrow space very quickly. Perhaps we would have greater success if we fished this method in water 200 to 300 feet deep.

You can have a real ball with this very "sporty" kind of light tackle casting in shallow water during late April, May, and early June. Hot spots are the big "flats" around creek outlets, rock piles, holes, and the like, where trout congregate. Figure 4 shows the erratic jigging action of handling the spoon.

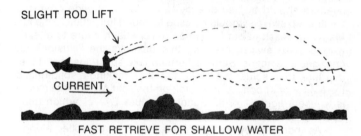

SLIGHT ROD LIFT

CURRENT

FAST RETRIEVE FOR SHALLOW WATER

NORMAL ROD LIFT

CURRENT

DARTING RETRIEVE FOR SHALLOW WATER

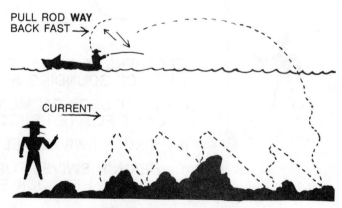

PULL ROD **WAY** BACK FAST

CURRENT

JIGGING RETRIEVE FOR DEEP WATER

FIGURE 4—How to "jig-spin" for trout

CHAPTER 6

TOP-LINE TROLLING TECHNIQUES AND TACKLE RIGS USING PLUGS, SPOONS AND DEAD BAIT

This is another deadly method, and a highly popular one, for catching all species of trout when they are in shallow water, or feeding close to the surface. You can use virtually any kind of rod and reel with light tackle or even a hand-line with heavy tackle and no sinker. Most sports-fishermen prefer to use the light tackle with fly rods and reels, spinning outfits, or level wind reels, and bait casting rods. The...level wind reels, equipped with the star drag, are...very popular for this sport. Since rainbows, salmon and brown trout are likely to be close to the surface after the lakers have gone deep, the wise trout fisherman usually has a top-line out while he's deep trolling for lakers durinng late June and July. As these three species move deeper, he can add weight to the top-line, and troll it down to 25 or 35 feet.

You will note in our sketches in Figure 5, I recommend moving up to a 10 lb. test line and leader. This is because the hard, smashing, surface strikes from heavy fish subject tackle to sudden excessive strain. Weak spots, such as knots, are more likely to break. The use of a "keel" as shown, is extremely important when lures revolve, and may twist the line. Additional weight can be attached to the keel when necessary to go deeper. Leaders should be tied directly to the lures, or wide open-type small snap swivels should be used to impart full action to the lure. Many successful trout fishermen never attach a lure to a leader with a snap swivel, claiming this destroys the "illusion" and changes lure action. Some fishermen take split rings, insert them in a lure, then solder the "split" together, making a solid ring, so the leader or spoon cannot catch on the split. My favorite method is to use a light #1 or #2 Sutton Shurluck Swivel, which I have opened up inside with a pair of ring-nosed pliers.

As indicated by the sketches, lures can be trolled along at the end of 6-10 foot leaders, or preceded by the smaller, shorter,

flasher blade units. These add more weight, and are no recommended for use with the lighter rods. However, thes combinations are sometimes terrific killers because of thei added visual attractiveness and vibration. Don't fail to try the bi streamer flies during this period. And, when everything els doesn't work, try a sawbelly curved on a Seneca gang hook a alone, at the end of a 10-foot leader.

By for, the most widely used lure for top-line fishing is th famous "Hemlock" Spinner. The ringed, double hook is remove the wire loop inserted in the dead sawbelly's mouth, pushe through the inner cavity and out the anus, after which the doubl hook is reattached to the loop. The wire can be bent slightly t give a twirling action.

Top-line trolling is usually more productive from dawn to th middle of the morning, an from mid-afternoon to darkness. O rough days it can be productive all day long.

One of the most deadly top-line trolling techniques for a species of trout, is to fish in very shallow water...from 2 to 6 fee deep...from one hour before dawn to two hours after sunrise...An if you're after the giant night-feeding brown trout, you can fis through until midnight or after. Incidentally, hundreds of Finge Lakes trout fishermen fishing this technique, swear by the famou little "Moon-eye" flutter spoon created by Ferd Lomb, available i a variety of finishes, including a bright fluorescent red, an "moonlight silver."

For top-line trolling, adjustable rod holders can be mounte on the "wings" or gunwales of your boat, pointed outward at a angle. These outside rods then ride like the "outriggers" ocean-fishing boats. Lines are less apt to get tangled, and a thir rod can be trolled from the center of the stern from 30 to 100 fee from the boat. On the "outrigger" rods, by the way, I usually let ou from 150 to 250 feet of line. Contrary to what a lot of "famous fishing writers say, for trout trolling I recommend trolling lure mostly at 150-foot distances or more.

Reel drags can be set under line breaking test strength hook the striking trout, and give him weight to work against as h runs.

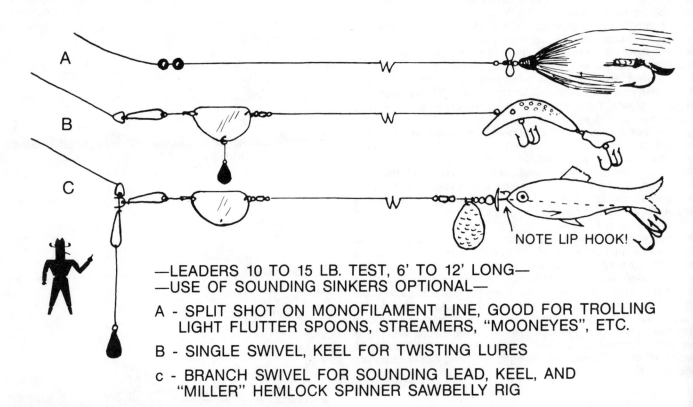

—LEADERS 10 TO 15 LB. TEST, 6' TO 12' LONG—
—USE OF SOUNDING SINKERS OPTIONAL—

A - SPLIT SHOT ON MONOFILAMENT LINE, GOOD FOR TROLLING LIGHT FLUTTER SPOONS, STREAMERS, "MOONEYES", ETC.

B - SINGLE SWIVEL, KEEL FOR TWISTING LURES

C - BRANCH SWIVEL FOR SOUNDING LEAD, KEEL, AND "MILLER" HEMLOCK SPINNER SAWBELLY RIG

FIGURE 5—Rigging for "top-line" trolling

VARY SPEEDS! VARY DIRECTIONS! VARY ROD ACTION!

You see guys trolling straight down the shoreline going "hell-bent for election," zipping over terrific hot spots one after another, like they had an early appointment at the other end of the lake! Conversley, you see others trolling along hour-after-hour, also in the one direction, at a snail's pace, heads drooping, eyes glassy or half-closed, in a state of semi-consciousness. Both are dead wrong !

Troll cross current...troll against the curent! Troll across the bars off and on. Zig-zag in and out...shallow then deep...on and off the shelves. Troll fast. Then troll slowly. Almost stop...then speed up. Work your rod in uneven varied strong jerks or hard jigs...fast then slow. Stop, let your lure sink to the bottom...then take off again. Make sharp turns... full circles. When I see a guy doing these things I know I'm watching a real trout fisherman!

Question: Did you ever study bait fish working in a lake? You never saw them swim in a straight line very far did you?

REMEMBER: Trout will often follow your lure for some distance waiting for it to dart up, down or sideways, before striking!

Yet, thousands upon thousands of so-called "expert" fishermen, including professional guides, insist upon trolling monotonously along, straight, at the same speed, with very little change of lure action. I guess that's why the conservation "professionals" report that 85% of the fish are not caught...they die of old age!

Of coruse, if you are deep-trolling with a hand-line at the same time you are trolling a top-line, you can't be working both outfits simultaneously. But, for deep trolling, as you will see in the next chapter, you should be "working" your boat, too. This automatically "works" your top-line to some extent. And, every once in awhile, reach over with your free hand, and work your top-line rod, with a few uneven strong jigs and long jerks, sometimes throwing it violently in a wide sweep from one side to the other.

Keep in mind, when you have 150 to 200 feet of monofilament line out, there's a lot of stretch in that line. You really have to work your line in strong, long motions to impart any motion at all to your lure. You might look like you're doing your morning setting-up exercises to your fishing pals, but let them laugh, while you catch the trout!

While trolling with a top-line rig, and a deep hand-line rig at once, you may get two fish on within seconds of each other! And the fish on the top-line is usually a wild and whopping rainbow.So now you've got a real picnic! Which should you bring in first? The top-line, of course. The top trout can run out all your line, and leave you groaning with a bare reel and no fish. So don't get confused. Wrap the hand-line around your arm a couple of turns, so the hand-line is held, but not too tightly, in case the deep trout wants to run. Then play your top trout on the rod carefully to net. Swat him a good whack with your "persuader," get him out of the net, and then play your deep trout to net. A good "double" is a great thrill, and you can get awfully excited and confused for a few minutes. Don't worry to much about that deep trout. Chances are he'll stay on, but you're almost sure to lose the top trout unless you play home quickly. It's always more simple, of course, if you're fishing with a pal. All you have to do is let him play the deep fish for you! Oh, yeah!

One more important thing about both top-line and deep trolling - when you catch a trout in a spot always go back over that spot at least once or twice trolling the same way. Don't just keep on going up the lake. Usually where there is one trout there's at least one more, and sometimes a whole school of them. Many, many times we "Pirates" catch our...limit in exactly the same spot...one on each pass over that spot.

CHAPTER 7

DEEP TROLLING TECHNIQUES WITH LIGHT AND HEAVY TACKLE RIGS USING PLUGS, SPOONS AND DEAD BAIT

Deep trolling is, of course, the traditional, and still most widely used method, of fishing for trout in the Finger Lakes. For that matter is probably true of all lakes throughout the American continent. There are three chief reasons for this. First, many of the "old timers" have always used the original deep trolling tackle set-up of straight wire and a spoon or plug, whether they were

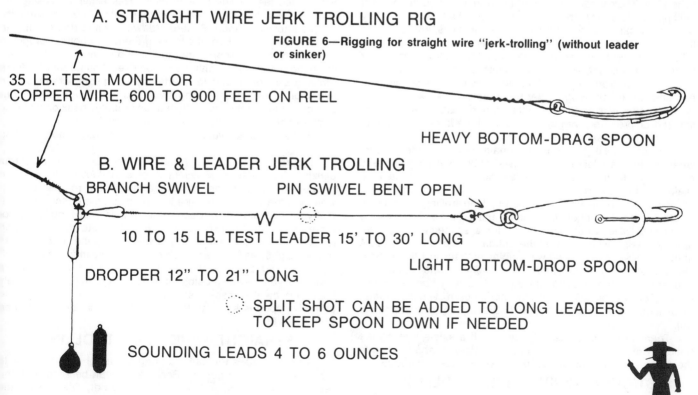

A. STRAIGHT WIRE JERK TROLLING RIG

FIGURE 6—Rigging for straight wire "jerk-trolling" (without leader or sinker)

35 LB. TEST MONEL OR COPPER WIRE, 600 TO 900 FEET ON REEL

HEAVY BOTTOM-DRAG SPOON

B. WIRE & LEADER JERK TROLLING

BRANCH SWIVEL   PIN SWIVEL BENT OPEN

10 TO 15 LB. TEST LEADER 15' TO 30' LONG

LIGHT BOTTOM-DROP SPOON

DROPPER 12" TO 21" LONG

SPLIT SHOT CAN BE ADDED TO LONG LEADERS TO KEEP SPOON DOWN IF NEEDED

SOUNDING LEADS 4 TO 6 OUNCES

FIGURE 6—Rigging for straight wire "jerk-trolling" (with leader and sinker)

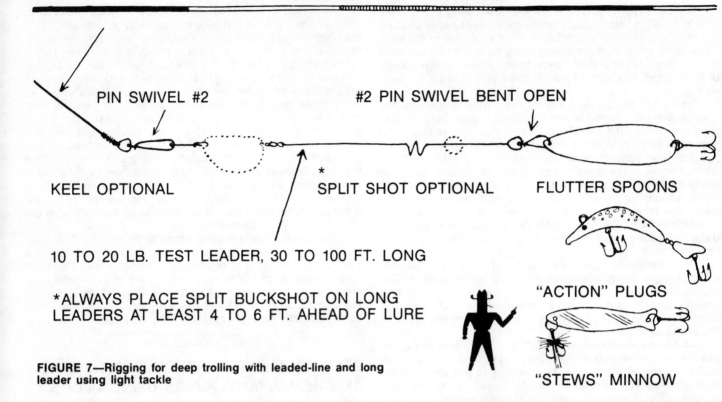

200 YDS. BRAIDED LEAD CORE LINE 18 LB. TEST METER-COLORED EVERY 20 YDS.

PIN SWIVEL #2   #2 PIN SWIVEL BENT OPEN

KEEL OPTIONAL   * SPLIT SHOT OPTIONAL   FLUTTER SPOONS

10 TO 20 LB. TEST LEADER, 30 TO 100 FT. LONG

*ALWAYS PLACE SPLIT BUCKSHOT ON LONG LEADERS AT LEAST 4 TO 6 FT. AHEAD OF LURE

"ACTION" PLUGS

"STEWS" MINNOW

FIGURE 7—Rigging for deep trolling with leaded-line and long leader using light tackle

fishing in the comparatively shallow water in May, or deep water in August. They just like it! Secondly, (and it's hard to imagine) many fishermen just will not believe, until they have the actual experience, that you can catch lunker lake trout, rainbows, salmon, and browns in the Finger Lakes on very light tackle. Third, (and I hate to bring this up), many trout fishermen unfortunately are not sports fishermen at all...they are "meat" fishermen. Their whole interest in deep trolling or drifting...with multiple leaders, and spoons, plugs, or live bait...is to fish only when they can "murder" trout in large quantities, and stock up their freezers for the season. A few even sell them illegally to restaurants and hotels around the area. They catch them two or three at a time, ignore legal creel limits, and may actually take home 20 to 30 trout per day! (Finger Lakes trout are delicious to eat, and are much sought after by gourmets everywhere. They have a tenderness and flavor that's hard to beat. When they are smoked or prepared with culinary skill, there is nothing finer in the world to please your taste buds.)

You see these guys only at certain periods of the season, when the trout are feeding ravenously. When the fishing slackens off and gets tough, they fold up their rigs and retire to the local "saloons" to play euchre.

There are basically two kinds of "deep-trolling"—trolling a single lure on, or right off, the bottom; and trolling a multiple-lure rig, having three or four leaders and lures, spaced about 20 feet apart, covering water right at the bottom, and at different levels above. This second method was originated back in 1880 by Seth Green, father of fish culture in America, who apparently understood "temperature plateaus" before they had thermometers! Today, this rig, with all its modern variations and innovations, is still called the "Seth Green" Rig (or thermocline rig).

There are several ways to deep-troll a single lure on the bottom. For the sake of simplicity, and clarity, I shall separate them into the three most successful widely used methods.

STRAIGHT-WIRE "JERK"TROLLING

This can be done by either a hand-line rig..., or by attaching a large capacity (600-900 feet) reel to a short, very stiff rod. Either

copper, or monel line can be used. Some fishermen use the simple hand-wind reels, while others have bought or built the "Victrola" reels which wind the line back on the reel automatically by the wound-up spring. Some also use the big-capacity salt water reels with a star drag, mounted on a short stubby, stiff rod that can stand the jerking. When fishing these wire lines without sinkers, or with very little weight, you must have 600 to 900 feet of line to work with. This eliminates using the famous A & S automatic reel...as it has only a 300-foot capacity.

As shown in Figure 6 there are two ways to rig up. You can see the "direct" method of attaching the heavy bottom-dragging "Pflueger Record" spoon right to the end of the wire. You "feel" the bottom at all times with the spoon itself. You bounce it off the rocks, gravel, or mud, in fast darts by jerking your wire quickly in two short jerks, and one long sweeping jerk. Then you let your arm or rod fall backward so the spoon wobbles back down to the bottom. This is a simple, inexpensive, easy, foolproof (but tiring) way to fish. And, it's very, very, effective for big bottom-feeding fish.

Figure 6 also shows a variation of this jerk-trolling method utilizing the added deceptiveness of a 10-foot leader and the greater action the leader imparts to the spoon. You use enough weight at the end of your wire to "bump" on the bottom, and you feel your way along. Your spoon usually rides several inches or more above bottom, except when you complete your "jerk" and let your arm or rod back down, in which case the spoon hits the bottom slightly as it settles. You'll probably lose more spoons with this leader rig, because they seem to snag on the bottom more often, but you may also catch more trout. Lure action is definitely improved by the leader, and you can use the lighter, more attractive spoons such as the Miller Trouter #9 and the Sutton Shurluck #66.

STRAIGHT WIRE "JIG" TROLLING

This method is the same as rigging up for jerk trolling with the 10-foot leader (Figure 6). Basic tackle can be either rod and reel, hand-wind reel, or "Victrola" rig. The only difference is the lure you employ, and the hand or rod action...you don't "jerk". The lure is what we call an "action" spoon, or plug. The spoon is a very light-weight "flutter" spoon with a treble hook such as the Miller Flutter-Lite #66 or #06, or the Sutton Shurluck #35. In the action plugs, the flatfish type of lure in white, silver, black, and red-and-white are most widely used. All you need to do is jig your line slowly up and down so the sinker "feels" the bottom, and let the action of the lure and the boat do the rest. (See Trolling Action later in this chapter.)

STRAIGHT LEADED-LINE OR WIRE AND LONG LEADER TROLLING WITH LIGHT TACKLE

Another method of trolling deep that is becoming more popular every year is illustrated in Figure 7. This involves using a medium stiff rod, a large capacity salt water reel with a star drag, and 200 yeards of meter-colored lead core line, and no sinker. For this line, I use and recommend the Gladding Special Mark-Five 18 lb. test, packaged in two 100-yard connected plastic dispenser spools. This smooth finished, braided line offers low resistance to water friction, and is amply leaded to sink readily. The metered colors change every 10 yards, enabling you to know accurately how deep you are trolling. This is particularly helpful when you are trolling off the bottom in deep water.

You can make your own accurate table of line lengths to trolling depths as follows: Turn on your depth finder, and then troll at desired trolling speed; troll in a 25-foot depth and leave out line until you hit bottom, then mark the number of colors of line you have out; repeat this at every 25-foot depth until you reach the maximum depth you wish to fish. You have 20 different colors to work with, which should take you down to about 150 feet. By adding additional footage of backing line you can get down to greater depths if you wish.

At the end of your leaded line you attach a 10-lb. test leader of at least 30 to 40 feet. Some fishermen use leaders up to 100 feet long. With this method you have no "sounding" lead or heavy sinker lead to content with. There is nothing to disturb the fish, and the long leader allows the spoon or plug to work with maximum action, with as near perfect illusion as possible. Since there is no heavy weight for you and the fish to fight against, this deep trolling method affords the finest in sporty light tackle deep trolling.

This same method is often used with a monel wire line, preferably as light as 20 lb. test, replacing the leaded line. When using a wire line on your reel, you should use a narrow, deep spooled reel, so your wire does not overlap horizontally causing "telescoping," and resultant jamming and kinking.

Whether you use wire, or leaded line, this deep trolling method is very effective. It not only provides thrilling light tackle sport, but it is the method used by some of America's "champion" trout fishermen to get really big lunkers of 35 to 50 lbs. They usually troll very very slowly, and use large plugs and spoons. Sometimes they bend the spoons in odd shapes to get more teasing action at the slow speeds. You'll see more on this in Chapter Eight.

THE FAMOUS "FLASHER" OR "CHRISTMAS TREE" RIG

Sometime around '50, some sporting goods jobber in the Finger Lakes area "got stuck" with a bunch of Davis Flasher Sets, shipped in from the West Coast. Nobody in New York State had ever used them for trout. A couple of Seneca Lake "Pirates" picked them up because they were cheap and decided to try them. The result was, to put it mildly, "utterly fantastic"! Using a sounding lead on a dropper, three-way swivel, hand wire line, and the flasher rig with a couple of cherry bobbers at the end, to which was attached a sawbelly impaled in a swirling curve on a "Seneca Gang" hook,...these guys caught trout so big...and in such numbers...that the word traveled like wild-fire...much to their dismay.

Today, probably more trout fishermen use this deep trolling rig on the Finger Lakes than any other method. It is still a deadly killer, although it is not nearly as effective as it was when it was new. Trout, particularly the big ones, get "wise" to lures just like bass do. That's why they grow big, and old. Each year, the flasher rig seems to decrease slightly in effectiveness. When you have anywhere from thirty to eighty boats trolling the same rig through a hot fishing area, it must look like a "Shrine Parade" to the fish! Many times while this is going on, I've trolled with a flasher rig along with the rest without getting strikes. Then I'd switch to

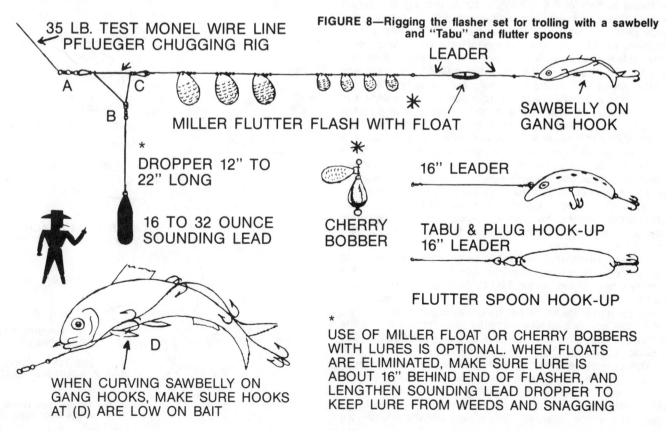

FIGURE 8—Rigging the flasher set for trolling with a sawbelly and "Tabu" and flutter spoons

35 LB. TEST MONEL WIRE LINE PFLUEGER CHUGGING RIG

LEADER

MILLER FLUTTER FLASH WITH FLOAT

SAWBELLY ON GANG HOOK

DROPPER 12" TO 22" LONG

16 TO 32 OUNCE SOUNDING LEAD

CHERRY BOBBER

16" LEADER

TABU & PLUG HOOK-UP 16" LEADER

FLUTTER SPOON HOOK-UP

WHEN CURVING SAWBELLY ON GANG HOOKS, MAKE SURE HOOKS AT (D) ARE LOW ON BAIT

* USE OF MILLER FLOAT OR CHERRY BOBBERS WITH LURES IS OPTIONAL. WHEN FLOATS ARE ELIMINATED, MAKE SURE LURE IS ABOUT 16" BEHIND END OF FLASHER, AND LENGTHEN SOUNDING LEAD DROPPER TO KEEP LURE FROM WEEDS AND SNAGGING

another lure combination and get strikes right away! When the trout are feeding greedily they'll hit the flasher rig like mad! Just ask Harry Howell and Ted Voight, the two friendly competitive restauranteurs from Geneva. At times they still get catches of trout on the flasher rig that make you turn green with envy. And, Herb Damico, another top fisherman and law officer of Geneva, moved his flasher fishing activities to Canandaigua Lake one summer, where the flasher rig was "fresher," and he really "murdered" the trout there all season long. I've often wondered how fishermen would do with this rig in other good trout lakes. The only report I've had on this concerns a pair of Finger Lakes fishermen who went to a Canadian trout lake last summer, used flasher rigs, and had to put big trout back in the lake every day.

There are three makes of flasher rigs on the market today designed primarily for this kind of trout fishing. (They are not to be confused with the much smaller "Christmas Tree" flasher rigs of Canada, widely used for catching "red trout.") They are the original Davis Flasher, the Outlaw Flasher, and the Miller Flutter Flash. These rigs run from 4 to 6 feet long. The three front flasher blades are about 5" long and 2½" wide, spaced about 5" apart. There is usually an intervening space of about 12", then 4 small trailer flasher blades of 2½" in length by 1¾" wide, spaced about 4" apart. All blades are swivel mounted on wire sections with fluorescent red beads used as spacers.

The original "Davis" Flasher has blades with a hand-hammered finish, blades on the "Outlaw" are a stamped dimple finish, and the Miller Flutter Flash has unique blades finished about 1/3 in smooth polished finish, and 2/3 in a hand-hammered finish. They are available coated in polished nickel, or brass, and a combination of brass on one side and nickel on the other. Brass seems to work best in clear water on bright days, while the silver produces best on dark days and/or in cloudy water.

The Miller Flutter Flash has several advantages I like. Sections are shorter for better, easier handling and storage. Each section is detachable so you can make up your own combination or flasher blades. And it comes complete with a bright fluorescent plastic float and leader, all ready to go. Incidentally, the Miller line also includes 6 different sizes and combinations, the smaller of which are effective on red trout, brook trout, rainbows, and bass.

Come to think of it, you might catch almost any species on these flashers. I've seen many fishermen pick up lunker bass, perch, pike, and have heard of big muskellunge being snared with them, too. One day while fishing for trout with Al Messner in about 50 feet of water with flasher rigs, he got a good strike, and played a nice "trout" into the net, which turned out to be a jack perch of close to 3 pounds! He really put up quite a fight.

The conventional way to rig up a flasher unit is shown in Figure 8. Most fishermen fish with 300 feet of 30 lb. test monel wire loaded on an A & S automatic reel. Others may fish these rigs on "Victrola" reels, or stiff rods and salt water type reels. Wire is attached to a Pflueger 3-way chugging rig at (A); the sounding lead of 12 to 16 ounces with a 17" to 21" leader or wire attached to dropper arm (B); and the flasher unit is attached, either alone or with a wire "spacer" to snap (C). Two floating cherry bobbers are connected in tandem to the end of the flasher to keep the bait from dragging bottom. The sawbelly is impaled on a Seneca gang hook, as shown, and the hook leader is attached to the end cherry bobber.

Other variations include leaving off the cherry bobbers and lengthening the leader or wire on the sounding lead. This gets the sawbelly closer to the bottom, and tends to give it more action. Short 8" to 12" leaders can also be attached to the end of the flasher unit and plugs and flutter spoons attached as shown. Two of the most popular, effective artificial lures for this rig are the famous Lutz "Tabu" made in Geneva, (imitation of a Sculpin), and the flutter spoon #35.

This rig is placed into the water carefully, after trolling motion is started, by dropping the sawbelly into the water first. This sawbelly must be spinning or twirling in the water. If it isn't twirling, remove it and draw up the "Seneca Gang" hooks to put more curve in the sawbelly. This is very important! After the

sawbelly is in the water, slowly drop in each section of blades, lower the sounding lead in, and make sure the rig is trolling straight, before lowering it to the bottom. Lower the rig steadily, but not too fast, until you feel your sounding lead hit bottom and the wire line goes slack. Then lift it up slightly and jig very slowly up and down, feeling the sounding lead hit bottom each time you lower your hand.

If your rig goes down too straight, and lacks "pulsating," twirling action when it's down...you may be trolling with the submarine current. Pull it up slightly and turn your boat immediately so you are trolling across or against the current. With the automatic type reels, the spring winds as you let out line, and unwinds, feeding the line back on the spool, as you bring your line in.

When trolling shallow water of 40 feet or less you can use a much lighter sounding lead to feel the bottom. Some men take off the sounding lead entirely and fish this rig just under the surface when the trout come in very shallow. This I can't quite understand. Why fish these heavy flasher rigs at the time you can get trout on light tackle?

THE "SETH GREEN" MULTIPLE RIG

This is the famous multiple lure rig I've talked about a number of times... With it you can fish from one to five lures spaced from the bottom or "deep" up to the surface. This is one of the oldest most effective ways to fish the trout of the Finger Lakes, and is still very widely used today. Seth Green's knowledge of lake waters and trout habits told him back in the 1880's that trout might be lurking at various depths. Lacking an accurate, dependable water

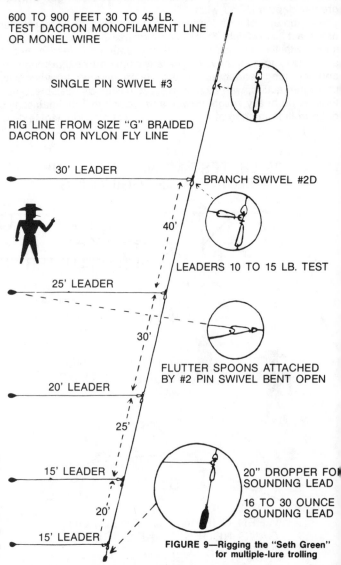

600 TO 900 FEET 30 TO 45 LB. TEST DACRON MONOFILAMENT LINE OR MONEL WIRE

SINGLE PIN SWIVEL #3

RIG LINE FROM SIZE "G" BRAIDED DACRON OR NYLON FLY LINE

30' LEADER

BRANCH SWIVEL #2D

40'

LEADERS 10 TO 15 LB. TEST

25' LEADER

30'

FLUTTER SPOONS ATTACHED BY #2 PIN SWIVEL BENT OPEN

20' LEADER

25'

15' LEADER

20" DROPPER FOR SOUNDING LEAD

16 TO 30 OUNCE SOUNDING LEAD

20'

15' LEADER

FIGURE 9—Rigging the "Seth Green" for multiple-lure trolling

depth thermometer, he did the next best thing...rigged up a long line, heavy sounding lead, and leaders spaced from 15 feet to 25 feet apart, with live sawbellies on the "snatch" type hooks. Early fishermen using this outfit rowed their boats very slowly, or drifted slowly. Many fishermen still fish this way from small rowboats. Quite a few prefer to do their "rig" fishing at night, hanging powerful lanterns out over the stern to attract schools of sawbellies, and hence the trout.

There are dozens of modern versions of this "Seth Green" Rig, involving all kinds of different spacings of the leaders, lengths of leader, types of line, and the like. Some use 10-foot leaders, some 15-foot leaders, some 30 or 40-foot leaders, etc., etc.

Let me cover here the most widely used, modern sporting Seth Green Rig, trolled at varying speeds, clear up to 7 or 8 miles per hour, with artificial lures. Starting with this, you can then very your leaders, spacings, lures and the like, all you wish to help you catch trout. Many "rig" fishermen make the mistake of not adjusting their rigs to fit changing conditions, and troll them in the same unvaried manner, fish or no fish. Others, like myself, keep 3 or 4 differently spaced hook-ups available in coils to meet wind, current and temperature plateau changes as they occur. If you are using a wire line, you can obtain sliding spacers and swivels which are located in position by a set screw. These can be moved up and down at various settings, and your leaders snapped on where desired.

Fighting a big 9 to 20 lb. trout on these rigs is much more of a sporting thrill than many think. Fishing with light flutter spoons, and light plugs with small hooks means your big trout will be hooked in the mouth, rather than down deep in the gullet. They are free to wage an all-out battle, and they really do. You just can't "horse" them in without losing them. After you slowly work the fish to the top you then have to play him in on a long 20 to 40 foot 10 lb. test leader...and that's a feat in itself.

It takes hours of study and patient practice, not only in learning to handle the rig proficiently, but in learning and improving lure action. Top rig fishermen like Ray Estes and Nick Groat of Rochester, who are credited with many improvements in rig fishing, design and produce their own spoons.

Figure 9 shows just how to rig up this modern, sporting Seth Green Rig for deep fishing. The main back-up line, to which the "rig" section is attached, is 600 to 900 feet of 30 to 45 lb. test Dacron heat-stretched monofilament or monel wire. This feeds on or off a spring-operated "Victrola," or on a salt water type level wind reel with a star drag. Those using a "Victrola" reel or level wind reel store their rig section, leaders and spoons in a box, or hooked together and wound on a discarded line spool. When in haste to land a fish we often wind up our leaders quickly on a block or cylinder of styrofoam plastic and insert the lure hooks in the plastic.

The A & S automatic reel can also be used, but its line capacity is limited to 300 feet, which restricts you to about 100 feet maximum depth when trolling slowly and about 75 feet when fast trolling. This same problem exists when hand trolling heavy bottom-bumping flasher rigs with this type of reel. The additional drag of the flasher rig makes it difficult or imposible to reach 100 foot depths.

The "rig" section of your Seth Green is made from two 25 or 30 yd. coils of fly line. This is level line size G, braided of solid Dacron or Nylon, finished to reduce water friction and to sink readily. The reason for using fly line is its ease of laying out in coils in the bottom of the boat or box without tangling, as you are bringing in a trout. Light-weight 3-way "branch" swivels, of the Sutton Shurluck type are attached to the end of the fly line, and spaced at intervals of 20 feet, 25 feet, 30 feet, and 40 feet up the line as shown in the sketch. 2-foot leader and sounding lead are attached to the end swivel. Weight of the sounding lead will vary according to trolling speed, winds, and currents from 16 ounces to 30 ounces. Leaders should be of Stren, or some "limp" Dacron or Nylon monofilament so they will lay flat when tossed in big coils. Nothing over 15 lb. test should be used, as the diameter gets too large. The bottom leader attached to the end swivel will be 15 feet long, the second leader 15 feet long, the third 20 feet long, the fourth 25 feet long, and the top leader should be 30 feet long. These extra lengths of leaders compensate for the "bow" or "belly" of the line, placing your lures not too far distant from each other vertically.

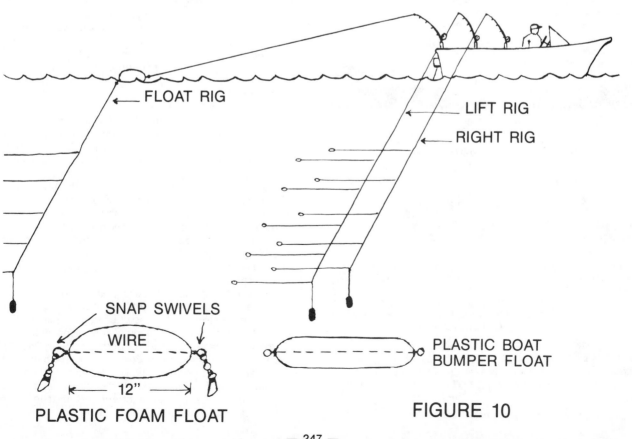

FLOAT RIG

LIFT RIG

RIGHT RIG

SNAP SWIVELS

WIRE

12"

PLASTIC FOAM FLOAT

PLASTIC BOAT BUMPER FLOAT

FIGURE 10

Whether leaders are stored in "laid" coils, or on plastic separately, or connected on spools...lures are attached to each leader, lures dropped into the water singly, leaders let out slowly, and attached to the branch swivels one at a time, starting with the first leader at the drop sinker.

When a fish gets on one of the spoons, you bring your line in on the reel until you reach your "rig." If your fish is on the top leader, handling is simplified. You just bring the fish in on the top leader and let the rest of the rig stay below. If your fish is on the bottom leader, you've got a real "picnic." You throw your fly line and leaders with spoons in big coils on the bottom of the boat, so each big coil lays on top of the other. When you come to the last leader you play your fish in to net or gaff. You should whack him on the "noggin" quickly with a persuader, before he has time to flop all over the boat, and mess up your line and leaders!

You should mark your main line every 20 yds. with some dye or colored split shot, and the like, so you can tell how much line you have out. You can then prepare tables, by trolling in known depths, which tell you how deep your bottom lure is running. Much of the time you'll be trolling in known depths, which tell you how deep your bottom lure is running. Much of the time you'll be trolling inwater as deep as 600 feet and you may want your bottom lure to run at 150 to 200 feet. Using the standard illustrated rig with a 30 ounce sinker you will find you have to put out 100 feet of back-up line, in addition to your rig section get down 125 feet.

Many of the most popular types of spoons and light plugs used in this method are: Minnnesota Pearl Wobbler, Quick-Strike 22, Miller 22, Miller 7, Sutton 44, Outlaw 65, Pine Valley 01, Quick-Strike 31 (swirl finish), Nivers 47, Sutton 35 (hammer finish), Quick-Strike 22 (swirl finish), Sutton 35, and Nivers 35. The small Flatfish or similar type lures are especially good for catching rainbows on the top leaders. As you put each lure in the water, try studying its action at various trolling speeds so you can see what the lure does.

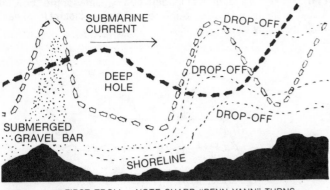

FIRST TROLL - NOTE SHARP "PENN-YANN" TURNS
SECOND TROLL - NOTE CROSS-BAR, CROSS-HOLE TROLL

FIGURE 11—Varying trolling directions and speed

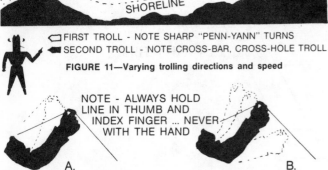

NOTE - ALWAYS HOLD LINE IN THUMB AND INDEX FINGER ... NEVER WITH THE HAND

A.
NORMAL EASY SOUNDING JIG, UP AND DOWN SLOWLY

B.
BAIT WORKING JIG-UP 2 SHORT JERKS, THEN DOWN

C.
DART AND FLUTTER BAIT WORKING JIG - PULL UP **FAST FIVE** LONG PULLS THEN LET BACK DOWN TO BOTTOM SLOWLY

D.
OFF-BOTTOM RISE AND FALL JIGGING - PULL UP **15** PULLS VERY SLOWLY, THEN LET BACK DOWN TO BOTTOM VERY SLOWLY

FIGURE 11—Varying trolling arm motions

VARYING TROLLING SPEEDS AND DIRECTIONS

Figure 11 suggests various ways of trolling your boat to get maximum natural action to your lures, to approach fish right, and get more strikes. These points were covered in Chapter Six and top-line trolling...but they are just as important in deep trolling... so I'll repeat them:

Troll across current...troll against the current. Troll across the bars...on and off the bars. ZIG-GAG in and out...shallow then deep...on and off the shelves. Troll fast...then troll slowly. Almost stop... Almost stop...then speed up. Work your arm or rod in UNEVEN slow, easy jigs. Make fast turns and easy jigs. Make fast turns and easy full circles. Pull your rig up to 15 feet or so very slowly...then let it down slowly.

USE YOUR DEPTH SOUNDER AND THERMOFISHOMETER!

In all deep trolling, your depth sounder and temperature gauge can save you time and wasted effort, by telling you exactly the depths you should troll to get most trout. By using your temperature gauge to check temperature plateaus, you can decide whether your standard rig is going to hit your various trout levels or not. You may decide to arrange two lower leaders closer to the bottom, to hit more lake trout, and place two top leaders closer to each other at the top to hit more rainbows, salmon, and browns. Without this device you are just guessing, hoping that one of the five leaders will hit at the right level.

CHAPTER 8

SECRET TRICKS FOR TAKING TROUT AND SALMON WHEN THEY ARE NOT FEEDING

This chapter title should also include "or when they are not hitting normal tackle rigs and lures." Actually, sometimes the trout are feeding, but are not feeding normally, and may be feeding where you are not reaching them. And, of course, there are often periods of time during the season when trout either don't feed much, or don't feed at all. This is covered fully in Chapter Three. The question is, "What can you do to tease trout into hitting when conditions are tough?" Times like these separate the real sport fishermen from the "meat" fishermen. Sports fishermen study, experiment, try old tricks and develop new ones. The "meat fishermen" fade out of the picture until the next "greedy" feeding period comes up.

The late Ted Cornish, to whom this book is dedicated, top trout fisherman and a leading dealer in trout tackle, has worked closely with me during tough fishing periods to find ways of getting trout to hit. Roy Japp, of Roy's Boat Livery on Seneca Lake, near Geneva, has also helped me experiment with various ideas and tackle. And, a number of the Seneca Lake "Pirates" have revealed some of their tricks to me. Naturally, these "secret" tricks don't work all of the time. But, you should try them, and experiment with new ideas you think up yourself. You'd be surprised to see some of the crazy combinations that work!

When fishing gets tough you've got to keep reminding yourself "why" trout kill and feed, and the "senses" they use to find food. For emphasis, I will repeat these points covered in Chapter Three:

*All trout respond with killing action out of hunger, fear (protectiveness), excitement, and competitive aggressiveness.

*All trout utilize the senses of sight, taste, smell, touch, and hearing (vibration) in their feeding and killing action.

You can appeal to hunger, or perhaps even stimulate hunger through all five of the senses. For example, live bait can be used to stimulate through sight, taste, smell, touch, and hearing. Dead bait stimulates through sight, taste, smell, and touch...with probably weak attraction by sight and no attraction by hearing because of reduced action (Trolling dead bait, of course, helps

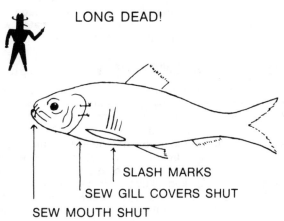

GILL COVERS OPEN
MOUTH OPEN

LONG DEAD!

SLASH MARKS

SEW GILL COVERS SHUT

SEW MOUTH SHUT

FRESHLY KILLED!

FIGURE 12—Tricks to make dead bait look alive

vercome this.) Artificial lures such as spoons and plugs
timulate by sight and hearing only...unless you "doctor" the lure
with an odor.

You can appeal to, or stimulate hunger, through many
standard fishing methods and lures. There isn't much you can do
about "fear" except hope that a fish will hit a lure to "kill" out of
self-preservation, such as protecting young, eggs and the like.
Some of the "secret" tricks are developed to stimulate hunger,
when ordinary methods fail. But, most tricks are developed to
timulate "excitement" and "competitive aggressiveness."

Varying trolling action, for example, helps to stimulate
"excitement," in addition to the basic appeal of the lure to hunger.
Using double "attractors" and "extra baits" and both "excitement" and "competitive aggressivenss" to the basic appeal of
hunger.

So, you see, if you are a "nut" like I am, that's the way you
think!

ADDING "LIVE" EYE AND ODOR APPEAL TO DEAD BAIT

Trout of all species will strike dead bait "still" fished as well
as trolled. As a matter of fact, for some unknown reason, trout will
often hit dead bait when they won't touch live bait! But dead bait
must have that "live" look, and odor.

Unless your dead sawbellies are old, and half-dehydrated
from the freezer you don't have to worry much about odor. But if
they are old, just grind or squash some of them, adding a little
water, and soak the whole ones in this smelly "mash" for an hour
or so before you put them on the hook. Some smart guys also add
a little smelly cheese to the mess for added odor attraction.

Mouths of dead sawbellies are very important! When
sawbellies die in nets, on your hook, and in your minnow bucket,
they usually die with their mouths wide open. They do not look
freshly killed to the trout. Keep a small needle and thread handy,
and sew the mouth shut with one stitch, cutting off the excess
thread (Figure 12). I also sew up the gills.

To add further appeal to fresh dead bait, some fishermen also
strike the sawbelly with three light close slashes of a sharp knife
down the side of the fish just behind the gill. Just break the skin
lightly. This releases a little blood, and gives the sawbelly the
appearance of having just been killed by another trout!

HOW TO HOOK SLOW, SHORT-HITTING TROUT AND TROUT THAT "MOUTH" THE BAIT

In Chapter Five we have already discussed the problem of
trout "mouthing" the bait when you are still fishing. You can strike
them hard and fast before they run too far and drop the bait. One
more trick on this, which I forgot to mention in Chapter Five, is to
hook the sawbelly through the dorsal fin instead of sewing him on

FIGURE 13—Trail-hook for slow hitters

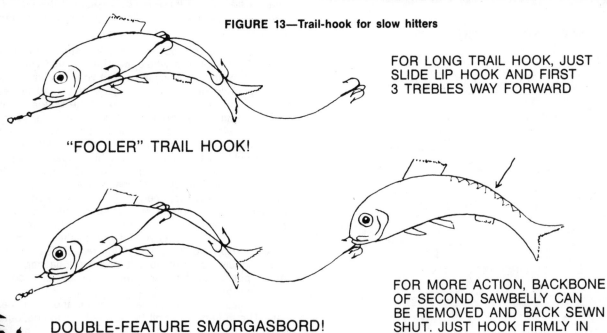

"FOOLER" TRAIL HOOK!

FOR LONG TRAIL HOOK, JUST
SLIDE LIP HOOK AND FIRST
3 TREBLES WAY FORWARD

DOUBLE-FEATURE SMORGASBORD!

FOR MORE ACTION, BACKBONE
OF SECOND SAWBELLY CAN
BE REMOVED AND BACK SEWN
SHUT. JUST HOOK FIRMLY IN
LIPS.

FIGURE 13—Two sawbellies for slow hitters and gluttons

with the gorge hook. You strike him just as soon as he grabs the bait, and you usually hook him in the mouth.

When you are trolling, and you keep getting slow, short hits, or the trout "mouth" the bait softly without getting a hook, there are several things you can do (Figure 13). First, use smaller size Seneca Gang hooks...they hook the fish faster, penetrate farther. Second, you can draw the first three treble hooks up the leader, and let the last treble hook trail behind several inches to snare the "late" hitter. Third, (and this is a real double feature humdinger), draw the first three treble hooks way up the gang hook leader, impale your curved, twirling sawbelly there, and then add a second sawbelly to the trailing hooks, hooked through the mouth! This not only hooks the late hitters, but it often stimulates a "gluttonous" trout to hit both baits, when he won't hit a single.

VARYING LURE ACTION

Most good trout fishermen know how important lure action can be...especially erratic, varying action. Most commercially made spoons and plugs are made for a certain continuing wiggle, wobble, or flutter, and to be trolled at an average moderate trolling speed. When you know it's smart to troll very, very slowly, you usually have to twist or bend spoons to get more action. Figure 14 shows some of these bent, and twisted variations of standard spoons. Conversely, when you want to troll very, very fast, you might get better action from the spoon by flattening the curve and twisting it ever so slightly.

Flatfish, and similar type lures have a standard rounded, slightly curved nose. ...many of us "whittle" these noses down to a flatter, more rectangular shape. This causes these plugs to wiggle normally for a distance, then suddenly dart off to the left or

NORMAL "88"

"GYPSY ROSE" CURVE

NORMAL "35"

"PEPPERMING" TWIST

NORMAL "31"

"HOT LIPS" MAVERICK

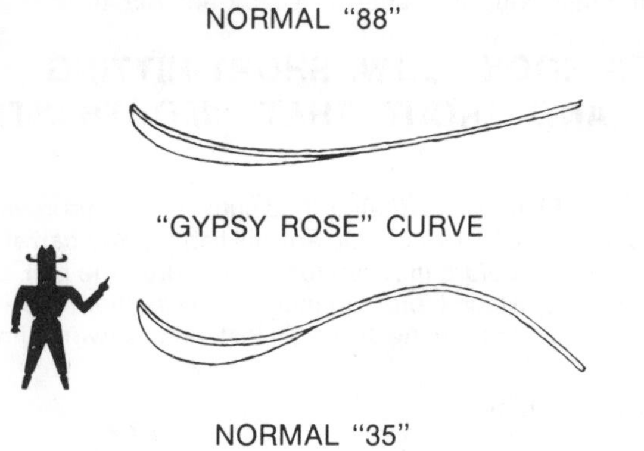

FIGURE 14—Bending spoons for increased action and very, very slow trolling

right. This happens only when you are fishing the lures off long 25 to 40-foot leaders.

MOSS-GREEN DYED LEADERS

The less conspicuous leaders are, the more trout hits you'll get. Leaders should always be of the smallest possible diameter in relation to the strength required. Clear, colorless, transparent leaders are usually standard. But, leaders in camouflage finishes are more effective, and leaders dyed a moss green seem to be quite important in getting more hits when the trout become "fussy." This is because you can't really "hide" a leader entirely from the fish, and a moss-green color is associated with his natural environment. Hence it arouses less alarm or suspicion.

ATTRACTING SALMONIDS WITH NOISE

Much of the time, trout can only see a few feet, due to the depth and clarity of the water they are in. Light falls off rapidly in the depths. They have to rely on the "sound" or "vibrations" of bait they pick up to find food. ... Scientists have made tests in tanks, and have proved that trout and other fish can "hear" food fish placed in the water from as far as 100 feet. They will rush in the direction of the vibrations long before they can see the bait. Alarming vibrations picked up by trout in a stream will scare them into hiding long before they see you. So why shouldn't they be sensitive to the vibrations of their own food supply? The standard multiple flasher or "Christmas Tree" rigs put up very strong vibrations in the water, which I'm sure is the big reason for their success, rather than the visual "flash."

Experiments along this line prompted Miller Lure Mfg. Co. Inc. at Springwater, N. Y., to introduce then years again the Miller "Vibra-Sonic" Flutter Flash... with two extra propellers on the set. These add further different "noise" wave vibrations to the flasher action, and have been proved to get trout when ordinary flashers fail.

THE "BIG THREE" DEADLY KILLERS WHEN TROUT ARE IN THE "DOLDRUMS"

All three of these methods are based primarily on stimulating hits by visual excitement, some noise, and competitive aggressiveness. Experienced stream trout fishermen will recognize instantly how these three methods parallel the use of multiple flies, and dropper attractor flies in getting stream browns and rainbows to hit.

1. Using a long top leader and flutter spoon trailing a flasher outfit...(Figure 15). The whole idea here is that you want to fish your flasher rig in the usual way but you also want to present a flutter spoon to the trout at some distance behind the flasher. You can vary the height of this spoon off the bottom to match the feeding depths of the trout. You splice a very small barrel swivel into your wire line above your flasher...from 3 to 15 ft. up (depending on how high off the bottom the trout may be hitting). This swivel must be small enough so it will feed through the guide on your automatic reel. Rig up a 10 or 20 lb. test leader from 35 to 100 ft. long with a heavy size 5 snap swivel at one end and a small pin swivel size No. 1 (opened wide) at the other end, for attaching your flutter spoon. You throw your spoon into the water, let your leader out straight, and snap it into one of the two barrel swivel eyes on your wire line as you let your flasher rig down slowly. If you wish to get your flutter lure riding very close to the bottom, the leader should be mounted 3 ft. above the flasher, and you will have to pinch on the leader a large split shot No. 5 about 8 to 10 ft. up the spoon.

The flasher rig does the attracting, and stimulates excitement. The trout may not hit the sawbelly on the rig, but suddenly along flutters your flashing spoon, all alone, and he smashes it. After several hits you can tell by the feel which lure the trout is on. If the trout is on the leader spoon, bring your wire in to the leader connection, wrap your wire around a cleat, and let the rest of your rig drag in the water as you play the trout to net on the leader. If he

SINGLE FLY ON DROPPER LOOP

SPLIT BUCKSHOT
6 FT. AHEAD OF SPOON

|← 8" →|

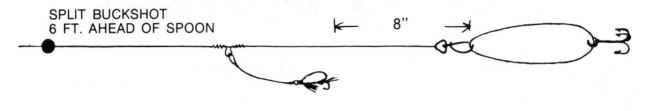

3-FLY CLUSTER TIED RIGHT ON LEADER

|← 8" →|

SINGLE FLY HUNG ON PIN SWIVEL

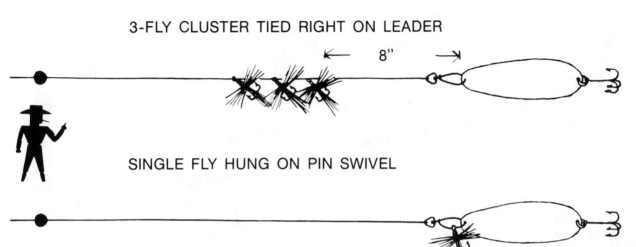

FIGURE 16—Adding flies and streamers ahead of or on flutter spoons

A. POOR VISIBILITY - POOR FEEDING

40 FT. TOP LEADER 3 FT. UP ON LINE

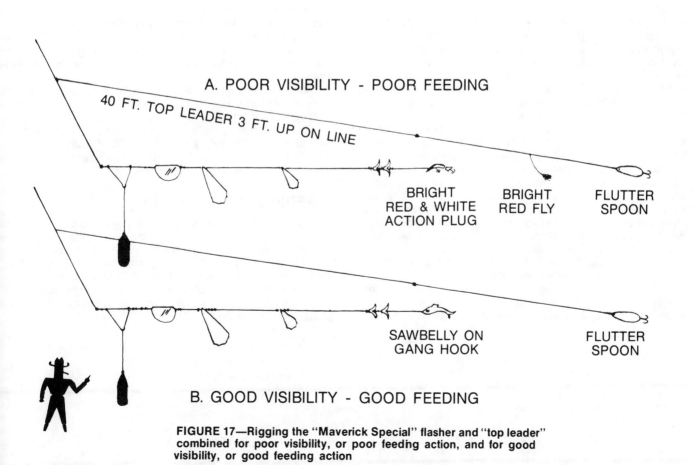

BRIGHT
RED & WHITE
ACTION PLUG

BRIGHT
RED FLY

FLUTTER
SPOON

SAWBELLY ON
GANG HOOK

FLUTTER
SPOON

B. GOOD VISIBILITY - GOOD FEEDING

FIGURE 17—Rigging the "Maverick Special" flasher and "top leader" combined for poor visibility, or poor feeding action, and for good visibility, or good feeding action

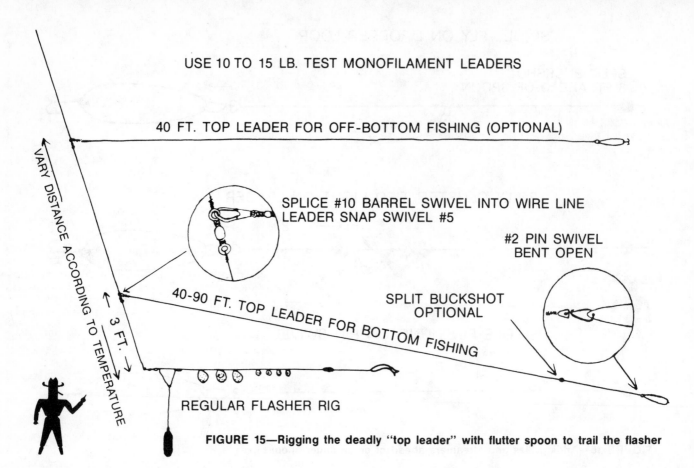

USE 10 TO 15 LB. TEST MONOFILAMENT LEADERS

40 FT. TOP LEADER FOR OFF-BOTTOM FISHING (OPTIONAL)

VARY DISTANCE ACCORDING TO TEMPERATURE

SPLICE #10 BARREL SWIVEL INTO WIRE LINE
LEADER SNAP SWIVEL #5

#2 PIN SWIVEL
BENT OPEN

40-90 FT. TOP LEADER FOR BOTTOM FISHING

SPLIT BUCKSHOT
OPTIONAL

3 FT.

REGULAR FLASHER RIG

FIGURE 15—Rigging the deadly "top leader" with flutter spoon to trail the flasher

is on the flasher rig, snap off your leader, snap it on a ring mounted somewhere at the stern of your boat, let it drag behind, then bring your rig and trout into the net. Every once in a while you'll get two trout on at once. Play the top leader fish to net first, then bring the lower one in.

2. Brilliant, brightly-colored lures and bright streamer flies as attractors...(Figure 16). Use the "top leader" and flasher rig as explained above. But, place a small size 10 or 12 barrel swivel, or dropper loop, in your leader about 14" ahead of your spoon pin swivel. Tie onto the swivel or dropper loop a short 4 or 5" leader and tie on this leader any of the bright, small red, red and white, yellow, or white streamers about size 12. Wet trout flies in any of these bright colors will also work well.

Instead of this, you can also obtain the small "Palmer" tied flies in the same colors with tiny size 12 treble hooks. These can be attached to the split ring at the end of your spoon.

At the end of the flasher unit, instead of using a sawbelly, tie on a leader 8" to 14" long and snap on brightly colored red and white, yellow, white, or bright green Flatfish or similar wiggling lures. (Some of us paint these with bright fluorescent pink and pearl nail polish.) When I'm using a bright plug on the flasher, I fish the leader spoon plain. The bright plug serves as an "attractor" and the spoon looks like a "natural."

3. The "Maverick Special" Trout Killer. (...Figure 17). This attractor-type, short, lightweight flasher rig is similar to the famous "Ford Fender" widely used in the West for trout, steelhead, and salmon. After testing this lure extensively last year, when trout fishing was in the "doldrums," I was so enthusiastic

about it, that Miller Lure Mfg. Co. decided make it and market it as I have redesigned it. Be sure to rig it up exactly as I have shown in Figure 17. Length of leader is very important, and you must use the keel.

You can fish this lure very, very slowly...or you can fish it very fast. You get two entirely different actions at these speeds.

This is a wonderful rig to use with a long top leader just 3 feet above it, as the short "Maverick Special" won't get tangled in the leader, as the larger flashers often do. I always use the top leader along with it.

When trout are feeding well and the water is clear you can use a twirling sawbelly on a Seneca Gang hook, or flutter spoon or Flatfish type lures in natural colors.

But when fishing really gets tough...the trout aren't feeding, and the water is "milky"...this "MAVERICK SPECIAL" rigged with brightly colored plugs, and the 40—ft. leader and flutter spoon will get trout when nothing else will.

EXPERIMENT YOURSELF!

These are just a few of the unorthodox "secret" tricks some of us have found productive when the going gets tough. When you run into difficult fishing periods, go back to the beginning of this chapter, review trout "senses" and "responsive killing and feeding action," and see what "combination salads" you can come up with. There is no greater fun, or feeling of accomplishment, than when you hit an idea that produces trout for you, while others are not getting hits.

DOWNRIGGERS IN THE FINGER LAKES

C. Scott Sampson

A downrigger in the Finger Lakes is used in a number of different ways that bring angler success. Those same methods on the Great Lakes would only result in lost tackle.

The major difference between the two waters is the species and size of the fish. Your chances of landing a chinook salmon on a "slider or cheater" rig is about as good as landing one on a even leader thermocline rig — slim and none.

The recording depth finders were the birth of frustration for many anglers but, it was this same frustration that has resulted in new techniques in downrigging that have been developed in and for the Finger Lakes.

I'm not saying that the traditional methods of copper line or thermocline rigs do not take fish, but, compared to the use of light tackle and downriggers, those methods seem to take the "sport" out of sport fishing. When the average Finger Lake salmonid is in the 2½ to 3 pound class, depending on the species, it has always seemed to me that a boat rod used with a thermocline rig was somewhat akin to using a 30-06 rifle for hunting squirrels.

The bread and butter fish of the Finger Lakes is the lake trout and while we can normally locate the fish by looking for the 48 degree water temperature where it meets the bottom structure, this is where the frustration begins.

As a general rule of thumb the slower the trolling speed the better for lake trout, but even this has exceptions. I have graphed out after trout, had them rise off the bottom to look at my offering as shown in black and white on the chart paper and then refuse to strike. I have increased speed like I am fishing for salmon and sometimes that works. Often it does not.

It is at this particular time that the angler is quickly separated from the fisherman, and it is at this time that the normal downrigger techniques have to be adjusted to bring success.

Consistent tonking of the bottom with a downrigger weight is one way to wake up trout, although it may also be an expensive way if the weight is caught and snapped off the cable. A less expensive way to excite fish but equally effective is to use a lure that will dive and dig into the bottom, kicking up the silt patterns that imitates a live bait fish feeding.

Lures such as the Flatfish, Canadian Wiggler, Fire Plug and Fishbacks all have a design that forces the lip of the lure to the bottom and the hooks ride free behind the body of the bait. That is the criitical issue in this type of fishing. A stick bait such as the Rapala or Rebel would be caught on the bottom in an instant because of the belly hooks that trail below the bait.

The normal rule of downrigging leader length is, the deeper you run the closer the bait or lure is to the bomb. While you will most often be fishing in the range of 80 to 100 feet of water that says that you should set the bait or lure close to the weight. Not in this case. Drop the flatfish type bait back 30 feet from the bomb so that it has plenty of opportunity to kick into the bottom. In fact, if you look at many of my lures you will see where the lips have been worn off in a similar manner to the toe of a kid's sneaker.

Setting the depth of the downrigger is also accomplished by feel rather than by counter and depth finder. When a depth finder says 100 feet and the cable meter says 100 feet you should be on the bottom. But, you are not. The cable is being pulled back at an angle away from the boat by the friction of the water as compared to the electronic depth signal which is going straight down. The lighter the bomb and the faster the boat speed, the greater this angle may be. You also have significant currents under the surface of many of the Finger Lakes which can effect this angle as well. Lower your downrigger until it hits bottom and then bring it back up 3 feet according to the meter.

I use 11 pound weights and often see a varience of 7 to 8 feet between the depth finder and the cable and both have been calibrated.

The best indication of the success of this method is the way that many of the lake trout have been caught. On many occasions I have brought trout to the net with the entire lure inside its mouth and propping the jaw open much like a northern pike spreader bar.

Cheater leaders have taken their name from the concept that an angler may only fish with no more than two lines with up to 15 hook points per line. In downriggers, that usually translates into two rods per angler and two baits. Or does it? The cheater is an extra leader or line that while separate, is attached to the main line and is legally a part of that line.

A cheater leader may be either fixed or left free to slide up and down the main line. It should not be much longer than your rod so that you can still play the fish to the net. I generally make up several leaders in advance of five to six foot in length for when the action is slow and I need that extra coverage.

The cheater is a monofilament line with a snap or a snap swivel on both ends. One snap connects to a bait or lure and the other hooks around the main monofilament line of the rod. In a free slider, the leader and bait will end up approximately half way between the surface and the downrigger release depth. The friction of the water bellies the line and the pull of the lure slides the lure to the furthest part of the main line curve without regard to depth.

In a fixed cheater, the angler selects the distance and uses a stacking release on the cable to lock the leader in place. The stacking release may be a commercial product such as the Clipper, Offshore or Roemer releases or it may be a simple rubber band that is looped around the downrigger cable, passed through itself and then the snap is passed around the main line and through the remaining loop of the band.

Rubber bands can also be broken and then tied in a simple overhand knot which is generally enough to hold the cheater in place. Experienced anglers will often leave a package of rubber bands in the sunlight to weaken them so that they will break with even lighter strikes and smaller fish.

When a fish takes the lure on the fixed cheater it has to open two releases. The one holding the cheater in place and the one holding the main line. This should suggest that you may need to set the release as light as possible. The leader then slides to the lure on the main line and stops and you play the fish on the rod and reel. There is no limit on the number of cheaters that you put out as long as you do not exceed the 15 hook points provision of the conservation law.

Most anglers will use only one cheater but there are times when a fixed and a slider in addition to the main line is advantageous.

Cheater placement can make a difference in angling success. I will often set a main line lure 15 feet from the bomb and use a large spoon such as a magnum Stinger as the terminal bait. Five feet above that release I attach the cheater with a smaller Stinger spoon. The setup looks like a larger fish is chasing the smaller fish. I have had days when all the trout taken have come only on the cheater. There is something competitive about fish and if they can beat another fish to a meal, they will.

The slider or free cheater simply gives you additional coverage and when fishing for lake trout on or near the bottom, the slider will often pick up a brown or a rainbow trout that is suspended in warmer water temperatures.

Color bombs, size and shape appear to be more of a personal preference than what will make a significant difference in the Finger Lakes. I personally lean toward the chartreuse or bright colors and I have been running fish-like bombs.

Ernie Lanteigne, when he was the DEC fisheries biologist in charge of Cayuga Lake, developed the trick of attaching large silver spoons without hooks and on a short leader to his bombs to act as an attractor. Lake trolls can also be used in the same way but you need to be careful of how much resistance you are adding. A large troll could pull your cables back and forth and possibly tanlge lines. Trolls also have the tendency to roll and you will need to set your main line release high enough over the bomb to be out of reach.

Attractors, bottom banging baits and cheaters can all help to increase your results on salmonids in the Finger Lakes but don't over look drastic changes of speed and depths of lures. On a slow day after placing my lures in a school of bait, I may release a rod and allow the lure to float to the surface. Sometimes that is just the change of pace that takes a trout.

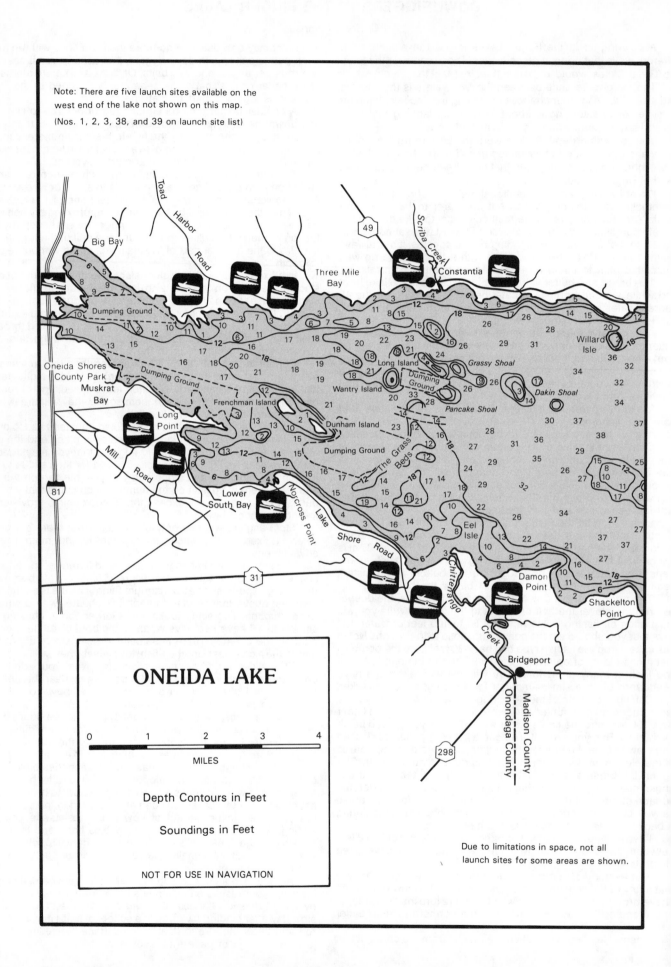

Note: There are five launch sites available on the west end of the lake not shown on this map.

(Nos. 1, 2, 3, 38, and 39 on launch site list)

ONEIDA LAKE

```
0        1        2        3        4
```
MILES

Depth Contours in Feet

Soundings in Feet

NOT FOR USE IN NAVIGATION

Due to limitations in space, not all launch sites for some areas are shown.

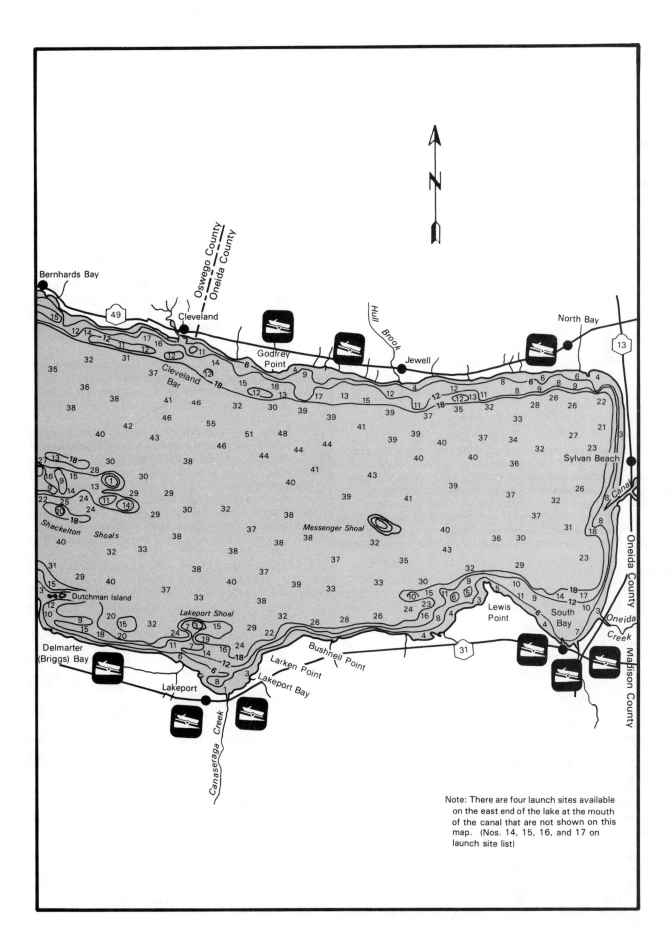

Note: There are four launch sites available
on the east end of the lake at the mouth
of the canal that are not shown on this
map. (Nos. 14, 15, 16, and 17 on
launch site list)

ONEIDA LAKE

map coordinates	43° 12' 25" 75° 55' 58"
USGS map(s)	Mallory, Brewerton, Cicero, Cleveland, Jewell, Sylvan Beach
location	10 miles northeast of Syracuse
access	Route 31 (southern shore), Route 49 (northern shore), Route 13 (eastern shore) Route I-81 (western shore)

Physical Characteristics

area	51,072 acres
shoreline	54.7 miles
elevation	369 feet
maximum depth	55 feet
mean depth	22 feet
bottom type	sand, silt, gravel, rubble
mean thermocline depth . .	Oneida Lake is nearly homothermal

Chemical Characteristics

water clarity	some turbidity due to suspended organic material and algae
pH	alkaline
oxygen	usually good throughout the lake. Localized areas of depleted oxygen levels occur during extended periods of hot, calm weather in the deepest parts of the lake.

Plant Life

Extensive weed beds are found in all of the major bays of the lake. The weed growth is especially luxuriant west of Constantia on the north shore and west of Chittenango Creek on the south shore. Numerous patches of weeds are also found: north of the dredged channel west of Wantry Island, north of Wantry Island, around Pancake Shoal, east of the dumping grounds, around Willard Isle and around Messenger Shoal.

Significant algae blooms occur here in the early summer.

Boat Launch Sites

1. Tri-Bridge Marina, Inc. - Route 81 and Weber Road, Brewerton. Double hard surface ramps, gas, marine supplies - fee.
2. Bradbury's Boatel - County Road 37, Brewerton. Hard surface ramp, marine supplies, gas - fee.
3. Big Bay Marina - RD 1, Camic Road, Central Square. Hard surface ramp, rentals, marine supplies, gas, bait, tackle - fee.
4. Charlies Boat Livery - McLoud Road, West Monroe. Single ramp, rentals, bait, tackle - fee.
5. Johnson Bay Marina - McLoud Road, West Monroe. Single hard surface ramp, rentals, gas, marine supplies, bait, tackle - fee.
6. DEC Fishing Access Site - at Three Mile Bay Wildlife Management Area off Toad Harbor Road, West Monroe. Gravel ramp, parking - no charge.
7. Constantia Cove - Route 49, Constantia. Double ramps, rentals, bait, tackle - fee.
8. Constantia Marina - Saint George St., Constantia. Single hard surface ramp, gas - fee.
9. Scott's Bait and Tackle - Route 49, Constantia. Single ramp, rentals, bait, tackle - fee.
10. Spruce Grove Marina - Route 49, Constantia. Single hard surface ramp, rentals, gas, bait tackle - fee.
11. DEC Fishing Access Site - off Route 49, one mile east of Cleveland. Multiple hard surface ramps, parking for 30 cars and trailers - no charge.
12. Kirshner's Fishing Camp - RD 1, Drive 18, Cleveland. Single hard surface ramp, gas, rentals, bait, tackle - fee.
13. Varner's Three Pines Boat Livery and Cottages - 2054 Lake Shore Road, RD #2, Blossvale. Single hard surface ramp, rentals, gas, bait, tackle - fee.
14. Pioneer Marina - Pioneer Avenue, Sylvan Beach. Single hard surface ramp - fee.
15. Skinner's Harbour - Sylvan Beach. Single hard surface ramp, marine supplies, gas - fee.
16. Holmes Marina - Oneida Street, Verona Beach. Hard surface ramp - fee.
17. Sylvan Beach Boat Yard - East Willow Avenue, Verona Beach. Marine Supplies, gas. There is an informal launch site adjacent to the marina where Route 13 crosses the canal - no charge.
18. Marion Manor - 104 RD #4, Canastota. Hard surface ramp, rentals, marine supplies, gas, bait, tackle - fee.
19. Oneida Lake Marina - Route 31, Canastota. Double hard surface ramp, marine supplies, gas, bait, tackle - fee.
20. Johnnie's Pier 31 Restaurant and Marina - RD #2, off Route 31, Canastota. Hard surface ramp - fee.
21. Hughes Harbor - off Route 31 on South Bay, Canastota. Single ramp (small boats only), rentals - fee.
22. Thrall's Lakeport Marina - Route 31, Lakeport. Double gravel ramps, rentals, marine supplies, gas, bait, tackle - fee.
23. Fremac Marine - Route 31, RD #1, Bridgeport. Single hard surface ramp, marine supplies - fee.
24. Doug's Rent-A-Boat - Palmer Drive, Bridgeport. Gravel ramp, rentals, bait, tackle - fee.
25. South Shore Fisherman Access Site - off Route 31, one mile east of Bridgeport. Double hard surface ramps, parking for 35 cars and trailers - no charge.
26. Fisher Bay Marina - 6114 Barrett Road, Bridgeport. Single hard surface ramp, marine supplies, gas, repairs - fee.
27. Anchorage Marina - 9503 Hitchcock Point Road, Bridgeport. Ramp, marine supplies, gas - fee.
28. Cayman Marina - 8414 Tuttle Road, Bridgeport. Single ramp, marine supplies, gas - fee.
29. Boats A-Float - Murry Drive RD #1, Clay. Single hard surface ramp, marine supplies, gas, bait, tackle - fee.
30. Maple Bay Marina - Lake Shore Road, RD #1, Clay. Single hard surface ramp, gas - fee.
31. Nelson's Boat Livery - 8534 Lake Shore Road, Clay. Hard surface ramp, rentals - fee.
32. Shady Grove Boat Livery - 8548 Lake Shore Road, Clay. Single hard surface ramp, rentals, marine supplies, bait, tackle - fee.
33. Captain's Cove - 6724 Lake Shore Road, Cicero. Double hard surface ramps, marine supplies, bait - fee.
34. Martino's Restaurant - Lake Shore Road, Cicero. Double gravel ramps - fee.
35. Spear Boat Livery - 5681 Lake Shore Road, Cicero. Single hard surface ramp, rentals - fee.
36. Aero Marina - Conway, Inc. - 9080 Beach Road, Brewerton. Single hard surface ramp, marine supplies, gas - fee.
37. Oneida Shores County Park - Bartell Road, Brewerton. Hard surface ramp open 6 a.m. to dark - fee.
28. Theisen Marine Sales - Theisen Road, Brewerton. Hard surface ramp, marine supplies - fee.
39. Brewerton Boat Yard - Bennett Street, Brewerton. Hard surface ramp, marine supplies, gas - fee.

Species Information

Walleye . . . . abundant; growth rate fair

Oneida and walleye. The two words are almost inseparable. There probably isn't a walleye fisherman worthy of the name in this part of the world that hasn't fished Oneida Lake, or at least seriously entertained the thought.

Oneida Lake's reputation as the finest walleye fishery in New ork State, and one of the finest in the United States, is based on very solid facts. Constant monitoring of the lake by the Cornell Research Station at Shackelton Point, under the direction of Dr. John Forney, and by the DEC gives a clear picture of the long term status of the fishery. In recent years the population of adult walleye in the lake has been as low as 200,000 and as high as 1,000,000. The state tries to maintain an average of 500,000 adult walleye. That comes out to an average of 10 walleye per acre. Imagine what the concentrations are when these fish are schooled up. It's nothing short of mind-boggling!

The walleye fishing on Oneida suffers from some of the same problems as perch fishing. Fluctuations in the size of the adult population seriously affect the quality of the fishery. Below 100,000 the fishing can be poor, especially if there has been a big hatch of bait fish in the lake. Above 500,000 it can be like fishing in a barrel, but the fish will be a bit small. But even with a large population of walleye the fishing can be adversely affected if the lake is overwhelmed by baitfish. A well-fed walleye, like a well-fed yellow perch, is not an easy fish to catch, no matter how good your presentation is. To minimize fluctuations the DEC changes the legal size limit on walleye caught here, reducing it from 15 to 12 inches when the fish become too numerous.

To guarantee a large population of walleye Oneida Lake is stocked each year to the tune of 100,000,000 fry, the vast majority of which are simply eaten. These fry come from the state walleye hatchery at Constantia, which supplies all of the walleye that are stocked in New York State. There is talk of building a facility at the hatchery for rearing fingerling walleye, which has been a dream of fishery managers for years. Recently developed rearing techniques now make this possible. When such a facility will go on line is anyone's guess, but it could be a boon to walleye fishing throughout the state.

The walleye in this lake grow rather slowly. A legal size fish (15 inches) is about 5 years old. Occasionally females will get up to 28 inches and tip the scales at 6 to 8 pounds, and that's about the limit for this lake. The reason the walleye grow so slowly here is that their diet consists largely of protein in the form of small yellow perch. While this might keep their growth rate down, it does wonders for their flavor. Oneida Lake walleye are especially sweet tasting because of their diet. Some people claim they are the best tasting walleye in the world! They could be right.

In a normal year Oneida Lake walleye spawn in late March and early April. Their spawning runs into the creeks and onto gravel bars are triggered by water temperatures in the low 40's. Usually the walleye have for the most part left the streams by opening day, but if ice-out has been late or the spring abnormally cold their spawning will be delayed and many fish will still be in the streams when the season opens. Significant runs of fish occur in all of the major tributaries of the lake including Scriba Creek, the Barge Canal and its tributary Fish Creek, Oneida Creek, Canaseraga Creek, and Chittenango Creek. A large number of walleye also run to the large gravel bars in the Oneida River or spawn on the gravel bars in the lake.

When walleye season opens the fish are often pretty sluggish due to cold temperatures and won't be biting very well, but by May 15 they will be pretty active.

There are conflicting opinions as to where the best fishing will be found come opening day. Tony Buffa, a highly regarded charter boat captain whose knowledge of this lake is the result of two decades of personally fishing on it, prefers the creek mouths or in the lake proper just in front of the creeks. He recommends fishing the mouths of Oneida Creek (due to poor access you should approach this area by boat), Canaseraga Creek and Chittenango Creek. The Sylvan Beach Pier at the mouth of the Barge Canal is also very productive. Unfortunately, the very best fishing area on the pier is posted due to disrepair and you can be ticketed for being there. Funds are being sought by the Oneida Lake Association to repair the pier, but in the meantime your best bet would be to fish from a boat in that area. There is a boat launch site nearby where Route 13 crosses the canal. When fishing in the lake in front of any of these creeks don't make the mistake of taking the words "in front of" too literally. Tony says the fish will normally be found in good numbers up to a quarter of a mile either side of the outflow.

Jigging is the most popular method for taking walleyes from the creek mouths. Most fish will be taken on 1/4 to 3/8 ounce bucktail jigs. The jig can be tipped with a worm or minnow or fished clean. Popular colors include black and white, brown and white, brown and yellow, and black and orange. Most of the water near the creek mouths is less than 10 feet deep. If you find that you have to move into water any deeper than this you might consider going to a half ounce jig.

Tom Chiotti, a senior aquatic biologist at the DEC region 7 office in Cortland who manages Oneida Lake, believes that the best early season fishing for big walleye takes place in waters up to 30 feet deep. He specifically mentions the waters around Dakin Shoal, Grassy Shoal, Pancake Shoal and Wantry Island as being especially good early on. The bar just west of Wantry Island is also productive just as the season opens. The same jigs that work in the shallows can also be used in these deep areas, the only difference being that they'll need to be at least a half ounce in size.

Aside from the creek mouths and shoals, good numbers of walleye will also be found early in the season on the shallow gravel bars of the lake and on rocky points. On the south shore of the lake Long Point is a very popular area come opening day. Located on the western end of Oneida, it is a finger of rock that extends quite a ways out from shore. This spot will hold walleye for about three weeks into the season. Some people like to troll this area, using Rebels and Rapalas in silver and black to match the gizzard shad, or in perch colors. On overcast or windy days you can flatline successfully here, but on calm, clear days you'll need to put a split-shot on your line to get down to where the fish are. If trolling isn't your game, anchor just off the point and work the area with jigs or cast with Rapalas.

Moving east along the south shore, other productive early season areas include Norcross Point, the gravel bars between Shackelton Point and Lakeport Bay, and Lewis Point. These are all very popular areas to troll in the first weeks of the season. The same holds true in these areas as on Long Point. On windy or overcast days the fish will move into the shallows, but on calm, clear days you need to move out into deeper water. In the case of Lewis Point the walleye will be found on the drop-offs around the point on calm days.

The north shore of Oneida Lake has extensive stretches of gravel and sand pockets, and practically the whole shoreline is good for trolling in the spring. The closer you are to a flowing tributary the better your chances are of being near a significant concentration of fish. Some of the streams that are dry beds in the summer have a flow in the spring due to run-off. An especially good area on the north shore is the Cleveland Bar, a quarter mile out from Cleveland. This bar has very good structure for walleyes. They like the shade that the deep water just off the bar provides and the easy access to food that the shelf itself offers. This particular bar is good for walleye all year long. Sometimes the fish will be there and sometimes they won't, but the Cleveland Bar is always one of the first areas you should check when looking for walleyes in this lake.

There are two areas on the north shore that deserve special attention. The first is Scriba Creek. This stream, which provides the water for the Oneida Hatchery, gets the third largest run of walleye of all the lake's tributaries (Fish Creek gets the largest, followed by Chittenango Creek). Unlike other streams where the fish can run upstream for miles, on Scriba Creek the walleye can only run up several hundred yards. They are prevented from moving further up by a dam. This means that the fish are forced to leave the stream almost as fast as they move into it. Some walleye will be found in front of the creek mouth early in the season, but the vast majority will move out to the shoals or spread out along the shore line of Three Mile Bay. Trolling the shallows of this bay in the month of May with 9S or 7S Rapalas is very popular and productive.

The second area is Big Bay. A lot of walleye spawn on the gravel bars of the Oneida River, and when these fish return to the

Carolyn Buffa with a stringer of Oneida Lake walleye. The walleye in this lake aren't big, but they are abundant and their flavor is superb. Photo courtesy Captain Tony Buffa.

lake many of them will hold over for a while in Big Bay to rest or feed. This bay is usually very productive for the first 2 to 3 weeks of the season. Trolling in Big Bay is very popular, but jigging will take just as many fish.

I've already mentioned the fact that Fish Creek at the eastern end of the lake gets the best spawning run of all the lake's tributaries. What I haven't told you is what these fish do when they leave the creek and move back out into the lake. Immediately after spawning tremendous numbers of walleye will converge on the sandy bottomed areas off Sylvan Beach. This information was relayed to me by Tony Buffa who has seen this phenomenon several times and has experienced the incredible fishing that can take place. If you're lucky enough to be in the Sylvan beach area when this occurs, forget the jigs and the Rapalas. Drifting worms right on the bottom will catch you all the fish you can handle. This isn't the kind of event you can plan on experiencing every year. It probably occurs more often before the season opens than after, and it only lasts a short period of time.

You might have the impression that, with a few exceptions, it's necessary to fish all of the areas described thus far from a boat. Certainly fishing from a boat has its advantages. Literally the whole of the lake becomes open to you, and some techniques such as trolling, can only be done from a boat. But much of this early season walleye fishing takes place in areas shallow enough to be accessible using nothing more than a good pair of chest waders. This is especially true of the east end of the lake.

The early season shallow water fishing only lasts three to four weeks. By early June the walleye will begin moving out toward the deeper areas of the lake. But don't get the idea that this is a sudden migration of fish from the shallows to the deep central portions of the lake. It's important to realize that this occurs in stages. Initially, the walleye are prompted to move off-shore by rising water temperatures, and they are only going to move as far as they need to in order to find amenable temperatures. They will spread out over the deeper portions of the lake only when their food base, which usually consists primarily of small yellow perch, move out of the shallows. These yellow perch spread out over the deeper areas of the lake and

become demersal, or bottom dwelling, in late June. Thus, for a period of several weeks the walleye are going to be found in areas fairly close to shore that have good structure and deep water nearby. The deep water provides shade and cool temperatures, while the structure, be it a sand bar or shoal, provides access to food. The proximity to the near-shore waters also allows the walleye to make foraging runs into the shallows at night to feed.

Once you have determined that the walleye have moved out of the shore areas, they will be found in most locations that incorporate the conditions described above. But there are some key areas to consider. Lakeport Shoal is very productive during this intermediate period. Work the south side of the shoal first, then concentrate on the north side.

Another important location at this time is the north side of Dutchman Island and the bar that extends off the east tip of the island. North of the island is shallow and mud bottomed and holds few fish of any type (Tony Buffa refers to it derisively as "Clam Bay"), but the south side is ideal for walleye.

Just north of Hitchcock Point, where Chittenango Creek empties into the lake, is a major shoal known as Eel Isle. This four acre shoal is marked off with a ring of buoys and is extremely trecherous to navigate over if you go inside of the markers. Parts of the shoal are only about two feet under water, but the edges quickly drop off to a depth of 10 to 20 feet, and hold good numbers of walleye through the month of June. An added attraction are the large patches of Oneida Lake pancakes which surround Eel Isle. Bait fish are drawn to the area by the freshwater shrimp that inhabit the pancakes, which in turn draw in walleye.

As stated earlier, the principle forage base of the walleye, small yellow perch, migrate out to the deeper portions of the lake around the end of June. This triggers a similar response in the walleye, and from the end of June until early September the bulk of the walleye fishing is going to take place in the deep open waters of the east half of the lake, or around the major shoals in the central and western portions of the lake.

When structure fishing, Shackelton Shoal is a key area to check. The shoal is denoted by buoys 121, 123, and 125. North of the buoys you have a deep water channel. South of the markers are two miles undulating shoals that Tony Buffa calls "walleye condominiums." Tony likes to drift fish over this shoal in a west wind, but Chuck Rogers at the Brewerton Bait Shop recommends an east wind, at least when fishing over the eastern tip of the shoal. Shackelton Shoal is such a fish haven that you can pick up walleye, yellow perch and smallmouth bass on the same drift. The walleye will hit on worms and Dixie spinners, while the perch and bass can be taken on crayfish.

Dakin Shoal, just north of buoy 128, is another good place to drift fish. It holds good numbers of walleye and smallmouth bass. The east end of this structure has a fairly abrupt drop-off which is especially productive when drift fished in an east wind.

A little west of Dakin are Grassy Shoal and Pancake Shoal. A deep narrow cut runs between these two shoals. This is an ideal area to drift fish over in an east wind, particularly when other areas aren't producing. The deep trough seems to be a natural holding area for walleye when lake conditions aren't good for fishing in other parts of Oneida.

Further west are Dunham Island and Frenchman Island. There is an excellent drift along the northeast side of these islands, where a fairly pronounced drop-off almost always holds fish. Walleye will at times be taken on the south side of the islands, but the drop-off is more tapered and holds fewer fish.

On the north shore of the lake are two sites that, while resembling the late spring holding areas discussed previously, will have significant numbers of walleye all summer long. The first, Cleveland Bar, has already been described. The second is Willard Isle, which is just southwest of Bernhards Bay. A very picturesque spot, it can be difficult to locate until you are almost on top of it. You'll know you're there when you see the terns standing on the isle. There are good drop-offs all the way around Willard Isle. The north side supports a sizeable grass bed. Yellow perch and smallmouth bass are commonly found in the shade of ese weeds, while the walleye are more often found on the south de, which as the greater drop-off.

The only significant piece of open water structure on the east d of the lake is Messenger Shoal, at Buoy 113. Messenger has e kind of structure that makes it impossible to get onto the nter of the shoal with anything but a very shallow draft boat. e shallow areas are marked by spar and can buoys. There are ry good weed beds that grow up along the edge of the shoal, oviding ideal structure for fish. Because of this, and because of e fact that it is essentially the only structure available to walleye the eastern end, there are almost always some fish on or very ar Messenger Shoal. There is also a lot of pancake around it, aking it even more attractive to the fish. Needless to say, this ould always be one of the first areas you investigate in the mmer months.

Though most of the walleye fishing after the end of June kes place far off-shore, there are conditions that can arise hich will bring the fish scurrying back to the near-shore waters. ne is the depletion of oxygen in the deep regions of the lake. rictly speaking, Oneida Lake does not have a thermocline, but it not truly homothermal. Some stratification does occur, rticularly in July and August during extended periods of calm eather. Normally, winds cause wave action, which charges the rface waters with oxygen and mixes them with deeper water yers. When this doesn't happen, decaying plant matter (algae) rns up much of the oxygen in the deeper layers. The walleye e then forced out of these areas. Many will make foraging runs to the shallows for short periods to feed.

Even if they don't have to contend with low oxygen levels, me walleye will leave the deep water and move into the near-ore waters at dusk and dawn to feed for short periods. This is ompted by the appearance in late July or early August of great mbers of baitfish along the shoreline, particularly gizzard shad.

In Tony Buffa's considerable experience, he has noticed that u are much more likely to catch a large walleye in the summer orking these shallows than you are fishing the deep open aters. The reason for this is probably the fact that when the zzard shad move on shore they are too large for the younger alleye to feed on. These smaller walleye are thus forced to main out in the open waters of the lake to feed on midge larvae d small yellow perch. The larger walleye find the gizzard shad ore efficient to feed on from an energy requirement standpoint d therefore will tend to remain in the shallows. During these eriods you should concentrate along near-shore weed lines, sing small crankbaits, such as the Rebel Double Deep Shad in llow perch or shad markings, or the Rapala Shad Rap.

Before getting into some of the techniques used to take alleyes from Oneida Lake in the summer months, I'd like to scuss for a moment some of the more common mistakes that e made by many anglers when they come here.

Probably the most common mistake that anglers make on is lake is being overgeared. You have to keep in mind that these e small fish, the vast majority of whom are going to weigh less an two pounds. Many people come here rigged up with 12 or 17 . test line, steel leaders and big snap swivels. That might be propriate on some lakes or rivers, but not on Oneida. These sh, which are not only small but line shy to boot, can be taken on to 8 lb. test line. Steel leaders really aren't necessary (walleye ave conical shaped teeth, which are not good for cutting, as pposed to the knife-edged teeth of a northern pike or chain ckerel which are designed for cutting), and if you're going to se a swivel use the smallest one practical.

Another mistake fishermen commonly make is to concen-ate too much of their effort in only one area. Just because one nd bar or drop-off was productive yesterday is no reason to esume that it will hold fish today. Walleye are not territorial and ll move where they must to find food. If an area that looks omising doesn't produce any action within half an hour, move a different area. There is no sense in fishing where the fish en't available.

Surprisingly, there are occasions when it's a waste of time to sh in areas that are literally carpeted with walleye! If you're

printing masses of fish close to the bottom on your recorder but not getting any hits, most likely you've located a school of walleye that have fed heavily and recently. Normally, the walleye will suspend when they are actively feeding. They might be just a little off the bottom, or they could be in the upper layers of the water column, but generally speaking, they will not be right on the bottom, though there are some exceptions to this. Usually when you are marking fish on the bottom they are well fed and resting, and a walleye in that condition can be almost impossible to catch. You can't induce them to strike by appealing to their sense of territoriality, by aggravating them or by threatening their young. It's best simply to move on and look for suspended fish.

But don't be satisfied with just any suspended fish. It can be great fun catching 20 or 30 walleye in a days outing, but at the end of the day, if you haven't caught any legal size fish you're still going to have that empty feeling in the pit of your stomach. The walleye in Oneida Lake school up by year class, so the fish in a particular school are all going to be roughly the same size. If you're picking up nothing but 13 or 14 inch walleye, difficult as it might be, you should move on.

Not paying attention to the weather is another common error that can make walleye fishing on Oneida Lake difficult. Because the lake is so shallow (average depth — 22 ft.) it and the fish in it are very responsive to changing weather conditions. The absolutely worst time to fish Oneida is when a sudden calm period follows several days of constant wind. This lake will lay flat very quickly and the walleye fishing will come to a halt almost immediately. The only alternative you have to getting off the lake is to go to deep trolling methods using lead core line or downriggers. You can get the fish to hit, but it isn't going to be very productive. They prefer to feed when the water is choppy.

The best time to fish Oneida for walleyes is when a few calm days are immediately followed by a rising barometer and a northwest wind. A 10 to 15 knot wind from this direction will give you a 1½ to 2 foot chop with just enough white water to mix in additional oxygen to a depth of about 12 feet. This brings the fish up off the bottom and the increased oxygen level apparently triggers a feeding response. This, plus the fact that the walleye have not fed for several days due to the just ended calm, can make for a fishing bonanza! About the only thing that can ruin the fishing under these conditions is if the lake has a big overabundance of baitfish, or it becomes too windy and kicks up a 2 to 4 foot chop.

Finally, human nature being what it is, it's not easy to set aside the tackle and techniques that only a week ago were working so effectively. But as the conditions on the lake change, it is critical that you respond to those changes by modifying your tackle and techniques accordingly. What worked so well on opening day will be entirely inappropriate by June 1.

It is usually unnecessary to troll for walleye after the third or fourth week of the season. Although there are fishermen who troll here all season long, there are more productive methods. From late May through early September the lion's share of the fish are going to be caught on Dixie spinners and drifted worms.

Tony Buffa prefers to drift worms and has refined the technique in a number of ways to make it exceedingly effective. The rig he uses is very simple. He ties a #4 gold Eagle Claw hook with a turned down eye to the end of a 6 lb. test line. The gold is important as it acts as an attractant. Using a three-way swivel, Tony attaches a 6 inch dropper line 18 to 24 inches above the hook. To the dropper line he adds split-shot, the exact amount depending on the speed of the drift and the depth.

When Tony starts his drift, he sets his rods in rod holders so that they are at a 45° angle to the plane of the water. He uses just enough weight on the dropper line so that at the start of the drift the worm is barely on the bottom and the line comes off the rod tip at a 90° angle. Initially, the worm will drift along the bottom, but slowly it will begin to rise due to the resistance of the water against the line. After two or three minutes the worm will have ascended to about mid-depth. It should then be reeled in and the drift started over. The advantage of this system is that it checks not only the near-bottom waters, but also the middle waters where feeding walleye often suspend.

When baiting the hook, Tony hooks the worm about ⅛ inch from the head. By not having a lot of worm bunched up on the hook you get a more natural presentation. When a walleye takes the bait, don't set the hook immediately. You'll only tear the hook out of the worm and give the fish a free meal. Wait five to ten seconds, allowing the fish time to take in all of the bait. Then set the hook.

Usually the above method is used in shallow water (10 to 20 feet) along shoals and bars. If you find that after drifting for a mile or so along a shoal you don't get any serious action, try moving out to deeper water (20 to 30 feet).

Drifting with Dixie spinners is another popular method for taking Oneida Lake walleyes in the summer. Tipped with a nightcrawler and slowly worked along the bottom these spinners can be nearly as productive as a plain drifted worm. The major drawbacks to using them is that you're apt to lose a few of these bottom bouncing rigs and they cost more than the equally effective #4 hook.

In recent years some fishermen have begun using down-riggers on Oneida. This equipment can be used throughout the deeper portions of the lake. Tom Chiotti points out that they are especially productive in the waters between buoys 109 and 111, 119 and 123 and 127 and 129. They are also useful for taking the suspended walleyes that move into the eastern basin in late August. However, most of the people I spoke with had reservations about using this type of equipment on this lake. They pointed out that the majority of walleye in the lake are so small that they often fail to release the line from the downrigger when they hit. They also thought that the use of so much sophisticated equipment was uncalled for given the fact that these fish are so readily available using much simpler rigs. They also felt this way about the use of side planers here. But there are times when downriggers are the only way to go. This is particularly true on calm days when drifting is impossible and the fish are in deep water.

Because of their ability to see in what we would consider to be near-total darkness, walleyes are as likely to feed at night as in the day. Beginning at dusk they start moving onto shallow portions of shoals or bars, or even up along the shoreline. They can be taken in a number of ways. Trolling the shallows with Rapala type lures is very effective. Before it gets too dark drifted worms will still catch fish, but at night Dixie spinners will be more effective. The blade of the spinner serves as an attractant by sending out vibrations that the fish can easily detect with its lateral line sense organ.

There is a small group of anglers here who fish in deep water at night for walleyes. The method they use is very similar to the one used on Keuka Lake and Canandaigua Lakae to take lake trout at night. A light is held over the water to attract bait fish, which in turn attracts the walleye. Dangling nightcrawlers, minnows or leeches over the side, they fish the entire water column. This method is very sporadic. You can go for hours without a hit, but if you manage to attract the attention of a foraging school of walleye the action can be mighty fast.

In early September there is a marked decline in the ability of drifted worms and Dixie spinners to catch walleye. Quarter ounce bucktail jigs, crankbaits and minnows (small silver shiners, buckeye minnows etc.) then become the bait of choice. These can be used in the same drifting or trolling mode as was used with drifted worms or spinners. Some anglers prefer to anchor over structure and fan cast with jigs or crankbaits or still fish with live minnows under a bobber.

The Cornell Research Station and the DEC have both indicated that there is evidence of a migration of walleye toward the deep open waters of the eastern half of the lake at the end of summer. The reason or reasons for this are uncertain. It might be in response to a need for cooler temperatures, or it could be a need to move closer to their principle spawning area, Fish Creek. A similar pre-spawn fall migration of walleye occurs in the Susquehanna River. This migration certainly does not involve all of the fish. There are so many walleye in Oneida that migratory

patterns are only vaguely discernable. These patterns are eve less well-defined when there is an overabundance of baitfish the lake, such as occured with gizzard shad in 1987.

In early October Oneida Lake begins to cool off. As it doe many walleye begin moving back toward the near-shore water By late October you will want to concentrate you're fishing effor in water 4 to 8 feet deep. The walleye will remain in thes shallows until the lake begins to freeze over.

While most near-shore areas will hold walleye in the fall, th most productive locations are where rocky points extend out in the water. Some of the best fishing will be found off Damon Poir Shackelton Point, Larkin Point, Bushnell Point and Lewis Poir These sites should all be checked when the south shore of th lake is choppy. Work each point with crankbaits or jigs for r more than 30 minutes. If you don't get any action in that amount time move on. It's almost guaranteed that a couple of these poin will have a feeding school of walleye on it when there is a cho along the south shore.

A very popular method on Oneida for taking walleye October and November is to go to a launch site and fish just shore in waders from 6 to 9 pm. Large numbers of walleye cruis the shoreline in the evening, searching for schools of minnow This is particularly effective in areas that have a stoney bottor

The pier at Sylvan Beach can be extremely productive in th fall. It's not uncommon for walleye to move into the lower reache of the larger tributaries, such as Fish Creek, to feed on minnow in the evening (6 pm - 9 pm). Bucktail jigs and small crankbaits perch colors are used to catch these fish as they migrate in an out of the stream. The same thing occurs to a lesser extent Cleveland and the pier there is very popular in the fall.

All of the areas mentioned above will be productive until th lake begins to freeze over, unless the lake is overrun by yello perch, white perch or gizzard shad. If yellow perch or white perc are the problem the fishing can be bad for up to a year. If gizzar shad are overabundant, the fishing could pick up again in the lat fall or early winter. Gizzard shad are not tolerant of co temperatures and a significant percentage will die off when th lake begins to freeze.

Oneida is one of the most popular lakes for ice fishing in Nev York State. Approximately 10% of the fishing activity here take place after the lake freezes over, resulting in about 20% of th annual catch. The lake normally freezes over and has safe ice b the first week of January, but in a really cold December safe ic will be formed by Christmas.

Access to the lake in the winter is limited at best. Priva marinas will occasionally allow parking, but it's not somethin you can count on. The best access is provided by the five publi launch sites on the lake. They are located at Godfrey Point, Thre Mile Bay, Oneida Shores County Park, Shackelton Point and th Route 13 bridge crossing of the Barge Canal at Sylvan Beach. I addition, there is a fisherman right-of-way, with parking, on Ta Bay off Route 49 and a fisherman parking area in Jewell. All these ares are good only if they are kept plowed. Anglers shoul be aware of the fact that on many of the perimeter roads off-roa parking is restricted, and is strictly enforced by the state and loca police.

Because many of the hard water fishing areas are quite distance from the access sites, especially after the fish move ou into deep water, some enterprising entrepreneurs have opene shuttle services. They use everything from flat bottomed boat towed by snowmobiles and tractors to canoes pulled by sma planes (air boats)! These services change from year to year. It's good idea to contact a bait and tackle shop in the area you wis to fish for current information on who is providing these service

Generally speaking, if the walleye fishing was good in th fall, it will also be good in the winter. The most productive period seem to be just as safe ice is forming over the shallows, and fron the end of February to ice-out. The interim period will certainly b productive if the season is good, but the fishing does drop o because the walleye become somewhat lethargic in mid-season

The shallow areas of the lake are the first to freeze over, an for a period of about two weeks they provide some of the bes

When ice fishing, warm clothing and protection from the wind are prime concerns. Portable shelters, such as the one pictured above, are easy to build. They serve as equipment lockers as well as wind breaks. For warmth, layered clothing works best. Photo courtesy Fred David.

walleye fishing of the season. The ice cuts off a lot of the sunlight, providing a haven for baitfish, which in turn draw in the walleyes. Nearly any bay that has a covering of ice will have some walleye cruising underneath, and some of them will provide truly outstanding fishing. Big Bay is often the first area on the lake to have safe ice. Its shallow depth (average depth 8 feet) and the relatively low influx of water from its tributaries cause the bay to cool off and freeze quickly. Walleye will be found in Big Bay for a period of about two weeks after firm ice forms. The walleye fishing in the bay during this period will be good, but not great. The shallows near Constantia, South Bay and the area around Lewis Point are also popular and productive early in the ice fishing season.

The utmost caution should be exercised when venturing out on this early ice. It may not have had time to build up to a safe thickness everywhere. Also, shifting winds can cause water pressure to build up under the ice, causing cracks.

The pursuit of walleye begins at daybreak over shoals or drop-offs. The true walleye connoisseur will also plan a few nights on the ice when the walleyes are reported to be active.

Not long after the bays freeze over the entire lake will develop a layer of ice. It doesn't take long for safe ice to form, and in a normal year Oneida will be covered by about two feet of ice by mid-season. Even in the dead of winter, however, you must be careful when venturing out on the ice. There are numerous springs that bubble up from the bottom of the lake. These can cause localized weak spots in the ice, and in some cases can actually cause small areas to melt completely.

When the lake becomes completely ice covered the shallow water ice fishing for walleyes comes to a halt. They quickly move out to deeper areas of the lake, often, but not always, around structure. Once they move off-shore the walleyes will always be found in deep water, no less than 25 feet and preferably 30 to 40 feet deep. And unlike the warmer months, they will almost never suspend. Even when feeding the walleyes will be within 6 to 10 inches of the bottom.

Usually the same areas that are productive in the summer months will also produce well in the winter. Noted winter hot spots include buoy 109, Messenger Shoal, the north side of Lakeport Shoal, the Cleveland Bar, Shackelton Shoal and the south side of Dakin Shoal.

One very popular area for winter walleyes that is not structure oriented is the deep water about one mile out from Sylvan Beach. As I noted earlier, there is evidence of a migration of some fish toward the eastern end of the lake in the late summer. They remain in the general area through the winter and much of the spring, providing some fine angling opportunities.

Some of the very best ice fishing takes place over large concentrations of pancakes. These craggy nodules are home to large schools of crustaceans, which are an important link in the food chain that ends with the walleye. These are especially productive areas when the bait fish populations are suppressed. Rather than being forced to range over wide areas of the lake, thus providing ready forage to the walleye, a disproportionately large percentage of the baitfish will be concentrated over these feeding areas, attracting the walleyes. Significant tracts of pancakes are scattered throughout the lake, but there are three particularly large concentrations. One is located north of the permanent base of buoy 130, another is found in the deep channel north of Shackelton Shoal, and the third is found 1½ miles straight out from Lestina Beach Road, just west of Lakeport.

Once you've determined the general area of the lake you want to fish, there are several things you can do to increase your chances of success. Naturally, locating the exact position of the walleyes would help. As is the case on most frozen lakes, one of the easiest ways to do this is to stick with the crowd. People don't usually gather where the fish aren't hitting. But beware! This can be a serious mistake. If enough people gather over a certain area, all of their activity (cutting holes, running snowmobiles etc.) can spook the fish and drive them right out of the area. This is especially possible in shallow areas. So make sure that people are still catching fish before you set your gear up.

Another aid to locating fish is the depth finder. These will help you locate the bigger schools and tell you what depth they are at if they are suspended. Most modern sonar units will read through clear, solid ice. You don' t have to cut a hole. Simply use a non-freezing solution, such as windshield washer fluid, to create a smooth bottomed puddle on the surface. The transducer will be able to transmit and receive signals clearly through this.

An important point to keep in mind before you set out in search of winter walleyes is that light affects them in the winter much as it does in the summer. They prefer to feed during periods of low light, i.e. dusk and dawn. Another period during which the fishing can be good is just prior to the arrival of an approaching winter storm. The rapidly decreasing light levels that accompany such storms has been shown to often trigger significant feeding activity in the fish.

There are two methods used to take walleye through the ice, and both are relatively easy to master. One is through the use of tip-ups. At one time these were much more common on the lake than they are today. But the advent of snowmobiling and the resulting mobility it gave ice anglers led to excess fishing pressure here and elsewhere. Now regulations stipulate that no more than five tip-ups may be used at a time, that the name and address of the owner must be on the tip-up, and the operator must be present when lines are in the water. Tip-ups baited with big buckeye minnows or silver shiners are highly effective. Some anglers on Oneida Lake feel that minnows are most effective early in the winter, though they will catch fish all season long.

Although removal of all tip-ups is necessary at the end of each outing, many fishermen continue to observe an unwritten rule that all tip-ups tilt to the north. This allows lost fishermen, especially during a whiteout, to establish direction. It is recommended that all fishermen include a compass as standard gear for winter fishing.

The other method used in taking walleyes here in the winter is jig fishing. This is a little more complicated than minnow fishing with a tip-up, but over the season it's also probably a bit more productive. When fishing with jigs in the winter use a fairly stiff 3 to 3½ foot rod, with extra large eyes to prevent ice build-up. Some people recommend 8 to 10 pound line for this type of activity, but the size of the fish in this lake really don't warrant line over 6 pounds. Though a few big females might tip the scales at 8 pounds in the winter, they are few and far between. If you are lucky enough to bring an especially big fish to the hole, don't make the mistake of trying to horse the fish up onto the ice with the light line. Gaff hooks are allowed here in the winter and make for a surer landing.

Of all the jigs used on Oneida, the Swedish Pimple is probably the most popular (½ - ¾ oz.). Half ounce bucktail jigs and Russian jigs also produce well here. All of these can be fished clean, or they can be tipped with various baits. Minnows (either whole or cut in half), perch eyes, and walleye eyes can all be used. These not only appeal to the fish taste-wise, but help to camouflage the hook. Mousey grubs or spikes, two maggot-like larvae, can also be used. Some jigs, such as the delicately balanced Jigging Rapala, should be fished clean, otherwise you won't get the proper action out of the jig. All of these lures should be fished as close to the bottom as possible to be near the walleyes, unless you've determined that the fish are suspended.

The technique used to fish a jigging spoon is simple. Rapidly flick the spoon upward with the rod tip. Before it can start to descend drop the rod tip down so that the spoon and line can free fall. You get better action out of the lure this way. The fish seldom hit when the spoon is on the way up. Most often they will strike while it's falling or just after it stops. If after a normal period of time the slack isn't taken out of your line, the odds are a fish has taken the lure on the way down. Set the hook with a sharp upward lift of the rod. If the lure does take out all of the slack, gently raise the rod tip to see if a fish hit after the lure stopped falling. If not, wait about 10 seconds and repeat.

Some anglers feel that the most effective jig is a small fraction-of-an ounce dot or fly, which mirror nymphs or shrimp. These tiny creatures are a mainstay of the walleye's diet in the winter. They claim that for consistent catches these ultra-small jigs are unbeatable.

Smallmouth Bass .... abundant; growth rate fair

Like most of the game species found in Oneida Lake, smallmouth bass here exhibit rather slow growth rates. A majority of the adult smallmouth are 13 to 15 inches, a size they don't reach until age 5. The few fish that reach 20 inches are old fish indeed!

What Oneida Lake smallmouth lack in size they more than make up for in abundance. In a way, smallmouth are almost a protected species on this lake. Because of the overwhelming popularity of walleye and yellow perch here, relatively few anglers who come here pursue the bass, leaving the fishery nearly untapped. Thus, there is a real bonanza awaiting those fish-erman who come here looking for a lot of action from these scrappy fighters. The fishing for smallmouth is outstanding on Oneida from the first day of the season to the last.

The vast majority of smallmouth taken on Oneida Lake are caught in water 5 to 15 feet deep. Occasionally they are caught by walleye fishermen trolling the deeper parts of the lake, but these are only incidental fish. The portions of this lake deeper than 15 feet have bottoms consisting primarily of silt, sand and mud, and in water over 25 feet are extensive areas of hard bottom carpeted by Oneida Lake pancakes. Bottom types such as these offer the fish little in the way of structure. You can easily tell if a smallmouth was taken from the depths of the lake. They are unusually dark in color, almost brown. It seems that their coloration is a response to their exposure to sunlight.

Typically, the smallmouth in Oneida Lake are going to be found close to shore, on the shoals or on the shallows around the islands. Especially good are waters over extensive areas of rock and rubble. Exceptionally good fishing is found on the dumping grounds at the western end of the lake. Because the lake is part of the barge canal system, a navigation channel had to be dredged on the western end of the lake. All of the dredgings, consisting largely of gravel and sand, had to be returned to the lake, and so were deposited in areas designated as dumping grounds. The one located between Oneida Shores County Park and Muskrat Bay offers some of the best smallmouth fishing on the lake. Just out from the launch ramp on Muskrat Bay are numerous small mounds of gravel and rubble. The bass can be found in great numbers around these mounds all season long. The dumping ground mentioned above and the one just south of Big Bay are the two to concentrate on. Those located east of Dunham Island and east of Wantry Island are not known for holding large numbers of bass. Nor are the small dumping grounds on the east end of the lake.

Aside from the western dumping grounds, smallmouth bass can also be found in good numbers on many of the rocky points that extend out into the lake, such as Lewis Point, or the points that extend off islands, notably Dunham Island, Frenchman Island and Dutchman Island. The breakwater off Cleveland, which must be approached by boat, is also good at times, as is the drop-off just outside of Three Mile Bay. As far as the shoals are concerned, excellent bass fishing can be had nearly anywhere among the pinnacles of Shackelton Shoal, around Messenger Shoal, Dakin Shoal, Lakeport Shoal, Eel Isle and Willard Isle. When fishing the shoals concentrate your efforts on areas where there is a distinct drop-off rather than a tapered decline of the bottom.

One thing to keep in mind when fishing for smallmouth bass here is that these fish are nearly as likely to be found in or near weed beds as they are over shoals or on rocky outcroppings. Contrary to what many people think, smallmouth are not at all reluctant to take up residence in weedy areas if the conditions are right.

Unlike some of the other lakes covered in this book, the techniques used to catch smallmouth bass on Oneida Lake are fairly straightforward and simple. Early in the season small bucktail jigs (⅛ ounce) are very effective on smallmouth when worked along developing weed lines and along rocky ledges. Small crankbaits also work very well.

In July and August the technique most commonly employed on this lake to catch smallmouth bass is drift fishing with live crayfish. The rig is simple. Hook the crayfish through the tail and attach splits shot directly to the line 18 to 24 inches above the hook. Be sure to use enough weight to get the bait down to the bottom. A little too much weight isn't really a problem, but too little could result in the crayfish drifting well above where the bass are feeding, and with a very unnatural presentation. This method will take smallmouth from all of the areas mentioned above.

The wind plays a very important role in this type of fishing. The direction and speed of your drift are dependant on the wind. It can also be a critical factor to consider when deciding on exactly where to fish. On very windy days, when the lake has a good chop, many crayfish are dislodged from their hiding places on the rocky shallows around shoals, bars and islands. Because of the wave dynamics this occurs primarily on the downwind side of shoals and bars, but on the upwind (i.e. windward) side of islands. The bass are instinctively drawn to these disrupted areas to pick up an easy meal. The same effect can be produced by dragging an anchor or cinder block over these areas like anglers do on Lake Ontario.

An important point to keep in mind is that, while drift fishing is a productive method all season long, crayfish should only be used as bait until the end of August. By early September minnows become the principle food source for the smallmouth bass, walleye and yellow perch in Oneida Lake.

Of course, there are techniques other than drift fishing that can be used to take smallmouth from this lake. Fly fishing is one alternative that can put you on to some very fast action. During periods of low light (dusk, dawn and overcast days) smallmouth often come into very shallow water to feed. Bluegill poppers are almost irresistable to these aggressively feeding fish. When the bass have moved back out into deeper water leech patterns in claret, black and white, and crayfish patterns can be used with deadly effect.

Normally the best smallmouth fishing on a lake of this type occurs in October and early November, when the fish go on a feeding binge to fatten up for the winter months. On Oneida Lake this usually holds true, but not always. Periodically this lake produces tremendous numbers of bait fish. When the bass switch from feeding on crayfish to feeding on minnows, this over-abundance of bait fish can make the fishing all but impossible. The most recent occurance of this was in the fall of 1987 when the lake was inundated with gizzard shad.

Yellow Perch . . . . abundant; growth rate good

In terms of sheer numbers yellow perch are the dominant species in Oneida Lake, far surpassing the numbers of walleye and smallmouth bass. The population of perch in this lake fluctuates considerably. The adult population has been estimated at various times to be as low as 1,000,000 and as high as 5,000,000. The latter figure occurred in 1981, at which time it was uncommon to come off the lake with less than 75 to 100 yellow perch. The adult population currently stands at 2,500,000 (November 1987).

Unlike most of the other species in Oneida Lake, the yellow perch here grow fairly quickly. This is because of the abundant forage in the lake. The perch feed heavily on zooplankton, insects and small fish. A typical three year old Oneida Lake perch is 8 to 10 inches long. But most perch here stop growing before they reach 13 inches because of forage restrictions.

The fact that yellow perch are abundant in Oneida Lake doesn't mean that they are always easy to catch. The fact of the matter is that these fish can be damned hard to catch. It's rarely worth your while to come here prior to late July if you're looking for big catches of yellow perch. Because of their vast numbers, you should be able to pick up a few fish in the spring and early summer, but the really good fishing isn't going to be had until at least the end of July. The reason for this has to do with the feeding habits of the perch and the amount of forage available to them. In the spring and early summer the fish will be dispersed throughout the lake, gorging themselves on the abundant zooplankton and insects. Before this forage base runs out they begin feeding on small fish, including their own young. The perch are very difficult to catch until these food sources run low, because they will be widely scattered and usually well fed. It isn't until they are forced to switch over to alternate food sources that the perch become catchable in any significant numbers. If their primary forage base is sufficiently large, it can last until the end of winter, which means that the perch fishing will be lousy for that whole season.

Typically, at least some of the perch will begin to school up by the end of July due to the need to seek out alternative food sources when the plankton density crashes. They begin to congregate in shallow weedy areas first. In most years they seem to show a preference for the weed beds in the western part of the lake. Big Bay, Three Mile Bay, the "Grass Beds," and the weed beds just west of Frenchman Island are all well known for good perch fishing at this time of year. In some years the perch school up in large numbers on nearly all of the weed beds of the lake.

Oneida Lake has an excellent population of smallmouth bass, but they receive relatively little attention from anglers. Though most of the smallmouth here are under 15 inches, lunkers like the fish pictured above are taken here each year. Photo courtesy Captain Tony Buffa.

This seems to correspond to periods when the adult population is very high, forcing the fish to spread out.

Crayfish are one of the food sources the perch will seek out if their primary forage base is diminishing. Thus the popularity of crayfish as bait in July and August. The crayfish will be found in the weeds and on the shoals. The perch show up on the shoals a bit later than on the weed beds. If they aren't gorged on other foods, the perch fishing on the shoals can be outstanding. Shackelton Shoal has the reputation for providing the best fishing at this time of year, but Dakin, Messenger, Lakeport and Pancake Shoals will all have good fishing if the conditions are right.

In late July and August the fish are going to be in shallow water (6 to 12 feet) and, if they are hungry, can be taken on a small crayfish drifted close to the bottom. Tony Buffa likes to hook them through the tail with a size 6 gold Eagle Claw hook. He feels that the extra little flash of color given off by the shiny gold hook serves as an attractant.

By mid-September crayfish are going to be difficult to find, for both the perch and the fisherman. The bait to switch to are small minnows. These can be fished in or among the weeds, and on the shoals.

Jigs are also highly effective for perch from September to ice-up. Small (1/8-1/16 oz.) deer hair jigs or Mister Twister type jigs in brown and white, black and white or yellow and green work well here. If you locate a large feeding school of fish, try casting or drifting a two jig rig. Double catches of perch won't be uncommon.

October is probably the best month for perch fishing on Oneida Lake. The perch are going to be schooled up for the most part, and feeding heavily in preparation for the cold winter months. They will be found along practically all of the deeper weed lines of the lake. Traditionally, the best fall perch fishing takes place along the weed lines in the Lower South Bay area. Jigs and minnows will continue to be the best baits, but you are going to have to modify your tactics slightly if you're using jigs. In the fall and early winter work the jig with a slow, deliberate stroke, rather than with a sharp pumping action. As the water gets colder the fish slow down and can't respond to the jig as quickly as in the summer.

Here's an important point to remember when fishing these weed lines in the fall. If you're catching a lot of perch on minnows or jigs and the action suddenly stops, more often than not the fish are still close by. Usually what happens is that the whole school of perch followed a school of minnows into the weeds. When this occurs, move your boat over the bed and locate an opening in the weeds. Fishing straight down in the pocket with buckeye minnows will take perch almost as fast as on the outer weed line.

The general tendency of the yellow perch is to move into increasingly deeper water in the fall and winter. However, there is a short period right at the start of the ice fishing season when large numbers of yellow perch can be found in the shallows. This occurs when safe ice has formed over the shallows, and before the rest of the lake has completely frozen over. The perch are drawn in by bait fish that seek shelter in the dimly lit waters under the ice. Key areas for this shallow water ice fishing include Big Bay, Lower South Bay, Delmarter (Briggs Bay), Lewis Point, South Bay, and the shallows off Verona Beach, Sylvan Beach, Cleveland and Constantia, and just northeast of Dutchman Island.

Most of the yellow perch caught in these shallow areas are going to be on the small side, usually no more than 8 inches. But they are available in vast numbers in some years. The big perch seldom move into the shallows, preferring instead to school up off the weed beds in 15 to 25 feet of water just as the lake begins to freeze. The hole a little north east of Dutchman Island is an especially productive area for these larger fish. In some years the school remains in the area all winter long.

Once safe ice has formed over the entire lake (this normally occurs by mid-January) the perch move out into increasingly deeper water. Species such as yellow perch and walleye are drawn to the deeper water by warmer temperatures and forage, primarily isopods amphipods and midge larvae. Once the perch have moved out of the shallows, the majority of them will be found in at least 25 feet of water, and often as deep as 30 to 40 feet. Normally they will be found close to the bottom, but occasionally they will be found suspended at various depths, possibly due to localized oxygen depletion on the bottom or because they are feeding on suspended schools of isopods.

Usually the same general areas that produced well in the summer will also produce well in the winter, but at greater depths. On the western end of the lake the deep water north of Frenchman Island, around buoy 130 and around Pancake Shoal are always highly productive areas. Dakin Shoal is also hot most of the winter. In the central portion of the lake the Cleveland bar, Shackelton Shoal and the previously mentioned hole north east of Dutchman Island are all choice locations. On the eastern end of the lake Messenger Shoal would be the area to concentrate your efforts on.

When scouting around for likely perch areas, keep in mind that they strongly favor two bottom types: mud/silt and pancake nodules. Most of the deep portions of the lake have mud/silt bottom. For information on where major concentrations of pancakes can be found see the section on ice fishing for walleyes.

The techniques used to take yellow perch are not very dissimilar to those used for taking walleye. The main differences are that the perch feed only during the day and the bait and lures that are used are smaller.

Fred David, an avid Oneida Lake ice fisherman, strongly recommends stopping into a local bait and tackle shop on the lake before heading out on the ice. There you can get up-to-date information on conditions, what's hot, and what's not. Fred is also the outdoor columnist for the Syracuse Herald-Journal and, along with Dominick Bello, the source of much of the ice fishing information that follows.

Tip-ups baited with small minnows will take plenty of perch on this lake. But their popularity has gone down since more restrictive regulations regarding tip-ups were put into effect several years ago.

Today, jigging is the principle method used to take perch on this lake. Standard equipment consists of a light 3 to 3½ foot jigging rod and an assortment of small jigging spoons, dots, and ice flies. Throw in a couple of the smallest bobbers you can get your hands on and a days supply of bait (mousy grubs, spikes

and small minnows) to tip your jigging spoons with and you're all set. Perch eyes can also be used to tip your spoons, but some anglers say that perch eyes aren't as productive here as on other lakes. Dressing the business end of your lure is important. It helps camouflage the hook and tastes good to the fish. Some fishermen substitute the live baits with artificial grubs or Uncle Josh's "Ice Flecks" and soak them in some type of fish attractant.

If yellow perch are your quarry, be sure to use 4 pound line. These fish hit very lightly in the winter, and anything heavier than 4 pound simply won't have adequate sensitivity.

When choosing your jigging spoons keep in mind that chartreuse and red are the two most successful colors. Black is also good, but few people seem to use black jigs here.

Dominick Bello has ice fished Oneida Lake for over 40 years, and during that time has developed specific lures and techniques to improve his booty ten-fold. His knowledge of fishing spawned the Islander Lure Company, which specializes in perch and panfish tackle.

Bello separates his techniques by depth: in shallow water he uses a unique underwater bobber method and in water over 12 feet he jigs. Ignoring the early perch fishing on the ice covered bays because they are too small, he doesn't pursue the perch until ice has formed over the deeper parts of the lake. Thus, he starts the season jigging for larger perch and only switches to his bobber method when these "keepers" finally move into the shallows in late February or early March.

"Always jig with a series of lures," Bello tells, "starting with the heaviest at the bottom, tying no more than 3 or 4 lures above it. Graduate in size a sixteenth to a quarter-ounce each lure. Baits of equal weight can be used in succession but always make them lighter than the bottom lure. This allows the heavier lures to fall or flutter to the bottom first, keeping the lures from tangling."

"Also, while it is wise to tie several jigging lures to the line, limit the rig to no more than 4 lures. When catching doubles or triples, if the fish are active after being hooked, and they usually are, the lures will catch on the underside of the hole and the pressure from the fighting fish will break the line, costing the fisherman the fish and perhaps several lures."

Bello suggests tying all lures directly to the line and to avoid using leaders. Winter-feeding fish can be finicky, sometimes only mouthing the bait. And they seldom move more than an inch after hitting. A two-inch leader will give the fish a 4-inch movement without the fisherman knowing he had a bite. With the line in direct contact with the lure every nibble is felt.

Most useful are small wire-like Fast Snaps. This allows the lure to be "tied" directly to the line and the sequence of lures can be changed without re-tying all the lures with numb fingers. Also, many ice fishing lures are metal willow-leaf design with the hole drilled in the lure and sold without split rings to tie a line to. It doesn't take long for the line to break on the sharp metal edges. Fast Snaps prevent lures from being lost.

Some winter jigging lures have turned-up eyes (ex. Baby Dippers) that keep the lure away from the line and easy to bite.

Spacing of lures is very important, according to Bello. The bottom lure should be a heavy spoon with a minnow-like design. Best is the Swedish Pimple or a Jig-N-Spoon representing a shiner or perch. This lure is generally for weight but large enough to attract a walleye, as well as perch. They are also used to thump the bottom when you begin fishing and every ten minutes to stir up the bottom, possibly releasing grubs from the lake floor. It is a natural instinct to tie lures 15 to 18 inches apart to give the rig depth, for catching upper-level fish as well as bottom feeders. If the fish finder is working it will detect suspended schools and a long string of lures will not be needed to cover all the depths.

"Closer-spaced droppers produce more fish," attests Bello, "but if the fish finder signals an occasional fish at the upper depths move the rig higher but generally, the fish will feed on the bottom."

Lure placement is important, but movement of the lure is equally important for keeping the fish interested, according to Bello.

"The first thing fishermen should do with all ice fishing lures

A mixed bag of fish from Oneida Lake. Catches like this are common when the fish are biting. Note the size of the panfish. Unlike game fish, species such as yellow perch grow rapidly here. Photo courtesy Captain Tony Buffa.

s to test their action in a tall glass or a tub of water. Each lure and set of lures reacts differently as it is jigged horizontally or vertically. Get a feel for the lure on the line and know what each lure is doing under the water. Once you have established the movement of each lure you can repeat it to "induce consistent strikes."

For deadly effective jigging Dominick Bello recommends using what he calls "the semi-suspended technique." The heavy bottom lure is allowed to rest right on the bottom and the upper lures are worked in one of two ways: either with a slack line or a tight line. In the first method the lures are worked by sweeping the line back and forth and vertically. If the line is tightened the lures can be worked by giving the line short strokes, causing the lures to twirl. Meanwhile, don't be surprised if a cruising walleye comes to pick up the lure resting on the bottom!

In the late winter the big perch move into the shallow parts of the lake, and Bello switches over to his special underwater bobber technique. Most ice fishermen use bobbers on the surface, and most of the time miss the bite because the wind is moving the bobber around, or it is icing up and becoming weighted down. An underwater bobber does not blow in the wind, nor does it ice up.

Using a bobber stop to keep the bobber 3 inches under water is beneficial in several ways. First, the bobber does not move unless there's a bite. Also, if the fish are feeding and taking the bait upwards instead of down, the bobber will float. Set the hook! Lastly, when the fisherman vibrates the line, the bobber swings from side to side, creating a tantilizing cadence to the lures below. With the bobber swaying from side to side you'll always know when you've got a bite because the bobber will stop swaying.

When using the above method, you want to use some sort of small slip bobber. If they aren't available, attach a small standard bobber to the line, but don't set the wire hook on the bobber back in the hole where it normally goes. Purposely set it off to the side so that it forms a hole through which the line can slide freely. The bobber will naturally float up as high as the bobber stop, but when you reel in it will slide down the line to the lure. The advantage to this is that, having already determined the proper depth to fish at when you put the bobber stop on your line, now all you need to do is drop your hook back in the water to find the desired depth. You'll know you're there when the bobber and the stop are 3 inches under water.

Largemouth Bass . . . . common; growth rate fair

Oneida Lake does offer some good fishing for largemouth bass, but their population is only a fraction of the size of the smallmouth population. The vast majority of largemouth are found in the western end of the lake. The most productive area by far is Big Bay, whose weed-choked waters hold numerous bass. But lesser populations can be found along the north shore of the lake as far east as Three Mile Bay. This section of the shore has numerous shallow cutbacks. These small weedy bays all hold fish. Largemouth can also be found along the south shore as far east as the mouth of Chittenango Creek. A particularly productive area on the south shore is just off the old trolley station at the end of South Bay. During bass tournaments this is one of the first areas the pros hit, and with good reason. It almost always gives up a good number of fish.

In the eastern portions of the lake, largemouth bass are only taken occasionally. Small populations exist in the larger weedy bays, such as North Bay and South Bay, but they really contribute little to the fishery. If you come out to Oneida Lake for largemouth bass, the west end of the lake is the area to concentrate your efforts.

Because their habitat is so restricted, the largemouth in Oneida Lake don't do a great deal of moving around. They are pretty much limited to the bays. Early in the season the bass will be located in the shallower portions of the bays and can be taken on small spinners. As the weeds develop the fish move out into slightly deeper water, to a maximum of about 15 feet. By early July safety pin type spinnerbaits, top surface baits and small, shallow running crankbaits will all be very effective.

Through the months of July, August and September many of the bays on Oneida Lake are thoroughly weed choked. Largemouth will often be found at the edge of small breaks in the weed cover, waiting in ambush for small fish. They can be taken on weedless plastic worms worked slowly through the weeds, or on spinnerbaits if the breaks are big enough. But anyone who has tried to coax an uncooperative largemouth out of this submerged salad knows that it can be as frustrating as it is exciting. To overcome some of the problems attendant to this type of fishing, some anglers employ a technique favored by tournament bass fishermen. Tony Buffa, who related this information to me, refers to the technique as "flipping" and has used it successfully during tournaments. The method is remarkably simple. Using a trolling motor equipped with weed cutters, take a shallow draft boat into the thick of the weed beds of an area like Big Bay. While one man carefully maneuvers the boat close to small openings in the weeds, the fisherman at the front of the boat stands ready to drop a plastic worm or Jig 'n-Pig in to the pocket of open water. Typically he is armed with a stiff rod and 17 pound test line. Only about 7 feet of line extends past the last eye of the rod. You're not casting at all, but literally dropping the lure into the water. Make sure your drag is set tight, for the moment you feel a fish hit the lure, you heave it out of the water, flipping the fish into the boat. This doesn't give the fish a chance to get tangled in the weeds. Needless to say, there isn't a great deal of sport in using this technique, at least in terms of fighting the fish, but it is extremely effective for catching the fish.

If you're looking for a more sporting method of taking largemouth from their weedy environs, try working buzzbaits, top water spoons or plastic worms along breaks in the cover or over slightly submerged weed growth. Dusk, dawn and overcast periods will provide the best action.

Generally speaking, Oneida Lake doesn't have a serious weed problem, thus it isn't necessary to bring in weed harvesters to cut navigation channels as is done on some lakes, such as Lamoka in Schuyler County. For the bass fisherman this is unfortunate, for the channels that are cut through the weeds often provide some of the best late summer largemouth fishing on the lake. Lacking this windfall, you might want to consider a trick I've seen used several times in Western New York. Locate an area likely to hold fish (Big Bay comes to mind) and, using a rake, scoop out a large opening in the weeds. Make the opening large enough to work a spinnerbait, small crankbait or buzzbait. The weeds don't have to be cut down to the bottom, but should be cut back far enough so that they don't interfere with the action of your lures. A day or two later you can work the cleared area for largemouth bass and panfish.

Additional Species

Oneida Lake is host to a large number of species that are of marginal importance to anglers. The lack of attention that these fish receive is often due more to their unsavory reputation than to their relative abundance. A case in point is the burbot. Known locally as ling or lawyer, this fresh water member of the cod family is a highly respected game fish in many parts of North America, but not on Oneida Lake. Caught in large numbers, through the ice, they are often just cast aside and left for scavengers. Doctor John Forney of the Cornell Research Station at Shackelton Point has a picture taken decades ago of an angler who built a shelter on the ice using nothing but frozen burbot! A more conventional

use would be to fillet the tail section of the fish, from the vent or back. The tail section of a burbot is a bit rubbery, but very tasty, somewhat reminiscent of bullhead. They are also good smoked (what isn't?). To catch burbot, fish close to the bottom with worms. Because they are most active in cold water they are most often taken through the ice.

Another species that often doesn't get a fair shake from anglers, at least in the north, is the channel catfish. Oneida Lake has a good population of these hard fighting and very palatable fish. Many of these are trophy size fish weighing up to 25 pounds. When you hook into a catfish you're not likely to mistake it for anything else. They put up a very powerful, deliberate kind of fight. On six pound line it can take up to a half hour to land a big cat—if it doesn't wear you or your line out first. Favoring deep water (25-40 feet), channel catfish are most often taken from the dredged channel adjacent to Shackelton Shoal or buoy 130. Worms drifted close to the bottom are the recommended bait.

In the spring, Oneida Lake offer some truly fine fishing for brown bullhead. The bullhead in this lake are good size, often weighing up to 2 pounds. Beginning just after ice-out they congregate in large numbers in the lower reaches of the lake's tributaries and in many of the shallow bays. They can be caught in these areas until early summer, but there is usually a 2 to 3 week period in the spring when the fishing for bullhead is nothing short of excellent! The most productive area is probably the lower reach of Canaseraga Creek and the bay at Lakeport, but good runs of bullhead also occur in the mouth of Chittenango Creek, the barge canal, Oneida Creek, South Bay, Big Bay and Big Bay Creek.

In recent years a very popular fishery has developed for black crappies. Known locally as calico bass, they are caught in good numbers in the early spring in many of the marinas and bays around the lake. By far the most productive area is Big Bay, where tremendous numbers are taken on minnows and small jigs. The crappie fishing is usually good for the four weeks following ice-out.

Surveys done in the 1920's suggested that chain pickerel and northern pike were nearly as abundant as walleye. However, the marshes and wetlands where these species spawned were drained for agricultural purposes or urban development. By the 1940's their populations were in serious decline. Today, chain pickerel and northern pike are rarely caught in Oneida Lake. Most are taken from the weed beds at the west end.

Tiger muskellunge, a hybrid relative of the pike and pickerel, are found in limited numbers in the lake. These sterile fish have never been stocked here; they are all escapees from the hatchery at Constantia. Weighing up to 20 pounds, these aggressive, toothsome predators are only taken rarely now, but they were more common in the 1970's and early 1980's. This was due to the fact that, as a result of Hurricane Agnes in 1972, holding ponds containing tiger muskie fry were flooded over, allowing many fish to escape in to Oneida Lake. With a life span of 7 to 10 years, these fish have left the fishery.

There are times of the year when brown trout make an appearance in Oneida Lake. They drop down into the lake in the winter and early spring from tributaries such as Fish Creek, Scriba Creek and Chittenango Creek. Every year someone reports taking a nice 5 to 7 pound brown through the ice. Unfortunately, these fish must be returned to the water — trout can't be taken legally here until April 1. More commonly, brown trout are caught by anglers trolling for walleye in the spring. The areas where these trout are taken most often include off the mouths of Scriba Creek and Chittenango Creek, and along Sylvan Beach and Verona Beach. The trout will remain in the lake until rising water temperatures force them to return to the cooler water of the streams.

White perch have become well established in Oneida Lake. They exhibit a good growth rate, getting up to 1¼ pounds. Scrappy fighters and good tasting, white perch usually travel in schools and can provide incredibly fast action when they go on a feeding binge. They haven't hurt the lake yet by their presence, but it's feared that if their population increases it could have a etrimental effect on the lake's other species.

Unlike most of the species found in this lake, pan fish are generally big. Bluegills and pumpkinseeds are platter size and meaty. In the shoal areas of the lake you often come across large schools of big pumpkinseeds. A stringerful of these can make for some fine eating.

Rock bass are plentiful in Oneida Lake. They can be found anywhere in the lake that has a rocky bottom. Disdained by many anglers, they are good fighters on ultra-light tackle and, when caught in the spring, very tasty. In the spring, check out the shallow bays, marinas, and near shore bars for hoardes of spawning panfish.

Rounding out the species you're liable to encounter in Oneida Lake are sheepshead, carp, silver bass, cisco, gar and bowfin.

General Information

The outstanding fishing enjoyed today by anglers on Oneida Lake has its origins in events that took place over 12,000 years ago. For Oneida is the last remnant of a vast body of water that geographers have named "Lake Iroquois," which was formed when glaciers blocked the waters of the St. Lawrence River. Many characteristics of Oneida Lake, from the many shoals and bars that serve as havens for fish, to the vast swamplands that surround it are attributable to glacial activity.

One unique aspect of this lake that may or may not be glacial in origin are the deposits of ferromanganese nodules known as "Oneida Lake Pancakes." Looking like a petrified pancake, these accretions contain varying amounts of iron, manganese, molybdenum, copper, zinc and about 15 other elements. Growing at a rate of about .04 inches per 100 years, some of these pancakes, which can reach up to 12 inches across, are nearly as old as the lake itself. Typically, pancakes are found in well aerated water between 20 and 30 feet deep. Large deposits of these nodules often form a transition zone between rocky shoals and mud flats.

Pancakes do play a role in the Oneida Lake fishery. In the summer months areas with extensive deposits of pancakes are host to a number of small crustaceans, most notably fresh-water shrimp. These serve as a forage base for baitfish, which in turn attract the larger yellow perch and walleye.

While glaciers played a major role in determining the nature of Oneida Lake, it is man who has been instrumental in determining what species of fish are found here. Before the arrival of white settlers in the region in the 1790's the Oneida and Onondaga Indians harvested the lake's vast populations of chain pickerel, northern pike, American eel and walleye. They also seined the lakes tributaries for spawning Atlantic salmon. But the species composition in the lake was radically altered by the activities of the white settlers. The first species to feel the impact were the salmon. The farming and logging operations of the settlers degraded the once high quality of the lake's tributaries. This resulted in unsuccessful spawning runs by the salmon, which disappeared by the mid-1800's.

The fate of the lake American eel fishery was sealed in 1916 with the completion of the Barge Canal system. Once harvested from the lake by the ton, the eels spawned in the Atlantic Ocean and migrated into Oneida Lake via Lake Ontario and the Oneida and Oswego Rivers. The locks and dams of the canal system almost completely cut off the upstream migration of the eels and those that were in the lake prior to the completion of the canal eventually died off or migrated out.

The most recent species to feel the impact of man's activities on Oneida Lake are the members of the pike family. As recently as the 1920's chain pickerel and northern pike were both shown to be nearly as common as walleye. Their populations collapsed when many of the marshes and wetlands contiguous to the lake were drained for agricultural purposes and urban development.

With the elimination of other large predators Oneida Lake's walleye population has thrived. The population of adult walleye has ranged from 200,000 to 1,000,000 over the past 15 years, with an average of about 500,000, or roughly 10 adult walleye per acre. The walleye benefit not only from the natural characteristics of the lake, which provides them with abundant forage and habitat, but also from the influence of man. Because of the great importance of the walleye fishery, it is closely monitored by the DEC, which operates the Oneida Hatchery in the Village of Constantia, and by the Cornell Biological Field Station at Shackleton Point. This field station, which as been contracted by the state to monitor the lake's fishery, is fortunate to have as its head Dr. John Forney, who is widely regarded as one of the top fisheries biologists in the world. The published research of Dr. Forney forms the basis for the management of walleye throughout the United States. The lake is also watched over by the Oneida Lake Association. Organized in 1945, the Association is a large group of private citizens dedicated to maintaining and promoting Oneida Lake as one of New York State's premier recreational resources.

NOTES: _____

_____

_____

_____

LAKE ONTARIO

(Webster Beach County Park to North Sandy Pond)
Contours in feet
Scale 1:80,000 (except for map of Oswego Harbor)

NOTE A

The lines that cover the maps for Lake Ontario are photographic artifacts of the Loran-C lines of position that are overprinted on all current nautical charts of this lake distributed by the National Oceanic and Atmospheric Administration (N.O.A.A.)

NOTE B

The maps contained in this book are not to be used for navigational purposes. The navigational charts which served as the basis for these maps can be obtained by contacting: Distribution Branch (N/CG33), National Ocean Service, Riverdale, Maryland 20737, (301) 436-6990. For current navigation regulations on Lake Ontario see the U.S. Coast Guart Pilot 6, or Weekly Notice to Mariners.

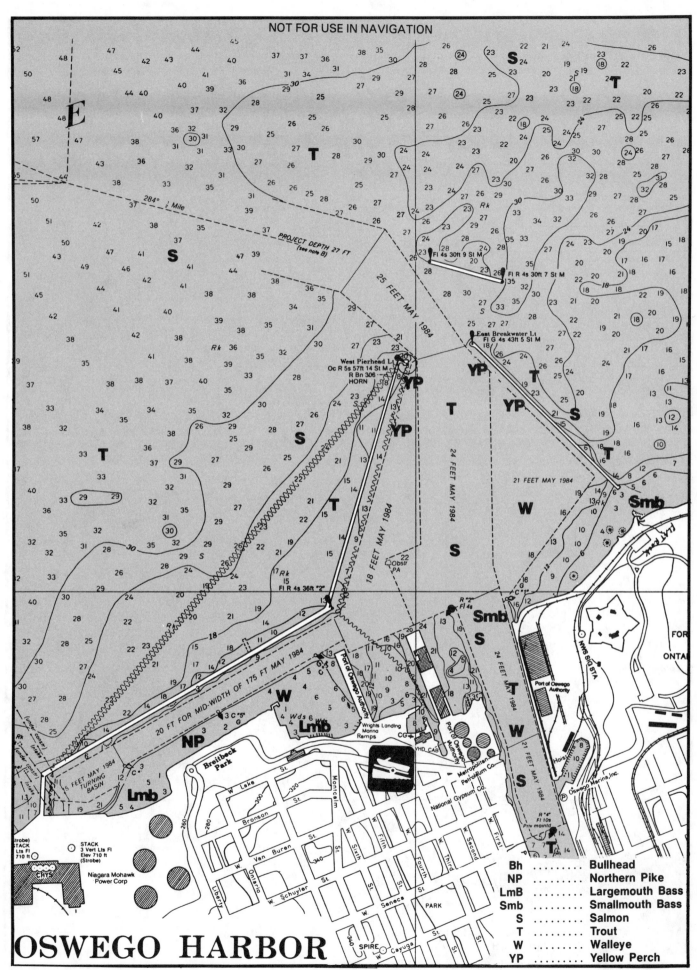

OSWEGO HARBOR

Bh	....	Bullhead
NP	....	Northern Pike
LmB	....	Largemouth Bass
Smb	....	Smallmouth Bass
S	....	Salmon
T	....	Trout
W	....	Walleye
YP	....	Yellow Perch

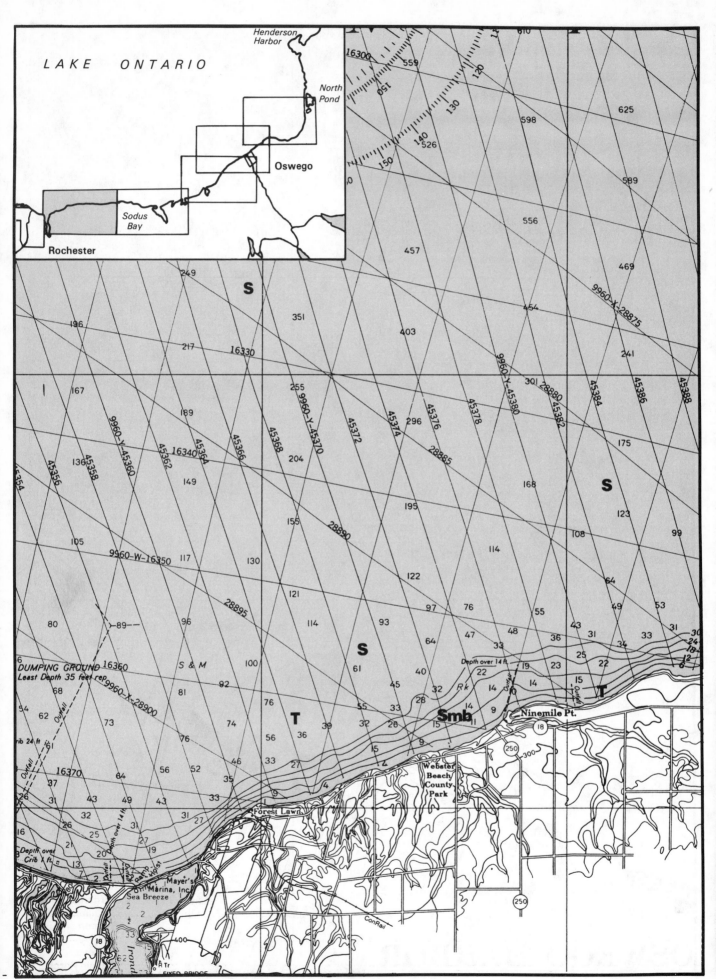

LAKE ONTARIO

Henderson Harbor

North Pond

Oswego

Sodus Bay

Rochester

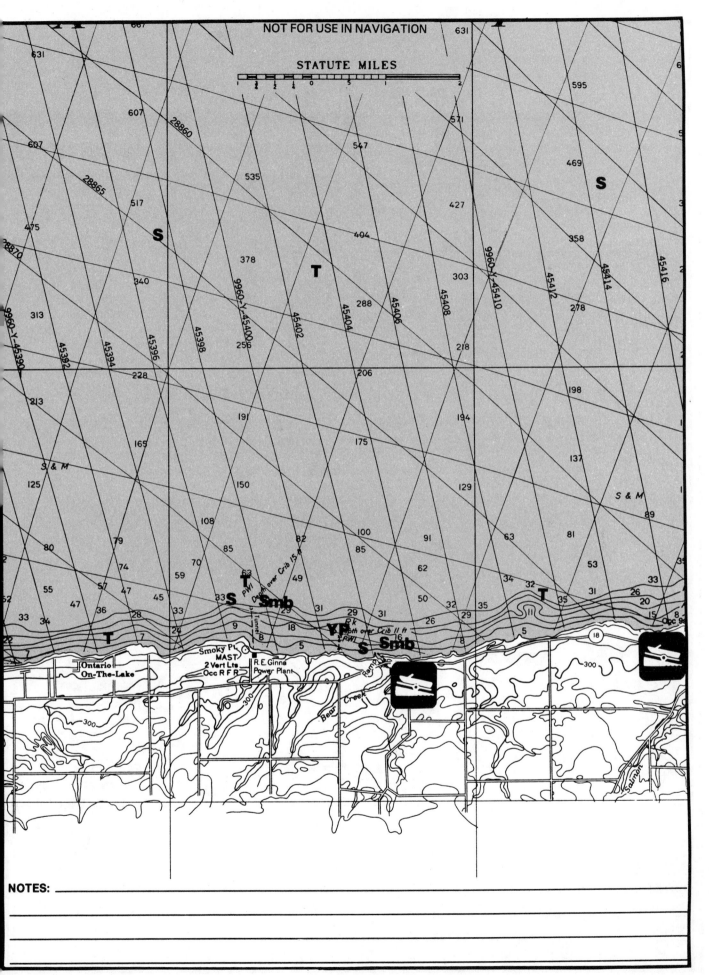

NOT FOR USE IN NAVIGATION

STATUTE MILES

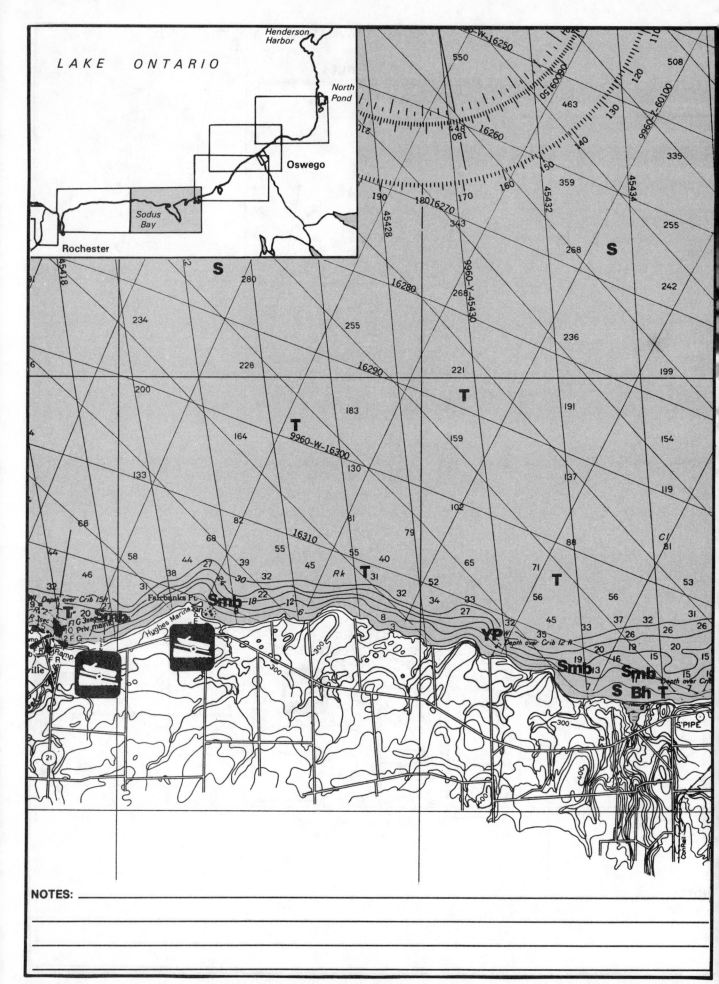

LAKE ONTARIO

Henderson Harbor

North Pond

Oswego

Sodus Bay

Rochester

NOTES: _____

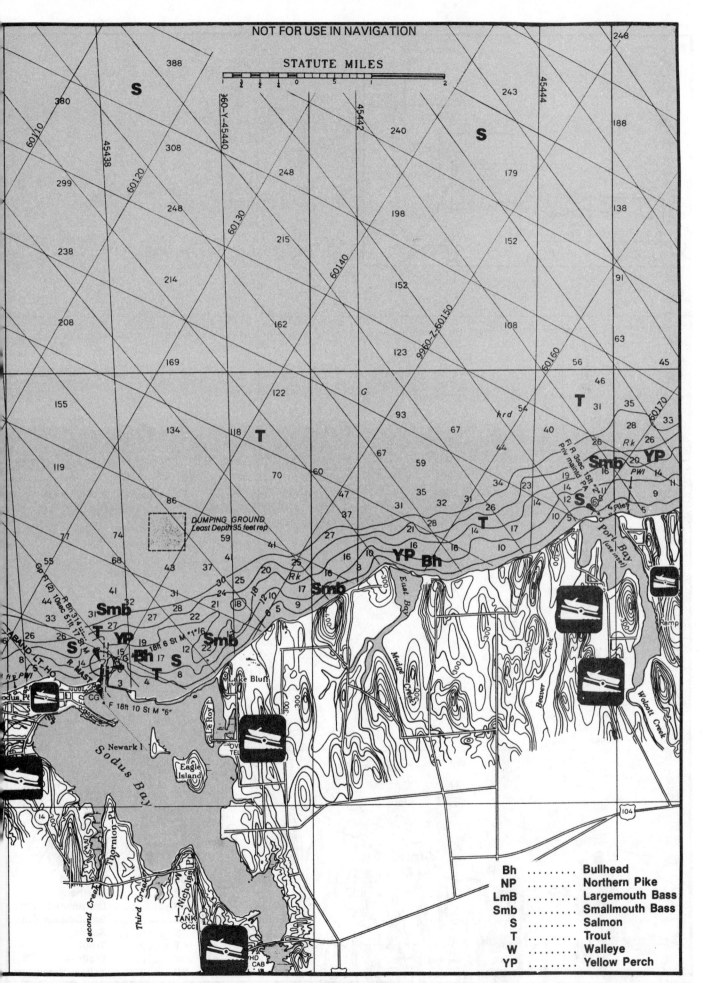

STATUTE MILES

DUMPING GROUND
Least Depth 35 feet rep

Port Bay
(use incel)

East Bay

Mudge Creek

Beaver Creek

Wolcott Creek

Sodus Bay

Newark I.

Eagle Island

Lake Bluff

Le Roy

Second Creek

Third Creek

Nicholas Pt.

Sodus Pt.

Bh	....	Bullhead
NP	....	Northern Pike
LmB	....	Largemouth Bass
Smb	....	Smallmouth Bass
S	....	Salmon
T	....	Trout
W	....	Walleye
YP	....	Yellow Perch

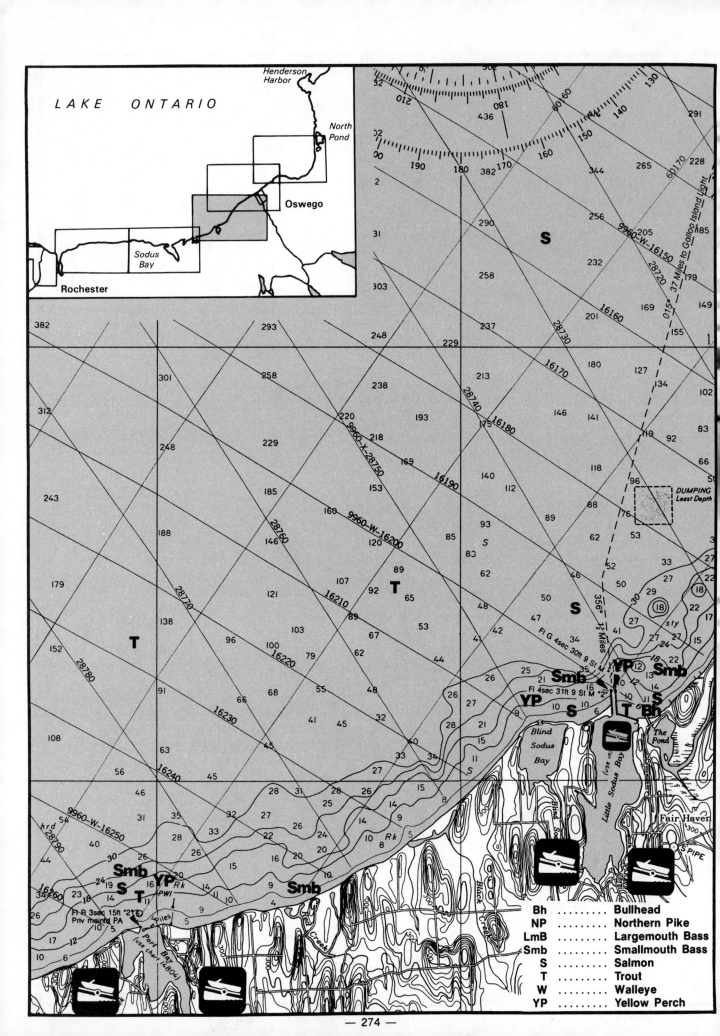

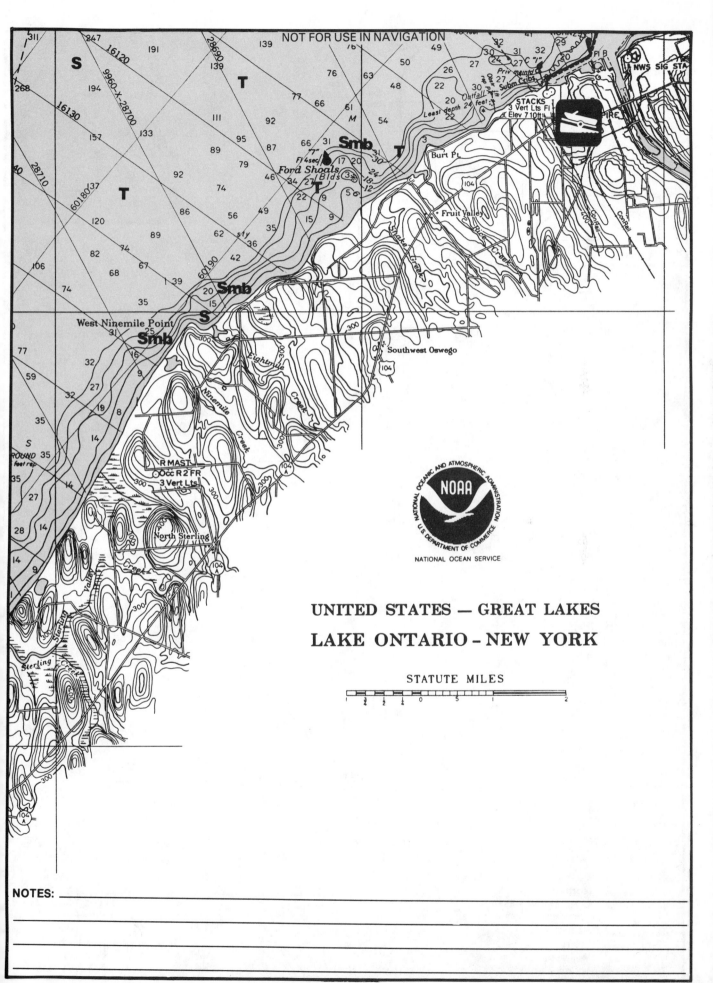

NOT FOR USE IN NAVIGATION

NWS SIG STA

STACKS
3 Vert Lts Fl
R Elev 710 ft

Burt Pt.

Fruit Valley

Smb

Ford Shoals
Fl 4 sec
"7"
Bld's

West Ninemile Point

Smb

S

Smb

Southwest Oswego

Eightmile Creek

Ninemile Creek

R MAST
Occ R 2 FR
3 Vert Lts

North Sterling

Sterling Valley Creek

Sterling Creek

NOAA
NATIONAL OCEANIC AND ATMOSPHERIC ADMINISTRATION
U.S. DEPARTMENT OF COMMERCE

NATIONAL OCEAN SERVICE

UNITED STATES — GREAT LAKES
LAKE ONTARIO – NEW YORK

STATUTE MILES

NOTES:

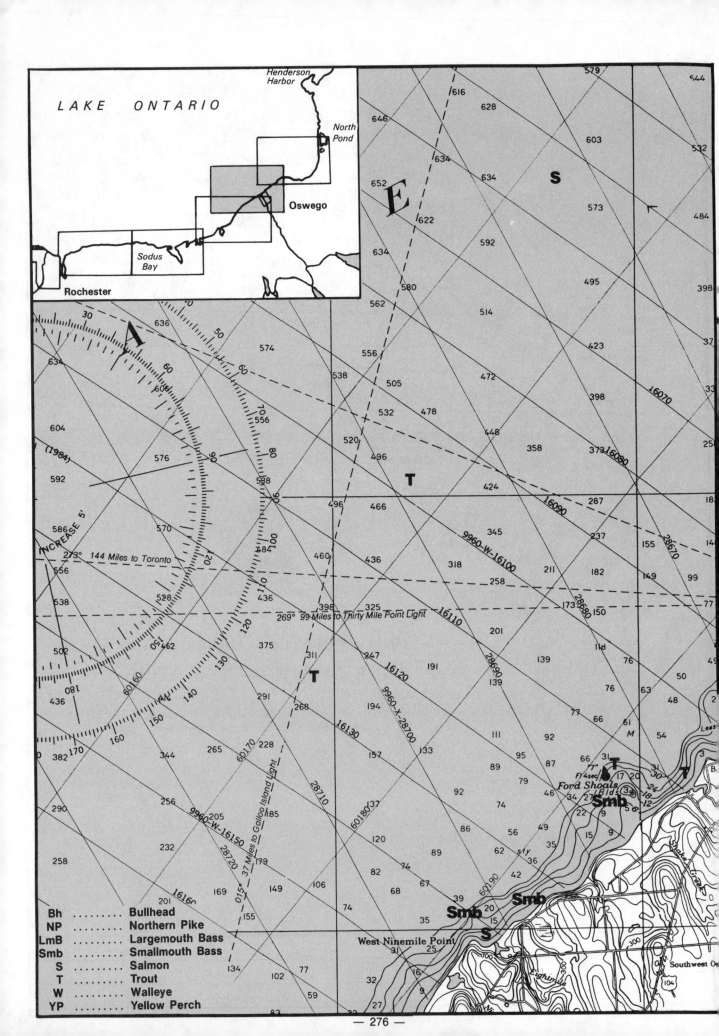

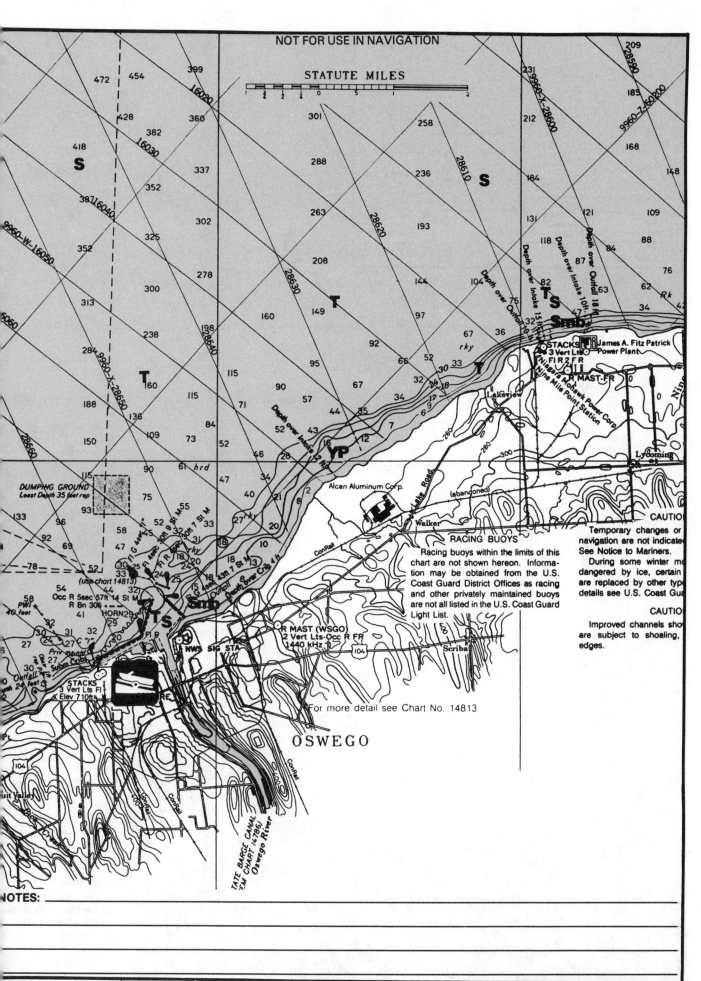

STATUTE MILES

RACING BUOYS

Racing buoys within the limits of this chart are not shown hereon. Information may be obtained from the U.S. Coast Guard District Offices as racing and other privately maintained buoys are not all listed in the U.S. Coast Guard Light List.

For more detail see Chart No. 14813

OSWEGO

CAUTION

Temporary changes or navigation are not indicate See Notice to Mariners.

During some winter m dangered by ice, certain are replaced by other typ details see U.S. Coast Gu

CAUTIO

Improved channels sho are subject to shoaling, edges.

DUMPING GROUND
Least Depth 35 feet rep

James A. Fitz Patrick
Power Plant

Niagara Mohawk Power Corp.
Nine Mile Point Station

Alcan Aluminum Corp.

Lakeview

Lycoming

Walker

Scriba

NWS SIG STA

R MAST (WSGO)
2 Vert Lts-Occ R FR
1440 kHz

STACKS
3 Vert Lts Fl
Elev 710 ft

STATE BARGE CANAL
EM CHART (4786)
Oswego River

NOTES:

— 277 —

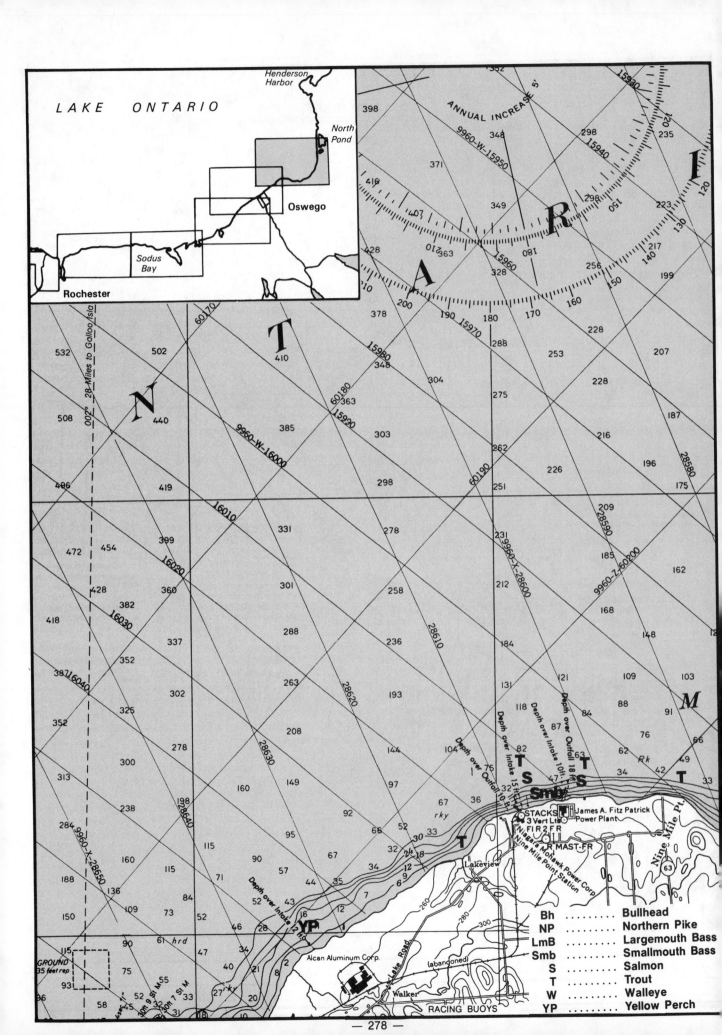

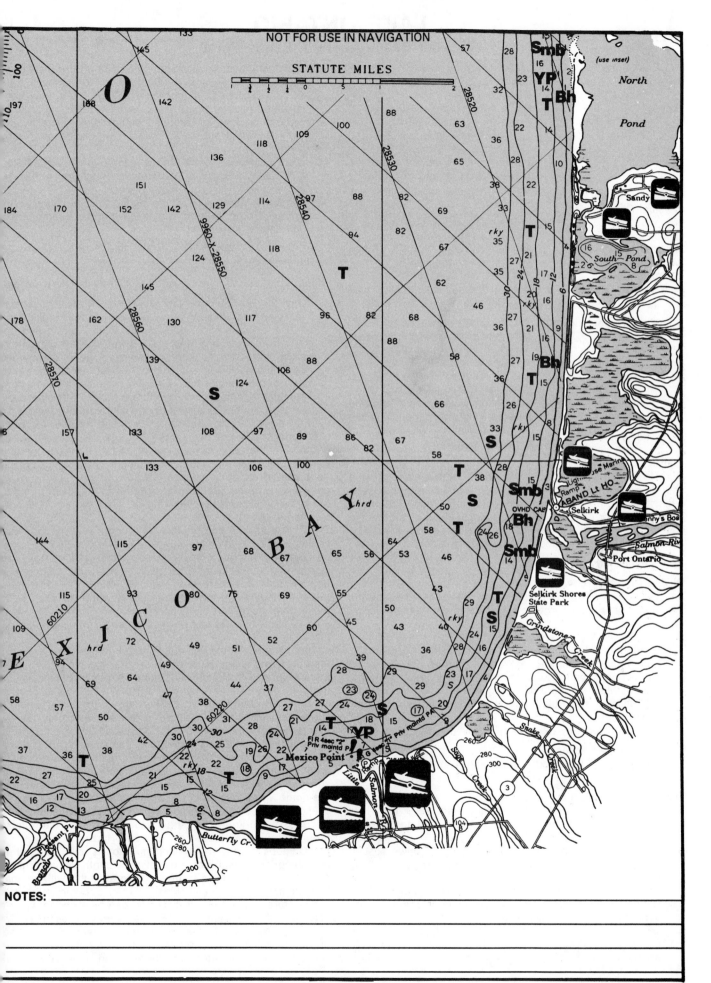

NOT FOR USE IN NAVIGATION

STATUTE MILES

NOTES: _____
_____
_____
_____

LAKE ONTARIO
(Webster Beach to North Sandy Pond)

N.O.A.A. Charts 14802, 14803
location . . . . Counties of Wayne, Cayuga and Oswego
access . . . . Route 104 provides the most convenient movement along the lake between Irondequoit Bay and the Village of Mexico; Route 3 provides the best access to the lake between Mexico and North Sandy Pond.

Physical Characteristics

area . . . . 3560 square miles (U.S. waters)
shoreline . . . . 356 miles (New York section)
elevation . . . . 245 feet
maximum depth . . . . approximately 780 feet
mean depth . . . . 276 feet
bottom type . . . . slate, gravel and sand interspersed with pockets of rock and rubble

Chemical Characteristics

water clarity . . . . generally clear; near shore areas are often muddy after storms
pH . . . . varies with location
oxygen . . . . good throughout the lake all year due to the seasonal turnover of top and bottom waters. Some bays and harbors might experience some oxygen depletion, but this is not generally a problem.

Plant Life

Due to its relatively hard, featureless bottom, unprotected shoreline and great depth, Lake Ontario has little rooted aquatic vegetation. What weed beds do occur are usually found in harbors, bays or off the mouths of streams. Algae, in the form of Cladophora, is often a problem in the shallow portions of the lake (5 - 25 feet) in the months of May, June and July.

Boat Launch Sites

Wayne County Section

1. Bear Creek - Town of Ontario ramp off Lake Road (Route 18); single ramp, no charge, town residents only, except during derbies.
2. Pultneyville Marine - east end of Hamilton Street, off Lake Road (Route 18) on west side of harbor in
3. Pultneyville Mariners - east side of harbor in Pultneyville. Single ramp, open to public only during derbies - no charge.
4. Hughes Marina - at Paradise Lagoon, off Lake Road (Route 18) 2 miles east of Pultneyville. Single ramp, rentals, gas, bait, tackle - fee.
    See also: Port Bay (page 148) and Sodus Bay (page 150).

Cayuga County Section

See entries for Little Sodus Bay (page 24) and the Pond (page 26).

Oswego County Section

5. Oswego Harbor - Wrights Landing Park, on West Third Street, City of Oswego. Multiple hard surface ramps, parking - fee.
6. Dowie Dale Campground - Route 104B, 13 miles east of Oswego just west of Mexico Point. Single ramp, gas, bait, tackle - fee.
7. Salmon County Campground and Marina - Mexico Point Road, off Route 104B. Double hard surface ramp, marine supplies, gas, bait, tackle - fee.
8. DEC Fisherman Access Site - at Mexico Point on east side of Little Salmon River, County Road 40 off Route 104B. Multiple ramps, parking - no charge.

9. DEC Fisherman Access Site - at Selkirk Shores State Park, miles west of Pulaski off Route 3 in Port Ontario. Sing launch site (beach launch) into Salmon River. May not b suitable for large boats. Park user fee after mid-May.
10. Lighthouse Hotel and Marina - end of Lake Road at mouth Salmon River. Hard surface ramp, marine supplies, gas, ba tackle - fee.
11. Clark's Cottages/Don's Marina - on County Road 5 off Rou 3 on Salmon River in Port Ontario. Single ramp, gas, ba tackle - fee.
12. Larrison's Marina - on Route 3 at north end of Salmon Riv Bridge in Port Ontario. Single hard surface ramp, rental bait, tackle - fee.
    See also: North Sandy Pond (page 88)

Species Information

Chinook Salmon . . . . abundant; growth rate excellent

Until recently, chinook fishing was essentially a late summ and fall event on Lake Ontario. Very few chinook salmon (als known as king salmon) were caught in the spring and ear summer. In fact, no one was really sure where the majority these fish were prior to August. However, recent creel cens figures from the DEC indicate that in the past several years angl success for this species has increased considerably in the sprir and summer months. This is due to two factors. First, there are tremendous number of chinook in the lake now, many more tha in the early 1980's. Secondly, because of the increasir likelihood of finding them, more anglers are actively seekir chinook in the spring and summer, rather than concentratir their efforts on the more predictable browns, lakers ar rainbows. This early season salmon fishery is in no wa comparable to the spectacular chinook fishing seen in the fa but it is a significant improvement over what was available only few years ago.

On the eastern end of Lake Ontario the best spring chinoc fishing will be found off the shores of Wayne County. The fish w be scattered, but good catches will commonly come from wat less than 100 feet deep. East of Wayne County chinooks a being caught with increasing regularity, but not in the numbe taken off Wayne County. The one area where chinook do n make up a major part of the spring catch is Mexico Bay, whe cold spring temperatures prevent the salmon from moving in ur mid-May.

In the summer, the chinook spread out over the lake.Thoug their preferred temperature range is usually given as 54° - 56° many charter boat captains are of the opinion that in the summ the chinook are most often found in 42° - 52° water. They a usually found further off-shore than brown trout, and further c the bottom than browns. There is still some controversy ov where the bulk of these fish are in June and July. It is known th many of them make their way into Canadian waters at this time But so many chinook are now in Lake Ontario that essentially a areas of the lake will have some salmon fishing during th summer months. Though these fish are widely dispersed, the are some areas that seem to produce more than their share salmon in the summer. The shelves and drop-offs just off of Litt Sodus Bay are known to attract salmon. So does the dumpir ground about 1 mile out from Oswego Harbor.

Chinook fishing really comes into its own around th beginning of August. For most of this month sexually matu salmon are engaged in a shoreward migration that will eventua find them near their natal streams. They become much mo temperature tolerant at this time and can be found in water a cold as 40° F or as warm as 60° F. Initially, they will be prey only boat fishermen. But, by the end of August phenomenal numbe of chinook will be staging off the mouths of tributaries or cruisir shallow near-shore waters, and shore bound anglers can partak

Due to the tremendous numbers of fish that have been stocked in Lake Ontario in recent years the quality of the fishing for chinook (king) salmon has improved greatly. In 1987 over 3,000,000 chinook were stocked in the lake! Many parts of Lake Ontario now enjoy good spring and summer salmon fishing as well as the traditionally good fall season.

Tony "Mike" Arlauckas, pictured at left, holds a 38 pound 14 ounce chinook salmon. An abundance of fish like this have turned Lake Ontario into one of the finest sport fishing lakes in the world. Tony operates Reel Lure'in Charter, one of the most successful charters on Lake Ontario. His boat is based at Shumway Marine in Rochester.

f this fishing bonanza.

The late summer salmon fishery is simply dominated by chinooks. They are larger, fight harder and far outnumber the coho salmon. Les Wedge of the DEC also feels that chinooks are more aggressive and less finicky than the current strains of coho being stocked in the lake. These fish will normally be found in deeper water during periods of high sun, moving closer to shore t dusk, dawn and overcast periods. By the first week of September the largest concentrations of fish will be found off the mouths of stocked tributaries. Needless to say, the greatest number of chinook will be found off the Salmon River, whose fall runs of chinook have become world famous. Other stocked tributaries on the eastern end of Lake Ontario include the Oswego River, Little Sodus Bay and Sodus Bay. While these areas will get the bulk of salmon, many fish will stray into unstocked streams. Unstocked tributaries known to hold stray chinook in the fall include Bear Creek, Maxwell Creek and Port Bay (Wayne County), Sterling Creek (Cayuga County), Little Salmon River, Grindstone Creek and North Sandy Pond (Oswego County). Spawning runs continue through November. There is no winter fishing for chinook salmon on Lake Ontario.

Coho Salmon............. common; growth rate excellent

Known also as silver salmon, coho are not nearly as abundant in Lake Ontario as their cousin, the mighty chinook salmon. There are several reasons for this. At the present time December 1987) the stocking program for cohos is in a bit of a lull due to budgetary cuts. The stocking level should soon return to a level of about 350,000 fish per year in the near future. But even with a return to previous stocking levels the number of coho being planted here is still dwarfed by the number of chinook released in to Lake Ontario and its tributaries. In addition, coho yearlings are not as likely to survive to maturity as are chinook.

Soon after ice-out coho will be found close to shore in search of forage fish and water temperatures that most closely approximate their preferred range of 50°-58° F. Areas that warm

up first, such as the mouths of major streams, warm water discharges from power plants and large piers near harbors all serve as attractants and are very productive early on. With regard to the portion of Lake Ontario covered in this book (Wayne, Cayuga and Oswego Counties) the spring fishing for cohos takes place west of Oswego. In years when coho are present in great numbers they make up as much as 50% of the spring harvest of salmonids from the shore of Wayne County. April is the peak of this spring fishery. Unlike chinook, coho tend to be a schooling fish, concentrating along particular areas of the shore. In Wayne County the major concentration of fish occurs at the Sodus Bay area. Lesser numbers of coho will also be found at West Nine Mile Point and the bay just to the east of the point. These latter areas are warmed by the outflow from Nine Mile Creek and Eight Mile Creek. Some coho will also be found around the near-shore warm water discharge of the Nine Mile Point power plant , at Little Sodus Bay and Port Bay.

As near-shore waters begin to warm into the mid-50's, coho start migrating toward deeper water. This takes place in late May and early June. By July the fish will be far off-shore, at least 3 to 5 miles out. During the months of July and August coho roam the open lake at random, showing little pattern other than preferring, when temperatures permit, the top 10 to 30 feet of water. In the eastern end of the lake there is essentially no summer fishery for cohos. Occasionally they will be found in this area in about 300 feet of water, associating with schools of bait fish. But this happens so infrequently that it really doesn't add much to the fishing opportunities. Even as far west as Wayne County summer cohos are an elusive fish requiring as much luck as skill to locate.

Coho fishing really picks up in mid to late August, when these fish begin moving shoreward in anticipation of their spawning runs. Unlike the situation in the spring when the fish will be found primarily west of Oswego, in the fall they home in on their natal streams which are all in the far east end of Lake Ontario (keep in mind that I am only talking about the waters off Wayne, Cayuga and Oswego Counties. There are other portions of the lake that are stocked with coho). As they move into Mexio

EMPIRE STATE/LAKE ONTARIO DERBY

Nothing demonstrates the success of the state's rejuvenation program for Lake Ontario any more than the phenomenal growth of the **Empire State/Lake Ontario Trout and Salmon Derby, Inc.** Known simply as ESLO, this tournament was founded by Dick Schleyer, a former Rochester area biology teacher and fishing enthusiast, in 1976. It's beginnings were modest. Competing for a grand prize worth $2,500, a total of 2884 entrants participated in the first derby. In 1977, the contest had to be cancelled due to the DEC's ban on fishing in Lake Ontario that year. But Schleyer was not to be denied his dream. Convinced that Lake Ontario could once again support a viable sport fishery, he and other businessmen and sportsmen pushed to have the fishing ban lifted. It was, and as they say, the rest is history. As the quality of the fishing grew, so did ESLO. Today, Schleyer and his son Rick operate what is recognized as the world's largest fishing derby. Now held in the spring, summer and fall, more than 32,000 anglers from all over North America compete annually for over $400,000 in guaranteed prizes, as well as for thousands of dollars worth of manufacturer's incentive prizes.

One of the many reasons that ESLO has been so successful is the fact that everyone who enters the contest has a very good chance of winning something, whether you're fishing from a pier, a dinghy or a fully outfitted charter boat. And you don't have to be an expert angler to win either. The rank and file fisherman often walks away with the top prize, which can be worth as much as $30,000!

There are an incredible number of ways to win in these derbies. Aside from the grand prizes, there are scores of awards for the largest fish in the major divisions: salmon, brown trout, lake trout and rainbow trout/steelhead. Then there are prizes handed out by the Kidney Foundation and Easter Seal, numerous manufacturer and dealer prizes and special awards. All totalled, there are over 8,000 chances to be a winner in the ESLO derbies!

It doesn't cost a fortune to take part in this exciting tournament. In 1987 the spring derby had an entry fee of $13.00, while the summer and fall contests were $12.00 each. The entry fee also entitles you to receive the ESLO Newsletter, an information packed brief that reviews past derby events and discusses important happenings on the lake.

Then there is "The Derby Gazette", put out twice a year and available free at many tackle shops and marinas ($3.25 by subscription). This newspaper is so filled with information on various aspects of Lake Ontario that it would take days to read it all. Many of the articles are written by some of the best anglers on the lake. In fact, many of the guest articles that appear in this book are reprints of articles that have appeared over the years in the Gazette. They are valuable sources of information on how to fish Lake Ontario successfully.

The positive impact that Lake Ontario's rebirth has had on the state's economy is tremendous. A significant part of this is due directly to ESLO. In a report prepared by the Wayne County Public Information Office and Sea Grant, it was shown that in 1986 the spring ESLO Derby generated over $4,800,000 in revenue for the lakeshore region of the state. Significantly, over half of this money was spent by anglers not residing in the lakeshore region (16.5% were from out-of-state). A total of 12,845 fishermen participated in the 1986 spring derby. When you consider the fact that over 30,000 anglers participate in the three derbies now held annually on the lake, the economic impact of ESLO assumes truly amazing proportions.

Although ESLO is a fishing for profit business, money is not the only concern of the people who run the operation. As early as 1970 Dick Schleyer was lobbying state agencies to recognize the economic and recreational value of Lake Ontario. This sense of commitment to upgrading one of the state's greatest natural resources has remained a part of ESLO throughout its existance. In 1985 it resulted in the formation of the ESLO Fishing Advisory Council (FAC). The FAC is funded entirely from derby entry fees and membership is free to all entrants. Designed to represent the broad-based interests of its members, which number well over 30,000, its board of directors is composed of charter boat associations, county representatives, commercial interests and fishing organizations. The lobbying of the FAC has been instrumental in getting federal, state and county aid for various waterfront projects, for the banning of gill nets on Lake Ontario and in getting the state to introduce Skamania steelhead into the lake.

To become a member of the Fishery Advisory Council all you need to do is participate in one of the ESLO Derbies. Walk-in registrations can be obtained at many tackle shops along the lake and in major cities of the state. Mail in registrations and other information about ESLO, the FAC and LEI (Lake Erie International Fishing Derby - the Lake Erie counterpart of ESLO) can be obtained by contacting:

ESLO
P.O. Box 23746
Rochester, New York 14692
(716) 272-0130

Here's one reason the ESLO Derbies are so incredibly popular. Captain John Roides of Rochester holds the 31 pound 12 ounce chinook salmon that won the $30,000 rig in the background. The largest fishing derby in the world, ESLO has a total annual prize package worth $400,000. Photo courtesy ESLO.

ay they again form big schools that are constantly on the move. itially, these schools can be found anywhere in the bay, from ear-shore waters to several miles out, depending on weather onditions. But by the first week of September they will be located ery close to the streams they will spawn in. They can remain ocked off the mouths of these streams for up to several weeks, aiting for the right conditions to trigger their spawning runs. It is uring this period that anglers experience the fantastic salmon shing for which Lake Ontario has become renowned. By the end f September the salmon will be found running in the streams. aturally, stocked streams are going to offer the best fishing (for formation on the great coho fishing in the Oswego River and almon River see separate entries for those waters), but coho do tray into unstocked streams. These runs last until late November. There is no winter fishery for coho salmon.

rown Trout.............. abundant; growth rate excellent

Not long after ice-out tremendous numbers of brown trout ill be found along the shoreline of eastern Lake Ontario, drawn by bait fish and favorable temperatures (50°-65° F). West of ine Mile Point browns can usually be found tight up against the nore by mid-April. However, east of Nine Mile Point Mexico Bay tays colder longer and the fish might not show up near shore ntil late April. When they come into the shallows north of the almon River they don't remain sedentary. There is a definite novement of browns northward along the shore, and they ometimes move as much as 3 or 4 miles per day, probably llowing favorable temperature conditions. Usually, though, rown trout are more likely than other salmonids to stay in the eneral vicinity of where they were stocked.

Nettings by the DEC have shown that in the spring browns an be taken practically anywhere along the shoreline west of the nouth of the Salmon River. North of the Salmon River the noreline fishing is not consistant. But even west of the river nouth some areas are better than others. Moving east to west ome of the more productive areas for brown trout in the pringtime include:

. Selkirk Shores State Park — This is a major brown trout tocking site. Public piers provide access to the lake.

. The western shore of Mexico Bay — The warm water outflow om several streams (Grindstone Creek, Little Salmon River, atfish Creek) creates a plume of warm water in this area rawing in salmonids.

. Sunset Bay — This small bay just east of Nine Mile Point lies utside of the fast shore currents of the lake and consequently varms up quickly. It's often possible to take browns here as early s mid-March.

. Nine Mile Point — This point is a cliff with 6 to 9 feet of water at s base. This is a good area to check when the fishing is hard.

. The Fitz Patrick power plant — The warm water discharge om this plant is very productive and popular in the spring. It's not ncommon to find over 100 boats congregated around the utflow.

. Nine Mile Point Station — This power plant has a discharge hat is close to shore and not well diffused, so the temperature lifference here is considerable. Excellent for browns in the pring.

. Lakeview — The small bay at Lakeview is usually just a little varmer than the surrounding waters, enough to bring in good umbers of brown trout. They congregate along the rocky ledges.

. Oswego Harbor — A number of factors combine to make this n excellent area for browns in the spring. The river itself is a fraw, this is a major stocking site and there are no less than four ignificant affluents in or near the harbor (2 warm water, 2 ewage). Check a current edition of N.O.A.A. chart 14813 to ocate these. The fishing in the harbor itself is especially good rom the mouth of the river down along the east wall of the harbor and in the slot where the current exists. During a strong wind

storm this harbor can still be safely fished.

9. Rice Creek — Brown trout are often attracted to the deep near shore waters off the mouth of this stream.

10. Ford Shoals - Very good early spring fishing here. The browns are often found right up on top of the shoal in 3 to 4 feet of water.

11. West Nine Mile Point — There is generally good trout fishing in this area due to the warm outflow of Eight Mile Creek and Nine Mile Creek. The small bay just east of the point is also very good. The big drawback to this area is that there are no launch sites nearby.

12. Little Sodus Bay piers — A plume of warm water builds up between the east pier and the mouth of Sterling Creek, attracting fish. Browns can be taken here as late as mid-June. This is also a major stocking site.

13. Port Bay — Smelt and alewives come into Port Bay to spawn, drawing in browns. This doesn't happen every year, but when it does the fishing can be very good.

14. Sodus Bay — A major brown trout area in the spring. Sodus Point is a stocking site. Great numbers of browns move into the channel and the bay to feed on alewives in May.

15. Salmon Creek (Pultneyville) — A stocking site, this area often has better than average fishing for browns.

16. Ginna Power Plant — The warm water discharge from this plant is best known as a site for excellent winter fishing, but good numbers of browns can also be caught here in the spring. Access to this area is poor.

Brown trout are much more tolerant of high water temperatures than other salmonids. Consequently, many of them will still be found close to shore after the rainbows, lakers and salmon have all moved out into deeper water. It's not until the end of June, when the thermocline has set up, that the brown trout move off shore in search of favorable temperatures. In the open waters of the lake they are usually found in water 56°-62° F. If conditions permit it they will remain in the general vicinity of the area in

Lucy Hinell, a secretary at the DEC's Cortland office, with 2 Lake Ontario brown trout. This lake offers some of the best brown trout fishing in the world! Photo courtesy Lucy Hinell.

You don't have to spend thousands of dollars to join in on the fishing action. There are hundreds of charter boat captains working on this lake, and their prices are usually quite reasonable. Pick your charter with care. Talk with tackle shops and marinas until you find a captain with a reputation for safety and efficiency, not just the ability to catch fish. Bill Kelley, pictured above, is one of the top charter boat captains on Lake Ontario.

which they were stocked. When searching for browns in the summer look for areas where the thermocline is no more than 30 feet from the bottom; the closer to the bottom the better. Obviously, you're not going to have to move too far off shore to find them. However, because of their strong preference for these conditions, brown trout will, if necessary, move great distances parallel to the shore to locate water with these requirements.

Because they are so predictable and abundant, brown trout are very susceptible to modern downrigging techniques. They can be taken in good numbers in June, July and early August, with the most productive summer fishing occuring from early July through early August.

In early August brown trout enter their spawning phase and stop feeding, making them essentially unavailable to anglers. Unlike spawning salmon, you're not likely to goad a spawning brown trout into striking. They remain in this state until late October or early November. As water temperatures begin to drop in the lake, they move closer to shore. By early October they will be found in great numbers in the shallows. When conditions are right they will make their spawning runs up streams and rivers.

Almost every tributary that has a flow into the lake will get a run of fish at this time, regardless of how small they are. See individual county sections for information on streams that get fall runs of trout. Approximately 60% of these spawning trout will die. Those that survive will return the following year as significantly larger fish. Brown trout in the 10 to 20 pound category will have survived several spawnings.

After spawning most of the browns will leave the streams and rivers and return to the lake. There are a few tributaries, though, that browns will hold over in. The lower Oswego River has respectable brown trout fishing in the late fall and winter, and to a lesser extent so do the Salmon and Little Salmon Rivers. Browns are also taken occasionally through the ice from Sodus Bay, Port Bay, Little Sodus Bay and North Sandy Pond. The fish that do return to the lake are somewhat scattered. Some are found fairly close to shore, while many probably move out into the deeper regions of the lake. For consistently good brown trout fishing in the late fall and winter, your best bet would be to concentrate on the warm water discharges of the power plants mentioned above.

Rainbow Trout/Steelhead . common; growth rate excellent

NOTE: The tributary systems of Lake Ontario are inhabite by several strains of rainbow trout, some stocked, some wild. It i possible for many of them to find their way into the lake prope where they are often referred to as "steelhead," the name given t lake-run rainbows. However, the true steelhead is a specifi strain of rainbow trout. Because most rainbows found in the lak are almost indistinguishable from true steelhead in terms o anatomy and habits, and to avoid unnecessary confusion, w have used the terms steelhead and rainbow trout interchangeabl when discussing Lake Ontario and those tributaries recognize as "steelhead" streams.

The yearly cycle of the rainbow starts in the early fall, whe they begin moving in close to shore, searching for favorabl water temperatures. They will be found within a quarter mile o shore from late September through early November, and ar readily taken using conventional trolling methods. By lat October many fish will begin moving into streams and rivers i anticipation of spawning. This movement into tributaries con tinues until early April, reaching its peak in March. Almost an stream that has an appreciable outflow into the lake will get a ru of fish, some more than others. Because many of the smalle streams are often closed off by a sand or gravel bar durin periods of low waterfall, you often have to wait for a significar amount of rainfall for them to break through to the lake. This i especially true in the fall. In the spring you can usually count o melting snow to keep the streams flowing.

Moving east to west, these are the streams that get majo runs of rainbow trout from November to April:

1. Skinner Creek — This small tributary of North Sandy Pond ha a population of wild steelhead. Adult fish begin returning to thi stream in early November. The fishing here can be good throug the winter and into the spring if the weather isn't too cold.

2. Lindsey Creek — This is another tributary of North Sand Pond that enjoys good runs of wild steelhead from Novembe through April if the weather holds out. Unlike Skinner Creek Lindsey Creek is closed to all fishing from October 1 throug November 30 (from Route 11 bridge to source) to protec

awning landlocked salmon. See regulations guide.

Little Sandy Creek — same as Lindsay Creek. If the weather cooperates, the steelhead fishing can be superb on this stream in December, otherwise you have to wait until spring. Wild steelhead of 20 pounds have been taken from this stream!

Salmon River — Rainbow trout can often be found near the mouth of this river as early as September. See article on page 79 for information on trout fishing here.

Oswego River — Very good fishing for rainbows here from late October through early May. See article on page 76 for information on trout fishing in the lower Oswego River.

Sterling Creek — Not fantastic, but the rainbow trout fishing here in the spring is certainly above average.

Sodus Bay piers — Sodus Point is a major stocking area for rainbows, and they home in on the bay in the late fall. The fishing is best in front of the bay or from the piers, not in the bay itself.

Maxwell Creek — For some unknown reason, Maxwell Creek unquestionably gets the best run of trout in Wayne County. They will be found in the lake not far from the creek mouth as early as October, providing some excellent fall fishing. By the spring, many of these fish will have moved into the creek itself making this by far the most productive stream in the county.

Because of selective breeding in the hatcheries, not all of the rainbow trout are going to spawn at the same time in the spring. Many of those that aren't spawning will often times be found in the lake close to shore in search of forage fish and warm temperatures. The preferred temperature range for these fish is 00-65° F. These shore-bound fish tend to orient off rocky points, piers, sharp drop-offs and shoals. They will also be found near areas of thermal mixing, such as stream mouths, warm water discharges from power plants and sewage outfalls (you can usually tell when you're near a sewage outfall by the grey color of the water). These are essentially the same areas where brown trout will be found in the spring. Refer to the section on brown trout for a listing of where many of these productive areas are located.

By late April, rainbows will begin to move off shore. Before they can break out into deep open water they become corralled behind what is referred to as a thermal bar. This bar is a temporary interface between waters of different temperatures. It is characterized by a rapid change in surface temperature over a very short distance, with warm near-shore waters quickly giving way to a steep "wall" of cold (39° F) dense water. Rainbows are strongly attracted to this thermal structure and stack up along the shoreward edge of the bar as it moves toward the center of the lake. The thermal bar finally disappears around the middle of June. While it lasts the trout fishing near the bar can be spectacularly productive.

When the thermal bar disappears (it doesn't really disappear. It is simply a stage in the development of the more permanent thermocline) the rainbows move out into the open waters of the lake. In the summer they can be extremely hard to find. They roam the open lake, at least 3 to 5 miles from shore, close to the surface, showing little tendency to concentrate in any particular area. Unlike the western half of the lake, where cold water upwellings are a common occurance, there is no significant thermal structure for these rainbows to orient to in eastern Lake Ontario. Thus, until they begin moving back toward shore in September, the fishing for rainbow trout can be difficult.

To help remedy this situation the state has started stocking several streams (Maxwell Creek, Oswego River and Big Stoney Creek) with the Skamania strain of rainbows. Normally, this strain of rainbows spawns in extremely long rivers where a long upstream migration to spawning grounds is necessary. Thus, their spawning cycle is somewhat different than other rainbows. Starting in June, Skamania begin moving back toward shore. They will be found a mile or less off shore, near the surface, from June through August. In late summer or early fall they start moving into streams, but won't spawn until the following spring.

Dan Van Alstine with a 23 pound 7 ounce steelhead. Photo courtesy ESLO.

These fish have been genetically selected for another interesting characteristic: They will not return to their natal streams to spawn until they have reached a weight of 10 or 11 pounds, their usual weight at maturity. Other strains of rainbows found in Lake Ontario are only 5 to 6 pounds when they begin making spawning runs. It is hoped that by stocking these fish here a consistent summer fishery for rainbows can be established in the lake.

Lake Trout .... abundant; growth rate excellent

Lake Ontario originally had an excellent population of native lake trout. Their eventual demise began in the 19th century with the settlement of large numbers of people on the southern shore of the lake. By the early 20th century a combination of commercial overharvesting and predation by lampreys had all but wiped out this once thriving population. The last recorded sport catch of native lake trout occurred in the 1930's.

In the 1960's advances in artificial rearing techniques and a commitment on the part of the state and federal governments to reestablish sport fishing in Lake Ontario resulted in a program for stocking lake trout here. Coupled with an ongoing lamprey control effort, the long term purpose of this stocking program is to reestablish a self-sustaining lake trout population. Naturally produced lakers have in fact been reported in recent years. If the program is successful it will be a major step in the rehabilitation of Lake Ontario.

The preferred temperature range of lake trout is 45°-55°. In the spring they move into shallow near-shore waters, drawn in by amenable temperatures and abundant forage fish. This takes place just after ice-out, which is important to remember, because ice-out does not occur on all areas of the lake at the same time. In a typical year the shoreline of the lake will be ice-free by late March in areas west of the Salmon River. Ice-out is somewhat later along the shore down lake of the Salmon River. The eastern tributaries of the lake originate on or near the Tug Hill Plateau and their outflow is especially cold for an extended period of time due to the great volume of snow that melts and runs off the plateau.

Nettings by the DEC have shown that lake trout can be found almost anywhere along the shore in the spring and can be taken by shore fishermen and boat fishermen alike. West of the Salmon River lakers are not harvested in numbers that are indicative of their abundance. This could be due to a number of factors. The fish could be moving a little further off-shore during the daylight hours due to their sensitivity to light. Or possibly the fishermen are concentrating their efforts on the more popular brown trout. This would seem to explain the fact that in April and early May lake trout do make up a significant part of the catch along the shore north of the Salmon River. Brown trout can't begin moving into that area until the end of April due to the cold temperatures, and anglers have to take what's available.

Though they can be taken practically anywhere along the shore of the lake in the spring, some areas can be especially productive. Check out the mouths of major tributaries, warm water discharges, major piers, sand bars and rocky points for the best spring action. This spring fishery lasts until the middle of May (end of May north of the Salmon River) when shore temperatures become too warm and the bait fish move off shore, forcing the lakers into deeper parts of the lake.

In the summer, lake trout are the bread and butter of Ontario's charter boat industry. When nothing else is hitting on the eastern end of the lake you can almost always count on taking a few lake trout. Because of their abundance and very predictable behavior they are very susceptible to modern downrigging techniques. To find them all you really need to do is locate water in the 45°-55° F range (53°-55° F is the optimum temperature range). Stay within that stratum long enough and you're sure to find some action. A majority of lakers are caught while suspended, but some fish are taken close to the bottom.

Beginning on October 1, 1987 new regulations went into effect for lake trout in Lake Ontario. The season now runs from January 1 to September 30. Possession is limited to fish less than 25 inches and greater than 30 inches. All other lake trout must be released. Daily limit: 3 lake trout per day.

Smallmouth Bass .... abundant; growth rate excellent

Lake Ontario has always been recognized as having superb fishing for smallmouth bass. And nowhere is this more true than in the eastern portion of the lake. Traditionally, areas such as Henderson Harbor and Chaumont Bay in the northeast corner of the lake were thought to hold most if not all of the really good smallmouth fishing. But in the past decade the stretch of shoreline along the southeast corner has also been shown to offer exceptional fishing opportunities for these scrappy fighters. Practically the entire shore line from Irondequoit Bay east to North Sandy Pond has the potential for holding bass. Areas offering exceptional fishing include (moving west to east):

1. Nine Mile Point/Webster Park — 4 miles east of Irondequoit Bay Outlet at terminus of Route 250; rock and boulder bottom.

2. Smokey Point — 5½ miles west of Pultneyville Habor; rock and

cobble bottom; discharge from Ginna power plant acts as a attractor.

3. Bear Creek Harbor — 3½ miles west of Pultneyville Harbor rock and cobble bottom.

4. Pultneyville Harbor — at intersection of Routes 18 and 2 good bottom structure, rock and cobble bottom.

5. Fairbanks Point — 1½ miles east of Pultneyville Harbor; goo structure, cobble and boulder bottom.

6. Boulder (Boller) Point — 2½ miles west of Sodus Poin boulder strewn bottom structure at 8 to 18 feet with good drop offs to 25 feet; excellent early season fishing and good summe fishing.

7. Maxwell Bay — 1¾ miles west of Sodus Point; fish directly o bay outlet; good early season and summer fishing.

8. Sodus Bay piers — at Sodus Point; good early season fishing from the piers or just in front of the bay in the lake; the fish ofter return to the area in early August providing very good fishing

9. Lake Bluff — 1½ miles east of Sodus Point; rock, cobble bottom, good structure beneath 4 to 25 feet of water; good earl season and summer fishing.

10. Chimney Bluffs — 3 miles east of Sodus Point; rock and cobble bottom; good early season and summer fishing.

11. Port Bay — north of Wolcott; directly off bay outlet the botton is cobble and rock from 15 to 30 feet of water; excellent summe fishing.

12. Red Creek — 2 miles east of Port Bay; fish off creek outlet and high bluff; excellent summer fishing in 15 to 30 feet of water

13. Fair Haven — fish east or west of outlet of Little Sodus Bay breakwalls at harbor entrance and off the outlet of The Pond a Fair Haven State Park are especially productive; silt and grave bottom.

14. West Nine Mile Point — 7 miles east of Fair Haven; irregula gravel bars off the mouths of Nine Mile Creek and Eight Mil Creek provide good summer fishing.

15. Ford Shoals — 4½ miles west of Oswego; productive fishing west to West Nine Mile Point and east to Oswego; mouth of Rice Creek and shoals off SUNY at Oswego are both very productive bottom along this stretch of shoreline is rocky.

16. Breakwalls at Oswego — at the entrance of Oswego Harbor good fishing on harbor side and lake side of breakwalls.

A lake trout with attached sea lampreys. Lampreys are still a problem in Lake Ontario. Attaching to the game fish with a rasping sucker-like mouth, they suck fluids out of the fish, retarding its growth and often killing it. Photo courtesy DEC.

. Flat Rock — just east of eastern Oswego harbor breakwall, off e Fort Ontario Historic site. Good smallmouth habitat around bmerged rocks. Boaters are warned to be cautious of shallow ater (less than 6 feet) with many submerged rocks near the irface.

. Nine Mile Point — 6 miles east of Oswego; fish close to rtical rock walls and around power plant discharge; rock and avel bottom; good fishing in summer and fall.

. Selkirk Shores State Park — 1 mile south of Salmon River; avel bottom; good summer fishing.

. Mouth of Salmon River — very good fishing where the sand it at the mouth of the river drops off to 10-15 feet; there is very od fishing in the summer where the current runs along the Ige of this drop-off; in August and September the bass can be und right in the mouth of the river in the evening.

. Entrance to North Sandy Pond — 6½ miles north of Port ntario; fish the entrance leading into North Sandy Pond; sand ottom. Boaters should be very cautious when navigating this hannel. Do not rely blindly on buoys — the configuration of the hannel can change almost daily.

Beginning in the late spring, when water temperatures are earing 50° F, smallmouth begin to school in shallow water along e lake shore, and in the lower reaches of many tributaries. They main in these areas through the spawning season. Later, ound the middle of June, rising temperatures force the bass to ek out cool, deeper waters. Their preferred water temperatures nge from 68° to 70° F, though they will at times be found in ater as warm as 75° F. They favor areas with a cobble or rocky ottom and are especially attracted to structures such as oulder-strewn shoals and submerged ledges. The greatest oncentrations of smallmouth occur in these areas during the onths of July, August and September, with some fish still vailable in early October.

Actively feeding fish will almost always be found in water ess than 45 feet deep. By the middle of October the smallmouth vill have migrated into deeper waters and will not feed very ggressively. Unlike some of the Finger Lakes, Lake Ontario has ever developed a winter fishery for bass.

There are three basic methods used to take smallmouth bass om Lake Ontario: trolling, drift fishing and still fishing, and they an be used in combination.

Some anglers consider trolling to be the most productive of hese techniques and troll throughout the season. But there are wo occasions when trolling is especially successful. The first is the early summer when the bass are moving out of the hallows and on to the shoals. For a period of a few weeks they re well dispersed on and between the two areas and locating heir precise location is difficult. Trolling allows the angler to over a great deal of ground, improving the chances of finding sh.

The second occasion when trolling is particularly called for is when an angler is fishing in waters he is unfamiliar with. Even hough it has been possible to identify individual areas as "hot pots," some of these "hot spots" are themselves the size of small akes. Usually an angler working over a new location is not going o know exactly where the fish tend to congregate. Trolling is good way to locate these spots.

Once you've located a productive area by trolling, don't just ry to commit it to memory. On a lake the size of Ontario this usually isn't feasible. Instead, mark the spot with a buoy (a plastic leach bottle will serve the purpose) attached to 45 feet of heavy tring and a weight. When a fish hits while trolling, toss the narker buoy overboard immediately, in the direction of where the ish hit. This will give you a pretty good idea of where a school of eeding smallmouth are located.

Because trolling, even at very slow speeds, puts extra stress n equipment, use slightly heavier equipment than you normally vould. Light to medium rods and reels should be used with 6 to 8 ound test line.

The major portion of the smallmouth's diet in Lake Ontario consists of crayfish and small minnows. Thus you want to troll with artificial baits that imitate these foods. Full-bodied sinking or deep-diving lures will produce the most fish if worked properly, but jigs and spinners will also take smallmouth. They can be trolled using flat lines or on short lines behind a downrigger weight.

A critical element in successful trolling is getting and keeping the lure as close to the bottom as possible without getting hung up on rocks or weeds. The smallmouth in this lake are seldom far from bottom. One way to ensure that the lure is at the proper depth is to start trolling, slowly letting out line. When enough line has been played out to get the lure to the bottom the rod tip will start dipping repeatedly as the lure bounces along the bottom. Don't let it do this too long or you could lose it. Reel in just enough line to make the rod tip stop jerking. The lure should then be just above the bottom.

In some portions of the lake a green algae known as cladophora carpets the bottom from mid-June through mid-August. If you're fishing in such an area, be sure to keep your lures riding above the algae and check them often for snagged plant debris.

The second technique used to take smallmouth on this lake is drift fishing. There are several variations to this method, all of which can be fantastically productive. This is especially true from late July through September when smallmouth are heavily concentrated on the shoals. Because drift fishing depends on the wind and the waves for speed and direction you are somewhat hostage to the whims of the weather. If the lake is too calm obviously you're not going to have a drift. If it's too windy and choppy you're going to be blown off the lake. Anglers I spoke to who specialize in drift-fishing recommend a south, southwest, west or west-northwest wind just strong enough to kick up a 1½ to 2 foot chop. Typically, ultralight tackle and 4 to 6 pound test

Captain Charlie DeNoto with a fine stringer of Lake Ontario smallmouth. DeNoto developed a technique he calls "Center Line Drifting" which often results in catches of 50 or more bass per outing. Photo courtesy Charlie DeNoto.

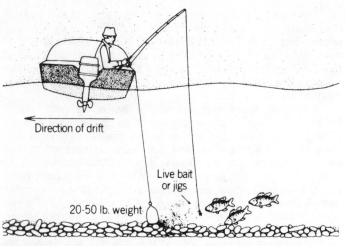

Direction of drift

Live bait
or jigs

20-50 lb. weight

One very successful drift technique is the anchor-drag method, also known as the center line drift method. From late July through September, the samllmouth's major source of food are crayfish (crabs) which are often present in large numbers on rocky lake bottoms. A drift or drag anchor is lowered to the bottom, not with the intention of stopping the boat's drift, but rather for the purpose of turning over stones on the bottom which expose the crayfish hidden beneath. This stirring up of the bottom by the anchor apparently attracts large numbers of smallmouth into the area to feed. Anglers fishing with live softshell crayfish or artificial jigs in the roiled waters behind the drag anchor usually experience faster action. Simple drag anchors can be made out of a cinder block, stones tied in nylon mesh bags, or a cement-filled plastic milk or bleach bottle.

line is used. Artificial baits, primarily jigs in black, brown or chartreuse, can be used, but live baits get more action. Crayfish (softshelled if at all possible), nightcrawlers and minnows, in descending order of preference, are the natural baits to use. Rigged on a #4 hook with just enough weight to reach the bottom the bait is dragged along the rocks and cobbles attracting the bass.

Charter boat captain Charlie DeNoto, who operates out of Port Bay, has developed a technique of drift fishing that he calls "center-line drifting." At times this method can be almost sinfully productive. More than once I've heard of parties coming back from a charter with Charlie having boated in excess of 50 smallmouth!

DeNoto's method takes advantage of the fact that, from late July through September, the smallmouth rely primarily on crayfish for food. These small crustaceans are often found in great numbers on bottoms that consist of rock and cobble. The key to center-line drifting is a 20 to 50 pound weight, which is attached to the gunwales amidships and allowed to drag along the bottom. This churns the bottom up, exposing crayfish, and creating what amounts to a chum line. The best smallmouth action occurs when you fish in the freshly roiled waters right behind the weight. Softshelled crabs are by far the best bait to use with this method, followed by worms, jigs and minnows.

A secondary function of the weight is to serve as a drag anchor, helping to control the speed of the drift. With a 1½ foot chop you can drift with the weight almost straight down. But if the wind picks up, causing you to drift too fast, feed rope out, letting the weight drag further and further behind the boat until your drift has been sufficiently reduced. Remember, though, that you want to be fishing on the far side of the weight, regardless of where it's positioned.

Center-line drifting is most productive in the waters just off the mouth of Port Bay, where the conditions are ideally suited to this technique. It can, however, be used on other parts of the lake that have a gravel or cobble bottom. It probably wouldn't be very productive in areas with a silt or sandy bottom, and it can't be

done in areas covered with large rocks or boulders because th weight would hang up.

The third method used to take smallmouth from Lake Ontari is still fishing. This is used when a concentration of fish has bee located, or when fishing over specific structures, such a boulders, ledges, etc. Ultralight rods and reels with 4 to 6 poun test line should be adequate. Live bait or artificials can be use depending on how and where you are fishing. Still fishing is mos effective when used in conjunction with trolling. Once concentration of fish has been located through trolling, the boa can be anchored and the area fished until the bass leave the are or stop feeding. Then resume trolling.

Much of the information used in this article was taken from the pamphlet "Angling for Smallmouth Bass in Lake Ontario, which was put together by Robert Buerger and Michael Voilan of the New York Sea Grant Extension Program. For information on how to obtain this and other Sea Grant publications se General Information.

Smelt . . . . abundant; growth rate good

Much of the success of Lake Ontario's rejuvenated salmonic fishery can be attributed to the huge forage base that exists in th lake. A large portion of this forage base consists of smelt, which are themselves sought by many anglers. Every spring, usually jus a few weeks after ice-out, unbelievable numbers of these small very tasty fish move in close to shore. They hug the bottom during the day, but at night move into shallow water (1 to 3 feet) and swim parallel to shore in schools that number in the millions seeking out streams in which to spawn. Anglers, armed with di nets and fishing by the glow of a fire or Coleman lantern, ca harvest almost unlimited quantities of smelt at the height of th run. Almost any stream mouth (unless closed off by a gravel bar) pier or stretch of shoreline will be productive, with angling opportunities limited more by poor accessiblity to the lake than by the availability of fish.

Yellow Perch . . . . common; growth rate good

Lake Ontario has always enjoyed a reputation for good perc fishing. At present, the yellow perch population is considerabl depressed compared to what it was in previous times, due t competition from alewives. But survivors from the strong yea classes of 1978 and 1982 are still to be found in good numbers i the eastern part of the lake, and at times the perch fishing can b down right good. And what these fish lack in numbers they make up for in size. Many of these fish run 1½ to 2½ pounds.

In the spring, yellow perch can be found in or near every major harbor or stream mouth and can be taken in goo numbers. At times you can still fill a 5 gallon pail with these fine tasting fish. Good spring perch fishing will be found at Sodus Bay (bay and piers), East Bay, Port Bay, Blind Sodus Bay, Little Sodus Bay, The Pond (Sterling Creek), Oswego Harbor, the mouth o Little Salmon River, North Sandy Pond and Deer Creek.

In the summer, the perch move out into the lake. To find them look for structure, preferably covered with algae (cladophora), i water no more than 50 feet deep. Many of the sites listed as hotspots for smallmouth bass are likely to hold some yellow perch. Other areas that should be checked out would be any o the locations marked on your Lake Ontario maps as PWI (potable water intakes). The perch seem to be attracted to the cribbing a the end of each intake, and some of these can be exceptionally productive. Perch can be found in these areas through the summer months, but the most productive period occurs in mid September. Minnows are the most productive bait.

In the late fall, yellow perch begin moving back into the larger bays to spend the winter. Bays that get a good influx of perch in winter include Sodus Bay, Port Bay, Little Sodus Bay, The Pond and North Sandy Pond. When the fish first move into these bays they can be very easy to catch. Later, many are harvested through the ice. See individual entries for fishing on the bays.

Walleye . . . . uncommon; growth rate good

Traditionally, walleye were an important fishery in Lake Ontario, but changes in the ecology of the lake have resulted in a drastic reduction in their numbers. The spawning in 1978 produced a fairly strong year class of walleye, and these fish have been providing the bulk of the fish caught in recent years. But their numbers are rapidly declining, and there is no indication that another strong year class will soon replace them. At present, there is very little open water walleye fishing in eastern Lake Ontario. Most of the walleye now caught are taken in or near the mouths of major streams or rivers, primarily those that have a healthy indigenous population of walleyes. Your best chance for taking a walleye from the east end of the lake would probably be at Oswego Harbor. The river has a very good population of these fish (the DEC claims that a state record walleye is swimming around in these waters) and they do find their way down to the harbor area. Lake-run walleyes are also drawn to the river mouth. Other areas that occasionally give up a walleye include Sodus Bay, Port Bay, Blind Sodus Bay, and North Sandy Pond, but these instances are becoming increasingly rare.

Additional Species

Aside from the major species found in Lake Ontario, a number of lesser fisheries exist whose combined importance can not be over estimated. Prominent among these secondary species are:

Brown Bullhead — Shortly after ice-out great numbers of these fine tasting fish will be found along the shore of the lake and in streams and bays. These lake-run bullhead are big, averaging about 1½ pounds. Outstanding fishing for them will be found in Sodus Bay, Little Sodus Bay, The Pond, the Oswego River, the Salmon River, Deer Creek and North Sandy Pond. These fish are not only good tasting, they are also practically free of the contaminants found in other species that inhabit Lake Ontario.

Black Crappie — Known also as strawberry bass, these delicately flavored fish are most easily caught in the spring and fall. From April through June large schools of crappies will move into bays and streams to spawn. The most productive areas in the spring are Sodus Bay, East Bay (when the barrier bar is open), Port Bay, The Pond, Little Sodus Bay, the Salmon River and North Sandy Pond. Summer heat will force them to move out into the lake during the summer. They are less active in the summer months and aren't easily caught. They become more active in the fall and can be taken in good numbers from near-shore waters of the lake if you can find them schooled up. In the winter, many of the bays along the lake provide fair to good ice fishing for crappies.

Rock Bass — At just about the time that apple trees are in blossom (late May) schools of rock bass will move into streams and bays to spawn. These scrappy fighters can be taken on live baits and small spinners in great numbers from Sodus Bay, Port Bay, The Pond, the Salmon River, Deer Creek and North Sandy Pond. In the summer, they can be found throughout the shallow portions of the lake near any type of structure: docks, shoals, gravel bars, downed trees and weed beds will all hold rock bass. Excellent table fare, many of the rock bass in Lake Ontario approach a pound in size.

White Perch — The spring spawning runs of white perch don't seem to be as massive in the eastern end of the lake as they are in areas to the west, such as in the Greece Ponds near Rochester. But they do provide some fine fishing in Little Sodus Bay, The Pond and North Sandy Pond. In the summer good catches are often taken from shoal areas at dusk and dawn, and from deep water in the daytime. These are a schooling fish, and when one is caught it's almost a certainty that great numbers of white perch are nearby.

Atlantic Salmon — Since 1983, Atlantic salmon have been stocked in Lake Ontario on an experimental basis, with a total of 49,000 yearlings being planted in Irondequoit Creek, Little Sandy

This gentleman is obviously pleased with the 12½ pound Atlantic Salmon he caught while fishing off Maxwell Creek. He was fishing aboard "The Fishin' Pole" charter, captained by John Kowalczyk, one of the top guides on the lake. The state plans on stocking tremendous numbers of Atlantics in Lake Ontario in the near future. Photo courtesy John Kowalczyk.

Creek and Lindsey Creek each year. The relatively small numbers involved in these stockings haven't really provided much of a fishery for this highly prized game fish, but it has resulted in two new state records for this species. It has also shown that it is possible to successfully reintroduce these salmon through a stocking program. In the near future, the State of New York and the Province of Ontario plan on dramatically increasing the number of Atlantic salmon stocked in the lake. Ontario tentatively plans a yearly planting of 350,000 salmon. The DEC hasn't yet decided on what level of stocking it will go to, but it will be enough to add a new and exciting dimension to the Lake Ontario fishing scene.

Also found in Lake Ontario are minor populations of largemouth bass, northern pike and channel catfish. Throughout the shallower regions of the lake are the ubiquitous carp, suckers and sheepshead.

General Information

Lake Ontario is truly a little giant. Though the smallest of the Great Lakes, it has nevertheless developed a well deserved reputation as one of the finest sport fishing waters in all of North America. It's deep, well oxygenated waters, productive littoral zone and numerous tributaries offer anglers outstanding fishing opportunities for a wide range of cold and warm water species.

Historically, Lake Ontario was a fishery of monumental proportions. Indians and early white settlers harvested vast quantities of the lake's native species, including Atlantic salmon, walleye, blue pike and lake trout.

Unfortunately, this bounty was doomed by a long series of ecological disasters, all of which were man-made. The destruction of spawning areas, overharvesting and the introduction of exotic species all combined to wipe out nearly all of the lake's game species. Those that remained were assaulted by toxins from industrial and municipal sources. By the late 1960's all that was left of this once great fishery was a bittersweet memory. In the words of Bill Abraham, a senior aquatic biologist for the DEC's region #8 office, "Before 1973, Lake Ontario was a good place to get your drinking water and dump your garbage."

In the late 1960's the first tentative steps were taken to turn this situation around. Programs were initiated to bring the problem of the sea lamprey under control, which was critical to the success of any stocking program. Then, taking their cue from the successful pioneering efforts of Michigan's early salmonid program, the State of New York and the Province of Ontario began stocking the lake with trout and salmon in 1968. Encouraged by the success of these early plantings, the scale of the program has increased steadily ever since. By 1986, over 8,000,000 trout and salmon were being stocked in the lake by New York and Ontario each year, and the dream of reestablishing a world class fishery had been achieved. Lake Ontario is now arguably the best lake for brown trout fishing in the world, and the quality of the chinook and steelhead fishing draws anglers from all over North America. And the miracle isn't over yet. Soon, biologists hope to establish a significant fishery for Atlantic salmon and the Skamania strain of steelhead.

Overshadowed by the spectacular trout and salmon fishing is Lake Ontario's warm water fishing. The narrow littoral zone of the lake has very good fishing for smallmouth bass, rock bass, bullhead, black crappies and white perch. If conditions are right the lake can also have some pretty respectable fishing for yellow perch. The many bays and creek mouths along the lake also provide good fishing for these and other species, and in the winter provide the bulk of the ice fishing on the lake.

Although the situation in Lake Ontario has vastly improved over the past two decades, it would be wrong to presume that all of the problems have been eliminated. Pollution is still a major problem here. The levels of pollutants in the lake have been declining for a number of years, but the levels of toxins found in many of the fish are still a concern to health officials. The state strongly recommends limiting your intake of most of the species caught in Lake Ontario. For a current summary of the state's health advisory regarding this lake consult your fishing regulations guide. For information on how to reduce the amount of contaminants found in the fish contact your regional office of the DEC or County cooperative extension.

Another problem that besets Lake Ontario is the lack of adequate public access, especially boat access. With the phenomenal growth of boating and fishing on the lake, the state has for a number of reasons been unable to keep up with the demand for additional facilities. And some areas of the lake will never have adequate launching capabilities due to the topography of the shoreline. County, state and federal agencies are looking at the problem, and new access sites are constantly being considered, but for the moment access to some portions of the lake are not adequate.

To accommodate those not familiar with the techniques of trout and salmon fishing on Lake Ontario, or who don't have the necessary equipment, a booming charter boat industry has developed. Operating out of every port on the lake, there are several hundred chart boat captains licensed by the Coast Guard to take you out in search of some of the finest fishing in the world.

Many of these captains are bonafide fishing pros who will not only help you catch fish, but will also teach you a great deal about how it's done. They can provide you with an experience you've not likely to forget. There are far too many licensed charters to list here, but many of them are affiliated with regional organizations. For information on what charters are available try contacting local marinas or one of the organizations listed below.

1. Eastern Lake Ontario
    Salmon & Trout Association
    6189 Ridgecrest Drive
    North Syracuse, New York 13212
    (315) 452-0636

2. Genesee Charter Association
    27 Topper Drive
    Rochester, New York 14622
    (716) 323-1147

3. Lake Ontario Charter Association
    P.O. Box 23291
    Rochester, New York 14692

4. Rochester Trout & Salmon Anglers
    796 DeWitt Rd.
    Webster, New York 13480
    (716) 671-7669

Additional information on fishing in central and eastern Lake Ontario can be obtained by contacting:

N.Y.S. Department of Environmental Conservation
6274 East Avon-Lima Road
Avon, New York 14414
(716) 226-2466

N.Y.S. Department of Environmental Conservation
P.O. Box 1169, Fisher Avenue
Cortland, New York 13045
(607) 753-3095

Sea Grant Extension Program
SUNY/Oswego
Oswego, New York 13126
(315) 341-3042

Lake Ontario Fishing Hot Lines

1. Jefferson County..........................(315) 782-266?
2. Oswego County ....(315) 342-587?
3. Wayne County............................(315) 483-4454
4. Monroe County ....(716) 467-732C
5. Orleans County ....(716) 682-4223
6. Niagara County..........................(716) 433-5606

The equipment and techniques used to locate and catch trout and salmon on Lake Ontario is a subject worthy of a seperate book. Rather than taking on such a task, I'vd chosen instead to reproduce the following articles. Written by some of the best anglers on the lake, and by biologists studying the dynamics of this fishery, these articles are realiable sources of information on various aspects of fishing on Lake Ontario. These articles originally appeared in either the ESLO Derby Gazette or as seperate publications issued by Sea Grant. Additional articles can be obtained by subscribing to the Derby Gazette or by contacting Sea Grant at:

New York Sea Grant Extension Program
Fernow Hall, Cornell University
Ithaca, New York 14853
(607) 255-2811

FINDING & CATCHING
SUMMERTIME BROWN TROUT
by Roger Lowden

Where do you find brown trout in Lake Ontario in the summer and how do you catch them? As recently as three years ago the majority of anglers who were unable to answer that question gave up on browns during this warm weather season. Now, however, due to the efforts of researchers and the success of an increasing number of fishermen who have applied advanced deep-trolling techniques, we know where and how to fish for summertime browns. Summertime, as defined for brown trout fishing purposes, is the period when the lake has warmed to the point where stratification (the formation of the thermocline) occurs. It lasts until brown trout "turn off," as they near their spawning phase, usually beginning in early August.

Researchers, led by Dr. James Haynes at SUNY College at Brockport, have shown that browns in Lake Ontario have a strong association with the thermocline when that magic band of cooler water is located within three miles of shore. If the thermocline is located 40 feet down, for example, brown trout will be there, especially where the thermocline intersects bottom. But the thermocline moves due to wind and weather and a few days later it may be 90 feet down. The browns will still be there if the bottom intersection is within about three miles of shore. If the bottom intersection is farther offshore, evidence indicates that brown trout will move laterally, paralleling the shoreline until they find the thermocline closer to shore. Haynes has documented lateral movement of individual brown trout up to 70 miles.

Using vertical gill netting techniques coupled with temperature profiles, Haynes found that 75% of brown trout were netted in or within 10 feet of the thermocline. Thirty percent were netted within 10 feet of the lake bottom, but 80% of those were caught where the thermocline intersected bottom. These nettings showed that browns are distributed in fairly equal numbers from about 48 degrees to about 68 degrees, that is, throughout the thermocline. Angling success, however, indicates that the most catchable fish—those that are actively feeding — are most often located in the warmer end of the zone. Experienced brown trout trollers concentrate their efforts in water from 56 to 62 degrees, although some fish are caught in water as warm as 70 degrees.

Based on this information, here is a game plan that will put you on summer browns. First, you'll need a boat equipped with tackle that will take your lines deep. Downriggers have the edge over other deep-trolling devices because they offer the most precise depth control. With the downriggers, you'll need line release devices to connect your line to the trolling weight or downrigger cable. Stacking releases (Roemer, Clipper, Walker, Offshore) are an advantage because they allow lines at various depths to cover the entire preferred temperature zone.

Next in importance is your choice of temperature sensing devices. Constant readout units, such as the Temp-Trol, Fish Hawk, Fishmate or Combinator (which measure the temperature at the trolling weight) are a definite advantage over hand-held units because the thermocline is constantly moving and changing.

A good depth finder is another important aid to summer brown trout fishing. In addition to showing fish and bait, the depth finder will help you locate bottom structure and will enable you to fish close to bottom without hanging up tackle if the occasion calls for tight-to-bottom fishing.

Your boat should also be equipped with a VHF or CB radio for safety's sake, as well as to share information. Many lake trollers are friendly fishermen who will help others find the daily pattern of depth, lure selection and color necessary for success.

Begin your brown trout trolling day by heading offshore until you are over a depth where you can find the thermocline. If there is any extensive bottom structure in the area, fish offshore from it as a starting point. Lower your temperature sensor (at trolling speed if it's a constant readout type) until you find 56 degree water. For brown trout that should be your deepest lure. Now raise the sensor slowly until it just reads 70 degrees and you've got the depth for your shallowest lure. In most cases, this range will be found in a relatively narrow band seldom exceeding 20 feet in width and often much narrower. Troll this temperature zone from the point where it intersects bottom to deeper water until you locate fish. Trolling speed should be moderate and, of course, turns and speed changes will often trigger strikes.

Most of the time, browns prefer smaller lures such as #2 and #3 Andy Reekers, Sutton West River, #1 Mepps spoons, #44 flutterspoons and small Alpena Diamonds and Evil Eyes. Brown trout seem to have a marked preference for green or chartreuse color combinations with white or silver, but like all fish, on certain days they can be very selective. So, it's wise to experiment with color combinations until you find the best one for that day. Combinations of yellow and red are good and sometimes black variations can be deadly. While spoons are currently the most popular brown trout offering, don't rule out small plugs. Some days they make the difference necessary to catch fish.

Line test for brown trout should be fairly light, usually no more than 10 pounds—lighter if you can handle it. The distance from the lure to the downrigger weight is a matter of personal choice. Browns will hit lures fairly close to the weight in deep water. If you prefer to run long lines, remember that some lures will run deeper as line is let out so it will be necessary to raise the downrigger weight to keep the lure in the strike zone and off the bottom.

Although browns tend to congregate in certain areas, there is a good lake-wide population that can be caught in mid-summer if you stick to the basic facts of brown trout behavior.

POWER PLANTS YEAR-ROUND
"HOT SPOTS"
by Dick Schleyer

If you're brave at heart and can't wait for mid-April when the lakes actively begin to come to life, you might consider the power plant "hot spots" as a major source of winter fishing activity.

Many serious, and indeed hearty, fishermen will have taken large numbers of trout and salmon throughout the winter months from the heated discharges of power plants on all the Great Lakes. These hot spots hold large concentrations of salmonids, bait fish and other forms of aquatic life.

Warm power plant outflows create a winter environment that sets the stage for an artificial ecosystem that is alive and active during the winter months. The normally cold inshore water has dispersed the salmonids and slowed their metabolism to the point where they feed infrequently making fishing poor at best. The exception to this occurs during winter thaws when runoff attracts steelhead, domestic rainbows, browns and immature salmon to the mouths of rivers and streams.

Increased water volume and temperature following thaws brings a run of steelhead into the rivers and streams providing exciting inshore winter fishing. Power plants that discharge directly into the lake from the shoreline create a high volume stream within the lake itself. The strong currents maintain a steady, regular flow into the lake. There is a minimal amount of dispersion from the area where it leaves the shoreline until it reaches 80 to 100 yards into the lake. That is where you want to fish. Anchor your boat at the edge of the stream current in the lake and fish much the same as you would fish a big stream. Cast your small to medium size spoons, plugs, egg sacs or bait (try jigging) and retrieve them to the boat through the current.

An aerial photo of the warm water discharge at the Ginna Power Plant. The lighter, warmer water serves as a strong attractant for bait fish & salmonids.

Spawning rainbows and browns are fooled into reacting to these currents as they do when seeking streams in which to spawn. They will also respond to the current even when the plant is shut down and the water being pumped into the lake is at near-lake temperatures. Some inshore warm water releases are located so that wading and pier fishing are possible as well.

Feeding salmonids, primarily brown trout, generally use the flow only when power is being generated and the water is warm. It is important that you fish for this species at plants (preferably nuclear) that are on-line and discharging a large volume of warm water. These outflows periodically produce excellent smallmouth bass, gizzard shad, lake catfish and silver bass after the lake warms in the spring.

The offshore discharging plants release their heated water from huge pipes well offshore and below the surface. This water is also released under great pressure and "boils" to the surface and disperses there. "Boils" or "bubbles," as they are sometimes referred to, are terrific fish attractors. You can fish this type of flow from anchored boats, casting, jigging or trolling though the bubbles. As with the shoreline discharge plants, the trout and salmon for the most part leave for more bountiful waters as soon as the lake temperature warms in April.

The good or bad of nuclear and fossil fuel power plants on the Great Lakes has been argued for years. Fishermen have come to accept this major intervention by man as an attractor and concentrator of various species of fish and have learned to capitalize on them to augment and extend their fishing seasons.

Fortunately, the game fish seem to move in and out of the temperature changes at will with less traumatization than was predicted by some biologist early on. The damage, which has been minimal, seems to occur when there are sudden shut downs at power plants during inshore cold water periods. The detrimental impact of power plants, especially nuclear, that discharge into river systems are another story and should not be confused with the results to date in the Great Lakes.

While launching can be a problem because of ice on ramps, some areas are sanding their ramps for better winter lake access. If the idea of dragging a small aluminum boat across the ice when necessary, to gain access to the lake appeals to you, don't forget that small boats afford little protection from the elements. The outdoor experts recommend a number of layers of clothing over heavier single layers to provide insulation and insurance against hypothermia. Use good judgement and caution.

There are a few charter guides available for this kind of fishing. Telephone calls to the ESLO/LEI weigh-in stations along Lake Ontario's and Erie's shorelines, or tackle stores on the other big lakes, can alert you to the times when fish concentrations are at their peek and whom you migh contact to arrange a winter charter.

SUMMER DEEP-TROLLING TIPS
(Adapted from Summer Salmonids in Lake Ontario, N.Y.S.D.E.C.,)

Often the difference between an empty cooler and a satisfying catch of trophy Lake Ontario salmonids can be attributed to seemingly minor details. Not specific to Lake Ontario is the often heard statement: 10% of the fishermen catch 90% of the fish. If you would like to be part of the 10% that get 90%, study and practice these secrets of the happy minority!

Lures

Since the major forage of summer salmonids in Lake Ontario is smelt and alewives, spoons and fullbodied plugs imitating bait fish are the logical choice. Silver is apparently the key color. Catches have been enhanced by the addition of red or green stripes, either painted or the stitch-on variety. One expert has recently found that luminescent (glow in dark) lures may make all the difference, especially when favorite silver varieties fail to produce.After talking with several experts, no one lure can be suggested as the lure to stock in your tackle box. The key points on lure selection are: color, trolling speed, action imparted by boat maneuvering and, importantly, the confidence you place in a particular bait. In short, an angler fishing with a lure in which he has little faith, tends to fish sloppily. He does not pay attention to the fine details that separate the fish catching minority from the unsuccessful majority.

Line

Because the visibility at summer preferred depths is often limited, line diameter is not as important as during the spring nearshore fishery. The experts recommend a line from 10-17 pound test. The actual line test will, in the end, depend upon the quality of line, individual skill and the downrigger line release. Breakage is most likely to occur at the time of a strike, just before the release trips.The amount of line trailing between the release d lure is a subject of much discussion. Unfortunately, there is ¬ subject of exact formula for fishing success, but there are a ¬w general guidelines that should be heeded. First, the ¬hallower the water, the more line that is required between the ¬re and boat. Most seasoned anglers feel this is simply a matter ¬ the boat spooking fish. Secondly, the type of lure will govern the ¬mount one can play out before he loses depth control. Flutter ¬poons tract stright but full-bodied plugs may dive or rise far ¬hough to send them out of the zone of preferred temperatures if ¬e length is excessive. Frequent turns will cause a change in ¬re action and running depth. The more line out, the less control.

In summary, a compromise between a "long line" and control ¬ust be reached. As a starting point, try these suggestions with ¬ur particular rig:

¬ater Depth	Lure Distance from Release
¬urface	150 feet
¬ feet	100 feet
¬ feet	75 feet
¬ feet	50 feet

¬emperature ¬pecies	Preference Range (°F.)
¬rown Trout	56 - 60
¬ainbow Trout	56 - 62
¬ake Trout	45 - 52
¬oho Salmon	55 - 62
¬hinook Salmon	55 - 62

¬elation to Thermocline

The thermocline is that layer of water in which a rapid change ¬f temperature takes place. This layer occurs in Lake Ontario ¬eginning in late June and can be found until September or ¬ctober. Typically, the thermocline is about 10 feet wide and ¬eflects a temperature change or drop of about 5°F. (58°F. to 53°F.) The salmonid species generally orient to the summer thermocline as follows:

Brown Trout .... no distinct orientation; can be found below, or above the thermo-cline.
Rainbow Trout .... Above
Lake Trout .... Below
Coho Salmon: .... Probably in and above
Chinook Salmon: .... in and above

Speed

The experts interviewed could not pin down a specific trolling speed that would guarantee success. Some days the fish seem to prefer a faster or slower presentation than other days. If one speed fails, try another. Don't get stuck in a grove. It is important that the lure is traveling at the speed for which it was designed. Remember that boat speed downwind is different than that upwind. However, they all agreed on technique—TURNS. The action imparted to many lures by turning apparently is irresistible to many lunker salmonids. Trolling in figure 8's or turning abruptly often brings strikes on slow summer days.

The Downrigger

Precise temperature/depth fishing has been stressed. The careful angler must be aware that his key piece of summer equipment, the downrigger may inject serious bias into an otherwise carefully calculated approach. First, check your counter to insure its accuracy at all depths. Prepare a correction chart if the actual depth does not correspond to metered depth.

Secondly, the angle of the downrigger wire line while being trolled will produce another source of bias. The faster you go and/or the more cable that is fished, the greater the deflection. A deflection from the stern of 30° will impart a 13 percent error in the actual fishing depth. A trolling weight of 10 pounds (standard weight 8 pounds) will alleviate some deflection. A recognition and understanding of this variable will allow the angler to adjust accordingly.

PLOT YOUR OWN COURSE
TO TROUT AND SALMON
by Mike Bleech

Do not follow the crowd unless you are satisfied with being ¬ne of them! When most boats are catching fish, it takes a ¬remendous amount of luck to come out on top by doing what ¬veryone else is doing. When the crowd is not having much ¬uccess, it makes no sense to mimic their efforts.

A lure change is one of the easiest ways to break with the ¬rowd. Most tackle shops along the salmon coast carry an ¬mpressive assortment of lures. There is good reason for this — ¬ive species of salmonids in the Great Lakes that numerous ¬anglers pursue. All five may be most receptive to completely ¬ifferent lures at any given moment and the most effective lure for ¬any of those species may change a few times each day. ¬Moreover, even when a particular lure gets hot, there may be ¬ome other lure that would be more attractive to larger fish!

Even a small boat can easily troll at least six lures, so it is ¬imple to be both conservative and bold with your lure choices at ¬he same time. With six lines out, for example, you can run four of ¬he currently "hot" lures and two oddballs.

During a spring outing in 1983, Craig Littlefield and I had ¬een smacking the fish on floating minnow lures, but on a couple ¬f lines we experimented with screw-tail jig bodies.

The first few cohos and most of the fish we caught that ¬morning fell for the screw-tails! The fish were less fussy about ¬what they hit after a couple of hours. But, if we had not ¬experimented with lures from the beginning we would have ¬missed the early action. No matter how effective a lure has been, ¬do not put all of your faith in!

Boats tend to bunch up and do the same thing when a few ¬ish are caught after a long spell of poor fishing. Word spreads ¬fast about the method used to take the first few fish, and soon ¬most anglers are copying that method. It is easy to see why that method accounts for nearly all fish caught for awhile. And the situation compounds itself. The action slows, while the rare fish caught is still taken with that method. This leads many anglers to believe it is the only method that works.

It is the trap of following the crowd! It is also a situation that puts the innovative angler at the advantage!

The crowd will continue to use the most recent productive method until the next successful method becomes common knowledge. The anglers who discover what it takes to turn the fish on will ride the gravy train alone, for a while.

During the first ESLO Brown Derby I met some new friends from my home state, Pennsylvania, while fishing out of Olcott. They were new to Lake Ontario fishing, and were full of questions. I supplied all the answers I could, while my strongest advise was to keep changing until something worked.

We had fair fishing that day as did most boats in our area, but nothing spectacular. Then we ran into our new friends. They were trolling at least twice as fast as any other boat. I headed my boat in their direction to inform them they were going too fast. They hooked and lost two fish before I could get within shouting distance!

While we trolled alongside them to get the story, they had a couple of more hits. They informed me that they had done as I suggested, changing every variable until something happended. It was when they tried to fast troll that the rods started popping.

Lucky for them they were too new to the game to realize they were trolling too fast!

One of the most consistently productive methods of breaking with the pack is trolling around the outside perimeter of a pack of boats. There are two lines of thought behind this. First, schools of fish move while packs of boats tend to stay in the same area.

Second, fish are believed to shy away from heavy boat traffic.

A pack of boats may be so large during a derby, it takes an hour or more to troll around the pack. The fish can be concentrated in one area, making most of the loop unproductive. Once fish contact is made, concentrate on that area working away from the pack. You may have located the route that the school is taking to leave the heavy boat traffic.

You may also find a clue to the direction the fish are taking by watching the pack of trolling boats. Most often catches will come from one area of the pack. If the action is happening in the outer, west end of the pack for example, this may be a signal that the school of fish is moving west and possibly deeper. Remember though that the result of such logic is merely an educated guess, not something to take to the bank!

"Don't be too sure of anything," advised one of my earliest mentors in Lake Ontario fishing. "Let those fish pick out what they want."

This applies to the depth factor, also. Salmonid anglers are very aware of the importance of temperature in fish location. In fact, many fish-finding formulas have their basis in temperature. Preferred temperature charts are printed on the back of lure packages, in magazines and in government literature. Unfortunately, fish cannot read!

The thermocline makes a good starting place in the search for trout or salmon, but that is all it is — a starting place.

In Lake Ontario, the thermocline has usually formed by early July. Before this time, the thermal bar (or thermobarriers) are the angler's primary temperature factor. Two and three years ago this factor was a hot thing. Savvy trollers were reaping big rewards by trolling along these thermal "fences," but it was a different story in the spring of 1985.

Numerous theories exist about why the thermal bar was less productive last spring; it really does not matter. Better to worry about where the fish **are** than to worry about why they are **not** somewhere else.

Still, temperature can be a big factor in locating trout and salmon, with two essential tools for taking full advantage of the temperature factor: a surface temperature gauge and a temperature probe. These tools will aid in locating fish, then help you stay with the fish as water temperature characteristics change.

Neither the thermocline nor thermal fences are constants. The exact location of a thermal fence or the depth of a thermocline can change significantly in the course of a day.

During a May, 1984 outing at Olcott, we located a huge school of cohos and lakers off the power plant over 180 feet of water. After steady action all morning, we returned to port for lunch, then we headed back to the same area we had fished in the morning. A pack of boats marked the location, but it was soon apparent that the action had ceased. There was no mystery to it. The surface temperature gauge showed that there was no longer a thermobarrier in the area.

We headed out, finding a thermobarrier over 240 feet of water. Even before the gauge revealed the fence, a coho slammed a lure off the planer board. We caught and released a dozen fish before the first boat broke from the pack and headed our way. By the time a dozen boats had joined us, the school had moved or dispersed.

We did not relocate the fish again that afternoon, but by breaking from the pack, we had action the other boats missed. The boats which had waited for someone else to find the fish experienced a dull afternoon.

There is a time to join the crowd. When everyone is catching fish, the high percentage shot is to do what everyone else is doing. But if you want to go for the gold, break with the crowd and set your own course for trout and salmon action!

Trolling plates are also popular on the Great Lakes. These devices attach to the lower units of motors. A metal plate is positioned behind the propeller, effectively reducing the thrust to the propeller. For many boats, this may be the best way to achieve desired trolling speeds.

Propellers can also play a part in speed control and most boat motors can operate with a variety of propellers. Generally, propellers with a large pitch are meant for speed while those with less pitch give more power. A propeller with pitch at the lower end of the range which a motor will safely handle will produce the slowest trolling speeds. For example if a 70 h.p. motor can be used with 15, 17 or 19 pitch props, then the 15 pitch would be best used for trolling. Be sure to carefully watch the tachometer with low pitch props, as too small a prop with too little pitch can allow an engine to develop to many rpm's.

One simple way to slow a boat's trolling speed is to drag a sea anchor. An effective trolling drag can be made by cutting a five-inch hole in the bottom of a plastic bucket. Some anglers drag a bucket from each corner of the transom, but care must be used to keep trolling drags clear of lines and propeller.

Serious Great Lakes salmonid anglers know the importance of matching trolling speed to tackle, and of making minor adjustments until a productive speed is found. But fishing remains a game of man against nature. No matter how carefully we handling the trolling speed factor, wind and waves will take much of the control away from us! No matter how scientific the angler gets, fish are still fish and nature has a way of reminding us that we are just men when we get too cocky.

HOW IMPORTANT IS COLOR SELECTION?
by Capt. Randy Snyder

The color pattern of the lures you pull are one of the most important things to consider when fishing for Lake Ontario trout and salmon. Purchase a few lures in different color patterns rather than different types of lures. If you cover the color patterns, you increase your chances of getting the fish to hit better than by switching to lures which have different actions in the water. A variety of colors of spray-paint comes in handy too.

We experienced this first hand in Michigan fishing for chinook salmon. Capt. Joe Burns, running the Chinook I, was having a super day right in front of the harbor at Manistee. Even though we were using the same size silver J-plugs, Capt. Joe was catching one fish after another while we remained fishless. A call on the VHF solved the mystery. Following Joe's suggestion, we painted the bottom half of our J-plugs blue and it worked like magic. We started boating chinooks.

While salmonids are very color conscious, they change their minds frequently, too. By mixing colors when you begin fishing, you can pin-point the preferred color of the day.

Using this theory, we started one outing using a spoon in every available color — green, blue, orange, gold and chartreuse. After boating two fish on the chartreuse striped lure, we switched to them exclusively and had fish on constantly. Then when we were just two fish shy of the day's limit, we replaced all the successful lures with different colors to test the theory. A half-hour later with no hits even, we switched back to all chartreuse and had two fish to make our limit for the day within 15 minutes.

We've proven the theory time and time again. Two summers ago while fishing off Hedges Nine Mile Point, my youngest son, Denny, and I were catching browns as fast as we could get the lines in the water on chartreuse fire dotted spoons. After boating our ninth fish of the day, we got a call from a friend our oldest son, Randy, was fishing with. They were just beginning to rig up and I suggested they use the lure that had proven so successful for us, but they didn't have that color on board. I gave them the lures off my rods only to discover when I got the tackle box out that I didn't have anymore of that color pattern.

Denny and I tried other color combinations to no avail while the other boat landed ten fish. Since they had their limit, they returned the lures and we caught our tenth to complete our daily limit, too.

Even the color of your cannon balls can make the difference between a great day and just another day riding around on the water. My preference for cannon balls is fluorescent green with fluorescent yellow running a close second. Mix the colors to begin with. By watching the chart recorder, you can distinguish the most effective color by observing which cannon ball the fish come up to look at more closely. We shorten our lures behind the preferred color, sometimes within two to three feet in back of the cannon ball. Colored weights not only get your lures down to the fish, they also act as an attractor.

When the fish aren't hitting, keep changing the color patterns of your lures until you find the right combination. Some days color won't make a difference but you won't know that until you try. Forget pink; it is the only color we can't get fish to hit, even though it looks great in the water. Spend your money on effective colors and experiment.

LAKE ONTARIO'S SPRINGTIME THERMAL BAR

Reprinted by Permission of the New York State Sea Grant

What exactly is the thermal bar?

Technically speaking, the bar is a temporary interface between different water temperatures in a freshwater body, occurring in spring. It is the zone at which inshore water temperatures greater than 39°F. meet offshore water temperatures less than 39°F.

What's so significant about it?

It's a general premise of nature that zones of change - "edges" - are attractive to animals. The thermal bar, because of the differences in water temperatures and densities around it, is a zone of dynamic change - a real change, apparently as far as rainbows are concerned. In one sense, the bar acts almost as a reef, attracting rainbows to it. In another sense, it acts like a corral, with rainbow "stacking up" just inshore of the bar in warmer (40°- 50° F.) water. The angler who can consistently find the bar and who can learn how to fish this natural feature may improve his or her rainbow catches.

What are the "dynamics" you say are occurring at the bar?

An elementary science lesson taught us that, at 32°F., water freezes into ice, which floats because it is less dense than water at other temperatures. The same lesson also taught us that water is most dense, or at its heaviest, at 39°F.

In spring, waters close to shore warm up first due to their shallowness and the influence of streamflow. As water reaches 39°F. it sinks to bottom, creating lake turnover effect. This zone of water, warming to 39°F. and sinking is, in fact, the bar, which slowly migrates offshore as the spring rains and sunshine provide much more of a "pool" of nearshore warm water.

When and how does the bar disappear?

Records show that one can expect Lake Ontario's thermal bar to migrate offshore throughout spring until the bar disappears or submerges, mid-lake, sometime in mid-June. When this occurs, theoretically no 39°F. water is found on the lake's surface.

How fast does the bar migrate?

A difficult question. If one assumes that it takes 2½ months for the bar to arise and then disappear, one could also divide 25 miles (the distance to mid-lake) by 75 days. This would result in an average movement of about 1/3 of a mile per day. But this is misleading. Weather changes, particularly wind, may move the bar hither and yon, as can lake phenomena like seiches, currents and internal waves. One thing seems certain, however. The bar moves offshore at a much slower rate in early spring; its offshore migration rate increases with the increasing solar radiation influence of late spring.

There is some evidence indicating that the rate of bar migration occurs faster over lake areas having a gradual offshore bottom gradient, and slower over lake areas having steep bottom inclines or sharp dropoffs.

How does the average fisherman find the bar?

An easy and accurate way to locate the thermal bar is to use a surface thermometer on your boat. When water temperature drops from, let's say, 45°F. to 39°F. (as the boat heads offshore), one can assume that the thermal bar has been found. This drop can occur in a short distance, measured in feet, or in a longer distance, measured in hundreds of yards.

On some occasions, the bar can actually be seen as a sharp change in water color, from greenish (inshore) to deep, dark blue. This change in color should not be confused with "mudlines" from stream flow. The bar is often quite visible from the air.

A "poor man's thermal bar finder" can simply be a person's eyes. Look for the color change noted above, along with a change in the surface ripple characteristics and the existance of floating debris. The bar's sinking water action often causes flotsam, such as dead forage fish, to collect atop the bar.

What is meant by a "Thermal Drop Off" or "Thermal Break?"

Whereas Lake Ontario is relatively featureless along its bottom, with little physiographic structure, the lake has an abundance of "structure" or variability when it comes to its temperature or thermal properties. The springtime thermal bar, which can attract and hold fish, is one such "structural feature." Furthermore, in addition to water temperature changes at the thermal bar, the lake often exhibits sharp drop-offs or breaks in temperature offshore. Examples of these features (beside the summertime thermocline, or that rapid layer of temperature change below warmer surface water) would be any area manifesting a fast decrease in surface water temperatures over a relatively short distance. For example, in 1983, anglers in May found a 3 or 4 degree change, from 47° F to 43° F, occurring in the lake's surface water temperature over a distance of ¼ mile . This was a thermal drop-off or break. What's important to note is the excellent catches of fish that occurred near this area of thermal change and others located over the past 2 years.

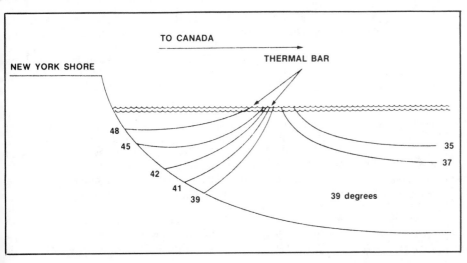

Simplified springtime thermal bar and temperature gradient illustration for Lake Ontario.

INCREASE YOUR ESLO CATCH . . .
TRY DODGERS
by Capt. Randy Snyder

Over the course of the fishing season, there are some periods where just pulling a straight lure doesn't seem to turn the fish on. When this happens, try dodgers as an attractor. When the thermocline is fickle and the fish are spread out with no set pattern to their feeding spurts, a dodger in front of your lure will produce fish most of the time. This is especially true in the Fall ESLO Derby as the big chinooks and cohos are scattered prior to schooling up.

There are many theories as to why dodgers in front of your lures attract fish. The two most likely reasons are noise and light reflection. The noise made by the back and forth swaying motion of the dodger is believed to represent a large fish swatting bait with its tail to stun the bait, thus making the bait easy picking. As the dodger passes nearby, the noise may lead the larger fish to believe that other fish are getting all the easy bait, thus they investigate and attack the lure.

Light reflecting off the dodger is another reason larger fish are attracted to the lures. When a dodger is working properly, the light produces an off-on effect as it is pulled through the water. Picture a flickering underwater light — now you see it — now you don't. I don't believe the dodger represents bait to the fish as some of the most effective dodgers are huge, much larger than the normal bait in the area, but it might appear as a small school of bait. Who knows?

I fished off Manistee, Michigan with one charter boat captain who put large, single hooks on both ends of his dodgers, claiming that huge chinooks will sometimes hit the dodger and not the lure. We didn't catch any chinooks on a dodger that week, but I have no reason to doubt his word. I believe though that when the kings do hit them, it's probably to kill something which has invaded their home territory.

Over the past years, I have been reluctant to stick with anything that I don't have full confidence in and dodgers were in that category. I've messed with them from time to time, but I never had the confidence to try them on a steady basis. However, that changed when I had the opportunity to fish with one of the best fisherman on the Eastern Basin of Lake Ontario in the Henderson area, Bill Foell from Tully, N.Y.

My knowledge of Bill's reputation came first by word of mouth from seasoned fishermen in that area, and then from fishing with him. Whenever Bill is around other fishermen, they lean into the conversation, hanging on to every word he says. This prompted me to pick Bill's brain about dodgers as he uses them almost exclusively for chinooks.

I could go on all day about the dodger combinations we talked about that day, but time and time again Bill stressed one basic method for successful chinook fishing with dodgers. Run an "O" dodger exactly four feet behind the downrigger weight and a squid or fly exactly nine inches behind the dodger. Over the years Bill has been fishing this set-up, it has produced more and bigger chinook on his rods. He uses only the chrome dodger and changes the color of the squid and fly, but the green squid and black fly appeared to be his favorite terminal lures. Bill also stressed that the slowest speed possible gets the best results when using dodgers. And believe me when I tell you Bill Foell KNOWS what he's talking about.

I decided to try Bill's four-foot, nine-inch method one day when the chinook fishing was slow. The slow period came during the 1984 Fall ESLO Derby. By changing over all downriggers, using Bill's method, our boat put three kings in the top twenty prize list, and the fourth would have been there but our client that day wasn't entered in the Derby. Those four fish alone gave me all the confidence I needed to use dodgers anytime, especially when the fishing's slow.

Bill offered me another tip on how to keep the fish off the wire after they hit, as almost every chinook you hook will wrap the monofilament around the downrigger cable when fishing so close to the weights and cables. After the fish is hooked, immediately hit the free spool lever to relieve the pressure on the monofilament. Then take the pole and run it around the cable from the outside to the inside of the cable. Bill said that nine out of ten times, the fish will wrap around the cable from the outside and by utilizing his suggestion, your success ratio is much greater; you don't cut or fray your lines.

I tried Bill's method and of all the kings we hooked on the dodger set-up last year, we lost two fish.

Try some dodger combinations when the action is slow. I think you will surprise yourself with the results.

LITTLE BOATS CAN CATCH BIG FISH!
SO ALL YOU HAVE IS A LITTLE BOAT . . .
by Gene Leonard

The anglers that enter the Spring ESLO Derby come from all walks of life. I've met doctors and day laborers, and men and women from just about every occupation in between. But one thing's for sure. They all have the same goal in mind — collecting that grand prize package for the largest fish entered.

Many entrants are fortunate enough to be able to fish from large, well equipped boats designed specifically for big water fishing. Charter boats and large private fishing craft will be out en mass to garnish the big money prizes. Some of these rigs cost many thousands of dollars, and the downriggers and other speciality equipment they carry can account for additional thousands.

Many others will stick to the shoreline, casting their lures in the hopes of striking it rich. If past results are any indication, these anglers will reap their share of the prizes, especially in the brown trout category.

But what about the other guys, — that group of anglers that own small boats with little or no expensive auxillary equipment. Should they, I mean we, a1count ourselves out of the competition for some really big prizes just because we don't have a bank of downriggers, marine radios and a Loran-C. Not on your life, we shouldn't.

The spring ESLO Derby comes at a time when the fish are both shallow and hungry. Lures don't have to be sent deep to be effective. In fact, lures trolled a few feet under the surface catch most of the prize winning fish. Small boats actually have many advantages over the larger boats when it comes to early season fishing.

First of all, there's land mobility. Besides being less expensive to operate, this might be the best argument for using small boats. They can be trailered long distances quickly, and without a lot of hassle. They can be off-loaded from even the smallest ramps. And from the ramp to the sound of "fish on" can be a matter of only a few minutes in many cases.

I've seen days when three pound trout were the rule at Sodus Bay and points east while Olcott and Braddocks Bay were literally swimming in twenty-pound kings. A one- or two-hour drive and quick launch, and anglers are right where the tackle busters are hanging out. This may be the best way to swing the odds of catching a major prize winning fish in your favor.

Sure we small boaters have to keep a close eye on the weather, but that's true for anyone venturing onto Lake Ontario, no matter what size boat they might be using. The larger boats will be able to go out on the big lake when high waves keep smaller boats in sheltered bays and inlets. But I can't begin to count the number of prize winning browns, rainbows and other sh species that have been caught inside Sodus Bay or Sandy Pond, and many of those "lucky" anglers were fishing from small boats.

Top line trolling is the most effective way to catch all of the various trout and salmon species in the early spring. The fish seek out warmer waters which, early on in the season are the surface waters found close-in to shore. Small boats are ideal for this style of fishing. Some rod holders, properly angled to help prevent line tangles, will allow three anglers to easily work six rods effectively.

The addition of one or two inexpensive downriggers can add versatility to the lure pattern. Dropping a couple of flutter spoons down 5 to 10 feet increases the odds of catching springtime browns. Just remember to keep lots of distance between the lures and the boat. Spring-run brown trout can be very skittish.

Add a couple of side planers and you create even more versatility. You can spread your lures to show them to more fish. By mounting the retrieval system on the bow, you, get it out of the boat occupants way while still keeping it handy for quick usage.

Maneuverability also has to be considered. A small boat can make tighter circles to stay over small schools of feeding fish. With a graph or LCD type depth recorder, small boaters can actually follow the fish with a lot less surface disturbance than the larger boats.

A small fishing rig allows anglers to reach more productive areas. Remember that spring run fish are in the shallowest, warmest waters. Small boats with outboard motors can go right into the shallows after them. The larger boats have to literally troll around the rocks if, that is, they can get in that shallow to begin with.

I've found it's easier to cast lures to the fish from small boats. I've seen times when casting to spring run fish was the only way to catch them. This usually occurs on those rare, dead calm days. Trolling, even in quiet boats, will tend to spook the fish right out of the area.

Small boats are ideal for fishing live bait. Many people associate the ESLO Derby with lures and trolling or casting. But sawbellies and smelt will account for quite a few trophy size trout and salmon.

Many small boaters will combine live bait fishing with some lure trolling, just to cover all the bases. They'll start out by trolling artifical lures for a couple of hours. When the activity drops off, they'll switch to drifting live sawbellies over the same areas they just finished trolling.

With a small boat, equipment organization is the key to success. Without it, a person moving a short distance like, say, to an active rod with a potential prize winning fish on, gets the distinct feeling he's passing through an obstacle course. But with everything in it's proper place, a small boat can be compared to a fine watch — it always seems to run smoothly.

One of the real keys with small rigs is practice. Having everything in its place is important, but having each person on board aware of the location of important items is even more so. With practice, finding stored items becomes routine.

So if it's possible, get your rig and your crew out several times before the start of the derby. Starting as much as a month ahead of time may just give you the edge in the big prize department.

Using a small boat is definitely better than no boat at all. It can also be a lot better than fishing from the large flashy cruisers. Sure, you can expect to get bounced around on choppy days. And rough water may keep you on shore while the big boys, those 25 plus footers, have gone fishing (and are getting bounced around).

But if you're lucky enough to land the winning king salmon in your little boat, then you'll take home the ESLO Grand Prize, and you probably won't have to worry about fishing in a little boat, ever again! Tight lines and good fishing.

LAKE ONTARIO SUMMER SALMON:
THEORIES ABOUND ON WHEREABOUTS

by Joe Swift

The whereabouts of salmon during the summer months was a topic intensely discussed by a gathering of over 120 top charter boat captains at the 1984 spring conference of the Lake Ontario Charter Boat Association (LOCBA) held in Rochester, N.Y. This savvy group of lake captains has been searching over the past few years to discover a pattern that indicates where salmon, particularly chinook, go during the months of June, July, and early August.

In spite of the fact that the combined New York and Canandian stockings of coho and chinook into the lake exceed 4 million per year, and despite the likelihood that these fish must feed regularly to reach the enormous size typical of salmon in this lake, angler catches of summertime salmon have been poor.

Captain Jerry Heffernan, a charter skipper working out of Wilson, New York, attests to the low summer catches of salmon. In a typical summer, less than 10% of Heffernan's catch is salmon. Nevertheless, when a charter insists that they want only salmon on a trip in June or July, he heads out to water depths of at least 325 feet and trolls on the lower side of the thermocline, concentrating most of his lures at the depth corresponding to 49°F.

It's worth noting that the majority of the charter captains attending the LOCBA spring conference was in agreement that chinook salmon seemed to prefer the far offshore, deep water at temperatures of 42° to 52° F. Interestingly, this hypothesis places salmon in Lake Ontario at temperature zones significantly below the 54° - 56° F range generally reported as "ideal" for salmon.

As with any group of individual thinkers, the charter captains have formulated several theories as to where salmon go in the summer months.

Captain John Oravec, the past president of LOCBA and a full time charter operator, speculates that it is possible for the salmon to concentrate (possibly in schools) in some remote regions of the lake where no one fishes. He also feels that, due to the deep, dark, black color typical of this lake's salmon, they must spend the majority of the summer in very deep water (maybe on or near the bottom) where they are sheltered from the sun's rays. This notion, known as the "Honey Hole Theory," does appear plausible. Certainly, the enormous size of the lake plus the fact that New York anglers seldom, if ever, venture into Canandian waters, make it extremely difficult to verify whether a particular spot or two exists holding many of the lake's resident salmon. A further complication is recognized by Oravec: the possibility of a "vertical migration" over a "Honey Hole" where the salmon reside on or near deep water structure during daylight hours and move upwards primarily at night to feed.

Captain Heffernan, on the other hand, believes that the "Honey Hole," if it exists, is highly transitory, with salmon strictly moving to seek the shallowest depths where they can find both forage fish and cold waters. And, since Canandian waters are on average cooler year-round than the more southern New York waters, the fish should, according to this "Moving Honey Hole Theory," migrate north or westwards during the summer.

Another theory proposed by this author and several other chapter skippers is known as the "Current Theory." The obviously strong migratory nature of Pacific Ocean salmon is cited here as the prime factor causing incessant wandering behavior. Attracted by the cold subsurface currents of the lake, in a manner not unlike the attraction exhibited by trout to a riff in a stream, the salmon are envisioned as seeking out and following underwater currents of the lake, as sources of evermoving, oxygen-rich waters. Owing to the fact that little is known about the lake's underwater currents, any influences they may have on salmon movements is strictly conjecture at present.

Another theory that is suggested by Dr. Mike Voiland, Sea Grant specialist and skipper of the Education Vessel *Ontario*, is known as the "Forage Theory." This theory acknowledges that the vast numbers of baitfish (or forage) are having a strong effect upon salmon behavior in Lake Ontario. Since alewives and/or smelt are presently available in large numbers virtually everywhere, and probably range to depths exceeding 200 feet, the salmon can be very selective as to what and when they eat. A lure may have little chance in competition with the overabundance of natural foods. It is submitted that the paucity of summer chinook catches in Lake Michigan prior to the mid-1970's was possibly caused by the lake's forage base exceeding the predator's needs. This theory also advances the notion that chinook may feed easily and heavily at dusk and dawn but then submerge into deeper, colder waters during daytime hours, and are effectively "off feed," as they digest and metabolize their forage much more slowly in the lower temperature water.

The final theory worth mentioning is one professed by Dr. Jim Haynes, biologist at SUNY Brockport and Sea Grant researcher, who has studied the movements of salmon over the past five years in Lake Ontario. Dr. Haynes uses miniature radio transmitters, surgically implanted or physically attached to the fish to follow and tract their movements. The purpose for this research is to pinpoint the movements of salmon, along with any seasonal migrations, and to identify habitat preferences, if any, that the salmon may have.

From his research, Haynes has discovered that these fish tend to be wide ranging and can travel, over short periods of time, much of the length and width of the lake. Because salmon in the Pacific Ocean can be found typically 1,000 miles or more apart just a month or so before schooling to spawn, plus the observation that Lake Ontario salmon do not inter-mingle with schools of brown trout or lake trout along the shoreline, **plus** the fact that his research teams could not find salmon in any shallow water estuary regions during four years of springtime electro-shocking/sampling, Haynes concludes that they disperse, more or less uniformly throughout the offshore regions. Hence, the name, "Dispersion or Density Theory."

As evidence of the dispersion tendency, Haynes cites the behavior of salmon that he tracked during the spring and summer of 1984. Twenty-three salmon were initially caught by co-operating anglers and radio tagged (by Haynes) in the western Canadian end of the lake. Within a few days, the fish dispersed widely, some travelling west, some north, and some east as far as Braddocks Bay and Rochester. Two of the original 23 salmon were lost from the study.

LITTLE THINGS MEAN A LOT
by Capt. Randy Snyder

One thing that stands out in my mind is how paying attention to details and the little things separate the good fishermen from the average angler. Thousands of examples could be cited but I'll try to isolate a few just to prove my point.

Condition of the angler's tackle is one of the most important factors of being a good angler. I try to have all my equipment in excellent condition. If my monofilament starts to show signs of frays or tends to be laying on the reel without memory, it immediately gets replaced. The worst thing to happen is to lose a big fish because five dollars worth of mono wasn't replaced when it should have been.

The condition of hooks is also important and probably second in importance to the condition of the line you are using. Test after test reveals that the average angler's hooks are very dull.

A good angler will almost always check each hook as he rigs it up, and if dull, he will sharpen it or replace it instantly. Many fish are not hooked due to dull hooks, and to be fishing for any type fish with dull hooks is almost a sin. Correcting the situation takes only a second.

My favorite method of sharpening them is as follows: using a small, flat coarse file, I hold the point of the hook away from me and run the file down each side of the hook seven or eight times, always stroking the hook from the barb to the point; lightly stroke the point from the barb to the point on the outside of the hook to finish the sharpening task. The results of such little effort will amaze you as the hooks will be almost needle sharp.

In putting the final strokes over the point of the hook, be careful not to roll the point over. With a little practice, you can become quite proficient at getting the hook ready in a hurry.

I purchase my hooks by the gross and before I use them, I sharpen each one. Almost every hook you will buy will have a small ball of plating covering the point. Very few hook manufacturing companies will ship hooks that are ready for the business end of the lure.

One of the biggest complaints of the average angler is that the fish weren't hitting but the fella the next dock over limited out. How can this be?

Sometimes the answer is very simple; the average angler if analyzed, probably set his favorite lure and pulled it for ten hours without changing color, size and the action of what he was using.

Chartering is very easy to do when the fish are hitting, but when they aren't is the time we captains earn our money. Very seldom do I leave lures in the water over one-half hour if they aren't producing. Without exaggerating, I'll bet I change lures and combinations over a hundred times in an eight hour trip on slow days. If I don't catch fish, it isn't because I haven't tried.

Details can mean a million different combinations. Do you know how far a certain lure will drop when trolled at different lengths behind the cannon ball? For instance, if you want your lure to run six to eight inches off bottom with a hundred feet of line out behind the cannon ball, how deep do you have to drop or run your cannon ball?

With every lure combo I run, I can tell you exactly where the lure will be in relation to the bottom with any amount of line out. Sometimes this six to eight inches off the bottom will make the difference in limiting out or just another boring day on the lake. Learning and remembering these combinations has taken years of on the water experimenting but the rewards are full fish boxes and satisfied clients.

Another important detail in fishing is the speed of the boat. I'm almost a fanatic about the speed of the boat as without the right speed your lures might just as well be in the tackle box. If you don't know what speed to run certain lures, you're wasting your time trying to fish with them. Spend some time watching your selected lure and see what it does at certain speeds.

Another detail which the average angler seems to overlook is the use of snap swivels on their lures. I never use a snap swivel unless I absolutely have to. My theory behind this is that it is extra junk that the fish can see as being not just right, thus they avoid your lure.

Picture yourself buying a hamburger and right smack in the middle you see a fly. Turn you off? You bet! Look at the swivel in the same sense that a person looks at the fly on his hamburger and it makes sense, doesn't it? Sure, it takes longer to tie a lure on every time you change it, but the extra work is often worth the effort.

I really believe the swivel was invented for the lazy fisherman so he doesn't have to tie knots. There are very few lures made today that have a swivel ahead of them to make them work right. Try running your lures without swivels and I'll bet your fish production will increase.

In summing up, I know details make the differnce between the average fisherman and the one who usually limits out day after day. For every step you take to catch fish, log it in a small notebook and over the winter months study your log. You'll be amazed at the little things you forget which will show up when reviewing your seemingly unimportant notes.

FINDING SALMON & TROUT IN LAKE ONTARIO

by James M. Haynes
(Reprinted by permission of the New York State Sea Grant)

Where do you catch salmon and trout in a 7500 square mile lake with an average depth of 280 feet and a bottom structure resembling a soup bowl? Millions of juvenile salmon and trout are stocked annually in Lake Ontario, yet anglers frequently ask this question. With funding and support from the New York Sea Grant Institute, the Research Foundation of the State University of New York (SUNY), and local anglers' groups, faculty and student researchers at the SUNY Colleges at Brockport and Fredonia are studying the movements, distribution, and habitat preferences of salmon and trout in Lake Ontario. By attaching radiotransmitters to fish and setting nets as far as 15 miles out into the lake, researchers are providing answers to both anglers' and scientists' questions about the ecology of salmon and trout stocked in Lake Ontario.

Beginning in the mid-1960s, the reintroduction of lake trout and the introduction of brown trout, steelhead/rainbow trout, and Pacific salmon (coho and chinook) to the Great Lakes have sparked remarkable interest and enthusiasm among anglers, recreational businesses, and fisheries biologists throughout the region. Major salmon and trout stocking efforts by Great Lakes states and provinces and U.S. and Canadian federal agencies are designed to establish a quality recreational fishery and to restore ecosystem balance in the lakes. Native lake trout were once abundant in all the Great Lakes, so a major fishery management goal is to re-establish self-sustaining stocks of lake trout. Other salmon and trout are stocked in an attempt to control, by predation, large invader populations of alewifes and rainbow smelt. New York alone is stocking five million salmon and trout annually, a number representative of other states and provinces.

The history of Great Lakes fisheries is a sad chapter in the history of man's exploitation and destruction of economically important natural populations and their environmental resource bases. As the Great Lakes region was settled in the early 1800s, commercial fisheries for Atlantic salmon (Lake Ontario only), lake trout, whitefish, lake herring, various ciscoes, walleye, and other fishes prized as high-quality food became profitable and grew. As fishery operations expanded and harvests increased, these highly sought-after species began to decline. Following the classic pattern of resource exploitation, instead of reducing fishing effort to ease pressure on commercially valuable fish stocks, effort was increased to maintain high harvest levels. In consequence, selected species populations in certain Great Lakes collapsed. The lake sturgeon was generally first. Because it damaged netting gear, deliberate attempts to eradicate it were made in all Great Lakes and were successful first in Lake Ontario by 1900.

At the same time over-exploitation was occurring, settlers in the Great Lakes region were building cities and industries and were substantially altering land and water resources. Vast hardwood forests that limited erosion, provided regular stream flows, and maintained cool temperatures in Great Lakes tributaries were cut down, and dams were built on streams to power mills. In Lake Ontario, because deforestation and damming prevented successful reproduction in tributaries, what may have been the largest Atlantic salmon population in the world was nearly extinct in 1870. Other species, notably warm-water fishes such as the walleye, were also greatly affected by development along Great Lakes bays and tributaries.

In the 1820s, the Erie Canal provided a commercial link from Lakes Erie and Ontario to the Hudson River and Atlantic Ocean. That link also permitted exotic species such as the alewife and possibly lamprey to reach Lake Ontario from the ocean. Alewives are voracious zooplankton (microscopic aquatic animals) feeders, and they quickly began competing with plankton-feeding native whitefish, ciscoes, and shiners (important food fish for some commercially valuable species). In the 1930s the Welland Canal connected Lake Erie to Lake Ontario. Within a decade lampreys and alewifs had invaded the upper Great Lakes, and

rainbow smelt, first introduced in Lake Michigan in the 1920s, spread to Lake Ontario. At the same time, human population and industrial growth throughout the region added ever-increasing amounts of raw sewage, chemicals, and industrial waste to lake waters.

Thus, Great Lakes fish populations were exposed to a disastrous array of pressures arising from man's use of the environment. In the 1920s, lake herring populations collapsed in Lake Erie and whitefish populations collapsed in Lake Huron. As fishing pressure increased, diminished fish stocks became more vulnerable to lamprey predation, and as commercial stocks collapsed in the various Great Lakes, both commercial fishermen and lampreys switched to the next available fishery stock with individual fish of largest size. Lake trout, burbot, whitefish, lake herring, and various ciscoes declined and collapsed, especially in the lower Great Lakes. At the same time, alewifes and smelt successfully displaced native forage fish stocks (primarily emerald and spottail shiners and deep water sculpins, the latter also pollution related), or, in the case of smelt, may have preyed on young-of-the-year lake trout. In the absence of native predators, alewife and smelt populations exploded throughout the Great Lakes. By the 1950s, commercial harvests consisted primarily of carp, drum, bullhead, and perch. Lake Erie was considered dying, and lake ecosystems, except for Lake Superior, were seriously out of balance. Despite the near absence of commercial fishing, lampreys and pollution prevented a resurgence of native predators while overabundant, unexploited alewifes and smelt formed windrows on Great Lakes beaches during their periodic die-offs.

Through the International Joint Commission for the Great Lakes, the U.S. and Canadian governments agreed to restore Great Lakes water quality by mandating municipal and industrial pollution control. Under these conditions, the Great Lakes Fishery Commission decided upon a two-pronged approach to restore health to Great Lakes fisheries: introduction of salmon and trout by stocking and lamprey control. Only recreational harvesting of salmon and trout is permitted in U.S. waters; Canada allows some commercial fishing for salmon and trout. However, it was not until substantial lamprey control was achieved by chemically treating lamprey spawning streams that salmon and trout populations in the Great Lakes grew large and vigorous. That increase generated great interest as fishermen crowded nearshore and tributary areas of the Great Lakes to catch the biggest fish they had ever seen.

Initially, anglers concentrated on spawning-run fish in tributaries: salmon in autumn, steelhead/rainbow trout in spring. As brown and lake trout numbers increased, fishermen learned their locations in nearshore lake areas and began to understand their habitat preferences. On Lake Ontario, both anglers and scientists became very interested in the location, distribution, and habitat preferences of stocked salmon and trout.

A large lake can be a very perplexing place for fishermen. Anglers know that fish often prefer to be near "structure," often associating with rocks or debris on bottom or with brush along shore, but Lake Ontario offers little such physical structure. The total area of the lake is immense compared to shoreline area, while wave action and nearshore currents scour beach and bottom zones, so little structure is available for fish. Furthermore, nearshore and surface water temperatures in Lake Ontario are above salmon and trout tolerance limits from late June through early September.

With minimal help from scientists, anglers learned the nearshore seasonal locations of Lake Ontario salmon and trout species by trial-and-error observation. In spring (ice-out to May-June), brown, lake, and steelhead/rainbow trout are found in cold water (36-50°F) very close to shore (often in two to three feet of water). In autumn (mid-September to early November), coho and chinook salmon ascend streams to spawn, brown trout are again very close to shore, and lake and steelhead/rainbow trout are in somewhat deeper water.

Obvious gaps in knowledge concerning the whereabouts of some species in certain seasons became evident. Aware of these gaps, anglers pressed scientists to study salmon and trout ecology in Lake Ontario. In particular, anglers desired knowledge about chinook salmon, the largest, most glamorous species stocked in the Great Lakes. Their accessibility to anglers on Lake Michigan in summer has helped establish an important, economically beneficial recreational fishery there. Anglers and recreational businesses wanted to see a similar fishery develop on Lake Ontario. As a result of these factors, the SUNY research group began studies to determine the seasonal locations and habitat preferences of salmon and trout in Lake Ontario. To do this we used two methods rarely used in Great Lakes fishery studies: radiotelemetry and vertical gill netting. We have documented seasonal movements of brown and steelhead/rainbow trout and Pacific salmon using telemetry. Vertical gill nets provide a method to determine precise depth and temperature preferences of salmon and trout in summer.

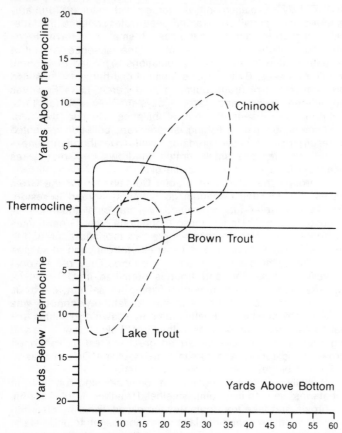

Relationship of lake and brown trout and chinook salmon to the thermocline and the bottom in summer. The vertical axis displays species position relative to the thermocline regardless of absolute thermocline depth and temperature. The horizontal axis displays the overall species distance from bottom.

Methods

Radiotelemetry has been used to study nearshore movements and stream selection by spawning-run salmon and trout in the Great Lakes, most notably with steelhead/rainbow trout in Lake Superior (University of Minnesota), coho salmon in Lake Michigan (University of Wisconsin), and coho and steelhead/rainbow in Lake Erie (SUNY Fredonia). In Lake Ontario we are examining salmon and trout movements in spawning and non-spawning seasons.

Radio receivers and transmitters were designed by the Bioelectronics Laboratory at the University of Minnesota and operate at 53 MHz. Transmitters (often temperature sensing) are

separately identifiable, and up to 100 can be distinguished simultaneously by receivers. Typically, 10 to 30 fish are tracked per season. Transmitter size depends upon battery size (larger batteries give longer life). Most transmitters are ¾ by 3-inch cylinders encased in epoxy, weigh about one ounce in water, and have an operational life of four to six months.

Salmon and trout are captured for radiotagging during periods when they move close to shore (spring and fall) using two methods: electroshocking or beach seining. A pontoon boat mounted with a generator and shocking booms creates an electrical field in the water. By moving slowing along shore in Lake Ontario or tributaries, salmon and trout are attracted into the field, stunned, netted, and placed in an aerated tank on board. A 650-foot beach seine (borrowed from the New York State Department of Environmental Conservation) is used to enclose pockets of water along the shore of Lake Ontario, thus trapping fish and permitting their capture.

Fish are tagged on site or kept for a period in holding cages to assure healthy condition. Before tagging, they are placed in an anesthetic solution to render them unconscious. Two methods are used to place transmitters on or in fish: external attachments near the dorsal fin and surgical implantation inside the body cavity. External transmitters have three wires embedded in their epoxy coating. A sharp needle is used to thread wires under the dorsal fin but above the major swimming muscles. Attachment wires are tied snugly against a plastic plate opposite the transmitter. Foam pads placed between transmitter/plastic plate and fish minimize tissue abrasion. A stiff antenna wire projects posteriorly from external transmitters. This technique is quick (about three minutes) and involves minimal trauma, but there is a risk that the fish will tear off the transmitters, especially while moving to spawn in streams.

Radiotransmitters are surgically implanted by incision in the belly area. Flexible antennae are inserted parallel to the main body axis, followed by the transmitter, and sutures close the incision. This technique requires more time (about eight minutes) and risk greater trauma but eliminate risk of losing transmitters. In fact, post-operative and subsequent field mortality is substantially higher among surgically tagged salmon and trout. In all tagging operations, fish gills are irrigated and antiseptic is applied to all attachment and insertion points to retard infection. Most surgically tagged and some externally tagged fish are held 12 to 24 hours to assure full post-tagging recovery.

After release, tagged salmon are tracked by truck, boat, or airplane, depending upon circumstances. When fish are within a mile of shore between Point Breeze and Irondequoit Bay, a truck mounted with Yagi antenna tracks them at half-mile intervals along shore. If fish are farther offshore in the same area or if we want to pinpoint their locations to obtain precise depth information, we track from boats mounted with Yagi antennae. When fish move out of the local study area, we use an airplane fitted with small loop antennae; a special, programmable scanning receiver tracks fish from the rapidly moving plane.

Vertical gill nets are rarely used in fishery studies because of the difficulty in setting and holding them in place over deep water. Their only previous use for salmon and trout in the Great Lakes occurred in Lake Erie at a maximum depth of 150 feet. In Lake Ontario we set vertical nets over depths ranging from 25 to 600 feet. Floating bars suspend nets (up to 150 feet long, from the water surface, while spreader bars at 25-foot intervals maintain standard 16-foot width. Net mesh sizes used are suitable for smelt, alewifes, salmon, and trout. Each time nets are set and retrieved, a temperature profile of the water column is taken at 6.5 foot intervals from surface to bottom. By comparing the depth at which fish are caught in a net with daily temperature profiles, the preferred temperatures of fish are determined.

Results

Several key questions about salmon and trout ecology in Lake Ontario are addressed in our study: 1) Where are chinook and coho salmon located in spring and summer? 2) Where are steelhead/rainbow trout located in summer and autumn? 3) What movements do lake and brown trout exhibit in their nearshore habitats? and 4) What are the seasonal movements and precise habitat preferences of all salmon and trout species in Lake Ontario? Our attempts to answer these questions were both rewarded and thwarted, depending upon the habits of each species.

Our research began by studying brown trout movement, behavior, and spawning stream selection in autumn 1980. Brown trout first appear near shore in autumn as water temperatures drop below 65°F. To our considerable surprise, brown trout, supposedly the most sedentary of the species stocked in Lake Ontario, moved as far as 70 miles in very shallow, nearshore waters while in spawning condition. Although several tagged fish seemed attracted to Sandy Creek (the tributary where most of our capture and tagging activities take place), no brown trout ascended the creek farther than one mile, despite the presence of suitable spawning areas farther upstream. No tagged brown trout were tracked entering other tributaries, indicating little reproductive success. While most tagged brown trout were stocked a few miles to the west two years before our study, one was stocked 50 miles to the east, confirming the extensive movement capabilities of brown trout in Lake Ontario. As nearshore and surface water temperatures drop below 39°F with the onset of winter, tagged brown trout move offshore to deeper, warmer 39°F water, where radio signals are reduced.

In spring 1981 we tagged more brown trout, several of which exhibited movements similar to those observed in fall 1980. However, most fish moved considerably farther east toward cooler water as summer approached. Brown trout continue to roam close to shore, investigating stream mouths and power plant outflows, until water temperatures exceed 65°F in June or July; then they begin moving offshore to deeper, cooler water where, again, radio signals are completely attenuated (at depths greater than 40 feet). One spring, brown trout tagged with a long-lived transmitter returned nearshore in autumn to their original area of preference, nicely confirming our hypotheses of nearshore and offshore movements based upon temperature preferences.

Once brown trout moved offshore in early summer, vertical gill netting found them associated with a wide range of temperatures. Most interesting is the strong degree of association brown trout exhibit with the thermocline, or zone of rapidly changing temperature in the water column. Intense summer sun heats the surface water of a lake but sunlight penetrates only to limited depths as solar energy is absorbed. The thermocline begins where the sun's energy has mostly been absorbed by surface waters, and a rather sharp decrease in water temperature (two degrees or more per yard) is observed with increasing depth. Thus, in summer, a lake is typically stratified with warm, less dense surface waters lying on cool, moderately dense thermocline waters that lie on the permanently cold, densest (39°F) bottom waters.

In Lake Ontario temperature stratification typically begins in late June and ends in September. Because the warmest layers of the water are near the surface and directly onshore, salmon and trout move offshore in summer to deeper waters and cooler, preferred temperatures. In Lake Ontario the thermocline is a dynamic zone that provides the only real physical structure for fish. As summer progresses the thermocline is driven deeper into the water column, although wind velocity and direction play a daily role in determining thermocline depth. In 1981-82 the average depth and temperature of the thermocline ranged from 10-98 feet and 46-65°F, respectively, and its width averaged 13 feet.

Brown trout association with the thermocline is strong, despite great variations in depth and temperature of that zone. Over 75 percent of brown trout were netted in or within 10 feet of the thermocline in summer 1981, a finding repeated in 1982. About 30 percent of brown trout were netted within 10 feet of the lake bottom, but 80 percent of those were caught there when the thermocline intersected the bottom. Brown trout are not found farther than three miles (usually in less than 100 feet of water)

offshore in any season and prefer to be as close to shore as possible given suitable water temperatures. Mean preferred water temperature, as defined by temperature sensing radio transmitters in spring and fall and by netting in summer, is 55°F for brown trout.

Steelhead/rainbow trout were radiotracked in spring 1981 and spring and fall 1982 and exhibited even greater movement than brown trout. Steelhead/rainbow were tagged as they ascended and decended spawning streams. Several successfully spawned, then returned to Lake Ontario and engaged in extensive movements along shore before moving to the open lake. An extraordinarily cold winter of 1981-82 delayed lake warming by four to six weeks compared to normal years. In 1981 nearshore lake temperatures reached 50°F by mid-May, and our tagged steelhead dispersed far out into Lake Ontario. In 1982 nearshore lake temperatures did not reach 50°F until mid-June, when steelhead again dispersed into the open lake.

In 1982 we confirmed the suspected importance of the "thermal bar" relative to the dispersal of steelhead/rainbow far out into Lake Ontario. The thermal bar is a zone of rapid horizontal temperature change extending toward shore at an angle from lake surface to bottom. As the lake begins to heat in spring, nearshore waters warm first. If water temperatures are measured at intervals while moving offshore, at some point over a distance of 200 feet or so surface temperature will drop markedly, typically from 45 to 39°F early in spring and 54 to 45°F farther offshore later in the spring. The thermal bar and other sharp horizontal temperature gradients act as a barrier that seems to pen steelhead/rainbow nearshore after they leave spawning streams. As nearshore surface temperatures approach 50°F and the thermal bar is "pushed" farther offshore (five to 20 miles), the steelhead/rainbow literally spill out into the open lake. Several steelhead bore temperature sensing transmitters that confirmed their presence in the thermal bar or other temperature gradient regions and the importance of the 50°F transition temperature. Two steelhead tagged in spring 1982 were later caught in Canadian waters many miles from their last known locations.

Steelhead/rainbow trout are notoriously net wary, and few have been caught in our vertical nets. However, acting on our research findings, in 1982 anglers sought out the thermal bar and caught steelhead near it. In summer they have fished five to 10 miles offshore, observed many large fish with depth sounders in 50-65°F water near the surface, and caught occasional steelhead/rainbow trout. Thus, it appears that steelhead behave in Lake Ontario just as they do in their native north Pacific Ocean waters. They are dispersing, open-water wanderers that do not concentrate in special open-lake or nearshore areas in summer. Consequently, they are difficult to find, and anglers must fish considerable distances offshore with larger boats and advanced electronic gear (depth sounders, loran-C navigation devices, temperature sensors). Many steelhead/rainbow move back nearshore in autumn and into tributaries to overwinter, movements documented by telemetry in fall 1982.

Lake trout proved difficult to radiotag because of their year-round preference for deeper waters than brown trout. We did tag

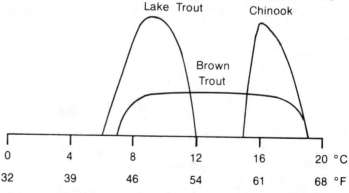

Summer temperature preferences of lake and brown trout and chinook salmon.

one each in spring and fall 1981. Both remained near their release areas for several days, then disappeared into deep water nearby, never to be heard from again.

Summer netting for lake trout was highly productive. They have clearly defined temperature preferences between 43 and 55°F. Like brown trout, many lake trout occupy the thermocline zone, but 35 percent were netted within 10 feet of bottom, indicating much stronger bottom orientation than brown trout. Most lake trout were netted in less than 100 feet of water, indicating that they too occupy narrow temperature preference bands as close to shore as possible in summer. We have netted, and anglers have caught, small numbers of lake trout far offshore and close to the surface (still in preferred temperatures), indicating that a portion of the population may be somewhat pelagic and wide ranging.

We have been unable to work effectively with coho salmon in spring or summer. They are currently rare in Lake Ontario because of very low recent stocking levels and poor post-stocking survival. Fall 1982 radiotagging studies revealed wide-ranging movements before selecting spawning streams.

Chinook salmon are the glamour fish of the Great Lakes, and a successful summer chinook fishery will vastly improve the economics of the Lake Ontario fishery. However, few chinook come nearshore in spring. Occasional nearshore strays are caught, and we tagged one such fish donated by an angler. The tagged chinook was released at 9:30 p.m., moved three miles east along shore, and swam toward mid-lake out of range by 1:00 a.m. We were unable to find the fish from Toronto to the St. Lawrence River by airplane and concluded it dispersed to deeper, open waters, a trait held in common with its cousins in the north Pacific. In fall 1982, radiotagged chinook displayed wide-ranging, predominantly westward movements in Lake Ontario before selecting spawning streams.

Because of the vast chinook stocking effort in Lake Ontario summer netting has been somewhat successful, despite chinook dispersal habits. In 1981 netting within three miles of shore, chinook salmon preferred temperatures from 57-63°F in areas in and above the thermocline. Netting in 1982 supports these findings, but only occasional chinook have been netted five to 15 miles offshore, indicating there is some concentration of chinook in nearshore thermoclinal areas, at least in late summer as onshore movements in preparation for fall spawning runs begin. Thus, it appears that the dispersing habit of chinook will make offshore fishing difficult but that, as numbers in the lake increase, nearshore thermocline areas may offer improved summer chinook fishing and spur the fishery, tourism, and economic boom hoped for by the Lake Ontario communities.

Radiotelemetry and vertical gill netting, fishery research techniques new to the Great Lakes, have helped researchers learn the locations, movements, and habitat preferences of salmon and trout in Lake Ontario. Radiotelemetry shows that salmon and trout move great distances during seasons when they are nearshore; summer netting reveals that steelhead/-rainbow trout and Pacific salmon are widely dispersed and far offshore, while lake and brown trout are concentrated in narrow temperature preference bands associated with the thermocline, lake bottom, and nearshore regions. Based on our experiences, we hope to design new research approaches to solve Great Lakes fishery problems and to help restore ecological and economic health to the Great Lakes region.

DIPSY DIVERS
NOT JUST ANOTHER FLASH IN THE PAN . . .
by Rob Birchler

When I think back on my first impression of Luhr Jensen's Dipsy Diver, it was a rather obnoxious looking little item which reminded me of a miniature U.F.O. And I must admit that I was quite skeptical to say the least, but let me tell you, I didn't have to put much time in with the Dipsys before they made a believer out of me.

Perhaps I should explain first exactly what a it is and what its functions are. The Dipsy Diver is an innovative trolling/diver planer which easily adjusts for a wide selection of depths and trolling positions. It's held in planing position by a weight molded into an adjustable base plate on the bottom and a fin with a built in release on top. It also comes with a snap-on "O" ring which the majority of fishermen prefer to leave on and can be used for attaining additional depth, thus making the Dipsy that much more versatile.

Basically the Dipsy dramatically increases your trolling span without interfering with your downriggers and allows you to fish a wide selection of depths without the assistance of lead weights or downriggers. Ontario is a big lake and by covering a wider area, you expose your lures to more potential fish—and that's the name of the game. The Dipsy also works as an attractor and is rapidly gaining a reputation for turning a slow day into a productive one. And I don't have to tell you that when the fishing's slow, every advantage helps.

Okay, so now we know what it is and what it does. So how do we use it? First, select the proper rod and reel. There are reels made specifically for this type of fishing, such as the Daiwa model 47-LC line counter reels. The standard downrigger rod is not recommended because of the pressure it receives from the pull of the Dipsy when it is in set position. A stiff rod such as Daiwa's SK-787HGL or SK-780HGL will handle the pull but not to the point of overkill once you have a fish on. It also allows you to clear your downriggers while trolling and landing a fish. Setting up a couple of rods and reels specifically for fishing divers saves a lot of time, too.

The standard line used is 20 lb. test which may seem on the heavy side, but you have a lot of pull until it trips and you don't want line stretch if you want to trip the diver yourself. Besides, and I can't tell you why, but when fish hit a Dipsy, they hit with vengeance. A snubber used between the diver and your lure helps cut down on break offs and can be purchased at most any shop that sells Dipsys.

The divers are available in three finishes: fire, kelly green and silver plate. Preference on color will vary according to conditions and on a given day one color may well outfish the other two with the reverse being the rule on another day. The standard size is 4 1/8 inch in diameter and the new "mini" is 3 1/4 inches.

So now that we've purchased everything we need and selected the color of the day, let's put it altogether. First, tie on the Dipsy and set the release to the proper tension. Next, snap the snubber to the back of the diver and tie on the leader. A 4 to 6 ft. leader seems to be the rule of thumb and though it is variable, the leader should be no longer than your rod so that you can bring the fish close enough to the boat to net.

Now, loosen the bottom screw and set the adjustable base plate as indicated between 0 and 3½, the 0 setting being the deepest. Maximum depth for the standard diver is 50 to 60 ft. and 30 ft. for the mini, depending on conditions. "Port" and "starboard" are clearly marked on the bottom of the base plate

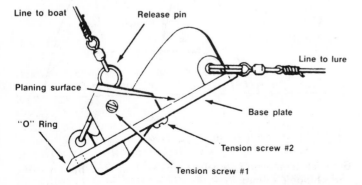

Line to boat

Release pin

Line to lure

Planing surface

"O" Ring

Base plate

Tension screw #2

Tension screw #1

and must be set according to the side of the boat you are running it from. Now, place your thumb firmly on the spool and put your reel in the free spool. Slowly allow the Dipsy to work its way away from the boat until you feel that the diver is where you want it.

It's important to note that the angle of the line from the boat to the water does not indicate the position of the Dipsy underwater due to the belly in the line, and how much line you let out is another variable. While it sounds vague, you should try different distances and depths until one starts producing. Keep in mind that just because you're graphing the majority of fish deep does not mean you won't catch fish above. Fish often leave their comfort zone to feed and chances are they will be the most aggressive.

A good example of this is the current New York State record brown trout that was taken by Jerry O'Keefe while fishing with Captains Jim Shouey and Don Chamberlain in the summer of '86. They were running their downriggers at 35 to 40 ft. when the big brown hit a Dipsy that was no deeper than 15 ft. By the way, that fish was an awesome 29 lbs. 15 oz.

Another technique you might want to try is running your Dipsys off planer boards. By doing this you're not limiting yourself to fishing the surface and it enables you to use your boards for more than shallow water fishing in the spring and fall. Another method that produces good results is to set a mini diver at 3, let out 20 to 30 ft. of line and clip it into an outside downrigger. Stacking releases should be used if you're trolling close to the bottom so you can keep the Dipsy running high enough to prevent it from hanging up on the bottom.

Dipsys can play a big part in lake fishing, though you'll have to put in some time before you become completely comfortable using them. But hang in there because the rewards will be well worth the effort and I'm sure that if you're not already, you'll become a believer, too.

SALMON-PRODUCING DOWNRIGGER TECHNIQUES

by Joe Swift

The scene when salmon return to their spawning waters is now becoming classic. Picture any of the rivers or larger streams gently flowing into Lake Ontario. Directly off the mouth is a fleet of about 100 boats that are actively circling across and near the outflow. The water depth ranges from about 5 to 25 feet and the water temperature is in the high sixties.

As you look beyond these nearshore boats, you notice another larger group of boats centered approximately one to two miles out. Although this fleet appears to be much larger, consisting of perhaps as many as 250 boats, they are less tightly bunched. In fact as you strain, you begin to notice a few boats on the horizon at the furthest reach of your vision. The offshore water depth ranges anywhere from about 90 to 350 feet deep. And although the top eighty or so feet of water is the same temperature as found onshore (high sixties) a defined thermocline, having temperature ranging from 62 down to 52F, usually occurs between 80 and 95 feet deep.

Action and excitement are now brought into this scene as you first see one of the offshore boats, after a long battle, land a king salmon. Instantly, another boat hooks onto one and you notice a silver shape jump about 200 yards astern of the boat. As you try to focus on this ongoing battle, you are distracted by the shouting of two excited fishermen who have caught an unquestionaly large chinook inshore and are working it to the net.

At this point, one realizes that, aside from the salmon, it is the downrigger that plays a major role in the drama that is unfolding before you. It is the downrigger that enables salmon anglers to effectively work their prey wherever and at whatever depth they are found.

Clearly, downrigging offers the versatility to light-line fish at virtually any depth. Given this, it is understandable that shallow water techniques are quite often different than those used offshore. Because mature salmon will often inhabit waters that are far warmer than their normal preferred temperatures of 51 to 56F, both techniques must be successfully mastered if the angler is to bring home consistent salmon catches.

Characteristic of the onshore, shallow water fishery is the need, at times, to place lures in close proximity to bottom structure or near the surface. The objective here is to present your lures effectively without continually hanging bottom or without loosing them to the propellers of heavy boat traffic commonplace in shallow-inhabited waters. Careful consideration must be given to the selection and rigging of lures.

Medium to large size flutter type spoons such as the Clearwater 171 Salmon Spoon, the Miller 22, the Sutton 38, and the Northport Nailer (modified to carry a single 4/0 stainless steel hook) are consistently good performers for near-bottom salmon trolling. By having the hooks ride upwards, occasional contacts with bottom result in surprisingly few snags.

When near bottom, it's helpful to adjust releases to trip with only a light pull on the lure by using a balance of rod loading (i.e.

bend) and release tension. Forces applied to the lure ranging between ¾ and 1 pound will trigger the release. With 12 to 20 pound test lines, this set-up has sufficient holding forces to adequately hook a fish and will readily trip upon any contact with bottom, weeds, or any other debris which is frequently encountered nearshore. Thus any fouled lure is immediately detected and quickly reset.

Most novice anglers use newly purchased releases right out of the package and set them once for all trolling. Unfortunately, many quickly find that this is a serious mistake. Any new release can have rough edges or spots in the mechanism that could make it work unpredictably. Thus, many first time uses of a release can, and often do, result in broken lines and lost fish. Fortunately, these can easily be avoided by working the release through a few dozen actuations before use. With those releases having swinging arm type mechanisms (such as the Black Marine, Big Jon, or Roemer Release) simply open and close the action twenty or more times on several tension settings. On the pressure pad or clip type releases (such as the Walker, Clipper or Offshore releases) cut off about 12 inches of the line you are intending to use and tie it into a loop. Load a portion of the loop into the release as though it were a normal fishing situation. Then pull evenly on the loop until it releases. Repeat this procedure several times until you are certain the release is working reliably. The release is now broken in and ready for its first use.

TROLL S-CURVE PATTERNS

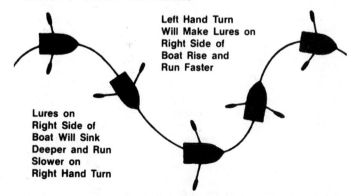

Left Hand Turn Will Make Lures on Right Side of Boat Rise and Run Faster

Lures on Right Side of Boat Will Sink Deeper and Run Slower on Right Hand Turn

An S-curve pattern will produce far more strikes than trolling a straight line. Every time your boat makes an inside turn the troll blades and trailing lure will work slower and deeper. On an outside turn the troll will rise in the water and the blades will spin faster. By trolling in S-curve patterns you will cause the troll and trailing lure to give off varied vibration patterns in the water, signaling to all nearby fish that something's in trouble and an easy meal is available.

The combination of the 12 inch loop of line and a fish "deliar" scale can conveniently be used to determine precisely what force is required to trigger the release. To do this, simply use the scale to pull on the loop and read the force (or weight) while tripping the mechanism. With the adjustable type releases, the method also enables one to very accurately set each and every release to exactly the same trigger force. As a rule of thumb, try to keep release trigger forces to about 10%, or less, of the line breaking strength.

Another point worth mentioning here is that most releases tend to deform the line within the contact region and thereby weaken it somewhat. It is important to use fresh line and try not to load the same portion of line into the release repeatedly.

Surface or near-surface fishing is perhaps the easiest way to fish for salmon. Almost any plug or spoon can be run, as can almost any lure/attractor combination. Here the main object is to effectively present several lures using downriggers and to avoid line tangles when in a trolling pattern. The best way to do this is by setting your lures in what is called "staggered and layered pairs".

This practical technique involves placing two similar lures (each on its own separate rod), at very specific depths and distances behind the boat by stacking the shallowest lures at the farthest position behind the boat above the deeper lures which are progressively closer to the downrigger cables. If one were to view this set-up out of the water it would look something like the multiple Chinese kites that are flown in the wind from a single string (the highest one is furthest away while the lowest kite is nearest the anchor point). Care must be taken here to position any diving or sinking lures only at the lower levels to prevent them from picking up a lower level lure on a turn.

As a rule, in shallow water, try to sweep the upper 50% of your water depth. For example, if fishing with three people in 30 feet of water using six rods, set two of the same lures (but usually different in color) at 2 to 5 feet down and 100 to 150 feet back another pair of perhaps different lures (also different in color) 6 to 10 feet deep 75 to 100 feet back and a third pair 10 to 15 feet deep 50 to 75 feet back. Then troll until you catch the first salmon. At that point, change half of the remaining lures to the color and style lure that caught the fish and also reposition the depths on the other rigs to run closer to where the fish was taken.

For chinooks, it is not necessary to use attractors (dodgers) on every line. What works rather well (if dodgers are used) is to place one at the shallowest and furthest back position and another deep and short. When using dodgers in line, you'll find it necessary to adjust your releases by an additional ¼ to ½ pounds to prevent false releases caused by the added drag of the attractor. Since mature salmon are sometimes found above well-defined thermoclines, these same surface riggings work for offshore located fish.

Once offshore however, it is generally a good idea to look for the most active salmon on or near the thermocline. Once you have pinpointed the depth of the thermocline, try to cover the temperature ranging from 52 to 62F, again, with equally spaced, "staggered and layered pairs" of lures as described. In deeper water however, the lure distance behind the cannonball can be shortened considerably (10 to 20 feet back for the deepest rigs and not more than 75 feet back for the shallowest running lures).

FISHING SECRETS
by Randy Snyder

When I was just starting to fish for lake trout back in the 50's, I made a deal with the owners of a particular marina on Seneca Lake to help during busy times in exchange for the use of a boat and motor which I couldn't afford to pay cash for. An hour before sunrise, I'd help fishermen get their boats and motors ready, run the gas pumps, dip bait, etc. You would think that just being around all these fishermen, I'd come up with a wealth of information, wouldn't you? Wrong!

The "locals" were so secretive they didn't share fishing tips with a person fishing in the same boat, that's how carefully they protected their secrets. One fellow in particular was a perfect prospect for a high ranking CIA position; actually wrapping his rigs in burlap bags, he'd hide them right up until it was time to slide them into the water.

What a difference a little help would have made if only one "local" had shared what I had to learn by myself. But I did learn one valuable lesson — I swore I'd go out of my way to help people learn how to catch fish, and I do.

One of the most rewarding aspects of owning and operating the Sea-ducer Charter Service is teaching new methods to old fishermen. And they never forget "who" helped them out and on some of my slow days, the very fishermen I once helped are more than eager to pass on information.

You don't think the Lake Ontario fishery would be as great as it is if everyone kept everything a big secret, do you? The more people who use and advertise their fishing successes, the more money the State will spend on the fishery as public response is what counts when the budgets are planned and the money is passed out. Most of us know that helping others promotes the fishery no matter where we fish . . . so here's a lesson I've learned that I'd like to share with you.

How many times do you come up empty when the rod jerks free of the downrigger release? It's happened to the best of us and it's frustrating, to put it mildly. If you haven't bothered to sharpen your hooks, do that first. Mine are always sharpened to needle quality, but we still used to miss an exorbitant number of hits at times and spent a lot of family time discussing it since our crew is family. And we finally reached a conclusion after going three for ten on a smooth-as-glass Lake Ontario day with no apparent reason for the missed hits.

The next day we tried adding an extra hook right over the original hook on one of our favorite spoons. Closing the ring of the trailer hook down with a pair of pliers, we had the lure with the original hook, plus a second hook trailing by approximately two inches. And our efforts paid off; we boated nine chinooks out of ten hits for the day — six of them hooked by the trailer hook only.

After several years of experimenting to overcome these short hits on plugs, we began to tie our own double hook set-ups. Tie 40-pound test dacron to the end of a swivel and extend a 3/0 treble hook to the business end. I tie the hook so that the ring of the hook is just passed the end of the plug, dropping the hook approximately 1½ to 2 inches behind where the original hook would normally end. Most chinooks we boat are hooked deep in the gullet and the lightly hooked ones are few and far between. The solution we found for "short" hits has proven to be effective and worth the time and effort.

Another "secret" I'd like to share with you is the excitement of trolling for chinook salmon at night. If you think just catching a chinook gets you excited, the first one you boat under pitch black conditions will make your blood boil, even though the first couple you hook will more than likely leave you talking to yourself about what you did wrong. But after a few of those episodes, your nerves will settle down and you're likely to be hooked on this method, too.

Experience has taught us that the first and last two hours of daylight are usually the most productive. Wherever you fish for chinook, there's likely to be a rush to get off the lake as the sun sets in the west and launches are clogged with boat traffic. You'll want to take this into account when planning your night fishing trips and launch accordingly.

The best conditions for night fishing chinook are a relatively flat lake with an overcast sky, trolling dead slow; I run two sea anchors instead of one to slow the boat down to the right speed. Don't forget to have a good spotlight handy and extra batteries, if it's battery operated. It's a must when you're ready to net your catch, or for charging lures such as the flourescent green-glo Jlugs (size 3) which was the preferred lure when I first began ight fishing chinooks off Manistee, MI in 1975.

Plugs are available now which allow you to insert a chemical ght stick to illuminate the body of the plug lasting up to eight ours. Though J-plugs are still successful, it's hard work etrieving and recharging them every half hour. With the light tick plugs, you spend the time you'd use repeating the recharge peration to concentrate on the details of working a particular tretch of the lake. You can also set your downriggers, then run top lines right over them so your chance of hooking up are doubled.

To hook a big chinook and land him in the daylight is something special, but to land one of these beauties in the dark is an experience which stands out all by itself. I will guarantee that your knees will be shakey when the fish is finally in the net and safely hoisted aboard.

Don't be afraid to experiment, and when you find a "better way," share it...there are plenty of fish in New York State lakes to go around. "Secrets" is a game that children play.

TROLLING SPEED CAN BE THE DIFFERENCE
by Mike Bleech

Trolling speed is but one of many variables that the salmonid roller must deal with. Any seasoned angler knows that a change n speed of less than one-half-mph can spell the difference between a number of hookups and just a few. Yet trolling speed is aken casually by some anglers and is misunderstood by even more.

To deal with trolling speed in an efficient manner, the angler must 1) understand what trolling speed is; 2) understand how to match terminal tackle to trolling speed; 3) know how to control rolling speed.

Trolling speed is the speed that the lures are moving through he water, but not necessarily the same speed the boat is moving. Currents, either on the surface or below, can cause the relative speeds of boat and lures to be different. For that matter, the lures n the spread may be traveling at different speeds, relative to the water. The wind, for example, can cause a surface current which would mean that lures run in that current, say from planer boards, would be traveling at a different relative speed than lures run below that current from downriggers.

Trolling speed for Great Lakes salmonids varies from the slowest possible speed to over 4 miles per hour. Any trolling speed over 5 mph is usually too fast. The standard trolling speed, if there is such a thing, is between 1½ and 3 mph. This is an over simplification, however, since the various salmonids react differently to trolling speed.

As a general guideline, salmon (especially in the spring) and steelhead are most likely to be turned on by faster trolling speeds while browns and lakers are more likely to be taken by a slower troll. Another general guideline is that trolling speeds for salmon and steelhead should also be slowed in water colder than 50 degrees.

It is important that you understand that speedometers and knot meters are not calibrated the same. You must understand your own instrument and not try to relate it to what you read or hear, just as you must match lures and attractors to the trolling speed. Few, if any, lures will perform acceptably throughout the salmonid trolling speed range. Most have an optimum speed range of somewhere in the neighborhood of 1½ mph. The most versatile lures in this context are the action plastic lures.

Dodgers are meant to wobble but when they spin, they are being trolled to fast. Spoons generally can be evaluated in the same way while plugs tend to have a broader operating range than lightweight spoons. The exception to this is the class of plugs commonly called the banana baits which give great action with the slowest trolling speeds.

It is important that you remember that all plugs must be perfectly tuned to achieve desired action under maximum trolling speeds. A few plugs are factory-tuned while many others include tuning instructions in the package. Lures should be tested alongside the boat with a minimum of six feet of line between the lure or dodger and the rod tip to allow freedom of movement similar to what it will have during use.

It is easy to understand what trolling speed is; control of the trolling speed is more difficult. Matching tackle to trolling speed takes time, effort and a good assortment of lures and attractors, but end result is worth the effort.

In order to control trolling speed there must first be some way to measure trolling speed! The only accurate way to measure trolling speed is to have a speedometer at the same depth as the lures in question. Such devices are on the market, but everything has a price — in addition to dollars and cents. There are speed devices that attach to downrigger balls which afford precise speed control down where the lures are, and some very good trolling speedometers which meter the speed of the boat. Granted, relative speed of lures may be different from boat speed, but these devices give the troller the ability to accurately gauge small changes in trolling speed. The ability to measure changes in trolling speed is far more important than measuring the actual relative speed of lures.

Why is it more important to measure change than the actual speed? Because the troller does not really care how fast the lures are traveling. What matters is how the fish react to the speed. If they're hitting, then it is important to measure absolutely no change in trolling speed. If the fish are not hitting it is important to measure small increases or decreases in trolling speed until a productive speed is found.

Tachometers are commonly used to measure changes in speed and some trollers watch the angle of the downrigger cables, while others rely on some mystical ability to sense speed. These methods are of limited reliability at best. Still, just knowing that minor trolling speed adjustments can be critical to success is an important bit of knowledge!

Many anglers have sadly learned that measuring the trolling speed is not enough — large motors will often not troll slow enough for salmonids. However, the new Evinrudes with big horses troll unbelieveably well, and auxiliary motor mounts are available, as is steering linkage to allow the small motor to be steered from helm.

THE LURE SPREAD
by Mike Bleech

One of the big keys to consistent success on Lake Ontario is a good spread of lures which gets all the lures you are allowed to run into the water without tangling. This spread covers a broad range of depths, distances from the boat, lure style and color to help the anglers zero in on the hot patterns. It catches the fish!

There are millions of salmonids in Lake Ontario — certainly one of the finest sport fisheries in the world. But there is a lot of water out there! The angler's job is to get a lure in front of a fish. Even with all the modern tools at the anglers' disposal; sonar, temperature probes and so on; it still boils down to covering as much water as possible.

The basic tools for attaining a maximum lure spread are: downriggers, planer boards and diving planes. The other ingredients of a good lure spread are accessories such as releases or rigging, and a thorough knowledge of the characteristics of the various lures.

What is the purpose of the downrigger? Most anglers would probably answer, "to get the lures deep." Dick Julylia, a respected field tester and innovator, taught me a better answer a few years back — an answer which gives the downrigger more than glorified sinker status. The downrigger, Dick pointed out, is a controlled depth trolling tool which provides precise depth control. It is the nucleus we will build the lure spread around.

Most small boats are equipped with two downriggers. Start the lure spread out right by mounting these with the arms pointed outward. With swivel bases they can be swung in for high-speed running or trailering. Using this set-up on my 16-foot boat and four-foot booms on my 'riggers,I get a spread of about 13 feet between the cables and I can run 1 or 2 more 'riggers in between.

The balls are set at different depths for two reasons. First, various depths are tried until fish contact is made. Second, even after the fish-producing depth band is found, depths of the balls are staggered by at least a couple of feet to avoid tangling. Deep-diving lures are usually run on the outside 'riggers when three or four lures are used, and in any case, on the deepest.

Dropper lines can be a major improvement to the lure spread by doubling the number of lures run from the downriggers. One dropper per 'rigger is the maximum which can be run without constant tangling. Droppers are attached to the main line, but are free to slide up and down. Set in position, they are attached to the downrigger cable by a special release.

Length of the droppers should be about five feet and they should be set at least five feet above the main line at the ball. The best lures for the droppers track straight, causing very little drag. Flutter spoons are a good choice. During mid-summer when most of the salmonids are deep, a dropper run well above the thermocline, using a bright red lure, is a good bet for steelheads.

Planer boards are the principle tool for the horizontal lure spread. With a pair of boards and a number of lines, a boat can troll a 200-foot-wide strip of water. This distance should only be attempted when the boat traffic is at a minimum, and up to six lines can be run off each board if conditions are right. Most use three lines off each board and cover about 100 feet and all about the same distance behind the release, approximately 10 to 15 feet. Since the tow line angles back, the outside lure will be furthest behind the boat. In most cases, when a fish is hooked it will swing clear of the other lines.

Many anglers look at diving planes as a tool for anglers who cannot afford downriggers. While they can be used successfully in place of 'riggers, they are much more than a substitute. Diving planes give the lure spread versatility.

Diving planes can get a lure at least as deep as 100 feet. Not with the control downriggers afford, but down there. Recent arrivals on the market are diving planes which go both down and out. When you want to get most of your lures down deep, but do not have enough 'riggers to handle them all, the down-and-out divers can supplement the vertical spread, by giving the deep lures horizontal mobility.

Small diving planes can be run off the planer boards. This set-up can be used to get lures down to about 35 feet, according to Capt. Jim Shouey who introduced me to this tactic during a productive outing last August. Thus, diving planes give the planer

boards vertical mobility. Bead chain weights are also very effective in accomplishing this.

Horizontal mobility for the deep lures and vertical mobility for the wide lures is certainly a lot more than a mere substitute for downriggers! A growing number of innovative deep trollers are using diving planes off their two downriggers to give a better deep troll.

So far in our treatise on the lures we have covered the tools which spread the lures. Now we will look at a sample spread. In this example the boat carries three anglers and is equipped with two downriggers and all the other tools mentioned so far. The thermocline is between 60 and 70 feet.

Since we are dealing with three anglers, we have six rods to work with, and since the thermocline is deep, we want most, but not all, of the lures to be deep. Many trollers would approach this situation by stacking two rods on each 'rigger, and this is fine. However, by placing just one rod on each 'rigger and adding a dropper, we have as many lures on the 'riggers and two extra rods to play with.

Down-and-out diving planes will take these two lines down into position. They will be covering water which cannot be reached with the 'riggers. The two remaining rods can be run as flat lines or off a planer board. Since there are only two lines, one board will be sufficient. A good set-up would be to run a small diving lure on the inside line. When one of these lines pops from its release, a steelhead will likely be the culprit.

Now, let's look at another example. This time the fish are near the surface, a typical spring situation. We will use the same boat and anglers as in the previous example.

One line is run from each downrigger, but there is no room for droppers in shallow water. While looking for a pattern, one of these lines should be short, 15 feet behind the ball and down about eight feet. The other line will be longer, say 50 to 70 feet back and down five. All lines should be changed (distance, depth, lure color and type) about every 15 minutes until a pattern is established. If cohos are in the area, an additional flat line can be added in between the 'riggers.

The remaining lines go out on the planer boards. Keep a variety of lures out there until fish contact is made. Some should be shallow-runners, and some deep-divers. With two rods on the 'riggers, two lines would be run from each board. Four lines could be run off one board, but this cuts the width of the spread which means only half as much water would be covered.

Too many trollers hold back on the purchase of the tools used in this work and adoption of these rather involved methods, thinking it too much effort for a Great Lake's method. The more adventurous have perfected these tactics, and found that they can be applied to almost all trolling situations in any large body of water.

Got the idea? Catching fish is like solving a puzzle, and there are many pieces to the fishing jigsaw. The good lure spread is only one piece of the puzzle, but it ties in other equally important parts. Pay careful attention to your lure spread. It will reward you with many fish!

FINDING A GREAT (LAKES) GUIDE
Reprinted by Permission of the New York State Sea Grant

The number of fishing guides offering services on Lake Ontario has mushroomed over the last three years. This presents a problem to many potential charter customers: How do you evaluate and select a charter service?

The key to making the wisest choice in the selection of a charter captain is simple. **ASK QUESTIONS!** Most good captains are open and willing to answer any questions and concerns you might have about a fishing trip. Don't hesitate to "talk turkey" (or chinook or brown trout) with a charter operator - it's the only way both you and the operator can hash out each other's expectations and responsibilities of the fishing trip.

Some basic questions should be answered before you decide on retaining a captain's services. These are: **Is the captain validly licensed by the U.S. Coast Guard to carry passengers for**

hire? Operators are required to possess and carry a Coast Guard license to carry 6 or less passengers for hire. Since there is no state licensing system, a federal license is the only way (and an easy way!) to determine if your captain is working legally and has passed the Coast Guard captain's exam. If there are any concerns, ask to see the license. **—Is the charter boat properly outfitted with the required safety equipment?** There is no required annual inspections that a charter boat must pass. As such, it is important to ascertain that the boat has the required flotation devices and emergency equipment. Look to see if the boat has a U.S. Coast Guard Auxiliary Courtesy exam sticker. It's not legally required, but does indicate that the captain has taken the time to have this voluntary inspection carried out. **—Is the boat adequately insured?** Again, there is no requirement here, but it may make you feel better to know that the boat and its operation is insured against passenger accidents. It also indicates that an insurer has screened the captain and the vessel to some degree and considers the charter business worthy of coverage. — **Does the boat carry a radio telephone?** It is not required, but a VHF-FM marine radio telephone is perhaps the safest and most reliable common communication device on the water. Radio channels are continuously monitored by the Coast Guard and most radios have a weather-band channel that constantly receives U.S. Weather Service broadcasts. CB radios do not offer these advantages and are limited in their broadcast range. — **Is the captain a member of any fishing, community or professional trade organization?** A captain who gives up time to be a member of a fishing group, a community board or professional charter boat association suggests by his involvement that he is responsible. For example, one charter boat group, the Lake Ontario Charter Boat Association has requirements of its members regarding licensing, insurance, vessel safety and radio equipment. — **Is the captain a skilled fisherman?** Obviously, not a question a customer would want only to ask of the captain. Ask around at tackle stores, talk to other fishermen and maybe some previous customers. There are numerous other questions that might be asked, including those related to price, payment and deposit, departure time, bad weather contingencies, refreshments and other boat rules. It's your money, so don't hesitate to ask. The good captain will want to answer these questions and have his potential clients understand all arrangements fully.

DOWNRIGGER FISHING
MORE FISH FOR YOUR FUEL

by Robert B. Buerger
and Christopher F. Smith

Fishing is more exciting than ever with the variety of modern equipment available for today's sport angler. From video screen depth finders to computer-assisted navigation aids, the sport-fishing industry has kept up-to-date on the latest technological advancements. The age-old quandary still faces the modern angler, however: how to get the fish to bite. For the boat sportfisherman, the problem can be more than just coming home empty-handed. Fuel and maintenance costs of operating a boat have risen drastically. The more time spent trying to locate and catch fish, the higher the cost of a day's sportfishing outing in energy and dollars. The successful angler today is the one who returns to port, not only with a well full of fish, but also with fuel remaining in the tank.

Innovations in sportfishing technology now enable you to increase your chances of finding and baiting certain fish. One technique that has proven successful for fish species sensitive to specific water temperatures is downrigging.

Most fish actively feed at or near a precise temperature range. The angler who knows and can gear his bait to the optimum range for his intended catch stands the greatest chance of success. When fish are in deep water, however, traditional flat lining will not hold the bait to the depth at which the fish are feeding. For years, some anglers have solved this problem by attaching heavy weights to their lines or using lead core line. Although this technique is proven effective, the excessive weight needed to lower the line to the appropriate depth minimizes much of the sporting "fight" of catching a fish; and even when the line is weighted, it becomes difficult to determine how deep it is running. Downrigging allows you to fish at specific depths without sacrificing the excitement of catching fish on light or medium tackle.

Downrigging: How it Works

The downrigger is a winch-type mechanism that feeds cable off a rotating reel through a guide system along an extension arm. A weight attached to the end of the cable draws it to the appropriate depth. Located near the bottom of the cable is the line release. The fishing line from an independent rod is attached to the release mechanisms on the downrigger cable.

By lowering the weight you can drop the line down to the desired depth. A meter is usually connected to the reel unit to provide a specific count of the amount of cable that has been released. At the desired depth the reel is locked into place.

The independent fishing rod is set in a holder either attached to the downrigger or placed directly behind it on the gunwale. A bow is placed in the rod by tightening the line between it and the release on the downrigger cable. When a fish "strikes," it pulls the line from the release on the cable and thereby sets the hook. As tension on the line is released, the rod appears to snap straight up and allows the angler to play the fish without excess line weight.

The downrigging unit is typically mounted on the stern or along the rear side of the boat. Figure 1 depicts a fully-rigged system.

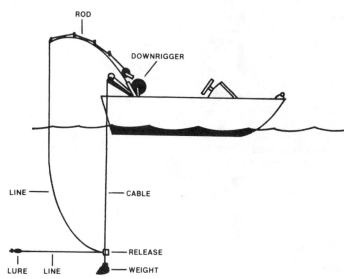

ROD

DOWNRIGGER

LINE — CABLE

RELEASE

LURE   LINE — WEIGHT

Figure 1 - Downrigger System

Basic Equipment

Downrigger design and construction vary with the manufacturer; however, all downriggers have some similar components. (See Figure 2.)

A. REEL—The wheel device on which the cable is coiled. Cable length capacity is usually up to 600 feet.

B. CRANK HANDLE—Device used to rotate the wheel to shorten or extend cable length. Manual cranks are standard, but more sophisticated units use electrically-powered cranks. Electric units raise and lower weight via a 12-volt motor. Power required to operate electric downriggers is minimal—usually about six amps for a 12 lb. weight. Some electric units shut off automatically when the weight reaches the arm on retrieval.

C. CLUTCH—Drag system that adjusts tension on the wheel. This allows cable to unravel when weight becomes entangled or caught on an obstruction. On some manual units it allows weight to be lowered quickly without use of a crank handle.

D. CABLE—Stranded stainless steel wire (approximately 150 lb. test) used to connect weight and reel. Line releases are placed on this cable. Special coaxial cable can be used that provides water temperature sensing (see temperature sensing section).

E. ARM—Extension tube or rod, usually between one to six feet in length, along which the cable runs and is supported. Some units have arms that are adjustable to various lengths. Arms that can be tilted up to the vertical position are available on some models.

F. GUIDE HEAD AND PULLY—Located at the end of the arm, the guide head and pully ensures smooth lowering and retrieval of the weight.

G. MOUNTING—provides for quick securing or release of downrigger unit. Many mounts have a swivel base that slides in or bolts down to a mounting plate to allow for different positioning and ease in connecting lines to release. Lock-in security mounts are an option available on some units.

H. WEIGHTS—Used to submerge line to desired depth. Weights are usually six to twelve pounds and come in numerous shapes and colors.

I. COUNTER—Usually attached to the reel, this provides accurate measure of the amount of cable that has been let out.

K. ROD HOLDER—The fishing rod attached to the downrigger is placed in this unit, which may be single or double-rigged.

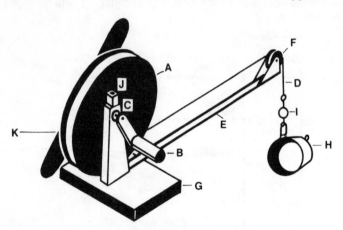

Figure 2 - Downrigger Components

Using the Downrigger System

Releases

Correct application of line release systems is essential for successful downrigging. Releases can be mounted (1) between a cable and a downrigger weight, (2) directly to a weight, or (3) at any location along the wire. The ability to attach the release at any point affords placement of more than one line on a single downrigger cable. "Stacking," illustrated in Figure 3, must be attempted with caution, as multiple hookups may cause line crossing.

Release designs vary in complexity, from a simple rubber band to plastic-molded, spring-set, adjustable tension mechanisms. Choice of type and design are dependent upon application. Adjustable tension releases are appropriate when high and slow speed trolling of lines having varying weights is expected over the course of a season, whereas less sophisticated releases are suitable for slow speed, light lure trolling. Correct release tension, best learned through experience, allows for release only when a fish bites the bait, and not when normal lure resistance occurs while trolling.

Releases should also be evaluated in terms of potential line wear. Some designs with flat, nonpointed surfaces, tend to distribute the "pinching effect"—a feature which minimizes line wear—over greater lengths of line.

With the variety of downrigger releases on the market today and the continual influx of new designs, you should consult an expert before choosing a release for your fishing needs.

When manufactured releases are not available, a rubber band may be substituted in the following way:

—Pull one end of a #12 rubber band through the other until it clinches down on your fishing line.

—Attach the rubber band loop to a snap-swivel located above the downrigger weight.

—If stacking lines, then repeat above and attach the other end of the swivel to the downrigging cable, using a second rubber band and snap.

Line from Release to Lure

The amount of line from the release mechanism to the lure is an important consideration when downrigger fishing. When you are fishing in shallow water, the boat may spook the fish; therefore, it may be necessary to locate the lure a greater distance behind the weight to enable fish to reenter the troll alley following passage of the boat. Generally, if you think fish are disturbed by boat movement, move the lure further from the release.

The greater the distance between lure and release, the greater the *line drop* after a fish "strikes." Line drop describes the slack period from the time the line is pulled free of the release to the time it comes taut to the tip of the fishing rod. At this time the lure is free-falling, possibly simulating prey that has been stunned as the result of an attack. If you are fishing for game fish that stun their prey and return to consume crippled bait, this could be to your advantage. If bait does not stall in the water after line drop, the game fish may think its prey has not been injured and is not catchable.

You may wish to use a dodger (Figure 3) between the lure and release to attract attention and impart movement to the lure or bait.

Lure Action

Another important consideration in downrigger fishing is the action of the lure. If your lure is of the diving type, the distance it will dive must be considered if stacking it next to nondiving lures or if fishing close to the bottom. A diving lure that would normally dive 10 to 15 feet if free trolled, will also dive 10 to 15 feet from the release point, with a downrigger. This should be taken into account when setting release position and weight depth.

Trolling Speed and Cable Angle

Trolling speed should vary according to type of lure, depth fished, and species sought. When trolling live or rigged baits, you should allow them to move as naturally as possible; therefore, a slower trolling speed is usually preferred. A faster speed can tear the hook, if not adequately secured, from the bait.

Artificial lures are normally trolled faster than live bait. As trolling speed increases, the angle of the downrigger cable off the

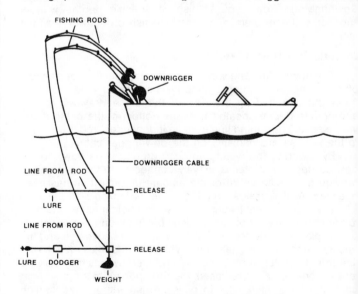

Figure 3 - Stacking Technique

stern also increases. As the boat moves through the water, the cable and weight tend to trail behind, which produces cable deflection.

To make accurate depth determinations for weights and lines, you might wish to use a paper-recording, fish-finding bathometer when downrigger fishing. Metal weights often appear as a solid black line on the paper. Consult a marine electronics dealer for details.

Temperature Sensing Equipment and Use

Water temperature is a primary determinant of fish distribution. Temperature may act to concentrate food organisms that attract fish, or may be a physiological barrier through which fish will not move. Generally, water temperatures decrease with increasing depth. As wind keeps the surface water layer well mixed and uniform in temperature, the temperature decreases rapidly within a sub-surface layer of water called the thermocline. During mid-summer months, the thermocline contains favorable dissolved oxygen and nutrient levels for fish and prey.

Knowledge of fish temperature preferences, coupled with the ability to measure temperature at various depths, can contribute to angling success.

Many types of water temperature sensing equipment are available. The simplest is a thermometer, used only to measure surface temperature, that can be hand-held over the side of a boat. A variation of the thermometer is a temperature sensor permanently mounted to the hull.

To measure temperatures at various depths, other instruments must be used. The coaxial temperature sensor system utilizes a special kind of downrigger cable which conducts an electrical signal from a sensor placed near the downrigger weight. As the weight is lowered, temperatures are read off a display unit on the boat. The hard wire sensor is similar to the coaxial sensor, but in this case the unit can be mounted at any point along the downrigger cable, and the signal is conducted along a separate wire. Several of these can be mounted on a cable to provide continuous temperature measurements at various depths. A third unit, the acoustic link, telemeters the temperature signal through the water from a dry cell-powered sensor on the downrigger cable to the display unit on board. No wire joins the sensor and display unit in this system. Yet another system uses insulated, coated, downrigger cable to transmit temperature information from a dry cell-equipped sensor attached to the cable, with water itself acting as the circuit ground. All of this equipment is flexible enough for practically any application, whether you are taking an isolated survey of the water column or a continuous reading at various depths while trolling.

Figure 4 illustrates types and uses of temperature sensing equipment. Consult marine and boating buyers guides to find equipment manufacturers.

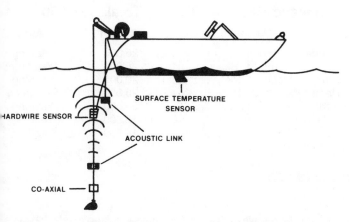

Figure 4 - Water Temperature Sensing Equipment

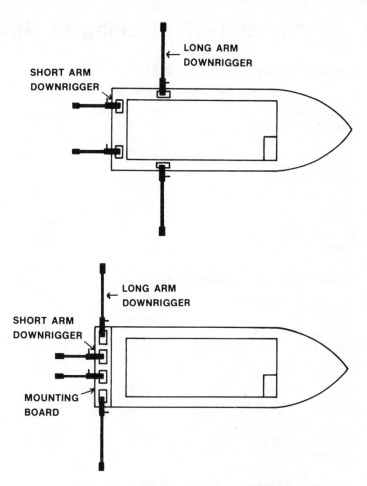

Figure 5 - Downrigger Layout Options

Mounting Boards

Downrigger bases are sometimes attached to mounting boards, usually placed atop the transom of a boat and containing four downrigger units and associated fish-finding electronics and equipment. Because each downrigger is equipped with its own mountable base, located at any point on the gunwale or transom of the vessel, mounting boards are not essential for downrigging.

Figure 5 illustrates two popular patterns for mounting four downriggers on a moderate size fishing boat. In general, downriggers with long arm extensions are used for side downrigger positions, and short arms are used for stern mounting. Common sense should be exercised when locating downriggers, so as to minimize potential interference with adjacent lines. When mounting electric downrigging units, you might wish to consult a qualified boat electrician.

Maintenance

Manufacturers generally outline any necessary maintenance required for various downrigger models. Because downriggers have moving and often electrical characteristics, visual maintenance and upkeep should be part of the cleanup routine following a fishing trip. Cables should be inspected for frays and kinks and replaced as necessary. Electrical cables should have no cracks and remain waterproof. Lubrication of pulleys, swivels, and snaps, etc. should be done often to prohibit corrosion and ensure smooth working characteristics.

Conclusion

Today's boat angler is faced with increasing operating costs due to rising fuel and maintenance expenses. The longer the time spent angling for fish the higher the costs. Downrigger fishing provides a way of locating and catching fish faster and thus saving fuel and money.

Proposed 1987 stocking of New York waters in Lake Ontario

Chinook Salmon - Total: 2,900,000

Location	Number	Age
Black River	2000,000	4 months
North Sandy Creek	100,000	4 months
South Sandy Creek	100,000	4 months
Salmon River	600,000	4 months
Oswego River	250,000	4 months
Little Sodus Bay	200,000	4 months
Sodus Creek	200,000	4 months
Genesee River	300,000	4 months
Oak Orchard Creek	300,000	4 months
Eighteenmile Creek	200,000	4 months
Lower Niagara River	250,000	4 months

Coho Salmon - Total: 350,000

Location	Number	Age
Black River	30,000	Yearling
North Sandy Creek	15,000	Yearling
South Sandy Creek	15,000	Yearling
Salmon River	90,000	Yearling
Oswego River	30,000	Yearling
Sodus Creek	30,000	Yearling
Genesee River	25,000	Yearling
Sandy Creek	30,000	Yearling
Oak Orchard Creek	30,000	Yearling
Eignteenmile Creek	30,000	Yearling
Niagara River	25,000	Yearling

Atlantic Salmon - Total: 49,000

Location	Number	Age
Lindsey Creek	11,000	Yearling
Little Sandy Creek	20,000	Yearling
Irondequoit Creek	18,000	Yearling

Brown Trout - Total: 500,000

Location	Number	Age
Ray Bay	38,000	Yearling
Henderson Bay	30,000	Yearling
Fairhaven Beach St. Pk.	35,000	Yearling
Oswego Harbor	38,000	Yearling
Selkirk Shores St. Pk.	35,000	Yearling
Hamlin Beach St. Pk.	38,000	Yearling
Irondequoit	25,000	Yearling
Genesee River	32,000	Yearling
Braddocks	25,000	Yearling
Webster	25,000	Yearling
Point Breeze	40,000	Yearling
Sodus	34,000	Yearling
Pultneyville	25,000	Yearling
Wilson	40,000	Yearling
Olcott	40,000	Yearling

Lake Trout - Total: 1,200,000

Location	Number	Age
Dablon Point	120,000	Yearling
Dablon Point	50,000	Yearling
Stoney Point	120,000	Yearling
Stoney Point	50,000	Yearling
Stoney Point	60,000	Fingerling
Selkirk	120,000	Yearling
Selkirk	50,000	Yearling
Selkirk	30,000	Fingerling
Hamlin Beach	120,000	Yearling
Hamlin Beach	50,000	Yearling
Hamlin Beach	30,000	Fingerling
Sodus	120,000	Yearling
Sodus	50,000	Yearling
Sodus	30,000	Fingerling
Niagara	120,000	Yearling
Niagara	50,000	Yearling
Niagara	30,000	Fingerling

Washington Steelhead - Total: 330,000

Location	Number	Age
Black River	20,000	Yearling
South Sandy Creek	25,000	Yearling
Salmon River	120,000	Yearling
Oswego River	15,000	Yearling
Genesee River	20,000	Yearling
Irondequoit Creek	24,000	Yearling
Salmon Creek	10,000	Yearling
Sandy Creek	13,300	Yearling
Oak Orchard Creek	20,000	Yearling
Fourmile Creek	13,300	Yearling
Keg Creek	11,100	Yearling
Twelvemile Creek	13.300	Yearling
Lower Niagara River	25,000	Yearling

Skamania Steelhead - Total: 82,000

Location	Number	Age
Stoney Creek	18,000	Yearling
Catfish Creek	10,000	Yearling
Oswego River	18,000	Yearling
Maxwell Creek	18,000	Yearling
Niagara River	18,000	Yearling

Domestic Rainbow Trout - Total: 138,000

Location	Number	Age
Henderson Bay	25,000	Yearling
Selkirk Shores St. Pk.	25,000	Yearling
Hamlin Beach St. Pk.	20,000	Yearling
Hamlin Beach St. Pk.	23,000	Fingerling
Sodus	20,000	Yearling
Wilson	12,500	Yearling
Olcott	12,500	Yearling

Grand Total: 5,349,000

These figures represent **projections** only. They are based on the best information available and constitute stocking levels that state fish culturists strive to attain. There is no guarantee against extenuating circumstances (fiscal problems, fish diseases, contaminant issues, manpower shortages, etc.) ultimately limiting the number of fish actually stocked in any single year. Likewise, conditions and hatchery production levels could result in additional fish being available.

CHINOOK SALMON

Common Names: Chinook, King Salmon

Identifying Characteristics:
—Green to grey back, turning silver on sides and belly; almost black during spawning
—Black mouth
—Large black spots found on back, dorsal fin, and entire tail
—15-17 anal rays

Habits and Habitat:
—Preferred temperature range 50°-58°; 54° ideal
—Less of a schooling fish than Coho salmon; found where the bottom and thermocline meet.
—Fish areas and depths where preferred temperatures are found. If waters are too cold, try the warmest waters available (such as in streams or off stream mouths)
—Spawn in fall in area streams and rivers; hottest time of year for catching "the big ones"

Tackle/Techniques:
—Spoons and spinners work very well, as do flatfish and J-Plugs. A change in color can often make a big difference.
—In streams and rivers, egg sacs are very effective. Live baits, such as night crawlers, minnows, or crayfish can often do the trick.

Local Hot Spots:
—Lake Ontario, Salmon River, Oswego River, Sodus Bay, Little Sodus Bay

(Oncorhynchus Tschawytscha)

ATLANTIC SALMON

(Salmo Salar)

Common Name: Landlocked or Atlantic Salmon

Identifying Characteristics:
—Back and sides are grayish-brown, becoming olive on sides
—Large dark spots scattered over body, but rarely on tail
—Bears a strong resemblance to Brown Trout, but (1) the upper jaw extends only to the rear edge of the pupil (2) has a single row of bottom teeth with no teeth on the roof of the mouth.

Habits and Habitat:
—Prefers cold, oxygen-rich waters
—One of the finest fighting sport fish in C.N.Y.
—There are populations of Atlantic Salmon which have been cut off from the ocean and so spend their entire lives in fresh water (Landlocked Salmon)
—Starting in September they move into their parent streams, but don't spawn until October or November
—Unlike other salmon, landlocked salmon don't always die after spawning

Tackle/Techniques:
—Same as for other salmon. Spoons and spinners, flies, and live bait all work well

Local Hot Spots:
—Finger Lakes (Cayuga, Hemlock, Keuka, Skaneateles, Owasco, Seneca); Fall Creek (Tompkins County); experimental stockings are presently being made in Lake Ontario.

BROOK TROUT

(Salvelinus Fontinalis)

Common Names: Brookie, Brook Trout, Speckled Trout

Identifying Characteristics:
—Dark body, olive to brown, with light spots scattered along its length
—Spots are irregular and wavey along the back, becoming progressively more circular towards the belly
—A few bright red spots surrounded by a blue ring are found on the sides
—Bottom fins are orange to pink, with a white leading edge followed by a dark stripe
—9-10 anal rays

Habits and Habitat:
—Prefers cold, clear waters; usually found in headwaters of streams and rivers
—Has very low tolerance for warm water or pollution
—Feeds on insects, worms, crayfish, etc.
—Spawns in fall

Tackle/Techniques:
—Excellent for fly-fishing. Can be taken on a variety of dry flys, wet flys or nymphs
—Small spoons and spinners
—Live bait, such as worms and crayfish

Local Hot Spots:
—Mad River, Beaver Creek, Fabius Brook, Factory Brook, Trout Brook, upper Cohocton River, Fall Creek, Cryder Creek, Cold Brook (Oswego County).

COHO SALMON

(Oncorhynchus Kisutch)

Common Names: Coho or Silver Salmon

Identifying Characteristics:
—Dark blue to green back, becoming bright silver on sides; turns reddish during spawning
—Black mouth with white gums
—Small black spots found on back, dorsal fin and upper half of tail (no spots on lower half of tail).
—13-15 anal rays

Habits and Habitat:
—Preferred temperature range 50°-58°; 54° ideal
—a schooling fish which prefers surface waters when temperature permits
—The first salmonid to move inshore in fall
—Fall spawning in area streams and rivers

Tackle/Techniques:
—Same as for Chinook

Local Hot Spots:
—Lake Ontario, Oswego River, Salmon River

RAINBOW/STEELHEAD TROUT

Common Names: Bow, Rainbow, Steelhead

Identifying Characteristics:

—Preferred temperature range 50°-65°; 60° ideal
—Coloring varies with environment in which the fish lives
—The migratory, lake-dwelling variety (steelhead) tend to be light and silver; can sometimes be confused with Coho salmon. The lateral color line of pink or red very faint, as are spots
—Stream-dwelling fish have many small, dark spots on body and upper fins, and especially on the tail. Body color varies from bluish to brown to olive green. Lateral line of pink or red can be very pronounced, especially during spawning
—White mouth and square tail
—10-12 anal rays

Habits and Habitat:

—Prefers cold, moving water
—Spawns in spring time, unlike other salmonids. Some hatchery-raised fish will occasionally spawn in fall
—Can tolerate a wide range of temperatures
—Often found near piers, rocky points, and sharp drop offs
—Feed on worms, crayfish and insects
—An excellent fighting fish

Tackle/Techniques:

—Can be taken in many different ways with a variety of baits
—Troll fast using large plugs or fluorescent spoons
—Natural baits such as egg sacs, worms, and crayfish work well
—Spoons and spinners are good in the fast water of streams and rivers

Local Hot Spots:

—Finger Lakes (except Honeoye, Conesus and Otisco), Lake Ontario, Naples Creek, Catharine Creek, Cayuga Inlet, Cold Brook (Keuka Lake Inlet), Salmon River (East Branch), Irondequoit Creek, Salmon River.

(Salmo Gairdneril)

BROWN TROUT

(Salmo Trutta)

Common Names: Brown, Brownie

Identifying Characteristics:

—Preferred temperature range 50°-65°; 60° ideal
—Found in a variety of waters, from streams and rivers to lakes and reservoirs
—Usually golden brown in color, with dark spots on entire body, but few or none on tail. Spots are often surrounded by faint, light halo. A smaller number of red or orange spots are scattered along the body.
—Squared, non-forked tail
—Can be confused with Landlocked Salmon (see)
—9-10 anal rays

Habits and Habitat:

—A suspending fish which doesn't wander greatly
—Often close to shore in shallow water (2'-3')
—Spawns in late fall
—Slightly less tolerant of warm water than Rainbow Trout
—Active at night, particularly in summer

Tackle/Techniques:

—Can be taken on variety of baits and lures, but care must be taken to present them as naturally as possible
—Live baits: worms, minnows, insect larvae, chubs, and smelt
—Flys: wooly worm, muddler minnow, and big millers, especially at night
—Lures: silver spoons and spinners, fluorescent colors, and minnow plugs
—Night fishing often good, especially in fall. Eggs, single and sacs, produce well

Local Hot Spots:

—Ninemile Creek (Onondaga County), Cohocton River, Virgil Creek, Mill Creek (Steuben County), Sodus Bay, Salmon River, Lake Ontario, Keuka Lake, Seneca Lake, Canandaigua Lake, Cayuga Lake, Otisco Lake.

CRAPPIE

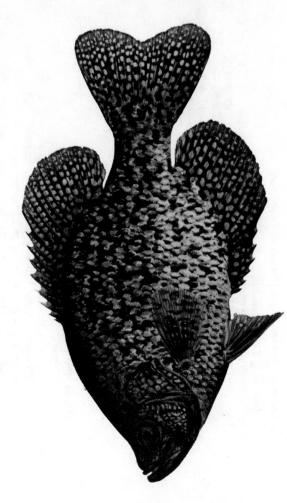

(Pomoxis Niaromaculatus)

Common Names: Crappie, Calico Bass

Identifying Characteristics:
—Back is green or olive, quickly becoming cream or silver on sides and belly
—Irregular dark blotches on sides and fins
—Anal fin virtually as large as the dorsal fin

Habits and Habitat:
—Found in lakes and ponds; prefer quiet waters
—Holds in weedy areas with rather clear water
—A schooling fish; spring spawning

Tackle/Techniques:
—Use light or ultra light equipment for most fun
—Small, live minnows work best. Put a bobber a few feet up from the bait and cast out. Wait until a school swims by.
—Small spinners also work well, as do Mr. Twisters
—Action with spring time school can be fast and furious
—Excellent eating

Local Hot Spots:
—Sodus Bay, Port Bay, Canandaigua Lake, Honeoye Lake West River, Whitney Point Reservoir, Seneca River, Waneta Lake, Cross Lake, Lamoka Lake.

LAKE TROUT

(Salvelinus Namaycush)

Common Names: Lake Trout, Lakers

Identifying Characteristics:
—A dark fish with light spots scattered over the head and sides
—Lower fins edged in white
—Tail deeply forked
—10-12 anal rays

Habits and Habitat:
—Preferred temperature range 44°-55°; 50° ideal
—Often found in very deep water (down to 300 ft.), particularly in summer
—When water temperatures approach freezing, they can be taken in shallows
—Spawn in fall

Tackle/Techniques:
—In early spring and late fall, cast from shore or shallow troll. A variety of spoons and spinners work well, as do flatfish and fireplugs. Live bait is also productive.
—The rest of the year, troll deeply using the above lures in combination with dodgers or cowbell attractors.

Local Hot Spots:
—Lake Ontario, Finger Lakes (except Conesus, Honeoye, and Otisco)

Common Names: Pumpkinseed, Sunfish, Sunny

Identifying Characteristics:
—Black gill flap with red tip
—Body olive to golden brown, turning yellow or orange towards belly
—Large side fins; small mouth
—Sides are mottled or lightly striped
—Light blue/green lines radiate back from mouth and eye region

Habits and Habitat:
—Prefer warm, weedy waters, especially in lakes and ponds
—Usually close to shore
—Hold near weeds, logs, docks, etc.

Tackle/Techniques:
—Best taken on ultralight equipment or with fly rod
—Nearly any small lure or natural bait works well, but worms are still best
—Good fishing for children in summer

Local Hot Spots:
—Finger Lakes (all), Sodus Bay, Waneta Lake, Lamoka Lake.

(Lepomis Gibbosus)

(Lepomis Macrochirus)

Common Names: Bluegill, Sunfish, Bream

Identifying Characteristics:
—Dark green to brown, becoming yellow or orange on breast
—Dark blue to almost black gill flap
—Dark blotch on the back of the dorsal fin
—Irregular vertical dark bars on sides

Habits and Habitat:
—Likes quiet, weedy waters
—Holds close to shore, hiding under docks and among vegetation
—Similar to Pumpkinseed, but tends more towards open areas

Tackle/Techniques:
—Same as for Pumpkinseed

Local Hot Spots:
—Goodale Lake, Sodus Bay, Finger Lakes (all) Waneta Lake, Lamoka Lake.

LARGEMOUTH BASS

Common Names: Largemouth, Black Bass

Identifying Characteristics:
—Dark olive green
—A dark band runs along the side the length of the body
—Deep notch between front and rear portion of dorsal fin
—Upper jaw extends beyond the back of the eye

Habits and Habitat:
—Prefers warm, sluggish streams or shallow, weedy lakes and ponds
—Likes mud bottoms
—Feeds on insects, frogs, worms, crayfish, etc.

Tackle/Techniques:
—Live baits, such as worms and crayfish, work well
—Try spinners or buzzbaits on surface, plastic worms on bottom
—Best on ultralight tackle or fly equipment

Local Hot Spots:
—Waneta Lake, Lamoka Lake, Redfield Reservoir, Park Station Lake, Sodus Bay, Port Bay, Little Sodus Bay, Finger Lakes (all).

(Micropterus Salmoides)

ROCK BASS

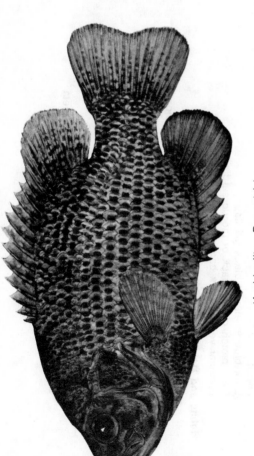

(Ambloplites Rupestris)

Common Names: Rock Bass, Redeye

Identifying Characteristics:
—Dark olive with white belly
—Red eyes
—Faint horizontal lines on sides, particularly towards belly
—Dark spot on gill flap, often edged with white

Habits and Habitat:
—Frequents deep, rocky streams and cool, clear lakes
—Often found in same areas as Smallmouth bass
—Can get abundant in some areas; if you get one, you can get a stringer full
—Scrappy and good eating

Tackle/Techniques:
—Most fun on ultralight equipment
—Will take flies, small spinners, and live bait

Local Hot Spots:
—Sodus Bay, Susquehanna River, North Sandy Pond, Finger Lakes (all), Lake Ontario.

WHITE BASS

Common Name: Silver Bass

Identifying Characteristics:
—Silvery green back, quickly turning silvery gray on side
—Small head, forked tail
—Thin, dark lines run horizontally across body
—Protruding lower jaw and yellow eyes
—Two section dorsal fin

Habits and Habitat:
—Prefer large, deep streams, rivers, and medium to large lakes
—Clear, quiet waters
—Usually in deep waters in daytime, shallows at twilight
—Often feed in dense, tight schools in shallow water right at the surface
—Feed on insects and other fish
—Spawn in streams May to August

Tackle/Techniques:
—Use light gear
—Live minnows or worms good
—Imitation minnow lures and Mr. Twisters produce well, as do small spinners
—The best time to catch them is when they're feeding in schools, often just off shore

Local Hot Spots:
—Lake Ontario, Sodus Bay.

(Morone Chrysops)

SMALLMOUTH BASS

(Micropterus Dolomieui)

Common Names: Smallmouth, Black Bass, Bronzeback

Identifying Characteristics:
—Pale green to golden bronze in color
—Dark, wavey bars run vertically along body
—The upper jaw does not extend back beyond the back of the eye
—Shallow notch between the front and rear portion of dorsal fin

Habits and Habitat:
—Prefers cold, clear water
—Found in rocky or gravelly lakes and streams
—Often in fast water or riffles
—Usually stays near bottom, but not too deep (usually 45' or less)
—Spring spawning

Tackle/Techniques:
—Crabs, minnows and worms work very well
—Small plugs and spinners work well
—Fish the shallows in spring, further out in summer and fall
—Fish near bottom
—Trolling, drifting or still fishing are all productive

Local Hot Spots:
—Susquehanna River, Fingler Lakes (all), Lake Ontario, Waneta Lake, Lamoka Lake.

CHAIN PICKEREL

(Esox Niger)

Common Names: Pickerel

Identifying Characteristics:
—Color varies from green to bronze
—Dark, chain-like markings along length of body
—Long, thin snout
—14-16 branchiostegal rays (slender bones which support soft part of gill cover; best seen from belly side of fish)
—Cheeks and gill cover completely scaled
—Dark vertical bar below eye

Habits and Habitat:
—Likes weedy, quiet waters
—Eats insects, worms, crayfish, and other fish
—Similar to Northern Pike, but not usually found where larger relatives (Muskie and Northerns) are present

Tackle/Techniques:
—Best taken on light spinning gear of fly rod
—Steel leader
—Natural baits such as minnows and crayfish
—Spoons, spinners, bucktails
—Can be ice-fished

Local Hot Spots:
—Finger Lakes (all), Lily Lake, Tioughnioga River, Waneta Lake, Lamoka Lake.

MUSKELLUNGE

Common Names: Muskie, Lunge

Identifying Characteristics:
—Green to light brown with cream belly
—No scales onn lower half of cheeks or gill covers
—Sides often have dark vertical bars or spots, on lighter background
—Head shaped like a duck's bill
—6-9 sensory pores on each side of lower jaw

Habits and Habitat:
—Prefers waters 60°-70°; 68° ideal
—A solitary, non-schooling fish
—Frequents clear, quiet, shallow areas of rivers and medium to large lakes
—Usually hangs near submerged weed beds or structure
—Most often in shallow water (15' or less)
—Individual fish tend to stay in one area

Tackle/Techniques:
—Best fishing in fall
—Use heavy gear and steel leaders
—Suckers, mice, and frogs are good as live bait
—Spinners and jigs work well, but think B—I—G
—Muskies are not very numerous and are difficult to catch; it's said a veteran angler can average about 30 hours of fishing per catch. If you're serious about getting one of these big tough fish, consider hiring an experienced guide.

Local Hot Spots:
—Waneta Lake, Otisco Lake, Loon Lake, Susquehanna River.

(Esox Masquinongy)

(*Stizostedion Vitreum Vitreum*)

Common Names: Walleye, Yellow Pike, Yellow

Identifying Characteristics:
—Largest member of perch family
—Big, glassy eyes which reflect light at night
—brassy to olive green on sides with light belly
—Dark, narrow bands run vertically on back and sides
—Silver or white tip on lower fork of tail
—Sharp spines on first dorsal fin
—Sharp canine teeth on jaws and roof of mouth

Habits and Habitat:
—Prefers waters 55°-70°
—A bottom dweller which frequently hangs near drop offs
—Often school, and tend to stay in one place and wait for passing food
—Mostly feed at night
—Spawn in early spring
—Often found in deep water

Tackle/Techniques:
—Fishing is best at night, and especially during late spring and fall
—Use live baits, or deep-diving plugs that resemble bait fish
—Spinners with worms, bright spoons
—Troll slowly and wait a few seconds before setting hook
—Bottom bouncing with jigs works well through the ice
—Great eating

Local Hot Spots:
—Otselic River (Broome County), Susquehanna River, Oneida Lake, Oneida River, Oswego River, Seneca River, Honeoye Lake.

NORTHERN PIKE

(*Esox Lucius*)

Common Names: Pike, Northern

Identifying Characteristics:
—Green to brown in color
—Light spots on dark background
—Entire cheek has scales, but only the upper portion of gill cover does
—Fins are heavily spotted or mottled in dark
—5 sensory pores found on each side of lower jaw

Habits and Habitat:
—A solitary fish that frequents cool, sluggish waters of lakes and streams
—Often found in shallow water over weed beds or structure
—Feed mostly on fish such as perch and suckers, but also on insects, crayfish, frogs, snakes, etc.
—Spawn in spring

Tackle/Techniques:
—Cast or troll using heavy gear with steel leaders
—Still fish with live suckers or perch
—Medium size spinners, spoons, and plugs work well
—Can be ice-fished

Local Hot Spots:
—Sodus Bay, Little Sodus Bay, North Sandy Pond, Owasco Lake, Cayuga Lake, Seneca Lake, Keuka Lake, Conesus Lake, Seneca River, Ox Creek.

WHITE PERCH

(Morone Americana)

Common Names:

Identifying Characteristics:
—Olive to blackish green back, fading to silvery green on sides
—Superficially resembles White bass, but usually has no stripes and is darker
—Compressed body with small head
—Very deeply notched dorsal fin
—Not a true perch

Habits and Habitat:
—Very similar to White bass

Tackle/Techniques:
—Same as for White bass

Local Hot Spots:
—Oneida Lake, Lake Ontario, Seneca River

YELLOW PERCH

(Perca Flavescens)

Common Names: Perch

Identifying Characteristics:
—Golden yellow on sides with olive green vertical bars
—Two separate dorsal fins
—Slight humpbacked appearance
—Moderately forked tail
—Many tiny teeth

Habits and Habitat:
—Prefers weedy, warm water lakes and quiet parts of streams
—Clear water
—A schooling fish; eats insects crayfish, etc.
—Stays shallow
—Inactive at night

Tackle/Techniques:
—Use light gear
—Most often taken on live bait just off bottom
—Troll with spinner and worm to locate school, then still fish with worms and small minnows
—Fish through ice with grubs or perch eyes
—Super eating, especially if caught ice-fishing

Local Hot Spots:
—Seneca Lake, Keuka Lake, Lake Ontario, Oneida Lake, Sodus Bay.

CHANNEL CATFISH

Common Names: Catfish, Channel Cat

Identifying Characteristics:
—Dark blue or olive on back, turning silvery on sides
—Small, dark irregular spots on body
—Deeply forked tail
—4 barbels on the chin, two on the snout, and one on each side of upper jaw
—24-30 anal rays

Habits and Habitat:
—Inhabits lakes and large rivers; often down stream from power dams
—Not usually in weed beds; prefers clean bottoms of sand or gravel
—Feeds mainly at night
—Bottom feeds on variety of fish, insects, crustaceans, etc.

Tackle/Techniques:
—Best night-fished
—Float bait, such as a strip of fish belly, downstream
—Fish on bottom with slip sinker, same as for Bulkhead
—Good eating

Local Hot Spots:
—Barge Canal System, Oswego River, Lake Ontario, Oneida Lake, Cayuga-Seneca Canal, Seneca River.

(Ictalurus Punctatus)

BROWN BULLHEAD

(Ictalurus Nebulosus)

Common Names: Bullhead

Identifying Characteristics:
—Yellow brown to chocolate brown
—Slender body with dark barbels
—Vogue, dark mottling on back and sides

Habits and Habitat:
—Prefers weedy, deeper waters of lakes and sluggish streams
—Found over both muddy and gravelly bottoms
—A bottom feeder with a diverse diet - insect larvae, mollusks, algae, etc.

Tackle/Techniques:
—Can be caught in very early spring
—Fish on bottom with slip sinker using worms, crabs, minnows or dough balls
—Handle with care - the spines are sharp
—Good eating
—Feeds mostly at night

Local Hot Spots:
—Lake Ontario, Sodus Bay, North Sandy Pond, South Sandy Pond, Finger Lakes (all), Cayuga-Seneca Canal, Seneca Canal, Seneca River, Oswego River.

WHITE SUCKER

Common Names: Sucker

Identifying Characteristics:
—Olive brown
—Cylinderical body
—Blunt snout; upper lip thinner than lower lip
—Large scales

Habits and Habitat:
—Found in almost any water condition - clear or muddy, fast or slow, clean or polluted
—Widely distributed
—Seems to prefer large streams and deep water im poundments
—A bottom-feeder whose diet consists of insect larvae, crustaceans, algae, etc.
—Spring spawning

Tackle/Techniques:
—Not a big fighter, but their flesh is good for patties and smoking
—Fish on the bottom with worms, dew worms, or dough balls
—They hit very lightly

Local Hot Spots:
—Lake Ontario, tributaries to Lake Ontario, Finger Lakes (all).

(Catostomus Commersoni)

SMELT

(Osmerus Mordax)

Common Name: Smelt

Identifying Characteristics:
—Greenish back with silvery sides
—Small and slender with forked tail
—Large Mouth
—Adipose fin between dorsal fin and tail

Habits and Habitat:
—Inhabit cool, medium deep waters of lakes
—Spring spawning, when they run up streams and rivers
—A schooling fish
—Spawn primarily at night

Tackle/Techniques:
—Best time to get smelt is during their spawning runs
—Go at night in early spring; the runs only last for a few days
—Use dip nets
—Can also be taken ice fishing using a strip of perch belly

Local Hot Spots:
—Lake Ontario, Salmon Creek (Tompkins County, Fall Creek, Sodus Bay, Grindstone Creek.

FRESHWATER DRUM

Common Names: Sheepshead

Identifying Characteristics:
—Grayish silver body
—Humped back and blunt snout
—Rounded tail
—Deep notch in dorsal fin, with very long rear section

Habits and Habitat:
—Found in large rivers and lakes
—Prefers clear waters, but tolerates turbid, silty areas
—Stays near bottom in 10'-40' of water
—Feeds on snails, mollusks, crayfish

Tackle/Techniques:
—Live baits such as worms, minnows and crayfish are good
—Spinners or small spoons
—Keep bait and lures near bottom
—A reasonably strong fighter, especially if large
—Good fishing even in mid-summer heat

Local Hot Spots:
—Lake Ontario, Cayuga-Seneca Canal.

(Aplodinotus Grunniens)

CARP

(Cyprinus Carpio)

Common Names: Carp

Identifying Characteristics:
—Olive green to bronze
—Long dorsal fin
—A pair of fleshy barbels on each side of upper jaw
—Large scales, each with a dark spot at its base and edged in dark
—Has cross-hatched pattern on sides

Habits and Habitat:
—Can tolerate a variety of aquatic environments, but prefers warm streams or lakes with muddy bottoms
—Feed on both plant and animal material
—Bottom feeders
—Tolerant of pollution
—A strong-fighting fish which can get quite large
—Spring-spawning

Tackle/Techniques:
—Use heavy gear
—Fish on bottom using a slip sinker
—Dough balls and worms work well

Local Hot Spots:
—Lake Ontario, the Barge Canal System, Sodus Bay, Finger Lakes (all), the lower portions of almost any large stream or river.

LOG SHEET

Date: / /

Time: _____

Stream/Lake Name: _____

Access Used: _____

Section Fished: _____

Species Name(s): _____

No. Caught: _____

Size (lbs./in.): _____

SITE CONDITIONS

Water Level/Flow: _____

Clarity: _____

Weed Growth: _____

ph: _____

Bottom Type: _____

Insect Hatches: _____

Range (Drift): _____

Tackle Used: _____

Method Used: _____

Comments: _____

_____

_____

_____

_____

WEATHER CONDITIONS

Barometer: _____

Wind Speed & Direction: _____

Humidity: _____

Cloud Cover: _____

Air Temp.: _____

Recent Rain Fall: _____

Cross Range: _____

LOG SHEET

Date: / /

Time: _____

Stream/Lake Name: _____

Access Used: _____

Section Fished: _____

Species Name(s): _____

No. Caught: _____

Size (lbs./in.): _____

SITE CONDITIONS

Water Level/Flow: _____

Clarity: _____

Weed Growth: _____

ph: _____

Bottom Type: _____

Insect Hatches: _____

Range (Drift): _____

Tackle Used: _____

Method Used: _____

Comments: _____

_____

_____

_____

WEATHER CONDITIONS

Barometer: _____

Wind Speed & Direction: _____

Humidity: _____

Cloud Cover: _____

Air Temp.: _____

Recent Rain Fall: _____

Cross Range: _____

LOG SHEET

Date: / /

Time: _____

Stream/Lake Name: _____

Access Used: _____

Section Fished: _____

Species Name(s): _____

No. Caught: _____

Size (lbs./in.): _____

SITE CONDITIONS

Water Level/Flow: _____

Clarity: _____

Weed Growth: _____

ph: _____

Bottom Type: _____

Insect Hatches: _____

Range (Drift): _____

Tackle Used: _____

Method Used: _____

Comments: _____

_____

_____

_____

_____

WEATHER CONDITIONS

Barometer: _____

Wind Speed & Direction: _____

Humidity: _____

Cloud Cover: _____

Air Temp.: _____

Recent Rain Fall: _____

Cross Range: _____

LOG SHEET

Date: / /

Time: _____

Stream/Lake Name: _____

Access Used: _____

Section Fished: _____

Species Name(s): _____

No. Caught: _____

Size (lbs./in.): _____

SITE CONDITIONS

Water Level/Flow: _____

Clarity: _____

Weed Growth: _____

ph: _____

Bottom Type: _____

Insect Hatches: _____

Range (Drift): _____

Tackle Used: _____

Method Used: _____

Comments: _____

_____

_____

_____

_____

WEATHER CONDITIONS

Barometer: _____

Wind Speed & Direction: _____

Humidity: _____

Cloud Cover: _____

Air Temp.: _____

Recent Rain Fall: _____

Cross Range: _____

LOG SHEET

Date: ___ / ___ / ___

Time: _____

Stream/Lake Name: _____

Access Used: _____

Section Fished: _____

Species Name(s): _____

No. Caught: _____

Size (lbs./in.): _____

SITE CONDITIONS

Water Level/Flow: _____

Clarity: _____

Weed Growth: _____

ph: _____

Bottom Type: _____

Insect Hatches: _____

Range (Drift): _____

Tackle Used: _____

Method Used: _____

Comments: _____

_____

_____

_____

_____

WEATHER CONDITIONS

Barometer: _____

Wind Speed & Direction: _____

Humidity: _____

Cloud Cover: _____

Air Temp.: _____

Recent Rain Fall: _____

Cross Range: _____

LOG SHEET

Date: ___ / ___ / ___

Time: _____

Stream/Lake Name: _____

Access Used: _____

Section Fished: _____

Species Name(s): _____

No. Caught: _____

Size (lbs./in.): _____

SITE CONDITIONS

Water Level/Flow: _____

Clarity: _____

Weed Growth: _____

ph: _____

Bottom Type: _____

Insect Hatches: _____

Range (Drift): _____

Tackle Used: _____

Method Used: _____

Comments: _____

_____

_____

_____

WEATHER CONDITIONS

Barometer: _____

Wind Speed & Direction: _____

Humidity: _____

Cloud Cover: _____

Air Temp.: _____

Recent Rain Fall: _____

Cross Range: _____

LOG SHEET

Date: / /

Time: _____

Stream/Lake Name: _____

Access Used: _____

Section Fished: _____

Species Name(s): _____

No. Caught: _____

Size (lbs./in.): _____

SITE CONDITIONS

Water Level/Flow: _____

Clarity: _____

Weed Growth: _____

ph: _____

Bottom Type: _____

Insect Hatches: _____

Range (Drift): _____

Tackle Used: _____

Method Used: _____

Comments: _____

_____

_____

_____

_____

WEATHER CONDITIONS

Barometer: _____

Wind Speed & Direction: _____

Humidity: _____

Cloud Cover: _____

Air Temp.: _____

Recent Rain Fall: _____

Cross Range: _____

LOG SHEET

Date: / /

Time: _____

Stream/Lake Name: _____

Access Used: _____

Section Fished: _____

Species Name(s): _____

No. Caught: _____

Size (lbs./in.): _____

SITE CONDITIONS

Water Level/Flow: _____

Clarity: _____

Weed Growth: _____

ph: _____

Bottom Type: _____

Insect Hatches: _____

Range (Drift): _____

Tackle Used: _____

Method Used: _____

Comments: _____

_____

_____

_____

WEATHER CONDITIONS

Barometer: _____

Wind Speed & Direction: _____

Humidity: _____

Cloud Cover: _____

Air Temp.: _____

Recent Rain Fall: _____

Cross Range: _____

LOG SHEET

Date: ___/___/___

Time: _____

Stream/Lake Name: _____

Access Used: _____

Section Fished: _____

Species Name(s): _____

No. Caught: _____

Size (lbs./in.): _____

SITE CONDITIONS

Water Level/Flow: _____

Clarity: _____

Weed Growth: _____

ph: _____

Bottom Type: _____

Insect Hatches: _____

Range (Drift): _____

Tackle Used: _____

Method Used: _____

Comments: _____

_____

_____

_____

_____

WEATHER CONDITIONS

Barometer: _____

Wind Speed & Direction: _____

Humidity: _____

Cloud Cover: _____

Air Temp.: _____

Recent Rain Fall: _____

Cross Range: _____

LOG SHEET

Date: ___/___/___

Time: _____

Stream/Lake Name: _____

Access Used: _____

Section Fished: _____

Species Name(s): _____

No. Caught: _____

Size (lbs./in.): _____

SITE CONDITIONS

Water Level/Flow: _____

Clarity: _____

Weed Growth: _____

ph: _____

Bottom Type: _____

Insect Hatches: _____

Range (Drift): _____

Tackle Used: _____

Method Used: _____

Comments: _____

_____

_____

_____

WEATHER CONDITIONS

Barometer: _____

Wind Speed & Direction: _____

Humidity: _____

Cloud Cover: _____

Air Temp.: _____

Recent Rain Fall: _____

Cross Range: _____